OPEN ECONOMY
MACROECONOMICS

OPEN ECONOMY MACROECONOMICS

Theory, Policy and Evidence

Ronald Shone

University of Stirling

Harvester Wheatsheaf

New York   London   Toronto   Sydney   Tokyo

First published 1989 by
Harvester Wheatsheaf
66 Wood Lane End, Hemel Hempstead
Hertfordshire, HP2 4RG
A division of
Simon & Schuster International Group

Printed and bound in Great Britain at the
University Press, Cambridge.

British Library Cataloguing in Publication Data

Shone, R. (Ronald), *1946–*
Open economy macroeconomics: theory,
policy and evidence
1. Macroeconomics
I. Title
339

ISBN 0–7450–0125–4
ISBN 0–7450–0214–5 Pbk

1 2 3 4 5 93 92 91 90 89

CONTENTS

PART I THEORY

PART II   POLICY

Part III   UK PROBLEMS

PREFACE

This book is the result of dissatisfaction with existing macroeconomics textbooks. Good as many of these are, they concentrate too much on the closed economy. At the same time, macroeconomics is often discussed in the abstract as if the institutional framework does not matter. Since much of macroeconomics is concerned with the short and medium terms of open economies, it appears to me that it is essential to deal with the open aspects of macroeconomics throughout the text and not leave it to the final few chapters. Furthermore, institutions do matter, particularly in the short and medium terms. I thus decided to write a book which dealt with theory, policy and institutions.

I discussed my dissatisfaction with existing works with Edward Elgar, formerly of Wheatsheaf. The same view had been expressed by a number of academics around the UK. Edward Elgar was accordingly keen to see such a book written. At this time I was switching from teaching microeconomics to macroeconomics. I had already been teaching a specialist course in international monetary economics at the University of Stirling, and the time was opportune to bring 'openness' to macroeconomics. Having, however, decided to embark on this project, I was aware that different academics have different needs; and thus Wheatsheaf conducted a small questionnaire in order to establish what macroeconomists would wish to see in an intermediate macroeconomics textbook. I wish to thank all those individuals who responded to this questionnaire.

Besides covering macroeconomics from an open perspective, the book has a number of other objectives. First, it is concerned largely with the UK economy. In other words, macroeconomics is discussed within the context of the UK economy. This is especially true of Part II, which is concerned with policy and Part III which is concerned with problems specific to the UK. In this respect there is a great deal of factual material supplied about the UK economy. This is deliberate. I find it very disheartening to hear undergraduates (and postgraduates) expounding on recent theories and yet having no idea about the magnitudes of basic economic indicators and parameters. This is even more true of institutions. The macroeconomy does not operate in a vacuum. Although it is desirable to have universal theories, it is most unlikely that economics will ever achieve these. I suspect that anything coming close to such a possibility will be a most uninteresting theory. Certainly, when it comes to policy discussion, it is impossible to consider such theories without referring to a particular economy and to a particular point in time.

The multiple aims of the book have made it quite long. Because of the desire to cover theory, policy and institutions it has been necessary to make choices and compromises throughout, the most obvious of which is the brevity of the theory in Part I. Linked to this is the choice of integration of theory and policy being left until Parts II and III. A student can only apply a theory once the theory is known. At the same time, it is almost impossible in macroeconomics to illustrate just one theory or one macroeconomic concept. In explaining the real world a number of macroeconomic ideas are usually required at the same time. Thus, Part I should be seen as setting down the bare essentials of macroeconomics in order to take up the discussion of policy later. Further theory will, therefore, be found in Parts II and III – although Part II in particular is referred to as 'policy'.

This book has taken almost four years to write, and in that time the material has been written on three different microcomputers using two different word processors. A variety of programmes have been used, such as spreadsheets, equation solvers, graphics packages and a variety of other statistical packages. I am grateful to all concerned for helping me, not only in the writing of this book, but also in becoming computer literate in the process.

I would like to thank my colleagues, past and present, who have helped me at various stages, especially Mick Common and Paul Hare for comments on early material. Thanks are due to Paul Hudson, Wolverhampton Polytechnic, who also read some of the early material. I would especially like to thank Alex Rebmann who read the whole manuscript and provided the most detailed comments I have ever received. Teaching invariably shows up weaknesses, and so I would like to thank all those students who have undertaken my courses in macroeconomics and international monetary economics and have forced me to clarify aspects of open economy macroeconomics. I would like to express my sincere thanks to my wife, Anne Thomson, for her understanding and patience during the writing of this book, especially in the final stages. At an emotionally weak moment she supplied a much needed encouragement. Finally, I would like to thank Sheila Shepherd for the excellent job of copy-editing; also thanks to Tony and, most especially, Margaret Thomson for their help in checking the proofs.

R. Shone
January 1989

FIGURES

TABLES

KEY VARIABLES

Variable	Description
£M3	broad definition of money (now M3)
σ	output–capital ratio
μ	technical progress (Chapter 18 only)
μ	expected capital gain/loss (Chapter 7 only)
a	real autonomous consumption
A	yield
AD	aggregate demand
a_L	labour productivity
$\hat{a}_L$	percentage change in labour productivity
APP_L	average physical product of labour
AS	aggregate supply
b	marginal propensity to consume
B	amount spent on bonds
bd	real budget deficit
BL_g	sterling bank lending to the government
BL_p	sterling bank lending to the UK non-bank private sector
bp	real balance of payments
bs	real budget surplus
c	real consumption
C_b	notes and coins held by the banks
cf	net capital inflow
cf_0	autonomous net capital inflow
C_p	notes and coins held by the public
D	bank deposits
D_L	demand for labour
drs	change in real foreign exchange reserves
e	real expenditure
E	earnings on a bond (Chapter 7 only)
E	effective exchange rate
E	employment
F	forward exchange rate
G	expected capital gain/loss (Chapter 7 only)
G	nominal (general) government spending
G_n	natural rate of growth
go	real government spending
G_p	sale of government debt to the non-bank private sector
G_w	warranted rate of growth
H_D	money base arising from government debt
i	real investment
IB	internal balance
im	real imports
im_0	real autonomous imports
i_0	real autonomous investment

I_{t-1}	information at the end of time period $t-1$
K	capital
$\hat{k}$	percentage change in Cambridge k
k	capital labour ratio (K/L)
$\hat{k}*$	percentage change in foreign country's k
L	volume of bank lending (Chapter 7 only)
L	labour
l_b	real central bank loans to the commercial banks
L_n	natural level of labour input
$\hat{M}$	growth of money supply
m	marginal propensity to import
$\hat{M}*$	monetary growth abroad
$M*$	money supply abroad
$M1$	narrow definition of money
M_b	commercial banks' deposits at the Bank of England
M_d/P	real demand for money balances
M_0	exogenous money supply
$M0$	money base
MPP_L	marginal physical product of labour
M_s	nominal money supply
M_s/P	real money supply
M_T	transactions demand for money
$n*$	optimal number of withdrawals
nx	real net exports
P	domestic price level
$\hat{P}$	actual inflation
$P*$	overseas price level
$\hat{P}*$	inflation abroad
P_m^*	foreign price of raw materials
P_b	price of a bond
P^e	expected price level
$\hat{P}^e$	expected inflation
P_b^e	expected selling price of a bond
P_g	average price of government spending
P_m	price of raw materials
PPP	purchasing power parity
$psbr$	real public sector borrowing requirement
$PSBR$	public sector borrowing requirement
$PSL2$	private sector liquidity 2
q	money multiplier
$\hat{R}$	percentage change in relative prices
R	return (Chapter 7 only)
R	relative price ratio (real exchange rate)
r	nominal interest rate
$r*$	overseas nominal interest rate
r^e	expected interest rate
r_n	natural rate of interest
s	standard deviation of bond earnings
S	spot exchange rate
$\hat{S}^e$	expected change in spot exchange rate
S_K	capital share in total output
S_L	labour share in total output
S_L	supply of labour
s_R	standard deviation of return
T	transactions balances
$T*$	optimal transactions balances
t_1	marginal rate of tax
t_0	real autonomous taxes
U	total unemployment

U	unemployment (%)
U_d	demand-deficient unemployment
U_f	frictional unemployment
U_j	job-search unemployment
U_n	natural level of unemployment
U_r	residual unemployment
U_s	structural unemployment
U_v	voluntary unemployment
$\mathbf{V}$	velocity of circulation of money
V	vacancies (Chapter 14 only)
V_s	suitable vacancies
V_u	unsuitable vacancies
$\tilde{W}$	wage inflation
Wl	wealth
W	nominal wages
w	real wages $(= W/P)$
wl	real wealth
w^e	expected real wages
w_n	real wage associated with the natural rate of employment
x	real exports
XB	external balance
x_0	real autonomous exports
y	real income
y_d	real disposable income
y^e	expected real income
y_f	full employment real income
y_n	natural level of real income
z	premium/discount on the dollar

Part I

THEORY

Chapter 1

INTRODUCTION

Macroeconomics is both exciting and frustrating. It is exciting because it is going through major changes; it is frustrating because it does not seem to be supplying the answers to the economy's pressing problems. Of course, these two aspects are not unrelated. When a subject does not appear to be supplying answers to policy questions, then there tends to be a detailed scrutiny of the theory underlying the subject. Some would say that when this happens the subject is in 'crisis', see Hicks (1974) and Bell and Kristol (1981). There are, of course, long periods of relative stability, when a subject is evolving and new ideas are related to old ideas, leading either to adaptation or to abandonment of the old in place of the new. There is little doubt that Keynesian economics, as embodied in the IS–LM–BP analysis, supplanted much of classical macroeconomics in college and university courses. However, four qualifications must be added to this statement. First, Keynesian economics did not *replace* classical theory, but, rather, gave a different emphasis; and because of the different emphasis, a different analytical apparatus. Second, classical economics was largely concerned (and still is concerned) with the long run; Keynesian economics was (and still is) concerned with the short run. This is a fundamental difference which leads to a totally different analytical framework of analysis. Third, Keynesian analysis has undergone a number of changes since Keynes launched his *General Theory of Employment, Interest and Money* in 1936. The changes include a synthesis between classical ideas and Keynesian economics – the extent to which real forces are emphasized and whether money is accommodating. The result has been a confusion of sub-groups: Keynesians, neo-Keynesians and post-Keynesians, to name the most prominent. The distinction between these groups is not always clear, see Davidson (1981) for one classification and Cross (1982) for a different one, based on the work of Lakatos, who distinguishes orthodox Keynesian, disequilibrium Keynesian, fundamental Keynesian and new Cambridge Keynesian! Fourth, in recent years there has been a revival of interest in classical ideas and classical analysis but this, too, has gone through a number of changes, which is not surprising. Keynesian economics supplanted classical economics, certainly as an approach to macroeconomics. This implies that classical economics was thought to have certain shortcomings which Keynesian analysis to some extent overcame. It follows, therefore, that any resurrection of classical economics would have to be adapted to deal with the early shortcomings *and* to demonstrate that the new analysis could deal, in turn, with the shortcomings of Keynesian analysis. The changes began with the Classical–Keynesian synthesis in which there was an attempt to provide a microeconomic foundation for Keynesian macroeconomics. In this analysis money, along with everything else, is important. But other economists, most notably Milton Friedman, argued that money mattered and that a stable monetary growth will best stabilize the growth in aggregate demand. This school of thought is now called the monetarist school. It is to be distinguished from the new classicists who emphasize rational expectations and market clearing. The new classicists emphasize supply, but not in the same way as the group labelled supply-side economists – who particularly emphasize tax incentives as a means of stimulating aggregate supply.

To the student of macroeconomics, it is these variety of schools of thought which leads to confusion and frustration. Furthermore, it has led to a major conflict in terms of policy, since many of the solutions suggested by the schools are often radically different – and can even be opposite! Although there are more than just two schools of thought, there is no doubt that Keynesians (as one group) and monetarists (as another) have dominated much of macroeconomics over the last 20 years or so.

Although there is quite a degree of disagreement between the different schools of thought, there is also much agreement. Even where there is disagreement, this may not be a qualitative difference, but, rather, a quantitative one over concerning the value of a particular parameter for instance. The more fundamental differences tend, however, to be concerned with basic assumptions and with the nature of *causation*. This is in marked contrast to the difference over the value of a parameter, which is an empirical question that can often, though not always, be resolved by statistical and econometric investigation. Causation, however, must be postulated within the theory and *cannot* be tested by econometric investigation (at least not at the present time). Causation is concerned with a knowledge (or belief) about how the world works. Economics may indicate, for example that x and y are related in some way. What it may not do, however, is reveal whether x is the cause of y, or y is the cause of x. Furthermore, the causation may be determined by *institutional* considerations. If this is the case, then what may appear to be true for one country, with one particular institutional framework, may not be true of another, with a different institutional framework. As we will see in Chapter 10 when considering money base control, a different view of the causation between the money base and the money supply is held by economists in the US than is perceived by economists in the UK. This could very well be simply a result of the differences in institutional banking in the two countries. It is interesting to note that there has been much debate over whether 'money matters', but very little of the debate concerns itself with institutions. It is as if 'institutions do not matter'. This is more surprising in the case of Keynesians than in that of monetarists. Keynesians are concerned with the short run. It follows, then, that causation and inter-dependence will be conditional on the institutions existing in that short-run period. For monetarists, this is less true since their concern surrounds the long run, where it is possible to change the institutional framework. However, this is rather hard to swallow. The banking structures, for example, in the UK and the US (as with every other country) have a long history: but they are different. A theory predicated on a particular view about banking structure cannot be universal. A theory that assumes the possibility of changing the whole structure of a country's banking is totally unrealistic.

While much of the analysis of this book applies to any country, other sections require the analysis to be placed within an institutional setting. For this reason it is necessary to choose a particular country. Where the discussion involves institutions, they will invariably refer to those in the UK – except where comparisons are being made. This is especially true when we consider policy. Monetary policy, fiscal policy, exchange rate policy, in fact all the policies discussed in Part II, will necessarily involve government. Although political scientists may discuss theories of government, when considering economic policy questions it is necessary to refer to *actual* governments. The structure of government in each country is different. Although each country may have a Central Bank, a Treasury, and various departments, this is as far as the similarity goes. Part of the aim of this book is to give the reader a minimal knowledge of the UK that is sufficient to place macroeconomic issues in context. Of course, this does not mean that there is no *theory* of policy which is not country specific; and, in fact, we take up this very point in Chapter 8. What it does mean is that Parts II and III are directed at the UK economy. Part I, containing the basic theory, although containing some information on the UK economy, is largely concerned with theoretical issues which are not country specific.

1.1 WHAT IS ASSUMED

The book assumes a first-year knowledge of macroeconomics, typical of any introductory textbook of economics (such as Lipsey (1983), Samuelson and Nordhaus (1983), Culyer (1985) or Begg, Dornbusch and Fischer (1987)). Because the book is fairly long in its present form, it was decided not to include a review of national income accounting in this chapter. Not only is this particular to a given economy, but it is also a very specialized topic, and to deal with it adequately would require a number of specialized definitions. The interested reader would do well to consult either Beckerman (1976) or, more recently, King (1986). Even so, the introductory textbooks just referred to will supply the necessary background on national income accounting. However, it must not be forgotten that national income accounting is a very recent development in economics, and owes much to the work of Stone (1966). Furthermore, national income accounting, as we now know it, is predicated on a view of the world which stems from Keynesian economics. It was Keynes' *General Theory* that stressed the components of expenditure (e.g., consumption, investment and government spending), and it was this work that led to the national income accounts in their present form.

As we demonstrate in this book, currently there is a reappraisal of Keynesian economics as to its relevance in the modern world. Consideration has turned to monetarism and supply-side economics. We will deal with both of these topics in this book. But, for the present, the point being made is that national income accounting does not give us much insight into these particular approaches to macroeconomics.

1.2 THE STATIC AND DYNAMIC MODELS AND EXPECTATIONS

Introductory textbooks on economics, as far as their macroeconomics is concerned, deal with a situation where prices are largely (although not wholly) constant. Where prices are allowed to change, the simple analysis of aggregate demand and aggregate supply is introduced. However, the underlying rationale for these relationships is not discussed in any great detail. There is even the danger that the treatment gives the student the impression that aggregate demand and aggregate supply are similar to (if not the same as) demand and supply in microeconomics. A very different rationale underlies *aggregate* demand and *aggregate* supply than underlies the demand and supply curves in an individual market. It is thus necessary to build up from the foundations and *derive* aggregate demand and aggregate supply. In many textbooks this is left to a very late stage. Here we do this immediately, in Chapter 2. This chapter begins from the simple income–expenditure model which encapsulates the goods market; introduces the money market and the balance of payments and then turns to aggregate supply, building this up from assumptions about production and the labour market. The goods market is embodied in what is called the IS curve; the money market is embodied in what is called the LM curve; and the balance of payments is embodied in what is called the BP curve. These three markets together give rise to an aggregate demand curve, which relates the price level to real expenditure. From postulating an aggregate production function, relating factors of production to output of the economy, and making assumptions about the pricing behaviour of firms in the economy, an aggregate supply curve is derived which relates the price level to real income. In equilibrium, real expenditure must equal real income: aggregate demand must equal aggregate supply. Thus, aggregate demand along with aggregate supply appears to determine the economy's price level and real income.

But this is not quite correct. By explicitly building up the model in Chapter 2, incorporating all these sectors, a number of assumptions must be made about changes in certain variables. For instance, a change in the price level (inflation) has either to be assumed zero, or held constant. The same is true of a change in the exchange rate. In the period since 1970 both the price level and the exchange rate have moved considerably. Inflation has increased and exchange rates have become volatile (especially since generalized floating began in 1973). These create dynamic changes within the economy which just cannot be ignored. When Keynes wrote the *General Theory* the problem was unemployment with little or no inflation. For much of the post-War period (at least up to the early 1960s), inflation was not a problem. In addition, exchange rates were pegged to the dollar and fluctuated over ranges only small – except for the odd periods when a currency was devalued or revalued. Hence, a theory which assumed zero inflation and zero changes in the exchange rate was a reasonable approximation to reality. But post-1970 changed all that. Inflation soared and exchange rates became very volatile. It is not surprising, therefore, that a theory based on zero inflation and zero changes in the exchange rate was felt to be inadequate.

But accepting these changes in the real world, two choices are open to the theorist: either change the theory to take account of these differences; or abandon the theory and replace it with another. Neo-Keynesian and post-Keynesian economics attempted to adapt the theory, while monetarism and new classical economics attempted to replace it. But this gives the impression that monetarists accept nothing of Keynesian economics, and vice versa. This is not true. It is usually a matter of emphasis and, as mentioned above, assumptions about causation.

In laying out the model in Chapter 2 we have explicitly incorporated the inflation and exchange rate changes variables, but we hold them constant. The reason for doing this is so that the *dynamic* assumptions one makes for the use of aggregate demand and aggregate supply are clearly set out. Thus, we refer to the model of Chapter 2 as the 'Static Model'. In Chapter 3 we allow inflation and exchange rates to change. We also allow other changes to take place. The simplest way to view the situation is to suppose that the aggregate demand curve and the aggregate supply curve shift over time. There is, then, a *moving equilibrium*. In particular, the price level will have a certain rate of change over time – but this is no more than inflation. These changes in turn are embodied in two relationships: on the demand-side we refer to the demand-pressure curve and on the supply-side we refer to the short-run Phillips curve. The result of inflation and real income changes depends on the combined interactions of these two relationships. Thus, Chapter 3 attempts to set up a 'dynamic model' which determines the rate of inflation and real income. Of course, by determining the rate of inflation, then, given the price level in the preceding period, this is a theory of price determination in each subsequent time period. Time is essential to the analysis – which is why it is a dynamic model.

But both inflation and exchange rate changes are not straightforward. Decision-makers form expectations about price changes and about exchange rate changes; and it is these expectations which often enter the analysis. Keynes in the *General Theory* basically assumed that expectations were exogenous. However, the 1970s clearly illustrated that expectations were far from exogenous, and that it was necessary to model these and incorporate them into the analysis. This has led to a growth of literature on the theory of expectations, which is by far the most significant change in macroeconomics (for good or bad) since 1945. Once again we have dealt with this topic very early in the book, namely in Chapter 4, rather than leaving it until later.

What all this means is that Chapters 2–4 are essential reading, and lay the foundation on which all later chapters are based. They set up the static and dynamic models which are used throughout, and discuss the various types of expectations formation which are often considered in different macroeconomic theories.

1.3 THE OPEN ECONOMY

As the title of this book indicates, an essential emphasis is the open nature of the economy. The UK economy is a very open economy. To ignore this fact is to make much of the analysis, if not pointless, certainly irrelevant. For far too long, macroeconomics has been taught by beginning with the closed economy and then, very briefly, commenting on a few ideas about the situation if the economy were open. In some cases the economy 'never gets opened', while in other situations students go away with the impression that most propositions which are true for a closed economy hold for an open economy. Much worse is when economists make pronouncements about 'the real world' based on theories for a closed economy. If the real world economy were closed, then all well and good. But if it is an open economy, then the statement should not be made, or it should be established as true for an open economy, or it should be appropriately qualified for an open economy.

There is little doubt that incorporating the openness of an economy leads to more variables and more interrelationships which must be simultaneously considered. However, by doing this from the outset and maintaining the discussion in terms of openness throughout, then a much better feel for economic relationships in an open economy will be obtained than if it were simply 'tagged on to the end of a course'. Accordingly, in this book the economy is opened immediately in Chapter 2. Some dynamic features are considered in Chapter 3, while Chapter 5 sets out some major concepts which are essential when considering an open economy. Because these features are discussed so early in the book, it means that international aspects of macroeconomics can be referred to throughout the remainder of the text.

Having set up the model, discussed expectations, and opened up the economy, we next turn to two major topics: the government budget, in Chapter 6, and the demand and supply of money, in Chapter 7. These chapters lay down the basics of Keynesian analysis and the monetarist criticisms, besides elaborating on fundamental macroeconomic relationships. In the final chapter of Part I we discuss the theory of economic policy. This chapter sets out the underlying rationale for the chapters in Part II, which concentrate very much on economic policy.

1.4 ECONOMIC POLICY

Fiscal policy and monetary policy have dominated much of the discussion in the last 20 years. Keynesian economics stresses, to some extent, the importance of fiscal policy in achieving full employment. Monetarists, on the other hand, emphasize the inflationary nature of passive monetary policy, and argue for monetary policy as the main approach to stabilizing *nominal* income. But what is the role of fiscal policy in an economy? We attempt to answer this question in Chapter 9. But three other major policy questions are considered there too: first, the present government's Medium-term Financial Strategy; second, whether governments should follow fiscal rules (and if so of what type); and third, the problems associated with the growing size of the public sector. The chapter concludes with the problems of achieving fiscal aims in an open economy. UK monetary policy, discussed in Chapter 10, has gone through major changes – not least in terms of institutional changes. But the main emphasis here is on monetary targeting and money base control. The chapter also emphasizes the difficulties of achieving monetary policy in the UK's open economy and why the exchange rate cannot be ignored when considering monetary policy. The often neglected topic of exchange rate policy is developed in some detail in Chapter 11, which emphasizes aspects peculiar to the UK – such as North Sea oil and whether Britain should join the European Monetary System.

The following two chapters, one on inflation and one on stabilization, deal most specifically with the failings of Keynesian economics in the 1970s. Inflation has been a major issue facing Western economies (and, even more so, Third World countries). In attempting to solve this problem it became essential to determine its cause. This led to a major debate on the cause, or causes, of inflation. However, there are also costs involved in reducing inflation which certainly cannot be ignored. Only if the costs are worth bearing is it appropriate to reduce inflation. But once it is agreed that inflation is to be reduced, the obvious next question is the type of policy to implement in order to achieve this goal. All these topics are dealt with, along with the difficulty of reducing inflation in the open economy of the UK. One of the difficulties with inflation, however, is the ability to stabilize the economy. However, exactly what do we mean by stabilization? The monetarists' dissatisfaction with Keynesian demand management of the economy has led them to propose rules; these rules are discussed in Chapter 13, along with those suggested by modern classicists. Because much of the literature concerning rules has come from the USA, there has been a tendency to discuss such rules for a closed economy. But if such rules are going to be proposed for the UK, which they have been, then it is essential to see how they would be applied in an open economy. Thus, it is not sufficient to state a monetary rule without considering a fiscal rule *and* an exchange rate rule that is consistent with it.

Although inflation could be said to be 'the' major problem of the 1970s, unemployment can equally claim to be 'the' major problem of the 1980s. Like other policy questions, that of unemployment is riddled with confusion – not least how to define it! Because aggregate supply (and the economic rationale for the Phillips curve) was poorly developed in most macromodels, the nature of unemployment has not been thoroughly analysed. This is not surprising. In the hey-day of Keynesian economics most economies were in a relative boom period and unemployment was not an issue. There followed a period of high inflation, which became the major issue to resolve. Only later, when *both* inflation and unemployment became prominent (stagflation), did macroeconomists turn their attention to unemployment. However, as Chapter 14 will illustrate, the analysis of unemployment is quite inadequate at the present time. One possible reason for this inadequacy is that a *macroeconomic* approach may not be the way forward. It may be that this issue can only be solved at the *microeconomic* level. This would, therefore, suggest policies towards industry. Thus, in Chapter 15 we have introduced a short chapter on industrial policy. Although it is unusual to include such a chapter in a macroeconomics textbook, the emphasis here is on fostering competition, the role of government in industry, privatization and the supply-side of the economy. In simple terms, this means shifting either the aggregate supply curve or the short-run Phillips curve (or both), to the right.

1.5 UK PROBLEMS

The final part of the book considers three particular problems which have faced the UK. Although not particular to the UK, they certainly have occupied the attention of policy-makers for much of the post-War period. Chapter 16 considers shocks. The analysis of shocks to an economy is fairly recent in the subject of macroeconomics. It is not, of course, unrelated to the fact that the 1970s was a very turbulent period for the world economy. But shocks can either be internally or externally generated. Do policy-makers approach these two types of shocks in the same way? Does it matter whether the shock is on the demand-side or the supply-side? Should shocks be accommodated or not? Do shocks have different impacts under a fixed exchange rate than under a flexible exchange rate regime? These are just some of the questions we attempt to answer.

In Chapter 17 we turn to the declining competitiveness of the UK economy. The UK economy has for many years been a very open economy. As such, it has become very dependent on international trade. If it suffers a decline in its competitive position, this inevitably means a decline in its welfare. But why has the UK suffered a decline in its competitive position? In trying to answer this question the issue broadens out into the question of deindustrialization, which requires a much longer time horizon for analysis. The same is also true of the final topic – namely, economic growth. Growth is generally considered to be a 'good thing', but it is necessary to discuss why. And once it is accepted as a 'good thing', it is then necessary to determine the sources of economic growth. To some extent this will explain why growth has slowed down and also how it can be increased. Some of the topics covered in Chapter 18 indicate the inadequate analysis of aggregate supply (which we referred to in relation to unemployment) – such as technical progress and the constraints on growth. But in the final analysis, should growth be an objective of macroeconomic policy?

1.6 THE USE OF APPENDICES

The present book contains a fair number of appendices, which are listed in the Contents, at the end of each chapter. Originally it was intended that the appendices should be contained in boxes incorporated in the text. However, some are quite long and would break up the text too much, albeit that the text was written so that it could be read without breaking off to read the boxes. On the other hand, the boxes do require some knowledge of the chapter contents. It was thus finally decided that the material should be contained in appendices and placed at the end of each chapter.

These appendices serve different functions. These are:

(a) to expand on a particular equation of importance;
(b) to elaborate on a particular point mentioned in the text;
(c) to illustrate points in the text by means of an example (usually a numerical example);
(d) to provide some factual detail about the UK economy; or
(e) to discuss a particular UK institution.

The fact that the appendices require knowledge of the text means that the text should, in general, be read before the appendices. Even so, the appendices themselves are quite self-contained – although occasionally one appendix will refer back to an earlier one (especially in the case of numerical examples).

1.7 PERCENTAGES AND HAT NOTATION

Throughout this book, we shall be using a 'hat' notation to denote a percentage change. A percentage change in the variable z, for example, can be written in many forms. In this book we shall denote the percentage change in the variable z, by $\hat{z}$, i.e.,

$$\text{Percentage change in } z \equiv \hat{z}$$

In Appendix 1.1, some useful properties of percentages are pursued.

APPENDIX 1.1 USEFUL PROPERTIES OF PERCENTAGES

Consider a variable z related to two other variables, x and y. Suppose we have the following product:

$$z = xy \tag{A1.1.1}$$

Then, taking natural logarithms, i.e. to base e, and denoted Ln, we have

$$\text{Ln } z = \text{Ln } x + \text{Ln } y \tag{A1.1.2}$$

Differentiating with respect to time, t, we have

$$d(\text{Ln } z)/dt = d(\text{Ln } x)/dt + d(\text{Ln } y)/dt \tag{A1.1.3}$$

However,

$$d(\text{Ln } z) = dz/z, \quad d(\text{Ln } y) = dx/x, \quad d(\text{Ln } y) = dy/y$$

Hence,

$$(dz/dt)(1/z) = (dy/dt)(1/x) + (dy/dt)(1/y) \tag{A1.1.4}$$

But each of these terms denotes the percentage change in the variable concerned over the time interval dt. In other words, $(dz/dt)(1/z)$ denotes the percentage change in the variable z over the time interval dt. Similarly for x and y. Defining

$$\hat{z} \equiv (dz/dt)(1/z)$$

and similarly for $\hat{x}$ and $\hat{y}$, we have the result that

$$\hat{z} = \hat{x} + \hat{y} \tag{A1.1.5}$$

If we have the relationship

$$u = x/y \tag{A1.1.6}$$

then, developing the analysis in a similar fashion, we get

$$\hat{u} = \hat{x} - \hat{y} \tag{A1.1.7}$$

If we have the relationship

$$y = a + bx \tag{A1.1.8}$$

then

$$\text{Ln } y = \text{Ln}(a + bx)$$

Totally differentiating,

$$d\,\text{Ln } y = d\,\text{Ln}(a + bx)$$

Hence,

$$dy/y = [1/(a + bx)] \cdot b \cdot dx = bx\,(dx/x)\,[1/(a + bx)] \tag{A1.1.9}$$

giving the result

$$\hat{y} = [bx/(a + bx)]\hat{x} \tag{A1.1.10}$$

We can summarize the important relationships in the following way:

1. If $z = xy$, then

   $\hat{z} = \hat{x} + \hat{y}$

2. If $u = x/y$, then

   $\hat{u} = \hat{x} - \hat{y}$

3. If $v = bx$, where b is a constant, then

   $\hat{v} = \hat{x}$

4. If $y = a + bx$, then

   $\hat{y} = [bx/(a + bx)]\hat{x}$

Chapter 2

THE STATIC MODEL

2.1 INTRODUCTION

One of the difficulties in analysing policy issues is that many interrelated factors must be analysed simultaneously. In the past ten years or so this way largely done in terms of an IS–LM–BP framework. But this model, in its simple version, assumes that prices are, constant. This is readily shown by examining how these relationships determine aggregate demand, which in turn relates prices to real income. Real income is determined only for a *given* level of prices. In this chapter we will construct an aggregate demand curve and aggregate supply curve, which together determine the price level and the level of real income. In so doing we will indicate how all the variables are related to each other and in what way the expected values of certain variables enter the analysis. For the static model discussed in this chapter, the magnitudes of these expected variables are assumed given from outside the system.

But even this model is incomplete. We will see that a number of relationships involve actual inflation, expected inflation, changes in productivity and expected changes in the exchange rate. The point is that these factors give rise to dynamic forces in the economy which lead to shifts in the various curves. Unless all these dynamic forces are absent, then we cannot establish the level of income. Put simply, dynamic forces will shift aggregate demand and/or aggregate supply. To complete the model we would need to model these dynamic forces, but we will not do this until the next chapter. There it is demonstrated that we can determine inflation and the level of income.

Although these two chapters portray the bare bones of the complete model, the remainder of the book will supply flesh to this skeleton. This procedure is useful because we can then concentrate on the macroeconomic issues which typify an open economy.

The main argument will be presented diagrammatically, while Appendix 2.1 will supply a mathematical specification. Occasionally, we draw on some results derived in Appendix 2.1 – especially when referring to the dynamic specification. The non-mathematical reader will be able to follow the argument if such statements are simply accepted.

2.2 THE IS–LM–BP MODEL

The IS–LM–BP model refers to the specification of three sectors of the economy:

(a) the goods market (the IS curve);

(b) the money market (the LM curve); and
(c) the trade sector (the BP curve).

Throughout, we will be concerned with variables in real terms. Thus real income, denoted y, is nominal income, Y, deflated by the price level, P, i.e.

$$y \equiv Y/P \qquad (2.1)$$

It is important to be clear from the outset whether variables are expressed in nominal or in real terms. As a guide, we will use lower case letters for variables in real terms and upper case letters for variables in nominal terms (with the exception of the interest rate and the exchange rate).

The goods market, which is at the heart of Keynesian economics, denotes the expenditure on goods and services. Total expenditure in real terms is the sum of real consumption expenditure (c), real investment expenditure (i) and real government expenditure (go). However, this refers to expenditure on goods and services regardless of whether they are produced at home or abroad. Although imports constitute part of home demand, such goods are not produced by domestic residents. Similarly for exports, which, although produced at home, are in fact consumed abroad. To arrive at domestic expenditure in real terms we must add the real value of exports (x) and subtract the real value of imports (im) – or, alternatively, add real net exports, $nx \equiv x - im$. Hence, real expenditure is given by:

$$e \equiv c + i + go + nx \qquad (2.2)$$

At the moment this is an identity. But now we must introduce some behavioural assumptions. We assume that real consumption is related to real disposable income (y_d). This gives the very simple consumption function of the form:[1]

$$c = a + by_d \qquad 0 < b < 1 \qquad (2.3)$$

If t denotes real taxes, and assuming taxes are a linear function of real income, i.e.

$$t = t_0 + t_1 y \qquad 0 < t_1 < 1 \qquad (2.4)$$

then we can re-write equation (2.3) in the form:

$$c = a - bt_0 + b(1 - t_1)y \qquad (2.5)$$

A more detailed discussion of the consumption function is provided in Appendix 2.2.

Real investment is assumed to be related to the *expected real rate of interest*, $(r - \hat{P}^e)$, i.e. the nominal interest rate, r, less the expected rate of inflation, $\hat{P}^e$. As the expected real rate of interest rises so the level of investment falls. Hence,

$$i = i_0 - h(r - \hat{P}^e) \qquad h > 0 \qquad (2.6)$$

A more detailed discussion of the investment function is supplied in Appendix 2.3.

Real government spending is assumed to be exogenous.

The trade account is less straightforward but is worth discussing from the outset. Consider, first, home imports. Real imports are assumed to rise with the level of real income. But equally important is the fact that imports will also rise if domestic prices rise relative to those abroad. Let the domestic price level be represented by P and the foreign price level in overseas currency by P^*. The foreign price level expressed in overseas currency can be converted to *domestic* currency by using the exchange rate, S. We define S in *indirect* terms (see Appendix 5.1) to be the number of foreign currency units per unit of domestic currency. If we are considering the United Kingdom (UK) as the home country and the United States (US) as the foreign country, then P^* is the foreign price in dollars while P^*/S is the price in sterling. The prices of domestically produced goods and services relative to the prices of foreign-produced goods and services is given by

$$R \equiv P/(P^*/S) = SP/P^* \tag{2.7}$$

The value of R is a measure of the competitiveness of home-produced goods and services relative to those abroad. The lower the value of R, the more competitive is the home country on world markets; the higher the value of R, the less competitive is the home country on world markets. (We will return to competitiveness in more detail in Chapter 17.) We can thus write the import function as

$$im = im_0 + my + gR \qquad 0 < m < 1, \quad g > 0 \tag{2.8}$$

We will assume that exports are related to an autonomous element, x_0 (which rises when income levels abroad rise) and to relative prices. When relative prices, R, rise, UK exports become less competitive and so decline. Hence,

$$x = x_0 - fR \qquad f > 0 \tag{2.9}$$

Subtracting equation (2.8) from equation (2.9) we obtain the following expression for real net exports ($nx = x - im$):

$$nx = (x_0 - im_0) - my - (f+g)R$$
$$= nx_0 - my - (f+g)R \tag{2.10}$$

where nx_0 denotes autonomous net exports, $(x_0 - im_0)$. We will refer back to equations (2.10) frequently. Notice that real net exports rise for a rise in autonomous exports, for a fall in income at home and for an improvement in the home country's competitive position (a fall in R).

This completes the set of behavioural assumptions for the goods market. All we require now is to state the condition for equilibrium in this market. This is where the level of real income is *equal* to the level of real expenditure, i.e. where $y = e$. If we substitute all the behavioural assumptions into the equilibrium condition, then we obtain the following expression for real income:

EQUIL B.
$Y = E$.
$$y = \frac{[a - bt_0 + i_0 + h\hat{P}^e + go + x_0 - im_0 - (f+g)R] - hr}{1 - b(1 - t_1) + m} \tag{2.11}$$

By combining all autonomous elements into one, i.e. define

$$z_0 \equiv a - bt_0 + i_0 + go + x_0 - im_0 \tag{2.12}$$

then we can re-write expression (2.11) in the form

$$y = \frac{z_0 + h\hat{P}^e - (f+g)R - hr}{1 - b(1 - t_1) + m} \tag{2.13}$$

One graph of equation (2.13), called the IS curve,[2] is the relationship between real income, y, and the nominal interest rate, r, and is illustrated in Fig. 2.1.[3] We note that it has a

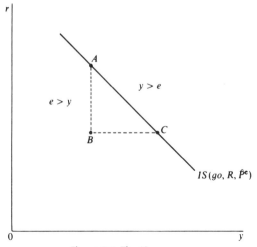

Figure 2.1 The IS curve.

negative slope, and it indicates, for a given level of expected inflation, what the level of income must be at each level of the *nominal interest rate* in order that equilibrium can be attained in the goods market. Consider any point on the curve, such as point A, which satisfies the condition that real expenditure equals real income. Now consider point B at a lower level of nominal interest rate, but the same level of real income as at point A. If the expected rate of inflation, $\hat{P}^e$, remains constant, then the lower nominal interest rate, r, means a lower expected real interest rate, $(r - \hat{P}^e)$. This will mean a rise in investment. This higher level of investment expenditure means that overall expenditure is greater than real income. However, the rise in investment will, through the multiplier effect,[4] raise the level of income until expenditure once again equals the level of income – as shown by point C. Hence, there is an inverse relationship between real income and the nominal interest rate such that equilibrium occurs in the goods market.

It should be clear that positions to the right of the IS curve denote situations where real income exceeds real expenditure. This follows from the fact that when real income remains constant, but the nominal interest rate increases, real expenditure declines (because investment is less at the higher rate of interest) and is less than real income.

What is important from equation (2.11) is that the IS curve is drawn relating real income to the nominal interest rate, and that it can only be drawn for a given expected rate of inflation and a given level of relative prices. Even if the expected rate of inflation were zero, we still must know relative prices, R. Relative prices are given (i.e. exogenous) if prices in both the home and foreign countries are given and if the exchange rate is given.

Equilibrium in the money market is obtained by equating the demand for real money balances with the supply of real money balances. The demand for real money balances, M_d/P, is positively related to real income and inversely related to the nominal interest rate – see equation (2.14) below. A more detailed analysis of the demand for money function is given in Chapter 7.

The real money supply, M_s/P, is equal to an exogenously given level of nominal balances, M_0, deflated by the price level – see equation (2.15) below.[5] Thus

$$M_d/P = ky - ur \qquad (2.14)$$

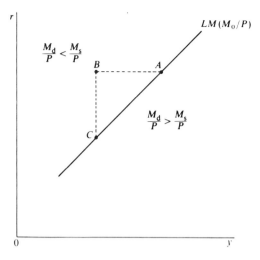

Figure 2.2 The LM curve.

where k and u are positive constants.

$$M_s/P = M_0/P \qquad (2.15)$$

Equating (2.14) and (2.15) we obtain the equilibrium result

$$r = -(M_0/uP) + (k/u)y \qquad (2.16)$$

Result (2.16) denotes a positive relationship between the nominal interest rate and real income. The graph relating the nominal interest rate, r, to real income, y, as specified by equation (2.16), is referred to as the LM curve, and is drawn in Fig. 2.2.[6] Consider point A on this curve. Now consider point B which is at the same interest rate, but a level of income which is lower than at point A. Since income is lower, then the demand for real balances must be less than the supply of real balances. In other words, to the left of the LM curve we have excess supply of real money balances. To restore equilibrium in the money market, interest rates must be lower in order to attract balances from interest bearing assets and into money, which is shown by point C. It is clear that there is an excess demand for money balances to the right of the LM curve.

It is important to note for our later analysis that the slope of the LM curve is given by k/u, and that the curve is drawn for a given level of *real* money balances. Since nominal money balances are assumed given (i.e. exogenous), this implies that real money balances are given only if the price level is known.[7]

Can we combine the IS curve and the LM curve and say that real income and nominal interest rates are determined by their intersection? The answer is, maybe! To see why this is so we must consider the balance of payments curve, the BP curve. This curve denotes equilibrium in the trade sector. We have already considered real net exports, nx. But the trade sector is not merely real net exports. The balance of payments in real terms, denoted bp, also includes the net *inflow* of capital, which we shall denote by cf (for net capital flow). Thus, in real terms we have

$$bp = nx + cf \qquad (2.17)$$

Let us state a simple expression for cf and then explain it. We make the behavioural assumption that

$$cf = cf_0 + v(r - r^* + \hat{S}^e) \qquad v > 0 \qquad (2.18)$$

where v is a constant and denotes the responsiveness of capital flows to changes in interest rates. The first term on the right-hand side of (2.18), cf_0, simply denotes an autonomous element. Since we are dealing with net capital flows, what matters is the interest rate differential, $r - r^*$, where r is the domestic nominal interest rate and r^* the nominal rate abroad.[8] A rise in the nominal interest rate at home relative to that abroad will mean an increase in the net capital inflow. Hence, v is positive. But simply taking $r - r^*$ does not take account of the cost of exchange risk. Suppose $r = 8\%$ and $r^* = 10\%$ (i.e. $r = 0.08$ and $r^* = 0.1$). This would imply a net outflow. But suppose the exchange rate is presently £1 $= \$2$. Suppose, further, that an individual expects sterling to appreciate by 5% (the dollar to depreciate by 5%). If he invested £1 abroad he would receive a return of 10% at the end of the period but would lose 5 percentage points of this as a result of the appreciation.[9] What he in fact requires is that the rate at home, r, exceeds the rate abroad *plus* the expected change in the exchange rate, where $\hat{S}^e$ in equation (2.18) denotes the expected percentage change in the exchange rate.

The balance of payments in real terms is therefore given by

$$bp = nx + cf$$
$$= (x_0 - im_0) - my - (f + g)R + cf_0 + v(r - r^* + \hat{S}^e) \qquad (2.19)$$

i.e.

$$bp = bp_0 - my - (f + g)R + vr - v(r^* - \hat{S}^e) \qquad (2.20)$$

where,

$$bp_0 = (x_0 - im_0) + cf_0 \qquad (2.21)$$

For equilibrium in the trade sector, we require that the balance of payments in real terms is zero. Setting $bp = 0$, we obtain

$$r = [-bp_0 + (f + g)R]/v + (m/v)y + (r^* - \hat{S}^e) \qquad (2.22)$$

From equation (2.22) we see that the slope of the BP curve is (m/v), which is positive. The curve is shown in Fig. 2.3. Again consider a point on the curve, point A. Now consider point B at the same level of nominal interest but a level of income which is higher than that at point A. At the higher level of real income net exports, nx will worsen because the level of imports will be higher at point B than at point A. Since the interest rate is still the same, there will be no change in the net capital flow position. Hence, the balance of payments will go into deficit. Equilibrium can be re-established by the rate of interest rising. This will not affect the net export position but will raise the level of net capital inflow. Hence, to the right of the BP curve, we have a situation of a deficit on the balance of payments; and to the left of the BP curve a situation of a surplus on the balance of payments.

The more responsive the net capital inflow is to the interest rate, i.e. the higher is the value of v, the less steep is the BP curve. In the extreme case of perfect capital mobility, v is infinite and the BP line is horizontal at $r = r^* - \hat{S}^e$. It is clear from equation (2.22) that the position of the BP curve is fixed only for a given level of interest rate abroad, r^*; a given relative price, R; and a given expected rate of change in the exchange rate, $\hat{S}^e$. In particular, the relative price, R, is given only where prices are given and the spot exchange rate, S, is given.

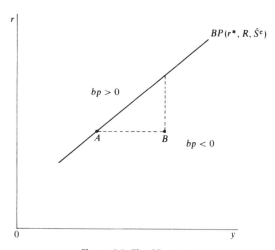

Figure 2.3 The BP curve.

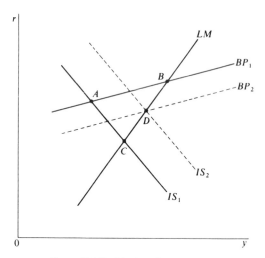

Figure 2.4 Positioning the economy.

We are now in a position to put all three curves on the one diagram, as shown in Fig. 2.4. Notice in particular that we have assumed that the price levels are constant in both countries; the exchange rate is constant; and, for the moment, we have assumed that $\hat{P}^e = \hat{S}^e = 0$. Given these additional assumptions, each curve is fixed. Now there is no reason for all three curves to intersect at the same r–y combination, and as drawn they do not do so. But which intersection prevails? Position A denotes the intersection between the BP curve and the IS curve. But point A denotes an excess supply of real money balances. Interest rates, being endogenous, will accordingly fall to establish equilibrium in the money market. In other words, the economy will gravitate towards point C. Point B cannot prevail either, because this denotes excess supply for goods, which will give rise to inventory accumulation unless interest rates fall and income falls. Point C *can* prevail because although the money market and the goods market clear, the balance of payments is in deficit. There is a net capital outflow. But where in the system is this money coming from? It is here that the model is incomplete. It must be assumed that the government has an accumulation of foreign exchange reserves which it is using to pay for the deficit. Of course, this situation can only be temporary because if it is repeated period after period, then the foreign exchange reserves will run out. We will return to this problem later.

We also show one other point in Fig. 2.4: from equation (2.11) (p. 14) we see that a devaluation of the exchange rate, a fall in S and hence a fall in R, shifts the IS curve to the right. This is because a devaluation leads to an improvement in the relative price position of the home country and hence to an improvement in net exports.[10] The new curve is given by IS_2. Furthermore, the BP curve moves down (i.e. to the right) for the same devaluation. This is because the improved net export position must be offset by a decline in the net capital inflow. This can only occur with a fall in the domestic interest rate. Since, in this model, the LM curve is independent of the exchange rate and nominal money balances are held constant, there is no reason for this curve to move. With a suitable exchange rate the curves IS_2 and BP_2 intersect the LM curve at point D – indicating that equilibrium is occurring in all markets simultaneously.

The model outlined so far is for a fixed exchange rate (S fixed), but it is readily adapted for a situation where the exchange rate is freely floating. We have already made the point that equilibrium on the balance of payments requires the sum of net exports and net capital inflows to be zero. Under a freely floating exchange rate, S will change continuously to establish this equilibrium result. In this sense, under a freely floating exchange rate the economy is always on the BP curve. In other words, the BP curve will always shift (due to a change in S) to bring about balance of payments equilibrium. To illustrate the point, consider Fig. 2.4, again with IS_1, LM and BP_1. In this situation there is deficit on the balance of payments. As we will explain more fully in Chapter 5, this will lead to a depreciation of the exchange rate. The result of this (just like a devaluation) is to shift the IS curve to the right and the BP curve down (to the right). When floating, therefore, the exchange rate will continue to float until a point such as point D is established.

2.3 THE MONETARIST–KEYNESIAN CONTROVERSY: EARLY VERSION

The IS–LM–BP model (or, as we will see, 'partial' model) was the basis of much controversy between monetarists and Keynesians. The crux of the debate was whether fiscal policy was more potent than monetary policy. Although we will take up policy issues in Part II, it is worth commenting on the formal aspects of the controversy. (Here the reader should sketch the cases being outlined for himself or herself.)

In the first instance, we need to know what is meant by 'being more potent'. What is usually meant by this term is: the policy which has the greatest impact on real income – monetary policy or fiscal policy? If the LM curve is fairly flat, then fiscal policy will raise the interest rate only a little but will have a substantial impact on income. In the extreme case where the LM curve is horizontal, there will be a full Keynesian multiplier impact on income. In Appendix 2.1 we derive the income multiplier with respect to a change in autonomous expenditure for a constant rate of interest, denoted k_{rc}; this is the full

Table 2.1 Relative slopes in the IS–LM–BP model

(a) Slopes of the IS and LM curves

	IS Vertical	IS Negative	IS Horizontal
LM vertical (classical)	$u = 0$ $h = 0$	$u = 0$ $0 < h < \infty$	$u = 0$ $h = \infty$ ◄――monetarist――► extreme classical
LM positive	$0 < u < \infty$ $h = 0$	$0 < u < \infty$ $0 < h < \infty$	$0 < u < \infty$ $h = \infty$
LM horizontal (liquidity trap)	$u = \infty$ $h = 0$ ◄―― Keynesian――► extreme Keynesian	$u = \infty$ $0 < h < \infty$	$u = \infty$ $h = \infty$

(b) Slope of the BP curve

Parameter value	BP curve	Type of capital mobility
$v = 0$	Vertical	No capital mobility
$0 < v < \infty$	Positively sloped	Some capital mobility
$v = \infty$	Horizontal	Perfect capital mobility

Keynesian multiplier just referred to and is given by

$$k_{\text{re}} = 1/[1 - b(1 - t_1) + m] \tag{2.23}$$

On the other hand, monetary policy – which shifts the LM curve – will have relatively little impact on income. If, however, the LM curve were vertical, then fiscal policy would have no impact on income, while monetary policy would have a significant impact on income.

Of course, the shape of the IS curve is not unimportant in establishing the impact on real income. Even if the LM curve were positively sloped, monetary policy would have no effect on real income if the IS curve were vertical: monetary policy would be impotent.

The relative impact of monetary and fiscal policy on real income thus seems to reduce itself down to establishing the relative slopes of the IS and LM curves. *This is a purely empirical issue.* However, it is quite clear from the equations we have presented, that the interest rate sensitivity of the investment function is crucial for the slope of the IS curve. If investment is not related to the real rate of interest ($h = 0$), then the IS curve is vertical and monetary policy is impotent. If the demand for money is independent of the rate of interest ($u = 0$), then the LM curve is vertical and fiscal policy is impotent. In general, we have some interest sensitivity for investment and the demand for money. Some extreme cases for the IS curve, the LM curve and the BP curve are outlined in Table 2.1.

Although it would appear that the controversy is about relative slopes, this would be to present the debate in too simplistic a fashion. Policy questions are very much about predictability – because through predictability there can be control. It is very difficult to control a variable if its level cannot be predicted. For prediction, however, *stable relationships* are necessary. The heart of the Keynesian system is the consumption function – one form of which we provide in equation (2.5), and more complex forms in Appendix 2.2. The consumption function was considered to be a stable relationship. The essence of the stability question is seen when we turn to the multiplier effects of a change in autonomous expenditure – such as government spending, go. The mathematics are provided in the appendices to this chapter; what matters here is that the multiplier is given by equation (2.23) above. The impact on income of a change in government spending is, therefore, $k_{rc} dgo$ (i.e., $dy = k_{rc} dgo$). This change in real income is predictable only if k_{rc} is a constant – and k_{rc} will be constant only if the parameters b, t_1 and m are constant.

Much of the analysis concerning the consumption function, outlined in Appendix 2.2, was to demonstrate that the marginal propensity to consume, b, was not constant. Even if we assume that the marginal rate of tax, t_1, is a constant – and is certainly within the control of government – then there is still the question of the stability of the marginal propensity to import, m. Monetarists have argued that the consumption function is unstable (b is variable). It is also the case that the more open an economy, such as the UK, the more likely the import function will also be unstable (m is variable). If either of these situations is the case, then the expenditure function will be unstable and predicting income changes using such multiplier formulas becomes hazardous.

But can monetarists fair any better? Monetarists contend that it is the demand for money function which is stable. If this is the situation, then, for a given interest rate, it is possible to predict the level of real income. But is the demand for money function relatively stable? We take up this issue in Chapter 7, particularly in Appendix 7.2. It does appear, however, that we are reduced to an empirical question once again: which is more unstable, the expenditure function or the demand for money function? It is not even clear how such a comparison can be made. These relationships are embedded within a system of equations; and it is impossible to consider one equation in isolation from the remainder.

In much of this early discussion of macroeconomics, the price level, P, was assumed constant, i.e. exogenous. However, it is clear that one source of instability in the economy arises from a variable price level. But the IS–LM–BP model is insufficient to determine the price level. We thus require a model which treats the price level as endogenous; and we discuss this in the remainder of this chapter.

We conclude the present section, however, with a numerical example which is set out in Appendix 2.4. Of particular note are (1) the diagrammatic representation of the two multipliers (k_{rc} and k_{rv} for constant and variable interest rate respectively) and (2) the result of a devaluation to establish all-round equilibrium.

2.4 AGGREGATE DEMAND

So far we have held the domestic price level constant. What happens to real income when the price level changes? To answer this question we note that the equilibrium condition in the goods market – given by equation (2.11), p. 14 – *is* related to the price level in so far as net exports are related to the competitive position of the economy, captured in the term $R = SP/P^*$. If we assume that the exchange rate is held constant and that prices abroad are held constant, then a rise in domestic prices raises R, leading to a decline in the domestic economy's competitive position, and hence to a shift left in the IS curve. In addition, the LM

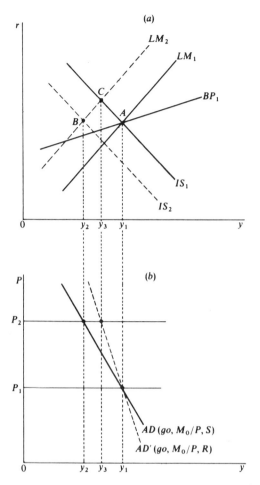

Figure 2.5 Derivation of aggregate demand.

curve is related to real money balances, M_0/P. When there is a rise in the price level, therefore, there is a decline in real money balances, and so the LM curve shifts to the left.

Since we are assuming a fixed exchange rate, although a rise in domestic prices also shifts the BP curve upwards, this is not relevant to establishing the level of income for a rise in prices. Why? Because we showed earlier that under a fixed exchange rate, the economy will gravitate to the position where the IS curve intersects the LM curve. We need only consider the new positions of the IS curve and the LM curve. (All the shift in the BP curve does is to change the balance of payments position.) This we have done in Fig. 2.5(a). We begin with all markets in equilibrium, as shown by point A. The rise in prices shifts IS_1 to IS_2 and also LM_1 to LM_2. The economy accordingly moves to position B where IS_2 intersects LM_2. In Fig. 2.5(b), we plot the various combinations of prices and income which are consistent with all this information. Thus at price level P_1, real income is y_1; while at price level P_2, real income is y_2.

The curve joining all such combinations is called the aggregate demand curve, denoted by AD. This curve denotes the P–y combinations which establish equilibrium in both the goods market and the money market. As can be seen from Fig. 2.5, this curve is downward sloping. It is important to note which variables have been held constant in constructing the *AD* curve. Specifically, real government spending is constant (because nominal government spending will rise by the same amount as a rise in the price level; and, similarly, it will decline for a fall in the price level). Since nominal money balances are assumed constant at M_0, then real money balances, M_0/P, fall for a rise in prices, and rise for a fall in prices. *This denotes a movement along the aggregate demand curve.* A change in nominal money balances, however, will shift the AD curve. Finally, we are assuming that the exchange rate, S, is held constant. This is important. A domestic price level which is variable but an exchange rate which is constant (with prices abroad also constant) implies a change in the relative price, R.

Figure 2.5 also shows the situation under a floating exchange rate system. We will deal with this more fully later, but for the present suppose the exchange rate, S, depreciates by the same percentage as the domestic price level, P, rises. This will leave the relative price ratio, R, unaltered. Hence, for a rise in domestic prices from P_1 to P_2 (Fig. 2.5), with R constant, the IS curve does *not* move, while the LM curve moves once again to LM_2. The economy accordingly moves to position C which denotes a higher level of income than that at position B for the same price change. We therefore have two aggregate demand curves: one for a fixed exchange rate and one for a fixed relative price (i.e. freely floating exchange rate):

1. $AD = AD(go, M_0/P, S)$ (2.24)
2. $AD' = AD'(go, M_0/P, R)$ (2.25)

AD is less steep than *AD'*, although both aggregate demand curves are downward sloping. Using the data in Appendix 2.4 we can obtain the following equations for aggregate demand (where $\hat{P}^e$ is set at zero):

1. $y = 34.5 + 7.2(1/P) - 4.2P$ for AD $S = 1, P^* = 1$
2. $y = 30.3 + 7.2(1/P)$ for AD' $R = 1$

It is not difficult to establish that an expansionary (contractionary) fiscal policy – that is to say, a rise (fall) in *go* – shifts the aggregate demand curve to the right (left); and that an expansion (contractionary) monetary policy – that is to say, a rise (fall) in nominal money balances – also shifts the aggregate demand curve to the right (left).

There is one final observation to make about aggregate demand which is relevant for later discussion: since the IS curve is drawn for a given expected rate of inflation, $\hat{P}^e$, then it follows that the aggregate demand curve must also be constructed for the same given expected rate of inflation. This is shown explicitly in Appendix 2.1. But we can capture the essence of the arguments by postulating a simple aggregate demand curve of the form

$$y = A_0 + A_1(1/P) + A_2\hat{P}^e - A_3R \qquad (2.26)$$

where A_0, A_1, A_2 and A_3 are positive parameters. For example,

$$y = 34.5 + 7.2(1/P) + 1.2\hat{P}^e - 4.2R \qquad (2.26')$$

which is derived from data in Appendix 2.4.

To see why A_2 is positive, consider a rise in the expected rate of inflation. In this situation investors would be expecting a fall in the real rate of interest. (Although the rise in expectations will raise the nominal interest rate – since it will lead to a shift to the right in the

IS curve – the rise in price expectations will be greater than the rise in the nominal interest rate so long as the LM curve is not vertical.) The rise in the real rate of interest will, in turn, entice firms to undertake more investment which, through the multiplier, will raise the level of income. Hence, there is a positive relation between $\hat{P}^e$ and y. Put another way: we do not know the level of investment until we know the expected rate of inflation, and we cannot know the level of income without knowing the level of investment! In this version of the model, therefore, we must assume that the expected rate of inflation is determined outside the model, i.e. it is exogenous.

Now that we have constructed the aggregate demand curve it should be clear why we cannot determine the level of income by means of the IS–LM–BP model. The level of income depends on what the price level is, as shown by the aggregate demand curve (either equation (2.24) or (2.25)). But it is clear from the analysis so far that we have two problems. First, aggregate demand on its own is not sufficient to determine the price level and the level of real income. Second, there are dynamic elements present – such as the expected rate of inflation and the expected change in the exchange rate – which will influence the economy over time. We deal with these dynamic elements in the next chapter. For the moment, we will assume all expected variables are exogenous. In the remainder of this chapter, we will provide a major missing element in the story to determine prices and income in a static model. Specifically, we will consider aggregate supply.

2.5 CLASSICAL AGGREGATE SUPPLY

Aggregate supply is less straightforward, but is worth discussing in some detail because many of the controversies and issues which occur in macroeconomics at the present time depend very much on such an understanding. How can we know how trades unions affect the rate of employment, and hence output, unless we include this in our model? Will a reduction in the marginal rate of tax lead to an incentive to raise the number of man-hours worked and hence to a rise in the level of output? Will a depreciation simply raise raw material prices and lead to inflation? Will changing expectations simply negate any influence the government may have in attempting to manage aggregate demand? These are just some of the problems we must deal with later in the book. For the moment, we will concentrate solely on constructing the aggregate supply curve and establish reasonably explicitly what it depends upon.

It is clear that real income, or output, must refer to the real value of goods and services produced in the economy. Such a supply of goods and services must be related to the employment of labour and capital and, also, to management. We can approach the issue by first considering the individual firm, which gives rise to the demand for labour. It is readily shown that the labour input consistent with the profit maximizing position for a firm is that level of labour input where the marginal cost of labour is equal to the marginal revenue product of labour.[11] With imperfections in both the labour market and the market for the product this can be expressed as

$$W[1 + (1/\phi)] = P[1 + (1/\eta)]MPP_L \tag{2.27}$$

where ϕ is the elasticity of labour supply and η is the elasticity of product demand. (With perfect competition in both labour and product market, we have the result that the money wage is equal to $P \times MPP_L$, i.e. the money wage is equal to the value of the marginal product of labour.)

Let us now suppose, along with the neoclassical economists, that we have an aggregate production function for the economy as a whole, given by

$$y = y(L, K) \qquad (2.28)$$

where $y \equiv Y/P$.

If we are dealing with the short run – that is to say, the time period over which the capital stock is constant – then $K = \bar{K}$ and we have simply that real income (output) is a function of labour:

$$y = f(L) \qquad (2.29)$$

If we make the further simplifying assumption that the marginal physical product of labour is proportional to the average physical product of labour,[12] i.e.

$$MPP_L = \alpha APP_L \qquad (2.30)$$

and we define

$$a_L \equiv y/L \qquad (2.31)$$

to denote labour productivity (i.e. the average product of labour) then

$$W = \mu a_L P \qquad (2.32)$$

where

$$\mu \equiv \alpha[1 + (1/\eta)]/[(1 + 1/\phi)] \qquad (2.33)$$

This means that the real wage, $w \equiv W/P$, is given by

$$w \equiv W/P = \mu a_L \qquad (2.34)$$

which is the economy's demand curve for labour.

The supply curve of labour arises from an individual's choice between income and leisure.[13] In the absence of taxes, the real wage denotes the individual's opportunity cost of foregoing leisure. Thus the individual will supply more hours, h, the greater the real wage,

$$h = h(w) \qquad (2.35)$$

In the aggregate we have

$$L_s = H(w) \qquad (2.36)$$

where L_s denotes the labour supply in terms of man-hours for the economy as a whole. This denotes, for a given wage, how many man-hours will be supplied by workers in the economy. So long as the economy's supply curve of labour is not backward-bending, we can express the real wage in terms of labour input, i.e.

$$w = H_{\bullet}^{-1}(L) = g(L) \qquad (2.37)$$

In other words, for a given supply of man-hours, this is the minimum wage that workers would accept. Hence, equation (2.37) denotes the aggregate supply curve of labour.

To summarize, the demand and supply of labour relating the *real wage* to labour is determined by the intersection of the two curves:

$$D_L: \quad w = \mu a_L \tag{2.38}$$

$$S_L: \quad w = g(L) \tag{2.39}$$

In this version of the model (the classical version), we have not introduced any price expectations. All variables are actual prices (and equal to expected prices, as we will show explicitly later). This does mean that the labour market is separated from the goods market, the money market and the trade sector. In other words, the demand for labour and the supply of labour together determine the real wage and the amount of labour which is employed in the economy. It is, of course, true that the remainder of the economy is dependent on the labour market. This classical labour market, along with our previous analysis is shown in Fig. 2.6.

Since the labour market, shown in Fig. 2.6(c), can be segmented from the rest of the economy, then the real wage (w) and the labour employed (L) is determined solely in this market – namely w_n and L_n. Given this labour employed, then we can use Fig. 2.6(c) to help determine the employment level in Fig. 2.6(d), i.e. L_n on the horizontal axis is translated into L_n on the vertical axis (since the line through the origin is 45°), which is the level of labour input on the vertical axis in Fig. 2.6(d). Given the level of labour employed (L_n), real income is determined from the production function $y = f(L)$ shown in Fig. 2.6(d), i.e.

$$y_n = f(L_n) \tag{2.40}$$

As drawn in the diagram this level of income is just sufficient to bring about an interest rate, r_n, which establishes equilibrium in the goods market, the money market and the trade sector.

In carrying out analysis, it is convenient to observe the situation in terms of *nominal* wages. This is shown in Fig. 2.6(a), where we have the labour market relating the nominal wage, W, to labour, L. The curves in Fig. 2.6(a) are derived by multiplying the curves in Fig. 2.6(e) by the price level for each level of labour. Thus, the demand curve for labour is denoted $\mu a_L P$ and the supply curve of labour is denoted $P_g(L)$. (Note in passing that a rise in the price level will, for a given level of L, shift demand to the right and supply to the left. Conversely for a fall in P.) At the money wage W_0 and price level P_0, the real wage is $w_0 = W_0/P_0 = w_n$ and the level of employment is L_n.

Suppose prices rise to P_1. As we see in Fig. 2.6(a) the demand and supply curves of labour rise by equal amounts and so the money wage rises by the same proportion as the rise in prices. The real wage remains the same. Hence the amount of labour employed remains the same. If we plot the relationship between the price level and the level of output generated, then we observe that at a price level of P_0 the level of employment is L_n. When the price level rises to P_1 the money wage rises to W_1 but the real wage remains constant. Hence, employment and output remain constant. This means that at the higher price of P_1 output is still y_n. This result is shown in Fig. 2.6(f). The relationship between the price level and the level of output (real income) is referred to as the *aggregate supply curve* (AS). Thus, under the classical assumptions discussed here, the aggregate supply curve is vertical at output level y_n. Notice, however, that this model still involves unemployment. If $\bar{L}$ denotes the total working population then $\bar{L} - L_n$ denotes *voluntary* unemployment at the equilibrium real wage w_n.

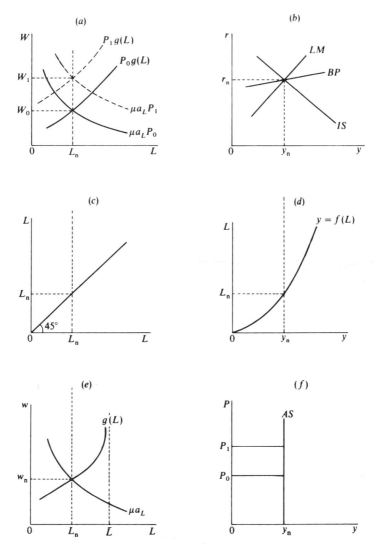

Figure 2.6 Classical aggregate supply.

At the higher price level, there is a fall in the level of aggregate demand (resulting from a leftward shift in both the IS and the LM curves). But this will result in some *frictional* unemployment. In a model with completely flexible prices – as is the assumption in the classical model – then prices must fall and return to their previous level. In other words, given aggregate demand and a vertical aggregate supply, only one price level can clear all markets simultaneously. Any price other than this price is only temporary and any unemployment over and above $\bar{L} - L_n$ is also only temporary.

This classical aggregate supply curve is sometimes said to be a long-run curve because it allows prices, output and employment to adjust. But care must be exercised here. As our analysis shows, this vertical aggregate supply curve is constructed under the assumption of a given capital stock and constant labour productivity. Are these suitable assumptions for the long run? In microeconomics, we usually assume that the long run is characterized by the ability to vary all factors of production – including capital. On the other hand, if we assume flexible prices and wages *and* that markets are quick to adjust, then the system will quickly gravitate to labour employed of L_n, income y_n and the price level P_0. This is assumed to take place in the short run with capital stock at $K = \bar{K}$ and labour productivity held constant.

What we can indicate, even within this simple framework, is that if labour productivity rises (a rise in a_L for given L), then the demand curve for labour will move to the right, the equilibrium labour employed will rise, and income will rise. Hence the vertical AS curve will move to the right. Similarly, when the capital stock rises, the demand curve for labour will move to the right and so too will the AS curve. We will return to this aspect in Chapter 14 when we consider in more detail the 'natural rate of unemployment'.

2.6 KEYNESIAN AGGREGATE SUPPLY CURVE

Keynes was very much in dispute over the classical version of the labour market, and hence about the shape of the aggregate supply curve. One way to approach Keynesian analysis is to postulate that workers make decisions about supplying themselves to the labour market (or decisions about how many hours to work) in line with expected real wages, where the expected real wage is the money wage deflated by the expected price level, i.e. $w^e = W/P^e$. The analysis becomes manageable by making two assumptions:

1. Employers know the wage charged and the price level, so

Let
$$w = \mu a_L \text{ or } W = \mu a_L P \tag{2.41}$$

2. Workers are unclear about price levels and use an expected price. Thus, the supply curve relates the expected real wage, $w^e = W/P^e$, to the level of employment, L, i.e.

$$w^e = g(L) \tag{2.42}$$

Since $w^e = (W/P)(P/P^e) = w(P/P^e)$, then

$$w = (P^e/P)g(L) \tag{2.43}$$

In the classical version it is clear that $P^e = P$ so that $w = g(L)$. Hence, one way to interpret the classical model is that workers and managers have perfect foresight as to the level of prices at all times – which is quite an heroic assumption.

In the Keynesian version, expected prices are exogenously determined. For the moment we will simply accept this assumption, but will return to expectations in greater detail in Chapter 4. The situation is shown in Fig. 2.7(*a,b*). We begin at point *A* with the price level at P_0, labour at L_0 and income at y_0. Suppose now that the actual price level rises to P_1. The demand curve for labour in the $W–L$ space moves from $\mu a_L P_0$ to $\mu a_L P_1$. (Notice that the vertical shift in the demand curve is $dP = P_1 - P_0$.) Now, given the assumption that suppliers of labour lack foresight we can make a number of assumptions. Suppose workers continue to recognize last period's price, P_0, as the relevant price. Then the supply curve in the $W–L$ space remains at $P_0 g(L)$. The economy accordingly moves from point *A* to point

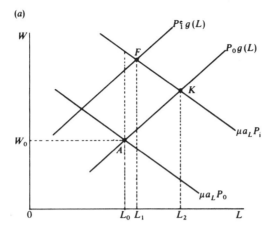

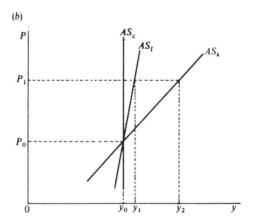

Figure 2.7 Keynesian aggregate supply.

K (this is the extreme Keynesian case of no foresight). Labour employed rises to L_2 and income rises to y_2. On the other hand, if they have some foresight – albeit imperfect – then they will assume a rise in the expected price level which will be less than the actual rise. Thus if P_1^e denotes the expected price level (which is less than P_1), then the supply of labour curve will move up to $P_1^e g(L)$ and the economy will move from point A to point F (some foresight). Hence, labour employed will still rise, to L_1; and income, too, will rise to y_1. In other words, the aggregate supply curve is upward sloping. The greater the foresight on the part of the labour supply, the steeper is the aggregate supply curve.

Keynes did make one further assumption and that was that the money wage was rigid in a downward direction. The money wage is W_0, which is historically given and is not explained within the model itself. For a rise in prices, we have the situation which we have just described. For a fall in the price level, however, the money wage does not decline, and so labour employed falls – and falls by more than it would have fallen if prices were flexible (because the supply curve is horizontal at the ruling wage, while the demand curve shifts to the left). Consequently, for prices below P_0, the aggregate supply curve is much less steep than that shown. The basic points still remain:

1. The aggregate supply curve is upward sloping.
2. The steepness of the AS curve depends on the foresight of those supplying labour.
3. The aggregate supply curve is dependent upon:
    (a) the level of labour productivity;
    (b) the level of capital stock;
    (c) the level of expected prices; and
    (d) the degree to which money wages are inflexible.

The result that the aggregate supply curve is dependent on the level of expected prices is quite crucial and is common to many formulations of the labour market – and not just to the Keynesian version. Given an exogenous expected price level, then the aggregate supply curve is determined. A rise in the expected price level on the part of those supplying labour (for whatever reason) will shift the aggregate supply curve upwards, i.e. a higher price is necessary to bring forth the same level of output. Note, however, that if those supplying labour are credited with perfect foresight (which, in some models, is assumed to be the case), then the aggregate supply curve is vertical.

The effect on the aggregate supply curve of a change in price expectations is illustrated in Appendix 2.5 by means of an arithmetical example.[14]

2.7 A SUMMARY OF THE STATIC MODEL

The crucial two elements in the static model are presented in Fig. 2.8. The upper diagram (*a*) represents the goods market, money market and trade sector, while the lower diagram (*b*) represents the aggregate demand and aggregate supply. It is worth recalling that aggregate demand is dependent on expected inflation, even if this is zero (i.e. $\hat{P}^e = 0$), while aggregate supply depends on the expected *level* of prices (i.e. P^e). Given a static situation, labour productivity is constant; the capital stock is constant; there is no expected inflation; and there is no expected change in the exchange rate. What we have shown, however, is a situation in which the equilibrium level of income is below the level determined by a vertical aggregate supply. This is what is meant by a Keynesian underemployment equilibrium.

If point *A* prevails in Fig. 2.8(*a*) and point *E* prevails in Fig. 2.8(*b*), then the price and income levels are determined. All markets are in equilibrium, and so there is no reason for the economy to move. Of course, this is because we have assumed that there is no inflation, and that the exchange rate just happens to give rise to a BP curve which passes through the IS–LM intersection. But there is no reason why this should generally be so. Furthermore, given the exogenous variables, there is no reason for the price level to change because there is no reason for the aggregate demand curve or the aggregate supply curve to shift.

The next step in the logic is not difficult to understand. Given such involuntary unemployment, the economy can be moved to its full employment level (i.e. to the level of employment such that only voluntary unemployment exists) by means of monetary and/or fiscal expansion. But once this is undertaken, it is no longer tenable to assume that expected prices remain fixed, expected inflation rates remain constant, or the expected exchange rate remains unchanged. Dynamic forces will come into the picture, and we must see how the

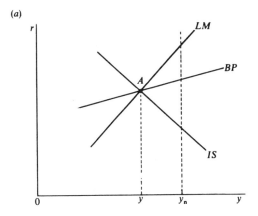

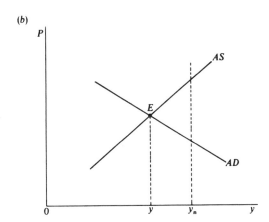

Figure 2.8 Summary of the static model.

economic system behaves when this happens. Furthermore, our treatment of aggregate supply is still too simplistic. It does not take account of taxation, the presence of trade unions or the presence of imported raw materials. Since much of the debate on *supply-side economics* is about these factors, it is essential that they are incorporated into the analysis. In the next chapter we will deal with a dynamic version of the model which will allow us to consider some of these difficulties, while other problems will be taken up in later chapters. Before we do this, however, let us just see how the economy has behaved in terms of prices and real income.

2.8 PRICES AND OUTPUT FOR THE UK

If the static model were a reasonably accurate description of the real world, then the price level would be fairly constant, and the level of real income would also be fairly constant – except for random shocks to the economy. A glance at Fig. 2.9 shows that this has not been the case for the period 1960–87. On the vertical axis, we have the retail price

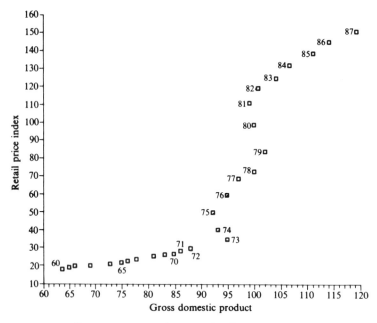

Figure 2.9 $P-y$ combinations for the UK, 1960–87.

index; and on the horizontal axis, we have an index for gross domestic product at factor cost and at constant 1980 prices – a representation of P and y respectively. Points on the diagram represent the intersection between the aggregate demand and the aggregate supply curves. A shift right (left) in aggregate demand will lead to a rise (fall) in the price level and a rise (fall) in output. On the other hand, a shift right (left) in aggregate supply only will lead to a rise (fall) in the price level but a fall (rise) in output.

From Fig. 2.9 we see that the price level remained fairly constant throughout much of the 1960s, while income rose. This would be consistent with a fairly flat aggregate supply curve and with an aggregate demand curve that was shifting to the right. A more plausible explanation, however, is a shift in aggregate demand to the right and a shift in aggregate supply to the right due to a rise in population. The 1970s and early 1980s, however, have shown quite a different picture. Prices have risen sharply while real income has shown a cyclical pattern around a fairly constant level. Although one explanation for this observation is a shift to the right in aggregate demand with aggregate supply almost vertical (the classical result), a more plausible explanation is a shift to the *right* in aggregate demand and a shift to the *left* in aggregate supply. These more plausible explanations will be justified later in the text, especially in Part II for aggregate demand shifts and Part III for aggregate supply shifts.

NOTES

1. This consumption function is one of the simplest that can be specified. If consumption is related to permanent income or to a person's income over his lifespan, then it will take more complex forms.

These differing forms, however, still relate real consumption to real income. See Greenaway and Shaw (1983), chapter 2, and Thomas (1984). Any change in prices will not affect such real variables. More significant, however, is the possibility that real consumption is related not only to real income but also positively to real money balances, M_0/P. This introduces a real balance effect into consumption behaviour, see Pigou (1943) and Patinkin (1948, 1959, 1965). When the price level rises then real money balances fall and so too does real consumption.

2. It is referred to as the IS curve for historical reasons. In a simple closed economy model with no government, equilibrium in the goods market can be expressed either as the condition where real income equals real expenditure, or where real savings equal real investment. In an open economy with no government, there is no requirement for investment to equal savings. What is required is that

$$s + im = i + x$$

where $s = y - c$.

3. The IS curve is just *one* possible construction from equation (2.11). For example, it is possible to construct a curve relating real income, y, to the level of competitiveness, R. With R on the vertical axis and y on the horizontal axis – and given the simple linear expressions in the text – the curve would have an intercept and slope given by

$$\text{Intercept } (R\text{-axis}) = \frac{z_0 + h\hat{P}^e - hr}{(f+g)}$$

$$\text{Slope } (y\text{-axis}) = \frac{-[1 - (1 - t_1) + m]}{(f+g)}$$

This line, too, would denote equilibrium in the goods market – but would be such that the nominal interest rate was constant.

4. A multiplier, in the most general terms, denotes the effect on an endogenous variable of a unit change in some exogenous variable – holding all other exogenous variables constant. In the model being developed, real income and the nominal rate of interest are endogenous variables. Since we are treating government spending as exogenous, then we can, for example, derive the income multiplier with respect to a change in government spending, denoted $\partial y/\partial go$. In this model, however, it is not possible to consider the income multiplier with respect to a change in investment. Why not? Since investment is related to the nominal interest rate, then a change in the nominal interest rate will lead to a change in investment. Hence, investment cannot be treated as an exogenous variable. On the other hand, it is possible to consider the impact on real income of a change in *autonomous* investment, i_0 (i.e. $\partial y/\partial i_0$).

There is no such thing as 'the' multiplier. For any given model, the total number of multipliers it contains is equal to the number of endogenous variables times the number of exogenous variables. (This does not include any derived multipliers.) On an elementary introduction to macroeconomic multipliers, see Lipsey (1983, chapter 36); Begg, Fischer and Dornbusch (1987, chapters 20 and 21); and Neal and Shone (1976, chapter 5).

5. We will consider the endogeneity or exogeneity of the money supply in Chapter 7.

6. It is referred to as the LM curve for historical reasons. The demand for money curve was referred to by Keynes as the *liquidity preference schedule*. So LM indicates equality between the demand for liquidity (money) and the supply of money.

7. In a model which takes account of wealth, Wl, then the demand for money equation is also a function of real wealth, $wl = Wl/P$. Thus,

$$M_d/P = ky - ur + nwl \qquad 0 < n < 1$$

i.e. a rise in real wealth raises the demand for real money balances but by less than the increase in wealth – since some of this increase is allocated to bonds and other assets. In this case, the LM curve becomes

$$r = -(M_0/uP) + (k/u)y + (n/u)wl$$

A rise in real wealth shifts the LM curve to the left.

8. In the discussion of capital flows, no account is taken of inflation at home and abroad. We have used only the uncovered interest parity condition. Capital flows are likely to respond to *real* interest differentials, which requires the Fisher condition to be met. See Levi (1983) and Hallwood and MacDonald (1986).

9. If you had £1 which you converted into $2 and then invested this in the US, you would receive at the end of the period $2.20. With a 5% appreciation of sterling (a 5% depreciation of the dollar) the exchange rate becomes £1 = $2.10. Converting your $2.20 back into sterling would give you a sum of £1.05. However, had you invested the £1 in the UK you would have ended with a sum of £1.08. The loss of £0.03 is 3 percentage points, namely

$$8\% - (10\% - 5\%) = 3\%$$

or

$$r - (r^* - \hat{S}^e) \cdot$$

10. A devaluation refers to an official change in the parity rate, e.g. Britain devalued sterling in 1967 from an official rate of £1 = $2.80 to £1 = `$2.40. A depreciation is where the exchange rate is floating and, say, the dollar price of sterling is falling due to market forces.

11. See Chapter 8 of *Applications in Intermediate Microeconomics*, Shone (1981).

12. If the aggregate production function is of the Cobb-Douglas type, then

$$y = aL^\alpha K^\beta$$

then $MPP_L = \partial y/\partial L = \alpha a L^{\alpha-1} K^\beta = \alpha(y/L) = \alpha APP_L$

13. See Chapter 2 of *Applications in Intermediate Microeconomics*, Shone (1981).

14. This example is adapted from Holbrook, reprinted in Teigen (4th edition, 1978, Chapter 1).

APPENDIX 2.1 SOME MATHEMATICS OF THE IS–LM–BP MODEL

(a) *The IS curve*

Substituting equations (2.5), (2.6) and (2.10) into the expenditure identity (2.2) and treating government spending, go, as exogenous we have

$$e = a + b(1 - t_1)y - bt_0 + i_0 - h(r - \hat{P}^e) + go + (x_0 - im_0) - my - (f + g)R$$

Substituting this into the equilibrium condition,

$$y = e \qquad (A2.1.1)$$

and solving for r in terms of y we get

$$r = \frac{z_0 + h\hat{P}^e - (f+g)R}{h} - \frac{[1 - b(1 - t_1) + m]y}{h} \qquad (A2.1.2)$$

where

$$z_0 = a - bt_0 + i_0 + go + x_0 - im_0 \qquad (A2.1.3)$$

Equation (A2.1.2) denotes all combinations of r and y that give rise to equilibrium in the goods market; in other words, the IS curve. The intercept on the r-axis and the slope with respect to the y-axis are indicated in Table A2.1.1.

Table A2.1.1 Intercept and slopes for IS, LM and BP curves

Curve	Intercept (r-axis)	Slope (y-axis)
IS	$\dfrac{z_0 + h\hat{P}^e - (f+g)R}{h}$	$\dfrac{1 - b(1-t_1) + m}{h}$
LM	$-\dfrac{M_0}{uP}$	$\dfrac{k}{u}$
BP	$\dfrac{-bP_0 + (f+g)R}{v} + (r^* - \hat{S}^e)$	$\dfrac{m}{v}$

(b) *The LM curve*

Substituting equations (2.14) and (2.15) into the equilibrium condition:

$$(M_d/P) = (M_s/P) \tag{A2.1.4}$$

we get

$$ky - ur = M_0/P$$
$$r = -(M_0/uP) + (k/u)y \tag{A2.1.5}$$

Equation (A2.1.5) denotes combinations of r and y that give rise to equilibrium in the money market. The intercept and slope of the LM curve are given in Table A2.1.1.

Notice that if the demand for real money balances is totally interest insensitive (i.e. $u = 0$), then the LM curve has an infinite slope; in other words, the LM curve is vertical (at income level $y = M_0/kP$).

(c) *The BP curve*

Substituting equations (2.10) and (2.18) into (2.17) and setting this equal to zero for equilibrium on the balance of payments, we have

$$(x_0 - im_0) - my - (f+g)R + cf_0 + v(r - r^* + \hat{S}^e) = 0$$

Or

$$r = \frac{[-bp_0 + (f+g)R]}{v} + \left(\frac{m}{v}\right)y + (r^* - \hat{S}^e) \tag{A2.1.6}$$

where $bp_0 = (x_0 - im_0) + cf_0$. Equation (A2.1.6) denotes combinations of r and y that give rise to equilibrium on the balance of payments. The intercept and slope of the BP curve are given in Table A2.1.1.

(d) *IS–LM intersection*

Since the economy will gravitate to where the IS curve intersects the LM curve, we can determine this solution by solving equations (A2.1.2) and (A2.1.5) for y and r, giving

$$y = \frac{[z_0 + h\hat{P}^e - (f+g)R] + (h/u)(M_0/P)}{1 - b(1-t_1) + m + (kh/u)} \tag{A2.1.7}$$

$$r = \frac{-(M_0/uP)[1 - b(1-t_1) + m] + (k/u)[z_0 + h\hat{P}^e - (f+g)R]}{1 - b(1-t_1) + m + (kh/u)} \tag{A2.1.8}$$

(e) *Multipliers*

A multiplier is the change in an endogenous variable brought about by a unit change in an exogenous variable. The most common multiplier to consider is the income multiplier with respect to a change in investment. In the model we have presented we cannot calculate such a multiplier with respect to total investment because investment is endogenous. We can, however, consider the impact on income of a change in autonomous investment, i.e. the result on y of a change in i_0. If we intend to hold the interest rate constant, then the multiplier impact on income of a change in autonomous investment can be established from equation (2.11); namely,

$$k_{cr} = 1/[1 - b(1 - t_1) + m] \qquad (A2.1.9)$$

Hence, for a change di_0 in autonomous investment, income changes by the amount

$$dy = k_{cr} di_0 \qquad (A2.1.10)$$

In diagrammatic terms the result (A2.1.10) measures the horizontal movement in the IS curve at a given rate of interest.

When we include the money market in the analysis, however, we know that the rate of interest cannot remain constant – except in the case where the LM curve is horizontal. What, then, is the change in income arising from a change in autonomous investment – but allowing the interest rate to change? This can be obtained from equation (A2.1.7). Since i_0 is part of z_0 then $di_0 = dz_0$. The change in income arising from a change in autonomous investment is, therefore,

$$k_{vr} = 1/[1 - b(1 - t_1) + m + (kh/u)] \qquad (A2.1.11)$$

Hence, for a change di_0 in autonomous investment, income changes by the amount

$$dy = k_{vr} di_0 \qquad (A2.1.12)$$

In diagrammatic terms, this measures the change in income from one equilibrium position (one intersection of the IS and LM curves) to another.

So long as u is not zero, it follows that

$$k_{cr} > k_{vr} \qquad (A2.1.13)$$

It must be remembered that this is only *one* particular multiplier. We can derive as many multipliers as there are endogenous variables multiplied by the number of exogenous variables.

It is also possible to construct *derived* multipliers. For example, we can construct a trade multiplier showing the change in net exports consequent on a change in autonomous exports. Certainly, we know that if autonomous exports increase, then this will increase the level of income through the multiplier expansion. But the rise in income will also lead to an increase in the level of imports. The question arises: will the net export position improve or deteriorate as a result of the increase in autonomous exports? The result is not too difficult to establish. First, consider the simple case with fixed interest rate. A rise in autonomous exports of dx_0 will lead to an increase in the level of income of

$$dy = k_{cr} dx_0 \qquad (A2.1.14)$$

The result on imports of this increase in income is

$$d(im) = m\,dy = mk_{cr} dx_0 \qquad (A2.1.15)$$

Hence, the change in the net export position, $d(nx)$, is

$$d(nx) = dx - d(im)$$

$$= dx_0 - mk_{cr} dx_0$$

i.e.

$$d(nx) = (1 - mk_{cr}) dx_0 \qquad (A2.1.16)$$

Similarly, if we consider the model in terms of a variable rate of interest, then the multiplier expansion of income is given by equation (A2.1.11), i.e

$$d(nx) = (1 - mk_{vr}) dx_0 \qquad (A2.1.17)$$

The net export multiplier, which we shall denote by k_{nx}, is given by

$$k_{nx} = (1 - mk_{cr}) \qquad (A2.1.18)$$

Or

$$k'_{nx} = (1 - mk_{vr}) \tag{A2.1.19}$$

If we substitute equations (A2.1.9) and (A2.1.11) into equations (A2.1.18) and (A2.1.19), respectively, we can see the derived multipliers in more detail. They are

$$k_{nx} = \frac{1 - b(1 - t_1)}{1 - b(1 - t_1) + m} \tag{A2.1.20}$$

$$k'_{nx} = \frac{1 - b(1 - t_1) + (hk/u)}{1 - b(1 - t_1) + m + (hk/u)} \tag{A2.1.21}$$

It can readily be established, using equations (A2.1.20) and (A2.1.21) that

$$k'_{nx} > k_{nx} \tag{A2.1.22}$$

so long as $k_{vr} < k_{cr}$.

(f) Fixed exchange rates

Under a fixed exchange rate system, equations (A2.1.2) and (A2.1.5) are sufficient to determine y and r. What, then, is determined in the trade sector and expressed in equation (2.17)? We have established that generally there will be a deficit or surplus on the balance of payments. This is readily established. Let $\bar{y}$ and $\bar{r}$ be determined by equations (A2.1.7) and (A2.1.8) respectively. Then from equation (2.17) we have

$$bp = bp_0 - m\bar{y} - (f + g)R + v(\bar{r} - r^* + \hat{S}^e) \tag{A2.1.23}$$

where $pb_0 = x_0 - im_0 + cf_0$. So long as prices at home and abroad are given and the spot exchange rate, S, is given (hence R is given), then all terms on the right-hand side of equation (A2.1.23) are given. Hence, equation (A2.1.23) gives the balance of payments: which may be positive (a surplus), negative (a deficit) or zero (equilibrium).

(g) Floating exchange rates

If the exchange rate is floating, however, then equations (A2.1.2) and (A2.1.5) are not in themselves sufficient to determine r and y. In this case the three equations, (A2.1.2), (A2.1.5) and (A2.1.6) must be solved simultaneously; they are sufficient to determine the three variables: y, r and S simultaneously. Notice in this case that all three curves – the IS curve, the LM curve and the BP curve – intersect at the solution values.

(h) The aggregate demand curve

In Section (2.4) it was pointed out that the aggregate demand curve was the relationship between y and P which preserved equilibrium in the goods market and equilibrium in the money market. These two equilibria are given by equations (A2.1.2) and (A2.1.5) respectively. In particular, the solution for income was given in terms of equation (A2.1.7). To show the relationship between y and P and other important variables explicitly, equation (A2.1.7) can be written in the form

$$y = \frac{z_0}{Q} + \left(\frac{hM_0}{uQ}\right)\left(\frac{1}{P}\right) + \frac{h\hat{P}^e}{Q} - \frac{(f + g)R}{Q} \tag{A2.1.24}$$

where $Q = 1 - (1 - t_1) + m + (kh/u)$. Or, more simply,

$$y = A_0 + A_1(1/P) + A_2\hat{P}^e - A_3 R \tag{A2.1.25}$$

where

$$A_0 = z_0/Q > 0$$
$$A_1 = hM_0/uQ > 0$$
$$A_2 = h/Q > 0$$
$$A_3 = (f + g)/Q > 0$$

Under a fixed spot exchange rate a variable P means a variable R. With S changing to compensate for the change in P then R is fixed. Hence, for a *rise* in P income must be less under a fixed exchange rate than under a floating exchange rate, as shown in Fig. 2.5 (p. 22). This conclusion, however, assumes $\hat{P}^e$ remains fixed – or, at least, the same under each regime.

APPENDIX 2.2 THE CONSUMPTION FUNCTION

In the text we simply stated that consumption was a linear function of disposable income. However, given the importance of the consumption function as a central relationship in aggregate demand, and its importance in terms of stabilization policy, we will briefly consider some extensions here.

Absolute income hypothesis

Equation (2.3) embodies what has become known as the absolute income hypothesis. Ignoring taxation throughout, the absolute income hypothesis simply states that current consumption is positively related to current income (where the relationship can be either linear or non-linear). The essential characteristic of this formulation is that the average propensity to consume, c/y, declines. Thus, if

$$c = a + by \tag{A2.2.1}$$

then it follows that

$$c/y = a/y + b \tag{A2.2.2}$$

and hence c/y will decline as income rises – approaching in the limit the marginal propensity to consume, b. However, empirical observation shows that the average propensity to consume does not decline. This has led to alternative specifications of the consumption function.

When observation is made of consumption in relation to income, there does appear to be a stable relationship over long periods, although this stability was less so in the 1970s. Three alternative theories were developed to account for this long-run stability: (1) the *relative income hypothesis* developed by Duesenberry (1949); (2) the *permanent income hypothesis* developed by Milton Friedman (1957); and (3) the *life-cycle hypothesis* developed by Modigliani and Brumberg (1954), Modigliani and Ando (1957) and Ando and Modigliani (1963). The first begins by making observations on the savings to income ratio, while the second and third hypotheses are based on intertemporal decisions. In other words, when individuals are planning current consumption they not only take account of current income, but they also consider future income and future consumption.

Relative income hypothesis

Duesenberry's relative income hypothesis begins by postulating that the average propensity to save, s/y, depends (linearly) on the present level of income relative to previous peak income, y^0. Thus,

$$s/y = a + b(y/y^0) \tag{A2.2.3}$$

Since

$$c/y = 1 - (s/y) \tag{A2.2.4}$$

it follows that the average propensity to consume is

$$c/y = (1 - a) - b(y/y^0) \tag{A2.2.5}$$

Unlike the absolute income hypothesis, the relative income hypothesis allows the average propensity to consume to vary in the short run, but will be constant in the long run. To see this long run result, assume income grows at a constant rate g, so that

$$y = (1 + g)y_{t-1} \tag{A2.2.6}$$

If $y_{t-1} = y^0$, then

$$y = (1 + g)y^0 \tag{A2.2.7}$$

Substituting (A2.2.7) into (A2.2.5) immediately gives,

$$c/y = [(1 - a) - b(1 + g)] \tag{A2.2.8}$$

Hence in the long run the average propensity to consume is constant and equal to the marginal propensity to consume.

Permanent income hypothesis

The permanent income hypothesis begins with the assumption that permanent consumption is proportional to permanent income, i.e.,

$$c_p = ky_p \tag{A2.2.9}$$

In simple terms, permanent income is the long period income which is generated such that wealth remains fixed. On the other hand, actual income, y, is composed of permanent income, y_p, plus transitory income, y_t, where transitory income simply refers to income arising from temporary and unanticipated occurrences (e.g., an unexpected wage increase or a bequest). Similarly, in any period, current consumption, c, is equal to permanent consumption plus transitory consumption. Thus,

$$y = y_p + y_t \tag{A2.2.10}$$

$$c = c_p + c_t \tag{A2.2.11}$$

Friedman made a number of assumptions: (1) transitory and permanent income were independent of one another. This means that transitory income is simply a random variable with a mean of zero; hence, for any group, income on average will equal permanent income; (2) transitory consumption is uncorrelated with both permanent income and with permanent consumption. Hence, for any income class, average transitory consumption will be zero, and actual consumption is equal to permanent consumption. Thus, for the population as a whole we have the relationship,

$$c = ky_p \tag{A2.2.12}$$

In order to test this theory and establish some of its implications it is necessary to convert the unobservable variable y_p into something that is observable. Friedman assumed that permanent income, based as it is on what individuals consider their future income will be, can be approximated by using an *adaptive* form of past permanent income. (We shall deal in detail with adaptive expectations in Chapter 4, so that we shall be very brief here.) It is assumed that,

$$y_{pt} - y_{pt-1} = a(y_t - y_{pt-1}) \qquad 0 < a < 1 \tag{A2.2.13}$$

where now variables are distinguished by their time period. Since equation (A2.2.13) can be expressed in the following way,

$$y_{pt} = (1 - a)y_{pt-1} + ay_t \tag{A2.2.14}$$

then y_{pt} can be expressed in the form of a distributed lag function,

$$y_{pt} = a \sum_{n=0}^{\infty} (1 - a)^n y_{t-n} \tag{A2.2.15}$$

Substituting equation (A2.2.15) into equation (A2.2.12) we have,

$$c_t = ka \sum_{n=0}^{\infty} (1 - a)^n y_{t-n} \tag{A2.2.16}$$

But even this is unwieldy for estimation purposes. Using the fact that,

$$(1 - a)c_{t-1} = ka \sum_{n=0}^{\infty} (1 - a)^n y_{t-n-1} \tag{A2.2.17}$$

Then,

$$c_t - (1 - a)c_{t-1} = ky_t \tag{A2.2.18}$$

Or

$$c_t = kay_t + (1 - a)c_{t-1} \tag{A2.2.19}$$

Three things can be deduced from equation (A2.2.19). First, the short run marginal propensity to consume is ka. Second, the long run marginal propensity to consume (derived from equation (A2.2.19) by setting $c_t = c_{t-1}$) is equal to k. Third, since $0 < a < 1$, then $ka < k$, hence the short run marginal propensity to consume is less than the long run marginal propensity to consume.

Life-cycle hypothesis

The life-cycle hypothesis developed by Ando, Brumberg and Modigliani is similar to Friedman's permanent income hypothesis, and is based on individuals maximizing a household utility function. Real consumption at time t is assumed proportional to the present real value of wealth at time t, $(W/P)_t$,

$$c_t = b(W/P)_t \tag{A2.2.20}$$

As with Friedman's theory, the problem is making (A2.2.20) operational. To do this an expression for the present value of real wealth is required. This can be shown to be composed of three things: (1) real household net worth at the beginning of period t, which we shall denote a_0; (2) current income, y_t; and (3) the present value of expected future labour income. With a lifespan of T years, then the present value of the remaining future labour income is $(T-1)y_t^e$, where y_t^e is expected labour income. Thus,

$$(W/P)_t = a_0 + y_t + (T-1)y_t^e \tag{A2.2.21}$$

The final problem is to eliminate the unobservable future labour income variable. It is possible to make a variety of assumptions about how this may be done, but here we will assume that the present value of expected labour income is proportional to present income, i.e.

$$y_t^e = \beta y_t \tag{A2.2.22}$$

Substituting equation (A2.2.22) into equation (A2.2.21) and substituting this result into equation (A2.2.20) we obtain

$$c_t = a_0 b + b[1 + \beta(T-1)]y_t \tag{A2.2.23}$$

In this model, the short-run marginal propensity to consume out of labour income is given by the coefficient of y_t, namely,

$$MPC = b[1 + \beta(T-1)] \tag{A2.2.24}$$

On the other hand, the average propensity to consume (c/y) can shift over time depending on the present value of assets, a_0.

Conclusion

In terms of our simple (linear) analysis, what these theories indicate is that consumption, besides being a function of disposable income, is also a function of real wealth – real wealth determining either permanent income or the present value of total resources. A rise in real wealth will raise consumption. Hence, we can postulate an alternative consumption function to (2.5) in the form

$$c = a - bt_0 + b(1 - t_1)y + q(Wl/P) \tag{A2.2.25}$$

where q is a positive constant. (It should be noted, however, that wealth will itself depend inversely on the rate of interest.) A rise in wealth with prices constant, will raise consumption and shift the IS curve to the right, and conversely for a fall in wealth. On the other hand, a rise in the price level will lead to a fall in consumption and hence a shift left in the IS curve. Conversely for a fall in the price level. This response of consumption to a change in the price level is known as the *Pigou effect*. As we will note later, the Pigou effect will have implications for the slope of the aggregate demand curve. The aggregate demand curve relates real income to the price level. With equilibrium in the goods market a function of price, along with equilibrium in the money market also being a function of price, this will result in a greater income response for a fall in price; in other words, a more price elastic aggregate demand curve.

APPENDIX 2.3 THE INVESTMENT FUNCTION

In equation (2.6) we expressed investment as a (linear) function of the real expected interest rate. In the following discussion we will assume that the rate of inflation (actual and expected) is zero. Given this assumption, investment is simply a function of the interest rate. In this appendix we attempt to do two things: first, to account for the inverse relationship between investment and the rate of interest; second, to consider more complex specifications of the investment function. Investment, however, is a complex topic and we cannot possibly do it justice here, so the reader would do well to consider a more intensive treatment of the topic, e.g. Junankar (1972), Nickell, S. J. (1978) and Pike and Dobbins (1986).

We begin by considering the *net present value* of a particular project, such as the purchase of some capital equipment. Suppose this project has a net return R_k from period $k = 1$ to period $k = N$. Further, we assume that the project is purchased at a cost C in the present, hence the net present value of such a project is given by

$$NPV = -C + \sum_{k=1}^{N} R_k/(1 + r)^k \qquad (A2.3.1)$$

If NPV is positive, which means the present value of the net returns outweighs the cost of purchase, then the firm should undertake the investment. (An alternative procedure is to establish the *internal rate of return* on a project, what Keynes called the *marginal efficiency of capital*. This is the value of the interest rate at which expression (A2.3.1) is equal to zero. If the internal rate of return exceeds the market rate of interest, then the project should be undertaken. There may, however, be some differences in the use of NPV as against the internal rate of return, see Hawkins and Pearce (1971), which we will not explore here.) Alternatively, if NPV is negative then the project should not be pursued. Hence, for a given rate of interest, projects will be ranked from the highest NPV to the lowest, and at the ruling rate of interest, only those projects for which NPV is positive will be undertaken. Put differently, capital purchases will be undertaken until the net present value of the last project is zero. Notice, in particular, that here we are relating the *capital stock* to the rate of interest.

Consider next a fall in the market rate of interest (a fall in r). For the same stream of net returns, this will raise the net present value of each project. Hence, a project which previously had a negative NPV may now have a positive NPV and will thus be undertaken. Certainly, all those projects which would have been chosen at the higher rate of interest will also be chosen at the lower rate. Thus the number (and present value) of investment projects will rise with a fall in the rate of interest, and conversely for a rise in the rate of interest. Consequently, there is a negative relationship between the capital stock and the rate of interest, what Keynes called the *marginal efficiency of capital schedule*. Also note that if there is a rise in the expected net return on all projects in subsequent periods, then this will raise the number and value of capital projects for a given rate of interest (a shift to the right in the marginal efficiency of capital schedule).

It is to be noted that so far we have dealt with the relationship between the rate of interest and the level of capital stock. But what we are interested in is the relationship between the rate of interest and the level of investment. Of course, the change in the capital stock denotes investment. However, this would be *gross* investment, which includes both replacement investment and *net* investment. What we are particularly interested in is the relationship between the rate of interest and net investment.

Consider Fig. A2.3.1, with the rate of interest at r_0 the capital stock is at its desired level, in which case there is no *new* investment – net investment is zero. On the horizontal axis we are measuring net investment or the change in the capital stock from the optimal amount – remembering that the origin

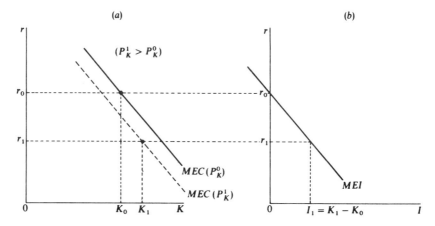

Figure A2.3.1 The marginal efficiency of capital and investment schedules.

is the desired capital stock. Now consider a fall in the rate of interest. We have already established that this will lead to a rise in the level of the capital stock, which is shown by the marginal efficiency of capital schedule, denoted MEC (Fig. A2.3.1(a)). However, if all firms in the economy attempt to expand their level of captial, then the price of capital goods will increase – and will increase for all firms. This rise in the price of capital goods will lower the marginal efficiency of capital on all projects. Accordingly, the level of new investment is less than that reflected in the marginal efficiency of capital schedule. The smaller additional increase in capital stock denotes the *marginal efficiency of investment* at each rate of interest, and is denoted by MEI in Fig. A2.3.1(b). It is the marginal efficiency of investment which denotes the investment schedule. The difference between the marginal efficiency of capital and the marginal efficiency of investment is that the latter takes account of the fact that as the rate of interest falls the price of obtaining capital goods will rise. From our present point of view, what matters is that there is an inverse relationship between investment (the marginal efficiency of investment) and the rate of interest.

The analysis so far, however, pays too much attention to the rate of interest as a determinant of investment, and gives no insight as to why the investment schedule may shift. Put another way, any variable that causes a shift in the investment schedule may be as important (or even more important) in determining the level of investment for the economy as a whole.

We have noted that a rise in the level of net returns shifts both the marginal efficiency of capital and the marginal efficiency of investment schedule to the right. In other words, a rise in net returns raises investment for a given rate of interest. However, in the aggregate, net returns on investment are not known. We accordingly require a *proxy* for net returns. A reasonable proxy for net returns is the current level of income, y. Thus, an alternative specification of the (linear) investment function is

$$i = i_0 - h(r - \hat{P}^e) + dy \qquad h, d > 0 \qquad\qquad (A2.3.2)$$

The presence of income in the investment function will *raise* the value of 'the' multiplier – see the Appendix 2.1.

But even the present discussion of investment is too simplistic. It would certainly seem to be the case that much net investment arises because of the gap between the actual and desired level of the capital stock; and furthermore, any investment undertaken to close this gap is only likely to represent a proportion of the gap. This approach has given rise to what is known as the *accelerator* theory of net investment, see Samuelson (1939), Goodwin (1951) and Eckaus (1953).

Other factors, too, have attracted attention. It has been argued that net investment is related to the level of profits. The higher the gross profits, the higher the retained profits (net profits less payments to shareholders less payments to government in the form of taxes) which are used for investment purposes. The underlying assumption is that investment funds can be obtained more easily from retained profits than from other sources, such as borrowing or issuing new equity. Furthermore, a rise in depreciation allowances, a fall in profits tax, or other tax benefits may have a sizeable impact on the level of investment. Such factors will, of course, shift the investment schedule specified in equation (A2.3.2) above, but they are not taken account of explicitly in the simple theory.

APPENDIX 2.4 IS–LM–BP MODEL: A NUMERICAL EXAMPLE

A number of points made in the text can be illustrated by means of a simple numerical example. The behavioural equations are as follows.

Goods market

$c = 4.75 + 0.75(y - t)$
$t = 3 + 0.3y$
$i = 35 - 2(r - \hat{P}^e)$
$go = 30$
$x = 10 - 5R$
$im = 20 + 2R + 0.2y$

Money market

$M_d/P = 0.25y - 0.5r$
$M_s/P = M_0/P = 3/P$

Balance of payments

$x = 10 - 5R$
$im = 20 + 2R + 0.2y$
$cf = 20.5 + (r - 15 + \hat{S}^e)$

Equilibrium conditions

Goods market
Money market
Balance of payments

$y = c + i + go + x - im$
$M_d/P = M_s/P$
$bp = 0$

Additional assumptions

The following variables are held constant at the values indicated.

Static assumptions

$S = 1$
$P = 1$
$P* = 1$

Dynamic assumptions

$\hat{S}^e = 0$
$\hat{P}^e = 0$

Given the model set out above it is possible to derive the following equations for the IS curve, the LM curve and the BP curve – all defined with respect to the nominal interest rate on the vertical axis and real income on the horizontal axis:

$$\text{IS curve} \qquad r = 25.25 - 0.3375y$$

$$\text{LM curve} \qquad r = -6 + 0.5y$$

$$\text{BP curve} \qquad r = 11.5 + 0.2y$$

The situation is drawn in Fig. A2.4.1. The IS curve intersects the LM curve at the following values:

$$y = 37.313 \qquad r = 12.657$$

However, at this level of income and interest rate the balance of payments is in deficit, $bp = -6.306$. Hence, the IS curve cuts the LM curve below the BP curve. Furthermore, the multipliers with constant interest rate (k_{rc}) and variable interest rate (k_{rv}) are given by

$$k_{rc} = 1.481 \qquad k_{rv} = 0.597$$

Fig. A2.4.2 illustrates the difference between the two multipliers for an increase in government spending from $go = 30$ to $go = 40$. For this higher level of government spending, the IS curve

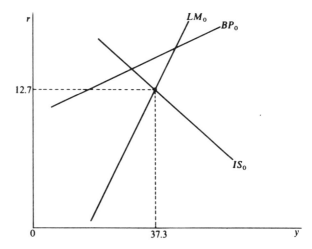

Figure A2.4.1 Equilibrium under a fixed exchange rate.

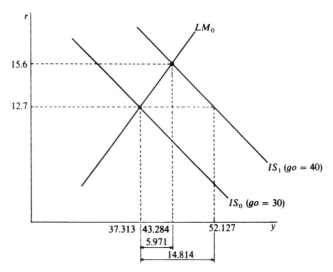

Figure A2.4.2 Effect on equilibrium of an increase in government spending.

takes the form

$$r = 30.25 - 0.3375y$$

We can summarize the results as follows:

	Initial position $(go = 30)$	New position $(go = 40)$
Equilibrium y	37.313	43.284
Equilibrium r	12.657	15.642
Income $(r = 12.7)$		52.1274
Change in income		
constant r		14.814
variable r		5.971

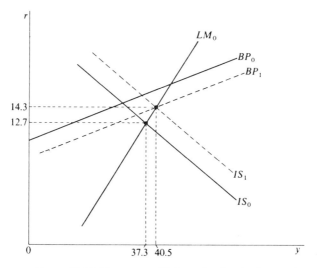

Figure A2.4.3 Effect on equilibrium of a devaluation.

Since the values above arise for an autonomous change in government spending of 10, it follows that the changes in income should be equivalent to the appropriate multiplier times 10, which is indeed the case.

A devaluation

It is possible to establish for this model the value of the exchange rate (S) which will establish equilibrium in all three markets simultaneously. Returning to $go = 30$, setting bp equal to zero and letting S become endogenous, the value of S establishing equilibrium in all three markets simultaneously is

$$S = 0.236$$

A devaluation of approximately 76.4%. The devaluation has no bearing on the LM curve, since this, in the present model, is independent of the exchange rate. However, both the IS and BP curves shift. The IS curve is a function of net exports, which itself is related to the relative competitiveness of the economy (R). A fall in S means a fall in R since $R = SP/P^*$. The result is a shift in the IS curve to the right (to IS_1) and a shift to the right of the BP curve (to BP_1), as shown in Fig. A2.4.3. The diagram is drawn for the following resulting IS and BP curves:

$$IS_1 \qquad r = 27.924 - 0.3375y$$
$$BP_1 \qquad r = 6.152 + 0.2y$$

The result is a rise in both the nominal interest rate and the level of real income to:

$$r = 14.253 \qquad y = 40.506$$

APPENDIX 2.5 AS AND PRICE EXPECTATIONS: AN ARITHMETICAL EXAMPLE

Let the short-run production function be given by

$$y = d_0 L - \tfrac{1}{2}d_1 L^2 \tag{A2.5.1}$$

Table A2.5.1 Aggregate supply and the expected price level

| | $P^e = 100$ | | $P^e = 120$ | |
P	L	y	L	y
60	2.6	38.7	2.5	37.5
70	2.7	39.7	2.6	38.5
80	2.8	40.6	2.7	39.4
90	2.9	41.3.	2.8	40.1
100	3.0	42.0	2.9	40.8
110	3.1	42.6	2.9	41.4
120	3.2	43.1	3.0	42.0
130	3.2	43.6	3.1	42.5
140	3.3	44.1	3.1	43.0
150	3.3	44.4	3.2	43.4

Partially differentiating this equation with respect to labour gives the marginal physical product of labour; namely,

$$MPP_L = \partial y / \partial L = d_0 - d_1 L \tag{A2.5.2}$$

Under marginal productivity theory, the real wage is equated to the marginal physical product of labour, hence the demand curve for labour is given by

$$w = d_0 - d_1 L \tag{A2.5.3}$$

In line with our discussion in the text, we assume that the supply curve of labour is a relationship between the expected real wage, w^e, and labour supplied. Taking a simple linear form:

$$w^e = l_0 + l_1 L \tag{A2.5.4}$$

i.e.

$$w = (P^e / P)(l_0 + l_1 L) \tag{A2.5.5}$$

We can equate equations (A2.5.3) and (A2.5.5) and solve for the equilibrium wage and the equilibrium labour – assuming, of course, that the labour market clears. Having solved for labour we can substitute this into equation (A2.5.1) to determine output. Since equation (A2.5.5) is a function of (P^e / P), then so too will be the level of output.

To see the relationship between P and y that arises in this model we continue the analysis in terms of an arithmetical example. Let the demand and supply curves of labour be given by

$$\text{Demand} \quad w = 20 - 4L \tag{A2.5.6}$$

$$\text{Supply} \quad w = (P^e / P)(-10 + 6L) \tag{A2.5.7}$$

Solving (A2.5.6) and (A2.5.7) for w and L and substituting L into equation (A2.4.1) to determine y, we can determine the level of y for each level of P, given P^e.

In Table A2.5.1 we give the calculations for L and y for each level of P – first for a value of $P^e = 100$ and then for a higher value of price expectations; namely, $P^e = 120$.

It can be observed from Table 2.5.1 that, first, for each value of P^e, as the price level rises so the level of output rises. In other words, there is a positive relationship between P and y – the AS curve is upward sloping. Second, the AS curve for $P^e = 120$ lies above the AS curve for $P^e = 100$. Hence, a rise in price expectations raises the AS curve. Third, whenever price expectations are fulfilled (i.e. whenever $P = P^e$), then the amount of labour employed is the same and the level of output is the same. Thus, when price expectations are 100 and the price level is also 100, then labour employed is 3 units and output is 42 units. When the expected price level is 120 and the price level is 120, then labour employed is once again 3 units and the level of output is again 42 units. Finally, within this arithmetical model, the natural rate of employment is 3 units and the natural rate of income is 42 units.

The framework can readily deal with taxes on wages. Assume that labour supply is determined by the net expected real wage, w_n^e. Then

$$w_n^e = (P / P^e)(1 - t_1)w \tag{A2.5.8}$$

where t_1 is the tax on wages. It is readily verified that this changes the coefficients in the labour supply equation, given by equation (A2.5.4) to $l_0/(1-t_1)$ and $l_1/(1-t_1)$ respectively; in other words, the labour supply equation takes the form

$$w = (P^e/P)[l_0/(1-t_1) + l_1 L/(1-t_1)] \tag{A2.5.9}$$

A rise in the marginal rate of tax, t_1, raises the absolute value of the intercept (on the w-axis) and raises the slope coefficient in equation (A2.5.9), so shifting the AS curve upward.

Chapter 3

THE DYNAMIC MODEL

In the preceding chapter we established that in a model with workers holding incorrect expectations about the current price level ($P^e \neq P$) and downward rigidity of money wages, it is possible for an equilibrium level of income to be determined which is other than at the natural level (y_n). However, for the model to be determinate it is necessary to assume that (1) expected inflation is zero ($\hat{P}^e = 0$), (2) there is no change in (labour) productivity ($\hat{a}_L = 0$), and (3) there is a zero expected change in the exchange rate ($\hat{S}^e = 0$). Under these assumptions the model determines the price level and the level of real income. Because of the assumption of zero inflation, the model is sometimes called a *fix-price model*. In such a fix-price model, there is nothing in the system to move the economy towards the natural rate of income, other than by government management.

In this chapter, we wish to investigate more thoroughly the dynamic elements which enter the analysis. What we intend to show is that it is not the level of prices which is determined in the system but, rather, the rate of inflation. Clearly, given the price level in the preceding period, and given that the system determines the rate of inflation, then the price level in the following period is determined.[1] To keep the analysis manageable we will continue to assume that the expected rate of change in the exchange rate is given. In this chapter, the intention is to concentrate on establishing the dynamic forces which determine the level of real income and the rate of inflation. Furthermore, the emphasis of this chapter, like the preceding one, is to lay out the bare bones of the dynamic model. In later chapters, we will use the model to analyse a number of issues and controversies in more detail.

It may help if we indicate where we are going in this chapter. As indicated in Chapter 2, the labour market plays a very crucial role in the determination of the aggregate supply curve. In Section 3.1 we look a little more closely at the demand for labour, and we argue that it does not only depend on the real wage but also on the level of expected income. Once again, to keep the discussion within reasonable bounds at this stage, we will assume that the expected level of income is determined exogenously. In Section 3.2 we consider in some detail a price-setting equation which not only relates the price level to wages and productivity (as we established in the last chapter) but also to the price of imported raw materials. By explicitly introducing raw material prices, we can establish, for this specification at least, the relationship between aggregate supply and the exchange rate.

In order to establish the relationship between price inflation and the level of income, we introduce two reaction functions. The first relates the rate of wage inflation to the gap between unemployment and its natural level. The second relates the unemployment gap (the gap between actual unemployment and the natural rate of unemployment) to the gap between income and the natural rate of income. This second reaction function is known as Okun's law. Hence, the procedure is to relate price inflation to wage inflation; to relate wage inflation to the unemployment gap; and, finally, to relate the unemployment gap to the income gap. Taken together the set of relationships implies that price inflation is related to the level of real income. This establishes what is called the short-run Phillips curve. In Section 3.3 we use this analysis to consider the dynamic model for an economy with an expected rate of inflation of zero.

This is not in itself sufficient to determine the rate of inflation and the level of income. In simple terms, it indicates dynamic forces only on the supply-side of the market. However, the pressure on prices to rise or fall because of changes occurring in the goods market or the money market, is not captured in the short-run Phillips curve. Such pressures from the demand-side of the economy are dealt with in Section 3.4. In this section, we provide the final piece of the puzzle. We show how demand pressures can be captured in terms of a demand-pressure curve, which relates price inflation to real income. The demand-pressure curve, together with the short-run Phillips curve, can determine the rate of inflation and the level of real income.

One simple way to think about the dynamic forces is as follows. Imagine the aggregate supply curve shifting over time. This shift would imply a rate of price inflation for each period. It is possible to relate this price inflation to the level of income – this is the short-run Phillips curve. But clearly, it is also the case that the aggregate demand curve can shift over time. This, too, will give a relationship between price inflation and the level of income – this is the demand-pressure curve. Together these determine the rate of inflation and the level of income.

If there is to be both a dynamic and a static equilibrium, then the rate of inflation determined by the short-run Phillips curve and the demand-pressure curve must be such that the IS curve and the LM curve are fixed and such that income remains at that level determined by the intersection of the short-run Phillips curve and the demand-pressure curve.

In Section 3.5, we consider in more detail the long-run Phillips curve which has attracted so much attention in the literature. This not only allows us to consider the traditional Phillips curve in the inflation – unemployment space, it also enables us to clarify the particular interpretation of 'long run' in this analysis. In the final section, we take a brief look at the UK economy over the period 1960–87 in the light of this dynamic model.

3.1 A RECONSIDERATION OF THE DEMAND FOR LABOUR

We commence our analysis by reconsidering the demand for labour. In Chapter 2, we established that the demand for labour was determined by the real wage or conversely, the wage demanded was given by

$$w = \mu a_L = d(L) \tag{3.1}$$

But it is also the case that if businessmen expect the rate of real income to decline (rise) persistently, then regardless of the real wage they will begin to lay off (take on) labour. Short-term changes over the business cycle are unlikely to lead to major changes in the demand for labour. In the short run, a rise in real income, and hence a rise in the demand for a firm's product, will be met out of inventories. But a short-run decline will lead to an accumulation of inventories. What we are here referring to is a persistent decline (rise) over the business cycle. Put another way, the demand for labour is a function not only of the real wage but also of the level of expected income. Expressing this as the relationship between the real wage and labour employed, we have

$$w = D(L, y^e) \qquad D_L > 0, D_{y^e} > 0 \tag{3.2}$$

The difficulty is that we must now explain how expectations about real income are determined. Also we would need to introduce inventories explicitly into the model. We will side-step both by assuming that they are exogenous. Given the assumption about expected income, a rise in the level of expected income will shift the demand curve of labour to the right, while a fall in the level of expected real income will shift the labour demand curve to the left.

3.2 THE RELATIONSHIP BETWEEN PRICES AND WAGES

In establishing this relationship we abstract from the problem of the expected level of income and assume a simple mark-up pricing. Let average cost be given by labour costs (WL) plus the costs of imported raw materials ($P_m Q_m$, where P_m is the home-price of imported raw materials and Q_m the quantity of raw materials used) divided by output, y. We assume that the quantity of imported raw materials used in production is proportional to output, i.e.

$$Q_m = \beta y \tag{3.3}$$

Average costs are thus

$$AC = (WL/y) + \beta P_m$$
$$= (W/a_L) + \beta P_m \tag{3.4}$$

where, again, $a_L \equiv y/L$. If price is a mark-up, π, over average cost, then

$$P = (1 + \pi)[(W/a_L) + \beta P_m] \tag{3.5}$$

We now make two assumptions:

(1) $P_m = P_m^*/S$ \tag{3.6}

where P_m^* is the foreign price of raw materials and S is the exchange rate.

(2) $P_m^* = c^* P^*$ \tag{3.7}

The second assumption asserts that the foreign price of raw materials is proportional to the foreign price level. Given the interpretation of R, as specified by equation (2.7), then

$$P_m = P_m^*/S = c^*P^*/S = c^*P/R \tag{3.8}$$

Therefore,

$$P = (1 + \pi)[(W/a_L) + (\beta c^*/R)P] \tag{3.9}$$

or

$$P = \frac{W}{[(1/(1 + \pi)) - (\beta c^*/R)]a_L} \qquad (3.10)$$

It is clear from this result that the price level is related to the wage level, W, productivity, a_L, the mark-up, π, and to the relative price at home and abroad, R.

In Appendix 3.1, we derive three cases in detail. Here we simply state the results.

Case 1 Labour productivity is constant and so too are relative prices and the profit mark-up. Under these assumptions we can think of the price equation as given by

$$P = a'W \qquad (3.11)$$

where
$$a' = 1/[(1 + \pi) - (\beta c^*/R)]a_L$$

which in turn means that the percentage change in the price level (the rate of inflation, $\hat{P}$) is equal to the rate of wage inflation, $\hat{W}$, i.e.

$$\hat{P} = \hat{W} \qquad (3.12)$$

Case 2 If we assume that the profit mark-up is constant and that relative prices at home and abroad are constant (i.e. $\hat{R} = 0$), but there is a change in labour productivity (i.e. $\hat{a}_L \neq 0$), then price inflation is equal to the rate of wage inflation less the percentage change in productivity, namely,

$$\hat{P} = \hat{W} - \hat{a}_L \qquad (3.13)$$

Case 3 If there is a change in wages, productivity and competitiveness, but assuming the profit mark-up is constant, then we show in Appendix 3.1 that price inflation can be expressed as

$$\hat{P} = \hat{W} - \hat{a}_L - a\hat{R} \qquad a > 0 \qquad (3.14)$$

These results are intuitively plausible. With mark-up pricing, if the only change to costs is wage costs, then prices will rise by the same percentage as wages ($\hat{P} = \hat{W}$). If labour productivity is rising, then only when wage inflation exceeds this will there be pressure on prices to rise ($\hat{P} = \hat{W} - \hat{a}_L$). Finally, if there is a rise in raw material prices, then this will affect most firms in the economy, and with mark-up pricing there will be a tendency for this increase in costs to be pushed onto the consumer and thus domestic prices will rise. For instance, if the spot exchange rate depreciates (S falls and hence R falls), then – under assumption (1) – this leads to a rise in raw material prices, which in turn raises home prices. Thus P and R are negatively related.

3.3 TWO REACTION FUNCTIONS

Thus far we have related price inflation to wage inflation. We must now relate wage inflation to unemployment and, further, unemployment to income.

What must be captured in the equation which expresses inflation as a function of the level of unemployment is how the state of unemployment creates pressure on wages to rise and

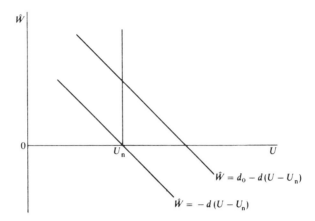

Figure 3.1 Wage–unemployment reaction function.

fall. Not only that, what must but also be included (even if only at a simple level) is how trades unions can push up the rate of inflation. If unemployment is less than the natural rate of unemployment (to be explained in detail in a later chapter), it could be argued that industry is overmanned or that the government has stepped in to raise the level of employment. In the first instance, the wage bill of firms is unnecessarily high; in the second case, pressure is being created in various sectors of the economy, and wages are being bid up as labour becomes more scarce. Hence wage inflation is negatively related to the unemployment gap, $U - U_n$. Similarly, if unemployment is greater than the natural level, there is slack in the economy and there will be pressure to bring wages down.[2] This would suggest a simple linear relationship of the form

$$\hat{W} = - d(U - U_n) \tag{3.15}$$

where d is a positive coefficient. This reaction function is shown in Fig. 3.1 by the line through the natural rate of unemployment, U_n. However, this is too restrictive. Trades unions have no other means of raising wages than to influence the value of d. A more convenient, and still simple, form is

$$\hat{W} = d_0 - d(U - U_n) \tag{3.16}$$

Thus, even when unemployment equals its natural rate it is still possible that there is wage inflation in the economy if trades unions are exerting power to raise wages. Thus, in this instance, d_0 is positive. Any attempt to curb the power of the unions can be interpreted as a fall in d_0. Furthermore, an *acceleration* in the rate of wage inflation is likely to be captured in a rise in d. This will result in the lines in Fig. 3.1 becoming steeper.

   If we are going to establish the equilibrium rate of inflation and equilibrium level of income, then we must further establish a relationship between unemployment and the level of income. This usually takes the following form:

$$U - U_n = - q(y - y_n) \tag{3.17}$$

where q is a positive coefficient. The point about this relationship is that if the level of real income is at its natural level, then so is the level of unemployment. In addition, the greater the gap between the level of income and the natural level, the greater is the gap between

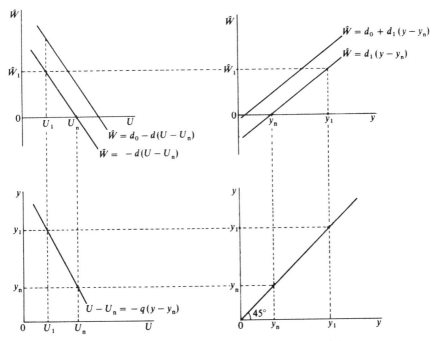

Figure 3.2 Derivation of the wage inflation–income relation.

unemployment and its natural level. This is more of an empirical relationship; it was first pointed out by Okun, and thus has become known as Okun's law. Of course, it is far from being a 'law', and it is not at all clear that the relationship is either this simple or even stable. An extended discussion of Okun's law can be found in Appendix 3.2. But here let us simply accept it.

We can substitute equation (3.17) into the wage inflation equation (3.16). Thus,

$$\hat{W} = d_0 - d(U - U_n)$$
$$= d_0 + dq(y - y_n) \qquad (3.18)$$

which gives the wage inflation equation in terms of income:

$$\hat{W} = d_0 + d_1(y - y_n) \qquad (3.19)$$

where $d_1 \equiv qd$.

Result (3.19) is a relationship between wage inflation and real income. The derivation of this wage equation is shown in Fig. 3.2. In this diagram we have constructed the wage–income relationship for the two wage–unemployment reaction functions drawn in Fig. 3.1.

It is now possible to substitute this result into each of the three cases we outlined above in equations (3.12), (3.13) and (3.14). Hence,

$$\text{Case 1} \quad \hat{P} = d_0 + d_1(y - y_n) \qquad (3.20)$$

$$\text{Case 2} \quad \hat{P} = d_0 + d_1(y - y_n) - \hat{a}_L \qquad (3.21)$$

$$\text{Case 3} \quad \hat{P} = d_0 + d_1(y - y_n) - \hat{a}_L - a\hat{R} \qquad (3.22)$$

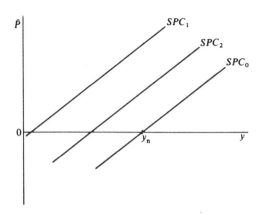

Figure 3.3 The short-run Phillips curve.

Each case gives a *positive* relationship between price inflation, $\hat{P}$, and the level of real income, y. Each case is a particular specification of the short-run Phillips curve (SPC). In Fig. 3.3 we have drawn SPC_0 to denote the relationship $\hat{P} = d_1(y - y_n)$; SPC_1 and SPC_2 denote cases 1 and 2 respectively. Case 3 is not drawn but it will lie above SPC_2 for, say, an appreciation of the exchange rate (namely, for a rise in S and hence in R) and below for a depreciation (namely, a fall in S and hence in R). We will frequently refer to Case 3 which typifies many economies through the 1970s and 1980s.

The relationship between the short-run Phillips curve and the aggregate supply curve can be illustrated more intuitively with the help of Fig. 3.4. In Fig. 3.4(a) we have an aggregate demand curve, AD, a short-run aggregate supply curve, SAS, and a long-run aggregate supply curve, LAS. In Fig. 3.4(b) we have a short-run Phillips curve, SPC_0. The economy is initially at equilibrium point E_0 with a price level of P_0 and income y_0. Note also that SAS_0 is drawn on the assumption that the nominal wage is W_0. Furthermore, we assume that expected inflation is also at zero.

Now suppose aggregate demand shifts to AD_1. The economy will move to equilibrium point E_1 and real income will rise to y_1. However, the rise in prices to P_1 will lower the real wage (to W_0/P_1). Workers will accordingly request a higher nominal wage in order to preserve their real wage. The real wage will be preserved if the nominal wage rises by the rate of inflation $\hat{P}_1 = (P_1 - P_0)/P_0$. This is so because $P_1 = P_0(1 + \hat{P}_1)$ and $W_1 = W_0(1 + \hat{P}_1)$, so $W_1/P_1 = W_0(1 + \hat{P}_1)/P_0(1 + \hat{P}_1) = W_0/P_0$. This will shift SAS to SAS_1. Note that SAS_1 must pass through point Z if wages rise by the same percentage as prices. However, this will move the economy from point E_1 to point E_2 in the upper diagram. The question we now raise is: how can the economy maintain the same higher level of output of y_1?

Since at point E_2 the level of income is below y_1, then it is necessary for aggregate demand to be raised, which is shown by AD_2. This will move the economy to point E_3 where AD_2 cuts SAS_1. But we know that SAS_1 is $\hat{P}_1$ percentage points above SAS_0 (since this was the increase in wages). Thus, P_2 is also $\hat{P}_1$ above P_1. However, at E_3 workers have nominal wages of W_1, which is based on a price level of P_1. Accordingly, they will raise their money wage by $(P_2 - P_1)/P_1 = (P_1 - P_0)/P_0 = \hat{P}_1$. This will shift SAS up once again by $\hat{P}_1$. This is exactly the result shown in the lower diagram by point B. Notice that if income were to be maintained at

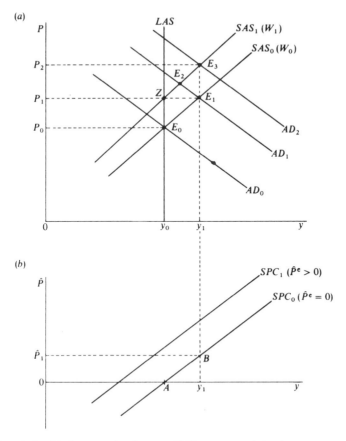

Figure 3.4 The relationship between the short-run Phillips curve and the short-run aggregate supply curve.

a higher level than y_1, AD would have shifted to the right by more than AD_1 and the price level, and hence the rate of inflation, would have been higher. This means that a higher level of income is related to a higher level of inflation, i.e. SPC is positively sloped in the $(\hat{P}, y)$-space.

Throughout this argument it is assumed that the expected rate of inflation is zero. Had the expected rate of inflation been positive, then workers would have built such expectations into their wage claims. The result would be a new SPC curve above SPC_0, shown by SPC_1. It must be above because the original Phillips curve is showing the result of maintaining income at some specified level and the resulting actual inflation – starting from an expectation of no inflation. If there is an expectation of inflation, then this would also be included in any wage claim. Hence $SPC_1(\hat{P}^e > 0)$ is above $SPC_0(\hat{P}^e = 0)$.

So far we have ignored price expectations. But it is possible to view the rate of price inflation as, say, Case 3 plus the expected rate of inflation. If the expected rate were zero, then we would have Case 3 exactly. If, however, the expected rate were positive, then we would expect the actual rate of inflation to be higher. If we included the expected rate of inflation, we have what is called in the literature the *expectations-augmented Phillips curve* (EAPC). Thus,

$$\hat{P} = d_0 + d_1(y - y_n) - \hat{a}_L - a\hat{R} + \hat{P}^e \tag{3.23}$$

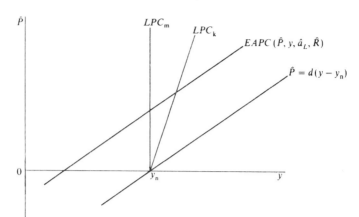

Figure 3.5 The expectations-augmented Phillips curve and the long-run Phillips curve.

We can simplify the result down to the following linear equation:

$$\hat{P} = C_0 + C_1 y - C_2 \hat{a}_L - C_3 \hat{R} + C_4 \hat{P}^e \tag{3.24}$$

where C_0, C_1, C_2, C_3 and C_4 are positive coefficients. The curve is drawn in Fig. 3.5 which relates the rate of inflation, $\hat{P}$, to the level of real income, y. This expectations-augmented Phillips curve is drawn for a given percentage change in labour productivity, a given percentage change in the real exchange rate and a given expected rate of inflation. (It also implies a given expected level of income.)

We have explicitly made the point that the Phillips curve which we have so far derived is a short-run curve. In the long run, price expectations are fulfilled, i.e. $\hat{P}^e = \hat{P}$. Substituting this condition into equation (3.24), we obtain

$$\hat{P} = \frac{C_0 + C_1 y - C_2 \hat{a}_L - C_3 \hat{R}}{1 - C_4} \tag{3.25}$$

If, as monetarists argue, the value of $C_4 = 1$, this curve is vertical, as shown by LPC_m in Fig. 3.5. It is vertical at the natural level of real income, however, only in the additional situation where $d_0 = 0$ and $\hat{a}_L = \hat{R} = 0$. If, as some neo-Keynesians argue, the value of C_4 lies between zero and unity, then there is also a positive trade-off between inflation and the level of real income (or a negative trade-off between inflation and unemployment) even in the long run, as shown by LPC_k in Fig. 3.5.

3.4 THE DYNAMICS OF AN ECONOMY WITH ZERO EXPECTED INFLATION

Before continuing with the model, let us pause for a moment to see how the model developed so far can be used to determine the level of prices and level of income when the expected rate of inflation is zero. In order to simplify the analysis, we will assume no change in the competitive position of the economy ($\hat{R} = 0$) and no change in labour productivity ($\hat{a}_L = 0$). This version of the model is captured in Fig. 3.6(a, b).

As illustrated in the diagram the economy is in equilibrium at real income level y_0 where the rate of inflation is zero. We assume throughout that the expected rate of inflation is zero.

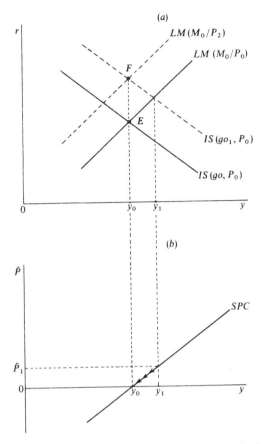

Figure 3.6 Dynamics of an economy with zero expected inflation.

This means that the short-run Phillips curve remains fixed. Given that the IS curve and the LM curve intersect at income level y_0 (and we will assume the BP curve passes through this intersection), then there is no reason for this level of income to change unless either the IS curve and/or the LM curve shifts. Given the assumption about exogenous real government spending and exogenous nominal money supply, the only thing that can change in the model is prices. But, as Fig. 3.6(b) reveals, at income level y_0, the rate of inflation is zero; and so prices do not alter.

Suppose now that real government spending is increased to go_1 in the next period only, i.e. a one-period increase in real government spending. This will initially shift IS to IS (go_1, P_0). This puts pressure on prices to rise. The level of inflation in the next period is $\hat{P}_1$. The economy moves over time. In the next period government spending returns to its former level of go. The initial rise in prices shifts the LM curve temporarily to the left as real money balances fall. With the return of government spending to its former level (the IS curve has returned to its initial position), price inflation will return to zero. As prices fall so the LM curve shifts right returning to its initial position. The economy returns to point E in the upper diagram, with a zero rate of inflation and income also returning to its former level of y_0.

Had there been a permanent increase in government spending, then the IS curve would have shifted to the right and remained there in subsequent periods. This would have raised the rate of inflation to $\hat{P}_1$ as before. This rise in inflation will shift the LM curve to the left. It will only stop moving when inflation is zero once again, which is at the higher price level of P_2. In this case the economy settles down at point F in the upper diagram, while inflation is zero and income returns to its former level of y_0.

The model has the property of converging on an equilibrium, partly because of the various assumptions about exogenous variables, but also because we have assumed a zero inflation rate to sustain income level at y_0. The model is, in fact, incomplete. It does not indicate a stable solution to inflation other than at a zero rate. Something is missing and we can make a partial guess at what this might be. The inflation rate so far is determined solely by the short-run Phillips curve. In other words, inflation is supply determined. This is clearly not the case in general. Inflation can also be created (and, hence, be determined) by demand pressure. What we also require to analyse is inflation arising from aggregate demand pressure.

3.5 THE DEMAND-PRESSURE CURVE

As the name implies, the demand pressure curve indicates the pressure on the price level arising from shifts over time in the aggregate demand curve.[3] In the preceding chapter we established the form of the aggregate demand curve, represented as equation (3.26):

$$y = \frac{z_0 + h\hat{P}^e - (f+g)R}{Q} + \left(\frac{h}{uQ}\right)(M_0/P) \tag{3.26}$$

where $Q = 1 - b(1-t_1) + m + (kh/u)$. If we consider changes, then

$$\Delta y = \frac{\Delta z_0 + h\Delta\hat{P}^e - (f+g)\Delta R}{Q} + \left(\frac{h}{uQ}\right)\Delta(M_0/P) \tag{3.27}$$

But

$$\Delta(M_0/P) = (M_0/P)(\hat{M} - \hat{P}) \tag{3.28}$$

so we can re-write equation (3.27) in the form

$$\Delta y = \frac{\Delta z_0 + h\Delta\hat{P}^e - (f+g)\Delta R}{Q} + \left(\frac{h}{uQ}\right)(M_0/P)(\hat{M} - \hat{P}) \tag{3.29}$$

If we assume price expectations remain constant ($\Delta\hat{P}^e = 0$) and that there is no change in the competitive position ($\Delta R = 0$), we can express equation (3.29) in the form

$$\Delta y = \frac{\Delta z_0}{Q} + \left(\frac{h}{uQ}\right)(M_0/P)(\hat{M} - \hat{P}) \tag{3.30}$$

i.e.

$$y = [y_{-1} + (\Delta z_0/Q)] + (h/uQ)(M_0/P)(\hat{M} - \hat{P}) \tag{3.31}$$

or, more simply,

$$y = D_0 + D_1(\hat{M} - \hat{P}) \tag{3.32}$$

where D_1 is a positive coefficient and D_0 depends on the change in autonomous spending (Δz_0).

The relationship between aggregate demand and the demand-pressure curve can be illustrated more intuitively with the help of Fig. 3.7(a,b). Initially we have an aggregate

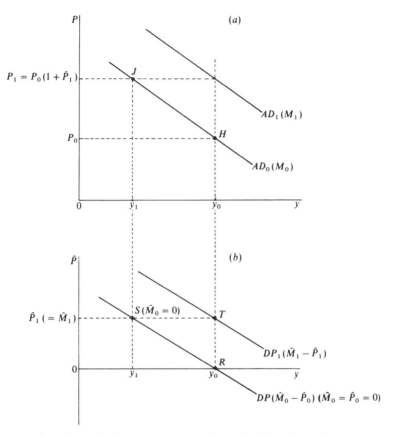

Figure 3.7 The relationship between aggregate demand and the demand-pressure curve.

demand curve AD_0 (Fig. 3.7(a)). This is drawn for a particular *level* of money stock, namely $M0$. The price level is P_0 and there is no inflation and no growth of money ($\hat{P} = \hat{M}_0 = 0$). Throughout we assume no exogenous shifts from fiscal policy. Since inflation and monetary growth are both zero, then there is no pressure to change income. This is shown by point R on DP_0 (Fig. 3.7(b)).

Now suppose for some reason that inflation were $\hat{P}_1$. In the next period prices would rise to $P_1 = P_0(1 + \hat{P}_1)$. With monetary growth still zero, this will mean a fall in real money balances and a movement up AD_0 from H to J, with income falling to y_1. This lower level of income can be maintained if nominal money balances are allowed to grow at the same rate as prices, namely $\hat{M}_1 (= \hat{P}_1)$. Put another way, any point on the DP curve indicates monetary growth *relative* to inflation. A fall in real money balances (higher inflation) must be associated with a lower level of income.

But DP_0 is based on the assumption that income is equal to y_0 at zero inflation and zero monetary growth. Return to point H with income at y_0. Suppose nominal money balances are growing at a constant positive rate $\hat{M}_1$. In period 1 the AD curve will move to AD_1. If income is to remain constant at y_0, then it follows that prices must rise by the same amount. Thus, at income level y_0 we have point T on DP_1. In other words, a higher monetary growth is represented by a DP curve to the right.

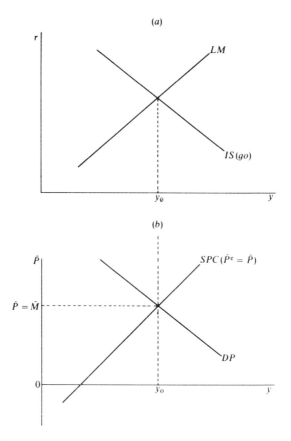

Figure 3.8 Constant inflation with constant monetary growth.

The dynamic version of the model is presented in Fig. 3.8(*a*, *b*). Initially, income is at y_0 and government spending is $\overline{go}$. With government spending held constant, the only reason for income to change from the point of view of demand pressure is if the money supply is growing at a faster rate than the price level. Suppose, then, the money supply growth is the same as the rate of inflation, i.e. $\hat{M} = \hat{P}$. Suppose further that the expected rate of inflation is given by $\hat{P}^e = \hat{P}$. This means that the LM curve remains stationary and so does the IS curve – assuming that the exchange rate depreciates to the same extent as the price change in order to keep R constant. The rate of inflation is determinate and positive. It can persist period after period with no change in real income – so long as expectations do not change, productivity does not change and the competitive position of the economy does not change! A simple numerical example is shown in Appendix 3.3.

The dynamics of the model are best appreciated by considering a change in real government spending, as shown in Fig. 3.9(*a*,*b*). First we will consider a one-period rise and then a permanent rise. We begin at point A in the lower diagram with inflation at the same rate as the growth of the money supply ($\hat{P}_0 = \hat{M}_0$) and income at y_0. The IS curve and the LM curve are given by IS_0 and LM_0 respectively. So long as there is no shock to the system this situation can be maintained since the IS curve and the LM curve remain stationary, the

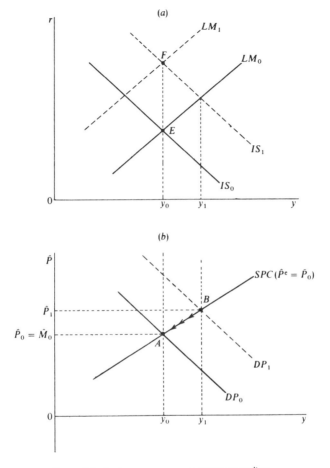

Figure 3.9 An increase in government spending.

demand-pressure curve and the Phillips curve also remain stationary and the actual rate of inflation is equal to the expected rate of inflation.

Now consider a one-period increase in government spending. In period 1 the IS curve shifts to IS_1 and the DP curve shifts to DP_1. In period 2 and subsequent periods the IS curve returns to IS_0 and the DP curve returns to DP_0. Although inflation initially increases to $\hat{P}_1$ (which temporarily shifts the LM curve left), this decreases to $\hat{P}_0$ and the economy returns to point E in Fig. 3.9(a) and to point A in the lower diagram.

In the case of a permanent rise in government spending, the IS curve moves to IS_1 and remains there. The DP curve shifts to DP_1 and the economy moves to point B in Fig. 3.9(b). However, now the rise in inflation shifts LM left. It will continue to shift left until inflation is brought down to its former level. The shift left in the LM curve shifts the demand-pressure curve left until it returns to DP_0. The rest is a movement to point F in the upper diagram and a return to point A in the lower diagram.

In the case of a one-period increase in the money supply, the LM curve shifts right to LM_1 for one period and then back to LM_0. Similarly, the DP curve shifts one period to DP_1 and then back again. Thus, with a one-period increase in the money supply, there is a

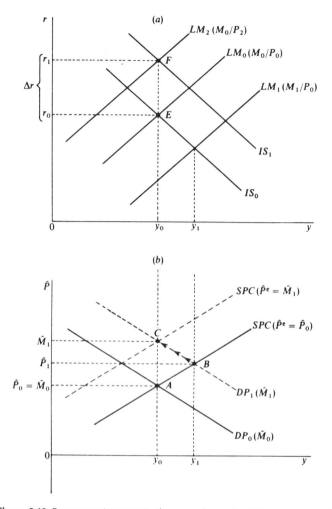

Figure 3.10 Permanent increase in the rate of growth of the money supply.

temporary rise in inflation, but the economy returns to its former equilibrium (point E in the upper diagram and point A in the lower diagram, Fig. 3.10).

In the case of a permanent shift in the money supply growth, to $\hat{M}_1$, say, the demand-pressure curve moves to DP_1, and the rate of inflation rises to $\hat{P}_1$, which is less than the growth of the money supply. The economy accordingly moves to point B in terms of Fig. 3.10(b). But now there is no reason for the economy to return to point A because the increase is sustained in each period.

Even so, the economy cannot remain at point B over the long run, the reason for this being that we have assumed a constant level of expected inflation. If the economy did move to point B, then the actual rate of inflation would exceed the expected rate of inflation. Market participants would soon realize this and so would revise their expectations upwards. We deal with this more fully later. For the moment it has *two* impacts: first, it means an upward shift in the short-run Phillips curve; and second, a rise in expected inflation will *lower* the expected real interest rate, which will lead to a rise in investment. The rise in investment, due to the revision of expectations, will shift the IS curve to the right. On the other hand, the shift upwards in the SPC will raise actual prices and thus will shift the LM curve left. The situation will stabilize once the IS curve has moved to IS_1 and the LM curve has moved to LM_2, i.e. a·movement to point F in Fig. 3.10(a) and point C in Fig. 3.10(b).

Why is this? The rise in inflation is now equal to the higher growth in money supply, and so real money balances are constant (hence there is no reason for any further movement in the LM curve). At point C actual inflation is equal to expected inflation and so there is no further movement in either the SPC or the IS curve. It is to be noted that the eventual rise in prices to P_2 denotes an inflation increase from $\hat{P}_0$ to level $\hat{M}_1$ (the distance AC in Fig. 3.10(b)). However, this increase is also the increase in expected inflation. It follows, then, that if income is to return to its former level of y_0, then the nominal interest rate will have to rise by exactly the rise in expected (and actual) inflation. This increase is represented by FE in Fig. 3.10(a), and the new interest rate is at the higher level of r_1. The economy has returned to an equilibrium, represented by points F and C, which can be maintained so long as no shocks to the system occur.

3.6 THE LONG-RUN PHILLIPS CURVE

At the end of Section 3.3, we referred to the long-run Phillips curve. In this section, the intention is to look more closely at this relationship. In particular we intend to show that 'long run' in the context of this analysis means a 'steady state' and that the long-run Phillips curve is only vertical at the natural level of income under special conditions.

The vertical long-run Phillips curve is usually derived for the very simple case. The usual derivation combines the result of case 1 (namely, $\hat{P} = \hat{W}$) and the simple wage inflation equation given in equation (3.7). Combining these and adding the expected rate of inflation, we have

$$\hat{P} = \hat{P}^e - d(U - U_n) \tag{3.33}$$

In the long run, the expected rate of inflation is equal to the actual rate of inflation. From this and equation (3.33), it follows that the rate of unemployment is equal to the natural rate. Regardless of the rate of inflation in the long run, there is no trade-off between inflation and unemployment.

The reasoning can be seen in terms of Fig. 3.11. We begin with the short-run Phillips curve SPC_0, which is drawn for a zero expected rate of inflation. Now suppose the government pursued a policy which kept the economy at an unemployment rate of U_1. If this was maintained, then the rate of inflation would be $\hat{P}_1$, which is greater than the level that people expected. Expectations would, accordingly, be revised upwards to the level $\hat{P}_1^e = \hat{P}_1$. This will, however, shift the short-run Phillips curve to SPC_1 (which is above SPC_0 by exactly the change in the expected rate of inflation). Unemployment will return to its natural level. If the rate of unemployment is maintained at U_1, then the actual rate of inflation will rise to $\hat{P}_2$, which is greater than the expected rate $\hat{P}_1^e$. Once again expectations will be revised upwards and unemployment will return to its natural level. So long as a policy is pursued to reduce unemployment below its natural level, the rate of inflation will

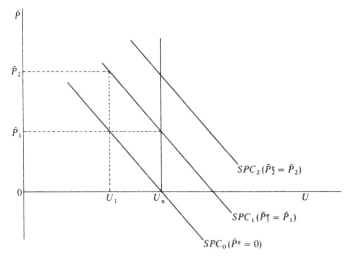

Figure 3.11 Acceleration in the rate of inflation.

accelerate. This acceleration in the rate of inflation arises because, in the long run, there is no trade-off between unemployment and inflation – at least in the version just presented.

It is clear from the foregoing analysis that 'long run' means that time period over which inflation expectations are brought into line with actual inflation. But let us consider this in terms of Case 3, namely, in terms of equations (3.14) and (3.16). If we substitute equation (3.16) into equation (3.14) and then add a term for expectations, we have

$$\hat{P} = z\hat{P}^e + d_0 - d(U - U_n) - \hat{a}_L - a\hat{R} \qquad (3.34)$$

If we set $\hat{P}^e = \hat{P}$, we have

$$\hat{P} = \frac{d_0 - d(U - U_n) - \hat{a}_L - a\hat{R}}{(1 - z)} \qquad (3.35)$$

It is clear from this equation that we require far more conditions to be met before we obtain a vertical long-run Phillips curve at the natural rate of unemployment, even if the period is long enough to bring expected and actual inflation rates into line. The set of conditions for a vertical long-run Phillips curve at the natural rate of unemployment are

$$
\left.
\begin{array}{l}
1. \ \hat{P}^e = \hat{P} \\
2. \ \hat{a}_L = 0 \\
3. \ \hat{R} = 0 \\
4. \ z = 1 \\
5. \ d_0 = 0
\end{array}
\right\} \qquad (3.36)
$$

Conditions (1)–(3) specify a *steady state*, i.e. a state where expectations are fulfilled and there is no change in productivity or in the real exchange rate. But even if there is such a steady state, a vertical Phillips curve requires conditions (4) and (5) to be met. Condition (4) means that expectations are *fully* anticipated. Neo-Kéynesians argue that expectations are not fully anticipated and thus $0 < z < 1$. But even if conditions (1)–(4) are met, there is no reason for condition (5) to be true.

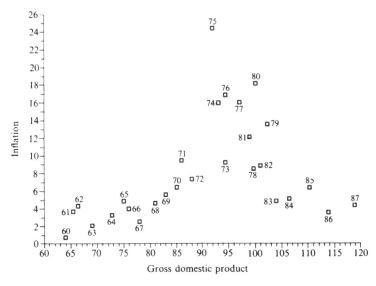

Figure 3.12 Scatter diagram of price inflation and real income in the UK, 1960–87.

The 'long run', when applied to the Phillips curve (whether vertical or not), refers to the *steady state*. This is clear when we recall that the capital stock is being held constant. In microeconomics, it is usual to define the short run as that time period over which at least one factor input is constant; the long run is the time period over which all factors of production are variable. In the present analysis, the long-run Phillips curve is for a constant capital stock. Put another way, the natural rate of unemployment in the steady state is for a given level of capital stock. This means that the time period is long enough for people to revise their expectations but not long enough for the capital stock to vary!

3.7 INFLATION AND OUTPUT FOR THE UK

It is not our intention at this point to discuss inflation, but it is worth seeing what the dynamic form of the model looks like for the UK economy. In Fig. 3.12, we present a scatter diagram for inflation and real income for the period 1960–87. Each point represents the intersection between the demand-pressure curve and the short-run Phillips curve. The path of observations over the 1960s is consistent with two possible explanations: (1) a shift right in the demand-pressure curve with a fairly flat and stable short-run Phillips curve; (2) alternatively, a shift right in both curves. As we note later, however, the short-run Phillips curve was fairly stable up until about 1967, and so the first explanation seems plausible. The 1970s, however, show a much more complex pattern. It is likely that both the Phillips curve and the demand-pressure curve were moving over this period. Furthermore, after the sharp rise in inflation, and the fall in output in 1975, there is a clear counterclockwise movement in the relationship between inflation and real income (if the information were displayed in the inflation–unemployment space, then the movement would be clockwise). The observations in Fig. 3.12 would indicate some major shifts in both the demand pressure curve and the short-run Phillips curve. Possible reasons for such shifts will be advanced later in the book – especially in Parts II and III.

NOTES

1. If the system determines the rate of inflation, $\hat{P}$, then given the price in the preceding period, P_0, it follows that the price in the next period, P_1, is also determined, since

$$P_1 = P_0(1 + \hat{P})$$

2. As it stands, this argument assumes that labour is homogeneous. A more complete model would need to relax this assumption. Furthermore, it would need to deal with the coexistence of both unemployment and vacancies – a point we will return to in Chapter 14.

3. There is no general consensus in the literature on the demand-pressure curve. It is *not* the same as the aggregate demand curve. The aggregate demand curve relates the price *level* to the level of real income; the demand-pressure curve relates the rate of *inflation* to the level of real income. This is discussed in some detail in Humphrey (1976).

APPENDIX 3.1 THE DERIVATION OF PRICE INFLATION

In this appendix the intention is to develop an expression for price inflation in terms of other variables, using the analysis developed in Chapter 3. We first derive an expression for $\hat{P}$ allowing wages, W, productivity, a_L, and the real exchange rate, R, to alter. We then consider some special cases which have arisen in various discussions of inflation.

We begin by using equations (3.5), (3.8) and (3.10) – which are listed again here:

$$P = (1 + \pi)[(W/a_L) + \beta P_m] \qquad (A3.1.1)$$

$$P_m = c^* P^* / S \qquad (A3.1.2)$$

which together give rise to

$$P = \frac{W}{[(1/(1 + \pi)) - (\beta c^*/R)]a_L}$$

Let

$$\theta = 1/(1 + \pi)$$

$$\varepsilon = \beta c^*$$

both constant. Note in particular, that we are assuming the profit mark-up, π, is constant. We will retain this assumption until the end of this appendix.

Hence,

$$P = W/[\theta - (\varepsilon/R)]a_L \qquad (A3.1.3)$$

Taking natural logarithms, i.e. to base e, and utilizing the results about percentages in Appendix 1.1, we have

$$\text{Ln } P = \text{Ln } W - \text{Ln}[\theta - (\varepsilon/R)] - \text{Ln } a_L \qquad (A3.1.4)$$

Differentiating totally,

$$d\text{Ln} P = d\text{Ln } W - d\text{Ln}[\theta - (\varepsilon/R)] - d\text{Ln} a_L$$

$$dP/P = dW/W - (da_L/a_L) - [(\varepsilon/R)/(\theta - (\varepsilon/R))](dR/R)$$

Using the hat notation developed in Appendix 1.1, we have

$$\hat{P} = \hat{W} - \hat{a}_L - [(\varepsilon/R)/(\theta - (\varepsilon/R))]\hat{R} \qquad (A3.1.5)$$

In the case where R is at the original level, we can simplify expression (A3.1.5) as follows:

$$\hat{P} = \hat{W} - \hat{a}_L - a\hat{R} \qquad (A3.1.6)$$

where

$$a = (\varepsilon/R)/[\theta - (\varepsilon/R)]$$

Case 1

The first case to consider is the simplest. Let productivity, a_L, and the real exchange rate remain constant. This means

$$\hat{a}_L = \hat{R} = 0 \qquad (A3.1.7)$$

Under the assumptions embodied in equation (A3.1.7), and recalling that we are also assuming the profit margin is constant, then expression (A3.1.6) reduces to the simple result

$$\hat{P} = \hat{W} \qquad (A3.1.8)$$

Case 2

In Case 2 we assume that the real exchange rate is constant, hence $\hat{R} = 0$. Then expression (A3.1.6) reduces to

$$\hat{P} = \hat{W} - \hat{a}_L \qquad (A3.1.9)$$

Case 3

In this final situation only the profit margin is held constant. Hence, we have exactly that given in expression (A3.1.6), namely,

$$\hat{P} = \hat{W} - \hat{a}_L - a\hat{R}$$

Notice also that the constant a is positive only if

$$\theta > \varepsilon/R \qquad (A3.1.10)$$

Allowing π to change

If π is also allowed to vary then

$$\mathrm{d}\,\mathrm{Ln}\,P = \mathrm{d}\,\mathrm{Ln}\,W - \mathrm{d}\,\mathrm{Ln}[\theta - (\varepsilon/R)] - \mathrm{d}\,\mathrm{Ln}\,a_L$$

i.e.

$$\hat{P} = \hat{W} - \hat{a}_L - \mathrm{d}\,\mathrm{Ln}[\theta - (\varepsilon/R)] \qquad (A3.1.11)$$

But

$$\mathrm{d}\,\mathrm{Ln}[\theta - (\varepsilon/R)] = \frac{\mathrm{d}\theta - \mathrm{d}(\varepsilon/R)}{[\theta - (\varepsilon/R)]}$$

$$= \frac{-(1+\pi)^{-2}\mathrm{d}\pi + (\varepsilon/R^2)\mathrm{d}R}{[\theta - (\varepsilon/R)]}$$

$$= \frac{-(1+\pi)^{-2}\mathrm{d}\pi + (\varepsilon/R)\hat{R}}{[\theta - (\varepsilon/R)]}$$

Hence,

$$\hat{P} = \hat{W} - \hat{a}_L - \frac{(\varepsilon/R)\hat{R}}{[\theta - (\varepsilon/R)]} + \frac{\mathrm{d}\pi}{(1+\pi)^2[\theta + (\varepsilon/R)]}$$

or

$$\hat{P} = \hat{W} - \hat{a}_L - a\hat{R} + bd\pi \qquad\qquad (A3.1.12)$$

where

$$a = \frac{(\varepsilon/R)}{[\theta - (\varepsilon/R)]} \quad \text{and} \quad b = \frac{1}{(1 + \pi)^2 [\theta - (\varepsilon/R)]}$$

APPENDIX 3.2 OKUN'S LAW

The second reaction function we considered in the text was the relationship between unemployment and the income gap. This relationship was first pointed out by Okun (1965) in the US, and by Godley and Shepherd (1964) in the UK. They argued that unemployment was related to excess demand in the goods market. As output expanded to reach its full potential, so employment would rise in order to produce this output. Hence, unemployment would fall. A *proxy* for excess demand in the goods market is the gap between income and potential income $(y - y_p)$, expressed as a percentage of potential income, y_p (although Okun took it as a percentage of actual income).

Using the concepts of the natural rate of unemployment and the natural rate of income, the latter being taken to be equivalent to Okun's potential income, then the relationship considered by Okun was

$$U - U_n = -q[(y - y_n)/y_n] \qquad q > 0 \qquad\qquad (A3.2.1)$$

where q is Okun's coefficient. Thus, if income was at its natural level (at full potential), then unemployment would be at its natural level. Any positive excess demand in the goods market would be reflected in income rising above its natural level which, in turn, would be reflected by a fall in unemployment below its natural level. For example, if income was 1% above its natural level, then unemployment would fall by q% points; while if income was 1% below its natural level, unemployment would rise by q% points.

What interpretation can be placed on Okun's coefficient, q, given in equation (A3.2.1)? If we assume that output (real income) is related to labour such that

$$y = f(L) \qquad\qquad (A3.2.2)$$

then,

$$dy = f'(L)dL \qquad\qquad (A3.2.3)$$

Dividing both sides by y, and re-arranging the right-hand side, we have

$$dy/y = [f'(L)(L/y)](dL/L) \qquad\qquad (A3.2.4)$$

But $f'(L)(L/y)$ is the elasticity of output with respect to labour, which we can assume to be a constant, denoted by β. In addition, we can treat the growth in employment (dL/L) as equal to the fall in the rate of unemployment, $(U - U_{-1})$. Hence, we can express equation (A3.2.4) as

$$\hat{y} = -\beta(U - U_{-1}) \qquad \beta > 0 \qquad\qquad (A3.2.5)$$

or

$$U - U_{-1} = -(1/\beta)[(y - y_{-1})/y_{-1}] \qquad\qquad (A3.2.6)$$

If, in the preceding period, unemployment was equal to its natural level and income was also equal to its natural level, then it follows

$$U - U_n = -(1/\beta)[(y - y_n)/y_n] \qquad\qquad (A3.2.7)$$

Comparing equation (A3.2.7) with equation (A3.2.1), we can interpret Okun's coefficient as equal to the reciprocal of the elasticity of output with respect to labour, i.e.

$$q = 1/\beta \qquad\qquad (A3.2.8)$$

In other words, q denotes the percentage rise in employment necessary to generate a 1% increase in output.

Although equation (A3.2.1) has been referred to as *Okun's law*, it is far from being a true 'law'. It is merely a regularity between the change in unemployment and the output gap. Even the estimate of q provided by Okun in his original work, namely $q = 0.3$, has been shown to be an underestimate for the US and should in fact be in the region of 0.4. Although there have been some further investigations into Okun's law for the US economy, e.g. Perry (1977) and Tatom (1978), little work has been done for the UK. The early work by Godley and Shepherd (1964) related output to employment rather than to unemployment, indicating that a 1% income above the natural (equilibrium) level was associated with a 0.5% rise in employment.

To the extent that this relationship is unstable or ill-defined (e.g., in not taking account of changes in productivity), then so too will be the short-run Phillips curve which is derived by employing such a reaction function. It could be argued that one reason why Okun's law is so popular is because of the analytical convenience that it affords: allowing, as it does, a link to be made between income and the rate of inflation. To this end we employ a simplified version of Okun's law in the text, namely,

$$U - U_n = -q(y - y_n) \qquad \text{(A3.2.9)}$$

APPENDIX 3.3 A NUMERICAL EXAMPLE OF DP AND SPC

Consider the following two reaction functions:

(1) $\hat{W} = -0.2(U - U_n)$
(2) $U - U_n = -0.95(y - y_n)$

where it is to be noted that we have not included a positive intercept in the first reaction function. These two equations give a wage equation of the form

$$\hat{W} = 0.19(y - y_n)$$

Using Case 3 of Appendix 3.1 in the form

$$\hat{P} = \hat{W} - \hat{a}_L - 0.26\hat{R}$$

we obtain the expectations-augmented Phillips curve:

$$\hat{P} = 0.19(y - y_n) - \hat{a}_L - 0.26\hat{R} + \hat{P}^e$$

For $y_n = 42$ a numerical expression for the expectations-augmented Phillips curve is

$$\hat{P} = [-8 - \hat{a}_L - 0.26\hat{R}] + 0.19y + \hat{P}^e$$

Consider now the demand-pressure curve. First note that we can obtain coefficients of the aggregate demand curve from equation (A2.1.24) in Appendix 2.1 of Chapter 2 (p. 37). Since $1/Q$ is simply the multiplier for a variable interest rate, this is equal to 0.597. Using equation (3.29), we can easily compute the following coefficients of the demand pressure curve:

$$\text{coefficient of } dz_0 = 1/Q = 0.597$$
$$\text{coefficient of } d\hat{P}^e = h/Q = 2 \times 0.597 = 1.194$$
$$\text{coefficient of } dR = -(f + g)/Q = -7 \times 0.597 = -4.179$$
$$\text{coefficient of } (\hat{M} - \hat{P}) = (1/Q)(h/u)(M_0/P)$$
$$= 0.597 \times (2/0.5)(3/1) = 7.164$$

Finally, assuming that income in the preceding period is equal to 42, then the demand-pressure curve is

$$y = 42 + 0.597dz_0 + 1.194d\hat{P}^e - 4.179dR + 7.164(\hat{M} - \hat{P})$$

Theory

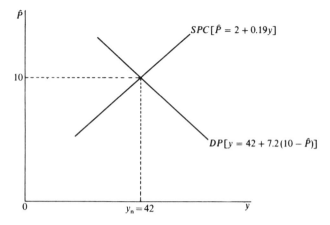

Figure A3.3.1 Equilibrium income and inflation.

We now make the following simplifying assumptions:

$$\hat{a}_L = 0 \qquad dR = 0$$
$$\hat{P}^e = 10 \qquad dz_0 = 0$$
$$\hat{M} = 10 \qquad d\hat{P}^e = 0$$

which give the following expressions for the demand pressure curve (DP) and the short-run expectations-augmented Phillips curve (SPC):

$$\text{DP:} \qquad y = 42 + 7.2(\hat{M} - \hat{P})$$
$$\text{SPC:} \qquad \hat{P} = -8 + 0.19y + \hat{P}^e$$

which under the simplifying assumption gives a solutions of

$$\hat{P} = 10 \qquad y = 42 = y_n$$

and is shown in Fig. A3.3.1.

Chapter 4

EXPECTATIONS AND MARKET CLEARING

It has been argued that one of the most significant changes in macroeconomics to have taken place over the past twenty or so years, has been in the area of expectations. Of course, expectations have been discussed in the past, most notably by Hicks in his *Value and Capital*, and by Keynes in his *General Theory*. The former, however, simply stated what condition must be placed on the elasticity of expectations in order to have a stable solution to an equilibrium system. On the other hand, Keynes treated expectations as exogenous. The major recent change has been in dealing with the *formation* of expectations. Other than treating expectations as exogenous, the most common treatment in the past was to assume that they were formed in an adaptive manner; that is to say, an adjustment was made to the error in the preceding expected value. We will deal with this in Section 4.2. Before doing so, however, we will discuss the meaning of 'expectations', in order that we can clearly see how the more modern treatment of expectation formation, in terms of 'rational expectations', is different from all that has gone before. We deal with rational expectations in Sections 4.3, 4.4 and 4.5.

One of the most characteristic features of modern macroeconomics, besides the formation of expectations, is that of market clearing. In simple terms, all transactions take place at equilibrium prices – where demand equals supply. Or, put another way, all transactions take place at market clearing prices. The reason for discussing this conceptual topic in this chapter alongside expectations, is that it is very difficult to separate the two concepts. More to the point, some authors attribute to expectations what is strictly attributable to market clearing.

4.1 WHAT DO WE MEAN BY 'EXPECTATIONS'?

What do we mean by 'expectations'? This may appear to be a simple question, but it is not. If the world was a place of certainty we would not need to have expectations – we would know exactly how variables are formed and exactly what values they take. Expectations, then, are concerned with unknown events. More specifically, they are concerned with unknown events in the future. A businessman may have expectations about future prices of his raw materials, the demand for his product, inflation and the future path of interest rates. He needs to form such expectations if he is to make sensible decisions. Similarly, in order to make decisions about consumption and saving, a consumer will need to formulate

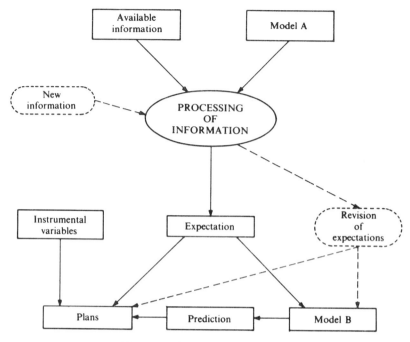

Figure 4.1 The expectations process.

expectations about his future income stream, the future path of interest rates and the rate of inflation in the future. Exporters and importers will need to consider not only the future path of interest rates at home and abroad, but also the expected appreciation or depreciation of the currency. Whenever there is an uncertain future, decision-makers are required to form expectations.

The expectation process is captured in Fig. 4.1, adapted from Frisch (1983). This diagram highlights a number of very important features about expectations which are worth discussing in some detail.

A decision-maker is thought of as a processing unit which combines the available information with some model. The model itself may or may not be well defined. By combining the available information with the model, an expectation is formed. This is usually an expectation about a particular variable, such as inflation, income, exchange rates, etc. By incorporating such expectations in a model – which may or may not be the same model as was used to process the information – a prediction is formed. A prediction involves no control over the variables as far as the decision-maker is concerned. A plan, on the other hand, is similar to a prediction except that the decision-maker has control over some instrumental variables. It is these variables which allow the decision-maker to plan, Frisch (1983) and Theil (1970).

Fig. 4.1 directs our attention to a number of questions:

1. Who is the processing agent?
2. Exactly how are expectations formed?
3. Does everyone process information in the same way?
4. For which variables are expectations being formed?

5. Is model *A* the same as model *B*?
6. Does everyone have access to the same information?
7. Does new information always lead to a revision of expectations?
8. How sensitive are predictions to different expectations formation?
9. How sensitive are predictions to different models used to derive predictions?

When expectations are treated exogenously, none of these questions are relevant. But more economists have come to realize that this is simply side-stepping the problem. Expectations play a major role in macroeconomic analysis and their formation must be dealt with explicitly. Once this is accepted, all the above nine questions are relevant!

So far we have made the point that expectations are about an unknown future event where the decision-maker processes information by means of a model in order to form the expectation. The model itself (model *A* in terms of Fig. 4.1) may be heuristic or it may be a formal economic or econometric model of the economy. Why is it necessary to incorporate a model at this stage in the process? The model provides a means of deciding which information is relevant – from all available information – and which is not relevant. This immediately raises the question of whether the *same* information is available to all market participants. Although in practice this may not be the case, it does seem reasonable to begin by assuming that the same information is available to everyone. If we do not assume this, then we can say very little, at the macroeconomic level, about expectations, in which case we revert back to treating them as exogenous. The assumption of identical information sets is not too unreasonable. Most information comes from government statistics, newspaper and television reports and other technical reports. It is obviously true that for some decisions one party in the decision-making process may have access to information not possessed by the others. But at the macroeconomic level this is less likely to be the case – except where governments persist in keeping some information secret.

The main difference of opinion between economists occurs over the type of information that is used in *forming* the expectation. Since most expectations in economics are concerned with specific variables, such as inflation, exchange rate changes and income (rather than events) we will concentrate on variables. In general terms we are concerned about the expected value of a variable, X say, denoted X^e. The question is whether expectations are based only on past values of the variable itself (expected and/or actual) or whether they are based on a whole set of information which may or may not include past values of the variable itself (expected and/or actual). As we will see in the next section, *adaptive expectations* is concerned only with past values of the variable itself and on no other information. But many economists have argued that this 'wastes' information. These economists, dubbed *rational expectations theorists* (RET), argue that where a variable is determined within an economic (or econometric) model, and where we require to determine the expected value of the same variable, it should be based on the same model that determines the variable itself. If this is done then the expectation is formed 'rationally'. Put simply, a 'rational expectation' is formed when the variable is determined by the same model and in the same way that determines the variable itself. Sargent and Wallace (1973) put it as follows:

> Expectations about a variable are said to be rational if they depend, in the proper way, on the same things that economic theory says that actually determine that variable.

Rational expectations, therefore, not only assume that more information is taken into

account, but also that a particular model is used to determine its value. We will deal with
this more fully in Section 4.3.

4.2 ADAPTIVE EXPECTATIONS

In effect, adaptive expectations mean that a decision-maker revises his previous expectations by a fraction of his forecast error. Let the variable be simply X, then

$$X_t^e = X_{t-1}^e + a(X_{t-1} - X_{t-1}^e) \qquad 0 < a < 1 \qquad (4.1)$$

where X_{t-1}^e is the preceding period's expectation, $X_{t-1} - X_{t-1}^e$ is the forecast error and a is
some fraction between zero and unity. If the decision-maker forecasts the preceding period's
value accurately, then there is no forecast error and the preceding period's expectation is
used for the current period's expected value. On the other hand, if the decision-maker
overestimates last period's value, then he adjusts his expectation downwards by a fraction of
his error, while if he underestimates last period's value, then he adjusts his expectation
upwards by a fraction of his error.

But having stated expectation formation in this way, there still remains the problem of
relating expected values to observable values – since expectations are non-observable. This
can be done by re-arranging equation (4.1) as follows:

$$X_t^e = aX_{t-1} + (1 - a)X_{t-1}^e$$
$$= aX_{t-1} + (1 - a)[aX_{t-2} + (1 - a)X_{t-2}^e]$$
$$= aX_{t-1} + a(1 - a)X_{t-2} + (1 - a)^2 X_{t-2}^e \qquad (4.2)$$

and so on. Then

$$X_t^e = aX_{t-1} + a(1 - a)X_{t-2} + a(1 - a)^2 X_{t-3} + \cdots + (1 - a)^{n-1} X_{t-n}^e \qquad (4.3)$$

and thus X_t^e is purely a function of past values of X, all of which are observable – except for
the final term (which we can ignore if we take it to be small). Note that the weight attached
to each preceding value of X declines in a geometric fashion. In general the jth weight,
denoted w_j, is given by

$$w_j = a(1 - a)^{j-1} \qquad (4.4)$$

and this weight depends on the value of a alone. The only thing we need is a value for
a – which can be obtained econometrically. However, what matters is whether the coefficient a is small (close to zero) or large (close to unity). If a is equal to unity, then the only
past value of the variable the decision-maker takes into consideration is the value of the
variable in the immediately preceding period. This follows from the fact that if $a = 1$, then

$$X_t^e = X_{t-1} \qquad (4.5)$$

On the other hand, if $a = 0$, then the preceding period's expected value is not corrected at
all. Where a lies between zero and unity, then the decision-maker has a 'long-term memory'
and all the past values of X are taken into account, with the most recent past being given
more emphasis. To see this, Table 4.1 presents the weights attached to preceding values of X

Table 4.1 Geometric weights for different adjustment coefficients

Period	Weights $a=0.75$	$a=0.5$	$a=0.25$
1	0.7500	0.5000	0.2500
2	0.1875	0.2500	0.1875
3	0.0469	0.1250	0.1406
4	0.0117	0.0625	0.1055
5	0.0029	0.0313	0.0791
6	0.0007	0.0156	0.0593

for different values of a. For a given value of a these weights apply to any variable which follows the adaptive expectations formulation – as specified in equation (4.1). It can be seen that the higher the value of a the more emphasis is given to the most recent past.

In static equilibrium, where the expected value equals the actual value for all time, t, then $X_t^e = \bar{X}$ for all time, t. Hence,

$$X_t^e = [a + a(1-a) + a(1-a)^2 + \cdots]\bar{X}$$

$$= a\bar{X}/[1-(1-a)]$$

$$= \bar{X} \tag{4.6}$$

In other words, if $\bar{X}$ is the equilibrium value, then, over time, the variable will converge on this equilibrium value sooner or later.

Whether we are dealing with price levels, inflation or exchange rates, any expected variable X_t^e can be analysed in terms of such adaptive expectations. However, they play a particular role in the models of inflation and exchange rates. In inflation models, the augmented short-run Phillips curve denotes the standard Phillips curve augmented by adding the expected rate of inflation to it. (Monetarists give this a coefficient of unity, while non-monetarists give it a coefficient between zero and unity.)

We have already shown that inflation is determined by the intersection of the short-run Phillips curve (SPC) and the demand-pressure curve (DP). However, when either or both also involve price expectations, then we require a third equation to specify exactly how these expectations are formed. If we assume an adaptive expectation, we can solve the system of equations.

Consider the following specification similar to the dynamic model that we developed in Chapter 3:

$$SPC: \qquad \hat{P}_t = 0.15[(y_t/y_n) - 1] + \hat{P}_t^e \tag{4.7}$$

$$DP \text{ curve:} \qquad \hat{P}_t = 10 - 0.45[(y_t - y_{t-1})/y_n] \tag{4.8}$$

$$\text{Expectations} \quad \hat{P}_t^e = a\hat{P}_{t-1} + (1-a)\hat{P}_{t-1}^e \tag{4.9}$$

The only difference between this specification and the model in Chapter 3, is that there we have a slightly different specification of Okun's law – closer, in fact, to his original specification. Equations (4.7)–(4.9) are based on equation (4.10) below, rather than on equation (3.17).

$$U_t - U_n = -q[(y_t/y_n) - 1] \tag{4.10}$$

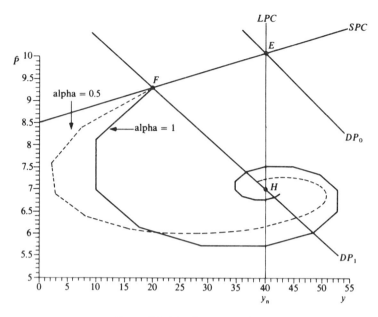

Figure 4.2 Adaptive expectations.

In other words, the unemployment gap is negatively related to the income gap as a proportion of the natural rate of income and we have assumed in equation (4.8) that $y_n = y_{t-1}$. The model is shown in Fig. 4.2.

The demand-pressure curve initially falls by 3 percentage points and the economy moves down the short-run Phillips curve. In the first instance the economy moves from point E to the point where SPC intersects DP_1, i.e. point F. This is determined by solving equations (4.7) and (4.8). But now the actual rate of inflation is less than the expected rate, and expectations are thus revised downwards in line with equation (4.9). This means, however, that the expectations term in equation (4.7) is now reduced, which means a movement of the short-run Phillips curve downwards. As inflation expectations are revised downwards, so the short-run Phillips curve moves downwards, eventually attaining long-run equilibrium at inflation rate 7% and real income at its natural level (i.e., $y = y_n$), shown by point H. As can be observed in Fig. 4.2 a spiral path occurs as the economy adjusts over time. With regard to the path taken over time, three observations are important:

1. The greater the value of the adjustment coefficient, a in equation (4.9), the *shorter* time it takes to reach long-run equilibrium.
2. The steeper the short-run Phillips curve the *shorter* the time it takes to reach long-run equilibrium.
3. Over the adjustment path we can observe:
   (a) falling inflation and falling output;
   (b) rising inflation and rising output; and
   (c) rising inflation and falling output.

Three main difficulties surround adaptive expectations.

1. Expectations formation is totally backward looking – depending as it does on $\hat{P}_{t-1}$ and $\hat{P}_{t-1}^e$. It takes no account of new information occurring now. The implication is that

market participants would make systematic mistakes whenever news indicated a higher or lower rate of inflation. What it means is that the information content is extremely limited: limited only to past values of the variable itself.

2. The coefficient, *a*, is not explained within an economic context. It is *ad hoc* and must be estimated. Some attempt has been made to allow *a* to vary.
3. Because *a* is *ad hoc*, it does not take account of the general equilibrium nature of models. In addition, such adaptive expectations must involve persistent forecasting errors. This means that the market is not efficient. Many monetarists believe that markets are efficient (such as the money market; the foreign exchange market; even, possibly, the labour market), and, furthermore, that such systematic errors cannot persist. As such, this particular formulation of expectations cannot hold – especially into the medium and long term.

Adaptive expectations are simple and allow expectations to be incorporated into econometric models in a fairly simple way (see Klein, 1972). Such expectation formation is certainly better than treating expectations as exogenous. However, such an approach clearly does not deal with all available information. If the government suddenly announced that it was going to go for a 'dash for growth', and that it would do this by reducing interest rates (expanding the money supply), then this information would make no difference to a decision-maker who formed his expectations in an adaptive manner. In fact, all information other than past prices would not, according to this formation, make any difference to the decision-maker. It was this inadequacy that turned economists' attention to a formulation of expectations which did take account of all (or most) available information.

4.3 RATIONAL EXPECTATIONS: MEANING[1]

The most significant change to occur in macroeconomics is the introduction of rational expectations. Rational expectations begin from the notion that market participants have information and acquire information, and that this information affects behaviour. Thus, price expectations, for instance, are conditional expectations – conditional on the information available at the end of period $t - 1$. In general:

$$X_t^e = E(X_t/I_{t-1}) \qquad (4.11)$$

i.e. the expectation of a variable X at time t is based on the information available at the end of time period $t - 1$. The basic issue is how to incorporate this information.

The difference between rational expectations and adaptive expectations, is that the latter involve systematic errors while the former allow no such behaviour. This does not mean that no mistakes are made or that no forecasting errors occur. Rather, it says that on average errors will cancel, and that market participants behave according to the true underlying structure. Two questions arise:

1. What is the true underlying structure?
2. What information can we assume?

The first major assumption is that market participants know both the entire structure of the model and all preceding variables relating to this model – endogenous and exogenous. Since

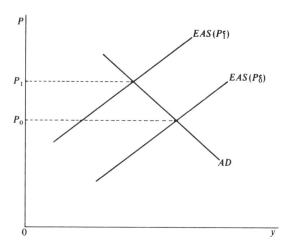

Figure 4.3 Price expectations and the AS curve.

the models are stochastic, then a second assumption must be made: namely, that market participants know the structure and properties of the random disturbances. In other words, they know the probability distribution of the random disturbances. These result in expectations being mathematical conditional expectations. The framework is of the 'as if' type where, in a world with readily available information which is quickly disseminated, people behave as if they knew the full model; otherwise systematic forecasting errors would creep in.

The observation about rational expectations is that the entire future path of a model must be assessed. This involves considering the time path of the endogenous variables, which in turn requires a clear statement of the model's dynamic behaviour.

It is worth noting that a rational expectation about a variable, X say, is the same thing as the prediction of X derived from the (a?) relevant theory. The problem is which theory – and hence which prediction? Although there is a variety of theories, each will specify a formal structure and, in particular, will predict values for endogenous variables. Where expectations enter the analysis, rational expectations theorists argue that the only consistent assumption is that they are formed in the way that the theory indicates the variable itself is formed. Although not obvious, this arises from the result that the mathematical expectation of a 'truly' random variable from its expected value (the expectation of the error), is zero. Thus, if $\varepsilon = X - E(X)$, then $E(\varepsilon) = E(X) - E(X) = 0$.

The essence of rational expectations is seen, first, in the type of model employed. For price expectations, this is basically the one which contains a typical AD curve and an expectations augmented AS curve, denoted EAS, as shown in Fig. 4.3. In particular, for any given EAS, price expectations are constant. A rise in price expectations shifts the EAS to the left (upward) and results in a rise in actual prices and a fall in real income. Hence, the higher the expected price level, the higher will be actual prices – assuming AD remains unchanged. (If AD is also a function of the expected price level, then what matters is whether the EAS curve shifts further to the left than the AD curve shifts to the right.)

Since expected and actual prices are related, how can theory determine the expected price level when the actual price level depends upon this expected level? In answering this

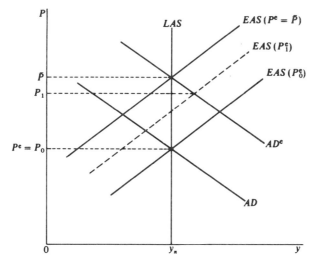

Figure 4.4 Price expectations in both AD and AS.

question, two key ideas must remain uppermost:

1. The expectation is about a *future* price.
2. The price is a prediction from the theory.

One problem is immediately apparent. Aggregate demand itself involves variables about which we form expectations, e.g. the money supply. Let us suppose we have done this, and have AD^e, as shown in Fig. 4.4. Beginning with P_0^e, our expectations are incorrect because the price level is P_1. Any price expectation other than $\bar{P}$ will be irrational since it will not be the outcome after all adjustment has occurred, as predicted by the theory. Only where $P^e = \bar{P}$ will actual prices equal expected prices. This in turn, is determined by the LAS curve which is vertical at y_n.

As long as any shift in aggregate demand is fully anticipated, then actual prices and expected prices will be the same. According to rational expectations theorists, differences can only occur as the result of unanticipated shifts in AD and/or EAS, i.e. as a result of unanticipated shocks to the economic system (see Parkin and Bade, 1982).

4.4 POLICY IMPLICATIONS OF RATIONAL EXPECTATIONS

One of the main reasons why there has been such attention paid to rational expectations theory is because it appears to have one most important policy implication: namely, that government policy is impotent. This implication is not concerned as to whether government policy is difficult to achieve – an empirical issue. On the contrary, it is a theoretical statement that government policy *cannot* succeed if individuals behave rationally!

The intuitive basis of this argument is as follows. If individuals behave rationally, then they will incorporate into their behaviour any adjustment to the economy which is undertaken by the government – as long as such policy is anticipated by decision-makers. If they do not do so, then they will make systematic errors. Since rational individuals do not make systematic errors, then it follows that anticipated changes in government policy must be part of their decision-making process. Since the behaviour of the economy is based on expected variables, and since expected variables incorporate policy behaviour on the part of the government, then the government cannot influence the real variables in the economy. In other words, government policy is impotent. However, all this is crucially dependent on the model (or the real world) having complete flexibility in prices and money wages.[2]

We can illustrate this policy conclusion by means of the model developed in Chapters 2 and 3. The heart of the model is the demand-pressure curve, equation (3.32), and the short-run Phillips curve, equation (3.24). The full derivation is presented in Appendix 4.1. Here we will simply state some of the more important results in order to illustrate the gist of the argument.

To keep the derivation simple, we will only concern ourselves with fiscal policy; hence, D_0 in equation (3.32) takes the form,

$$D_0 = y_{-1} + (\Delta go/Q) \tag{4.12}$$

It is therefore possible to conceive of D_0 as a policy variable. (Had we been concerned with monetary policy, then D_0 would equal $y_{-1} + (h/uQ)[\Delta(M_0/P)]$, with no real change in the argument to be presented.) We further assume that productivity is unchanging ($\hat{a}_L = 0$), and there is no change in the competitiveness of the economy ($\Delta R = 0$). Given these assumptions, equations (3.32) and (3.24) can be written in the simpler form,

Demand pressure $\quad y = D_0 - D_1 \hat{P} \tag{4.13}$

Phillips curve $\quad\quad y = E_0 + E_1 \hat{P} - E_2 \hat{P}^e + u \tag{4.14}$

In equation (4.14) we have: (1) expressed the Phillips curve as y in terms of $\hat{P}$;[3] and (2) we have also added a random error term, u, to the short-run Phillips curve. By doing this we are adding uncertainty to the economic system – but only on the supply-side of the economy. It is possible to include uncertainty on the demand-side of the economy, but this will not add anything to the arguments to be developed.

We can solve equations (4.13) and (4.14) for $\hat{P}^e$ and y, as shown in Appendix 4.1. The results show that the expected inflation rate, $\hat{P}^e$, depends on the expected value of the policy variable, i.e. on $E(D_0)$. Furthermore, we show that the rate of inflation, $\hat{P}$, and the level of real income, y, depend on

1. The level of the policy variable, D_0.
2. The deviation of the policy variable from its expected value, $D_0 - E(D_0)$.
3. The error term, u.

It is *not generally* the case that income will deviate from its natural level only if there are random variations in aggregate supply, or if government policy deviates from what is expected, as suggested by Carter and Maddock (1984, p. 96). Besides the obvious possibility that there may be uncertainty on the demand-side, this result requires, further – in the present model – that

$$E_1 = E_2 \tag{4.15}$$

$$E_0 = y_n \tag{4.16}$$

Condition (4.15) is the usual monetarist assumption that the coefficient of inflation expectations is unity (i.e., $C_4 = 1$). Condition (4.16) is somewhat arbitrary – although necessary for derivation of the conclusion!

Appendix 4.1 also considers two policy rules: one active and one passive. Combining the policy rule in the model developed, and once again assuming equations (4.15) and (4.16), it can be shown that the deviation of income from its natural level is simply a function of the error term in the policy equation and the error term in the short-run Phillips curve. In other words, only unanticipated random shocks – either on the supply-side or due to actual government policy – will cause real income to deviate from its natural level. This is true whether the policy is an active one or a passive one. It does appear, however, that the conclusion is loaded in favour of a monetarist (non-market interventionist) result! In particular, there is no reason why assumptions (4.15) and (4.16) should be true. If not, then the level of real income will also depend on the expectation of the policy variable, $E(D_0)$, besides the uncertainty in the short-run Phillips curve and the uncertainty attached to the policy rule followed. Furthermore, as we have already pointed out, the result only follows under the assumption of complete price flexibility. It could be argued that it is this assumption which leads to policy impotence rather than the assumption of rational expectations *per se*.

The conclusion that

> *systematic aggregate demand policy can never be effective if expectations are formed rationally* (Carter and Maddock, 1984, p. 101, original italics)

cannot be sustained – except under some very rigid (monetarist) assumptions.

4.5 COMMENTS AND CRITICISMS OF RATIONAL EXPECTATIONS

Is the assumption of rational expectations a sensible one to make about behaviour? We noted that Keynes avoided the issue by assuming expectations to be exogenous. He could then change expectations and see how the system was affected by such a change, but expectations themselves were given. Adaptive expectations did allow some change to be made in expectations, but these were backward looking and assumed that forecasting errors were not corrected.

In many respects it is not a question of considering the weaknesses of rational expectations theory (RET) in isolation, but, rather, to see if it is 'better' to treat them as exogenous or by some *ad hoc* method – as in adaptive expectations. By 'better' we must see if it accounts for results which cannot be accounted for by alternative theories. Let us simply go through the list of criticisms.

1. It is assumed that the model is known. But which model? Economists cannot agree between themselves how to model the economy – or parts of it. Monetarists, in particular, stress that it is 'their' model which is correct. Rational expectations are then framed in these terms. Earlier we showed that the system arrived at a solution because it was assumed that the LAS curve was vertical at the natural rate of real income. This is part of the 'correct model'. In other words, the whole model is involved in the analysis – and not simply rational expectations. It is, however, possible to have a Keynesian model which involves rational expectations. But this has been little analysed, since neo-Keynesians rarely accept rational expectations.

2. Monetarists have two crucial assumptions:

   1. Markets clear quickly.
   2. Expectations are formed rationally.

There is a tendency in the literature to attribute some of the dynamic results to the second assumption. However, a more careful consideration of the models reveals that it is the first assumption which is the crucial one. If, for instance, we assume that markets clear quickly, but we also assume that expectations are of the adaptive type, then we still arrive at the same solution. The path actually taken is different, but not the end result. But monetarists are usually concerned about the long run and where the economy will settle. If the above is true, then it is possible to argue that precise formation of expectations is of little conse-quence to the long-run equilibrium. This is not true of the short run, but few short-run models involving rational expectations exist.

A careful consideration of policies suggested by monetarists are not about rational expectations, but, rather, about ensuring that markets *do* in fact clear quickly. Again we see the world being changed to conform to the theory!

3. Rational expectations are dependent on taking account of all relevant information. Price movements are supposed to adapt quickly and easily to any new information. But for which market is this true? The only markets are for stocks and for foreign exchange – the two classic examples of markets which are perfectly competitive. But rational expectations theory is concerned with price expectations and the labour market. The reality is that wage contracts operate over different time periods, and are negotiated at different times of the year. How can wages be adjusted quickly to new information? Again, we see it is the assumption that markets clear quickly which is highlighted, rather than the assumption of rational expectations. Even so, the information in forming rational expectations is not the same across labour markets. Only in the long run will such adjustments be possible and so only in the long run will such an assumption be reasonable. But we are also concerned with the short and medium terms.

Counterarguments

1. A consistent macroeconomic theory, consistent with microeconomic behaviour, must assume maximizing (i.e., optimising) behaviour. Expectation formation must also do the same. Hence,

> rational expectations is the application of the principle of rational behaviour to the acquisition and processing of information and the formation of expectations.
>
> (Carter and Maddock, 1984)

Any other assumption about expectation formation is outside the usual microeconomic paradigm. So why assume it for other behaviour?

2. Do we need to assume a model? Rational expectations theory assumes no forecast error. Then if people behave in this way, using all relevant information, they behave *as if* they know the model – and the correct one, for if it was not correct then forecast errors would involve a systematic component. The more efficient the market, and the more readily information is disseminated, the more this is true. But what of other less efficient markets? Here the law of large numbers is invoked where, in the aggregate, individual irregularities cancel each other out.

3. Although for global stability, all paths lead to equilibrium – whether expectations are formed rationally or not – in the explosive case it is an empirical question when and whether the path is explosive and what can be done about it.

4. Rational expectations theorists recognize that if governments follow rules which they then change, it will take time for the new rule to be recognized – unless announced. In this case there will be systematic forecast errors. But this can be overstated, especially when the rule involves a lag structure. Where the new policy is announced, then the criticism is no longer valid. However, this in turn, depends on a belief in the policy being pursued. The Chancellor of the Exchequer, Sir Geoffrey Howe, announced a money growth rule which was rarely ever met. But a merit claimed by rational expectations theorists is that these difficulties are explicit and not implicit; and no matter how difficult, they must be taken into account. Such rational expectations are at present in their infancy.

5. Information is not costless. In typical economic terms, it is worth acquiring up to the point where the marginal benefit equals the marginal cost. The problem is to model the information available. Again, rational expectations theory makes this need explicit, e.g. whether different individuals have access to different information. At present models are too simplistic – but at least they recognize the need. The point is not to abandon the models but, rather, to further the research.

NOTES

1. The literature on rational expectations is now becoming quite voluminous. An elementary introduction can be found in Shaw (1984), while a more detailed and advanced discussion (but still at undergraduate level) can be. found in Begg (1982), Sheffrin (1983), Carter and Maddock (1984), Attfield *et al.* (1985). Useful articles on the subject are by Kantor (1979), Buiter (1980), Lawson (1981), Colander and Guthrie (1981), Maddock and Carter (1982), and Demery and Duck (1984). The strongest exponents of this approach in the UK are Minford and Peel. Their arguments can be found in Minford and Peel (1983). This list, however, is by no means exhaustive.

2. Strictly, the policy impotence is more a result of price flexibility than of the assumption of rational expectations.

3. In equation (3.24), letting $\hat{a}_L = \hat{R} = 0$, then

$$\hat{P} = C_0 + C_1 y + C_4 \hat{P}^e$$

which on re-arrangement gives

$$y = (-C_0/C_1) + (1/C_1)\hat{P} - (C_4/C_1)\hat{P}^e$$

i.e.

$$y = E_0 + E_1\hat{P} - E_2\hat{P}^e \qquad E_1, E_2 > 0$$

APPENDIX 4.1 POLICY IMPLICATIONS OF RATIONAL EXPECTATIONS

The model in Chapter 3 consists of a demand-pressure curve and a short-run Phillips curve, given by equations (3.32) and (3.24) respectively. Thus,

$$\text{DP:} \qquad y = D_0 - D_1\hat{P} \qquad D_1 > 0 \tag{3.32}$$

$$\text{SPC:} \qquad \hat{P} = C_0 + C_1 y + C_4\hat{P}^e \qquad C_1, C_4 > 0 \tag{3.24}$$

In order to make comparisons with other works, we can re-arrange equation (3.24) to express y in terms of $\hat{P}$ and $\hat{P}^e$. Thus,

$$y = -(C_0/C_1) + (1/C_1)\hat{P} - (C_4/C_1)\hat{P}^e$$

or

$$y = E_0 + E_1\hat{P} - E_2\hat{P}^e \qquad E_1, E_2 > 0 \tag{A4.1.1}$$

If we now add uncertainty to specification (A4.1.1), and time subscript the variables, we have the model

$$DP: \qquad y_t = D_0 - D_1\hat{P}_t \tag{A4.1.2}$$

$$SPC: \qquad y_t = E_0 + E_1\hat{P}_t - E_2\hat{P}_t^e + u_t \tag{A4.1.3}$$

It is important to note that

$$D_0 = [y_{-1} + (\mathrm{d}go/Q) + A_1(M_0/P)\hat{M}] \tag{A4.1.4}$$

We are, then, treating D_0 as the policy variable. If we have only fiscal policy, then

$$D_0 = [y_{-1} + (\mathrm{d}go/Q) \qquad \text{since } \hat{M} = 0 \tag{A4.1.5}$$

If we wish to consider only monetary policy, then

$$D_0 = y_{-1} + A_1(M_0/P)\hat{M} \tag{A4.1.6}$$

The model embodied in equations (A4.1.2) and (A4.1.3) can be solved for $\hat{P}_t$ and y_t. Equating (A4.1.2) and (A4.1.3) and solving for $\hat{P}_t$, gives

$$\hat{P}_t = \frac{D_0 - E_0 + E_2\hat{P}_t^e - u_t}{(D_1 + E_1)} \tag{A4.1.7}$$

Substituting result (A4.1.7) into equation (A4.1.2) we can solve for y_t. Hence,

$$y_t = \frac{D_0 E_1 + D_1 E_0 - D_1 E_2\hat{P}_t^e + D_1 u_t}{(D_1 + E_1)} \tag{A4.1.8}$$

However, both $\hat{P}_t$ and y_t are related to expected inflation in period t, i.e. to $\hat{P}_t^e$. It is here that we invoke the rational expectations assumption. This assumption is that the expected value of a variable is determined in the same way that the variable itself is determined within the model. In other words, the model determines inflation by equation (A4.1.7), so to obtain the expected value of inflation in period t we simply take the expected value of $\hat{P}_t$ given in equation (A4.1.7). In doing this we make two assumptions:

1. $E(\hat{P}_t^e) = E(\hat{P}_t/I_{t-1}) = E(\hat{P}_t) = \hat{P}_t^e$ \hfill (A4.1.9)
2. $E(u_t) = 0$ \hfill (A4.1.10)

where $E(.)$ refers to the expectations operator.

Now taking the expectation of equation (A4.1.7) we have

$$E(\hat{P}_t) = \frac{E(D_0) - E_0 + E_2\hat{P}_t^e - E(u_t)}{(D_1 + E_1)}$$

i.e. using assumptions (1) and (2),

$$\hat{P}_t^e = \frac{E(D_0) - E_0 + E_2\hat{P}_t^e}{(D_1 + E_1)}$$

Solving for $\hat{P}_t^e$ we get

$$\hat{P}_t^e = \frac{E(D_0) - E_0}{(D_1 + E_1 - E_2)} \tag{A4.1.11}$$

Thus, the expected rate of inflation, $\hat{P}_t^e$, depends on the expected value of the policy variable, $E(D_0)$, and parameters

Result (A4.1.11) only gives the value of the expected rate of inflation under rational expectations. We have yet to determine the actual rate of inflation, given in equation (A4.1.7). Substituting result (A4.1.11) into (A4.1.7) gives

$$\hat{P}_t = \frac{(D_1 + E_1)(D_0 - E_0) - E_2[D_0 - E(D_0)] - (D_1 + E_1 - E_2)u_t}{(D_1 + E_1 - E_2)(D_1 + E_1)} \tag{A4.1.12}$$

Notice in result (A4.1.12) that the expected rate of inflation depends on the deviation of the policy variable from its expected value and on the error term.

It is also possible to solve for y_t under rational expectations. Substituting equation (A4.1.11) into equation (A4.1.8) we get,

$$y_t = \frac{D_1[E_1 D_0 - E_2 E(D_0)] + D_0 E_1(E_1 - E_2) + D_1 E_0(D_1 + E_1) + D_1(D_1 + E_1 - E_2)u_t}{(D_1 + E_1 - E_2)(D_1 + E_1)} \tag{A4.1.13}$$

In order to compare this result with those of Carter and Maddock (1984, p. 96) we can make two *special* assumptions,

1. $E_1 = E_2$
2. $E_0 = y_n$

Under these two assumptions, the rational expectations result can be expressed:

$$y_t - y_n = \frac{E_1[D_0 - E(D_0)] + D_1 u_t}{(D_1 + E_1)} \tag{A4.1.14}$$

Under these assumptions, therefore, the deviation of income from its natural level is related to the deviation of the policy variable from its expected value and the error term.

We can also derive the inflation rate under these special assumptions, namely,

$$\hat{P}_t = \frac{D_0 D_1 + E_1 E(D_0) - (D_1 + E_1)y_n - D_1 u_t}{D_1(D_1 + E_1)} \tag{A4.1.15}$$

which is the result given in Carter and Maddock (1984, p. 95).

Policy rules

We now consider two policy rules: one active and one passive. Let these be given by,

Active:	$D_0 = G_0 D_{t-1}^0 + G_1 y_{t-1} + G_2 \hat{P}_{t-1} + v_t$	(A4.1.16)
Passive:	$D_0 = G_0 D_{t-1}^0 + w_t$	(A4.1.17)

Taking expectations, we have,

Active:	$E(D_0) = G_0 D_{t-1}^0 + G_1 y_{t-1} + G_2 \hat{P}_{t-1}$	(A4.1.18)
Passive:	$E(D_0) = G_0 D_{t-1}^0$	(A4.1.19)

Substituting equations (A4.1.16) and (A4.1.18) into equation (A4.1.13) gives the result for the active rule of,

$$y_t = \frac{D_1 E_0}{(D_1 + E_1 - E_2)} + \frac{(E_1 - E_2)E(D_0)}{(D_1 + E_1 - E_2)} + \frac{D_1 u_t + E_1 v_t}{(D_1 + E_1)} \tag{A4.1.20}$$

Under the special two assumptions that (1) $E_1 = E_2$ and (2) $E_0 = y_n$, result (A4.1.20) reduces to

$$y_t - y_n = \frac{D_1 u_t - E_1 v_t}{(D_1 + E_1)} \tag{A4.1.21}$$

which is the result given in Carter and Maddock (1984, p. 99).

The passive rule is readily derived. Under this condition $G_1 = G_2 = 0$ where G_1 and G_2 are the coefficients in equation A4.1.16. Since result (A4.1.21) does not involve either of G_1 or G_2, then we immediately have the result for the passive rule of,

$$y_t - y_n = \frac{D_1 u_t - E_1 w_t}{(D_1 + E_1)} \qquad (A4.1.22)$$

which is the result given in Carter and Maddock (1984, p. 99).

Chapter 5

BALANCE OF PAYMENTS AND THE EXCHANGE RATE

Britain is an open economy and as such the trade sector plays a major role. Whether this role is one of a constraint on domestic policy or whether it is an engine for growth will be taken up later. What we intend to do in this chapter is set out the major aspects of the market so that we can take up the relevant issues later.

It will be useful at the outset to indicate where we are going in this chapter. In the first section we will lay out a simple set of accounts which not only indicate the trading position of the country (in this case the UK), but which also lay down the more usual notation for dealing with aspects of trade in a macroeconomic setting. Furthermore, these accounts help us to explain what is meant by external equilibrium – or what is more usually called balance of payments equilibrium. In so doing we relate the balance of payments accounts to the concepts of demand and supply of foreign currency. By doing this we can also see what equilibrium means in terms of the exchange rate. Having established the meaning of equilibrium on the balance of payments, in Section 5.2 we investigate the implication of balance of payments equilibrium in the IS–LM framework. In this section particular emphasis will be placed on distinguishing responses with respect to the current account, or net exports, and responses with respect to the capital account.

With the growing acceptance of monetarist views it is useful to clarify these for an open economy. Two of the main concepts employed in monetarist arguments are the purchasing power parity theorem and the interest parity theorem, which are dealt with in Sections 5.3 and 5.4 respectively. It will be seen that these impose a mixture of a long-run concept and market efficiency. It must be recalled that monetarist ideas arose in large part to explain the inflation of the late 1960s and 1970s. The IS–LM–BP model was an analytical device that was useful for analysing Keynesian underemployment equilibrium with no inflation. When analysing the 1970s and 1980s, however, we must include floating exchange rates and inflation at home and abroad. This involves more dynamic considerations, most especially the expectations-augmented Phillips curve which includes the possibility of real exchange rate changes. We deal with this in Section 5.5.

While analysing the main analytical elements necessary for a thorough understanding of open economy macroeconomics, a number of more practical features of the foreign exchange market will also be discussed – largely in the appendices in order not to detract from the main argument. Hence, we discuss spot and forward exchange rates and the function of the Exchange Equalization Account. Each of these has some implications for the analytical treatment, but all are important in their own right. Furthermore, in Appendix 5.4 we also outline the stop–go policies of the 1950s and 1960s because of the important role played by the balance of payments.

Table 5.1 The balance of payments accounts: main categories

	Exports of goods and services	x
−	Imports of goods and services	im
=	Current balance	$nx = x - im$
+	Net capital flows	cf
=	Balance of payments	$bp = (x - im) + cf$
=	(−) Change in reserves	$- drs$

Note: $nx + cf + drs \equiv 0$

5.1 BALANCE OF PAYMENTS ACCOUNTS AND EQUILIBRIUM

The balance of payments accounts for a country show the trade in goods, services and capital between residents of a country with the rest of the world. Table 5.1 sets out a very simple set of accounts in real terms for the UK which will be useful in our discussions.

The current balance, or net exports (nx), is the difference between the export of goods and services (x) and the import of goods and services (im). When many commentators refer to 'the' balance of payments they often have this in mind. Although net exports are most relevant for considerations of a country's competitive position, as we will see in Chapter 17, it is not necessarily the most relevant for discussions of the exchange rate or policies towards unemployment: capital flows must also be taken into account.

Capital flows, as recorded in the UK accounts, have gone through a number of changes, which we will not discuss here.[1] However, at the present time net capital *inflows* (capital inflow less capital outflow) are presented with no division between short- and long-term capital – largely because in the present climate of world trade the distinction is almost meaningless. In Table 5.1 we have labelled this cf. The balance of payments in real terms, denoted bp, is the sum of net exports plus net capital inflows, i.e.

$$bp \equiv nx + cf \tag{5.1}$$

The UK current account balance (net exports) and the balance of payments for the period 1963–87 is presented in Table 5.2. (Notice that this table includes the balancing item, denoted e, for errors and omissions.)

The line in the accounts can be drawn at any point that is of interest to the person concerned. But why draw a line? The point is that the line distinguishes imbalances between items above it. If we are concerned about private motives for trading in goods, services and capital, then we would draw the line after net capital flows, as we have done in Table 5.1. The item below the line is (minus) the change in the reserves, denoted $- drs$, which must accommodate the items above the line. This is as it must be because the accounts are simply a recording of all debits and credits and, taken as a whole, they must balance, i.e.

$$nx + cf + drs \equiv 0 \tag{5.2}$$

How do we interpret equilibrium in the foreign trade sector? At first glance it may appear to be where exports equal imports ($x = im$). However, this in fact is not a sensible way of interpreting equilibrium. Is it a balance of forces or merely a situation where the value of exports equals the value of imports? To clarify the forces in operation, and hence to clarify

Table 5.2 UK balance of payments in real terms, 1963–87, £ million (1980 = 100)

Year	Current balance $nx = x - im$	Private net capital flows[a] cf	Balance of payments $bp = nx + cf$	Balancing item e
1963	610	−351	259	−420
1964	−1759	−627	−2387	−47
1965	−347	−288	−635	180
1966	554	−1649	−1095	−416
1967	−1199	−1369	−2568	941
1968	−1069	−2737	−3806	−559
1969	1854	−31	1824	1441
1970	2874	3332	6206	−202
1971	3601	6356	9957	875
1972	591	−1505	−914	−2388
1973	−3132	5434	2302	406
1974	−8049	6971	−1078	359
1975	−3096	3689	593	−33
1976	−1500	312	−1188	517
1977	−162	8136	7974	4855
1978	1292	−6115	−4823	2892
1979	−712	1572	860	577
1980	3035	−2347	688	−334
1981	6026	−7799	−1773	−429
1982	3687	−3763	−76	−1296
1983	2953	−3603	−651	1009
1984	1506	−5415	−3909	3816
1985	2314	−3732	−1418	3161
1986	31	−6403	−6371	8571
1987	−1102	7762	6661	621

[a] Includes net investment, net lending etc. to overseas residents by UK banks, and net lending overseas by UK residents other than banks and general government

Source: Economic Trends, Annual Supplement 1988 and *Economic Trends,* March 1988

the meaning of equilibrium in the foreign trade sector, it is useful at this point to introduce the exchange rate.

Let S denote the $/£ spot exchange rate – the spot dollar price of sterling (e.g. $1 = £2). (The practical aspects of spot and forward quotations are presented in Appendix 5.1.) Consider now the demand and supply curves for *pounds*, as illustrated in Fig. 5.1. The demand for sterling arises from British exports of goods and services and capital inflows; similarly, the supply curve of sterling arises from British imports of goods and services and the outflow of capital.[2]

Now if we assume instantaneous adjustment in the foreign exchange market, the exchange rate will settle down at S_0. This would constitute a balance of forces and hence equilibrium in the foreign exchange market. But how does this translate into the accounting concepts we outlined in Table 5.1? To see this consider a disequilibrium exchange rate, namely S_1. At this exchange rate the quantity of sterling demanded is q_1^d, while the quantity supplied is q_1^s. But which quantity is eventually realized?

If there were no external agency and all demands and supplies referred to *private* transactions, then the short side of the market must prevail. Although private suppliers are willing to provide q_1^s pounds, only q_1^d is being demanded and this will thus be the quantity that is realized. The fact that a number of suppliers will not find buyers will put pressure on the exchange rate to fall (for sterling to depreciate). Had the exchange rate been below the equilibrium level, then there would be a number of demands of sterling which would go

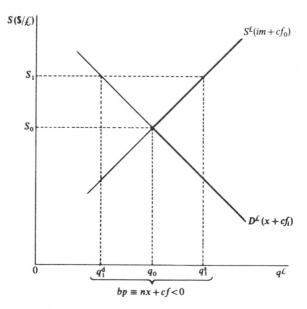

Figure 5.1 The demand and supply of sterling.

unsatisfied. This in turn would put pressure on the exchange rate to rise (for sterling to appreciate). Only at equilibrium S_0 would all demands and supplies be met. If the exchange rate were quick to adjust, then S_0 would be the exchange rate observed and q_0 the demand and supply of sterling observed. This is a *flex-price model* of exchange rates.

An alternative model is a *fix-price model* of exchange rates in which a disequilibrium can (temporarily) be maintained so long as an external agency (such as the Central Bank) enters the market. In other words, the demand and supply curves still refer to *private* transactions, but the realized quantity of sterling at the fixed exchange rate S_1 is determined by both private motives *and* Central Bank intervention. To see this, again assume that the exchange rate is fixed at S_1. At this exchange rate there is an excess supply of sterling of $q_1^s - q_1^d$. The exchange rate S_1 could prevail if the Central Bank demanded the excess. In this case, all suppliers would find buyers (q_1^d private funds and $q_1^s - q_1^d$ funds from the Central Bank). If, on the other hand, the exchange rate were fixed below the equilibrium rate, then this rate could be maintained only if the Central Bank applied sterling.

The fix-price model just outlined is the one that is relevant to the fixed exchange rate period. What is important is to relate this disequilibrium which is sustained by the intervention agency into its equivalent in terms of the balance of payments accounts. This is readily done with the help of Fig. 5.1. At the exchange rate S_1 the supply of sterling exceeds the demand. Since all supply is satisfied (partly by private funds and partly from Central Bank funds), then the sterling value of imports plus capital outflow for investment into overseas assets exceeds the sterling value of exports and capital inflow for investment in UK assets. In other words, net exports plus net capital inflow is negative, i.e.

$$bp \equiv nx + cf < 0 \tag{5.3}$$

Returning to the exchange rate S_1, it is clear that the balance of payments deficit can be realized only if someone other than foreigners demands the additional sterling. The additional sterling is being demanded by the Central Bank (strictly the Exchange Equalisation Account – see Appendix 5.2). This should not be too difficult to understand. If the overall balance of payments is in deficit, then this constitutes an excess demand for dollars (hence an excess supply of pounds). Domestic residents want dollars in exchange for sterling in order to acquire goods, services and capital from abroad. The extra dollars (over and above what comes in from the sale of UK exports and capital inflows) come from the UK's exchange reserves. To be specific, suppose the deficit is £100 million and the exchange rate is £1 = $2. Then domestic residents require $2 million. Only if the Bank of England demands the equivalent of £1 million can domestic residents have their desires fulfilled. Since we are making the assumption that private demands for goods, services and capital are met, then the Bank of England experiences a fall in its exchange reserves of $2 million. Of course, the Exchange Equalisation Account now has an additional £1 million. What it does with this can have significant consequences for the economy – a point made in Appendix 5.2.

To summarize the argument up to this point, if we consider the foreign exchange sector in terms of the exchange market, equilibrium is where the demand for sterling is equal to the supply of sterling (or where the demand for foreign exchange is equal to the supply of foreign exchange). Such an equilibrium can be specified equivalently as:

$$bp \equiv nx + cf = 0 \tag{5.4}$$

Or

$$drs = 0 \tag{5.5}$$

With instantaneous adjustment in the foreign exchange market, the balance of payments, bp, would always be zero and the change in the reserves, drs, would also be zero. Deficits and surpluses in the foreign trade sector can only be realized if the government steps in and alters its reserve position. This would certainly be the case with a fixed exchange rate, but it can also be the case under a floating exchange rate where the government either deliberately intervenes in the foreign exchange market ('dirty floating') or if it evens out excessive fluctuations in the exchange rate ('leaning against the wind'). What is clear from Table 5.2 is that the UK balance of payments has rarely been in equilibrium – under either a fixed exchange rate period (1948–72) or a floating exchange rate period (1972 onwards).

One other point is worth mentioning in relation to the equilibrium conditions (5.4) and (5.5). Equilibrium condition (5.4) indicates the requirements for 'above the line' and above the line items refer to private intentions to trade in goods, services and capital by private residents. The change in the reserves, on the other hand, denote accommodating movements. However, governments often have desired positions about their level of reserves (or the exchange rate – or both). Any movement of reserves to achieve a desired position implies corresponding movements in the above the line items – which are then accommodating the reserve changes. Furthermore, the change in a country's reserve position has implications for the level of money stock in the country, a point we will elaborate on later. For the moment, all we need to note is that if the level of reserves rises, for whatever reason, the domestic money supply will rise (but not necessarily by the same amount). Similarly, a fall in the level of reserves leads to a fall in the domestic money supply (but not necessarily by the same amount). For an open economy, therefore, it does not make sense to assume that the money supply is exogenously given.

Although we have discussed the nominal exchange rate, S, in this section, it is important to realize that we are dealing with a model in *real* terms. The question can be put in the following way. Under a floating exchange rate system, what are the alternative equilibrium conditions

$$bp \equiv nx + cf = 0 \qquad (5.6)$$

$$d(rs) = 0 \qquad (5.7)$$

determining? It is in fact the *real* exchange rate, $R = SP/P^*$. This can either be considered as a measure of competitiveness (which we expand on in Chapter 17) or as the nominal exchange rate adjusted for the two countries' price levels.

5.2 MORE ON THE BP CURVE

In Chapter 2 we established the following results for the items on the balance of payments:

$$nx = (x_0 - im_0) - my - (f + g)R \qquad (5.8)$$

$$cf = cf_0 + v(r - r^* + \hat{S}^e) \qquad (5.9)$$

$$bp \equiv nx + cf \qquad (5.10)$$

It is useful when doing comparative statics with the IS–LM–BP framework to also see explicitly what is happening to the balance of payments, both current account (net exports, nx) and capital account (net capital flows, cf). The situation is shown in Fig. 5.2.

Consider point A on the BP curve in Fig. 5.2(a). This point is for interest rate $r = r_0$ and real income $y = y_0$. At interest rate r_0 net capital flows are zero and we have also assumed that at income level $y = y_0$ net exports are also zero. Now consider point B, which is to the right of point A. At this higher level of real income, $y = y_1$, real imports rise giving rise to a deficit on the current balance, $nx < 0$. Since the domestic interest rate remains at $r = r_0$, then there is no reason why net capital flows should alter. To re-establish equilibrium on the balance of payments interest rates must rise. But by how much? They must rise by that amount which attracts net capital flows of cf_1. This amount of net capital inflow is just sufficient to compensate for the deficit on the current account, as shown by the fact that $nx + cf_1$ in Fig. 5.2(c) cuts the horizontal axis at income level y_1.

In Fig. 5.2 we also show that the less responsive net capital flows are to interest rate changes (the steeper the schedule in Fig. 5.2(b), such as cf') the steeper the BP curve, as shown by BP' in Fig. 5.2(a), which corresponds to cf' in Fig. 5.2(b) and $nx + cf_2$ in Fig. 5.2(c). Put conversely, the more responsive net capital flows are to interest rate changes the flatter the BP curve. In the limit, with perfect capital mobility, the BP curve is horizontal. What this implies is that the domestic interest rate cannot diverge from the foreign interest rate, r must equal r^*. If the domestic interest rate exceeded the foreign interest rate, capital would immediately flow in and the rise in the money supply would bring down the domestic interest rate until it was in line with that abroad; while if the domestic interest rate fell below the rate abroad capital would immediately flow out, so reducing the domestic money supply and raising the domestic interest rate. (One point of interest is whether the BP curve is less or more steep than the LM curve. We take up this point in Appendix 5.3.)

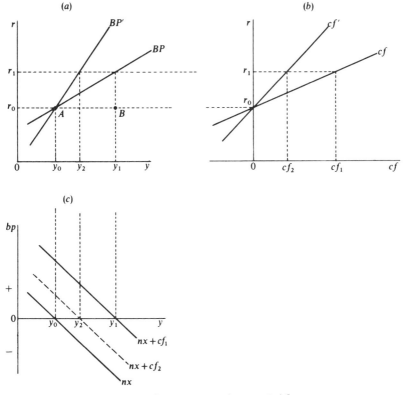

Figure 5.2 The BP curve and net capital flows.

Before leaving Fig. 5.2 it is worth noting that net exports are a function of real income, y, and the real exchange rate, R. The slope of the nx schedule is given by the marginal propensity to import, m; while a change in the spot exchange rate, S, with prices at home and abroad constant, will shift the net export schedule. A devaluation (a fall in S) will shift the net export schedule upwards because a devaluation will lead to a rise in exports and a fall in imports; a revaluation, on the other hand, will shift the net export schedule downwards. Hence, a devaluation will shift the BP curve downwards (to the right) and a revaluation will shift the BP curve upwards (to the left). What implication does this have for a floating exchange rate system? If the exchange rate appreciates or depreciates just sufficient to compensate for the inflation differential, i.e. if $\hat{S} = \hat{P}^* - \hat{P}$, then the real exchange rate will remain unchanged, i.e. $\hat{R} = 0$. In this instance a floating exchange rate will not alter the real net export schedule and so the BP curve will remain unchanged. If, however, the spot exchange rate does not change in line with the inflation differential, then the BP curve will move. Which direction the BP curve moves in will depend on whether the spot exchange rate is changing in excess of the inflation differential or less than the inflation differential. We will discuss this point later.

Two further results can be deduced from Fig. 5.2, as follows:

1. A rise in interest rates abroad will shift the net export plus net capital inflow schedule ($nx + cf$) upwards as a result of an increased capital outflow. This will result in the **BP** curve moving upwards (leftward).

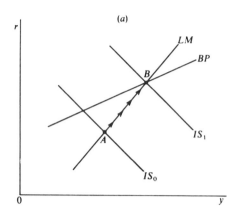

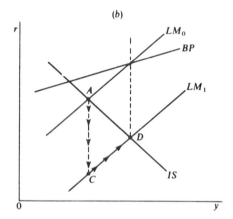

Figure 5.3 Fiscal and monetary policy under a fixed exchange rate.

2. A rise in the expected depreciation/appreciation of sterling, i.e. a rise in $\hat{S}^e$, will lead to an upward (downward) movement in the net capital flow schedule, and hence an upward (downward) movement in the BP curve.

The analysis so far is a warning that when considering fiscal or monetary policy the implications for the balance of payments cannot be ignored. To see why this is the case, consider the situation in Fig. 5.3, where the economy is initially at point A – an underemployment equilibrium and a deficit on the balance of payments. For the moment we will assume a fixed exchange rate and prices at home and abroad constant (which implies that the real exchange rate is constant and so the BP curve is fixed). Full employment can be achieved by using fiscal policy, monetary policy or a combination of the two. Let us take the two extremes for comparison.

Suppose the government implemented an increase in investment grants to stimulate industry. For the moment we will assume that this is financed from a sale of bonds (i.e., we are dealing with a pure fiscal expansion). This will shift the IS curve to IS_1, as illustrated in Fig. 5.3(a). But how does the economy get from equilibrium point A to equilibrium point B? We have made the assumption that the money market is the quickest to clear. At the ruling interest rate there will be a stimulus to income. The rise in income will lead to an increase in the demand for real money balances which in turn will lead to a rise in the interest rate. The movement of the economy is, therefore, along the LM curve from *A* to *B*. If, on the other hand, the government increased the money supply, then there would be a shift to the right of the LM curve, to LM_1, and the economy would move from *A* to *D*. What will be the path of the economy in this instance? At the initial interest rate there is excess supply in the money market. Given the assumption about quick clearing in the money market, this leads to a fall in interest rates and the economy moves to point *C* in the first instance, as shown in Fig. 5.3(*b*). The fall in the interest rate leads to excess demand in the goods market. This in turn leads to a rise in income. As income rises so too does the transactions demand for money. This leads to a movement along LM_1 from point *C* to point *D*.

Although the outcome with regard to the level of real income is the same, the path the economy traverses over time is quite different. Furthermore, the stimulus to aggregate demand arising from investment grants not only raises income but also leads to an equilibrium on the balance of payments (at least as shown in the diagram, although what matters is that such a stimulus will improve the balance of payments position). The reason for this is that investment not only stimulates the level of exports, but the rise in the interest rate leads to a capital inflow which compensates for any short-fall on the current account which occurs because imports rise as income rises. When we turn to monetary policy we see that the rise in the money supply has worsened the balance of payments position. This is because of two additive effects. First, the rise in income leads to an increase in imports. Second, the fall in the rate of interest leads to a fall in the net inflow of capital. Both the rise in imports and the fall in net capital flows worsens the balance of payments. This analysis is basic to an understanding of the stop–go policies of the 1950s and 1960s, especially in the UK. These policies are outlined in Appendix 5.4.

The analysis so far presented is very Keynesian in orientation. It assumes a fixed price level at home and abroad, which can be typified by a horizontal aggregate supply curve. Furthermore, the spot exchange rate is also assumed fixed. These assumptions together imply that the real exchange rate, $R = SP/P^*$, is constant. The main attention has been on stimulating aggregate demand by either monetary or fiscal policy. The fact that a country such as the UK has only limited reserves does mean that any attempt at trying to achieve full employment leads to difficulties on the balance of payments. But the model we presented in Chapters 2 and 3 indicated that inflationary pressure can arise on both the demand- and supply-sides of the economy. This was certainly the case in the late 1960s and 1970s. Furthermore, the Bretton-Woods System broke down in the early 1970s and many countries were floating their exchange rates by 1973. The IS–LM–BP framework accordingly became less relevant as a means of analysing the economy. We must turn, therefore, to alternative approaches which attempt to take account of price changes and a floating exchange rate.

5.3 PURCHASING POWER PARITY

Purchasing power parity stands in a central position of monetarist theories of the determination of the exchange rate. In essence it relates the bilateral exchange rate to the prices in each country. Two forms can be distinguished: the *absolute* purchasing power parity (absolute PPP) and the *relative* purchasing power parity (relative PPP). Absolute PPP is concerned with explaining the *level* of the exchange rate while relative PPP is concerned with explaining the *change* in the exchange rate.

The absolute PPP is deduced from the *law of one price*. If the same good is available in both the UK and the US, then, tariffs, transport costs and other distortions aside, the two goods will sell for the same price after translation through the spot exchange rate. Thus let p denote the price in sterling, p^* the price in dollars and S the dollar price of sterling (\$/£). Hence, the commodity selling for p in the UK will sell for Sp in the US. If $Sp > p^*$, then no one in the US will purchase the UK good. If $Sp < p^*$, then people in the US will purchase the imported good. If they are the same good they must sell for the same price. If they do not there will be profits to be made and goods will flow until a single price prevails. Hence, for a single commodity we have

$$Sp = p^* \quad \text{or} \quad S = p^*/p \tag{5.11}$$

If this is true for all commodities, then the price level in the two countries can also be related by the expression

$$SP = P^* \quad \text{or} \quad S = P^*/P \tag{5.12}$$

In other words, in the absence of transport costs, trade impediments and other market imperfections, the level of the bilateral exchange rate is determined by the ratio of the price level in the two countries.

Relative PPP is more concerned with explaining changes in the exchange rate, $\hat{S}$. Using equation (5.12) and taking percentage changes (see Appendix 1.1) we have

$$\hat{S} = \hat{P}^* - \hat{P} \tag{5.13}$$

Hence, a rise in prices at home relative to those abroad leads to a fall in the exchange rate ($\hat{S} < 0$), i.e. to a depreciation of sterling. Conversely, a fall in home prices relative to those abroad leads to an appreciation of the exchange rate.

Much has been written on both the absolute PPP and the relative PPP,[3] but sufficient has been said to relate the concepts to monetarists' views.

We begin with an extreme formulation which asserts that the demand for money is a stable function of income and is independent of the interest rate. There will be no loss if we take the demand for money equation in the Cambridge form $M_d = kPy$. Furthermore, the same assumption is made for both the home and the foreign country. Again let us take these to be the UK for the home country and the US for the foreign country. Thus,

$$M = kPy \qquad \text{applies for the UK} \tag{5.14}$$

$$M^* = k^*P^*y^* \quad \text{applies for the US} \tag{5.15}$$

If we invoke absolute PPP, then we can substitute equation (5.14) and equation (5.15) into equation (5.12), which gives us

$$S = (M^*/k^*y^*)/(M/ky) \tag{5.16}$$

It is revealing, however, to use relative PPP. In so doing we note that we can express equations (5.14) and (5.15) in growth terms as follows:

$$\hat{M} = \hat{k} + \hat{P} + \hat{y} \qquad \text{for the UK} \tag{5.17}$$

$$\hat{M}^* = \hat{k}^* + \hat{P}^* + \hat{y}^* \quad \text{for the US} \tag{5.18}$$

Now substituting equations (5.17) and (5.18) into equation (5.13) we have

$$\hat{S} = (\hat{M}^* - \hat{M}) - (\hat{k}^* - \hat{k}) - (\hat{y}^* - \hat{y}) \tag{5.19}$$

Hence if the money supply is growing at home relative to that abroad, the home currency depreciates. Similarly, if the home country's income is growing less than that abroad, then this too leads to a depreciation of the exchange rate. Since k is the reciprocal of the income velocity of circulation of money, then such velocities can be revealing in explaining volatile exchange rates and major depreciations during hyperinflationary situations.

Some monetarists would go further. In the long run, with income in both countries at their natural levels (hence $\hat{y} = 0$ and $\hat{y}^* = 0$), the major cause of exchange rate changes is simply changes in the money supply. Hence, in the long run excessive growth in the money supply not only causes inflation but also results in a depreciating exchange rate. As shown in Appendix 5.5, the present analysis is also used to explain world inflation in terms of the growth in the world money supply.

The present analysis is long run for two reasons. First, the demand for real money balances is assumed, in the long run, to be related only to real income. Second, absolute (or relative) PPP is only likely to hold in the long run.

How, then, do monetarists explain short-run movements in exchange rates? The explanation comes from considering the asset market, in particular interest rate parity. To this we now turn.

5.4 INTEREST RATE PARITY

We can approach the phenomenon of interest rate parity by considering under what conditions a UK investor would invest (say £1) in the UK or in the US. If she invested in the UK she would earn $£(1 + r)$ at the end of the period, which we will assume is 3 months. Alternatively, the money could have been invested in the US. The £1, if changed into dollars at the spot exchange rate S, would give S dollars. If she now invested this in the US for three months, then her dollar return would be $\$S(1 + r^*)$. However, she runs the risk that the exchange rate may change in the intervening period. To illiminate such an exchange risk she can sell dollars forward at a rate F (see Appendix 5.1 on the meaning of forward exchange rates). This would then give her $(S/F)(1 + r^*)$ pounds sterling in three months' time.

If

$$(1 + r) > (S/F)(1 + r^*)$$

then she would invest in the UK. If, on the other hand,

$$(1 + r) < (S/F)(1 + r^*)$$

then she would invest in the US. Money would cease to flow only when equality is achieved, i.e. only when

$$(1 + r) = (S/F)(1 + r^*) \tag{5.20}$$

Equation (5.20) denotes the interest parity condition. It is, however, more useful to express it slightly differently. We define the premium/discount on *sterling* as

$$z = (F - S)/F \tag{5.21}$$

Substituting equation (5.21) into equation (5.20) we obtain

$$z = \frac{r^* - r}{1 + r^*} \tag{5.22}$$

However, if the product zr^* is very small, we have the approximate result,

$$z = r^* - r \tag{5.23}$$

It is convenient to think of the premium/discount, z, as the cost of covering forward. Thus, interest parity requires that the interest differential be equal to the cost of forward cover. Whenever this is not the case, funds will flow between markets until the condition is met. If we assume, as we did generally for the money market, that funds flow quickly and that the money market is quick to clear, then this condition will more generally be met – even in the short run.

But what use is this result to our present analysis? To see the implication of the interest parity condition, and how it relates to relative purchasing power parity and market efficiency, we begin by considering two more general demand for money equations which incorporate interest rates. More specifically we deal with the equations in terms of rates of growth, but now interest rates enter as changes, dr and dr^*, for the home country and the foreign country respectively.[4] Hence,

$$\hat{M} = \hat{P} + \hat{y} - adr \qquad \text{for the home country} \tag{5.24}$$

$$\hat{M}^* = \hat{P}^* + \hat{y}^* - adr^* \quad \text{for the foreign country} \tag{5.25}$$

where for simplicity we have assumed that the coefficients of r and r^* are the same. If we now include the relative purchasing power parity condition specified in equation (5.13), and substitute equations (5.24) and (5.25) into this, we obtain

$$\hat{S} = (\hat{M}^* - \hat{M}) - (\hat{y}^* - \hat{y}) + a(dr^* - dr) \tag{5.26}$$

It is at this point that we must turn to the interest parity condition given in equation (5.23). Interest parity states that the interest rate differential is equal to the cost of forward cover, where the latter term (using the indirect quotation of exchange rates) is $z = (F - S)/F$. Now consider the expected future spot rate for, say, three months ahead. Let this be denoted S^e. If the foreign exchange market is efficient, and assuming investors are risk neutral, then the three months' forward rate would equal the expected three months' spot rate, i.e.

$$F = S^e \tag{5.27}$$

If we now substitute equation (5.27) into the parity equation (5.23) and take differences,[5] we have,

$$(dr^* - dr) = \hat{S}^e - \hat{S} \tag{5.28}$$

Hence,

$$\hat{S} = (\hat{M}^* - \hat{M}) - (\hat{y}^* - \hat{y}) + a(\hat{S}^e - \hat{S}) \qquad (5.29)$$

which on re-arrangement gives,

$$\hat{S} = \frac{(\hat{M}^* - \hat{M}) - (\hat{y}^* - \hat{y})}{(1 + a)} + \frac{a\hat{S}^e}{(1 + a)} \qquad (5.30)$$

Hence, in the short run the spot exchange rate is not only determined by the relative rates of growth of the money supplies and the relative growth rates of the two countries, but also by the expected appreciation/depreciation of the exchange rate. If the exchange rate is expected to depreciate ($\hat{S}^e < 0$), then the spot rate itself will also do so. Of course, the exact path of the short-run exchange rate depends on how these expectations are formed. We discussed a number of features of expectations in Chapter 4, but one formulation which gives rise to the concept of overshooting is presented in Appendix 5.6.

It is to be noted that the short-run explanation of exchange rate changes given in equation (5.30) is consistent with the long-run solution we have already given. To see this, we note that in the long run, expectations are fulfilled, a point we emphasized in Chapter 4, hence

$$\hat{S} = \hat{S}^e \qquad (5.31)$$

If we also have a stationary economy, with income at its natural level – as monetarists usually conceive their long-run stationary economy, then

$$\hat{y} = \hat{y}^* = 0 \qquad (5.32)$$

In the long-run stationary economy, therefore, the change in the exchange rate is found to be equal to the relative difference in monetary growth, i.e., substituting equations (5.31) and (5.32) into equation (5.30) we have

$$\hat{S}_L = (\hat{M}^* - \hat{M}) \qquad (5.33)$$

In the more realistic case we have examined in this section it will be noted that the long-run solution often quoted by monetarists, and expressed explicitly in terms of equation (5.33), involves *three conditions*:

1. relative purchasing power parity (equation (5.13));
2. interest rate parity (equation (5.23));
3. market efficiency (equation (5.27)).

International trade economists have been looking into all three conditions. The general evidence is that neither the first nor the second holds; although there is some evidence that the third condition holds.[6] The major difficulty, however, is in explaining short-run movements in the exchange rate, and here the role of exchange rate expectations is vital.

5.5 THE PHILLIPS CURVE FOR AN OPEN ECONOMY

It will be noted that the monetary models outlined in the two preceding sections are largely long-run models and certainly down-grade everything other than monetary influence on the

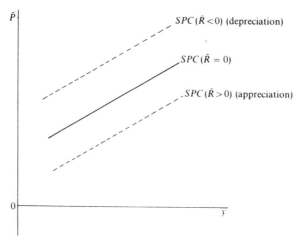

Figure 5.4 The SPC and exchange rate changes.

exchange rate. What the analysis does do, however, is indicate that there is a rather complex link between inflation, interest rates and exchange rates. This link is important in the consideration of policy. We have already shown that a pure fiscal expansion raises income and raises the rate of interest. Pure monetary policy raises income but lowers the rate of interest. Both these policies are expansionary as far as aggregate demand is concerned: both move the demand-pressure curve to the right and so raise the rate of inflation. There is, however, a need to consider whether there is a differential impact on the short-run Phillips curve.

We can do this by considering the form of the short-run Phillips curve we derived in Chapter 3 (equation (3.14) on p. 51). If for the present argument we ignore any change in productivity, then we can write the short-run Phillips curve as

$$\hat{P} = d_0 + d_1(y - y_n) - a\hat{R} \tag{5.34}$$

An appreciation of the real exchange rate ($\hat{R} > 0$) leads to a movement to the right in the short-run Phillips curve, while a depreciation of the real exchange rate ($\hat{R} < 0$) leads to a leftward movement in the short-run Phillips curve. In Fig. 5.4 we have drawn three such short-run Phillips curves, one where $\hat{R} = 0$, one with the exchange rate appreciating and one with the exchange rate depreciating.

Now let us return to the two possible policy options, a pure fiscal stimulus and a pure monetary stimulus, with floating exchange rates. In each case we are assuming that the stimulus applied moves the demand-pressure curve by the same amount. In the absence of any exchange rate changes the short-run effect is to move the economy from point A to point B in both instances, as shown in Fig. 5.5(*a*) and (*b*). However, in the case of the fiscal stimulus the short-run Phillips curve moves to the right. Why is this? The fiscal stimulus raises interest rates and raises income. The rise in income worsens the net export position but leads to an increase in capital inflows. If capital is responsive to interest rate changes, then this will lead to an overall improvement in the balance of payments. The surplus on the balance of payments will in turn lead to an appreciation of the exchange rate. This in turn will move the short-run Phillips curve to the right. The economy will, in the short run, move from point A to point C.

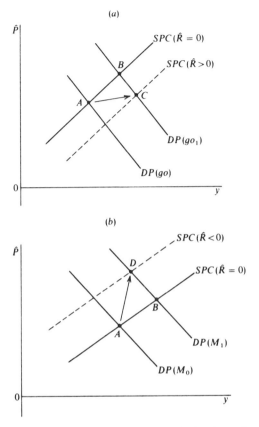

Figure 5.5 Policy options, the SPC and exchange rate changes: (a) fiscal stimulus; (b) monetary stimulus.

What is the effect of a pure monetary stimulus? The monetary stimulus raises income but lowers the rate of interest. The rise in income reduces net exports and the fall in the rate of interest reduces the level of net capital inflows. The combined result is an unambiguous deterioration in the balance of payments. Under a floating exchange rate regime, this will lead to a depreciation in the exchange rate. The depreciation will move the short-run Phillips curve to the left. The economy accordingly moves, in the short run, from point A to point D.

It must be emphasized that both points C and D are short-run solutions. In the case of monetary expansion the long-run solution is that the exchange rate will depreciate by the same extent as the increase in the growth of the money supply. The same is not true, however, for the fiscal stimulus since in the long run there is no reason for any change in the nominal money supply. This is not the end of the story, however.

In the case of a monetary expansion, inflation will rise in the short run by more than the monetary expansion because of the depreciation of the exchange rate. When expectations are included in the analysis, these too will be revised upwards and so further shifts to the left in the short-run Phillips curve will take place. On the other hand, the fiscal stimulus leads to a fall in the rate of inflation and this could lead to a revision of expectations downwards.

The conclusion one comes to from this analysis is that the exchange rate plays a vital role in moving the economy to a final equilibrium position. Furthermore, where that final equilibrium position happens to be depends very much on whether the economy is being stimulated (or depressed) by monetary or fiscal policy. Finally, the short-run path of the economy is very different for the two policy options.

NOTES

1. The UK balance of payments accounts have gone through two major changes: one in 1970 and a second in 1976, Allin (1976). The major change was in 1970. Prior to that date the accounts were divided into the current balance, the balance on long-term capital and the balance of monetary movements. The current balance plus the balance on long-term capital (both items to be taken as 'above the line') was referred to as the *basic balance*. In 1970 the accounts were divided into the current balance, the total currency flow, and official financing. The reason behind the change was the growing difficulty of determining which was a short-term capital flow (a monetary movement with less than one year to maturity) and which was a long-term capital flow (usually taken to refer to maturities in excess of five years). The change in 1976 shifted the borrowing in foreign currencies by public sector bodies from above the line to below the line, in recognition of the fact that these were largely accommodating transactions.

2. The two classic articles on exchange rate determination using demand and supply are by Haberler (1949) and Robinson (1947). A more modern and thorough treatment can be found in Chacholiades (1978).

3. See for example Officer (1976), Katseli-Papaefstratiou (1979) and McKinnon (1979).

4. The fact that interest rates enter as changes in percentage (and *not* percentage changes) is because interest rates are already expressed in percentage terms. The justification for equation (5.24) is as follows, where we consider only the domestic economy. Let

$$M_d = kPy^b e^{-ar}$$

Taking natural logarithms,

$$\mathrm{Ln}\, M_d = \mathrm{Ln}\, k + \mathrm{Ln}\, P + b\,\mathrm{Ln}\, y - ar$$

since $\mathrm{Ln}\, e = 1$. If we now totally differentiate this expression we get,

$$d\,\mathrm{Ln}\, M_d = d\,\mathrm{Ln}\, k + d\,\mathrm{Ln}\, P + b(d\,\mathrm{Ln}\, y) - a\,dr$$

Using the hat notation developed in Appendix 1.1, we have

$$\hat{M}_d = \hat{k} + \hat{P} + b\hat{y} - a\,dr$$

If $\hat{k} = 0$ (which arises if the income velocity of circulation of money is constant) and $b = 1$, then we have expression (5.24) (p. 98). Exactly the same analysis is used in deriving expression (5.25) for the foreign country.

5. In deriving result (5.28), notice that $(1 - z) = S/F = S/S^e$ if $F = S^e$. Taking natural logarithms we have

$$d\,\mathrm{Ln}(1 - z) = d\,\mathrm{Ln}(S/S^e)$$

But z is small, then $\mathrm{Ln}(1 - z) \sim -z$. Hence,

$$-z = \mathrm{Ln}(S/S^e) = -(r^* - r)$$

Totally differentiating, we have

$$d\,\mathrm{Ln}(S/S^e) = -(dr^* - dr)$$

Or

$$\hat{S}^e - \hat{S} = dr^* - dr$$

which is precisely equation (5.28) in the text.

6. On the empirical testing of PPP see Katseli–Papaefstratiou (1979) and Edison (1987). On a test of interest rate parity see Glahe (1967) and Hodjera (1973). The literature on testing foreign exchange market efficiency is growing, but a useful introduction can be found in Hallwood and MacDonald (1986) – which also covers purchasing power parity and interest rate parity.

APPENDIX 5.1 SPOT AND FORWARD EXCHANGE RATES

The foreign exchange market determines the exchange rate, i.e. the price of one currency in terms of another. However, a distinction must be made between the *spot* exchange rate and the *forward* exchange rate. The spot exchange rate refers to the exchange of two currencies (most usually in the form of bank drafts) for 'immediate' delivery. In practice this means within two business days. The forward rate is the price agreed now for the future buying or selling of a currency in terms of another. By 'future' is meant anything greater than two working days. Hence, there are as many forward rates as there are time periods. In practice it is common to find quotations for 30-days, 90-days and 180-days forward.

With the exception of sterling, it is conventional to quote exchange rates as the number of domestic currency units per US dollar – i.e. the price of the dollar in terms of domestic currency. Hence, if the German Deutschmark is quoted as 2.5000, this means that 2.5000 Deutschmarks are being exchanged for 1 US dollar. In practice, sterling is quoted the other way round – in other words the quotation is the number of US dollars for £1 sterling. Thus, if sterling is quoted as 1.5000 this means that £1 is exchanged for $1.5000 units of US dollars. Notice that the British convention is to quote the price of *sterling* in terms of dollars, while other countries quote the price of a *dollar* in terms of domestic currency. *Throughout this book we have employed the British convention in terms of quotations, and hence in the derivation of the formulae.*

The point of emphasizing the different ways of quoting exchange rates is because it is most ambiguous to refer to a 'rise' in the exchange rate. If the dollar price of sterling rises, then sterling is appreciating against the dollar – or, equivalently, the dollar is depreciating against sterling. A depreciation of sterling is reflected in a *fall* in the number of dollars per £1 (in the text, a fall in S). On the other hand, a depreciation of the Deutschmark, given the European convention of quotation, will mean a *rise* in the number of Deutschmarks per $1.

A given exchange rate has two quotations: a buying price (or 'bid' price) and a selling price (or 'offer' price). For example, $/£ rate on Wednesday 15 January 1986 was 1.4400–1.4410. This means transactors would be willing to buy pounds for $1.4400 or sell pounds at $1.4410. The *spread* simply refers to the difference between the buying price and the selling price. The size of the spread reflects the cost, profit and risk attached to the transaction. In practice only a *point-spread* is quoted. In the example just given, a call of 0–10 would be given.

It is not the practice, however, to quote the forward rate in full. The forward rate is simply quoted in terms of the difference from the spot rate. But it is here where the different conventions of quotation can cause some confusion. When more is paid for forward delivery than for spot delivery of a *foreign* currency (European convention), then the foreign currency is said to be at a *premium*. If less is paid for forward delivery than for spot delivery of a foreign currency, then the *foreign* currency is at a *discount*. But notice also that if the foreign currency is at a premium (discount), this means that the domestic currency is at a discount (premium). Now although the British convention is to quote the dollar price of sterling, premiums and discounts are quoted on the *dollar*. Suppose, therefore, that the spot exchange rate between the dollar and sterling is $1.4405 (the mid-point of Wednesday's spread). Further, suppose the dollar is at a premium (more sterling is paid for $1, or less of dollars are paid for £1 sterling). We might, then, have the one month forward quotation of 0.0064–0.0062 (or, rather, a call of 64–62 points). This is referred to as the *swap premium*. Notice that there has been no quotation of the forward rate. This can be calculated implicitly from the quotations. Since the dollar is at a premium, then sterling is at a discount. Hence, the forward rate for sterling is 1.4405 less 0.0064 (i.e., 1.4341) on the bid side, 1.4405 less 0.0062 (i.e., 1.4343) on the offer side. In other words, a dealer would pay a rate of $1.4341 for each £1 delivered to him in one month's time, and would offer to deliver sterling at $1.4343 in one month's time.

It is much more convenient to express the swap margin as a percentage per annum in order to compare it with annual interest rates. The European convention would be to take the swap margin as a percentage of the spot rate and annualize this. Again, however, because of the way the British quote their exchange rate, the swap margin is taken as a percentage of the forward rate and then annualized. The cost of forward cover (British convention, i.e. using the *indirect* quotation), expressed as an annual rate is given by

$$z = \frac{(F - S)}{nF} \times 100$$

where n is the fraction of the year for which the forward quotation is given. In the example we have been pursuing, let F be the mid-point of the bid-offer spread. Then $F = 1.4342$, which is the rate for a 30-day period. Hence, $n = 30/365$, which means

$$z = \frac{(1.4342 - 1.4405)}{1.4342} \times \frac{365}{30} \times 100 = -5.34\%$$

Hence, the cost of forward cover at an annual rate is 5.34%.

APPENDIX 5.2 EXCHANGE EQUALIZATION ACCOUNT

The exchange equalization account (EEA) was set up in 1932. Although part of the Bank of England, it is technically in the control of the Treasury. The purpose of the account has been to intervene in the foreign exchange market in order to stabilize the exchange rate. In addition, the account manages all net foreign exchange transactions by altering its asset holdings. In particular, the account holds all the UK's foreign exchange reserves. Because the EEA is a government account it is an integral part of the Exchequer's financing mechanism. It is this feature which complicates the relationship between official intervention in the foreign exchange market and the domestic money supply. However, in attempting to clarify this relationship it must be pointed out that in 1971 there was a change in the *procedure* of the workings of the EEA with regard to Treasury bill transactions – although this makes no analytical difference to its effect on the money supply. Finally, in attempting to clarify the relationship between balance of payments deficits/surpluses and the money supply it is necessary to consider (1) first round effects (or direct effects), and (2) ultimate effects (or net effects), which take account of the financing mechanism. Since sterling floated in 1972, we can use pre-1971 to analyse the situation under a fixed exchange rate and the procedure of the EEA with regard to Treasury bill transactions, while considering post-1971 in terms of floating exchange rates under the revised EEA procedures.

Pre-1971

Consider a deficit on the balance of payments totalling £100 million. This means that domestic residents are importing goods, services and capital in sterling terms in excess of what they are receiving from the export of goods, services and capital. With a *fixed* exchange rate, the Bank of England would have to demand sterling (supply foreign currency) equal to this difference. The EEA would obtain the foreign currency from its exchange reserves, which would fall (in sterling terms by £100). However, residents would be paying for the foreign exchange reserves with sterling, transferring £100 million sterling bank deposits to the EEA. The result of this would be a fall in the cash base. Pre-1971, however, the EEA did not simply sit on this £100 million, but, rather, purchased UK Treasury

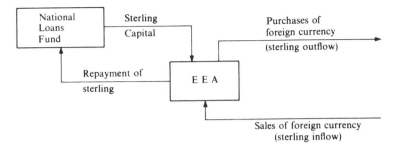

Figure A5.2.1 The EEA and inflows and outflows of currency.

bills supplied by the Bank of England. If nothing else was undertaken, then this would result in a fall in the money supply of £100 and a contraction of the domestic banking system. *This is the first round effect.*

The question arises, however: 'What does the Bank do with the additional £100?' If, for instance, the Bank should increase the total money supply by £100 by engaging in open market operations, then the final result is *no* change in the money supply and no contraction of the domestic banking system – although there will still be a reduction in the level of foreign exchange reserves and a new Treasury bill issue of £100 million to the EEA, together with a decline in domestic borrowing of £100 million. In other words, the government has a decline in domestic debt to match its decline in foreign assets. This offsetting action on the part of the authorities with respect to the money supply is called *sterilization*, and here we have a situation of perfect sterilization. Had the authorities increased the money supply at the second stage by less than the value of the sale of Treasury bills, then the money supply would not have been fully offset.

A similar but opposite situation occurs with a surplus on the balance of payments. In this case the EEA sells Treasury bills back to the Bank of England in order to obtain the sterling required to purchase foreign currency. A surplus of £100 million would lead to a first-round effect of an increase in the money supply of £100 million. The liquidation of Treasury bills that arises as a consequence of the surplus would lead to an increase in government domestic debt to match the increase in its foreign assets. The ultimate effect on this depended on which sector took up these Treasury bills. If, for example, the non-bank sector took up the Treasury bills, then they would transfer £100 million to the government account. There would, in this instance, be no *net* increase in the money supply. The increase would have been totally sterilized.

Post-1971

Since 1971 this procedure of buying and selling Treasury bills by the EEA has been discontinued. When foreign currency is now sold and sterling is received from domestic residents, this is now paid directly into the National Loans Fund. The acquisition of sterling from domestic residents in this way enables the government to finance some of its spending. In other words, it reduces the central government's need to borrow sterling domestically (i.e., it reduces the domestic component of the PSBR). Conversely, if there is a surplus on the balance of payments and a need to purchase foreign exchange, then the sterling required for this will come from the National Loans Fund, and so will raise the domestic borrowing requirement of the PSBR. The only difference between this procedure and that prior to 1971 is a book-keeping one with regard to Treasury bills. Analytically, the two procedures are identical. Thus the procedure is now more direct and does not involve the intermediate buying or selling of Treasury bills. This direct relationship is illustrated in Fig. A5.2.1.

Turning now to the situation under floating; in a situation of clean floating there is no need for government intervention. Any sterling being sold is purchased by another participant in the market (either resident or non-resident). However, the net monetary effects depend (as before) on the precise financing mechanism. Consider a surplus on the balance of payments. This means that non-residents are demanding sterling (selling foreign currency) in excess of the supply (demand). If the foreign currency is sold to other UK residents, then there is no net change in the banks' reserve assets, or eligible liabilities, and hence no change in £ *M* 3. Had the sale of foreign currency been to non-residents who supply the sterling, then this too would have no effect upon reserve assets or eligible liabilities, since such transactions do not in any way involve the Bank of England. However, there is a rise in £ *M* 3 as the sterling acquired by the non-resident (which is excluded from £ *M* 3) is switched into the account of a UK resident (which is, of course, counted in £ *M* 3). This is just one difference and many others are considered by Llewellyn, Llewellyn *et al.* (1982, chapter 4).

The essential conclusions are two in number (if eurosterling intermediation is ignored):

1. With official intervention in the foreign exchange market the monetary effects of the balance of payments is *not* measured by the change in external reserves.
2. The domestic money supply is *not* immune from external transactions when the exchange rate is allowed to float freely.

The reasons for these two conclusions, as we have attempted to show here, are: first, the extent to which transactions in public sector debt are involved; and, second, the extent to which sterling bank deposits are switched between residents and non-residents.

Finally, it is worth pointing out that the changes in UK banking instituted in 1980–81 (see Appendix 10.3) in no way affect these conclusions.

APPENDIX 5.3 RELATIVE SLOPES OF LM AND BP CURVES

In the text it was demonstrated that both the IS curve and the BP curve were positively sloped. What is not so obvious is the importance this has for exchange rate policy in response to a fiscal expansion. Here we consider a fixed exchange rate system similar to that which operated prior to the collapse of the Bretton-Woods system.

The situation is shown in Figs A5.3.1 and A5.3.2. In both these diagrams the economy is initially at point *A* with all three markets in equilibrium. In Fig. A5.3.1 net capital inflows are not very responsive to interest rate changes, which results in the BP curve being steeper than the LM curve. In Fig. A5.3.2, however, net capital inflows are quite responsive to interest rate changes, resulting in the BP curve being less steep then the LM curve.

Now consider a fiscal stimulus which shifts the IS curve from IS_0 to IS_1. In Fig. A5.3.1 this leads to a movement of the economy from point *A* to point *B*. But point *B* represents a *deficit* on the balance of payments. Although the rise in interest rates attracts more capital, this is not sufficient to counter-balance the fall in the current account which results from the rise in imports – the rise in imports occurring as a result of the rise in income. On the other hand, the same fiscal stimulus represented in Fig. A5.3.2 moves the economy from point *A* to point *C*. But point *C* represents a *surplus* on the balance of payments. This arises in the present situation from the fact that the rise in interest rates raises the net capital inflow more than is sufficient to swamp the deterioration in the current account.

What exchange rate policy is required to re-establish equilibrium in all three markets? In the case of Fig. A5.3.1, the policy is one of *devaluation*. This will move the IS curve to the right, to IS_2, and the BP curve to the right, to BP_1. The economy moves from point *B* to point *D*. In the case of Fig. A5.3.2, the policy is one of *revaluation*. This will move the IS curve to the left, to IS_2, and the BP curve to the left, to BP_1. The economy moves from point *C* to point *E*.

It is to be noted that under a fixed exchange rate system, a fiscal stimulus will lead to a lower rise in both income and interest rates the greater the interest sensitivity of net capital flows. Furthermore, the exchange rate response may be a revaluation rather than a devaluation.

The different result arising from a fiscal expansion does not occur in the case of a monetary expansion. The reason is as follows. A monetary expansion will reduce interest rates and raise income. The fall in interest rates will reduce the net capital inflow, while the rise in income will raise imports and cause a deterioration in the current account. There is, therefore, an unambiguous deficit on the balance of payments regardless of the interest sensitivity of net capital flows. The exchange rate policy

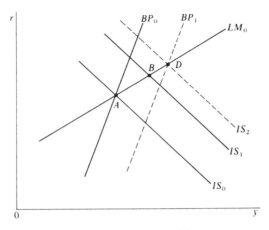

Figure A5.3.1 Fiscal stimulus with low capital flow interest – sensitivity.

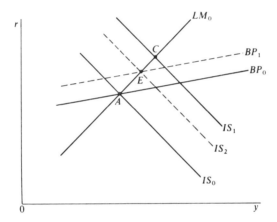

Figure A5.3.2 Fiscal stimulus with high capital flow interest – sensitivity.

response necessary to re-establish equilibrium in all three markets simultaneously is, therefore, a devaluation. The only difference that arises is the *extent* of the devaluation.

APPENDIX 5.4 STOP-GO POLICIES OF THE 1950s AND 1960s

As Keynesian economics became better known and began to influence government policy, it was considered that the solution to unemployment, when the economy had less than full employment, was to expand aggregate demand – usually by means of fiscal expansion – and when there was too much aggregate demand to cut it back. In simple terms, a pure fiscal expansion shifts the IS curve to the right and so shifts AD to the right. In this period prices were fairly stable and AS was considered approximately horizontal. Thus the fiscal expansion was going to fall on employment and output. What then was the problem?

The problem occurred with the balance of payments. As income rose so did the level of imports and this led to a growing deficit on the *current account*. The situation is shown in Fig. A5.4.1. To the extent that a pure fiscal policy is being pursued (a bond-financed increase in *go*, so that only the IS curve

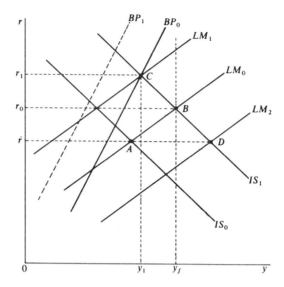

Figure A5.4.1 Stop–go policies of the 1950s and 1960s.

shifts, as explained fully in the next chapter), then there is also a rise in interest rates. This in turn will attract short-term capital into the economy – since the exchange rate was, during this period, held fixed. To some extent this inflow of capital could offset the deterioration in the trade account, but the extent of this depends on the interest elasticity of net capital inflows – a point emphasized in Appendix 5.3. In this situation the economy moves from point A to point B – where we have assumed point B is at the full employment income level, $y = y_f$ (although not necessary for the analysis) and a low interest rate sensitivity for net capital inflows (which was more likely in the 1950s and 1960s). Thus, point B shows a larger deficit on current *and* capital account than point A, and this has arisen purely because of the worsening on current account.

In fact, with no intervention by the authorities the economy will move to point C. Why is this? The deficit at point B will mean a loss of reserves. This loss will result in a fall in the nominal money supply and, with prices constant, will lead to a shift in the LM curve to the left until it cuts the IS curve at point C, which is also *on* the BP curve. Although income is smaller than the full employment level $(y_1 < y_f)$ interest rates are higher $(r_1 > r_0)$. Generally, however, this automatic adjustment did not take place!

During the 1950s and 1960s fiscal policy was dominant and monetary policy passive. Generally, interest rates were held fairly constant. What is the result of this? Fiscal expansion shifted the IS curve to IS_1 but because the government wanted the interest rate to remain constant at $\bar{r}$, the money supply was *increased*, so shifting the LM curve to LM_2 – i.e. the economy moved from point A to point D. The deficit on the balance of payments is much larger at point D than at points A, B or C. By holding the rate of interest constant, the net capital inflow also remains constant. However, the rise in income leads to a rise in imports and so raises the deficit on the current account. Furthermore, it is possible that the economy is overexpanded, with real income rising above the full employment level, which can only put pressure on prices to rise.

With a growing deficit the country's reserves of foreign exchange is depleted by ever larger amounts. Since the UK could not be allowed to run out of reserves (or else it could not honour its trading commitments) something had to be done. But what? It could allow interest rates to rise to attract short term capital inflows. But this had two implications. First, it would reduce investment. Second, it meant a fall in the money supply and hence less impact on employment and output. Certainly, there was a rise in Bank Rate during crisis periods. At this time the exchange rate was taken as sacrosanct and would not be changed. The only thing left was a general deflationary package. This shifted the IS curve and the LM curve to the left. However, tight monetary and fiscal policy led to a fall in income and to a rise in unemployment. When this became too unpalatable and once the balance of payments became less of a problem, the economy was once again expanded. Hence the term 'stop–go'.

The basic problem with 'stop–go' was that the government had too many objectives (full employment, no inflation and balance of payments equilibrium) and too few instruments to achieve them (basically only fiscal policy). Monetary policy was purely accommodating – or could be considered as being used to maintain a target rate of interest. Fiscal policy was being used in an attempt to achieve full employment *and* balance of payments equilibrium. Full employment generally required a fiscal expansion, while balance of payments equilibrium required fiscal contraction. Clearly, both could not be achieved simultaneously. (We consider this problem in more detail in Chapter 8.)

The problem was compounded during crisis periods. An expected devaluation led to an increase in net capital outflows (a devaluation from £1 = \$2 to £1 = \$1 meant obtaining \$2 and then converting this back into £2, thus making a profit of £1). An expected devaluation thus shifted the **BP** curve upwards (from BP_0 to BP_1), and hence the deficit at point *D* worsened. This led to an even greater loss in the reserves. Higher interest rates were not enough. A devaluation was necessary, and this occurred in 1967. This shifted IS to the right and BP downwards, so attempting to achieve both a full employment level of income and a balance of payments equilibrium.

The point was that fiscal policy could now be used to achieve full employment income, and devaluation could be used as a means of achieving balance of payments equilibrium.

APPENDIX 5.5 A SIMPLE MONETARIST MODEL OF WORLD INFLATION

A simple monetarist model of world inflation can also be developed. Let M and M^* denote money supply at home and abroad in sterling and dollars respectively – these being the only two countries in the world. Demands in home currency units are similarly given by $M_d = kPy$ and $M_d^* = k^*P^*y^*$. Expressing all relationships at the world level in dollars, we have

$$\text{World supply of money:} \quad Mw = SM + M^* \tag{A5.5.1}$$

$$\text{World demand for money:} \quad Dw = SkPy + k^*P^*y^* \tag{A5.5.2}$$

Finally, from absolute purchasing power parity we have

$$Pw = SP = P^* \tag{A5.5.3}$$

Equating (A5.5.1) and (A5.5.2), and using (A5.5.3), we obtain

$$Mw = SkPy + k^*P^*y^*$$
$$= (ky + k^*y^*)Pw$$

Taking natural logarithms, we have

$$\text{Ln}\,Mw = \text{Ln}(ky + k^*y^*) + \text{Ln}\,Pw$$

Totally differentiating, we get

$$dMw/Mw = [1/(ky + k^*y^*)](k\,dy + k^*dy^*) + dPw/Pw$$

Hence,

$$\hat{M}w = [ky/(ky + k^*y^*)]\hat{y} + [k^*y^*/(ky + k^*y^*)]\hat{y}^* + \hat{P}w$$

But it is readily shown, using the fact that money demanded equals money supplied in each country, that

$$\beta = SM/Mw = ky/(ky + k^*y^*)$$

$$(1 - \beta) = M^*/Mw = k^*y^*/(ky + k^*y^*)$$

Hence,

$$\hat{P}w = \hat{M}w - [\beta\hat{y} + (1-\beta)\hat{y}^*] \tag{A5.5.4}$$

In a long-run stationary state where output in each country is at its natural level, $\hat{y} = 0$ and $\hat{y}^* = 0$, from which it follows that

$$\hat{P}w = \hat{M}w \tag{A5.5.5}$$

i.e. world inflation is a result of world monetary growth.

APPENDIX 5.6 EXCHANGE RATE EXPECTATIONS AND OVERSHOOTING

Since floating exchange rates there have been attempts to explain why the exchange rate may move so dramatically on occasions in excess of what is required: in other words, there is a tendency for the exchange rate to overshoot. In this appendix a model of exchange rate overshooting will be considered, which is an adaption of Dornbusch's model (1976).

We begin by assuming, first, that the home country is small and that there is perfect capital mobility. This means that the interest rate at home, r, is equal to that abroad, r^*, less the expected percentage change in the exchange rate, $\hat{S}^e$. Thus,

$$r = r^* - \hat{S}^e \tag{A5.6.1}$$

where,

$$\hat{S}^e = (S - S^e)/S^e \tag{A5.6.2}$$

and where S is defined as the ratio of overseas currency to domestic currency (e.g., \$/£, where the UK is the home country and the US the foreign country).

Second, in the long-run, purchasing power parity is assumed to hold. Hence,

$$R = SP/P^* = 1 \qquad \text{or} \qquad SP = P^* \tag{A5.6.3}$$

and in equilibrium $\hat{S}^e = 0$ so that $r = r^*$.

Third, income is assumed constant at its full employment level, i.e.

$$y = y_n \tag{A5.6.4}$$

and thus all adjustment falls on prices, interest rates and the exchange rate.

Fourth, we assume that the expected exchange rate change is altered in proportion to the deviation from purchasing power parity. Let S_p denote the spot exchange rate in equilibrium (i.e., PPP), then

$$\hat{S}^e = -a[(S - S_p)/S_p] \qquad a > 0 \tag{A5.6.5}$$

This means that if the spot exchange rate is above the purchasing power parity rate, a depreciation of the home currency is expected; while if the exchange rate is below that of the purchasing power parity rate, then an appreciation is expected.

Fifth, and most importantly, we assume that the money market is very quick to clear while the goods market takes time.

With these assumptions the aim is to show, first the equilibrium in P–S space, i.e. the price level on the vertical axis and the spot exchange rate on the horizontal axis. When this is done, we can then consider the result of an increase in the money supply.

Consider, first, the money market. Using equation (2.14) and substituting in equations (A5.6.1), (A5.6.4) and (A5.6.5) we have

$$M_d/P = ky - ur$$
$$= ky_n - u(r^* - \hat{S}^e)$$
$$= ky_n - ur^* - ua[(S - S_p)/S_p]$$

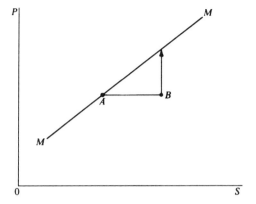

Figure A5.6.1 Equilibrium in the money market under flexible exchange rates.

Equating the supply of real money balances (M_s/P) with the demand for real money balances (M_d/P), and treating the nominal money supply as exogenous and equal to M_0, then

$$M_0/P = ky_n - ur^* - ua[(S - S_p)/S_p]$$

or

$$M_0/P = (ky_n - ur^* + ua) - ua(S/S_p) \qquad (A5.6.6)$$

Equation (A5.6.6) denotes a positive relationship between the price level and the spot exchange rate, and is shown by the line MM in Fig. A5.6.1. Any point on the line MM denotes combinations of P and S for which there exist equilibrium in the money market. The positive relationship can be verified as follows. Take a point A on the curve MM. Assume there is an appreciation of sterling (a rise in S). This will move the situation to point B. But now the exchange rate is above its purchasing power parity level, and hence there will be an expectation of a depreciation $(\hat{S} < 0)$. This will lead to a *rise* in $r^* - \hat{S}^e$, which in turn means a rise in r, as assumed in equation (A5.6.1). At the higher rate of interest, the money market will be in disequilibrium, there being an excess supply of real money balances. To re-establish equilibrium in the money market, the price level will have to rise, so reducing real money balances. It follows, therefore, that there is a positive relationship between P and S representing money market equilibrium.

Now consider equilibrium in the money *and* goods market combined. To establish this we first take the equilibrium condition in the goods market, embodied in equation (2.13). If we assume that expected inflation is zero $(\hat{P}^e = 0)$, then we have

$$[1 - b(1 - t_1) + m]y_n = z_0 - (f + g)R - hr \qquad (A5.6.7)$$

Defining

$$D = [1 - b(1 - t_1) + m]$$

then

$$Dy_n = z_0 - (f + g)(SP/P^*) - h(r^* - \hat{S}^e)$$

i.e.

$$Dy_n = z_0 - (f + g)(SP/P^*) - hr^* - ha[(S - S_p)/S_p] \qquad (A5.6.8)$$

Equation (A5.6.8) denotes equilibrium in the money and goods market (and is accordingly similar to the aggregate demand curve). In Fig. A5.6.2 we represent this equilibrium in the P–S space, and denoted GM. The line GM is negatively sloped. To see why this is the case, begin at point A denoting money and goods market equilibrium. Let the exchange rate depreciate (S falls), moving the situation to point B. The depreciation of the exchange rate improves the competitive position of the economy and so stimulates aggregate demand. However, with income at its natural level this will lead to a disequilibrium in the goods market, which can only be rectified by a rise in the price level. Hence, GM is negatively sloped.

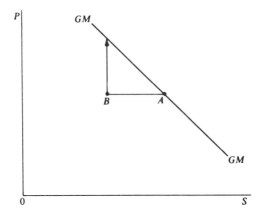

Figure A5.6.2 Equilibrium in both money and goods markets under flexible exchange rates.

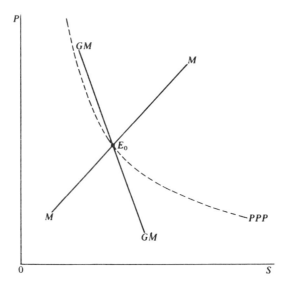

Figure A5.6.3 Equilibrium with purchasing power parity established.

The whole model is represented in Fig. A5.6.3, where we have combined the MM curve and the GM curve. We have also included the locus of points which represent purchasing power parity. From condition (A5.6.2) we know that $SP = P^*$. Since we are holding the price level abroad constant, $SP = P^*$ represents a rectangular hyperbola in P–S space. We have labelled this PPP in Fig. A5.6.3. This diagram shows all round equilibrium.

Now consider the situation in Fig. A5.6.4, where we have supplied the workings of the model in terms of both IS–LM and MM–GM. The situation is initially at point A in Fig. A5.6.4(a) and E_0 in terms of Fig. A5.6.4(b), and there is no expected change in the exchange rate ($\hat{S}^e = 0$) because PPP is satisfied. Thus the price level is at $P = P_0$ and the domestic interest rate is at r_0. Now assume there is a rise in the money supply from M_0 to M_1. This shifts the LM curve to $LM(M_1/P_0)$ and the MM curve to $M'M'$. A number of results can be noted at this stage. Because we assume a quick adjustment in the money market and a sluggish adjustment in the goods market, the immediate impact is a depreciation of the exchange rate from S_0 to S_1 and a fall in the interest rate from r_0 to r_1. The economy moves from point A to point B in terms of Fig. A5.6.4(a) and from point E_0 to point E_1 in terms of Fig. A5.6.4(b).

However, the depreciation of the exchange rate will lead to an improvement in the competitive position of the home economy (since P is temporarily constant at P_0 and the price level abroad is

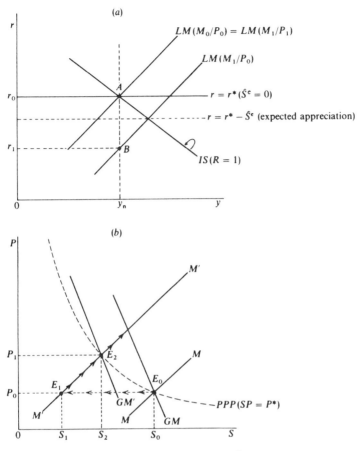

Figure A5.6.4 Exchange rate overshooting.

constant by assumption, then $R = SP/P^*$ will fall). This will raise net exports and so stimulate aggregate demand, temporarily shifting the IS curve to the right. But since real income at its natural level is constant in the long run, then the rise in aggregate demand must lead to a rise in the price level. The rise in the price level will in turn reduce the level of real money balances, so shifting the LM curve to the left. As prices rise, there is a movement up the $M'M'$ curve. The movement up the MM' curve indicates both a rise in prices *and* an appreciation of sterling (an appreciation which was expected by the market since the exchange rate fell below its PPP level). It is to be noted that the rise in prices occurs because of the assumption made about income. At point B the goods market is in disequilibrium. Rather than adjusting income, the excess demand manifests itself in a rise in prices. The rise in prices will shift the LM curve to the left, and reverse the improvement in the country's trade competitiveness. As this happens interest rates will rise, so shifting the GM curve to the left. The system will come to a stop when the price level rises to P_1, shifting the LM curve to $LM(M_1/P_1)$, $[= LM(M_0/P_0)]$, and the IS curve returns to its former position (since in the long run there will be no change in the real exchange rate – no change in R). It is to be noted that the economy has returned to a long-run (static) solution: income has returned to y_n, purchasing power parity once again holds, but at the higher domestic price level of P_1, and the domestic interest rate has returned to r_0 (with no expected change in the exchange rate).

The most characteristic result of this analysis is that the exchange rate *overshoots* its long-run result, as does the interest rate. Initially one would observe the interest rate falling dramatically and the exchange rate depreciating markedly. This would then be followed by a period of rising interest rates and an appreciating home currency.

Chapter 6

THE GOVERNMENT BUDGET

The government plays a major role in the modern economy, and no treatment of macroeconomics would be complete without some detailed analysis as to how it functions and how it influences the economy. The role of government is too broad a topic for this book. Here we will concentrate solely on the government budget: government receipts in terms of taxes and government spending in various forms. In 1987, government expenditure (central and local government) constituted 48.4% of gross domestic product – by no means a small component.

It is useful from the outset to see what makes up the government budget and the changes in its composition over time. Table 6.1 sets out general government receipts and expenditure in real terms for the period 1960–87. Government receipts arise from taxes: direct taxes on income (including national insurance contributions), and indirect taxes, such as VAT. The other component is trading income, rent, royalties, etc. Together these are denoted by t (in real terms) throughout this chapter. Government spending arises from four main areas: first, current expenditure on goods and services, such as health, education and defence; second, capital expenditures on the country's infrastructure, such as roads, schools and hospitals; third, transfer payments, such as pensions, unemployment benefits and student grants; and fourth, interest payments on outstanding debt. Finally, there is a component of net lending, to such organizations as the nationalized industries.

In terms of the analysis presented in this chapter we will consider only three components of government spending, current and capital expenditure (denoted g_c in real terms), transfer payments (denoted tr in real terms) and the interest payment on outstanding debt (denoted ip in real terms),[1] i.e.

$$go = g_c + tr + ip \tag{6.1}$$

In so far as direct tax is on income, a large component of taxes will be directly related to income. To the extent that national insurance contributions are considered as a form of tax, a change in this can be analysed in terms of a change in the marginal rate of tax. Indirect taxes, being based on expenditure, are not related to income and can be considered in the form of an autonomous element. This allows us to consider taxes as a simple linear function of income. By taking this approach we can consider fiscal expansion or contraction of the economy in some detail and lay the foundations for analysing fiscal policy, which we do in Part II.

In the first section of this chapter we define the budget surplus (or deficit) – both in terms of the actual surplus and in terms of full employment. As we will see, this latter measure of

Table 6.1 General government receipts and expenditures, 1960–87 (figures at 1980 prices £ million)

Year	Receipts — Taxes, national insurance, etc. contributions	Receipts — Trading income, rent royalties, interest, etc.	Expenditure — Goods and services: Final consumption	Goods and services: Gross domestic capital formation	Current and capital transfers: Current grants and subsidies	Capital transfers	Debt interest	Net lending etc.	Total	Real budget surplus bs
1960	38 916	4589	22 763	4530	11 586	462	5486	3235	48 062	−4557
1961	41 631	4586	23 711	4815	12 551	472	5728	3341	50 617	−4400
1962	43 719	4927	24 368	5186	12 990	567	5544	3111	51 767	−3121
1963	43 939	4829	25 145	5414	13 799	595	5848	2741	53 544	−4775
1964	46 122	5225	25 896	6614	13 838	704	5939	3728	56 719	−5372
1965	49 513	5525	27 091	6729	15 071	820	6075	4277	60 064	−5025
1966	52 417	5933	28 360	7334	15 457	820	6354	4441	62 765	−4415
1967	57 156	6236	30 610	8349	17 684	1749	6660	5606	70 657	−7265
1968	61 657	6812	31 106	8836	19 244	2815	7265	4876	74 142	−5674
1969	65 595	7325	30 751	8672	19 008	3229	7398	3828	72 886	35
1970	68 893	7662	32 599	8831	19 426	2873	7308	4435	75 472	1083
1971	66 507	7959	33 968	8527	19 507	3008	6904	5673	77 587	−3120
1972	65 855	7892	36 106	8494	22 177	2522	7003	5001	81 303	−7556
1973	67 798	8300	37 762	10 414	23 210	2762	7534	4329	86 010	−9912
1974	72 817	9180	40 617	10 691	27 280	2656	8480	5555	95 278	−13281
1975	75 187	8837	45 219	9753	27 971	2355	8072	7315	100 685	−16661
1976	74 692	9228	45 403	9107	28 479	2398	8887	3974	98 247	−14327
1977	73 354	8912	42 706	7052	28 008	2223	9111	535	89 634	−7368
1978	75 303	9079	44 698	6267	30 979	2740	9490	2458	96 631	−12248
1979	79 607	9585	45 882	6028	32 339	2205	10 229	4189	100 873	−11681
1980	82 464	10 211	49 027	5550	32 891	2193	10 873	3542	104 076	−11401
1981	86 054	10 251	49 570	4029	34 994	2118	11 354	2528	104 593	−8288
1982	87 753	10 317	49 826	3588	36 366	2304	11 502	2298	105 886	−7816
1983	90 634	9680	51 913	4748	37 733	2790	11 162	634	108 980	−8666
1984	92 446	9640	52 394	4848	39 523	2846	11 812	−1251	110 173	−8086
1985	95 154	10 265	52 350	5101	40 443	2333	12 348	−1232	111 342	−5923
1986	98 098	8813	54 439	4987	40 512	2120	11 751	−2767	111 041	−4131
1987	101 945	8686	55 732	4520	40 562	1994	11 522	−4360	109 969	661

Source: Economic Trends, Annual Supplement, 1988 Edition and May 1988

the budget surplus is important when attempting to *measure* whether fiscal changes are expansionary or contractionary. In Section 6.2 we consider the balanced budget theorem. In the past considerable attention was given to the balanced budget multiplier, but this became less relevant as governments persisted in running budget deficits. In the 1980s, however, there has been a strong move, both in the UK and in the US, to attempt to balance the budget. What is not clear from much of the discussion is whether this is meant to equate the level of government spending with the level of tax receipts; or whether it is meant to change government spending only in line with the change in tax receipts. As we will see, these are not the same thing. In Section 6.3 attention centres on how the budget surplus/deficit is financed. This financing of the budget surplus/deficit constitutes a constraint on fiscal (and, one might add, monetary) policy. In Section 6.4 we turn to the much debated topic of wealth effects. A further constraint on the budget arises from a view about the desired size of the public sector. We turn to this issue in the final section of this chapter.

6.1 THE BUDGET SURPLUS

The government receives income in the form of taxes. Let t denote *real* taxes, both direct and indirect. Since, in particular, direct taxes are related to real income, we can write this in the simple form

$$t = t_0 + t_1 y \tag{6.2}$$

where t_0 denotes real autonomous taxes and t_1 is the marginal rate of tax. Further, let g_c denote real current and capital government expenditure, tr denote real transfers, and ip the real interest payment on outstanding debt. Hence, total real government spending as defined here is $g_c + tr + ip$. Accordingly, the budget surplus (in real terms) is real tax receipts less total real government spending, i.e.

$$bs = t - g_c - tr - ip \tag{6.3}$$

or

$$bs = t_0 + t_1 y - g_c - tr - ip = (t_0 - g_c - tr - ip) + t_1 y \tag{6.4}$$

The real budget surplus for the UK for the period 1960–87 is shown by the final column in Table 6.1.

If real government spending is treated as exogenous, and given, and assuming real transfers and the interest payment on outstanding debt are also constant, say at $tr = tr_0$ and $ip = ip_0$, then we can write equation (6.4) in the simple linear form

$$bs = bs_0 + t_1 y \tag{6.5}$$

where

$$bs_0 = (t_0 - g_c - tr_0 - ip_0).$$

Equation (6.5) is shown in terms of Fig. 6.1 by the line *BS*, where it is clear that the real budget deficit, *bd*, is no more than the negative of the real budget surplus, i.e.

$$bd = -bs \tag{6.6}$$

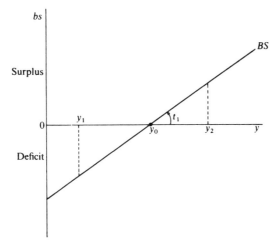

Figure 6.1 The budget surplus/deficit.

A *balanced budget* is where government spending plus transfers plus the interest payment on outstanding debt is equal to tax receipts, i.e where

$$bs = 0 \tag{6.7}$$

In terms of Fig. 6.1, for real income less than y_0 the budget is in deficit, while for income above y_0 the budget is in surplus. Notice, in particular, that the intercept is given by $bs_0 = (t_0 - g_c - tr_0 - ip_0)$ and the slope is given by the marginal rate of tax, t_1. A rise in government spending on current or capital account, or a rise in transfers, lowers the budget surplus line and raises the level of real income at which the budget is balanced. Similarly, a fall in the marginal rate of tax also raises the level of real income at which the budget is balanced. In the first case the rise in government spending must be matched by a rise in tax receipts if the budget is to be balanced. With tax rates constant, this can only occur if income rises. In the second case, a fall in the marginal rate of tax also lowers tax receipts (but not necessarily by the same magnitude as in the first example). The budget can only be brought into balance, assuming government spending is unaltered, if income rises to compensate for the fall in the marginal rate of tax.

One must be careful when interpreting Fig. 6.1. All that is specified is the budget surplus/deficit. There is no analysis as to what level of real income the economy will tend towards. All we can say from the diagram is that if we know the level of real income, we can then establish from equation (6.4) what the real budget surplus or deficit will be.

The difficulty is highlighted in terms of Fig. 6.2. The economy is initially at real income y_1 on the schedule marked BS_1, with the budget balanced. Now suppose the marginal rate of tax is raised. This will pivot the budget surplus line to BS_2. Is this rise in taxes a fiscal expansion of the economy or a fiscal contraction?

To answer this question we require a measure of fiscal expansion/contraction. Suppose we decide to use the *actual* budget balance to measure this. If there is a budget surplus we assume there has been a fiscal contraction, while if there is a budget deficit we assume there has been a fiscal expansion. Suppose that the rise in taxes reduces income to the level y_2, as indicated in Fig. 6.2. At this income level there is a budget deficit (denoted bd_2). This would

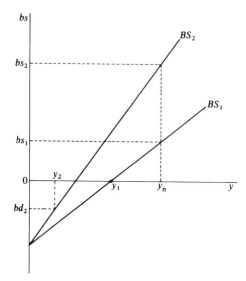

Figure 6.2 Measuring fiscal stance.

thus suggest that the rise in taxes is expansionary! The reason for this result is not hard to see. As drawn, the substantial fall in income will lead to a large fall in real tax receipts, even though the marginal rate of tax is higher than it was previously.

Suppose, therefore, that we decide on an alternative way of measuring fiscal expansion/contraction. Suppose we decide to measure the budget surplus/deficit at the level of full employment (or what we can refer to as the natural rate of income). Again referring to Fig. 6.2, at income level y_n the budget surplus rises from bs_1 to bs_2. Using this measure we would conclude that the tax rise has been contractionary. In fact, on this basis, all we are required to do is agree on a fixed level of real income on which to base the comparison – whether this be full employment or a high level of employment.

The ideas so far highlighted are illustrated in Appendix 6.1 by means of a numerical example, using the information contained in Appendix 2.4. The information in both Appendices 2.4 and 6.1 will be utilized further in the present chapter.

Although the full employment budget surplus is appealing it is not without its own problems. First, the measure is totally independent of what brings about the change. In other words, it does not distinguish between a change in taxes, a change in expenditure or a change in transfers. As we will see in the next section, the impact on income of a change in expenditure is greater than the impact on income of an equivalent change in taxes or in transfers. It has been suggested, therefore, that a weighted measure be formed (a weight of 1 for government spending and a weight of t_1 for taxes or transfers).

Second, no distinction is made between direct or indirect taxes and so the impact of these two is assumed to be the same. A change in the marginal rate of tax on income is therefore supposed to have the same impact on the economy as a change in the rate of VAT! Other distinctions are also discussed (such as the differential impacts of trade). What is clear, however, is that all differentials are ruled out in this simple framework because, effectively, the model is a *single* good economy, i.e the economy only produces 'output' y.

To use the full employment budget surplus as a measure can be misleading in situations where unemployment benefits, for example, are altered. In this situation the full employment budget surplus remains unaffected (since there is no change in employment). However, the actual measure of the budget surplus will depend on the level of unemployment that exists. This can be overcome to some extent by taking a measure at some high level of employment (but not full employment) but the measure then becomes decidedly arbitrary.[2]

6.2 THE BALANCED BUDGET THEOREM

Adam Smith said long ago that governments should be as prudent as the private family. Just as an individual cannot live beyond his means, so too with governments. He said,

> What is prudence in the conduct of every private family, can scarce be folly in that of a great kingdom.

From this quotation a number of people have inferred that Adam Smith recommended a balanced budget. However, after Keynes' *General Theory* it was considered 'right' (although not necessarily prudent) to run a budget deficit in order to achieve full employment. In the 1980s there has been a return to the views of Adam Smith: namely, that governments should balance their budgets.

The literature on balanced budgets is often confusing. It confuses two separate ideas. Namely, a balanced budget and a balanced budget *change*. To be specific:

1. A *balanced budget* is where government expenditure (including transfers and debt repayment) is equal to tax receipts, i.e. where

$$g_c + tr_0 + ip_0 = t \quad \text{or} \quad bs = 0 \tag{6.8}$$

2. A *balanced budget change* is where the change in government expenditure is matched exactly by a change in government receipts, i.e where

$$dgo = dt \tag{6.9}$$

Clearly, if (1) holds true initially, then (2) will imply that (1) holds true after the increase in government spending. However, if (1) is not true, satisfying (2) does not necessarily imply that $bs = 0$ after the change.

It is important to keep (1) and (2) clearly distinguishable. In much of the political discussion about balanced budgets, the one being referred to is (1). On the other hand, much of the economic discussion of the balanced budget multiplier – to be presented in a moment – is in terms of (2). In practice the issue is complicated even further by discussions of the desired size of the public sector. What is not often made clear is that the idea of a desired size of the public sector imposes a constraint on the level of income at which the budget is balanced under definition (1). We will return to the issue of the size of the public sector in the final section of this chapter.

The idea of a balanced budget multiplier is very straightforward: it asks what is the effect on income of *changing* government spending in line with the *change* in taxes ($dgo = dt$). It might be thought that income will not change at all, in which case the multiplier would be zero. As it turns out, this is not the case.

We begin with the equilibrium condition in the goods market embodied in equation (2.11) and re-written here:

$$y = \frac{[z_0 + h\hat{P}^e - (f+g)R] - hr}{1 - b(1 - t_1) + m} \qquad (6.10)$$

The change in income arising from the change in government spending is simply the multiplier k_{rc}, i.e.

$$dy/dgo = 1/[1 - b(1 - t_1) + m] = k_{rc}$$

It is when we turn to taxes, t, that difficulties arise. In general we have, for the change in taxes,

$$dt = dt_0 + t_1 dy + y dt_1 \qquad (6.11)$$

If the change in taxes arises solely from a change in the autonomous component, namely t_0, then we obtain the result, as shown in Appendix 6.2:

$$dy = \left[\frac{1 - b}{1 - b(1 - t_1) + m}\right] dgo \qquad dt = dt_0 \qquad (6.12)$$

On the other hand, if both the autonomous element and the induced tax changes are allowed – the induced tax changes arising from the change in income – we have the 'long-run' result, shown in Appendix 6.2:

$$dy = \left[\frac{1 - b}{1 - b + m}\right] dgo \qquad (dt_0 = dgo - t_1 dy) \qquad (6.13)$$

The intuition behind the increase in income when there is a balanced budget change is as follows. The rise in government spending will have the full multiplier impact on national income. However, the tax increase is partially offset because the change in disposable income leads to a change in consumption weighted by the marginal propensity to consume. In other words, a one-unit decline in disposable income will lead to a fall of b in consumption. Since the marginal propensity to consume is less than unity, the fall in income from the tax cut must be less than the rise in income from the increase in government spending. The end result, therefore, is a rise in income. The mathematics outlined in Appendix 6.2 merely indicates that the extent of the rise in income depends on the assumptions being made.

It will be noted that neither result (6.12) nor result (6.13) are unity. On the contrary, both multipliers are less than unity. In all realistic cases, income will rise/fall with a balanced budget increase/decrease in government spending, but by less than the change in government spending. The often quoted result that 'the balanced budget multiplier is unity' arises from two extreme assumptions (or, from too restrictive a model). If the marginal rate of tax is zero *and* the marginal propensity to import is zero, then the multipliers in (6.12) and (6.13) become unity. Such extreme assumptions are not very appealing when dealing with a modern open economy.

It is clear from equation (6.10) that the multiplier k_{rc}, and the balanced budget multipliers derived in Appendix 6.2, are obtained for a *constant* rate of interest. When allowance is made for the money market, the multiplier is smaller and includes a term indicating responses in the money market. This multiplier is derived in Appendix 6.3. What is clear, however, is that the balanced budget multiplier is even further reduced. Only in very naive models is the balanced budget multiplier unity. The conclusion we come to is that in general the balanced budget multiplier is less than unity.

It will be noted that discussion of the balanced budget multiplier is done solely in terms of balanced budget *changes*. However, much of the debate in the 1980s concerns balancing the budget, i.e. achieving $bs = 0$. Of course, if we begin from a balanced budget position and initiate a balanced budget change, then bs is still zero and income can be raised. The arguments for pursuing a balanced budget, in terms of $bs = 0$, however, have nothing to do with the balanced budget theorem. We will take up the issue of a balanced budget in Section 6.5.

6.3 FINANCING THE GOVERNMENT BUDGET

So far we have discussed the government budget simply in terms of receipts less government spending. For most years, as Table 6.1 makes clear, the UK government has had a budget deficit. The question we wish to consider in this section is: exactly how is the excess of spending over tax receipts financed?

In attempting to answer this question it is important to distinguish stock and flow equilibria.[3] A stock equilibrium refers to the desired holdings of stocks of money, bonds and other assets. In other words, equality between the demand for stocks and the supply of stocks. Flow equilibrium, on the other hand, refers to flow demand for goods and services (over, say, a year) with the flow supply of goods and services. In the context of the IS–LM–BP model, flow equilibrium refers to equilibrium in the goods market (a point on the IS curve). Flow equilibrium does not imply that stocks are at their desired level; hence flow equilibrium does not imply stock equilibrium. On the other hand, stocks can only be maintained at their desired level if flow demand is matched by flow supply, since this will mean there is no addition to the level of stocks. In other words, stock equilibrium implies flow equilibrium.

We have made the point that flow equilibrium refers to equilibrium in the goods market (a point on the IS curve). But in the present context what is meant by stock equilibrium? Consider a situation where stocks are at their desired position – both the stock of money and the stock of bonds. Now if the government is running a budget deficit which is financed either from increased money or from an increase in bonds, then the stock equilibrium must be disturbed. This in turn will lead to changes in the goods market as market participants attempt to re-establish stock equilibrium. Such a stock equilibrium can only occur when all government spending ($go = g_c + tr + ip$) is being financed from taxes (t). Stock equilibrium, therefore, implies a balanced budget ($bs = 0$).

Effectively, there are only three ways in which the government can finance their spending:

1. from taxes;
2. by borrowing from the Central Bank;
3. by borrowing from the public.

Hence, a budget deficit can only be financed either by borrowing from the Central Bank or borrowing from the public. In the former case this means printing more money – raising the money base $M0$ (explained more fully in the next chapter). In the second case it means issuing more bonds in the hope that the public will purchase them and so supply the government money in return. Let $d M0$ denote the nominal change in the money base and dB the nominal *value* of the change in the bond issue,[4] or in real terms $d(M0/P)$ and $d(B/P)$ respectively. Then the budget deficit $(bd = -bs)$ is

$$bd = g_c - t + tr + ip = d(M0/P) + d(B/P) \qquad (6.14)$$

If government spending is financed solely from taxes, that is to say the budget is balanced, then $g_c + tr + ip = t$ and $d(M0/P) = d(B/P) = 0$. If, on the other hand, the government financed the deficit solely by means of borrowing from the Central Bank, then $g_c - t + tr + ip = d(M0/P)$ and $d(B/P) = 0$. Alternatively, if the budget deficit is financed by means of borrowing from the public then $g_c - t + tr + ip = d(B/P)$ and $d(M0/P) = 0$. This is usually referred to as a pure fiscal expansion because the budget deficit has been financed solely by borrowing from the public with no change in the money supply. Let us analyse each of these cases in turn.

(a) Tax financed increase in government spending

In Fig. 6.3 we begin at point A with income at y_0 and a balanced budget $(g_c + tr + ip = t)$. Now suppose government spending is raised by dgo and that this is financed solely from additional taxes, dt. In Fig. 6.3 we have assumed that taxes were raised by changing only the marginal rate of tax, t_1 (rising from t_1 to t_1'). The rise in government spending, other things constant, will move the IS curve from IS_0 to IS_1. Income will rise to y_1 and there will be a budget deficit of bd_1. However, this cannot be the final outcome because it ignores how the resulting budget deficit is being financed. If it is financed by an equal change in taxes, then the final outcome is at point H in Fig. 6.3(b) and point C in Fig. 6.3(a). At income level y_2 the new level of taxes just matches the new level of government spending, and so point H represents a balanced budget position. The extent of the rise in income from y_0 to y_2 depends solely on the balanced budget multiplier, and this we have already established is positive but less than unity.

(b) Money financed increase in government spending

In this case there is an increase in government spending which is financed by an increase in the money supply. The situation is shown in Fig. 6.4 Again the initial position is point A, with income at y_0 and a balanced budget. Government spending rises by dgo which, other things being equal, moves the IS curve to IS_1. But if the budget deficit which results (denoted bd_1 in Fig. 6.4) is financed by borrowing money from the Central Bank, then the money base will rise and so too will the money supply. As the money supply rises, the LM curve moves to the right, which also raises income. The rise in income will raise endogenous taxes and so reduce the budget deficit. But so long as a deficit remains, the money supply will continue to increase. The money supply will stop changing only when the budget is balanced – at point D in Fig. 6.4(a) and point J in Fig. 6.4(b). In this instance a money financed increase in government spending leads to a rise in income from y_0 to y_3, which exceeds the rise in income y_0 to y_1.

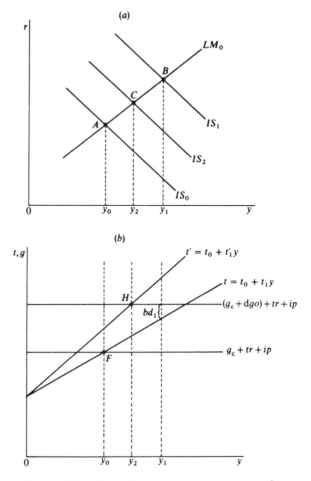

Figure 6.3 Tax financed increase in government spending.

(c) A bond financed increase in government spending

This case is probably the most complex of the three forms of financing. The situation is shown in Fig. 6.5. The economy is initially at point A with income at y_0 and a balanced budget. Let government spending rise again by dgo which, other things being equal, moves the IS curve to IS_1. The rise in income leads to a budget deficit of bd_1. Now suppose this deficit is financed by the issue of more bonds to the public. Two consequences occur as a result of this financing. First, the increase in interest payment on the outstanding debt will raise disposable income, which in turn will lead to a rise in consumption. This in effect is an exogenous shift in the IS curve, which moves further to the right. Second, the interest repayment on the national debt can no longer be ip, but, rather, is $ip + d(ip)$. Hence, there is a further movement in total government expenditure. The situation will only settle down when the IS curve reaches IS_4 in Fig. 6.5(a) and the total government expenditure schedule cuts the tax schedule at point K. Both point E in Fig. 6.5(a) and point K in Fig. 6.5(b) are for

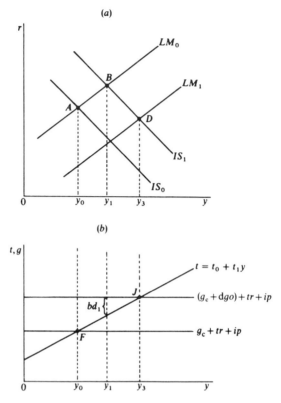

Figure 6.4 Money financed increase in government spending.

income level y_4. At this income level the budget is once again balanced. (In this analysis we have assumed that there are no portfolio effects on interest rates and that no crowding out occurs.)

The three forms of financing can conveniently be compared in terms of Fig. 6.6. A balanced budget increase in government spending gives rise to a movement from A to C in Fig. 6.6(a) and F to H in Fig. 6.6(b). On the other hand, the money financed increase in the budget deficit leads to a movement from A to D in Fig. 6.6(a) and F to J in Fig. 6.6(b). Finally, a pure fiscal expansion where the budget deficit is financed from bond sales will move the economy from point A to point E in the upper diagram and from point F to point K in the lower diagram. All lead to a rise in real income – but not to the same extent. It is clear from Fig. 6.6 that the bond financed increase in government spending is the most expansionary in that it raises income the most. However, it also has the greatest impact in raising interest rates. The rise in income resulting from the rise in government spending results in a rise in the transactions demand for money. This in turn leads to a rise in the interest rate (a movement up the LM curve from A to B). However, the additional rise in income resulting from the additional interest repayment on the national debt leads to a further increase in the transactions demand for money, and hence to a further rise in the rate of interest (a movement up the LM curve from B to E).[5]

The conclusion we come to is that, of the three forms of financing, a balanced budget increase in government spending has the least impact on income, while a bond financed increase in government spending has the greatest impact on income. However, the money

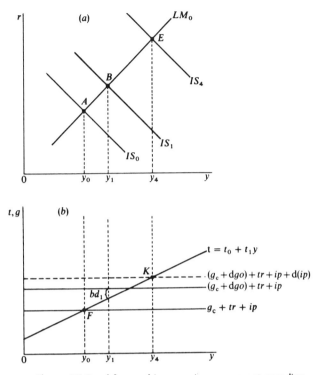

Figure 6.5 Bond financed increase in government spending.

financed impact and the bond financed impact may not be as indicated in Figs. 6.4, 6.5 and 6.6. The reason for this arises from the fact that we have neglected to consider one stock variable – namely, a country's wealth. If real money balances and/or real bonds constitute part of a country's wealth, then both a money financed increase in government spending and a bond financed increase will lead to a rise in the level of wealth. We consider this wealth effect in the next section.

Equation (6.14) is an important equation and must always be true – consequently it is considered as a constraint on government policy. In monetarist literature, however, it is considered as a short-term result. Why a short-term result? Issuing bonds will simply lead to taxes in the future in order to pay interest on the outstanding debt. In the long run, the only means of paying for a continued budget deficit (so the argument goes) is by continually altering the money supply. In the long run, therefore,

$$g_c - t + tr + ip = d(M0/P) \qquad (6.15)$$

We will use this result in later chapters when considering monetary policy in combination with fiscal policy.

6.4 WEALTH EFFECTS

The government budget constraint illustrated the fact that the IS curve and the LM curve are interrelated. However, there is another reason for their interrelationship which we have

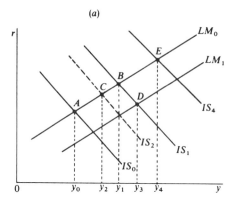

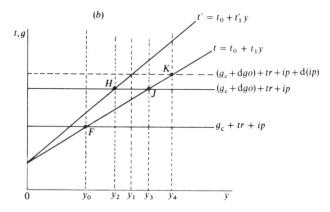

Figure 6.6 Comparing the methods of financing.

so far ignored. In order to appreciate this further connection we must define the private sector wealth position of the economy. In simple terms we can define private sector wealth (a stock), $wl_p = Wl_p/P$, as the sum of physical capital stock, ks, the real value of money holdings, M/P, and the real value of bond holdings, b; i.e.

$$wl_p = Wl_p/P = ks + (M/P) + b \qquad (6.16)$$

In the case of a tax financed increase in government spending the wealth position of the private sector remains unchanged. However, both a money financed and a bond financed increase in government spending will raise the level of private sector wealth (assuming the price level remains constant). Assuming initially that the private sector were in a stock (and hence a flow) equilibrium, this will no longer be the case. Consider first a money financed increase in government spending. The rise in the money supply, prices assumed constant, will lead to a rise in real private sector wealth. However, there is no reason to assume that individuals will wish to hold *all* the additional wealth in the form of real money balances. To the extent that they do not, there will be impacts in the goods market and in the market for bonds. Both these impacts will lead to a rightward movement in the IS curve (a positive wealth effect). The result is shown in Fig. 6.7. Since the wealth effect is positive the effect of monetary expansion as a means of financing government spending is greater than was indicated in the preceding section.

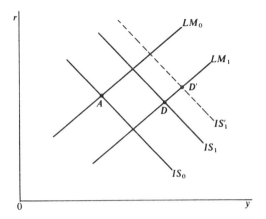

Figure 6.7 Money financed increase in government spending and the wealth effect.

In the case of a bond financed increase in government spending, there will be a rise in bonds and hence a rise in private sector wealth. Again, there is no necessity for the rise in wealth to be held solely in terms of bonds. To the extent that individuals diversify their portfolios, there will be impacts in the goods market and in the money market. In the goods market there will be a rise in consumption, and hence a rightward movement in the IS curve (a positive wealth effect). In the money market there will be a rise in the demand for money. With a fixed supply of money balances, equilibrium in the money market can be restored only by a rise in the rate of interest. In other words, the LM curve moves to the left (a negative wealth effect). The final result of the wealth effect under a bond financed increase in government spending is to raise the rate of interest. Its impact on real income, however, is uncertain. The result on real income depends on the elasticity of consumption with respect to wealth in comparison with the elasticity of the demand for money with respect to wealth. If the latter outstrips the former, the leftward shift in the LM curve will outweight the rightward shift in the IS curve, with the result that real income will be less than indicated in the previous section (y_5 rather than y_4). This situation is illustrated in Fig. 6.8.

The wealth effect just alluded to has led to a further dispute between Keynesians and monetarists. Keynesians, although acknowledging the existence of the wealth effects, consider them to be small. Monetarists, on the other hand consider them to be large and important. (For a consideration of the debate, see Dow and Earl, 1982, chapter 9.)

6.5 SIZE OF THE PUBLIC SECTOR

In the 1980s attention turned to the size of the public sector, with governments being concerned that it was too large. In Appendix 6.4 we consider some measures of the size of the public sector. We will take up the policy aspects of the size of the public sector in Part II; here all we wish to do is consider one formal aspect of it in relation to the budget surplus. The question we wish to raise is: will the pursuit of a balanced budget be consistent with some desired size in the public sector?

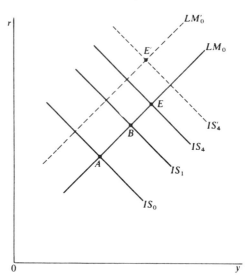

Figure 6.8 Bond financed increase in government spending and the wealth effect.

Suppose we measure the size of the public sector as the ratio of real government spending to real income, i.e.

$$z = go/y \qquad (6.17)$$

If z^* denotes the desired size of the public sector (e.g., 0.20, as suggested by the Friedmans (1980), or 0.25 as suggested by Burton, 1985), then it follows that $go = z^* y$. The situation is shown in Fig. 6.9(a, b). The tax schedule is given by t, government spending initially by go and $z^* y$ denotes the level of government spending in relation to real income which preserves the desired size of the public sector (Fig. 6.9(a)). In Fig. 6.9(b) we have drawn the budget surplus. Given go, the budget is balanced at income level y_0 where BS_0 cuts the horizontal axis. However, given the desired size of the public sector z^*, such a balanced budget is not considered desirable – in the sense that it implies a public sector larger than that desired (i.e., go lies above $go = z^* y_0$). It would appear that one solution is to reduce government spending to go_1 (since $go_1/y_0 = z^*$). However, this is not appropriate. The reduction in government spending will reduce income through the multiplier process and income could be at y_1 denoting a balanced budget but still too large a public sector. A quite opposite solution is to raise government spending to the level go_2. The result is a new budget surplus line, denoted BS_2, and a balanced budget can be achieved at income level y_2. The reason for this result is that the rise in government spending raises income by more through the multiplier process. The result is to reduce the ratio of go/y because y is expanding more than go.[6] The danger inherent in the first policy is to lead to the mistaken view that a reduced size in the government sector automatically means lowering go. This not only leads to a recessionary policy, but can also have quite the opposite effect in terms of *relative* size. What it will succeed in doing is reducing the *absolute* size of the public sector.

What is clear from Fig. 6.9 is the possible conflict between objectives. The desired size of the public sector adds yet an additional constraint on government policy other than pursuing a balanced budget and financing any further deficits or surpluses.

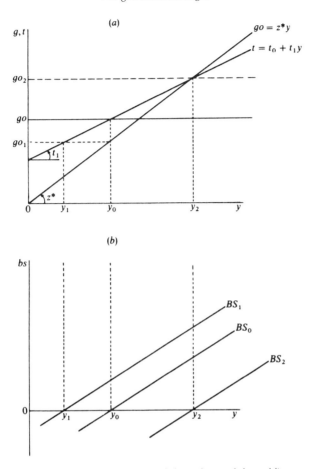

Figure 6.9 Budget deficit/surplus and desired size of the public sector.

NOTES

1. In our theoretical development we do not distinguish net lending. It could be considered as a component of net transfers (*tr*). However, it is an item which has been growing. The analysis could readily be extended by considering net lending (*nl*, in real terms) as separate, so that total government expenditure becomes,

$$go = g_c + tr + ip + nl$$

2. See Okun and Teeters (1970) and Blinder and Solow (1974) for some early analysis, and Savage (1982) for measures in the UK of high employment budget surpluses.

3. Flow equilibrium can be likened to a bath of water where the inflow from the tap is equal to the outflow down the drain – which will maintain the water level constant. On the other hand, stock equilibrium can be likened to the desired level of water in the bath. If the water is not at the desired level, then either the inflow must be increased or the outflow decreased or some combination of the two. However, once the water has reached the desired level, then the inflow must equal the outflow if the desired level is to be maintained (which can, of course, mean zero inflow and outflow). This

illustrates the point that a stock equilibrium implies a flow equilibrium, while the converse is not necessarily true.

4. Suppose the government issues a bond which pays £100 each year in perpetuity (where the £100 is sometimes called the coupon value). The present value of such a bond is the sum of the discounted coupons. Thus, if the rate of interest were r, and the coupon value were C, then the present value would be

$$PV = \sum_{n=1}^{\infty} \frac{C}{(1+r)^n} = \frac{C}{r}$$

Thus, if the rate of interest were 10% and the coupon value were £100, then an individual would be prepared to pay £1000. In this example, the value of the bond issue would be £1000 or the present value ($B = C/r$ in the text). On the other hand, the *real* value of the bond would be B/P or C/rP.

5. The change in the national debt is a change in the wealth position of individuals. The impact of this wealth effect is in some dispute between monetarists and Keynesians, see, for example, Dow and Earl (1982, Chapter 9).

6. For a determinate solution for go, then it must be the case that $t_1 < z^*$. If this is not true, then it is not possible to achieve a balanced budget at the desirable relative size of the public sector!

APPENDIX 6.1 BUDGET SURPLUS: A NUMERICAL EXAMPLE

From the information contained in Appendix 2.4 we can derive the following results:

$$t = 3 + 0.3y \tag{A6.1.1}$$

$$go = 30$$

$$bs = t - go = -27 + 0.3y \tag{A6.1.2}$$

The level of income which clears the money market and the goods market is $y = 37.313$ and at this level of income the budget surplus is given by

$$bs = -27 + (0.3)(37.313) = -15.806 \tag{A6.1.3}$$

Hence, there is a budget deficit. It is to be noted that for the tax structure embodied in equation (A6.1.1) the level of income that would balance the budget is $y = 90$, which is obtained by setting $bs = 0$.

Now let the tax rate rise to $t = \frac{1}{3}$. The new levels of income and budget surplus which clear the goods market and money market are

$$y = 36.765 \quad \text{and} \quad bs = -14.745 \tag{A6.1.4}$$

The situation is shown in Fig. A6.1.1, where the rise in the tax rate pivots the budget surplus line from BS_1 to BS_2.

With government spending maintained at $go = 30$, the rise in the tax rate would lead to an increase in tax revenue at the same level of income. But the equilibrium level of income falls. However, in the present example, the fall in income is not sufficient to offset the rise in revenue from the increased tax rate, and overall tax revenues rise from the initial value of $t = 14.194$ to $t = 15.255$.

The question still remaining, however, is whether the situation is expansionary or contractionary. Assuming full employment income (the natural level of income) is $y_n = 42$, then the full employment budget surplus changes from,

$$bs_n = -14.4 \quad \text{for } t_1 = 0.3 \tag{A6.1.5}$$

to

$$bs_n = -13 \quad \text{for } t_1 = 1/3 \tag{A6.1.6}$$

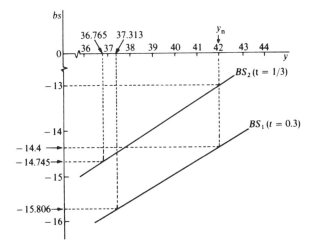

Figure A6.1.1 Budget surplus and a rise in the marginal rate of tax.

In both situations the government stance is expansionary. However, it is less expansionary at the higher tax rate.

APPENDIX 6.2 BALANCED BUDGET MULTIPLIERS

The balanced budget multiplier refers to the change in income arising from a change in government spending matched by an equal change in taxes. Thus, if dy denotes the change in income, dgo the change in government spending and dt the change in taxes, such that $dgo = dt$, then

$$dy = K_b dgo \text{ given } dgo = dt \tag{A6.2.1}$$

where K_b is the balanced budget multiplier.

The total change in income arises from two sources: (1) the change in government spending, and (2) the change in taxes. We can express this in the form

$$dy = (\partial y/\partial go)dgo + (\partial y/\partial t)dt \tag{A6.2.2}$$

But $dgo = dt$, hence,

$$dy = [(\partial y/\partial go) + (\partial y/\partial t)]dgo \tag{A6.2.3}$$

Results (A6.2.1)–(A6.2.3) apply in all the cases we are about to consider.

Case 1

There is only autonomous taxes, hence $t = t_0$ ($t_1 = 0$). Thus, $t = t_0$ and $dt = dt_0$. From equation (6.10) we have

$$\frac{\partial y}{\partial go} = \frac{1}{1 - b + m} \qquad \text{since } t_1 = 0 \tag{A6.2.4}$$

$$\frac{\partial y}{\partial t_0} = \frac{-b}{1 - b + m} \qquad \text{since } t_1 = 0 \tag{A6.2.5}$$

Hence, substituting results (A6.2.4) and (A6.2.5) into (A6.2.3) we have

$$dy = \left[\frac{1}{1-b+m}\right] - \left[\frac{b}{1-b+m}\right]dgo$$

$$= \left[\frac{1-b}{1-b+m}\right]dgo$$

The balanced budget multiplier in Case 1 is, therefore,

$$K_b = (1-b)/(1-b+m) \qquad\qquad\qquad (A6.2.6)$$

Note that $K_b = 1$ only when $t_1 = 0$ *and* $m = 0$.

Case 2

In this situation we have $t = t_0 + t_1 y$.

Case 2(a) A short-run change in taxes

In this instance we consider the change in taxes arising solely from a change in the autonomous component, t_0. Hence, $dgo = dt = dt_0$. From equation (6.10) we have

$$\frac{\partial y}{\partial go} = \frac{1}{1 - b(1 - t_1) + m} \qquad\qquad (A6.2.7)$$

$$\frac{\partial y}{\partial t} = \frac{-b}{1 - b(1 - t_1) + m} \qquad\qquad (A6.2.8)$$

Hence, substituting results (A6.2.7) and (A6.2.8) into (A6.2.3) we obtain

$$dy = \frac{1}{1 - b(1 - t_1) + m} - \left[\frac{b}{1 - b(1 - t_1) + m}\right]dgo$$

$$= \left[\frac{1-b}{1 - b(1 - t_1) + m}\right]dgo$$

The balanced budget multiplier in Case 2(a) is, therefore,

$$K_b = (1-b)/[1 - b(1 - t_1) + m] \qquad\qquad (A6.2.9)$$

Which is not equal to unity even if $m = 0$.

Case 2(b) Long-run change in taxes

But why have we referred to Case 2(a) as short run? The reason is that any change in government spending and autonomous taxes will lead to a change in income. This change in income will induce a further change in tax receipts, through the term $t_1 y$. It is no longer the case, therefore, that taxes equal government spending when we take account of such induced changes. To take account of such induced changes we must note that

$$dt = dt_0 + t_1 dy \qquad\qquad\qquad (A6.2.10)$$

where we are assuming there is no change in the marginal rate of tax, t_1. We still require $dt = dgo$, so we can express the autonomous change in the form,

$$dt_0 = dt - t_1 dy = dgo - t_1 dy \qquad\qquad (A6.2.11)$$

Substituting (A6.2.11) into equation (A6.2.3) we have

$$dy = (\partial y/\partial go)dgo + (\partial y/\partial t)(dgo - t_1 dy)$$

$$= [(\partial y/\partial go) + (\partial y/\partial t)]dgo - t_1(\partial y/\partial t)dy$$

Substituting equations (A6.2.7) and (A6.2.8) into this result, we have

$$dy = \frac{1}{1 - b(1 - t_1) + m} - \left[\frac{b}{1 - b(1 - t_1) + m} \right] dgo + \frac{bt_1 dy}{1 - b(1 - t_1) + m}$$

i.e.,

$$[1 - b(1 - t_1) + m] dy - bt_1 dy = (1 - b) dgo$$

$$[1 - b + bt_1 + m - bt_1] dy = (1 - b) dgo$$

$$dy = [(1 - b)/(1 - b + m)] dgo$$

In other words, the long-run multiplier is, once again,

$$K_b = (1 - b)/(1 - b + m) \qquad (A6.2.12)$$

which is independent of the marginal tax rate t_1, but is only unity if the marginal propensity to import is zero, i.e. if $m = 0$.

Cases 1 and 2 can be verified using the model developed in Appendix 2.4. Since we are dealing with constant interest rate throughout, we can set $h = 0$, which makes the goods market independent of the money market. For Case 1 we make the further assumption that $t_1 = 0$. Solving we obtain an equilibrium value for income of $y = 112.222$. Taking each change in turn we have,

new level of y resulting from go rising by $10 = 134.444$

new level of y resulting from t_0 rising by $10 = 95.556$

Hence, the changes in income are

$$134.444 - 112.222 = \quad 22.222$$

$$95.556 - 112.222 = -16.667$$

$$\text{Total} \qquad 5.555$$

Using result (A2.6) we have

$$K_b = (1 - b)/(1 - b + m) = (1 - 0.75)/(1 - 0.75 + 0.2)$$

$$= 0.25/0.45 = 0.5555$$

Hence,

$$dy = K_b dgo = (0.5555)(10) = 5.555$$

For Case 2 we set $t_1 = 0.3$ and $h = 0$. Solving for income, we obtain $y = 74.815$.

Case 2(a)

Taking each change in turn,

new level of y resulting from go rising by $10 = 89.630$

new level of y resulting from t_0 rising by $10 = 63.704$

Hence, the changes in income are

$$89.630 - 74.815 = \cdot\ 14.815$$

$$63.704 - 74.815 = -11.111$$

$$\text{Total} \qquad 3.704$$

Using result (A6.2.9) we have

$$K_b = (1 - b)/[1 - b(1 - t_1) + m]$$

$$= (1 - 0.75)/[1 - 0.75(1 - 0.3) + 0.2] = 0.25/0.675$$

$$= 0.37037$$

Hence,

$$dy = K_b dgo = (0.37037)(10) = 3.704$$

Case 2(b)

With $h = 0$ and $t_1 = 0.3$, equilibrium income, as before, is $y = 74.815$. At this level of income, tax receipts are $t = 25.444$. Hence, setting the new tax receipts at $t = 35.444$ and $go = 40$, a rise of 10, it is possible to establish that the income level which generates this new level of taxes is $y = 80.370$ (which can be verified by noting $t_0 = 11.333$). Hence, the change in income, in the 'long run', is

$$dy = 80.370 - 74.815 = 5.555$$

Using result (A6.2.12) we have,

$$K_b = (1-b)/(1-b+m) = 0.5555$$

Hence,

$$dy = K_b dgo = 5.555$$

Consequently, the 'long-run' result is independent of the marginal rate of tax.

APPENDIX 6.3 BALANCED BUDGET IN IS–LM FRAMEWORK

In Appendix 6.2 we discussed the balanced budget multiplier, but only for the goods market. In other words, the interest rate was assumed constant and investment was thus exogenous. This, however, is not generally the case. Any autonomous change in the goods market will shift the IS curve, which in turn will alter the rate of interest. The change in the rate of interest will alter the level of investment, which will then have repercussions for the overall change in income and interest rate.

In what follows we will utilize the results we developed in Appendix 6.2. We begin with the general result (A6.2.3) of Appendix 6.2, which indicated that for a change in government spending, dgo, equal to a change in taxes, dt, we have

$$dy = [(\partial y/\partial go) + (\partial y/\partial t)]dgo \qquad (A6.3.1)$$

We further showed in Appendix 2.1 (equation A2.1.7) that the equilibrium level of income (where *IS* intersects *LM*) is given by

$$y = \frac{[z_0 + h\hat{P}^e - (f+g)R] + (h/u)(M_0/P)}{1 - b(1-t_1) + m + (kh/u)} \qquad (A6.3.2)$$

Using result (A6.3.2) we can briefly reproduce the balanced budget multipliers.

Case 1

$t = t_0$ ($t_1 = 0$), thus $dt = dt_0$. From result (A6.3.2), and remembering that

$$z_0 = a - bt_0 + i_0 + go + x_0 - im_0 \qquad (A6.3.3)$$

we have

$$\frac{\partial y}{\partial go} = \frac{1}{1 - b + m + (kh/u)} \qquad \text{since} \quad t_1 = 0 \qquad (A6.3.4)$$

$$\frac{\partial y}{\partial t_0} = \frac{-b}{1 - b + m + (kh/u)} \qquad \text{since} \quad t_1 = 0 \qquad (A6.3.5)$$

Substituting equations (A6.3.4) and (A6.3.5) into equation (A6.3.1), we obtain

$$dy = \left[\frac{(1-b)}{1 - b + m + (kh/u)} \right] dgo \qquad (A6.3.6)$$

Consequently, in this instance the balanced budget multiplier is

$$K_b = (1 - b)/[1 - b + m + (kh/u)] \tag{A6.3.7}$$

which is different from unity. However, since (kh/u) is positive, then this balanced budget multiplier is *smaller* than that outlined in Appendix 6.2.

Case 2

Following the same lines of analysis as given in Appendix 6.2, and utilizing equation (A6.3.2) we have the results for the general case $t = t_0 + t_1 y$, of

$$K_b^S = (1 - b)/[1 - b(1 - t_1) + m + (hk/u)] \tag{A6.3.8}$$

for the short run; while the long-run balanced budget multiplier is,

$$K_b^L = (1 - b)/[1 - b + m + (kh/u)] \tag{A6.3.9}$$

Both results (A6.3.8) and (A6.3.9) are smaller than the equivalent results shown in Appendix 6.2, but are also different from unity.

APPENDIX 6.4 SIZE OF THE PUBLIC SECTOR

There has been a growing literature on the size of government spending in relation to its absolute level, its level relative to income, and the growth of both absolute and relative sizes. The early literature attempted to explain the growth in government spending over fairly long historical periods, see Peacock and Wiseman (1961), Gupta (1967), Veverka (1963), and White and Chapman (1987). Of particular attention was 'Wagner's Law', which stated that government spending tends to rise with economic activity. Certainly, a cursory look at Table A6.4.1, which gives figures for real general government spending, *go*, which is the total of government spending on goods and services, transfers, debt interest and net lending, along with real GDP at factor cost for the period 1964–87, indicates a rise in government spending relative to GDP from 40.7% to a peak of 54.4% in 1982 and falling thereafter. These figures can be compared with 1890 when it was 8.9%, 1920 when it was 26.2% and 1960 when it was 36.4% (see Burton, 1985).

These studies in turn gave rise to questions of measurement. How should the size of government spending be measured? The issue of measurement became most prominent in the UK in the 1970s when a variety of measures were used, not least by government publications, see Brown and Jackson (1986), Stibbard (1985), Imber (1983), Beeton (1986) and White and Chapman (1987).

Like many economic aggregates, there is no 'right' way to measure government size. This is because the government can be viewed from many angles, each with a particular measure attached to it. One view is no better than another.

Although there are many ways to measure government spending, official figures concentrate on general government expenditure and the public expenditure planning total. General government expenditure is by far the most common, and is certainly the favoured one when performing international comparisons. In addition, it became an important aggregate in the UK government's Medium-term Financial Strategy. But even before the Conservative government's MTFS, the 1970s had seen a shift of emphasis from controlling physical resources towards financial control of public sector corporations. The result of this was to *exclude* the capital expenditure of nearly all public corporations and replace it by government finance to them in the form of grants and loans, Stibbard (1985). Thus, the ratio for pre-1977 in Fig. A6.4.1 is greater than that for the series 'General government expenditure' which involves the post-1977 definition. In addition, a further distinction was made in 1977 with regard to the public expenditure planning total – the main difference with other aggregates was its treatment of debt interest. However, whatever measure is used, the historical pattern of government spending is more or less the same: it has been rising secularly. The three *relative*

Table A6.4.1 Total government expenditure as a percentage of GDP at factor cost 1964–87

Year	Real total general government expenditure go	Real GDP at factor cost y	go/y
	(£ million 1980 prices)		%
1964	56 627	139 071	40.7
1965	60 032	141 914	42.3
1966	62 649	144 749	43.3
1967	70 716	149 614	47.3
1968	74 121	154 081	48.1
1969	72 812	153 414	47.5
1970	75 498	159 011	47.5
1971	77 630	165 512	46.9
1972	81 342	172 397	47.2
1973	93 898	200 791	46.8
1974	95 175	183 646	51.8
1975	100 734	187 556	53.7
1976	98 181	190 923	51.4
1977	89 658	187 283	47.9
1978	96 688	199 588	48.4
1979	100 831	202 182	49.9
1980	104 076	199 658	52.1
1981	104 557	194 573	53.7
1982	105 862	194 519	54.4
1983	108 976	203 702	53.5
1984	110 160	207 244	53.2
1985	111 353	214 960	51.8
1986	111 041	219 545	50.6
1987	109 969	227 381	48.4

Note: Figures after 1970 involve new presentation of government accounts
Source: *Economic Trends, Annual Supplement* 1986, 1988 and May 1988

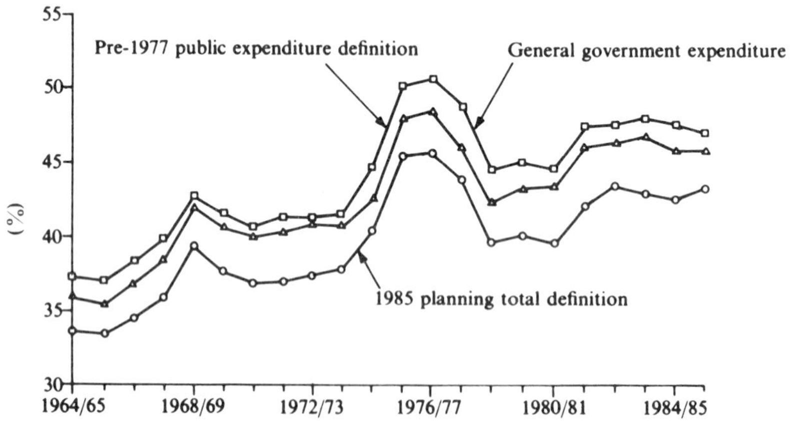

Figure A6.4.1 Three relative measures of UK government spending. *Source*: Stibbard (1985), Table C.

measures for the UK just referred to are illustrated in Fig. A6.4.1, and they show a similar pattern even if they differ in detail. Furthermore, a similar pattern is shown by all OECD countries. The rise in government expenditure illustrated in the diagram has, some argue, now reached such a high level that the tax burden it entails is too excessive, much of government spending is wasteful and in general the role of government should be considerably reduced.

Chapter 7

THE DEMAND AND SUPPLY OF MONEY

The model presented in Chapters 2 and 3 only briefly sketched the monetary sector. There was a simple demand for money schedule which related real money balances to the level of income and inversely to the rate of interest. The supply of real money balances was simply treated as exogenous. Equilibrium in the money market was established by equating the demand for real money balances with its supply – and, diagrammatically, is embodied in the LM curve. In this framework, monetary policy is often conceived of as simply a shift in the LM curve – monetary expansion leading to a rightward shift and monetary contraction as a leftward shift in the LM curve. If this was all there was to it, then why is there so much controversy surrounding monetary policy?

In trying to answer this question it is necessary to consider the determinants of the demand and supply of money in more detail. The demand for money has been quite thoroughly investigated, see for example Laidler (3rd edn, 1985) and Cuthbertson (1985). But it must be constantly kept in mind that,

> We study the demand for any item mainly so that we may make predictions about the
> consequences of changes in its supply. (Laidler, 1985, p. 3)

Only recently has the supply of money been considered in any depth. One reason for this is that the demand for money can be considered primarily from a theoretical point of view. The supply of money, however, is very much a product of the institutional framework of the economy under investigation. By treating the money supply as exogenous, such institutional dependence is irrelevant. Once the money supply is considered as endogenous to the system (i.e. the money supply is dependent on variables determined by the system – such as the rate of interest or the level of real income), then it does matter what the institutional framework happens to be. Furthermore, the *effectiveness* of monetary policy cannot be assessed independently of the institutional environment. Finally, and most importantly, the effectiveness of monetary policy will be influenced by how open the economy happens to be. Again it is important to stress that consideration of the demand for money is not much influenced by the fact that an economy is open. On the other hand, the openness of the economy does influence the supply of money. In this chapter both these influences – the institutional environment and the openness of the economy – will be considered.

7.1 THE DEMAND FOR MONEY

Why do people demand money balances? In the first instance it is because they require money for everyday purchases: the purchase of newspapers, transport to work, lunch, etc. However, our concern is with the economy as a whole. Considering transactions in the economy, it is clear that the value of what is purchased must be equal to the value of what is sold. This is an identity which must always be true. Let M denote the total stock of notes and coins in the economy. Does this constitute the value of what is purchased, say over a year? Clearly not. First, money is a *stock* and the value of what is purchased over a year is a flow. Second, a particular note or coin can be used in a number of different transactions as it circulates round the economy. If we let V denote the average velocity of circulation of money – that is to say, the average number of times money circulates over a period of time – then the total value of money required for purchases over a period of time is MV. (Notice that MV is a flow and denotes the value of purchases over a specified period of time, say a year.)

Now consider the other side of the coin, namely the value of goods and services sold. If T denotes the transactions in goods and services over a specified period of time and P the average price level, then (in the aggregate) PT represents the value of goods and services produced. Since the value of what is purchased must equal the value of what is sold over a specified period of time, it follows that

$$MV = PT \qquad (7.1)$$

If T is considered in terms of real income, y, and the velocity of circulation, V, as the *income* velocity of circulation, then identity (7.1) can take the form $MV = Py$. If, further, we let $k = 1/V$ and assume k is constant, the transactions demand for money, denoted M_T, can then be expressed in the Cambridge form,

$$M_T = kPy \qquad (7.2)$$

Alternatively, the transactions demand for *real* money balances is,

$$M_T/P = ky \qquad (7.3)$$

The reasoning behind equation (7.2) is straightforward. If money income generated over a year is given by $Py = Y$, then individuals will require a fixed proportion of this to purchase the goods and services produced. So long as the average income velocity of circulation remains constant, there will be sufficient transactions balances for the purchase of the goods and services produced over that year. Notice also that a *lower* income velocity of circulation of money means a higher transactions demand for money (since k is higher for a lower value of V). Whether V is, in fact, a constant remains to be seen (and we take up this point in Appendix 7.1). For the moment it should be noted that V (and hence k) will depend very much on the institutional framework of pay, e.g. whether the majority of the working population are paid weekly or monthly and whether they are paid in cash or through a bank balance.

So far it would appear that real transactions balances depend only on real income. Such a view, however, presupposes that all pay is in the form of cash and that individuals do not hold part of that cash in the form of interest bearing accounts – such as a deposit account. In a society where workers are paid weekly this would be a reasonable approximation. (In fact, in a number of developing countries the only demand for money is for transactions purposes and the relationship between the demand for money and income is fairly close.) However, in a more modern capitalist society where individuals are paid weekly and monthly, and where the majority are paid by means of bank transfers, equation (7.2) is not the most suitable specification of the transactions demand for money.

Suppose an individual is paid monthly by a bank transfer – in real terms equal to z. For ease of exposition, assume that this transfer goes into the individual's deposit account which earns an interest of $r\%$ per month. If the individual withdraws (is total income over the month in regular intervals, he will withdraw z/n each time he carries out one of the n withdrawals. If spending is assumed to take place evenly over the period during which the individual is holding cash, then the average cash holdings is $(z/n)/2 = z/2n$. The interest forgone by holding such cash must be $rz/2n$. There is, however, another cost. Each withdrawal involves a transactions cost with the bank. If c denotes the transactions cost, then the individual will incur nc costs over the month. Hence, the total cost incurred by the individual is

$$TC = nc + (rz/2n) \qquad (7.4)$$

What is the optimal number of withdrawals for this individual, which we shall denote n^*? This can be obtained by minimizing expression (7.4) with respect to n. The result is[1]

$$n^* = [rz/2c]^{1/2} \qquad (7.5)$$

Since the average demand for transactions balances is given by $z/2n$, if equation (7.5) is substituted into this we obtain the optimal transactions balances (T^*) of

$$T^* = [cz/2r]^{1/2} \qquad (7.6)$$

The conclusion drawn from this analysis is that for individuals, their optimal transactions demand for money, T^*, is positively related to their real income and inversely related to the rate of interest (on bonds).[2] In addition, the greater the transactions cost the greater the transactions demand for money. In the aggregate the same basic dependence should also be the case; namely, transactions demand for real money balances is positively related to real income and inversely related to the interest rate.

So far the only motive we have discussed for holding money is for transactions purposes. Keynes, in particular, put forward three motives for holding money: (1) for transactions purposes, (2) for precautionary purposes, and (3) for speculative purposes. Our discussion so far indicates that the demand for real transactions balances is largely dependent on real income, and that there may be some sensitivity to interest rates. However, what about the remaining two motives?

People will tend to take more money out of their accounts than they actually need for *known* transactions in case some unexpected purchase is necessary. The precautionary demand for money arises because of an uncertain future. The amount withdrawn for precautionary reasons must be weighed against the loss in interest that such a withdrawal will involve. The optimal withdrawal for precautionary purposes by an individual is where the marginal benefit from the increased liquidity is equal to the marginal cost of the withdrawal. Since the marginal cost of the withdrawal involves the rate of interest, it is clear that the optimal amount of precautionary balances will be related to the rate of interest. Furthermore, the higher the rate of interest the higher the marginal cost of the withdrawal

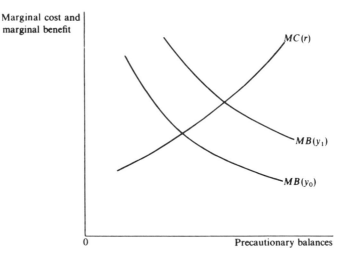

Figure 7.1 Optimal holdings of precautionary balances.

and hence the lower the precautionary demand for money. In addition, the marginal benefit from increased liquidity is for a *given* level of real income. The higher the level of real income the higher the level of money balances that can be held for the same marginal benefit (i.e., the marginal benefit schedule is further to the right for a higher level of real income, as shown in Fig. 7.1). Hence, the optimal holding of precautionary balances will be higher the higher the level of income.[3]

In the discussion so far it has not been clear whether money is substitutable with other assets. This is an important point because it leads to different formulations of the demand for money. It is common to find monetarist models which are based on the assumption that money is not highly substitutable with other assets. Some Keynesians (or neo-Keynesians), on the other hand, do assume a degree of substitutability between money and other assets. Once we move away from thinking about money in isolation and consider it merely as one asset in a spectrum of assets, then theory begins to define the demand for money in terms of the outcome of a *portfolio choice*. A typical portfolio choice model is that of Tobin (1958).

In Tobin's model there is zero inflation, and a consumer is assumed to hold his wealth in terms of either money, M, or bonds, B, or some combination of the two. Bonds have an interest payment of r, while money has a zero interest (i.e., money is a risk free asset with a zero return). A bond in perpetuity has a price P_b equal to the yield, A, divided by the rate of interest, i.e. $P_b = A/r$. Let P_b denote the *purchase* price and let P_b^e denote the *expected selling* price. In fact, the expected selling price is dependent on the expected interest rate, i.e. $P_b^e = A/r^e$. Accordingly, the expected capital gain or loss, G, is given by

$$G = \frac{P^e - P_b}{P_b} = \frac{r}{r^e} - 1 \tag{7.7}$$

The total earnings on a bond, denoted E, will be the interest rate at the time of purchase plus the capital gain (or less the capital loss), i.e

$$E = r + G$$

Tobin assumes that the capital gain, being dependent on some expected interest rate, is a random variable which is normally distributed with mean, μ and standard deviation s. In

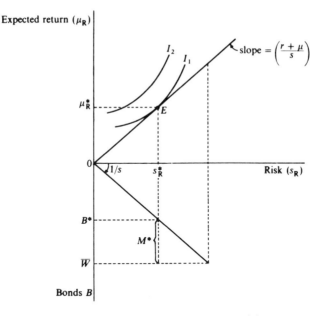

Figure 7.2 Tobin's liquidity preference model.

this model, s is used as a measure of risk.[4] Since G is normally distributed then so is E (since E is a linear function of G). The mean and standard deviation of E are

$$E(E) = r + E(G) = r + \mu$$

$$\mathrm{Var}(E) = \mathrm{Var}(G) \qquad \text{hence } SD(E) = s$$

where $E(.)$ denotes the expected value, $\mathrm{Var}(.)$ the variance and $SD(.)$ the standard deviation.

Now suppose B denotes the amount of money spent on bonds then the total return, denoted R, is given by

$$R = BE$$

But since E is a random variable then so is R, and because E is normally distributed then so is R. The mean and standard deviation of the distribution of R are:

$$E(R) = \mu_R = BE(E) = B(r + \mu)$$

$$\mathrm{Var}(R) = s_R^2 = B^2 \mathrm{Var}(E) = B^2 s^2$$

$$s_R = Bs$$

From this final result we have

$$B = (1/s)s_R \tag{7.8}$$

and from the $E(R)$ we have

$$\mu_R = B(r + \mu) = [(r + \mu)/s]s_R \tag{7.9}$$

Equation (7.9) gives the trade-off between the expected return, μ_R, and the risk, s_R, and is drawn in the upper section of Fig. 7.2.

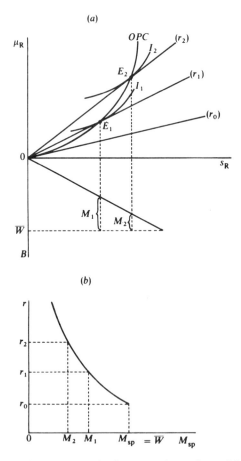

Figure 7.3 The derivation of Tobin's speculative demand for money.

Equation (7.8) is drawn in the lower section of Fig. 7.2. For a given risk of capital gain, s given, if all wealth is invested in bonds, then $B = \bar{W}$ and this sets the vertical line on the right of Fig. 7.2. Given both μ and s, along with the interest rate r, we see from equation (7.9) that the slope of the line in the upper section of the diagram is $[(r + \mu)/s]$.

Also shown in Fig. 7.2 is the individual's preference structure. The individual is assumed to have a utility function based on the return he gets from bond purchases, i.e. $U = U(R)$. Now if $U(R)$ is quadratic and, as we have so far assumed, R is normally distributed, then it can be shown that $E(U)$ depends upon the expected return μ_R and the risk s_R. Whether the individual is risk-averse, risk-neutral or a risk-taker depends on the shape of his utility function.[5] As drawn in Fig. 7.2, the individual is assumed to be risk-averse.

The individual will maximize his expected utility, which means that he will move to the highest possible indifference curve in Fig. 7.2, subject to the budget constraint. Thus the individual will hold B^* of his wealth in the form of bonds. Since there are only two assets, this also means that he will hold $M^* = \bar{W} - B^*$ of his wealth in the form of money. With this particular portfolio he expects a return of μ_R^* with a risk of s_R^*.

We can now derive the speculative demand for money balances more precisely. This is shown in Fig. 7.3. At interest rate, r_1, equilibrium is at point E_1. At the higher interest rate,

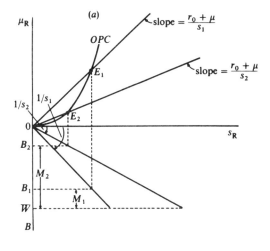

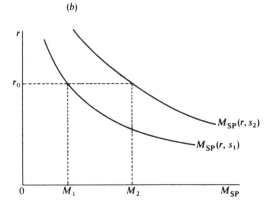

Figure 7.4 A change in the speculative demand for money.

r_2, equilibrium is E_2. Given the preference structure and the constraint for this individual, the demand for money falls from M_1 to M_2. If we assume the interest rate is parametric, i.e. can vary continuously, then the optimum portfolio curve (OPC) can be derived, as shown in Fig. 7.3. From this can be constructed the speculative demand for money schedule. As can be observed from the diagram, this curve is downward sloping, i.e. there is an inverse relationship between the demand for speculative money balances and the rate of interest.

This analysis is quite useful in illustrating the impact of a change in the risk. Suppose the government is pursuing some policy which investors see as a rise in the level of risk; in other words, a rise in s for any given return r_0. The result of this is shown in Fig. 7.4(a, b). The line in Fig. 7.4(b) pivots from that with a slope of $1/s_1$ to that with a slope of $1/s_2$. Since wealth remains constant at $\bar{W}$ and given the OPC curve, equilibrium moves from point E_1 to E_2 and the demand curve for speculative money balances moves to the right (since the interest rate remains constant at r_0). This should not be surprising. If investment in bonds becomes more risky, then at any particular interest rate individuals are more prepared to hold part of their wealth in the form of money.

It should be apparent from the foregoing discussion that all three motives for demanding money effectively lead to the same conclusion: the demand for real money balances is positively related to real income and inversely related to the rate of interest. The fact that individuals have all three motives and that there is no objective way of separating these individual components in practice, means simply that we can say that the total demand for real money balances is positively related to real income and inversely related to the rate of interest. This is captured in the equation we utilized in Chapter 2, namely

$$M_d/P = ky - ur \qquad k > 0, \quad u > 0$$

We can go one stage further, however. As the discussion of the speculative demand for money revealed, the level of wealth possessed by the individual matters. In other words, the speculative demand for real money balances is for a *given* level of real wealth, Wl/P. A rise in real wealth leads to a rise in the demand for speculative balances and hence a rise in the demand for real money balances. As we will see later, this particular relationship between the demand for real money balances and the level of wealth has become a central aspect of the crowding out debate. It is, therefore, worth bringing out the wealth effect explicitly as follows:

$$M_d/P = ky - ur + n(Wl/P) \qquad\qquad k > 0, \quad u > 0, \quad n > 0 \qquad\qquad (7.10)$$

Notice that for a rise in real wealth there is a rise in the demand for real money balances. With a constant supply of real money balances this means a shift to the left in the LM curve.

The demand for real money balances embodied in equation (7.10) is a much more simplified version than that proposed by Milton Friedman in his book *The Quantity Theory of Money – A Restatement* (Friedman, 1956). Here Friedman not only divides the interest rate into three parts (interest paid on money, interest paid on bonds and the interest paid on equities) but includes a term denoting the fraction of human to non-human wealth. What matters for our present discussion is that both Friedman and Tobin recognize that real wealth can influence the demand for real money balances. Where the difference lies is in terms of what can be substituted for money. In Tobin's analysis it is bonds, while in Friedman's analysis it can be between money and commodities as well as money and bonds.

Before leaving the demand for money, one further elaboration is worth mentioning. Earlier, when discussing the transactions demand for money, we considered the quantity theory of money. In particular, we considered the income velocity of circulation of money, defined as

$$\mathbf{V} = Py/M_s \qquad\qquad (7.11)$$

(Notice that we have assumed that the demand for money is equal to the supply of money.) In the Cambridge form we have $k = 1/\mathbf{V}$. But suppose the income velocity of circulation of money is not a constant but rises with the rate of inflation. In other words, the greater the rate of inflation the more people spend money and convert it into consumer goods and real assets. As in earlier chapters, let $\hat{P}$ denote the rate of inflation. Then we are now assuming

$$\mathbf{V} = \mathbf{V}(\hat{P}) \qquad \mathbf{V}' > 0$$

Alternatively,

$$k = k(\hat{P}) \qquad k' < 0$$

Hence, the demand for real money balances becomes

$$M_d/P = k(\hat{P})y - ur + n(Wl/P) \qquad\qquad (7.12)$$

A rise in the rate of inflation lowers k and so reduces the demand for *real* money balances. This in turn leads to a shift in the LM curve to the right even in the $r - y$ space.

Is there any evidence of a variable velocity of circulation of money? This is considered briefly in Appendix 7.1.

7.2 DEMAND FOR MONEY: STABLE OR UNSTABLE?

So far we have considered a static demand curve for real money balances, summarized in equation (7.12). The usefulness of this equation, however, is dependent on the stability of the demand for money equation. It must be emphasized that a stable *relationship* does not mean constant values for variables. What it does mean is that for given values for the independent variables the value of the dependent variable can be predicted with a reasonable degree of accuracy. However, if the relationship is unstable, it will not be possible to predict the dependent variable with any accuracy, given values of the independent variables. Let us, therefore, specify the demand for money equation in a stochastic form:

$$M_d/P = ky - ur + v \qquad (7.13)$$

where v is a random variable. Notice in particular that the instability of equation (7.13) may, to some extent, have already been accounted for. First, equation (7.13) does not take into account real wealth, Wl/P, and so the equation may involve an omitted variable. Second, equation (7.13) assumes a constant k. But we have already argued that k is inversely related to the rate of inflation, $\hat{P}$. In so far as inflation rose in the 1970s, this too is a misspecification. Of course, we could consider

$$M_d/P = k(\hat{P})y - ur + n(Wl/P) + v' \qquad (7.14)$$

where, again, v' is a random variable. However, there would be difficulty in estimating such an equation because of the high correlation between inflation and the rate of interest.

The problem of instability can be seen in terms of Fig. 7.5. Here two alternative assumptions are made. In Fig. 7.5(a) the money supply is assumed to be exogenous. Given this assumption, and given an unstable demand for money equation, then interest rates will vary between r_1 and r_2. In Fig. 7.5(b) we assume the government is pegging the interest rate at $\bar{r}$. Given an unstable demand for money, then the money supply must vary between M_1 and M_2 if $\bar{r}$ is to be maintained. It is of major concern to the authorities, therefore, whether or not the demand for money is unstable. In Appendix 7.2 we consider some of the evidence.

7.3 THE SUPPLY OF MONEY

In the model outlined in Chapters 2 and 3 the money supply was treated as exogenous. This is far too simplistic and does not allow a proper understanding of the problems faced by governments in pursuing monetary policy. Furthermore, by treating the money supply as exogenous, monetary policy is totally independent of the institutional framework within which it is conducted.

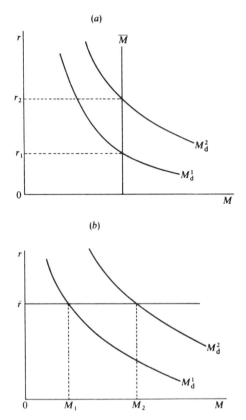

Figure 7.5 A problem of money demand instability.

It is well known that banks can create money. It is also the case that the only 'producer' of money is the government. But we must be careful in our choice of words. Governments supply money in the form of notes and coins, labelled $M0$, and sometimes called high-powered money. Banks cannot print any notes of their own (here we ignore the Scottish banks) or mint any of their own coins. What they can create, however, is additional bank deposits. To the individual who owns these bank deposits they are, effectively, money. It is common, therefore, to consider the money supply as comprising currency held by the public plus deposits with the banks, labelled $M1$. As soon as this is done the question arises as to whether all deposits are included – current account and deposit account (time) deposits. The reasons for including time deposits is because they can be readily transferred into current account deposits and used for immediate transactions (although banks can request up to 14 days' notice). The difficulty of definition becomes even more of a problem when non-bank financial intermediaries, such as building societies and finance houses, are also considered. Building societies now offer chequing facilities, and to all intents and purposes are like banks. The major difference is that the bulk of building society funds are for house loans. The creation of deposits will, therefore, depend on the size of the non-bank financial sector and the leakage to it from the banks. Fig. 7.6 supplies the various definitions of 'money supply' used in the UK, showing how they are related to one another.

Before discussing some of the theoretical issues it is important to realize that the financial system is a complex interlinking of financial institutions. It can be thought of as a pyramid, at the top of which is the Central Bank, the Bank of England, and below this are the main commercial banks – the 'big four': Lloyds, Barclays, National Westminster and the Midland. These banks operate a branch banking system throughout the UK. Below these are a variety of non-bank financial intermediaries (NBFIs), such as building societies, finance houses, friendly societies, etc.

Financial institutions, of which commercial banks are a significant part, play a major role in channelling savings to borrowers. During any period of time the economy will be composed of *potentially* deficit and surplus units. Such units can take on deficits and surpluses because of the presence of financial institutions. These institutions issue their own liabilities to savers and use the funds they receive to lend to borrowers. Hence, financial intermediaries increase the range of financial instruments which can be used by savers and borrowers; they offer tailor-made liabilities to fit savers' preferences; and, finally, they lend funds on differing terms in order to meet the needs of particular types of borrowers (Bain, 1970). Different financial institutions usually specialize in one form of liability to their customers – commercial banks offering current and deposit accounts; insurance companies offering insurance facilities; and, building societies offering mortgages. In recent times, however, the degree of diversification of their portfolios has been increasing. But what matters is that their *major* business will impose a certain constraint on the form that their portfolio can take.

Because of the expansion of non-bank financial institutions and the greater diversification of the portfolios of banks and non-banks, control of the broader definitions of money outlined in Fig. 7.6 is made more difficult.

It is possible to capture many of the institutional features just discussed, and also to lay down a framework within which to discuss a number of the debates surrounding monetary policy, by first considering the *money multiplier*. In simple terms this is the relationship between the narrowest definition of money, the money base $M0$ (or high-powered money), and a broader definition of money – $M1$, $M2$, etc. For the moment let us simply talk of the 'money supply' and label it M_s. Then the relationship we are considering is simply

$$M_s = qM0 \tag{7.15}$$

where q is the money multiplier.

The money base, $M0$, the narrowest definition of money, is composed of notes and coins. Such notes and coins can be held by the public, denoted C_p, the banks, denoted C_b, and the commercial banks' deposits at the Bank of England, denoted M_b. The total money supply depends on which definition we choose to consider. Let this be $M1$. Then $M1$ is composed of notes and coins held by the public and sight bank deposits, denoted D. Thus,

$$M0 = C_p + C_b + M_b \tag{7.16}$$

$$M1 = C_p + D \tag{7.17}$$

We now introduce some *institutional and behavioural assumptions* (which may of course be inaccurate!). First we assume commercial banks must hold a cash/deposit ratio of e, i.e.

$$C_b = eD \tag{7.18}$$

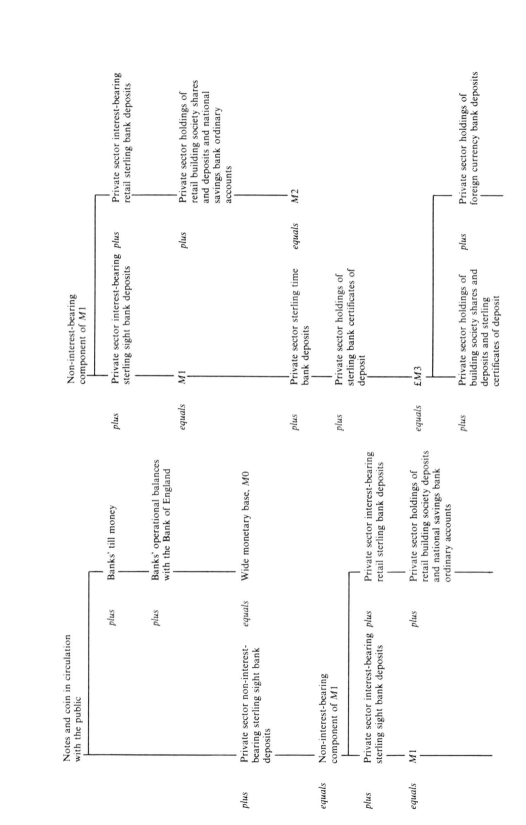

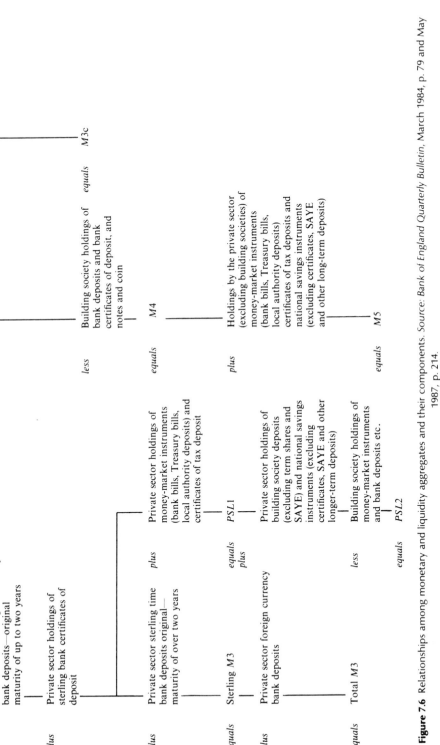

Figure 7.6 Relationships among monetary and liquidity aggregates and their components. *Source: Bank of England Quarterly Bulletin, March 1984, p. 79 and May 1987, p. 214.*

Second, the public hold a fraction of their deposits in the form of cash, i.e.

$$C_p = gD \tag{7.19}$$

Finally, we assume that the commercial banks hold a proportion of their deposits at the Bank of England. Let this be f, then

$$M_b = fD \tag{7.20}$$

Substituting equations (7.18), (7.19) and (7.20) into equations (7.16) and (7.17) and taking the ratio $M1/M0$, we have,

$$\frac{M1}{M0} = \frac{C_p + D}{C_p + C_b + M_b} = \frac{gD + D}{eD + gD + fD} = \frac{1 + g}{e + g + f}$$

Hence,

$$M1 = \left[\frac{1 + g}{e + g + f} \right] M0 \qquad \text{or } M1 = qM0 \tag{7.21}$$

Furthermore, it is possible to derive a relationship between deposits and the money base. Thus,

$$D = M1 - C_p$$

$$D = \left[\frac{1 + g}{e + g + f} \right] M0 - gD$$

$$(1 + g)D = \frac{(1 + g)\, M0}{(e + g + f)}$$

i.e.,

$$D = M0/(e + g + f) \tag{7.22}$$

Notice that if $g = f = 0$, then (7.22) reduces to $D = M0/e$, in other words, deposits can expand by a multiple of the reserve base. Equation (7.22), however, indicates that the multiple credit creation is less than this because of the leakages to the public who require to hold cash, and the leakage into the reserves that must be held at the Bank of England. Thus, if $g = 0.2$, $e = 0.05$ and $f = 0.01$, then the multiplier is $q = 4.6$ and the creation of deposits is 3.8.

Even result (7.21) is too simplistic and does not take account of a number of other important institutional considerations. It is possible to derive a similar result taking into account the fact that individuals hold both current and deposit accounts (see Dow and Earl, 1982, chapter 5). However, a more significant leakage is private sector funds deposited with non-bank financial intermediaries. This leakage is considered in Appendix 7.3, where we establish the following relationship between a broader definition of money, namely $M3$, and the money base, $M0$:

$$M3 = \left[\frac{1 + g + \mu\beta}{(e + f)(1 + \mu\beta) + (g + n\beta)} \right] M0 \tag{7.23}$$

where μ denotes the fraction of deposits which the NBFIs have with the commercial banks, β the fraction of deposits the private sector hold with the NBFIs rather than the commercial banks, and n the fraction of deposits held by the NBFIs as reserves.

The importance of equation (7.23) is that without a knowledge of the coefficients, it is impossible to know whether the money multiplier in equation (7.23) is greater or less than the money multiplier in (7.21). In other words, an expansion in the money base may raise the money supply in terms of $M1$ or $M2$ but may either not raise £$M3$ to the same extent or may raise it more than $M1$ or $M2$. The different impacts on the alternative money supplies arises because of the presence of non-bank financial intermediaries included in equation (7.23).

The money multiplier, in the form $M_s = qM0$, is usually considered as an interpretation of the money supply. The first thing to note about this formulation of the money supply is that it is independent of the rate of interest. The reason for this should not be hard to see. The formulation assumes that banks, non-banks and the public operate up to the full limit of their ratios. In other words, there is no limit on the availability of funds. Furthermore, the analysis presupposes that the ratios are constant. Neither of these assumptions is true. We will discuss the relationship between the money supply and the rate of interest in the next section. What is important about equation (7.21) or equation (7.23) is its stability, for only then can the government predict the effect on the money supply of a given change in the money base. The stability of the money supply thus depends on the stability of q, which in turn depends on the stability of the various coefficients. Hence,

$$\hat{M}_s = \hat{q} + \hat{M}0 \qquad\qquad (7.24)$$

$$= \hat{M}0 \qquad \text{if and only if} \qquad \hat{q} = 0$$

Although the reserve ratio, e, is set by the Bank of England, there is no compulsion for the commercial banks to hold reserves as low as indicated by such a ratio. There is evidence that banks are risk averse and hold slightly more than this. In this case e is no longer constant, and the legal reserve ratio is simply a *lower bound*. In addition, there is no reason for the public to have a fixed cash to deposit ratio. This will also mean that the relationship between the changes in the money base and changes in the broader money supply is not one-to-one, that $M1$, $M3$, etc., will vary independently of $M0$ because of variations in q. Some idea of the extent of variations in the money multiplier are provided in Table 7.1.

The major criticism, however, against either equation (7.21) or equation (7.23), as a formulation of the money supply, is that it treats the commercial banks as purely passive. The result of this is that the money supply is taken to be independent of the rate of interest. If banks, like other firms, are considered as profit-maximizing institutions, then it would be the case that the money supply is related to the rate of interest. To this we now turn.

7.4 MONEY SUPPLY AND THE RATE OF INTEREST

There is no reason why banks, and other non-bank financial intermediaries, cannot be considered as profit-maximizing institutions. Of course, in doing this there must be some licence in giving meaning to 'output'. In the case of the commercial banks it is convenient to think of 'output' as deposits, D. The resource costs incurred by a bank are positively related to the volume of deposits and additional costs arise in the form of interest payments on deposit accounts *relative to interest rates offered elsewhere*. Hence, total costs are positively related to the level of deposits and positively related to the interest rate on time deposits.

Table 7.1 Estimates of changes in UK money
multipliers, 1977–87

Year	$\hat{q}1$	$\hat{q}3$	$\hat{q}3c$	$\hat{q}4$	$\hat{q}5$
			(%)		
1977	6.8	−5.5	−5.8	−0.1	−2.3
1978	0.9	−0.2	−0.2	−0.4	0.1
1979	0.2	4.2	3.8	5.6	6.2
1980	−3.7	10.8	10.9	9.4	6.4
1981	12.5	19.6	22.5	15.1	8.2
1982	7.1	4.7	6.8	7.7	7.8
1983	5.4	5.3	7.5	7.5	7.2
1984	13.1	7.7	10.1	11.1	10.8
1985	13.3	8.6	5.8	8.1	7.8
1986	17.2	14	17.1	10.9	10.3
1987	17	16.9	14.5	10.6	9.9

Note: Each column is computed by taking the rate of growth of
the appropriate money stock and subtracting the rate of growth
of notes and coins (which constitutes about 90% of the 'wide
monetary base')

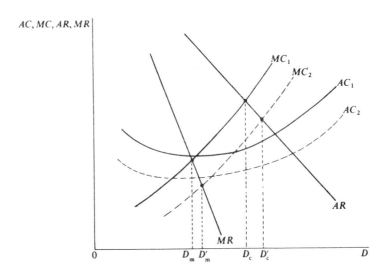

Figure 7.7 Commercial banks treated as firms.

From total costs it is possible to derive average and marginal costs. The relationship
between average costs and deposits and marginal costs and deposits is taken to be typical of
a firm. For the industry taken as a whole, average and marginal costs are assumed to be U-
shaped, as shown in Fig. 7.7. Since total costs are specified for a given interest rate on time
deposits, it is to be noted that both the average cost and marginal cost curves are drawn for
a particular rate of interest on time deposits. A rise in the interest payment on time deposits
leads to a rise in the average and marginal cost curves.

The revenue received by a bank arises from the bank charges on each current account
deposit (sometimes called sight deposits) and from the interest rate received on all loans.
A rise in the level of deposits, therefore, will lead to a rise in the level of revenue for a given
level of bank charges. If the ratio between sight deposits and time deposits remains fixed,

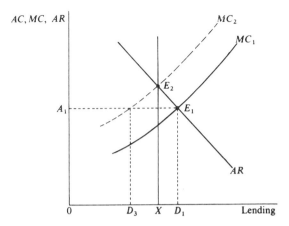

Figure 7.8 A constraint on bank lending.

and with a constant rate of interest on loans, it follows that the *firm*'s average revenue (equal to marginal revenue) remains constant. However, the *industry* demand curve for credit is downward sloping, as shown in Fig. 7.7. This is because, other things equal, the public will demand more credit from the banking system only if the banks make it more attractive to do so by lowering the interest payment on loans. If the industry is a competitive one, then the industry demand curve is equal to the marginal revenue curve, and the industry will maximize profits where marginal cost is equated with average revenue (equal, in this instance, to marginal revenue). If the industry is monopolistic or is colluding in any way, then there will be an average revenue and a marginal revenue curve – just as in a typical monopoly. Both situations are shown in Fig. 7.7, where D_c represents deposits under perfect competition and D_m deposits under monopoly.

Given MC_1 and the *competitive* industry demand curve for loans, the industry will expand deposits up to point D_c. On the other hand, if the industry is typified by monopoly, then for marginal costs, MC_1, the industry will expand deposits up to D_m, where marginal cost cuts marginal revenue. (Of course, it assumes that cost conditions would be the same for both situations.) Now what happens when interest rates rise? Here we must be careful which interest rate we are referring to. In the macrocontext we are usually referring to government policy, so it is convenient to think of the rate of interest as that on Treasury bills. Suppose, therefore, that the interest rate on Treasury bills rises. This will reduce the relative interest rate on time deposits, which will reduce total costs (since costs are positively related to the relative interest rate.) This results in a fall in the average and marginal cost curves (shown by AC_2 and MC_2 in Fig. 7.7), which leads to a *rise* in the level of deposits (whether under perfect competition or under monopoly) and, more significantly, to a rise in the money supply. Consequently, there is a positive relationship between the money supply and 'the' rate of interest.

Both results, however, presuppose that the commercial banks are not constrained in any way. Consider next a situation where the commercial banks are in perfect competition ($AR = MR$), as shown in Fig. 7.8. We begin with an equilibrium position given by point E_1, where costs are A_1 and deposits are D_1. Suppose now that the Central Bank sells securities, so reducing the money supply by reducing the monetary base $M0$. This in turn will lead to less bank deposits, say $0X$. At the initial interest rate, implied by the cost A_1, there is an excess demand for credit of XD_1. This will result in the banks competing among themselves for the limited reserves and deposits. In order to attract such loans the banks will raise the interest payment on time deposits. The result will be a rise in the marginal cost curve. The cost curve will continue to rise until MC_2, where it intersects the downward sloping demand curve at the level of deposits of $0X$. It is possible, in the short run, for banks to leave their interest rates unaffected – implied by A_1. If costs do rise by those implied in MC_2, then loans will fall below $0X$, to D_3.

It is clear from Fig. 7.8 that the degree to which interest rates rise will depend on the interest elasticity of the demand for deposits by the public. Furthermore, if the Central Bank does not wish interest rates to rise, then it must raise the level of base money.

The analysis of banks as profit-maximizing institutions has led to the suggestion that money base is not an exogenous variable, but, rather, that the level of bank lending is exogenous, Coghlan (1978). Using the definitions in the previous section we have:

$$D = L + C_b + M_b \tag{7.25}$$

$$M = D + C_p$$

$$C_p = gD$$

where L is the volume of bank lending. But

$$C_b + M_b = (e + f)D$$

$$M = D + gD = (1 + g)D$$

Hence, (7.25) can be written,

$$D = L + (e + f)D$$

or

$$D = L/[1 - (e + g)]$$

Hence,

$$M = \left[\frac{(1 + g)}{1 - (e + f)} \right] L \tag{7.26}$$

This means that if banks can secure reserves, then the money supply becomes a function of such bank loans as the banks find it profitable to meet. What equation (7.26) means is that if, from an initial profit-maximizing equilibrium condition with no excess reserves, the demand for bank loans rises, then the banks will bid for the deposits and reserves to meet such demand. In the process interest rates on bank deposits will rise. This in turn would lead to an increased differential between interest rates on bank deposits and those on, say, government securities. What the outcome will be depends on the interest sensitivity of the demand for bank deposits and the response of the authorities to the rise in interest rates on bank deposits relative to those on government securities. In this case the money base becomes endogenous and determined by the banks' portfolio decisions.

7.5 MONEY SUPPLY IN AN OPEN ECONOMY

So far we have dealt with the money supply in what is essentially a closed economy. As we will see when considering monetary policy in Chapter 10, the UK Conservative government have had great difficulty in controlling the money supply in the UK. One reason for this is the fact that the money supply is influenced by what happens to international trade – in particular, what is happening to the level of reserves. In Chapter 5 we demonstrated that the balance of payments on current and capital account is equal to official financing and that this in turn is the same as the change in the level of overseas reserves. Suppose the country is running a balance of payments surplus on current and capital account. This means that receipts exceed payments and there is a rise in the level of the country's reserves. But such reserves are a part of the money base (high-powered money). A rise in the level of reserves is thus a rise in the level of high-powered money. Conversely, a deficit on current and capital account on the balance of payments leads to a fall in the country's reserves and a concomitant fall in the level of the money base. Of course, the government may not like the resultant change in the money base and may offset such changes. For instance, a surplus may be offset by reducing other categories of high-powered money. Similarly, a deficit may be offset by raising the level of high-powered money from other sources. This process of altering the level of the money base to offset changes in the country's foreign exchange reserves is called *sterilization* (see also Appendix 5.2).

It is important, therefore, to break down *a change in* the money base into its component parts. This can be done in a variety of ways, see Llewellyn (1982). One useful categorization is to consider the change in the money base in terms of the following four components:

1. A change in the money base induced by the government borrowing requirement – in other words, a rise in the money base required to pay for some part (or all) of the excess of government spending over taxes. In real terms this is denoted $d(H_D/P)$.
2. A change in the level of reserves arising from balance of payments transactions, and in real terms denoted drs.
3. A change in the level of money base arising from government action to sterilize the effects of the reserve changes. If μ denotes the proportion of reserves offset, then the change in the money base for sterilization purposes is μdrs.
4. A change in the Central Bank loans to the banks, and in real terms is denoted dl_b.

Hence, the change in the money base, $d(M0/P)$ is equal to:

$$d(M0/P) = d(H_D/P) + drs - \mu drs + dl_b \qquad (7.27)$$

$$= d(H_D/P) + (1 - \mu)\, drs + dl_b \qquad (7.28)$$

We can, however, usefully elaborate this one stage further. The change in the money base required to pay for some of the excess of government spending over taxes arises from the budget deficit, which in real terms is $(go - t_1 y)$. Let a proportion β of this deficit be paid for by the government borrowing money from the Central Bank, then

$$d(H_D/P) = \beta(go - t_1 y) \qquad (7.29)$$

Substituting equation (7.29) into (7.28) gives

$$d(M0/P) = \beta(go - t_1 y) + (1 - \mu)\, drs + dl_b \qquad (7.30)$$

Since we already have a money supply equation of the form,

$$M_s/P = q(M_0/P) + jr$$

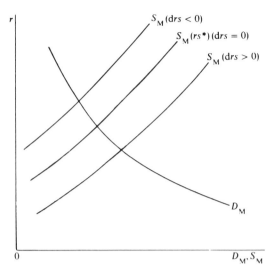

Figure 7.9 The money supply and a country's reserves.

then substituting equation (7.30) into this gives us an expression for the *change* in the supply of money, namely

$$d(M0/P) = q\beta(go - t_1 y) + q(1 - \mu)\,drs + qdl_b + jdr \qquad (7.31)$$

What is important to note about equation (7.31) is that the change in the money supply depends on the level of real income, a change in the foreign exchange reserves, a change in Central Bank loans to the commercial banks and a change in the interest rate which arises from Central Bank open market operations. To appreciate the open economy features of this result consider the demand and supply of money in Figure 7.9. Let $S_M(rs^*)$ denote the money supply with the level of exchange reserves at some desired amount rs^*, such that $drs = 0$. Suppose now that there is a deficit on the balance of payments so that drs is negative. This fall in the level of reserves leads to a fall in the money base (and even if partially offset) will lead to a fall in the money supply. Hence, the supply curve of money shifts to the left, to $S_M(drs < 0)$. Alternatively, a surplus on the balance of payments leads to a rise in the level of reserves and to a rightward shift in the supply curve of money, to $S_M(drs > 0)$.

What is the implication of this result for the LM curve? It means that the LM curve is drawn for a zero change in the level of foreign exchange reserves. A deficit on the balance of payments means an LM curve to the left, while a surplus on the balance of payments means an LM curve to the right. The result is that there is no longer a single aggregate demand curve, but, rather, a series of aggregate demand curves (Fig. 7.10(a)) depending on the change in the level of foreign exchange reserves, as illustrated in Fig. 7.10(b).

The conclusion we draw from this analysis is that aggregate demand is responding to dynamic forces arising from the changes in the level of a country's reserves. This in turn means that the degree of instability of aggregate demand depends on the extent to which the Central Bank engages in sterilization and what the desired level of reserves the government has in mind. What is often overlooked is the connection between the equilibrium level of income and the rate of inflation (in terms of the intersection between the demand-pressure

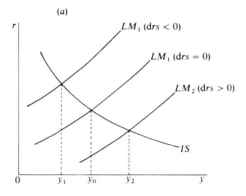

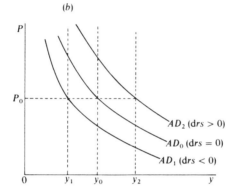

Figure 7.10 A change in reserves and the AD curve.

curve and the short-run Phillips curve) and the desired level of reserves and the change in the level of reserves. This association can lead to a policy conflict which we will investigate in Chapter 11.

NOTES

1. Partially differentiating equation (7.4) with respect to n and setting the result equal to zero, we have

$$\partial TC/\partial n = c - (rz/2n^2) = 0$$

which gives the optimal value for n, denoted n^*, of

$$n^* = [rz/2c]^{1/2}$$

Since $T = z/2n$, then the optimal transactions demand for money, denoted T^*, can be determined by substituting n^* for n. Doing this, and simplifying the algebra, gives the result

$$T^* = [cz/2r]^{1/2}$$

2. If there is an interest payment on money balances, i say, as distinct from an interest payment on bonds, denoted r in the text, then the inventory model for holding money can be written in the form (Cuthbertson, 1985)

$$T^* = [cz/2(r-i)]^{1/2}$$

If i and r are related, which occurred in the UK after the introduction of competition and credit control, then it is possible to vary i when r varies. For a criticism of the inventory model, first outlined by Baumol (1952) and Tobin (1956), see Sprenkle (1966).

3. For a more detailed discussion of the three motives for holding money and how the literature has dealt with them, see Laidler (3rd edn, 1985), chapter 6 and Cuthbertson (1985), chapters 2 and 3.

4. The capital gain/loss, denoted G, is a random variable which is assumed to have a normal probability distribution with mean μ and standard deviation s. Thus

$$G \sim N(\mu, s)$$

The standard deviation is the spread about the mean μ, and so can be considered as a measure of the risk.

If $Y = a + bX$, then given

$$X \sim N(\mu, s)$$

it can be shown that

$$Y \sim N(a + b\mu, bs)$$

In the text $E = r + G$ (i.e., $a = r$ and $b = 1$), so that

$$E \sim N(r + \mu, s)$$

5. See Hey (1979) for a discussion of risk-aversion and the implications for the shape of indifference curves.

APPENDIX 7.1 INCOME VELOCITY OF CIRCULATION OF MONEY

Much of the analysis of the demand for money is based on the idea that the transactions demand for money can be expressed in the form $M_T = kPy$ or $M_T = kY$. The coefficient k is the reciprocal of the income velocity of circulation of money, i.e.,

$$k = 1/V$$

Thus the constancy of k depends on the constancy of the income velocity of circulation of money. But does it matter whether the income velocity is constant or variable? It does, because a variable income velocity of circulation of money will lead to an unstable demand curve for money, which in turn will raise problems for monetary management.

In Fig. A7.1.1 we present three charts of the income velocity of circulation of money in the UK during the period 1963–87. Each graph is defined as Y/M_s, where Y is GNP at market prices and M_s denotes $M1$, $M3$ and $M3c$ respectively. As can be seen from the diagram, the income velocity of circulation of money has been far from constant. Income velocity in terms of $M1$ especially has shown a gradual rising trend over much of the period, rising from 4.2 to a peak of 7.4 in 1980. The trend for the broader definitions of money is not so clear. One other striking feature from the chart is that the income velocity with respect to the narrow definition of money has a cyclic pattern which is not so clearly demonstrated in the broader definitions of money. (For a thorough discussion of the velocity of circulation of money, with international comparisons, see Bordo and Jonung (1987)).

What may account for this pattern? Since V is defined as the ratio of money income to nominal money supply, then V will rise whenever money income is rising more than the nominal money supply. One possible reason is because interest rates have been rising over the same period. A rise in interest rates lowers the real demand for money which in turn will raise the income velocity of circulation of money. A further reason for the rise could be people's expectation that inflation will continue. If this is the case people expect the value of money to fall and consequently spend it that much quicker. However, there are also institutional reasons which may account for the rise in the

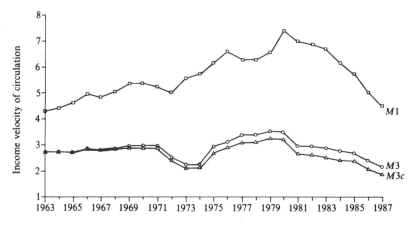

Figure A7.1.1 Income velocity of circulation of money

income velocity of circulation of money. These include (Goodhart, 1984):

(a) improvement in communications;
(b) the change to a more urban society;
(c) an increased growth and stability of the banking system;
(d) the emergence of non-bank financial intermediaries; and
(e) technical developments in the mechanism for transmitting payments.

It is not possible to ascribe the changes in the velocity to each of these categories or to distinguish their influence from that arising from interest rate changes or inflation rate changes. However, such institutional changes are fairly steady and gradual – although the advent of electronic banking may be one of the most significant institutional changes which will affect the velocity in the 1980s. (See Goodhart, 1984, chapter V, section 4.)

APPENDIX 7.2 THE INSTABILITY OF THE DEMAND FOR MONEY FUNCTION

A major plank of monetarist literature is that a rise (or fall) in nominal money supply will lead to a rise (or fall) in nominal income. In other words, changes in the money supply are transmitted into changes in nominal income. However, such a causation (from M_s to Y and not Y to M_s) is dependent on the stability of the demand for money. This is an empirical question.

In order to establish whether the demand for money is unstable, there is thus a need to undertake econometric investigation. Such empirical studies have concentrated on two aspects:

1. the appropriate functional form;
2. which variables should be included in the equation.

The analysis in this chapter indicates that the demand for real money balances depends on real income, possibly the rate of interest and possibly the level of real wealth. One way to test whether interest rates and real wealth are significant in explaining the demand for real money balances is to include these variables in a regression equation and test the significance of the coefficient. If the coefficient is statistically significant, then this indicates that the variable concerned is significant in partly explaining the dependent variable, namely the demand for money. One major difficulty is obtaining data on real (or nominal) wealth. In the first instance, therefore, most studies concentrated on relating nominal demand for money to nominal income and the rate of interest. Thus the standard regression equation took the form:

$$M_d = \beta_0 + \beta_1 Y + \beta_2 r + v \tag{A7.2.1}$$

where v is a random variable.

Since attention centred on the elasticity of the demand for money with respect to income and to the rate of interest, the equation was usually specified in logarithmic form – in other words, the variables in equation (A7.2.1) denote the logarithm of M_d, the logarithm of Y and either r or the logarithm of $(1+r)$ (*note* $\log(1+r) \sim r$).

A stable demand for money could therefore be interpreted as one in which the coefficients in equation (A7.2.1) were significant and stable and that variations in Y and r accounted for most of the variation in M_d. The difficulty with this interpretation is that it is too naïve. Distinctions must be made between short- and long-term interest rates and, at the very least, some consideration must be given to the lagged structure of some of the variables. These complications, and others, have been taken into account in a number of studies on the demand for money. Studies on the demand for money in the UK include those by Artis and Lewis (1976, 1984), Grice and Bennett (1984), Goodhart (1984, chapter II) and Patterson (1987).

What conclusion can we draw from these studies as to the stability of the demand for money in the UK? As has often been the case, the period of the 1950s and early 1960s indicated a stable demand for money. Equation (A7.2.1) (in logarithmic form) was the typical form used in these early studies. It was the turbulent 1970s that gave rise to doubts about the stability of the demand for money and led to further specifications of the demand for money equation. The basic belief was that the demand for money was a stable relationship but was probably mis-specified (e.g., wealth in addition to income should be included, or a more elaborate lag structure had to be specified.) An alternative view, however, was that market clearing does not take place in the money market and so it is not possible to equate the demand and supply of money (a necessary condition for empirical tests of equation (A7.2.1)). Such an approach was taken up by Artis and Lewis (1976). The evidence on the stability of the UK demand for money for the period after 1970 is not conclusive. It would appear, therefore, that to predicate monetary policy on the belief that the demand for money is a stable relationship may be unjustified.

APPENDIX 7.3 MONEY MULTIPLIER IN THE PRESENCE OF NON-BANK FINANCIAL INTERMEDIARIES

A major leakage from the banking system is to the non-bank financial intermediaries (the NBFIs), such as building societies and finance houses. The private sector besides depositing funds with the commercial banks can also deposit funds with the NBFIs. These institutions in turn will have reserve ratios, but also will deposit some of their funds with the commercial banks.

Let N denote the private sector funds received by the NBFIs. If a fraction, n, of such funds must be maintained as reserves, denoted R_n, then

$$R_n = nN \tag{A7.3.1}$$

Suppose that the NBFIs deposit a fraction, μ, of such funds with the commercial banks, then such non-bank deposits, D_n, are given by

$$D_n = \mu N \tag{A7.3.2}$$

Finally, we suppose the private sector is willing to hold a fraction, β, of its deposits with NBFIs, i.e.

$$N = \beta D_p \tag{A7.3.3}$$

The banking sector, as before, is typified by the following ratios:

$$C_p = q D_p \tag{A7.3.4}$$

$$C_b = eD \tag{A7.3.5}$$

$$M_b = fD \tag{A7.3.6}$$

where it should be noted that in this framework we are assuming the cash held by the public is a fraction of private sector deposits, the banks cash ratio and the ratio of deposits with the Bank of England are both with respect to total deposits, D, i.e.

$$D = D_p + D_n \tag{A7.3.7}$$

In the present situation, the money base, $M0$, and $M3$ (the old sterling $M3$) are defined as

$$M0 = C_b + M_b + C_p + R_n \tag{A7.3.8}$$

$$M3 = C_p + D \tag{A7.3.9}$$

What we require is the revised multiplier, q, the ratio of $M3/M0$. In obtaining this ratio it is useful first to consider an expression for deposits. Substituting equation (A7.3.3) into equation (A7.3.2) and then substituting this result into equation (A7.3.7) we obtain,

$$D = (1 + \mu\beta)D_p \tag{A7.3.10}$$

Expression (A7.3.9) can therefore be written

$$M3 = gD_p + (1 + \mu\beta)D_p = (1 + g + \mu\beta)D_p \tag{A7.3.11}$$

Similarly, we can re-arrange equation (A7.3.8) as follows:

$$M0 = eD + fD + gD_p + nN$$

$$= (e + f)D + gD_p + n\beta D_p$$

$$= (e + f)(1 + \mu\beta)D_p + (g + n\beta)D_p$$

i.e.,

$$M0 = [(e + f)(1 + \mu\beta) + (g + n\beta)]D_p \tag{A7.3.12}$$

Taking the ratio of equations (A7.3.11) and (A7.3.12) we have for the money multiplier, q,

$$q = \frac{M3}{M0} = \frac{(1 + g + \mu\beta)}{(e + f)(1 + \mu\beta) + (g + n\beta)} \tag{A7.3.13}$$

Chapter 8

THEORY OF ECONOMIC POLICY

Before we begin Part II on economic policy, it is worth considering the theory which underlies it. This is important. One of the main statements made by the UK Conservative Party since 1979 is that it is not the job of government to achieve certain objectives; rather, the aim of government is to create a *climate* for growth and development. This is in marked contrast to UK policy formation in the period 1945–79, which was based on the idea that it was the responsibility of governments to achieve certain stated objectives. These objectives were usually:

(a) full employment;
(b) low inflation;
(c) balance of payments equilibrium (or surplus);
(d) growth; and
(e) a more equitable distribution of income.

Of course, not all objectives were simultaneously pursued. Also, at different times one particular objective took precedence over the others. However, once it is agreed that governments have certain objectives to achieve, it naturally follows that the next step is to consider what instruments governments have at their disposal for achieving such objectives: that is, what *instruments* they have for achieving a set of *targets*. This conception of policy into targets and instruments dominated analysis in many countries from 1945 until the late 1970s and early 1980s.

In this chapter we will consider the theory of policy that was set out in terms of instruments and targets. This is a useful beginning because it allows us to see how management of the economy was carried out in the main during the post-War period. However, we will also outline its shortcomings. This is necessary because we need to see why the framework was inadequate for dealing with the period after 1970. We will conclude by considering alternative theories of economic policy.

Once we consider policy in terms of instruments and targets, then a number of obvious questions arise, such as the following:

1. What targets are there?
2. What instruments are there?
3. Can an instrument become a target?
4. Must instruments/targets be quantitative in nature?
5. Is it necessary to assign particular instruments to specific targets?

6. If the answer to (5) is, 'Yes', then on what basis is the assignment to be carried out?
7. Can microeconomic instruments be used to achieve macroeconomic objectives?
8. Must targets be independent of one another?
9. Must instruments be independent of one another?
10. Does uncertainty make any difference?

These are just some of the questions we will deal with in this chapter.

8.1 TARGETS AND INSTRUMENTS

The objectives of economic policy usually refer to specific variables, e.g. employment (or unemployment), inflation, the balance on the balance of payments, and the growth of GNP. A fairer distribution of income, although it may be captured in the Gini coefficient, is not dealt with in such a quantitative manner. Put another way, the government has target variables: 3% unemployment, 5% inflation (or even a zero rate of inflation), and so on. Although macroeconomic variables – such as inflation, unemployment and the balance on the balance of payments – can be reduced down to simple aggregates, this is not true of all government objectives. We have already alluded to a fairer distribution of income, but the same applies to competitiveness. As we will see in Chapter 17, there are various measures of 'competitiveness', but in no way would any of these indices be made an objective of policy. The reason is not difficult to see. Some objectives are more about 'concepts' than they are about variables. Thus, governments may want a 'fairer distribution of income' (a conceptual objective), or an economy which is 'more competitive on world markets' (a conceptual objective).

Even where it is possible to reduce objectives down to specific variables, these may hide multidimensional aspects of the underlying problem. For example, suppose an objective is to reduce unemployment down to 3%. Let us suppose that this has been achieved. However, it may be achieved with all the unemployment occurring in the north; or all the unemployed being male; or all the unemployed being school leavers. In other words, the *composition* of the 3% unemployment cannot be irrelevant to the achievement of the objective. Composition is not the only consideration. The time scale for achieving the objective is also important. The effects of achieving a zero rate of inflation in five years is quite different from achieving the same objective over a period of, say, fifteen years. In other words, objectives cannot be considered independently of the time scale necessary for their achievement.

There are certain instruments that a government has which it can use to achieve its agreed set of targets. Some are specific – such as the marginal tax rates, money supplies, government spending and the exchange rate. But others are not so specific – such as a prices and incomes policy. When the government can manipulate specific instruments, we talk of instrument variables. An important consideration, however, is the *degree* to which the government can control the variable in question. In the case of the marginal tax rate, for example, it has complete control; but this cannot be said of the money supply. The government controls only high-powered money – but this is not the same as the money supply. The money supply also involves bank lending, and this is only partially affected by bank ratios laid down by the Central Bank. However, it is possible for the Central Bank to exert non-quantitative pressure on the commercial banks in an attempt to control the expansion of credit. Certainly this has been done in the UK. But it cannot be modelled in any obvious way – and, hence, the impact of such control cannot be predicted with any accuracy.

The money market provides another important illustration of the difficulty of deciding whether a variable is an instrument at any moment of time. To illustrate this point consider the following scenario. Suppose the government wishes to control inflation by means of the money supply – a policy we shall consider in Part II. This would suggest that the money supply is an instrument (what is often now called an *intermediate target*). However, Central Banks can either determine the money supply or the rate of interest but not both. Hence, in this example the rate of interest must be whatever is the outcome of the stated money supply. But suppose there is an outflow of capital to the USA for some reason. The government may wish to stem this outflow. How can they do this? By forcing up UK interest rates? But they can only do this by restricting the money supply. In other words, they must relinquish, temporarily, their use of the money supply as an instrument for the achievement of inflation. This has been a typical feature of the post-War period in the UK – the government vacillating between control of the money supply and control of the rate of interest. What this example illustrates is the importance, the necessity, of having *independent* instruments for the achievement of various targets.

What is also illustrated by this example of the money market is the confusion between instruments, intermediate targets and ultimate targets (objectives). Some clarification is provided in Appendix 8.1.

We can illustrate the use of instruments and targets by means of the multiplier results we derived in Chapter 2. This example also has the merit of illustrating the importance of stability in economic relationships. We begin by reminding the reader of the equilibrium level of income in the IS–LM model; that is, the level of income determined by demand conditions for a given price level. This is equation (8.1).

$$y = \frac{[z_0 + h\hat{P}^e - (f+g)R] + (h/u)(M_0/P)}{1 - b(1 - t_1) + m + (kh/u)} \tag{8.1}$$

The multiplier with respect to a change in the autonomous component, z_0, is,

$$k_{vr} = 1/[1 - b(1 - t_1) + m + (kh/u)] \tag{8.2}$$

Consider now a target level of income, denoted y^* – which for this illustration we shall assume is greater than the equilibrium level of income given by equation (8.1). Suppose the government intends to achieve this target level of income by means of government spending. Hence, the target variable is real income, y, and the instrument variable is government spending, *go*. The remaining variables, although important in determining the level of income, are irrelevant from the present policy point of view.

Now ask the question: 'What change is necessary in government spending in order to move income from level y, given in equation (8.1), to income level y^*?' Since government spending is a component of z_0, then we can consider the level of *go* (and hence z_0) that is consistent with the target level of income y^*. Since we are holding constant inflation expectations, the exchange rate, the price level at home and abroad and the money supply, then we can simplify equation (8.1) as follows:

$$y = k_{rv}go + k_{rv}a_0 \tag{8.3}$$

where we have utilized equation (8.2) and combined all constant terms under the one term, a_0. Similarly, we can express the target level of income as

$$y^* = k_{rv}go^* + k_{rv}a_0 \tag{8.4}$$

Subtracting equation (8.3) from (8.4), we obtain

$$y - y^* = k_{rv}(go - go^*) \tag{8.5}$$

Defining,

$$dy \equiv y - y^* \tag{8.6}$$

$$dgo \equiv go - go^* \tag{8.7}$$

Then, the change in government spending, dgo, necessary to achieve the target level of income is

$$dgo = dy/k_{rv} \tag{8.8}$$

What is shown by result (8.8) is that if the government is going to achieve its target, it must:

1. Forecast the discrepancy between income level y and the target level of income, y^*;
2. estimate the multiplier, k_{rv}.

The first involves forecasting models of the economy, while the second involves large scale macroeconometric models of the economy – such as the Treasury Model.[1] Notice also, that predicting the change necessary in government spending not only depends on estimating the multiplier, k_{rv}, but also on determining how stable it is. If the multiplier can vary between certain limits, then so too can government spending necessary to achieve the target level of income. (This, of course, assumes the forecast is accurate – which it is unlikely to be.)

The present example illustrates what is called a *fixed target model*. Although we have considered only one target and one instrument, the point extends to larger policy models. A fixed target model involves a set of targets (denoted T) and a set of instruments (denoted I). Thus,

$$\text{Targets} \qquad T_1, T_2, \ldots, T_n \tag{8.9}$$

$$\text{Instruments} \qquad I_1, I_2, \ldots, I_m \tag{8.10}$$

where n denotes the number of targets and m the number of instruments. In any analysis, it may or may not be the case that the number of instruments equals the number of targets. Furthermore, in a fixed target model, the targets are simply specified. How the decision-maker decides on these set of targets, or the level that such targets should take, is not determined within the policy model.

8.2 SOME PRINCIPLES OF FIXED TARGET MODELS

Given just one instrument and one target, then it follows that the number of instruments equals the number of targets, and there is no uncertainty or ambiguity about which

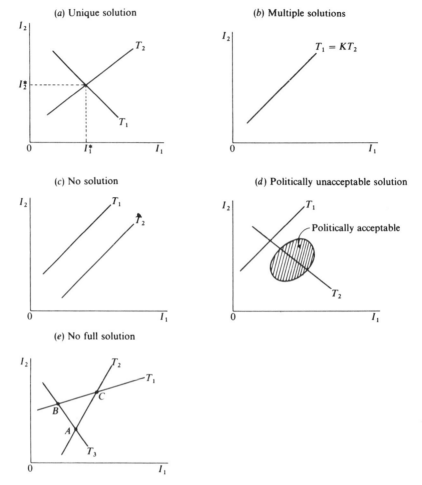

Figure 8.1 Targets and instruments: various possibilities.

instrument to attach to which target. Suppose, however, that there are three targets: T_1, T_2 and T_3. How many instruments are required to achieve these three targets?

In a classic work Tinbergen (1956) demonstrated that, in a fixed target model, it is necessary to have as many independent instruments as there are independent targets. Let us state this as a principle:

Tinbergen Principle (TP)
In a fixed target model, if there are n independent target variables, then there must be n independent instrument variables (i.e., $n = m$).

The importance of the instruments and targets being *independent*, and that the number of instruments must equal the number of targets, is illustrated in Fig. 8.1. The diagram also illustrates that these conditions are necessary but by no means sufficient. In each diagram, on the axes we have instruments I_1 and I_2. The targets, denoted T_1, T_2 and T_3, are drawn as straight lines. Each line denotes the combination of the two instruments necessary to achieve that particular target. In Fig. 8.1(a), therefore, there are two instruments to achieve the two targets. The solution is to set the two instruments at levels I_1^* and I_2^*, respectively.

In Fig. 8.1 (*b*) the two targets are not independent of one another – $T_1 = kT_2$ (i.e., target T_1 is proportional to target T_2). In this case there is a multiplicity of solutions for the instruments which will achieve both targets. On the other hand, Fig. 8.1(*c*) illustrates the situation where there exists no solution (in this case the instruments are in some fixed relation to each other). Fig. 8.1(*d*) illustrates a situation where a solution exists, but that it is not politically acceptable. Finally, Fig. 8.1(*e*) shows the situation where there are three targets and only two instruments. As drawn, there is no possibility of achieving all three objectives at the one time. Any two can be achieved; but this does mean abandoning one of the targets. If a decision-maker does have three independent targets, then Tinbergen's principle indicates that there is a need for another instrument which is *independent* of the first two.

Tinbergen's principle is concerned only with *consistency*. But even this has its uses. The stop–go policies of the 1950s and 1960s, which we discussed in Appendix 5.4, typified inconsistent policies. Governments generally relied on government spending as the only policy instrument. However, they had, at the time, two policy objectives: (1) full employment, and (2) balance of payments equilibrium (inflation at the time was fairly low). To raise income to the full employment level meant a rise in government spending. But a rise in income led to a rise in imports, and hence to a deterioration in the current balance. (At the time the capital account was not considered as important and all attention was on the current account.) To improve the current balance meant that government spending had to be cut. But a cut in government spending meant a rise in the level of unemployment. In other words, the use of one instrument (government spending) was insufficient to achieve the two objectives (full employment and balance of payments equilibrium).

Later it was considered that monetary policy could be used to help achieve a consistent set of policy objectives. In this case it was assumed that the balance of payments was responsive to the rate of interest through the capital account. Given a fixed exchange rate (and fixed prices at home and abroad), the only two obvious policies were fiscal policy and monetary policy. The two instruments were considered to be, for example, government spending (fiscal policy) and the rate of interest (monetary policy). It is, then, theoretically possible to achieve the two objectives of full employment – often referred to as *internal balance* – and balance of payments equilibrium – often referred to as *external balance*. In other words, it is possible to find a consistent set of policy instruments which would achieve internal and external balance.

Three difficulties arose over the use of such policies. First, even if the decision-maker had two instruments for the achievement of two targets, Tinbergen's principle does not indicate to the policy-maker how this could be achieved. Second, macroeconomic developments in the late 1960s indicated that monetary policy and fiscal policy are not independent of one another – they are linked through the government budget constraint. We have dealt with this in Chapter 6. Third, much of the analysis arose in terms of a fixed price level. Once inflation enters the scene – and its reduction (elimination?) becomes a third objective – then Tinbergen's principle does indicate that a third independent instrument is necessary. In effect, there was the need to consider the assignment of instruments to targets; and, second, a search for a set of independent policy instruments to achieve the three generally accepted targets of full employment, price stability and balance of payments equilibrium. We take up these developments in Part II; here we will continue with the underlying theoretical problems.

8.3 THE ASSIGNMENT PROBLEM

Tinbergen's Principle (TP), outlined in the preceding section, is deficient in two respects. First, even if there are as many independent instruments as there are targets, this does not guarantee a solution. Even if a solution exists, it does not guarantee that it is economically meaningful (e.g., it may imply a negative exchange rate); or that it is politically acceptable (e.g., it may imply 25% unemployment). Second, it does not indicate how, if at all, we should assign the instruments to the targets. Suppose, for instance, that we have two independent instruments, I_1 and I_2, and two independent targets T_1 and T_2. All Tinbergen's principle tells us is that there is a level for I_1 and I_2 which will achieve the two targets. But if we are to achieve the two targets we must consider the *process* of doing so.

One possibility, favoured very much by control engineers, is to

> ... discover what pattern of combination of simultaneous use of all available weapons (instruments) would produce the most preferred pattern of combination of simultaneous hits on all the desirable targets.   (Meade, 1978, p. 426)

This is basically a restatement of Tinbergen's principle. In the case of two instruments and two targets, it recognizes the fact that instrument I_1 effects both T_1 and T_2, and similarly for instrument I_2. But to arrive at a solution, a policy model must be established which links the instruments to the targets – and such that the model can be explicitly solved. This is no easy task. Furthermore, at the practical level all government bodies engaged in managing the economy are required to know what all other departments are doing. Although the approach is theoretically sound, it is impracticable.

The other extreme has also been suggested. We can state this as follows

> *Complete Decentralized Assignment (CDA)*
> Pair instruments and targets so that each instrument adjusts to the disequilibrium in one and only one distinct target.

What implications does this have? It means no two targets respond to the same instrument and no two instruments affect a single target. But it is clearly too general. With two instruments and two targets it tells us that we should assign one instrument to achieving one of the targets and the other instrument to achieving the second target. But it does not indicate any criterion for assigning which instrument to which target. For instance, should I_1 be assigned to T_1 or to T_2?

Two principles for assignment have been proposed in the literature. The first, and most widely known, is Mundell's *principle of effective market classification* (PEMC) (Mundell, 1962). The second was suggested by Meade in his Nobel Prize Lecture, what we call here *Meade's responsibility principle* (MRP), (Meade, 1978).

Mundell's PEMC states

> *Principle of effective market classification*
> Each policy instrument should be paired with the policy objective (target) over which it has the most relative influence.

To illustrate this principle, consider the achievement of two targets: (1) an income level y^* (say, income at the full employment level); and (2) balance of payments equilibrium ($bp = 0$). These two targets can be thought of as internal balance and external balance. Next consider

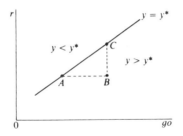

(a) Internal balance

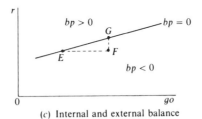

(b) External balance

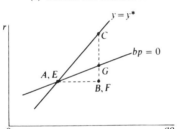

(c) Internal and external balance

Figure 8.2 Internal and external balance.

two instruments: fiscal policy (in the form of government spending, *go*) and monetary policy (in the form of the rate of interest, *r*). Throughout we assume that the price levels at home and abroad are constant and the exchange rate is constant. The situation is captured in Fig. 8.2, which has instruments on the axes and the targets as lines. The first thing we must establish is the slopes of the 'target lines'. First, consider the target income level y^* in Fig. 8.2(a). We begin at point A such that the target level of income prevails. Now consider a rise in the level of government spending, the rate of interest remaining constant. The situation moves to point B. The rise in government spending will cause income to rise through the multiplier effect. Income will accordingly be greater than the target level of income. What must happen to the rate of interest to re-establish the target rate of income? Income must be reduced. A reduction in income will occur if the money supply is reduced. A reduction in the money supply, in turn, will raise the rate of interest. A movement to point C will thus re-establish income at the target level. Hence, there is a positive relationship between the two instrument variables (*go* and *r*) along the line $y = y^*$. (In other words, the internal balance line is positively sloped.)

Next consider Fig. 8.2(b), denoting balance of payments equilibrium (or external balance). Begin at point E, such that the balance of payments is in equilibrium. Now consider a rise in government spending, the rate of interest remaining constant. The situation moves to point *F*. The rise in government spending will cause income to rise through the multiplier effect. The rise in income will cause a rise in the level of imports of goods and services and, at the given rate of interest, will result in a balance of payments deficit (since there is no change in the net flow of capital). What must happen to the rate of interest in order to re-establish balance of payments equilibrium? Clearly, there must be a rise in the rate of interest in order to attract more capital inflow which will finance the worsening current account position. Hence, again, there is a positive relationship between the two instruments (*go* and *r*) along the target line *bp* = 0. (In other words, the external balance line is positively sloped.)

In Figure 8.2(*c*) we have placed the two curves together. We have drawn them such that the line denoting the income target (internal balance) is steeper than the line denoting the balance of payments target (external balance). Why is this? For any increase in government spending there is a rise in income through the multiplier effect. Let this rise in income be d*y*. As far as the income target is concerned, the rate of interest must rise in order to reduce income by this full amount. However, when we turn to the balance of payments situation, the rise in income of d*y* will lead to an increase in the level of imports of only *m*d*y* (where *m* is the marginal propensity to import). Since the marginal propensity to import lies between zero and unity, then it follows that

$$m\,\mathrm{d}y < \mathrm{d}y \tag{8.11}$$

Hence, the rise in the rate of interest to correct for the rise in imports (*m*d*y*) must be smaller than the rise in the rate of interest to correct for the change in income (d*y*).

It follows, then, that the line denoted *bp* = 0 is less steep than the line denoting *y* = *y**. Furthermore, the more mobile capital, the less the interest rate needs to rise in order to attract the necessary capital inflow to correct for the deficit on the current account. With perfect capital mobility, the line denoting the balance of payments target is horizontal (i.e., the external balance line is horizontal) – at the rate of interest ruling abroad. A number of the ideas on internal and external balance are highlighted by means of a numerical example in Appendix 8.2.

We are now in a position to consider alternative assignments. Suppose the monetary authorities are assigned the task of achieving external balance (*bp* = 0) by means of manipulating the rate of interest; and that the treasury is assigned the task of achieving internal balance (*y* = *y**) by means of manipulating government spending. The situation is shown in Fig. 8.3(*a*). The economy is initially at point *A* – where neither target is being achieved. If the monetary authorities raise the rate of interest in order to achieve balance of payments equilibrium, then the economy moves to point *B*. However, this aggravates the situation with regard to the income target. Accordingly, the government raises the level of government spending, taking the economy from point *B* to point *C*. The resulting increase in income, which arises from the increased government spending, increases the level of imports and leads to a worsening on the trade account. The monetary authorities accordingly raise the rate of interest in order to attract capital to finance the deficit on current account. This takes the economy from point *C* to point *D*, and so on. What we see from Fig. 8.3(*a*) is that each round requires less and less adjustment, and that the system will eventually converge on the 'bliss point' *Q*.

Now consider the reverse assignment rule. In other words, suppose monetary policy was used to achieve internal balance (*y* = *y**) and government spending to achieve external balance (*bp* = 0). The situation is shown in Fig. 8.3(*b*). The economy is situated at point *E*.

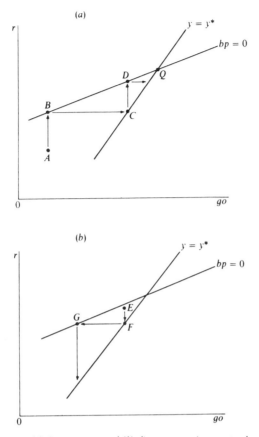

Figure 8.3 (a) Convergent and (b) divergent assignment rules.

The interest rate is lowered by the monetary authorities in order to stimulate income. The economy moves from point E to point F. The rise in income, however, leads to a worsening state of the trade account. In order to reduce the level of imports, government spending must be reduced with this particular assignment. The economy moves from point F to point G. And so on. What we see from Fig. 8.3(b) is that each round takes the economy further away from the 'bliss point' Q.

What causes the difference in the reactions? We note that in both parts of Fig. 8.3, the internal balance line ($y = y^*$) is steeper than the external balance line ($bp = 0$). This means that government spending has more of a relative impact than the rate of interest on achieving the target income level than it does in achieving balance of payments equilibrium. Of course, with only two instruments and two targets, this implies that the interest rate has more of a relative impact on the balance of payments than does government spending. What Mundell's PEMC thus tells us is to assign fiscal policy to the income target (since it has the greatest relative impact) and monetary policy to the balance of payments target (since it has the greatest relative impact). What Fig. 8.3(b) illustrates is that Mundell's PEMC is violated.

The analysis just presented has two major short-comings. First, it strictly applies to a situation where there are two instruments and two targets. 'Relative impacts' become far less precise once the number of instruments and targets exceeds two. Second, the framework was set up to deal with a world where there was little or no inflation. Whether inflation becomes another target or not, what it does do is lead to movements in the target lines constructed in, for example, Fig. 8.3. In other words, the target lines become unstable during inflation.[2] A point illustrated by the numerical example in Appendix 8.2.

In the presence of inflation, another assignment rule is called for. Meade suggested one assignment (1978), which he analysed in his Nobel Prize Lecture. This can be stated as follows,

Meade's Responsibility Principle (MRP)

> Place one instrument in charge of one particular authority with the responsibility of hitting as near as possible one well defined target.

Since the early 1970s three problems have occurred in most economies: rising unemployment, inflation and balance of payments problems (especially deficits). If decision-makers have the three objectives of (1) full employment, (2) stable prices, and (3) balance of payments equilibrium, then Mundell's PEMC is not very helpful.

Given the Tinbergen principle, we now have three targets, and thus three independent instruments are required. Even if we accept the complete decentralized assignment principle (CDA), we still need to assign instruments to targets by some means. Given that Mundell's PEMC is inadequate, what principle can be utilized? This is what Meade addressed himself to in his Nobel Prize Lecture. The principle he annunciated is given above, in what we have called Meade's responsibility principle (MRP).

The basic idea is that a given bureaucratic machinery will imply a 'natural' matching between certain institutions and targets. For instance, the Bank of England manages the country's foreign exchange reserves, and so is a 'natural' choice for achieving balance of payments equilibrium. Since we associate monetary policy with the Bank of England, then we assign monetary policy to the achievement of the balance of payments, and the Bank of England takes *responsibility* for the achievement of this objective. Similarly, it is 'natural' (although possibly less so) for the Treasury to achieve full employment. Since the Treasury has the budget as the obvious instrument, fiscal policy should be assigned to achieving the target level of income, and the Treasury takes *responsibility* for the achievement of this objective. The general idea is illustrated in Fig. 8.4, where A_i is the ith authority, I_i the ith instrument and T_i the ith target. Consequently, the assignment of I_i to achieving T_i is indirect, because of I_i's link with A_i. In the present example we have the same assignment rule as suggested by Mundell.

Since Meade separates the objectives of full employment and price stability, it is 'natural' for the Prices and Income Board to be responsible for the achievement of price stability. In this approach, it is not necessary for all the instruments to be quantitative in nature. What we now have is three government bodies using whatever instruments are within their jurisdiction to achieve the stated objectives. Any failure is then placed with the authority concerned. Meade particularly emphasizes the importance of a government body taking *responsibility* for a particular objective. On a practical level, if a stated objective is not being achieved then the government can at the very least request the reasons why it is not from the appropriate authority.

This is not a trivial point. Consider the position taken by the UK Conservative government since it took office in 1979. Its major objective is the fight against inflation. It has given the Bank of England *and* the Treasury the task of achieving this: the Bank by

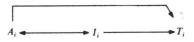

Figure 8.4 Meade's assignment.

controlling the growth of the money supply, and the Treasury by reducing the public sector borrowing requirement – which constitutes a large element in the growth of the money supply. The pound sterling was floated in June 1972 and, theoretically at least, the exchange rate can change so as to establish equilibrium on the balance of payments. But what about the employment situation? In the long run, it is possible, so monetarists would argue, that zero inflation can occur at the natural level of unemployment. The present government is arguing that inflation and unemployment can, therefore, be solved simultaneously – so long as the growth in the money supply is controlled. Let us suppose that the long-run situation is true (although how long is the long run?). What about employment in the short run and medium run? It is implicit that the government itself is responsible for the short-run employment situation because implicit, if not explicit, is that no policy instrument (or no authority) is responsible for the achievement of full employment in this period. Monetarists argue that this is the 'cost' of achieving a zero inflation in the long run. But are the costs worth it? Is another strategy possible which involves less cost? We will take up some of these aspects in Part II.

8.4 FLEXIBLE-TARGET POLICY MODELS

Tinbergen's approach to policy modelling, and the assignment principles suggested by Mundell and Meade, are concerned with fixed target models. In other words, the framework treats the targets as given. A more complete policy model, however, must include an analysis of the chosen targets and the level of these targets determined by decision-makers. Put another way, what is the optimal combination of policy targets and how are these to be achieved? This question led to a series of policy models of the *flexible* type.

In broad terms, the approach assumes that the decision-maker has a welfare function. This welfare function has as its components the variables with which the decision-maker is concerned (e.g., inflation, unemployment and the balance on the balance of payments). The aim is to maximize the decision-maker's welfare subject to the fact that the variables contained in the welfare function are related to one another through the economic system. Exactly how the variables are related is captured in terms of an economic model. Hence, the framework specifies the target variables in terms of the components of the welfare function, while the economic model contains instrument variables and other variables which are irrelevant from the policy point of view. The fact that the economic model has some variables which are irrelevant from the policy point of view means that there can be some degree of choice as to the policy instruments – but exactly what this choice is depends on the model chosen and on the institutional considerations which are incorporated.

The framework can be seen in terms of Fig. 8.5. The economic model is captured in terms of our demand-pressure curve and short- and long-run Phillips curve. The welfare function is given by a series of 'indifference curves', which we have labelled W_0, W_1, etc. In Fig. 8.5(*a*)

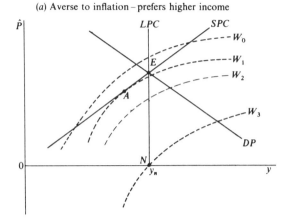

(a) Averse to inflation – prefers higher income

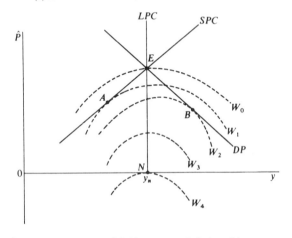

(b) Averse to inflation – prefers higher income only up to $y = y_n$

Figure 8.5 Desired solutions in a macromodel; (a) averse to inflation; (b) more y preferred up to $y = y_n$.

and 8.5(b) we have assumed that the decision-maker is averse to more inflation – in other words, the less the rate of inflation the higher the level of welfare. However, in Fig. 8.5(a) we assume that the higher the level of real income the higher the level of welfare; while in Fig. 8.5(b) we assume that welfare is raised for higher income levels only up to income level $y = y_n$; thereafter welfare declines for higher levels of income. Fig. 8.5(b) is attempting to capture the idea that the decision-maker wishes to run the economy at a level determined by the natural rate of income (or the natural rate of unemployment).

In Fig. 8.5(a) the short-run equilibrium (point E) denotes the lowest welfare position; furthermore, the short-run optimal solution (point A in both figures) would require some policy adjustment on the part of the decision-maker. However, Fig. 8.5(b) illustrates that there are two possible short-run policy solutions (point A and point B). If the aim is to maximize welfare, then policy solution B is preferable to the policy-maker than policy solution A (at least as drawn here). In both cases, however, the long-run solution is the same (point N, at income level $y = y_n$ and inflation at zero). This is not surprising given the assumptions surrounding the two alternative welfare functions. Given that the aim is to

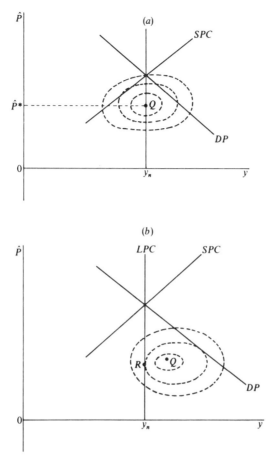

Figure 8.6 Desired solutions and long-run conflicts in a macromodel: (a) high income, preference structure; (b) high employment preference structure.

reduce inflation as much as possible and given that the long-run solution must lie on the long-run Phillips curve, it follows that point N must be the long-run solution.

It is possible to have somewhat different preferences, as illustrated in Fig. 8.6(a) and (b). In this case the indifference map forms concentric curves around a 'bliss point' (point Q). In Fig. 8.6(a) the 'bliss point' lies on the LPC, and so this point is feasible, given the model as embodied in the long-run Phillips curve. In Fig. 8.6(b), however, point Q is not on the long-run Phillips curve and so cannot, given the model, be attained in the long run. The long-run solution is given by point R. The main difference between Fig. 8.6(a) and (b), is that in the latter case the decision-maker will always feel that he can improve on the situation (that point Q is preferable to point R). There is nothing inherent in the structure of the decision-maker's preferences which says that the 'bliss point' would be (or should be) on the long-run Phillips curve.

The flexible-target approach, just outlined, was pioneered particularly by Theil (1964). What we have discussed here is only the flexible-target model with no uncertainty. It is possible to extend this analysis to deal with uncertainty, but this takes us beyond the scope of this book.[3]

8.5 OTHER APPROACHES TO POLICY-MAKING

The view that we have expressed about policy-making thus far is a *normative* one. A model of the economy is specified and then this is used to indicate how the economy can be improved in order to approach the desired target.[4] This does involve a very special view about government behaviour. In particular, the models – whether Keynesian or monetarist – treat government spending as exogenous. In other words, government spending is determined by factors outside the model. Thus, once an objective is specified – as in the fixed-target model – then what the government ought to do can be determined. What governments actually do is not really considered in this framework. The same basically applies in the case of flexible-target models. The approach provides *decision rules* which governments may wish to follow.

The normative approach, which is at the heart of Keynesian macroeconomics, quite naturally leads to the idea that governments can use various instruments to stabilize the economy. When income is below its potential, governments can implement policies, such as fiscal expansion, to bring the economy to its full potential. When the economy is above its full capacity output and there is pressure on prices to rise, governments can implement opposite policies. We will deal with stabilization in more detail in Chapter 13. The point we are attempting to highlight, however, is that the present approach presupposes that governments can in fact carry out such stabilization. Such a view has not been universally accepted. In the very early days of Keynesian economics (*circa* 1943), Kalecki took issue with the view that government spending could be treated as exogenous and used to stabilize the economy on the lines of Keynesian demand management. Although demand expansion was universally accepted when the economy was below its potential (because this would mean gains by both workers and capitalists), the same could not be said of an economy at full employment. Kalecki felt that in this instance capitalists – but not workers – would urge a deflation of the economy. The reason why capitalists wanted to deflate the economy was in order to curb the power of workers and trade unions which increased during such periods of full employment. We see from this brief discussion that Kalecki was attempting to *explain* government spending – and not simply treating it as exogenous to the economic system.

Alternative policy models begin with the idea that governments aim at maximizing their voting, i.e. their objective is to remain in power. In the earlier analysis the decision-maker was assumed to have a welfare function which had target variables as its arguments. In the present analysis the welfare function is in terms of votes – and it is the number of votes which is being maximized. More specifically, the aim is re-election, and the probability of this is greater the greater the lead in the opinion polls. In other words, the government's lead in the opinion polls is used as a *proxy* for the probability of being re-elected. The next step is to see what determines the government's lead in the opinion polls. The majority of studies relate such a lead to the state of the economy – where 'state of the economy' is captured in such variables as real income, the price level, the rate of unemployment, etc. The relationship between government popularity and the state of the economy has been called a *support* or *appraisal* function, Mosley (1984).

One extreme view is that governments do not have welfare functions: they do not maximize anything at all! Such a view leads to a description of what a particular government actually does in various situations. The tendency here is to argue that government policy is simply responding to situations as and when they occur. This is certainly the view expounded in Dow (1964), Brittan (1971) and Blackaby (1978). However, with the move from Keynesianism to monetarism – especially by UK and US governments – there is no doubt that government policy does have an underlying philosophy. Although this philosophy may not be captured in terms of a maximizing function, it does suggest that economic policy is not purely *ad hoc*. It could be argued that looking at government policy in terms of instruments and targets, is simply a very narrow view of government economic policy – which is limited in so far as it does not take account of government objectives other than target variables, and does not take account of the underlying philosophical stance of the government in power. But to do this would require an extremely elaborate framework (model?) which would, most likely, be intractable.

8.6 RATIONAL EXPECTATIONS AND ECONOMIC POLICY

We made the point in Chapter 4 that rational expectations theorists have argued that governments are impotent. If individuals behave rationally, then they take account of government action in their decision-making and consequently counteract any impact such government policy may have. If such a view is taken, then there is no requirement for governments to attempt to stabilize the economy (as Keynesians would suggest) or to attempt to improve the lead in the opinion poles. In fact, rational expectations theorists would argue for very little government manipulation of the economy – other than for safety and law and order. When government policy is being pursued it should be of the type which involves rules rather than discretion. We will take up this debate in more detail in Part II, but what matters for the present is that when expectations are formed rationally, optimal policies still exist but they differ from those in which expectations are treated as exogenous. The theory indicates that policy rules must be specified by the policy-makers. The policy rules may be simple or complex, but what is important is that the rules must be known by the public. Given such knowledge on the part of the public, it is assumed to follow its behaviour in accordance with its own objectives. A different rule will lead to different behaviour on the part of the public. It is then (theoretically) possible to determine the optimal policy rule.

Finally it is worth noting that the instruments-targets approach has been criticized on the grounds that governments do not maximize anything. A pragmatist would have to say, in the case of rational expectations, that no government would openly stipulate its policy rule – and, if it did, it is almost certain that the electorate would not believe it. It should also be remembered that the rational expectations approach is an extreme model which indicates what governments ought to do. It is a *normative* approach to policy just as much as the instruments-targets approach.

NOTES

1. See Cuthbertson (1979), Keating (1985), Wallis *et al.* (1985) and Appendix 13.2.

2. Both the internal and external balance lines move when prices change. A rise in prices causes the internal balance line ($y = y^*$) to move to the *right*, while a rise in prices causes the external balance line ($bp = 0$) to move to the *left*. The result is a rise in both the interest rate and government spending necessary to maintain both internal and external balance.

3. See Peston (1974) and Gapinski (1982), Chapter 7.

4. Levačić (1987) has criticized economists in this respect for concentrating on too narrow a view of the economic policy-making process. The rational decision-making procedures outlined by economists do not take account of the distributional conflicts that the political system attempts to resolve (and resolve differently from the market mechanism). Furthermore, 'it also neglects the institutional context in which economic policy is made and how this affects policy outcomes'. (p. xi)

APPENDIX 8.1 TARGETS, INSTRUMENTS AND INDICATORS

See Fig. A8.1.1 for a representation of this appendix.

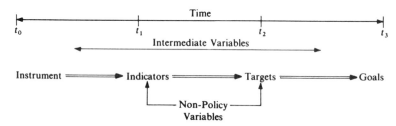

Figure A8.1.1 Targets, instruments and indicators

Goals, objectives, ultimate targets

These denote the main variables about which policy is ultimately concerned. They include:

(a) high level of employment;
(b) low rate of inflation;
(c) balance of payments equilibrium; and
(d) satisfactory rate of economic growth.

(Sometimes a more equitable distribution of income is included in the above list.)

Targets, intermediate target, intermediate variables

These are variables which lie closer to goals and have a fairly predictable effect on goals. They include:

(a) bank reserves;
(b) level of short- and long-term interest rates; and
(c) total money supply.

There are four criteria for being a (intermediate) target:

(a) must be affected by the policy instruments with a shorter time-lag than is involved in goals;
(b) must be readily observable with little or no delay;
(c) must be stably related to one or more goals of policy; and
(d) non-policy influences on it should be separable from the policy influence, and be identifiable.

Target variables can either be concerned with *quantity* or with *price*, e.g.

Quantity	*Price*
money supply	short-term interest rates
money base	long-term interest rates
domestic credit	equity yields
expansion	

Indicators

These indicate the direction and strength of policy. Indicators should:

(a) be observable;
(b) be close to the instruments of policy;
(c) have a stable relationship with the instruments of policy;
(d) be influenced primarily by policy action and to a much lesser degree by non-policy variables. Or, it must be possible to separate policy and non-policy influences on the indicator; and
(e) have a stable and close relationship to the target of policy.

Some of the same variables listed for intermediate targets have been suggested for instruments. Others include banks' assets and liabilities and short-term interest rates.

Instruments

These are variables on which the government can operate in order to influence goals through their effect on instruments and (intermediate) targets. They include:

(a) open market operations;
(b) special deposits; and
(c) the Bank's discount rate (i.e. MLR).

APPENDIX 8.2 INTERNAL AND EXTERNAL BALANCE: A NUMERICAL EXAMPLE

Internal balance is the condition of full employment at zero inflation (although this is a very extreme definition of internal balance, we will retain it in this example). External balance is the condition of a balance of payments equilibrium, i.e., $bp = 0$. In this example we will utilize the IS–LM–BP model outlined in Appendix 2.4, with some minor changes.

The full employment level of income is taken to be $y^* = 42$ (equal to the natural level in other examples). We begin with a situation of internal and external balance, namely the conditions:

$$y = y^* = 42 \text{ and } \hat{P} = 0 \qquad \text{internal balance}$$
$$bp = 0 \qquad \text{external balance}$$

The only difference between the equations in Appendix 2.4 and those given here are the following:

1. $go = 37.85$
2. $cf_0 = 25.4$ hence,
   $cf = 25.4 + (r - 15 + \hat{S}^e)$

All remaining equations and parameters are as specified in Appendix 2.4.

Given the parameter values just specified, the goods market, the money market and the balance of payments are all in equilibrium, i.e. the IS curve, the LM curve and the BP curve intersect one another at the same point. The equilibrium values for the interest rate and level of real income are,

1. $r = 15$
2. $y = 42$

The *internal balance* line denotes combinations of the interest rate and the level of government spending (the two chosen instrument variables) at which $y = y^* = 42$ (and inflation is zero, i.e, $\hat{P} = 0$). The *external balance* line denotes the combinations of the interest rate and government spending for which $bp = 0$. From the parameter values given we can derive the following internal and external balance equations (each expressing the rate of interest in terms of the level of government spending):

$$\text{internal balance:} \qquad r = -3.925 + 0.5go \qquad \text{(A8.2.1)}$$

$$\text{external balance:} \qquad r = 7.985 + 0.186go \qquad \text{(A8.2.2)}$$

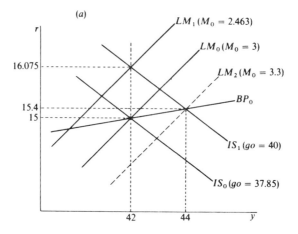

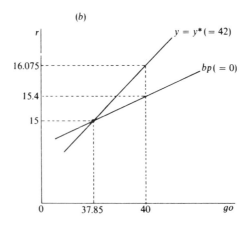

Figure A8.2.1 Result on internal and external balance of a rise in government spending.

Solving equations (A8.2.1) and (A8.2.2) gives the values for the instrument variables, namely,

1. $r = 15$
2. $go = 37.85$

It is to be noted, as mentioned in the text, that the slopes of both the internal and external balance lines are positive. Furthermore, the external balance line is *less steep* than the internal balance line. In particular, a rise in government spending from 37.85 to 40 will require a rise in the interest rate from 15 to 16.075 in order to maintain internal balance, but a rise from 15 to 15.4 to maintain external balance. All these results are shown in Fig. A8.2.1(a, b), where it is also noted that to maintain internal balance for a rise in government spending requires the nominal (and real) money supply to fall from 3 to 2.463; while for the same rise in government spending, the money supply must rise to 3.3 in order to maintain external balance. Hence, the difference in the response on the interest rate.

Next consider the result of a rise in the *actual* rate of inflation, say from zero to 5%. The situation is graphed in Fig. A8.2.2 and is based on the following results. The internal and external balance lines become:

$$\text{internal balance} \quad r = -4.1 + 0.5go \quad\quad\quad (A8.2.3)$$

$$\text{external balance} \quad r = 8.113 + 0.186go \quad\quad\quad (A8.2.4)$$

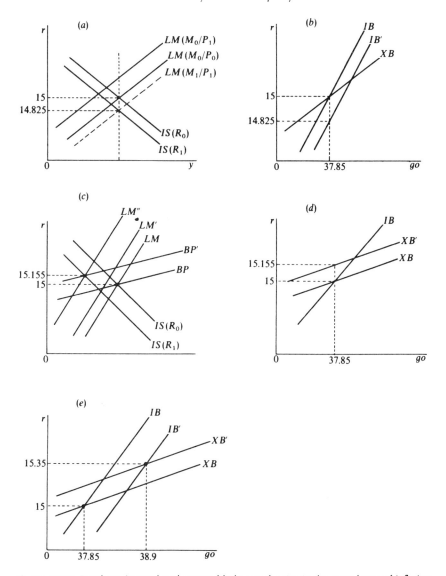

Figure A8.2.2 Result on internal and external balance of a rise in the actual rate of inflation.

Comparing equation (A8.2.3) with (A8.2.1) and equation (A8.2.4) with (A8.2.2) it can be seen that the internal balance line shifts down (to the right) while the external balance line shifts up (to the left). This situation is shown in Fig. A8.2.2 in terms of both the IS–LM–BP framework and in terms of instruments and targets. It is clear from Fig. A8.2.2(e) that inflation (or a rise in inflation) results in a rise in both the nominal interest rate *and* the level of real government spending necessary to maintain both internal and external balance. For the parameters given, the interest rate rises from 15 to 15.35 and real government spending rises from 37.85 to 38.90.

Part II

POLICY

Chapter 9

FISCAL POLICY

What is fiscal policy? How easy is it to implement? How do we measure the extent of fiscal policy? What is the link between fiscal policy and (1) monetary policy or (2) exchange rate policy? Who is responsible for the achievement of fiscal policy? What have been the major changes in fiscal policy since 1964? What is the role of fiscal policy? Is there a case for fiscal policy rules, and if so, what are they? Why is it that Keynesians favour centralized fiscal control while monetarists argue for no government control on efficiency grounds? Is there a logic behind the UK government's Medium-term Financial Strategy? These are just some of the questions we need to address in this chapter.

The topic of fiscal policy is a broad one and we must keep the discussion within bounds. Thus the main emphasis of this chapter is to consider the role of fiscal policy and what difficulties have been encountered in achieving such a role. In doing this we will inevitably consider a number of the questions raised in the preceding paragraph. In order to make the discussion concrete we will consider UK fiscal policy in particular, for only then can we consider specific difficulties which a government has encountered in trying to pursue its fiscal aims. Furthermore, it is not possible to discuss fiscal policy in the abstract. Countries have been imposing taxes and handing out subsidies for many years. Institutions in individual countries have arisen which are different in structure, function and organization. In addition, the aim of different governments is not the same.

This does not mean that the theory we have developed so far is totally irrelevant. On the contrary, we will consider fiscal policy in the light of the theory we have so far laid down – especially in the light of our analysis of Chapter 6. This point is worth stressing. The way one looks at policy is predicated on some model or other – whether formal or heuristic. Not only is this true of fiscal policy, it will be true of all the policy discussions in this part of the book. But we begin with an interpretation of fiscal policy and its role.

9.1 DEFINITION AND ROLE

In simple terms fiscal policy may be defined as any measure that alters the level, timing or composition of government spending and/or tax payments. This, however, is too broad. Under a fixed exchange rate system, any change in the exchange rate will alter the flow of trade and hence alter the tariff receipts from imported commodities on which duties are paid. But this would not be classified as fiscal policy – even though the measure altered the level of tax receipts. On the contrary, it would be treated as trade policy. But we can treat this effect on government taxes as *indirect*. What we are concerned with when we consider fiscal policy is *direct* measures which alter the level, timing or composition of government spending and/or tax payments.

It is possible to be more precise about the meaning of direct measures if we incorporate the institution which is responsible for implementing fiscal policy; namely, the Treasury. The British Treasury, although a Whitehall department, has functions which are not laid down by statute. The result of this is that its powers and responsibilities are a subject of confusion and argument, Brittan (1971).[1] However, from our present point of view, such confusion and argument resides within Whitehall rather than with the role of the Treasury in setting taxes and controlling government spending. Where the confusion and argument does impinge on our discussion is with regard to the role of, for example, the Medium-term Financial Strategy (MTFS), first introduced in the March budget of 1980.

The Treasury undertakes three forecasts of the economy during any one year, the most important being in February immediately prior to the budget. But more recently it has set out a Medium-term Financial Strategy. What is important about this strategy is that it was not so much a plan as a statement of government objectives. It did not, however, contain any information as to how these objectives would be achieved. We will discuss the MTFS in Section 9.4; the point being made here is that the Treasury not only takes responsibility for taxes and government spending, but it is also involved in setting policy objectives. How the various functions are dealt with within the Treasury is outlined in Appendix 9.1.

Even if we agree that fiscal policy broadly denotes measures undertaken by the Treasury which directly influence the level, timing and composition of government spending and/or tax payments, this does not indicate the *role* of fiscal policy. In other words, should fiscal policy be trying to achieve anything?

One of the major roles of fiscal policy has been in terms of stabilization. But exactly what is being stabilized? Is it the stabilization of aggregate demand or is it the stabilization of income? These are clearly not the same thing. Stabilization of aggregate demand refers to reducing fluctuations in the aggregate demand curve. On the other hand, as we indicated in Part I, income is determined by the short-run Phillips curve and the demand-pressure curve. Income stabilization, therefore, is not just a question of aggregate demand. The idea that income stabilization and stabilization of aggregate demand were one and the same arose from the simple analytics of aggregate demand and aggregate supply in which the aggregate supply curve was horizontal at some predetermined price level. Any instability in aggregate demand, therefore, would manifest itself in terms of an unstable income level. Where aggregate supply is upward sloping, and where account is taken of inflation, then we must distinguish between stabilization of aggregate demand and stabilization of income.

Although we will consider stabilization in more detail in Chapter 13, another consideration that must be borne in mind is the time period over which fiscal policy can be used to stabilize aggregate demand and/or income. If, as neoclassicists argue, the long-run aggregate supply curve is vertical at the natural level of income, then there is no need to attempt to stabilize income, since this will occur anyway. Of course, this does not rule out whether it is advisable to attempt to stabilize income in the short and medium terms. There is some evidence (see Demery and Duck, 1984, p. 20) that fiscal policy is effective in the short run but that it has little or no impact on income in the long run. The authors further conclude that there is some *prima facie* evidence for regarding fiscal policy (and monetary policy) as an instrument for income stabilization.

Another role of fiscal policy is in regard to the *distribution* of income or output, and not simply in the level of income or output. For example, it is possible for fiscal policy to discriminate in favour of investment. Such distributional questions involve value judgements on the part of the decision-makers.

The distributional role of fiscal policy is just part of a larger debate of what *is* the role of government in managing the economy. This even begs the question of whether a government should, in fact, attempt to manage the economy. We pointed out a moment ago that income stabilization and demand stabilization were often used synonymously. In the eyes of some people, fiscal policy was also synonymous with demand management of the economy. But this involves three premises, Blackaby (1979*a*):

1. The economy requires to be managed.
2. What has to be managed is aggregate demand.
3. The way to manage aggregate demand is by means of fiscal policy.

None of these propositions are obviously true. The first proposition involves a belief that a managed economy is somehow better than an unmanaged economy. The second proposition grew out of Keynesian macroeconomics which to a large extent underplayed the supply-side of the economy. The third proposition was also an outgrowth of Keynesian economics which stressed the importance of fiscal policy over monetary policy as a means of managing aggregate demand. That it is not the only way to influence aggregate demand, or the most significant way, is one of the controversies between Keynesians and monetarists.

The point being advanced here is that the role of fiscal policy must be seen in the broader context of the role of government.

An important feature of most Conservative governments has been that they see their role as improving efficiency. For example, under Mr Heath, the Conservative aim was to improve efficiency by changing the structure of taxation. What is significant about this approach to fiscal policy is that it is essentially thought of in *microeconomic* terms. However, in Heath's later period of office, when inflation rose and became a more prominent problem, policy switched to more macroeconomic solutions. Although the problem of inflation turned governments' attention to macroeconomic solutions, there have always been two completely opposing views about the allocative role of fiscal policy: one is that fiscal policy can be used to improve the performance of the economy, namely 'interventionism'; while the second is that markets are basically efficient and that the economy can be improved by keeping tax distortions down to an absolute minimum, namely the philosophy of 'neutrality'.

There is little doubt that Conservatives lean towards 'neutrality', while Labour leans towards 'interventionism'. The different philosophical approaches was clearly shown in the 1960s and 1970s. Labour's interventionist approach was clearly illustrated when it took office in 1964 under Harold Wilson, introducing corporation tax, capital gains tax and a selective employment tax. When the Conservatives came to office in 1970 under Mr Heath, they abolished the selective employment tax and modified corporation tax. When Labour returned to power in 1974, a policy of interventionism was again pursued, and when Mrs Thatcher came to power in 1979 a policy of non-intervention was followed. This constant oscillation between two extremes has led to greater political uncertainty in the UK and such reforms and counter-reforms have adversely affected industry, a point we will return to in Chapter 15.

We can summarize the various roles of government as follows:

1. To raise taxes to finance government spending.
2. As an instrument of stabilization.
3. As an allocative instrument.

9.2 BRIEF SUMMARY OF UK BUDGETARY POLICY 1964–87

The aim of this section is to briefly set out some of the major changes which have taken place in the UK with regard to budgetary policy since 1964.[2] Between 1964 and 1987 there have been two Labour administrations (1964–1970 and 1974–1979) and two Conservative administrations (1970–1974 and 1979–1987). Initially we will simply set out the changes and then go on to consider some broader features of budgetary policy in the light of these details.

1964–70 Labour

Prior to 1964 the dominant view was that taxation was too high (a view held by most Conservative governments). Furthermore, the view was also held that taxation should be used as a means of demand management. After 1964, however, the background to taxation policy was one of taxation to pay for rising public sector spending, considered necessary for the achievement of economic and social objectives. Fiscal policy became more interventionist and was used more explicitly as a means of income redistribution. At the time, increases in income tax were ruled out because of their adverse affect on savings and investment, and the main tax to be introduced was the selective employment tax, introduced in 1966. While in 1965 the company tax system was separated from the personal by the introduction of corporation tax (at 40%), and a double taxation on distributions was also introduced (with companies being made responsible for deducting the standard rate of income tax at source).

Throughout the period the balance of payments was a constant problem, and to a large extent dominated budgetary policy. After the devaluation of sterling in November 1967 a number of fiscal adjustments were implemented in order to release resources so that expenditure switching could take place. Taxes were increased in the 1968 budget, corporation tax was raised by $2\frac{1}{2}$% and in 1967–68 a special surcharge on investment income was added to surtax.

1970–74 Conservatives

When the Conservatives came to power in June 1970 they overturned a number of the tax changes implemented by preceding Labour administrations. One of their major aims was to simplify the tax structure, which they did in the 1973 budget by replacing income tax and surtax with a unified system of personal taxation, the 30% standard rate on earned income being redefined as the 'basic' rate, and a 75% maximum rate was set. They abolished purchase tax and selective employment tax (in two steps, in 1971–72 and 1973–74) and replaced these with a value added tax (introduced in 1973–74), which initially applied at a single rate of 10%, and brought Britain someway towards harmonization with the EEC. It was also supposed to make stabilization policy more effective. Finally, the same corporation tax rate applied to both distributed and undistributed profits, so abolishing a certain degree of double taxation.

1974–79 Labour

During this period Labour also introduced a number of major tax changes. Two new taxes were introduced: a petroleum revenue tax in 1974 and a development land tax in 1976. Furthermore, in 1975 the Labour government abolished estate duty and replaced it with a capital transfer tax. As inflation grew the government turned to two new innovations. First, it granted some income tax concessions in return for TUC support for a wage restraint. Second, personal allowances set against income tax liability were index linked (i.e., they were increased each year in line with the rise in the Retail Price Index over the previous calendar year). There were also a number of social reforms, including a new tax rate of 25% on the first £750 of taxable income in 1978, and in 1979 the system of child allowances was phased out and replaced by a system of child benefits of a fixed amount per child.

1979– Conservative

The major change in budgetary policy undertaken by the incoming Conservative government was a switch from direct to indirect taxation. The two main features of this were: first, a reduction in the basic rate of income tax from 33% to 30% (and, in 1986, to 29%); and, second, to increase value added tax to 15%. There was also a basic aim to reduce government expenditure. This was done within a Medium-term Financial Strategy, which was implemented in 1980. A major government expenditure is grants to local authorities. At the time, central government had no control over the current expenditure of local authorities, and so it exercised control indirectly by setting *cash limits*. These were first introduced in 1974–75 on certain central and local government building programmes. In 1976 they were linked to the rate support grant and supplementary grants paid to the local authorities. Furthermore, in the same year, cash limits were set on the capital expenditure of local authorities and nationalized industries. Thus, cash limits are a means by which the central government can *indirectly* control the expenditure of local authorities and nationalized industries. A further measure implemented by the Conservative government as a means of reducing expenditure on nationalized industries was to carry out a policy of privatization, a policy we will discuss in more detail in Chapter 15.

The budgetary changes just outlined only give a historical record. What is equally important is to see these changes as part of wider general trends in policy and different philosophical outlooks. The Labour administration of 1964 used fiscal policy as a means of achieving economic and social objectives: a 'healthy' foreign balance, stable prices and full employment; social justice for the needy, a fair distribution of taxation and the sound planning of public expenditure as a means of achieving sustained economic growth. At the time the aim was to achieve some sort of planning of the economy, embodied in the National Plan.[3] As a consequence, fiscal policy was more interventionist and there was a greater emphasis on income redistribution. Pressure on sterling mounted in the early years of Labour's administration, and policies were pursued (especially credit restraint) to transfer resources to the balance of payments without a cost to employment. Rising government spending continued and there was continued pressure on sterling. Sterling was eventually devalued in November 1967. At the same time, a policy of expenditure switching was implemented (see Chapter 8).

The period was characterized by an interventionist policy, rising government expenditure (see Fig. 9.3) and a recurring balance of payments problem. The major adjustment of the economy, which was considered necessary to safeguard the balance of payments, fell on private expenditure. The major new tax introduced was the selective employment tax. Cuts in expenditure were depended upon to deal with the balance of payments problem. As the private sector became depressed, so income fell and so, too, did imports.

When the Conservatives came to power in 1970 they saw that government intervention led to a rise (and, in their opinion, too high a level) of public spending. Furthermore, they believed the level of taxation was also too high. Conservatives have generally given more emphasis to the possible disincentive effects of high marginal tax rates. But a change in the marginal rate of tax has both an income effect and a substitution effect, which influence an individual's leisure in opposing ways: for a rise in the marginal rate of tax the substitution effect raises leisure hours (reduces hours worked), while the income effect reduces leisure hours (raises hours worked).[4] The Conservatives' policy is one of reducing the marginal rate of tax and raising the income tax and surtax thresholds. In line with its general principle of less taxation, the Conservative administration undid a number of the taxes implemented by preceding Labour administrations. Furthermore, there was some attempt to rationalize the tax structure.

It could not be said, however, that Conservative policy did not pursue a demand management approach. Demand management continued, albeit more cautiously, and was aimed at keeping demand roughly in line with productive potential. Growth became a major priority. With growth having been stimulated by measures taken in the 1971 budget, the momentum was continued with further measures in the 1972 budget (with a prospective rise in the rate of growth of 2 percentage points). But, as noted above, when the economy was stimulated a balance of payments deficit was the inevitable result. This difficulty was to be met if necessary by floating the exchange rate. As it turned out, pressure on sterling forced Britain to leave the snake (see Appendix 11.2), and in June 1972 sterling was allowed to float.[5] At this time inflation began to rise substantially, as did the rate of unemployment, convincing economists and policy-makers alike that the stability of the Phillips curve had broken down.

With the return of Labour in 1974 inflation became a major priority. However, from a fiscal point of view, the most important features of this period were: first, the income tax concessions given in return for TUC support for wage restraint; and, second, the fact that personal allowances set against income tax liability would be automatically index linked. Even so, a number of the fiscal policies pursued by the Labour administrations during this period were directed at a fairer distribution of income, especially the alleviation of the poverty trap. Once again, there was a general return to an interventionist policy, although the crisis in 1976 led the IMF to impose certain constraints on government fiscal and monetary policy.[6]

After the return of the Conservative government in 1979 there was once again a reversal of policy. There was a move to indirect taxation with income tax being reduced as a means of stimulating incentives, and an increase in VAT as a substitute. There was a definite objective to reduce government spending, both in terms of its growth and as a proportion of GDP. In line with this policy, one of the most significant changes was the introduction of cash limits as an indirect means of controlling the expenditure of local authorities and nationalized industries. Furthermore, there was a move to medium-term financial planning.

Given such changing budgetary policies since 1964 and such differing attitudes towards tax and government spending between Conservative and Labour, is there any evidence of changing fiscal stance over the period? Of course, fiscal *stance* is not the same as fiscal *policy*. Essentially, the latter involves using an econometric model to compare the actual path of the economy with some simulated path based on policy assumptions, such as holding fiscal instruments constant. Fiscal stance, on the other hand, measures 'the impact of all changes in government receipts and expenditure, other than those which arise directly from fluctuations in aggregate activity'. (Biswas *et al.*, 1985, p. 55) Thus, fiscal policy is but one determinant of fiscal stance. Even so, there has generally been a desire to have a single indicator of fiscal stance. We discussed some of these and the difficulties attached to them in Chapter 6; here our intention is simply to discuss what such typical indicators reveal about the period 1964–84.

Indicators of fiscal stance have been computed for the UK by Biswas *et al.* (1985), from which the following comments are based. Fig. 9.1 shows two graphs based on yearly data, one for the unadjusted fiscal deficit as a percentage of GDP (at market prices), and labelled *UD* (for unadjusted deficit). The second graph shows the same fiscal deficit, but adjusted for different weightings of government expenditure and taxes and also cyclically adjusted as a percentage of GDP (at market prices), and denoted *WD* + *CD* (for weighted deficit and cyclically adjusted deficit combined).[7] It would appear that, in general, fiscal stance has been countercyclical, with two exceptions. The first was under the Barber boom of the early 1970s when expansion reinforced a strong cyclical upturn. The second was in 1980–81 when a contractionary fiscal stance reinforced a sharp downturn. The downward movement of the *WD* + *CD* graph after 1980 would suggest that the *level* of budgetary stance continued to be deflationary to the end of the period covered by the data.

What is most characteristic of this brief summary is the two opposing approaches to budgetary policy as a means of managing the economy; and the fact that the economy has been put through a rather long period of reform and counter-reform. Part of the reason for this is because fiscal policy has been a major instrument ('the' major instrument) in achieving too many simultaneous objectives. Prior to 1979 the major emphasis of fiscal policy was on balancing short-run demand. The success or otherwise of such stabilization will be discussed in Chapter 13, but it should not be concluded that a medium-term strategy is the necessary alternative. The history of this period indicates that at various times medium-term policies have been pursued, usually under Conservative administrations which attempted to stimulate economic growth. During such periods short-term stabilization has been compromised. It is not at all obvious that there has been any improvement. A more concerted medium-term policy, as under the Conservative administration after 1979, requires more justification, and we will consider this in Section 9.4.

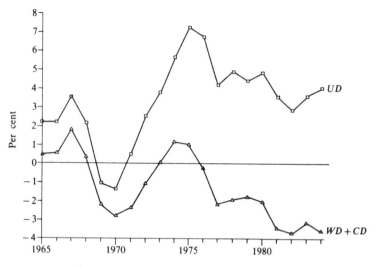

Figure 9.1 UK indicators of fiscal stance, 1965–84.

9.3 THE PSBR AND THE MONEY SUPPLY

It was pointed out in Chapter 6 that the government budget constraint links monetary and fiscal policy very closely. The budgetary decisions we have just discussed in the preceding section determine the size of the public sector borrowing requirement (PSBR), while monetary policy determines how the PSBR is to be financed. The connection between the PSBR and the money supply is worth discussing for two reasons. First, it helps in coming to a fuller understanding of the government budget constraint and seeing in what sense it *is* a constraint. Second, it lays down some useful background for discussing the Conservative government's Medium-term Financial Strategy.

Table 9.1 provides a summary of the counterpart to changes in sterling $M3$ (now denoted $M3$, see Fig. 7.6) in relation to the PSBR for the period 1963–86. Of course, these figures give pure accounting conventions.

Analysis of the figures begins by approaching the accounts in terms of three definitions lying behind the flow of funds, Cuthbertson, (1985).[8] Expressed in the changes in money terms (all sterling) they are: (1) the change in sterling $M3$; and, (2) the PSBR. Combining these we derive an expression for the change in sterling $M3$ and the PSBR. Thus,

$$d\pounds M3 \equiv dBL_p + dBL_g + dC_p \tag{9.1}$$

$$PSBR \equiv dG_p + dC_p - dRs + dBL_g \tag{9.2}$$

combining equations (9.1) and (9.2) we get

$$d\pounds M3 \equiv PSBR - dG_p + dRs + dBL_p \tag{9.3}$$

where

$\pounds M3$ = sterling $M3$;

BL_p = sterling bank lending to the UK non-bank private sector;

Table 9.1 Relationship between M3 and PSBR, 1964–87

£ million

Year	PSBR (1)	Purchases by UK NBPS of public and central government debt (2)	External and foreign currency financing of public sector (3)	Banks' sterling lending to UK NBPS (4)	External and foreign currency transactions of UK banks (5)	Net non-deposit sterling liabilities (6)	Domestic counterparts (7)	External and foreign currency counterpart (8)	M3 (9)
1963	834	1	..	..	..	..	..	..	1052
1964	980	−122	−87	..	..	..	..	..	654
1965	1170	0	5	..	..	..	..	..	887
1966	949	115	9	..	..	..	..	..	432
1967	1844	−304	−8	..	..	..	..	..	1239
1968	1252	310	13	..	..	..	..	..	1044
1969	−534	−92	−163	..	..	..	..	..	299
1970	−51	−58	−53	..	..	..	..	..	1494
1971	1320	−2312	−137	..	..	..	..	..	2412
1972	1950	−780	−173	..	..	..	..	..	4835
1973	4093	−1406	−116	..	..	..	..	..	6591
1974	6452	−858	19	..	..	..	..	..	3313
1975	10162	−5528	−1020	−365	−4	−392	4268	100	1215
1976	8938	−5711	−2963	3407	997	−1125	6634	−1966	3533
1977	5463	−8417	5531	3188	−1654	−337	234	3877	3769
1978	8436	−6035	−985	4698	1560	−972	7099	575	6703
1979	12681	−10959	641	8585	−3531	−768	10307	−2890	6653
1980	11823	−9435	−11	10025	−633	−1169	12413	−644	10595
1981	10590	−11325	−1069	11405	916	−1211	10670	−153	9295
1982	4924	−10590	−1323	17556	−1592	−1460	11890	−2915	7515
1983	11635	−10819	−1568	13590	−719	−1952	14406	−2287	9480
1984	10240	−11148	−1617	17140	−1987	−2182	16232	−3604	9847
1985	7526	−7784	−3139	20951	500	−3013	20693	−2639	15058
1986	2300	−3544	−1953	30755	−488	−3775	29501	−2441	23051
1987	−1398	−479	6131	38651	−3668	−4640	36813	2670	34624

Note: The relationship between columns is 7 = 1 + 2 + 4; 8 = 3 + 5; 9 = 6 + 7 + 8 (however, there appear many discrepancies in the official figures as recorded here)

.. indicates data not available

Source: *Economic Trends, Annual Supplement* 1988, and *Financial Statistics*.

BL_g = sterling bank lending to the government;
C_p = cash held by the non-bank private sector;
Rs = sterling from the sale of foreign currency reserves;
G_p = sale of government debt to the non-bank private sector.

What identity (9.3) illustrates is that the change in £$M3$ can come about through fiscal changes (PSBR), debt sales to the non-bank private sector (dG_p), dealings in the foreign exchange market (dRs) and by the Central Bank influencing bank lending to the private sector, which it does through interest rate changes.

In the period to 1979 the PSBR was not used as an instrument of policy – nor as an intermediate target. What appeared to be the case was that monetary policy and fiscal policy were set independently of one another. The former was determined by the Bank of England and the latter by the Treasury. Of course, what identity (9.3) reveals is that something had to be the residual if this accounting definition was to be preserved – which it had to be . If £$M3$ is a policy objective (an intermediate target) and the PSBR is determined by fiscal policy, this leaves dG_p, dRs and dBL_p. However, the Bank of England did not wish long-term interest rates on government debt to fluctuate. This constrains the change in debt sales to the private sector (dG_p). Furthermore, under a freely floating exchange rate there is (theoretically at least) no change in the reserves (d$Rs = 0$). Hence, it follows that the residual had to be sterling bank lending to the non-bank private sector. The money supply could therefore be altered by the government engaging in open market operations. A reduction in the money supply could be achieved by the government selling Treasury bills to the non-bank private sector. This would reduce the deposits of the commercial banks and also the bankers' balances at the Bank of England, which would in turn lead to a rise in interest rates. The rise would be further enhanced as commercial banks attempted to obtain 'cash' by selling short-term bills – which would be accepted by the Bank of England at the penal rate if the public would not take them up. The rise in interest rates reduced the demand for advances and hence the money stock.

There are three difficulties with the argument just advanced. First, it implies that the commercial banks were fully loaned up and hence when the government engaged in open market operations banks were forced to sell short-term bills. As we discussed in Chapter 7, commercial banks are profit maximizing institutions which have a spectrum of assets and liabilities. It is not at all clear that banks are fully loaned up in practice. Second, the argument does not take account of the presence of the discount houses which act as intermediaries between the commercial banks and the Bank of England. Nor for that matter does it take account of the presence of non-bank financial intermediaries which, as we discussed in Chapter 7, have a bearing on the money multipliers. Third, although in theory a freely floating exchange rate leads to a zero change in the reserves, this is far from true in practice. As the market adjusts there is a resultant buying or selling of foreign exchange reserves. Depending on the adjustment in the foreign exchange market, this could be quite small. On the other hand, any deliberate intervention in the foreign exchange market, either to influence the trend rate or to iron out excessive fluctuations, would lead to a change in the reserves arising from a deliberate policy. We return to this point in the final section of this chapter.

What we conclude from this section is that it is not possible for a government to pursue independent monetary and fiscal policy. Furthermore, the more objectives a government has the more equation (9.3) becomes constrained. As we discuss in Section 9.5, a monetary rule also requires a consistent fiscal rule. But consistency between a monetary and fiscal rule is not sufficient. Equation (9.3) illustrates that a change in the reserves can influence either £M3 or the PSBR and hence consistency would also require an exchange rate rule. What we must look into later is exactly what these rules might be.

9.4 THE MEDIUM-TERM FINANCIAL STRATEGY

In the UK after 1979 there was a conscious move away from short-term demand management of the economy to medium-term policies (and with it an emphasis on supply-side policies). The policies carried through under two Conservative parliaments, under the leadership of Mrs Thatcher, became known as the 'Thatcher Experiment'.[9] It was, it must be emphasized, a series of policies with implications for all sectors of the economy. It is not the intention here to analyse the experiment as a whole. All we wish to do is concentrate on the Medium-term Financial Strategy (MTFS) introduced in the March budget of 1980.

Although it is referred to as a 'financial strategy' it was not a strategy at all. It was no more than a statement of the government's objectives. The budget of 1980 set a target rate of growth for sterling $M3$ (7–11% for 1980–81, 6–10% for 1982–83; and 4–8% for 1983–84). Furthermore, it set a target for the PSBR as a percentage of GDP. This was to decline from its $5\frac{1}{2}$% figure for 1978–79 to $3\frac{3}{4}$% in 1980–81 to $1\frac{1}{2}$% in 1983–84. It in no way outlined how these objectives would be obtained. (It would be a strange 'strategy' indeed which simply said 'we will take the Island' but did not outline a plan to carry it out!) It did, however, have one important element, and that was the underlying causal beliefs of the government (or, more accurately, the Treasury).

The general steps followed in setting out the MTFS are as follows (Budd, 1984, p. 14):

1. The government makes assumptions about (a) the desirable and feasible path for inflation, and (b) the growth of nominal income.
2. It determines what monetary growth is consistent with the growth in nominal income.
3. It decides what path for the PSBR is consistent with the growth of the money supply and with its desire to reduce interest rates.

It is likely, of course, that some iterations are allowed for.

The MTFS had three basic premises underlying it; these are follows:

1. There is a predictable and causal relationship between changes in the growth of £M3 and inflation.
2. Public sector borrowing is the prime determinant of the growth in £M3.
3. Public sector borrowing levels are the prime determinant of interest rate levels.

We have discussed the first proposition elsewhere, but it is central to all the thinking of the Thatcher experiment. The second proposition is by no means self-evident. In the preceding section we established the link between a change in the money supply and the PSBR. But this is an accounting relationship. It is quite a different matter to say that the PSBR is the *cause* of changes in the money supply. Even taking a simple correlation between changes in the money supply and the PSBR for data given in Table 9.1 we get 0.002, which indicates no significant (linear) correlation.[10] Furthermore, a regression cannot establish causation. It is quite possible to construct a scenario where both £$M3$ and the PSBR are changing, but changing because of changes in the pattern of trade (and hence in the reserves). Finally, it may be the case that the PSBR has a certain degree of influence on the level of interest rates, but it is not the *only* thing which determines interest rates, as we explained in Chapter 7. Thus, it is not surprizing to find commentators saying such things as: 'Experience was very shortly to suggest – or confirm – that all three propositions were of doubtful validity.' (Keegan, 1984, p. 145)

Now although the validity of the three propositions is doubtful, there is one additional element of the strategy that requires mention. It could be argued that the MTFS was more a means of dealing with expectations, which was why it emphasized the *medium* term. If people believed that the government would succeed in bringing down the rate of growth of sterling $M3$ and that they would reduce the level of the PSBR as a percentage of GDP, then this in turn would most likely bring down the expected rate of inflation, which would in turn bring down the actual rate of inflation. Thus, it does not matter whether any of the three propositions actually hold; what matters is that people believe that as a package, they will bring down the rate of inflation. The view that rational expectations (see Chapter 4) underlay the MTFS was given by Alan Walters when he wrote:

> The idea, based on the concepts of rational expectations, was that the announcement of these target rates of growth of the money supply etc. would induce entrepreneurs, investors and workers to adjust their behaviour to the new policy as though it were a *new* reality. (Quoted from Holmes, 1985, p. 53)

By the budget of 1982 the MTFS was still operating but the original targets had been relaxed and the strategy was interpreted more flexibly. In addition, rather than concentrate solely on sterling $M3$, a number of monetary variables came in for discussion ($M1$, £$M3$ and $PSL2$) with no clear idea as to how policy was to be assessed in relation to some or all of them. On the other hand, the growth targets for the PSBR stayed closer to what was laid down in the 1980 budget. What remained clear, however, was that the target for the PSBR in relation to GDP was determined largely by the government's objective about monetary growth. With the relaxation in targeting of sterling $M3$, more attention switched to the target for the PSBR, and it could be argued that the PSBR, far from supporting sterling $M3$, began to supplant it as the main objective of policy, Savage (1980). Of course, the targets being discussed within the MTFS were not about objectives – in the sense of referring to such things as inflation, unemployment, balance of payments, etc. – but, rather, were concerned with *intermediate* targets considered necessary for the achievement of final objectives. The success of such a policy thus depends upon whether there exist stable statistical relationships between intermediate targets and final objectives.

Later budgets reiterated the importance of the MTFS, but introduced some amendments. In 1983 the budget gave target ranges for $M1$, £$M3$, and $PSL2$. But it also mentioned the exchange rate as an important indicator. By the budget of 1984 attention switched to monetary aggregates $M0$ and £$M3$ (since $M1$ appeared to be growing too rapidly), and we find the rather vague phrase that there would be a commitment to 'maintain the main thrust' of the MTFS. In 1985 the exchange rate re-appeared in the list of monetary indicators subject to policy surveillance, a point we will pursue in Section 9.7. Furthermore, it was in this year that a target was first set for money GDP, although the reason why this should become an indicator was not given.[11] Although the 1985 budget was a reassertion of the faith in the MTFS, its justification was brought somewhat into doubt by the pronouncement that 'there is nothing sacrosanct about the precise mix of monetary and fiscal policies required to meet the objectives of the Medium-term Financial Strategy' which contradicts the notion that there is a relationship between the budget deficit and the rate of growth of the money supply. By autumn of 1985, $£M3$ was abandoned as a target variable and it became clear that the exchange rate would begin to play a more important role in the MTFS. In the budget of 1986 a target range was given for $£M3$, which was at a much higher level than was expected, but no target was set beyond 1986–87. However, target ranges were set for $M0$, with a falling target range over the coming years. It is revealing to note that once again the link between monetary growth and the rate of inflation was stressed. Mr Lawson, the then Chancellor of the Exchequer, once again stressed the importance of reducing the growth of money GDP. What was clearly hoped was that this reduction would come about through a reduction in the rate of inflation rather than a decline in the rate of growth of real output. This, however, was more a belief than based on any hard evidence.

In the early years of the Conservative administration the PSBR became a cornerstone of the MTFS, and certainly had persistent targets set for a decline in the PSBR as a percentage of GDP. Although the PSBR is difficult to predict, its target value had remained quite constant. However, this was achieved largely through a 'fiscal adjustment' which was made in each budget. Even so, by 1986 the PSBR became a rather meaningless figure because of government sales of public sector assets. Central privatization proceeds rose from £377 million in 1979–80 to £2091 million in 1984–85, and was projected to rise to £4750 million in each of the years 1986–87 to 1988–89 (King, 1986, p. 26).

The fact that the government set target growths for the PSBR in relation to GDP (the ratio *PSBR–Y*) made the strategy difficult to justify on logical grounds. There had, of course, been growing arguments linking inflation to the growth of the money supply. But exactly what this implied about the *PSBR–Y* ratio was not at all clear. Miller (1981, 1982) had made some attempt to place a logical reasoning on the strategy, but this was very much an ex-post rationalization. (His argument was that on some extreme assumptions the fiscal plans could be interpreted as a strategy for balancing the *inflation adjusted* budget.) The basis from the government's point of view was the belief that the main component of $£M3$ was the PSBR and that to bring down the growth in $£M3$ the PSBR had to be reduced. How this became translated into a particular level for *PSBR–Y* is more difficult to justify. In Appendix 9.2 we present one attempt to justify the fiscal component of the MTFS, based on the paper by Congdon (1984), and discussed in some detail in Budd, Dicks and Keating (1985).

The conclusion that one inevitably comes to about the MTFS is that it was based on a series of beliefs which had only a thin underlying rationale. Initially the monetary target became important in itself, rather than the final objective on which it was supposed to operate – namely inflation. But the particular indicator of monetary stance was constantly changing. Although the PSBR as a percentage of GDP remained a target, this became meaningless with the sale of government public sector assets. The belief that the exchange rate could be left to market forces was explicitly buried in 1985 when Nigel Lawson said that 'benign neglect is not an option'. What can be said in favour of the MTFS is that it imposed a certain discipline on the government with regard to its spending (some, of course, would say too stringent a discipline) and that this in turn affected people's expectations with regard to future rates of inflation.

9.5 FISCAL RULES

With the rise in monetarism, especially in the UK and the USA, there has been considerable interest in the use of rules as an alternative to demand management of the Keynesian type. We will discuss the more general debate of rules versus discretion in Chapter 13 on stabilization. Here our concern is more narrow. What we wish to consider is whether any fiscal rules have been suggested, what they are, and why these particular rules have been suggested. In so far as we are concerned about why particular rules have been suggested, a major element of this is *consistency* of different policy rules. Economic policy is a mix, in particular, between monetary, fiscal and exchange rate policy. There has been a number of rules suggested for monetary policy, which we will discuss in the next chapter, but fiscal and exchange rate policy have had far less attention. We consider exchange rate rules in more detail in Chapter 11. What, then, are the fiscal rules which have been suggested?

Let us begin with an extreme situation. Suppose we have a government that wishes to attain a long-run stationary steady state. What would be the characteristic features of this long-run stationary steady state? Because the economy is long run, then it would be on the long-run Phillips curve with income at the natural level. Since we are dealing with a *stationary* steady state, real income would not be growing. If it was a true steady state, then inflation would be zero and prices would be constant. But this could occur in the long run only if there were no growth in the money supply. Hence, the nominal money supply would be constant. Hence, the LM curve (which is a function of real money balance, as we showed in Part I) would be fixed. To sustain the situation in the long run at a stationary steady state, real interest rates must be constant (and since inflation is zero this means nominal interest rates would need to be constant). If they were not, then investment would change and so, too, would income. Forces would be set up to bring income back to its former level, and the same would be true of the rate of interest. But the rate of interest can remain constant only if there is no further issue of government debt (where we are assuming some already exists). This, of course, means that there can be no further financing of government spending from the issue of government bonds. This particular rate of interest is the 'natural' rate of interest (in the Wicksellian sense[12]). What it means in terms of the static and dynamic model we developed in Part I, is that the IS and LM curves intersect at the natural level of income and the natural rate of interest. The demand-pressure curve and the short-run Phillips curve intersect on the horizontal axis at the natural level of income. The situation is shown in Fig. 9.2(*a,b*). With no shocks to the system, this situation can continue indefinitely.

What are the implications of this result for fiscal policy? For the moment let us ignore the fact that a government deficit can be financed from changes in the reserves or from the sale of public assets. This means that the only means of financing the budget deficit is either by raising high-powered money or issuing new government bonds. But both of these have been ruled out in our long-run stationary economy. It follows, then, that for such an economy we require that all government spending be matched by tax receipts, i.e.

$$g_c + tr + ip = t \tag{9.4}$$

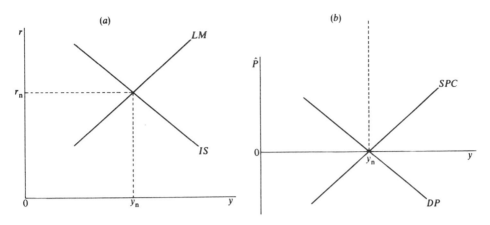

Figure 9.2 Equilibrium in a long-run stationary economy.

where all variables are in real terms and follow the notation of Chapter 6. Of course, equation (9.4) is no more than a balanced budget.

Let us just return to the two provisos we made: (1) selling off public assets; and (2) financing government spending from a change in the reserves. The sale of public assets is clearly a one-off event and cannot continue in the long run since very soon all assets would be in private hands. This, then, can only be a short-run financial arrangement. Turning to the second. If we consider a two-good, two-country world, and that both countries are in a long-run stationary state, then it follows that inflation in both countries is zero and hence the price level in both countries is constant. By the condition of absolute purchasing power parity (see Section 5.3), the exchange rate is constant and determined by the ratio of the two countries' prices. Furthermore, in this very special case interest parity should hold. Interest rates in the two countries are constant, as explained above. The exchange rate is constant. There should, then, be no divergence between the spot and forward exchange rates. The forward premium would be zero and (real) interest rates would be the same in the two countries (the Fisher condition[13]). There would therefore be equilibrium on the balance of payments and there are no reserve changes! Thus, even for an open economy in a long-run stationary state, we still arrive at the rule for fiscal policy as one of a balanced budget.

We have laboured this result because it is by far the most common (and popular) fiscal rule which has been advocated. What is not so often made clear are the conditions under which it is true. One fiscal rule is, therefore

Fiscal Rule 1A
Set fiscal instruments such that the budget is balanced.

This rule holds whether the economy is closed or open – although if open it requires that all countries are in a long-run stationary state with zero inflation and following the same fiscal rule. (Also note, that in terms of the MTFS, if the budget deficit is approximately equated with the PSBR, then this fiscal rule implies a PSBR as a percentage of GDP of zero!)

As we pointed out in Chapter 6, there are a number of shortcomings in just looking at the budget deficit or surplus. One alternative that has been proposed is the full-employment budget deficit or surplus, which we also discussed in Chapter 6. Using this definition of a budget deficit or surplus, a slight variant on Fiscal Rule 1A is possible by setting a full-employment balanced budget rule (or what in the US would be high employment balanced budget rule). Thus, we have an alternative

Fiscal Rule 1B
Set fiscal instruments so that the full employment budget is balanced.

There is, of course, the more practical problem attached to Rules 1A and 1B of whether the balance should be achieved each year, over the business cycle, or over some arbitrary period, such as five years.

We demonstrated in Part I that even in the long run there is no necessity for inflation and the growth in money supply to be zero. With a vertical Phillips curve at the natural rate of income, inflation can be determined by governments. What must be the case, in the long run, is that the rate of growth of money supply must equal the rate of growth of inflation. In other words, the demand-pressure curve and the short-run Phillips curve intersect on the long-run Phillips curve at the point where the rate of monetary growth is equal to the rate of inflation. In this case the budget need not balance; on the contrary, the deficit is equal to the level of high-powered money which generates a rate of growth of money supply equal to the chosen rate of inflation.

We thus arrive at a second (long-run) fiscal rule, namely

Fiscal Rule 2A
If inflation in the long run is targeted at some particular (positive) level, then set fiscal instruments such that the budget deficit is equal to the growth in high powered money that is consistent with the target rate of inflation.

Or, in terms of the full-employment budget deficit

Fiscal Rule 2B
If inflation in the long run is targeted at some particular (positive) level, then set fiscal instruments such that the full-employment budget deficit is equal to the growth in high-powered money that is consistent with the target rate of inflation.

However, care must be exercised in interpreting these results. In the first instance it implies that there is a fixed relationship between the money supply, say £$M3$, and high-powered money i.e. £$M3 = qM0$, as discussed in Chapter 7. Thus, if inflation is set to grow at 5%, then high-powered money can grow at 5% (so long as q is constant), which in turn is the size of the budget deficit which can be financed from this expansion in the money base. If there is no fixed relationship between the money base and such broad definitions of the money supply, then it is no longer clear what 'consistency' means and, hence, exactly which rule is being followed.

Even if there is a fixed rule between the money base and a broad definition of money, the rule can only hold for an open economy under further restrictions. First, the exchange rate must be freely floating. If this were not so then it is quite possible for deficits (or surpluses) to occur on the balance of payments which will lead to decreases (or increases) in the domestic money supply, and so prevent the rule operating. Second, with freely floating exchange rates, exchange rate changes will be determined by relative purchasing power parity (relative PPP), i.e. $\hat{S} = \hat{P} - \hat{P}*$ (see Chapter 5). But by interest rate parity and market efficiency (see Chapter 5), $\hat{S} - r* - r$. Combining these two results means that $r - \hat{P} = r* - \hat{P}*$, i.e. there must be equal *real* rates of interest.[14] But if inflation is a policy target, then there is no reason why relative PPP should hold and no reason why real interest rates would be equalized. This, in turn, would lead to capital flows and hence a problem for the monetary rule being advocated and followed. To avoid this likelihood, it would be necessary to coordinate macroeconomic policy between trading countries. Not only would this mean losing sovereignty over monetary policy, it would also mean constraints on fiscal and budgetary policy. In particular, the different countries would require to have consistent fiscal policies, and hence consistent fiscal rules. It is apparent, therefore, that any fiscal rule of the kind suggested under Rules 2A and 2B would only succeed for an open economy under rather stringent conditions. If these conditions are not met, and there is no reason to believe they would be in today's world, then it does not follow that abiding by such a rule would be any improvement on the present attempts at demand management.

It is also worth noting the implication of Rule 2B for the MTFS. For a target rate of inflation, this would imply a certain rate of growth for high-powered money (equal to the rate of growth of broad money). If the PSBR is equated with the budget deficit, this implies a certain level of PSBR relative to the full-employment level of income. Hence, the $PSBR-Y_f$ ratio, where Y_f is the full-employment level of GDP, must be consistent with the chosen rate of inflation. Furthermore, the target rate of growth for nominal GDP (Y) must not be inconsistent with these other conditions!

What might a rule be for a growing economy? Here we shall be fairly brief. In a growing economy it is approximately true that

$$£\hat{M}3 = \hat{P} + \hat{y} \qquad (9.5)$$

If $£M3 = qM0$, and if q is constant, then it follows that

$$£\hat{M}3 = \hat{M}0 \qquad (9.6)$$

Hence, the growth of money base consistent with a target rate of inflation is

$$\hat{M}0 = (\hat{P}^* + \hat{y}) \qquad (9.7)$$

where $\hat{P}^*$ is the target rate of inflation. In this economy there is no bond financed budget deficit; all budget deficits are financed from increases in high-powered money consistent with the target rate of inflation. Hence, the budget deficit is equal to

$$bd = dM0 = M0 \cdot \hat{M}0 = M0(\hat{P}^* + \hat{y}) \qquad (9.8)$$

We have, therefore, a third fiscal rule

Fiscal Rule 3
Set fiscal instruments at such a level that the budget deficit is equal to

$$bd = M0(\hat{P}^* + \hat{y})$$

Notice that this result is consistent with our discussions above. Under Rules 1A and 1B, both $\hat{P}^*$ and $\hat{y}$ are zero, and hence the $bd = 0$. Under Rules 2A and 2B, $\hat{y} = 0$ and there is a target rate of inflation of $\hat{P}^*$, hence the budget deficit is given by

$$bd = M0 \cdot \hat{P}^* \qquad (9.9)$$

To see these results in line with the MTFS which we discussed above, suppose the real PSBR is written psbr, and is approximately equal to the real budget deficit, bd. Then the real psbr relative to the natural rate of income, y_n, is given by,

$$bd/y_n = psbr/y_n = (M0/y_n)(\hat{P}^* + \hat{y}_n) \tag{9.10}$$

which is very similar to a result given by Congdon (1984).

However, for a growing economy result (9.10) does not take account of the fact that it is an open economy. In other words, result (9.10) either applies to a closed economy, or only holds for an open economy under additional restrictions, although we will not discuss these additional restrictions here.

9.6 SIZE OF THE PUBLIC SECTOR

In Section 6.5 we briefly introduced some ideas on the size of the public sector. Here our intention is to pursue the discussion from a purely policy perspective. There is no doubt that in the 1980s there was a strong move in both the UK and the US, as well as in a number of European countries, to reduce the size of the public sector. The reason for this was the observation that in many Western countries there was a rise in the size of the public sector – no matter how it was measured. This seemed to support 'Wagner's law' – namely, that public spending tends to grow faster than the rate of the economy in general. In more specific terms, the ratio of government spending to income tends to rise. Of course, in establishing whether this is true, even in a statistical sense, it is necessary to come to some agreement on what is to be included in government spending and which particular level of income should be used in the denominator. Even so, there has been quite a dramatic rise in the ratio of government spending to GNP for the UK, rising from 8.9% in 1890 to 30% at the beginning of the Second World War, Burton (1985), and to a peak of 54.4% by 1982, falling thereafter. A similar pattern can be found in most European countries. Such a rise in government spending relative to income would occur if the elasticity of government spending with respect to income were greater than unity. For the period 1960–87, using annual data on general government spending and GDP at factor cost, both deflated by the RPI, the elasticity is 1.48, which is slightly greater than that indicated by Levitt (1984), although he considers the period 1961–82.[15]

A closer look at the period since 1964 shows not only that the ratio of general government spending to GDP (at factor cost) has been rising, at least up until 1982, but that it has risen cyclically, as shown in Fig. 9.3. It must be pointed out, however, that there has been quite a difference in the movement of components of government spending over this period, as shown in Table 9.2. The most notable rise has been in transfers (not including interest payment on national debt). Levitt (1984) indicates that the second major source of the rise in government spending relative to GDP is from the *relative price effect*. In other words, the average prices of government spending have risen more than the general price level, so that even with a constant volume, nominal government spending to nominal GDP will rise. This readily follows from the fact that if

$$g = G/P_g \quad \text{and} \quad y = Y/P \tag{9.11}$$

where P_g is the average price of government spending, P the general price level, G nominal government spending, g real government spending, Y nominal GDP and y real GDP, then

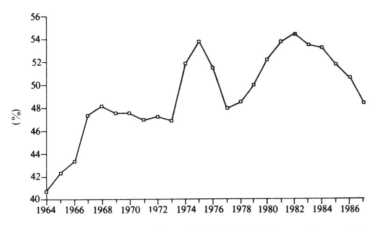

Figure 9.3 General government spending to GDP (*fc*), 1964–87 *Source: Economic Trends.*

Table 9.2 The components of UK government spending, 1964–87 (percentage ratios with respect to GDP at factor cost)

Year	Expenditure on goods and services g_c/y	Current and capital transfers tr/y	Debt interest ip/y	Net lending, etc. nl/y	Total government expenditure g/y
1964	23.3	10.4	4.3	2.7	40.7
1965	23.8	11.2	4.3	3.0	42.3
1966	24.6	11.2	4.4	3.1	43.3
1967	26.1	13.0	4.5	3.7	47.3
1968	25.9	14.3	4.7	3.2	48.1
1969	25.7	14.5	4.8	2.5	47.5
1970	26.1	14.0	4.6	2.8	47.5
1971	25.7	13.6	4.2	3.4	46.9
1972	25.9	14.4	4.1	2.9	47.2
1973	26.2	14.1	4.1	2.3	46.8
1974	27.9	16.3	4.6	3.0	51.8
1975	29.4	16.2	4.3	3.9	53.8
1976	28.6	16.2	4.7	2.1	51.5
1977	26.6	16.2	4.9	0.2	47.9
1978	25.6	17.0	4.8	1.1	48.5
1979	25.7	17.1	5.1	1.9	49.8
1980	27.4	17.6	5.5	1.7	52.2
1981	27.5	19.1	5.8	1.2	53.7
1982	27.4	19.9	5.9	1.2	54.4
1983	27.8	20.0	5.5	0.3	53.7
1984	27.6	20.4	5.7	−0.6	53.2
1985	26.7	19.9	5.7	−0.6	51.8
1986	27.1	19.4	5.4	−1.3	50.6
1987	26.5	18.7	5.1	−1.9	48.4

Source: Economic Trends, Annual Supplement, 1986 and May 1988

$$G/Y = (P_g \cdot g)/(P \cdot y) = (P_g/P)(g/y) \qquad (9.12)$$

Thus, G/Y will rise if P_g rises relative to P for a given value of g/y.

Conservatives have always been concerned about the size of the public sector, even more so under Mrs Thatcher. The focus on the size of the public sector became acute when in

1976 the Treasury announced that government spending was approaching 60% of GDP. As it turned out, this figure was a mistake but it did highlight the problem, assuming one saw it as a problem.[16] The main worry was that a high level of public spending would be a threat to individual freedom as the state encroached more and more on the allocation of economic resources. This theme was prominent in the speeches made by Mrs Thatcher and Sir Keith Joseph during the period 1975–79.

In the MTFS, introduced in 1980, a clear series of reductions in planned government spending were laid out, with a reduction in volume terms over the four years 1979–80 to 1983–84. As a means of ensuring this, cash limits were imposed, as Section 9.2 outlined. If spending rose beyond the cash limits, then the volume would have to be reduced. In 1981–82 the first cut in the volume of spending occurred, since until then it had simply been a question of reducing the planned levels of previous administrations. As it turned out, general government spending as a percentage of GDP actually rose relative to the level when the Conservatives came to power in 1979! By 1984 there was a change in strategy. The aim was to hold government spending in real terms. The ratio of government spending to GDP could still be reduced if the rate of inflation was held constant and low and there was a rise in output (which together would mean a rise in nominal GDP, arising largely from a growth in output, and a fall in the $G–GDP$ ratio[17]). As it turned out, planned government expenditures were not achieved and, as has persistently happened in the past, actual levels exceeded planned targets. From the evidence to date there does not seem any reason to suppose that such overshooting of planned targets will not persist into the future.

In 1983 Mr Nigel Lawson was quite concerned about the spending levels of his colleagues, and called for a national debate on the question. Burton (1985) points out that this was an implicit statement of failure to curb the spending plans of his own colleagues and that the pressures to raise government spending were just too great. It appears that so long as there is not an overall commitment to a reduction in government spending, then Wagner's law will continue to hold sway.

A similar debate was taking place in the USA. There the debate crystallized in 1982 into a Senate resolution on a constitutional amendment. It was in two parts: first, that budgets should be balanced; second, that government spending as a percentage of GDP be set at 20%. These two policy proposals are often suggested as a 'package', but they should be seen as quite distinct. One can readily oppose a balanced budget (see Rules 2A and 2B in the preceding section), and still support a constraint on government spending. Even if one accepted a constraint on government spending, however, there is no reason to believe that a figure of 20% is at all meaningful. But such a (combined) proposal is not confined to the US. Burton (1985) has suggested that the UK governments should balance their budgets and that government spending should be confined to 25% of GDP.

It is possible to give some justification for a limit to be set for the ratio of government spending to GDP, whether a balanced budget is accepted or not. But this must be predicated on the belief that a smaller role for government is necessary. Consider, first, a balanced budget. All this means is that government spending must equal taxes. This can be at a high level of government spending and taxes or a low level of government spending and taxes. The former would imply a large role for government and a high $G–GDP$ ratio, while the latter would imply a low $G–GDP$ ratio (unless one believed that spending by governments would raise national income by more than the private sector could – although the converse is often assumed). It follows, therefore, that a constraint on the role of government would require not only a balanced budget but a curb on the level of government spending, which could be achieved by setting a ratio of $G–GDP$. But suppose one does not accept that an economy must follow a balanced budget. Consider, then, Rule 3 above. Here the budget deficit is proportional to the target rate of inflation plus the rate of growth of output. The higher the target rate of inflation the greater can be the budget deficit, but the greater the budget deficit the greater the $G–GDP$ ratio. Hence, to prevent the role of government expanding too greatly it is possible once again to impose a limitation on government by setting a ratio for $G–GDP$ along with a target for the rate of inflation. Although a more complicated policy mix, in theory it should be just as feasible as setting a balanced budget and a fixed $G–GDP$ ratio. (It may even be more practicable in this case to set a target for the $PSBR/GDP$ ratio, see Appendix 9.2.)

The conclusion one arrives at is that there is nothing to justify a balanced budget analytically, especially for a growing open economy. Nor is there any analytical reason for curbing the role of government. There is a philosophical belief, of course, that the role of government should be as minimal as possible, but whether this can be translated into a $G–GDP$ ratio of 20% or 25% is not at all clear. Setting a ratio has the merit of imposing a simple external discipline on the policy-maker and acts very similar to cash limits. But there are other ways to impose discipline and it is not at all clear that this is the most suitable way to do so. If the question is truly one about discipline, then the debate should be carried out in these terms rather than by trying to find some theoretical justification for a constant $G–GDP$ ratio.

9.7 FISCAL POLICY IN AN OPEN ECONOMY

It was thought that if a country pursued sound internal policies, then the exchange rate could be left to freely float and be determined by market forces. This, to some extent, is true in the long run. The problem is that in the short and medium terms the exchange rate influences the domestic price level and, to some extent, price expectations. As a consequence, sound internal policies may become very difficult to implement. This became clear in the UK and, from about 1982 onwards, there were various references to the necessity of taking account of exchange rate movements in various MTFSs. It was explicitly mentioned in the 1985 budget when Mr Lawson said that 'benign neglect was not an option'. He went on to say

> This is why I have repeatedly argued that it is necessary to take the exchange rate into account in judging monetary conditions. There is no mechanical formula which enables us to balance the appropriate combination of the exchange rate and domestic monetary growth needed to keep financial policy on track. But a balance still has to be struck, and struck in a way that takes no chances with inflation.
>
> (Quoted from Budd, 1985, p. 14)

The unfortunate response (at least for the government) to this remark was that people in the City attempted to work out what target rate the government had for the exchange rate, despite repeated comments by the government that it had no such target rate. For a government so keen to reduce inflationary expectations, this only introduced more un- certainty into the system.

There was a further difficulty with the government's stated aim with regard to the exchange rate. It had indicated that it would distinguish between external and internal influences on the exchange rate, Budd (1985). If the influence arose from external sources, such as a rise in US interest rates or a change in OPEC oil prices, then there would be no necessity to change monetary policy. On the other hand, if the exchange rate was itself responding to changes in the PSBR or to monetary growth, then this would necessitate a change in monetary and/or fiscal policy. But there are three difficulties in carrying out such a policy. First, it is very difficult to know why the exchange rate is changing, and so it is very difficult to establish whether it is changing because of internal or external influences. Second, even if the exchange rate change is external, it will undoubtedly influence the price level in the short and medium terms. Third, changes in the exchange rate are seen as signs of fluctuating economic health, whether rightly or wrongly. As a result, in 1985 the government decided to take account of exchange rate movements *whatever their cause.*

Although there was no target set for the exchange rate in the budget of 1986, it was believed at the time that interest rate policy was largely determined by the objective of holding sterling, and hence import prices, at a level which would bring inflation down.

What is clear from these remarks is that the exchange rate began to play a more prominent, if rather obscure, role in the mix of policies pursued under the umbrella of the MTFS. What is not clear is the precise role, if any, of the exchange rate. In our discussion of rules, it became clear that a *long-run* policy rule for the exchange rate which would be consistent with monetary and fiscal rules is one of purchasing power parity. But, as we pointed out in Chapter 5, purchasing power parity has a number of shortcomings. Furthermore, in an open economy such as that of the UK, there would also need to be interest rate parity. But interest rate parity is established by combining arbitrage, hedging and speculation. These in turn can influence the exchange rate in the short and medium terms and create a divergence from purchasing power parity. This divergence in turn, as Nigel Lawson discovered, can undo any success of other 'sound' domestic policies for bringing down the rate of inflation.

What is clearly lacking, both at theoretical and practical levels, is any clear analysis of the link between the exchange rate and the domestic price level. This is no easy task. For one reason, it will depend very much on the pricing policies of firms, which in turn depends on the competition that firms face, either at home or abroad. Some work has been carried out on the role of the exchange rate in relation to monetary and fiscal policy, for example by Artis *et al.* (1984) and by Currie (of which some preliminary reports are noted in Currie, 1985*a*), but much more work needs to be done on the relationship between exchange rate policy and monetary and fiscal policy.

NOTES

1. There has been a growing interest in the workings of the Treasury in relation to economic policy. Besides Brittan (1971) it is also discussed in Keegan and Pennant-Rea (1979), Mosley (1981, 1984), and Browning (1986).

2. More detailed discussions can be found in Price (1978) for the period up to 1974; while for the period after 1980 it is useful to consult the IFS budget briefs.

3. When Labour came to power in 1964 it set up a rather elaborate planning machinery. However, the National Plan, although an important document, did not lead to any clear planning of the economy because of the many shortcomings in the plan – not least because of certain inconsistencies.

4. The relationship between taxes and hours worked has been fairly extensively researched, especially at the University of Stirling, under Professor C. V. Brown. Many of the results can be found in Brown (2nd edn, 1983).

5. The snake was an arrangement of EEC currencies which shortened the exchange rate movements of cross-parities. This was necessary after the Smithsonian agreement of December 1971, which widened the band for currency movements *vis-à-vis* the dollar. See Appendix 11.2.

6. A detailed discussion of the 1976 crisis can be found in Fay and Young (1978), see also Appendix 11.3.

7. The weighted fiscal deficits are derived by weighting components of government spending and components of tax receipts. If $\mathbf{w}_1$ denotes a vector of weights for government spending components and $\mathbf{w}_2$ a vector of weights for tax components, then the weighted budget deficit (WD) can be expressed as

$$WD = \mathbf{w}_1 G - \mathbf{w}_2 T$$

The cyclically adjusted budget deficit (CD) is derived by adjusting the budget deficit ($G - T$) by a factor which takes account of the income gap (y_{gap}) and a vector of yield elasticities (**e**). Thus

$$CD = (G - T) + y_{gap} \cdot \mathbf{e} \cdot T$$

where y_{gap} is the difference between the actual income level and the trend level as a percentage of the trend level, Biswas *et al.* (1985).

8. For a discussion of the flow of funds see Bain (1973), Bank of England (1972), and Cuthbertson (1985).

9. The literature on Mrs Thatcher's economic experiment is becoming quite voluminous. See, for example, Holmes (1985), Pratten (1982), Keegan (1984), Buiter and Miller (1981), Minford and Peel (1981), Hodgson (1984), Kaldor (1983), Coutts *et al.*(1981), Craven and Wright (1983), Frazer (1982), Reddaway (1982), Ward (1982), Matthews and Reddaway (1980), and Thompson (1986).

10. The regression of the change in $M3$ (the old £$M3$) on the PSBR for annual data 1963–87, is given by

$$dM3 = 6329.0 + 0.0771 \, PSBR \qquad R^2 = 0.0019$$
$$(2460.1) \quad (0.3711)$$

where the figures in brackets are standard errors. This would appear to indicate an extremely weak link. However, both series have major time trends. If, therefore, we introduce a time trend, T, into the regression we obtain (with standard errors in brackets)

$$dM3 = - 3721.2 - 0.9764 \, PSBR + 1170.5T \qquad R^2 = 0.8314$$
$$(1408.8) \quad (0.1859) \qquad (112.4914)$$

Not only does the coefficient of the PSBR have the correct sign, but it is also not significantly different from *unity*. Also, the correlation is much higher.

11. Samuel Brittan had argued for such an indicator in his *How to End the Monetarist Controversy* (1981).

12. The natural rate of interest as discussed by Wicksell is dealt with in Patinkin (1965).

13. The Fisher condition is discussed in Levi (1983).

14. This in turn would have implications for the size of outstanding national debt in the two countries.

15. The regression of $\log(G/P)$ on $\log(GDP/P)$ for annual data at 1980 prices for the period 1960–87 is

$$\log(G/P) = -6.5611 + 1.4827 \log(GDP/P) \quad R^2 = 0.9685$$
$$(-10.3825) \quad (28.2839)$$

where the figures in brackets are t-values. For the same sample period, the elasticity for final consumption is lower (1.3245) as it is for debt repayment (1.3769), while for transfers it is much higher (2.1839) – a slightly different numerical result from that of Levitt (1984), but in the same direction. It is worth noting that introducing a dummy for political influence is found to be insignificant – a result typical of other studies.

16. For a detailed discussion of this see Sir Leo Pliatzky (1982).

17. Since

$$G/Y = (P_g/P)(g/y)$$

then taking percentage changes, denoted with a circumflex, we have,

$$(\widehat{G/Y}) = (\hat{P}_g - \hat{P}) + (\hat{g} - \hat{y})$$

If the government holds g constant ($\hat{g} = 0$) and if P_g and P are held in line and the government are successful in lowering both $\hat{P}_g$ and $\hat{P}$, then (G/Y) can be reduced by an increase in output (a rise in y).

APPENDIX 9.1 THE TREASURY

Organization

The Treasury is one of the oldest departments of the State, but in terms of numbers employed it is one of the smallest. It is a policy-making department which has few executive duties that bring it into contact with industry or the public. Even its contact with the financial markets is conducted mainly through the Bank of England. Historically, its primary duty has been to control the expenditure of public funds; but today one of its main tasks is

> to manage the economy of the United Kingdom so as to achieve the economic objectives laid down by Ministers and approved by Parliament. (The Ball Committee)

The organization of the Treasury is governed by its functions, and as these change so does its organization (see Brittan, 1971; Keegan and Pennant-Rea, 1979; and Browning, 1986). There have been a number of re-organizations (1962, 1964, 1968, 1975, 1981), with 1975 reflecting a major change in organization. Under the 1975 changes, the Treasury was grouped into four sectors. Three (the Overseas Sector, the Domestic Economy Sector and the Public Services Sector) were headed by a Second Permanent Secretary, while the other was headed by the Chief Economic Adviser. However, under Mrs Thatcher, the Treasury has been 'pruned down', and the latest organization is set out in Fig. A9.1.1. In comparison to the organization after 1975, it has no prices and incomes policy and the number of sectors and number of Second Permanent Secretaries has been reduced from three to two; the Domestic Economy Sector has disappeared and Fiscal Policy and Home Finance are now managed at the Deputy Secretary level; while Industry is now under Public Expenditure. Finally, since the Civil Service Department was disbanded in 1981, this has now come under the responsibility of the Treasury.

The Treasury has been constantly under siege in the post-War period. In 1964 Labour tried to hive off part of the Treasury to the Department of Economic Affairs, which was meant to be a medium-term planning agency. Of particular significance was the setting up of the Central Policy Review Staff, or 'Think Tank', which was implemented by the Conservatives in opposition in the 1960s and retained by Labour when it was returned to power in 1974. The 'Think Tank' has on occasions served the

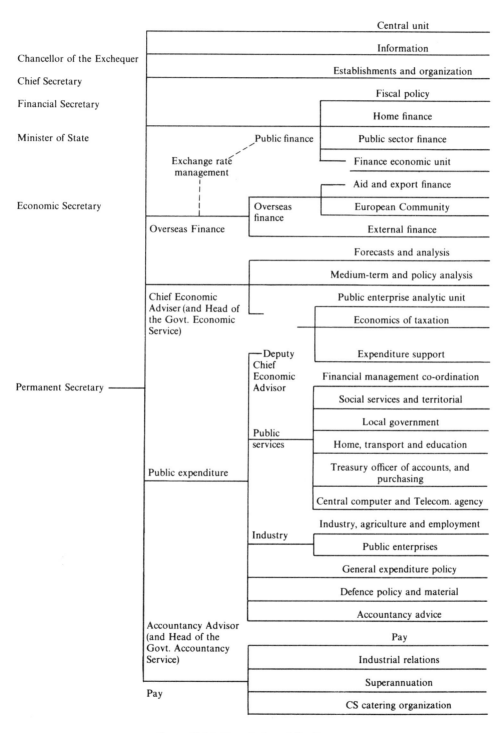

Figure A9.1.1 Organisation of the Treasury.

Prime Minister in opposition to the 'Treasury view'. At times there has been a loss of confidence in the Treasury, the most notable occasion being in 1976 (see Appendix 11.3 on the sterling crisis of 1976), when the Treasury also suffered a defeat at the hands of the Bank of England over the approach to monetary policy. Notwithstanding this crisis, the Treasury is a main force in economic policymaking in the UK

> The Chancellor and his senior officials continue, both constitutionally and in practice, to be the most *consistently* dominant direct Government influence on economic discussions in Cabinet, and on such sensitive economic decisions as may be taken by the Prime Minister and Chancellor, without reference to full Cabinet. (Keegan and Pennant-Rea, 1979, p. 81)

Budget forecasting

But, of course, one of the main functions of the Treasury is to prepare the budget – and because this is an on-going process throughout the year, and repeated every year, it is to some extent ritualistic. In each year there are two main forecasting rounds: September–October and December–January, with a subsidiary one in June. Evaluating and recommending policy options is closely tied to these forecasting rounds – hence, their importance. Central to the whole operation is the Treasury model (see Appendix 13.2). The first round consists of collecting and inserting the latest economic data into the model. While this is going on, the Policy Co-ordinating Committee will check the policy assumptions which are to be used in the current forecasting round. These will include changes to existing policy instruments and the possible inclusion of new policy instruments. If the Chancellor is interested in some particular policy change, he can make his views known at this stage so that its implications can be investigated by means of the model. The model is then run under a variety of assumptions which provide simulations of the main economic variables. Included in this exercise is a 'no-change' situation (i.e., a forecast is made on the assumption that present policies are continued without change). After consulting experts in other departments (especially the Inland Revenue, the spending ministries and the Bank of England), a forecast is made of what will happen over the next year, and this constitutes the 'central case'. Projections are then made of the economy if policy were altered in specific ways. The results are presented in the form of 'ready reckoners', i.e. forecasts of what would happen to the economy if just one policy instrument were allowed to alter by some handy conventional amount (such as 1%). These 'ready reckoners' are then combined into policy packages, which the Chancellor may or may not wish to consider for use in his budget.

APPENDIX 9.2 SOME SIMPLE ANALYTICS OF THE MTFS

Here the intention is to derive an expression for the $PSBR/Y$ ratio, which plays such a prominent role in the MTFS. In doing this we shall use the following notation:

ND = national debt
IP = interest payment on the national debt
BD = budget deficit
$PSBR$ = public sector borrowing requirement
Y = nominal GDP
P = domestic price level
y = real GDP
$\hat{P}$ = inflation
$\hat{y}$ = growth in real output

We begin by assuming that the rate of interest is constant. This is a reasonable long-run steady state assumption. Under this assumption a constant debt interest–income ratio (a constant IP/Y) implies a constant debt–income ratio (a constant ND/Y). We can express this constant debt/income ratio as follows:

$$ND/Y = a \qquad a > 0 \tag{A9.2.1}$$

Given expression (A9.2.1), it follows that

$$dND = a \, dY \tag{A9.2.2}$$

But the change in the debt is the same as the budget deficit. Hence, it follows that

$$BD = a \, dY \tag{A9.2.3}$$

Since the budget deficit can be approximated by the PSBR ($BD = PSBR$), then substituting the PSBR for the BD and dividing both sides by nominal income we get,

$$PSBR/Y = a \, dY/Y \tag{A9.2.4}$$

But nominal income $Y = Py$, and hence,

$$dY/Y = \hat{Y} = \hat{P} + \hat{y} \tag{A9.2.5}$$

Substituting expression (A9.2.5) into equation (A9.2.4) we arrive at the simple result

$$PSBR/Y = a(\hat{P} + \hat{y}) \tag{A9.2.6}$$

So long as the *PSBR–Y* ratio is maintained equal to the right-hand side of expression (A9.2.6), then the *IP–Y* ratio will remain constant.

However, result (A9.2.6) cannot be the situation for a long-run stationary economy. For such an economy the rate of inflation must be zero ($\hat{P} = 0$) and so too must be the growth in real output ($\hat{y} = 0$). It follows, then, that for a long-run stationary economy we have the result

$$PSBR/Y = 0 \tag{A9.2.7}$$

This implication was noted by Odling-Smee and Riley (1985), but they argue for a non-zero result, even in the long run. However, for a growing economy where the target rate of inflation is $\hat{P}*$, we have the result

$$PSBR/Y = a(\hat{P}* + \hat{y}) \tag{A9.2.8}$$

The usefulness of result (A9.2.8) is to note that given various (intermediate) targets expressed in the MTFS, the debt–Y ratio (coefficient a) cannot be a constant. To see who this is so, first note that in 1984 the debt–Y ratio was approximately equal to 0.5. Now consider the target rate for the *PSBR–Y* ratio to be 3.25% (the target rate set for 1984). Furthermore, suppose inflation is zero and output grows at 2%, so nominal GDP also grows at 2%. Then it follows from equation (A9.2.8) that

$$a = 3.25/2 = 1.625 \tag{A9.2.9}$$

Hence, the debt–Y ratio must rise.

Although result (A9.2.8) is fairly extreme it does highlight some of the policy debate. But it also indicates that in some discussions the equation is overdetermined! What it indicates is that if a target is set for the *PSBR–Y* ratio and nominal GDP growth, then the debt–Y ratio must become the residual outcome, otherwise the expression is overdetermined.

Chapter 10

MONETARY POLICY

In the UK, since about 1979, monetary policy has replaced fiscal policy as the major element in macroeconomic policy-making. The aim of this chapter is two-fold: first to outline why the change in macroeconomic policy took place; and, second, to outline exactly what form monetary policy has taken in the UK.

More than any other topic, monetary policy *cannot* be discussed in isolation from the institutional framework in which it is conducted. There are, of course, some theoretical notions which are independent of such institutions, but once we turn to actual policy and how it is actually applied, then it is necessary to be country specific and to take account of the institutional structure of that country. In this chapter we confine ourselves exclusively to the UK. This point cannot be stressed too often. The monetary system, and, more broadly, the financial system in the UK is quite different from those in the US and other European countries. Banking in the UK developed as a branch banking system and although the Bank of England was only nationalized in 1949 it has always played a pivotal role in the UK monetary system.[1] Because of the important (and changing) role of the Bank of England, we present in Appendix 10.1 some comments on the History and Role of the Bank of England (or what we will often refer to as the Bank).

But exactly what is monetary policy? How easy is it to implement monetary policy? How do we measure the extent of monetary policy? Why is it that only after 35 years has monetary policy come to replace fiscal policy in the UK? Who is responsible for achieving monetary policy? What is the relationship between monetary policy and the institutional framework in which it must operate? What were the two major banking reforms (the first in 1971 and the second in 1980–81) and how significant were they? What is the role of monetary policy? Is there a case for monetary rules, and if so, what are they? Why is the definition of money so important in the debate over the efficacy of monetary policy? Why is the stability of the demand for money function so important to the monetarist position? These are just some of the questions we need to address in this chapter.

10.1 DEFINITION AND ROLE

Monetary policy has sometimes been said to be 'concerned with financial variables: the supply of money, the flow of credit and interest rates', Struthers and Speight (1986), p. 284. In fact, this interpretation lists the *instruments* of monetary policy.[2] The theory of policy, outlined in Chapter 8, provides a common framework within which to discuss the definition of, and influence of, monetary policy. In terms of instruments and targets (including intermediate targets)

> Monetary policy could be defined as changes in those instruments which have, on some principle, been classified as monetary instruments; the effects of monetary policy can then be identified, in two stages, with the effects of monetary actions on the intermediate variables and the effects of changes in these upon the goal variables of the system.
>
> Artis (1978)[3]

It must be clear, however, that this interpretation of monetary policy presupposes a policy analysis in terms of instruments and targets. But even if one accepted such a framework, as we pointed out in Chapter 8, it is not clear whether a monetary variable is an instrument or a target; nor does it follow that all *actions* can be reduced to instruments/targets. For example, a certain degree of monetary influence is exercised by the Bank of England over the commercial banks and other financial institutions in the form of 'prudential control' which can hardly be reduced down to a specific instrument, but it is no less a part of monetary policy (and since the elimination of many other controls, this can now be said to be a major means of operating monetary policy). Even so, the setting of monetary targets has now become the norm.

Before continuing our discussion it is worth emphasizing the meaning of 'target' in this context. In the instruments – targets policy model discussed in Chapter 8, target referred to *ultimate* target, i.e. growth, inflation, unemployment and balance of payments. The point is that instruments do not affect targets directly but, rather, affect them through intermediate variables. Money supply is such an intermediate variable. The policy instrument for influencing this variable is open market purchases and sales of government securities (such as Treasury Bills). It is even possible to subdivide intermediate variables into policy indicators and intermediate targets (see Appendix 8.1). Where an intermediate variable lies closest to the instrument variable (rather than the ultimate target variable) then this is referred to as an *indicator* because it is supposed to indicate the direction and strength of the instrument variable. For instance, if open market purchases are undertaken to influence the money supply (an intermediate target), then it is possible to see the influence of this policy by looking at short-term interest rates. Thus, short-term interest rates become an indicator of monetary policy. This example also illustrates that an *intermediate target* is supposed to lie closer to the ultimate target variable (rather than the instrument variable). A further aspect of the distinction between indicators and intermediate targets is illustrated by this example. An indicator is supposed to respond quite quickly to the instrument variable, while an intermediate target has a longer time period before it becomes affected.

But why introduce such complications into the analysis of policy? The reason is that it can be very difficult to see the influence of a policy on the economy independently of other factors. Indicators, it is argued, can help distinguish the influence on intermediate targets of the policy rather than non-policy influences which also happen to influence the intermediate target. See Saving (1967); Bain (3rd edn, 1980), chapter 8; Brunner and Meltzer (1969); and Pierce and Tysome (1985), chapter 11. One feature of indicators which is worth mentioning is the use of Domestic Credit Expansion (DCE) as a monetary policy indicator. This concept is a generalization of the money supply indicator for an open economy, and was much favoured by the International Monetary Fund. In fact, the Fund, when lending money to participating countries often set DCE targets – thus converting a monetary indicator into a monetary target.[4]

What, then, is the role of monetary policy? One simple answer to this question is to say that it is to achieve some of the final objectives or goals. A narrower view, in the light of the comments made so far, is to say that its role is to achieve a set of intermediate targets, the purpose of which is to achieve some ultimate goals. This is an important distinction when considering the *effectiveness* of policy. It may be possible to achieve some intermediate target but not necessarily a final objective. Under the first role the policy is ineffective, while under the second it is effective. The reason is not difficult to see. The transmission goes from policy instrument to intermediate target (possibly via some indicator) and then to the final objective. The effectiveness of the first link in the chain (between the instrument and the intermediate target) by no means guarantees the second link (between intermediate target and final objective). Furthermore, the achievement of an intermediate target is not an end in itself but merely a means of achieving some final objective.

But what is the final objective? In the early 1950s and 1960s the main objective of macroeconomic policy was the achievement of full employment output (the price level being assumed constant – which at the time was not unreasonable). Under the assumption of a constant price level, the analysis is readily conducted in terms of the IS–LM model outlined in Chapter 2. In simple terms, fiscal policy could be used to shift the IS curve while monetary policy could be used to shift the LM curve. In such a framework the role of monetary policy (along with fiscal policy) was to achieve full employment output. Thus, in terms of Fig. 10.1, if the economy were situated at point A on IS_0 and LM_0, then full employment output, y_f, could be achieved in any one of three ways: (1) A fiscal expansion, shifting IS to IS_1 (the economy moving from A to B), (2) by means of a monetary expansion, shifting LM to LM_1 (the economy moving from A to C); and (3) by means of a policy mix, shifting IS to IS_2 and LM to LM_2 (the economy moving from A to D). In terms of the policy objective, each is successful (B, C and D all achieve $y = y_f$); the major difference is to interest rate. However, as Chapter 3 made clear, there will in fact be dynamic forces set up which will be different in each of the three cases. These, in turn, are likely to lead to different long-run results. As for the effectiveness of monetary policy in comparison with fiscal policy, we discussed this in Section 2.3 and it is based on the relative slopes of the IS and LM curve (and in an open economy *also* on the slope of the BP curve).

However, this is a static analysis. When we turn to the 1970s, when inflation became a major problem, this framework is no longer applicable. Even the analysis in terms of aggregate demand and aggregate supply is not sufficient because this must assume that dynamic forces are not operating. As we will discuss in a moment, the late 1970s and 1980s have been characterized by setting rates of *growth* in money supply figures. Although much of the policy surrounds a reduction in the rate of growth of the money supply, there *is* still a growth. The point is that when the model is set up in real terms, which we did in Chapters 2 and 3, the LM curve is related to real money balances (M/P). Thus, even with a positive rate of growth of money supply, so long as this rate of growth is equal to the rate of growth of price inflation, then the LM curve will remain stationary (in the r–y space). We discussed the significance of all this in Chapter 3. What we must direct our attention to here is the change in policy objective in the late 1970s and 1980s and the change in the policy assignment that took place when the Conservatives took office in 1979.

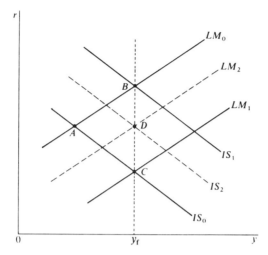

Figure 10.1 Policy measures to achieve full employment.

In line with monetarist arguments, outlined in Part I, the Conservative government believed that there was a strong positive association between monetary growth and inflation. Thus, if the ultimate objective was to reduce the rate of inflation, it was necessary to reduce the rate of growth of the money supply. Thus the second link in the transmission chain discussed above was changed from money supply and real income to monetary growth and inflation:

$$M_s \longrightarrow y \qquad \text{1950s and 1960s}$$

$$\hat{M}_s \longrightarrow \hat{P} \qquad \text{mid-1970s and 1980s}$$

Having accepted this chain of causation, the logic is unassailable. To achieve the ultimate objective it is necessary to achieve target growth rates of money supply. Hence, money supply growth became a monetary (intermediate) target of policy. Exactly how such a target could be achieved – whether through money base control or interest rate control – will be taken up in a later section.

The important point being made, of course, is that even if an instrument – target model is accepted, which instrument to be assigned to which target depends very much on the particular economic approach to macroeconomics one accepts; and this, in turn, will determine what role is to be played by monetary policy. In order, therefore, to fully understand monetary policy in the UK, it is necessary to consider what brought about the change in role just alluded to.

10.2 THE CHANGING ROLE OF MONETARY POLICY IN THE UK

With so much talk of monetary targets these days it may be tempting to think that they have been the basis of monetary policy throughout the post-War period. But this is not in fact the case. It was not until after the *Radcliffe Committee Report* (1959) that monetary aggregates were compiled and published. For much of the 1950s and 1960s the major concern of the monetary authorities was to preserve an 'orderly' gilt-edged market arising from the growing national debt. If the government wished to borrow on favourable terms, they would manipulate the financial sector through open market operations in order to achieve their desired interest rate. In other words, they would let the money supply be whatever was necessary to achieve their desired rate of interest. But from our theoretical analysis the essential point about monetary policy (along with fiscal policy) was to achieve a full employment level of income – at least during this period. It was generally considered at the time that interest rates did not substantially affect the level of investment and, consequently, monetary policy was not very effective in influencing the level of income through its affect on the level of investment. This view was certainly held by the Radcliffe Committee. Thus, monetary policy played a subordinate role to fiscal policy.

Because of this the two aspects of the monetary authorities as financier of the national debt and as implementer of monetary policy did not appear to be in conflict. But this was not the case. For part of the 1950s and 1960s, sterling and the balance of payments became a major concern for the government. Short-term interest rates were used by the monetary authorities as a means of manipulating the external position. Thus, *Bank Rate* was used to signal to the market the intentions of the monetary authorities and as a means of attracting short-term capital (a feature captured in the Mundellian analysis we developed in Chapter 8 when discussing internal and external balance). However, such a policy of raising Bank Rate to attract more international capital also made borrowing on the national debt expensive for the government. The conflicting aims of the authorities in trying to reduce the servicing of the national debt and as the authority to implement monetary policy was a recurring feature of the post-War period.

But why was a change in Bank Rate effective in terms of influencing domestic liquidity? It must be appreciated that during this period the Bank of England imposed a 30% liquidity ratio (later reduced to 28%) and an 8% cash ratio on the commercial banks. So long as the commercial banks maintained these ratios, then the Bank could influence the commercial banks by changing the assets available to them. It was this institutional framework which led to the analysis of money multipliers, which we developed in the second half of Chapter 7. However, the Bank Rate was only one instrument of policy during this period. It was also supplemented by changes in hire purchase regulations and in quantitative and qualitative control on bank advances.

In the 1960s a further instrument of policy was used, namely 'Special Deposits'. These were deposits of the commercial banks held at the Bank of England. They were 'special' in the sense that they were *not* included as part of the commercial banks' liquidity. Hence, a call of special deposits by the Bank would reduce the liquidity of the commercial banks which would, in turn, mean that their liquidity ratios fell below the legal required limits. Hence, they would have to adjust their portfolio position by calling in loans or reducing the level of advances that they would have formerly made to the private sector. Special deposits, therefore, were means of reducing excess liquidity in the system without having to adjust short-term interest rates.

In summary, monetary policy was subordinate to fiscal policy and was dominated by control of interest rates in order to service the national debt. Where bank rate was changed this was largely because of external circumstances. This fits in fairly well with the Keynesian orthodoxy which dominated policy-making throughout this period. Furthermore, there was no dissention from the view that the main objective of policy (largely fiscal with monetary accommodating it) was to achieve full employment.

However, there was a growing number of Chicago economists putting forward a view that money mattered and that monetary policy should play a more dominant role in stabilization, the major exponenont of which was Milton Friedman (although Robert Mundell had been arguing the same from the point of view of international trade). What is interesting from the point of view of UK monetary policy is that these arguments were not so influential. Their impact came indirectly via the International Monetary Fund. The Fund had for some time been very much influenced by monetarist arguments, especially as applied to countries with balance of payments problems. In the late 1960s when Britain needed to borrow from the IMF the government agreed to reduce the rate of monetary growth which the IMF requested. In a second letter of intent[5] the government agreed to set a target for Domestic Credit Expansion for 1969–70. What this meant, of course, was that the government had to some extent to relinquish its control over nominal interest rates.

This occurred at a time when there was growing awareness that the type of monetary control operating throughout the 1950s and 1960s was not working. In addition, the constant barrage of controls and the interest rate cartel that the commercial banks operated had led to little competition and to market inefficiencies and distortions. It was felt that there was a need for monetary reform. This came in 1971 with Competition and Credit Control (CCC). We will discuss this, and the later reforms of 1980–81, in a later section, but what they did was to increase the competition in the banking system and remove many of the controls on lending (a quantity adjustment) and to place more reliance on changes in interest rates (a price adjustment). The 1971 reforms were a failure and one of the basic reasons for this was the fact that to work the Bank needed to control interest rates. It appeared either that the Bank was unwilling to do this or that it was incapable of doing it through the market mechanism. Accordingly in December 1973 the Bank introduced a *quantitative* control in the form of supplementary special deposits, or what became known as the 'corset'. This was undoubtedly a departure from CCC, and we will leave it to Appendix 10.2 for a further analysis. Suffice to say that it was probably effective in the early years but became less effective over time – and it was eventually abandoned in 1980.

One argument that has been advanced is that CCC was not really a failure but was introduced at a time when many macroeconomic relationships were changing. The Phillips curve had broken down around 1967 and inflation in the 1970s had begun to be a major problem, especially after the Barber boom of 1971–72, whose increase in the money supply filtered through into price changes about eighteen months later – which, in addition, coincided with the first major increase in oil prices. The consumption function, the most important relationship in the Keynesian framework, was also becoming unstable. The demand for money function, although initially showing some degree of stability, also showed signs of becoming unstable (see Appendix 7.2). In Britain much econometric work was done on improving estimates of the consumption function, by introducing wealth and taking account of inflation (in addition to improving the econometric specification and the lag structure of the function). On the other hand, in the US more attention was being directed to improving the specification of the demand for money function, although this was soon followed in the UK.

The 1970s also illustrated the conflict which could arise in an open economy under a floating exchange rate between monetary policy and competitiveness. In the mid-1970s there was a considerable influx of capital as domestic interest rates rose relative to those abroad (the analysis of which we discussed in detail in Chapter 5).

However, the inflow of capital, if left unchecked, would lead to a sterling appreciation. But such an appreciation, however, raised export prices and lowered import prices, so leading to a deterioration in the competitive position of the UK on world markets. In order to avoid this the authorities intervened in the foreign exchange market. However, such intervention undermined the domestic monetary policy that was being pursued and so intervention was abandoned in the autumn of 1977.

As inflation became the major difficulty faced by many countries, more attention was given to the link between monetary growth and the rate of inflation. More economists were coming round to the view that inflation was, in Friedman's words, 'a monetary phenomenon'. The analytical arguments underlying this statement have been presented in Part I. What matters from our present point of view is that if they are correct, then a means of controlling inflation is to control the rate of monetary growth. Accordingly, in the 1970s we see more attention being paid to monetary growth targets as a means of bringing inflation under control. Although monetary targets were announced in Healey's budget of 1976, it was not until Margaret Thatcher came into power in 1979 that they became an essential feature of monetary policy. In fact, as we outlined in the last chapter, the targeting of monetary growth was an essential element in the Medium-term Financial Strategy. But having decided to set monetary targets the next problem is exactly how this is going to be achieved. We take up this particular debate in a later section.

What can we conclude from the period of the 1970s? Conclusions are difficult because the period involved too many changes – domestically, world wide, institutionally, theoretically and politically. As the circumstances changed, the policies previously adopted were found wanting. There was a search for an alternative approach. Monetarism seemed to offer that alternative. More than that, monetarists in general also favoured the workings of the market over government intervention. Since this view is consistent with Conservative policy in the UK, it is not really surprising that it was taken up, and so after 1979 monetary policy took on a new significance and replaced fiscal policy as the major component of macroeconomic policy in the UK.

10.3 THE BANKING REFORMS OF 1971 AND 1980–81

With the increase in credit controls throughout the 1960s and the interest rate cartel of the commercial banks, there was a view that the banking system was not sufficiently competitive. Furthermore, the distortions created by the repeated controls favoured the non-commercial banks over the commercial banks in so far as the controls largely applied to the latter. Over this period, therefore, there was a growth in the secondary banks – for example, foreign and overseas banks, merchant banks and acceptance houses.

The result was a major banking reform, introduced in September 1971, under the title of *Competition and Credit Control* (CCC). The reform fell into three main parts, as follows:

1. Most of the distorting controls were abolished. Quantitative restrictions on bank advances were removed and the interest rate cartel was abandoned.

2. Other controls were lightened and also were extended to other institutions. The 8% cash ratio and 28% liquidity ratio were replaced by a $1\frac{1}{2}$% cash reserve ratio and a $12\frac{1}{2}$% reserve asset ratio. These were new ratios which applied first to all banks and were later extended to finance houses.

3. A commitment to competition and market forces was agreed.

Whether $£M3$ became a target of the policy was unclear. Some attention was certainly paid to credit flows, as the flow of funds approach became more prominent, in which case the money supply acted more like an indicator. Furthermore, the bank rate (in existence for more than 270 years) was replaced by the minimum lending rate (MLR). The MLR was determined by the rate of discount for Treasury bills plus $\frac{1}{2}$% and rounded up to the nearest $\frac{1}{4}$%, and so the MLR would *normally* follow market rates. However, if the authorities wished to give a lead to the market, the formula was temporarily suspended. The aim, of course, was to make the MLR far more flexible than its predecessor, the bank rate, but, at the same time, it lost its 'announcement effect'.

Soon after the introduction of CCC it appeared to be failing. There is not sufficient space here to discuss the reforms and its shortcomings in any detail (see Gowland (1978), Artis and Lewis (1981), Hall (1983) and Spencer (1986)), but by June 1972 the pound was forced to leave the 'Snake' (see Appendix 11.2) and sterling was floated. In December 1973 the supplementary special deposits scheme (the 'corset') was introduced, which was a quantitative restriction (see Appendix 10.2), which could be considered as quite a break from the spirit of CCC. In addition, the supervisory role of the Bank was extended over more financial institutions, while more *prudential* control was later exercised by the Bank. Also during the 1970s the authorities acknowledged that fiscal policy had implications for the money supply and that the PSBR was recognized as one of the components of sterling $M3$. This link in turn led to more attention being paid to 'cash limits' on certain kinds of public expenditure (see Chapter 9). What this meant was that the PSBR became part of monetary policy. Notwithstanding all these changes, it could be said that control was still being exercised by means of interest rates and direct controls.

When the Conservatives took office in 1979 there was a radical change of direction.[6] There was a move to a medium term strategy, embodied in their Medium-term Financial Strategy (discussed in Section 9.4), of which targeting of money supply took a central position. The PSBR was to be kept consistent with the monetary growth targets, which in turn implied further cash limits to be imposed on certain public expenditures. At the same time, however, academics were debating the efficacy of the actual monetary control being exercised by the Bank of England. Monetarists, in particular, were advocating money base control, which we will discuss in more detail in the next section. As a result the government issued a consultative Green Paper, HM Treasury (1980), on monetary control. As it turned out, the government did not introduce money base control, but it did implement a number of changes over the period 1980–81, a summary of which is provided in Appendix 10.3.

In essence, these reforms did not involve major changes. The authorities continued to influence the counterparts of the money stock using short-term interest rates – and it could be said that interest rates were the sole remaining monetary instrument for achieving monetary control, and reflected the authorities' belief that quantitative controls were ineffective. The changes were, however, a move in the direction of money base control, even though the Bank continued to use interest rate control in its operations. That interest rates remained the means of control is evidenced by the fact that the authorities had money supply targets which, along with the exchange rate, were taken as intermediate targets. The success of these changes depended upon two things: first, whether the authorities could meet the targets set for money supply (although which money supply is a moot point); and, second, whether the Bank would allow interest rates to perform their market-clearing function.

As noted, the reforms of 1980–81 were a move to money base control. This debate, which to some extent is still going on, is worth commenting on in more detail. This we do in a later section. But why was the Bank so reluctant to take up money base control? There are a number of reasons, but one is worth commenting on here. The UK is an open economy and, as we showed in Chapter 5, there is a close link between interest rates and exchange rates. The importance of the exchange rate within the overall medium term strategy of the Conservative government was recognized in the budget of 1983, when the exchange rate entered the set of indicator variables. This aspect of the debate we shall also deal with in later sections.

10.4 WHICH MONETARY TARGET?

Over the last few years there has been considerable controversy over which monetary aggregate the authorities should attempt to target – assuming, of course, that it does wish to target 'the' money supply. In considering this controversy, three questions must be examined:

1. Why should the authorities wish to have a monetary target?
2. Which monetary aggregate (or set of aggregates) should be targeted?
3. How successful are the authorities at achieving their targets?

In answer to the first question, it really depends on whether 'money supply' is considered as an indicator or an intermediate target. As an intermediate target we have already argued that the money supply is important because of its association with the rate of inflation. In this case what matters is which monetary aggregate is the one most closely associated with the rate of inflation. In other words, if there is a strong belief that 'the' money supply is the cause of inflation, then what matters is that monetary aggregate which has the strongest association with the rate of inflation. Taking this line of reasoning, it would appear that the most appropriate monetary aggregate is the one which leads to general purchasing power, since it will be this aggregate which leads to the demand for goods and services. The most appropriate monetary aggregate in this instance would appear to be £$M3$ (now $M3$). However, even this is not at all obvious. There is an argument in favour of $PSL2$ (the current $M5$). It should be recalled that $PSL2$, unlike £$M3$, includes building society deposits. To the extent that building societies have been extending the range of business that they undertake, and most especially the extent to which they offer chequing and 24-hour machine with-drawals from accounts, it would be difficult to argue that such accounts do not contribute to the overall level of aggregate demand. Since it is the level of aggregate demand which matters for inflation, then it follows that a case can be made for the broad aggregate $PSL2$ ($M5$). Whether £$M3$ ($M3$) is chosen or $PSL2$ ($M5$), what matters is the intermediate target which has the strongest association with the ultimate target of inflation.

If, on the other hand, the monetary aggregate is seen more as an indicator of policy, then what matters here is the monetary aggregate which has the strongest association with the instrument of monetary policy. If this line of reasoning is taken, the importance of obtaining a strong and predictable relationship with the instrument of policy is obvious. If, as seems to be the situation in the UK, monetary policy is largely conducted by means of interest rate control, then it follows that the most suitable indicator is the one which has the strongest and most predictable association with short term interest rates. It would appear that it is the narrow definitions of money, such as $M0$ and $M1$, which act as 'best' indicators of such monetary control.

A detailed analysis of the late 1970s and 1980s readily reveals the authorities constantly changing the monetary aggregate which they considered 'in some sense' to be important – always, however, in terms of *rates of growth*. In 1976, when monetary targeting first took place, Dennis Healey (the then Chancellor of the Exchequer) targeted on $M3$, and later this was changed to £$M3$. Sterling $M3$ was the main monetary aggregate in the early years of the Conservative administration. In the early 1980s the confusion between intermediate target and indicator became apparent. Sterling $M3$ was invariably in excess of its target ranges and did not apparently 'indicate' the stance taken by monetary policy. As such, the targets for monetary growth became somewhat useless, except as an indication of intent. What the authorities were looking for was a monetary indicator. Thus, in the budget of 1982 a single target range was set for the three monetary aggregates $M1$, £$M3$ and $PSL2$. The authorities also indicated that they were monitoring a number of other monetary aggregates, e.g. $M0$, non-interest bearing $M1$ and $PSL1$. In addition, the exchange rate entered the list of indicators. Furthermore, in 1983 the Chancellor indicated that the narrow definition of money, $M1$, which was supposed to be the closest working definition to transactions balances, was becoming a poor measure of money held for transactions purposes. In addition, he stated that they would be giving greater weight to $M0$ in their assessment of monetary conditions. What is revealing, however, is that the argument was not that this was a better predictor of monetary policy, but, rather, that the narrow monetary aggregates were better indicators of inflation. This view was pursued in the 1984 budget when a target range for $M0$ was explicitly set for the first time. There appears, then, a shift in treating $M0$ from being an indicator of monetary policy to being an intermediate target. By autumn of 1985 £$M3$ was abandoned as a target variable, although in the budget of 1986 the target range for £$M3$ was set, and set at a particularly high level. However, the target was set only for the financial year 1986–87, with no growth targets set for later years. On the other hand, there was a re-statement of the importance in the narrow monetary aggregate $M0$, where growth targets were set for later years (at a declining rate).

It is fairly clear from this brief summary of events that the monetary authorities, and/or the Chancellors, have no clear idea of the link between monetary aggregates and inflation, nor which monetary aggregates act best as indicators of monetary policy. Even more, it would sometimes appear that monetary aggregates have become important in themselves rather than as a means of reducing inflation or as an indicator of monetary policy.

Whether the aggregates act as intermediate targets or indicators, we raised the question of whether the authorities have been successful in achieving them. The answer, in general, is no. We have not got the space here to go into the details of why the authorities failed to achieve their targets, but Table 10.1 gives the target ranges and the outcomes. For a more detailed account of the reasons for failure see Hall (1983), Llewellyn *et al.* (1982), and

Table 10.1 UK monetary targets, 1976–87

Target period	Monetary aggregate	Target range	Actual outcome
		percent p.a.	
April '76–April '77	£M3	9–13	7.7
April '77–April '78	£M3	9–13	16.0
April '78–April '79	£M3	8–12	10.9
October '78–October '79	£M3	8–12	13.3
June '79–April '80	£M3	7–11	10.3
June '79–October '80	£M3	7–11	17.8
February '80–April '81	£M3	7–11	18.5
February '81–April '82	£M3	6–10	14.5
February '82–April '83	£M3	8–12	11.1
	M1	8–12	14.3
	PSL2	8–12	11.3
February '83–April '84	£M3	7–11	9.4
	M1	7–11	14.0
	PSL2	7–11	13.1
February '84–April '85	£M3	6–10	11.6
	M0	4–8	5.5
April '85–April '86	£M3	5–9	16.5
	M0	3–7	3.3
April '86–April '87	£M3	11–15	20.9
	M0	2–6	6.1

Source: *Bank of England Quarterly Bulletin*, various issues.

Spencer (1986). However, in part, it was this lack of success in achieving stated monetary targets that led to a move to an alternative aggregate: in the hope, no doubt, that this would be more successful!

10.5 MONEY BASE CONTROL

Before discussing the debate on whether monetary control should be via interest rates or via the money base, it may be worth commenting on why the government may want to control the money supply at all.

Although Keynes did not underestimate the importance of money, neo-Keynesian analysis stresses the importance of fiscal policy as a means of demand management of the economy. But monetarists have argued, not surprisingly, that monetary policy is more effective in achieving macroeconomic ends. However, the particular end in view is not quite the same. Early stabilization policy, which we will discuss in detail in Chapter 13, was concerned with achieving a full employment level of income. However, monetary policy has become associated with achieving a low (or even zero) rate of inflation. The connection is most easily seen by using the Cambridge Quantity Equation we outlined in Chapter 7, namely,

$$M_d = kPy \tag{10.1}$$

where M_d is the demand for money, k is the reciprocal of the income velocity of circulation of money, P is the general price level and y real income. If the money market is quick to clear, then $M_d = M_s$ so that

$$M_s = kPy \tag{10.2}$$

It is supposed that in the long run k is constant (however, see Appendix 7.1) and y is at its 'natural' level. Hence, any increase in the money supply must manifest itself in an equal increase in the price level. Thus, taking percentage changes in equation (10.2) we have

$$\hat{M}_s = \hat{k} + \hat{P} + \hat{y} \tag{10.3}$$

which, under the assumptions that $\hat{k} = 0$ (the velocity of circulation of money is constant) and $\hat{y} = 0$ (income is at its natural level), means that

$$\hat{P} = \hat{M}_s \tag{10.4}$$

Notice an important behavioural assumption introduced into equation (10.4) which can very easily be overlooked, i.e. we have *assumed* that the causation runs from money supply growth to inflation and not vice versa: it is assumed that it is the increase in the money supply which *causes* the increase in the price level. Can the causation run the other way round: from inflation to monetary growth? Yes it can! As the price level rises the monetary value of transactions rises. There is, then, a greater need for money balances to engage in such transactions if money is to act properly as a medium of exchange. The point is, however, that 'money supply' is determined institutionally by the Bank of England and the financial system as a whole. There is in general no reason to suppose that the money supply so created is sufficient (or more than sufficient) for the transactions needs of the economy. Furthermore, as we outlined in Chapter 7, the transactions demand for money is only one reason for holding it. Even so, there is no reason to suppose that the supply of money will match the demand for money.

But returning to our argument of why control the money supply, it readily follows from equation (10.4) that if the objective is to control inflation, then it is necessary to control the money supply. As we have just noted, however, this proposition depends on a number of assumptions, as follows:

1. There is a stable demand for money.
2. The income velocity of circulation of money is constant.
3. There is no growth in real income.
4. The causation runs from money supply to the price level and not vice versa.
5. The demand for money is interest insensitive.

Consequently, a monetarist would argue that controlling inflation requires control over the money supply. If, of course, inflation is caused by other factors – such as trade union pressure – then it does not follow that controlling the money supply will control inflation. It is for this reason that the *end* must be constantly kept in mind. It is the control of inflation which is the primary objective, at least of the present Conservative government in the UK; and control of the money supply is simply an intermediate target for the control of inflation. Even if control of the money supply was possible and/or successful, whether this will control the rate of inflation depends very much on what causes inflation. But for the moment let us suppose that there is a strong link between the money supply and inflation. The question still remains as to how the authorities can control the money supply and which money supply is the appropriate one to control.

In Chapter 7 we established various relationships between monetary aggregates (such as $M1$ and $£M3$) and the money base, $M0$, each derived under the assumption that there was a multiplier relationship between the money base and the specified monetary aggregate. In other words, in general we have,

$$M_s = qM0 \qquad (10.5)$$

where q is the money multiplier. If we take percentage changes of (10.5) we have,

$$\hat{M}_s = \hat{q} + \hat{M}0 \qquad (10.6)$$

and furthermore, if q is constant (so $\hat{q} = 0$), then it follows that the growth in the money supply ($\hat{M}_s$) is equal to the growth in base money ($\hat{M}0$). There is, however, a further assumption involved in the analysis and that is that the causation runs from the money base to the money supply. In other words, if the authorities wish to reduce the money supply, then all they need to do is reduce the level of $M0$ in the system. This, of course, presupposes that $M0$ is purely exogenous and determined by the monetary authorities and not itself responding to the level of money supply in the overall system. Goodhart (1984), for example, has raised doubts over the causation running from $M0$ to M_s, and has argued that in the UK at least, the causation runs from M_s to $M0$! Thus, $M0$ rather than determining the money supply is endogenous to the monetary system.

The argument about money base control is fairly straightforward. Assuming a relationship along the lines of equation (10.6), and noting that base money ($M0$) is within the control of the monetary authorities, then it should be easier for the authorities to control the money supply by controlling the level of money base than by controlling interest rates. Since $M0$ is under the control of the authorities, so the argument goes, then in order to control M_s all that is needed is to control $M0$ and to do this all that is required is to predict the value of the money multiplier q.[7] With the assumed causations (between $\hat{M}_s$ and $\hat{P}$ and between $\hat{M}0$ and $\hat{M}_s$), then if $\hat{P}^*$ is the target rate of inflation this would imply, according to equation (10.4), a target for money supply of $\hat{M}_s^*$; and, according to equation (10.6), would imply a target for money base of

$$\hat{M}0^* = \hat{M}_s^* - \hat{q} \qquad (10.7)$$

What this analysis illustrates is that if money base control was going to work, then a reserve requirement would need to be placed on the commercial banks (and other financial institutions if intermediation was going to be avoided). However, this could be mandatory or non-mandatory. There has been some difference of opinion about which of these alternatives is appropriate, e.g. Griffiths (1979) supported a non-mandatory approach, while Gowland (1982) argued that the system would not work unless it was mandatory. The argument against mandatory ratios was the worry that they may impose too precise a control, leading to quite large and volatile movements in short-term interest rates. A second worry, which arose out of the response to the 'corset', was that banks may try to avoid the penalties implied by such a scheme by some artificial means of adjustment – an example of 'Goodhart's law'.[8]

If banks conform to the money multiplier formula in equation (10.5) – whether for prudential reasons or because it is mandatory – and if there is no uncertainty in the system

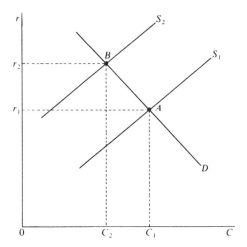

Figure 10.2 Money base control and interest rate control with no uncertainties.

(which is most doubtful), then it is possible to argue that money base control and interest rate control are conceptually the same, a point of view expressed in the Green Paper. The situation is shown in Fig. 10.2. On the vertical axis we have the rate of interest on loans (denoted r) and on the horizontal axis the quantity of credit (denoted C). The demand curve for credit is denoted D and the supply curve denoted S. Assume the banking system is in equilibrium at point A with interest rate r_1 and credit of C_1. Now suppose the authorities wish the amount of credit in the system to be C_2. They can achieve this in one of two ways. Either they can control interest rates, which in terms of Fig. 10.2 means raising the rate of interest to r_2. Initially, this will lead to a disequilibrium in the money market. But as the banking system competes for available deposits, the supply curve for credit will shift to the left until it reaches S_2. Alternatively, the Bank could simply reduce base money sufficient to reduce credit to C_2. This would shift the supply of credit to S_2. At the initial interest rate there would be excess demand for credit. The interest rate would rise, and rise until it reached r_2, so eliminating the excess demand. In both situations the end result is point B.

But this is far too simplistic, and certainly not the way it would be likely to operate in the UK financial system. To illustrate the difficulty, consider the situation in Fig. 10.3, where we have two alternative demand curves for credit, D_1 and D_2. We begin at the equilibrium point A with interest rate r_0 and credit C_0. First consider interest rate control. If the authorities wished to restrict credit to C_1, then the interest rate would need to be raised to r_1 if demand were D_1, and r_2 if demand were D_2. Any interest rate lying between r_1 and r_2 would mean a level of credit below C_1 if demand were D_1, and above C_1 if demand were D_2. If money base control were used and the supply curve of credit shifted to S_2, then the actual amount of credit arising in the system, determined by the intersection of demand and supply, would be E in the case of demand D_1 and F in the case of demand D_2. In general, this range of credit (around the desired level C_1) would be narrower than that from some arbitrary interest rate between r_1 and r_2. On the other hand, the interest rate would have a greater range of variation, a point emphasized by Foot *et al.* (1979).

However, some economists, such as Artis and Lewis (1981), argue that money base control will give the banks a more positive and active role in monetary control than the

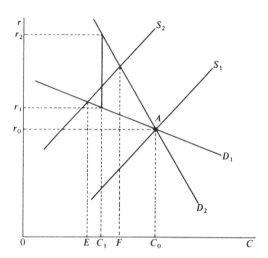

Figure 10.3 Money base control and interest rate control in the presence of uncertainties.

passive role under interest rate control. Griffiths (1979), although admitting that money base control would mean more frequent changes in the rate of interest, argues that there is no reason to suppose these would be large. This, he felt, would be better than the older, large and infrequent changes in Bank Rate. One argument against money base control, certainly in the UK context, is the fact that it would require institutional changes,[9] which some see as undesirable in themselves. On the other hand, this does presuppose that the present system and its institutional arrangements are in some sense desirable, even though they include market distortions.

Four reasons have usually been advanced against the implementation of money base control:

(a) the resultant fluctuations in interest rates;
(b) the possibility of the Bank relinquishing its role as 'lender of last resort';
(c) the institutional change involved; and
(d) the fact that it would lead to intermediation throughout the eurosterling market.

We will consider each of these briefly.

1. This is the mirror image of interest rate control. The situation is illustrated in Fig. 10.4. Suppose there is money base control. If we assume that the relationship $M_s = qM0$ holds, then if base money is $\bar{M}0$ the money supply would be $\bar{M}$. If, therefore, the demand for money could vary between M'_d and M''_d, then the rate of interest would vary between r' and r''. This does not necessarily mean large fluctuations, but it does imply frequent and small changes in interest rates. The question then arises of whether small and frequent changes in interest rates or frequent changes in the money supply is more detrimental to the economy.

2. The Bank would need to relinquish its role as 'lender of last resort', or at least it could not always act as lender of last resort without defeating the object of its money base control. Since loans from the Bank as 'lender of last resort' are for seven days, where this does

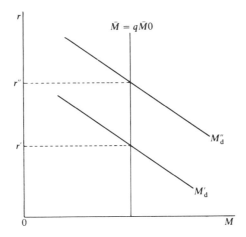

Figure 10.4 Money base control and variable interest rates.

operate in some form or other, it would mean that the Bank would have to determine the money base from week to week.

3. The introduction of base control would require a change in the definition of reserve assets, which, it appears, would lead to a loss of business for discount houses. This in turn would result in mergers and a desire to diversify their business. Another institution that would be affected is that of the jobbing firms, which deal with gilt-edged stocks. See Foot *et al.* (1979).

4. Money base control would lead to commercial banks seeking funds in the eurosterling market, i.e. from sterling held by non-UK residents. This would give a stimulus to the growth of the eurosterling market. It need not necessarily mean, however, that the eurosterling market will expand, except to the extent that the authorities impose controls on the banking system.

One feature of the money base sometimes overlooked for an open economy is that for it to operate effectively the exchange rate must be freely floating (and one might add that the exchange market would need to clear quickly). We will deal with the open economy aspects in the next two sections; suffice it to say here that for an open economy the level of reserves constitutes part of the money base. Hence, any change in the level of reserves will also mean a change in the money base. A freely floating exchange rate with no market intervention and quick market clearing would mean, in theory at least, no change in the level of reserves, and hence no change in the money base from this source.

It is quite clear from the foregoing discussion that there is no agreed view on which type of control is the most appropriate. The issues are complex; they depend on the level and source of uncertainty in the banking system; they depend on the openness of the economy and the type of exchange rate system being operated; and, not least, they depend on the institutional structure of the economy. The debate over money base control versus interest rate control cannot be based on an abstract economy: in this debate the institutions matter.

10.6 MONETARY POLICY IN AN OPEN ECONOMY

A useful beginning is to consider the effects of monetary policy under fixed and floating exchange rates *where all markets are free to adjust*. The situation is illustrated in Figs 10.5 and 10.6. Consider, first, Fig. 10.5, illustrating the situation under a fixed exchange rate. It is to be noted that in this analysis we have assumed a fair degree of capital mobility. (In other words, the BP curve is less steep than the LM curve – see Appendix 5.3 for the implications of different assumptions concerning the relative slopes of LM and BP.) In Fig. 10.5(*a*) the economy is assumed to be in equilibrium at point *A*, with all markets in equilibrium. Furthermore, the economy is in long-run equilibrium, as illustrated in Fig. 10.5(*b*), with the rate of inflation equal to the rate of growth of the money supply and income at its natural level.

Now consider a pure monetary expansion. The result of this depends on whether it is a one-off event, or whether there is a general increase in monetary *growth*. If it is a one-off event, the initial impact is a shift in the LM curve to the right, to LM_1 and a shift in the demand-pressure curve to DP_1. The economy moves to point *C* in the upper diagram, resulting in a temporary deficit on the balance of payments. The reason for this is the rise in income results in a deterioration in the current account (goods and services), while the fall in the rate of interest reduces net capital inflows. However, given this is a one-off event, in the next period the LM curve moves back to LM_0 and the demand-pressure curve also shifts back to its initial position. The short-run Phillips curve should not alter so long as there has been no revision of price expectations.

Next, consider a permanent increase in the money supply. Again the LM curve shifts to LM_1 in the first period and the demand-pressure curve moves to DP_1. However, over time, there are a number of dynamic forces in operation. Let us first try to identify these forces and then see how they interact. First, the permanent rise in the money supply means that there will continue to be a deficit on the balance of payments for a number of periods into the future. Second, there will be a rise in the rate of inflation from $\hat{P}_0$ to $\hat{P}_1$. Third, under free market forces with no government sterilization of the money supply, the deficit will result in a reduction in the money supply. This will result in a shift to the left in the LM curve (relative to LM_1). Fourth, the rise in the rate of inflation will have three (or possibly four) effects. It will reduce the competitive position of the economy on world markets which will (1) shift the IS curve to the left; (2) raise the BP upwards (to the left); (3) reduce the level of real money balances in the economy, so shifting the LM curve to the left; and (possibly) (4) raise the level of inflationary expectations, which will shift the SPC curve upwards (to the left).

Where the economy actually settles will depend on the relative strengths of each of these dynamic forces. If we take one extreme case where adjustment in the money market is very quick relative to other markets, and especially relative to the impact of inflation, then the fall in the money supply resulting from the deficit will move the LM curve back to its initial position (along with the DP curve). The balance of payments will then be self-correcting. This analysis explains the view that balance of payments problems are temporary so long as market forces are left to operate. Under different assumptions about relative adjustments in the different markets, it is quite possible that a vicious circle sets in. The initial deficit leads to a fall in the money supply and a leftward shift in the LM curve. However, the rise in the

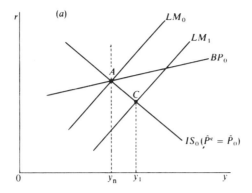

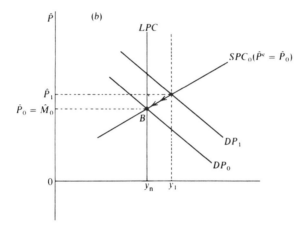

Figure 10.5 Monetary policy under a fixed exchange rate.

rate of inflation shifts the IS curve left and the BP curve left. Furthermore, if there is a revision upwards of price expectations, then the shifts in IS and BP curves arising from a declining competitive position will be that much greater. The result is a continuing deficit and a continuing decline in national income, with the economy trapped in a vicious circle of decline. In these circumstances it is not true to say that a deficit is a temporary phenomenon.

Next, consider a floating exchange rate, shown in Fig. 10.6(a,b). Here we only consider a permanent increase in the money supply growth. Again the balance of payments goes into deficit and inflation rises. Under this regime, however, the deficit will give rise to a depreciation in the exchange rate which will leave the competitive position of the economy unchanged if it is equal to the increase in the rate of inflation. Although a fairly extreme assumption, we will take it to be true. Under this assumption, there will be no shift in the IS curve and no shift in the BP curve – both of which are functions of the competitive position of the economy (variable R as used in Chapters 2 and 3). There will, however, be a leftward shift in the LM curve arising from a decline in the money supply (resulting from the deficit) and the fall in real money balances (arising from the increase in the price level). The

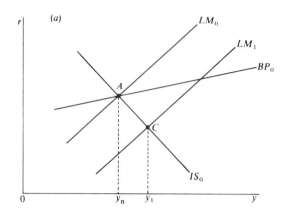

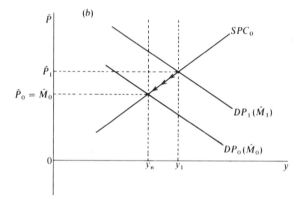

Figure 10.6 Monetary policy under a flexible exchange rate.

economy will accordingly move back to position *A*, with the demand-pressure curve returning to DP_0. Here we see the argument that a deficit (or surplus) on the balance of payments is only a temporary phenomenon.

Of course, in practice the different markets adjust at different rates and there are complex lags in the structure of the various markets. As we pointed out in Appendix 5.6, these can give rise to the problem of overshooting. Furthermore, the 'temporary' deficits and surpluses can last for quite a long time – possibly too long to be left to *automatic* adjustments.

One of the objectives of this section has been to point out the rather complex link between the various sectors of the economy, and, in particular, to illustrate the point that monetary (or fiscal) policy cannot be considered as if the economy is closed. The results, and most especially the dynamic adjustments that take place, are quite different for an open economy. Furthermore, the type of exchange rate regime, although it may not influence the final outcome (at least under free markets), will influence *where* within the economy the adjustment will take place. If the exchange rate is fixed, for example, then all the adjustment must fall on prices and output (and hence employment). On the other hand, if the exchange rate is flexible, then some adjustment will fall on the exchange rate. This may alleviate or aggravate the situation. In addition, the movement of interest rates over the adjustment period can have important implications for the long-run growth of the economy.

With this analysis in mind, let us return to UK monetary policy and consider why the government have had such difficulty in achieving its monetary target and why the openness of the economy has such an important bearing on this.

10.7 MONETARY TARGETS AND EXCHANGE RATE INDICATOR

The present Conservative government, very much like preceding governments, has found to its cost that it cannot ignore the exchange rate. The simplistic textbook idea that under a freely floating exchange rate the balance of payments will look after itself is simply misleading in the real world of policy. The essential element in the complex linking of monetary policy and exchange rate policy is the interest parity result we developed in Chapter 5. Interest parity, it will be recalled, links interest rates at home and abroad with the cost of forward cover on the foreign exchange market. If money supply is targeted in order to achieve an inflation target, and if the PSBR is made consistent with this – which is the aim in the UK – then there will be implications for interest rates, exchange rates and the country's reserves. In particular, the effects on the exchange rate will then ramify through the economy, affecting the goods market and even the labour market.

To see this point consider the following scenario. Suppose the government restricts the growth in the money supply in order to bring down the rate of inflation. If the reduction in monetary growth is greater than the reduction in the rate of inflation, then there will be a decline in real money balances and interest rates will be forced up. However, this reduction in the growth of money can be achieved in a variety of ways, which we discussed in Chapter 9. But suppose it arises from a reduction in the PSBR. What are the implications of these policies for the trade sector? The reduction in output arising from this policy will undoubtedly reduce the level of imports and could improve the current account (although it must be emphasized that this may be at an overall reduced level of imports and exports). In addition, the rise in interest rates will attract inflows of capital (or reduce net outflows). On both accounts, therefore, there will be an improvement in the balance of payments. However, this will lead to an appreciation of sterling under a floating exchange rate system. Such an appreciation will raise export prices and lower import prices, and hence reduce the competitiveness of UK exports on world markets. It would appear, then, that the monetary policy being pursued would be at the expense of UK exporters.

Consider a different scenario. Suppose the UK government reduces the growth in the money supply and reduces the PSBR in line with this, just as before. Now suppose that the government is successful in its aim and inflation is falling. In this case it can ease its monetary restraint and let interest rates fall. This in turn will stimulate industry and begin to bring the economy towards its natural level of output; at least that is what is supposed to happen, in theory. But suppose that at the same time the US is following a policy of restraint which is raising US interest rates. This will attract funds out of the UK and into the US. The increased net outflow of capital will worsen the balance of payments, regardless of what might be happening to the current account. As a result, there will be a depreciation of sterling. This depreciation will raise import prices and lower export prices. Since imports are a major element in the general price level (and noting that many imports are inputs into other commodities), then this will raise the general price level at home. It is quite possible for this impact to swamp the initial policy pursued by the UK government. In this case, the fall in output and employment would all have been in vain!

These two scenarios are purely illustrative, but they do capture a number of the events of the 1980s. Of particular importance is the fact that domestic monetary policy cannot be set independently of what is happening in the rest of the world – especially in those countries with which the UK trades. Furthermore, the *actual* movement in the exchange rate will occur as the outcome of a number of factors happening simultaneously, not least the changes in exchange rate expectations – which under floating become more important. The fact that the exchange rate is responding to a series of simultaneous events both at home and abroad, makes it very difficult to see exactly what the relationship is between the setting of monetary targets and an appropriate exchange rate policy. What is clear, however, is that for the UK monetary policy and exchange rate policy (and, one might add, fiscal policy) cannot be treated as independent of one another.

NOTES

1. See Sayers (1964).

2. Struthers and Speight (1986) make this explicit: 'Monetary policy operates on its ultimate targets via changes in the quantity of money, changes in interest rates, and direct control of one or more forms of credit.' (p. 304)

3. Artis (1978) also makes the point that the sequence can be viewed in reverse, 'and attention focused upon the response of monetary instruments to deviations in the goal variables from their preferred values'. (pp. 259–60)

4. Thus, when Britain borrowed from the IMF in the 1976 crisis, the Fund imposed targets for DCE.

5. Reprinted in Wadsworth (1973).

6. Thompson (1986) has argued that it was not as radical as first thought because the constraints imposed on policy-makers was so great that, *ipso facto*, the approach was not so different.

7. See Schiltknecht (1981) for a discussion of how the Swiss National Bank attempted to predict q.

8. Goodhart's law states that any attempt by the Bank of England to regulate or tax one channel of banking business will quickly lead to such business being conducted through an alternative channel which is not bound by the same controls.
9. Some of these are discussed in Foot *et al.* (1979).

APPENDIX 10.1 HISTORY AND ROLE OF THE BANK OF ENGLAND

The Bank of England is the Central Bank of the UK. It has its origins with the Charter of 1694, which allowed it to form a joint-stock company, being set up to raise funds for the British government. From its beginnings it grew rapidly, largely because it was the banker to the government. As a consequence its notes soon became widely accepted in London. Partly because of this, other banks began to deposit their gold holdings with the Bank. The result was that the Bank of England soon took on the role of the 'bankers' Bank'. However, its status as a central bank was only conferred with the Bank Charter Act of 1844, when it became the monopoly producer of bank notes in the UK (with the exception of the Scottish and Irish clearing banks, which issue their own notes – although they have a major backing of Bank of England notes).

In line with this monopoly, the note issue function was separated from other activities of the Bank – leading to an Issue Department and a Banking Department – a division that remains to the present day. As the Bank's standing grew, it took on the role of stabilizer of the banking system. It did this by guaranteeing to purchase bills issued by other banks. As a consequence, it took on the role of 'lender of last resort' – a most important function for stability. Thus, by the beginning of the twentieth century, the Bank had already taken on what is generally considered to be the main functions of a central bank, namely:

(a) the sole issuer of bank notes;
(b) banker to the government;
(c) banker to the other domestic banks;
(d) lender of last resort; and
(e) the repository of the country's gold holdings.

On the other hand, its role in monetary policy was fairly limited (but growing), in part because it was still a private joint-stock company at the beginning of the twentieth century. It was finally nationalized under the 1944 Bank of England Act. As a result of the nationalization the Bank became subject to the authority of the Chancellor of the Exchequer, and became unambiguously an institution of government. Thus it quite clearly took on the role of 'implementing government monetary policy'. It is worth stressing that monetary policy is the responsibility of the government. The government acts through the Chancellor of the Exchequer (head of the Treasury along with the Prime Minister), and the Bank's role is advisory – albeit an important advisor. Once the broad outlines of monetary policy have been decided, the Bank's role is to implement it. The unconstitutional nature of the Bank has, at times, led to signs of conflict between the Governor and the government of the day (especially under Lord Cromer in the mid-1960s), but more recently the Bank's influence is pursued more behind the scenes – note that the Governor sees the Chancellor of the Exchequer once a week and the Prime Minister at regular intervals.

In the process of nationalization the government acquired the whole of the Bank's capital. However, it did not lay down the precise role and functions of the Bank in the Act. The Bank simply carried on doing what it had always done – since it had a supreme reputation in the world of banking. While there was financial stability, the Bank's imprecise role was not a problem. On the other hand, in the late 1970s and 1980s, when there was some imprudent banking and (in some parts of the world) bank collapses, the Bank's 'supervisory role' needed spelling out more explicitly, which was done in the Banking Act of 1979. This role also became important as the number of bank mergers increased, and as a number of private companies attempted to enter the financial sector through take-overs. The latter, in particular, required the approval of the Governor of the Bank of England.

In carrying out the government's monetary policy, the Bank undertakes borrowing for the government by issuing new gilt-edged stock. Outstanding government debt is bought and sold on the stock exchange. The Bank can influence this market itself by selling new government stock, so influencing long-term interest rates. By engaging in open market operations it can influence the short-term rates of interest. In the past it did this through the minimum lending rate (MLR, before 1972 the same as Bank Rate), i.e. the rate at which the Bank would re-discount Treasury bills. Not only did this raise the cost of borrowing for the discount market, but it acted as a major signal to the market that the Bank wanted to see a rise in short-term interest rates. The banking reforms of 1980–81 (see Appendix 10.3) abandoned the formal announcement of MLR, and replaced it with an undisclosed market equivalent – but with the option of re-introducing it if the circumstances seemed necessary.

Since the abandonment of fixed exchange rates in 1972, and most especially since exchange controls were removed in 1979, the exchange rate has become a major indicator of government policy. As pointed out in Appendix 5.2, the Exchange Equalization Account (EEA), which is administered by the Bank, carries out the excess buying or selling of foreign exchange on behalf of the Treasury. This account has a bearing on the PSBR. More significantly, there is a very close association between exchange rates and short-term interest rates. Although in the early years of the Medium-term Financial Strategy it was thought that the exchange rate could be left to float freely, the view now (mid-1988) is that short-term interest rates and exchange rates must be *jointly* managed. This, of course, makes the day-to-day management by the Bank that much more difficult.

The most significant change in the Bank of England's role in the post-War period has undoubtedly been its supervisory one. To a large extent this arose from the secondary banking crisis of 1973–75. The crisis broke two days after a series of measures were introduced on 17 December 1973 (which included the 'corset'), when the collapse of Cedar Holdings, a Section 123 bank, was predicted. Already, at the end of November, London and Country Securities, also a Section 123 bank, had run into liquidity difficulties. The Governor called an emergency meeting of some 40 banks and institutions, which resulted in a support package which became known as the 'lifeboat'. By 1975 a total of 26 secondary banks and finance houses called on the 'lifeboat' for help. Although a major banking crisis was averted, the situation did reveal the inadequate supervisory regulations of the Bank in such matters. The result was the Banking Act of 1979.

The Act involved a two-tier system of regulation: one giving supervisory powers over the deposit taking institutions, the other giving the Bank the power to determine which institution was a 'recognized bank' and which a 'licensed deposit taker' – although (after the Bank's rescue of Johnson Matthey Bankers) this distinction was later abolished. In addition, in December 1985 it was announced that a Board of Banking Supervision was to be set up within the Bank. The Board is advisory to the Governor, who can oppose the Board's advice, but must inform the Chancellor of the Exchequer if he does so. Finally, it is worth noting that the supervisory role of the Bank, and most especially the role of the Governor, has become far more important now that London is a financial centre open to the world markets.

APPENDIX 10.2 THE 'CORSET'

In 1973 the money supply (especially $M3$) had been growing rapidly, partly as a result of Competition and Credit Control, a rise in inflationary expectations and as a result of arbitraging – and despite the call for substantial special deposits. Banks had been bidding competitively for deposits and assets. The result was a general rise in nominal interest rates. At the time nominal interest rates were already high, with the minimum lending rate at 13%. The Bank of England did not want further rises in interest rates. Accordingly, in December of 1973 the Bank of England introduced a Supplementary Special Deposit Scheme, what later became known as the 'corset'. In the Bank's view

> The arrangements should therefore restrain the pace of monetary expansion, including the pace at which banks extend new facilities for bank lending, without requiring rises in short-term interest rates and bank lending rates to unacceptable heights. (Bank of England, 1974, p. 37)

Thus, the scheme was a non-market monetary control mechanism which constrained the growth of bank credit creation by imposing limits and penalties on the growth of interest-bearing eligible liabilities, and applied to all institutions which fell within the regulations of Competition and Credit Control. A maximum target growth rate was set for interest-bearing eligible liabilities, the figure being 8% per annum of the average value of such liabilities held violated this target, then it had to pay a supplementary special deposit to the Bank of England. The amount deposited at the Bank of England was on a graduated scale. If the excess was 1%, then 5% of it had to be supplied to the Bank; if the excess was 1–3%, then the penalty rose to 25%; while for deposits in excess of 3%, the penalty became 50%. It is clear, therefore, that the penalty was very progressive. As with ordinary special deposits, such funds could not be included in the institution's calculation of its reserve base; at the same time, such deposits earned no interest. The cost to the institution, therefore, was the interest foregone.

From the point of view of the authorities, the scheme was simple and flexible. In particular, flexibility was achieved by changing the length of the period in which the control was to be applied; varying the acceptable growth in interest-bearing eligible liabilities; changing the size and number of tranches above the allowable rate at which penalties would be imposed; and changing the rate imposed for these higher tranches. Furthermore, at the time of implementation it appeared to be an effective device for controlling the growth of the money supply. Certainly, following its introduction the growth in the money supply fell markedly.

The 'corset' was a quantitative control which distorted the competitive market (and was totally at odds with the spirit of CCC). When first announced, it was intended to be only a temporary measure, but it turned out to be far from temporary, and lasted until June 1980. As the distortionary effects of the control began to take effect, institutions found two basic ways around the controls. The first was the substitution of liabilities not subject to the controls. In particular, banks increased bank acceptances (i.e., bills of exchange which were accepted within the banking system). Of course, the banks charged a fee for such acceptances. But, more significantly, such acceptances were not included in the interest-bearing eligible liabilities that were subject to the 'corset'. The second leakage was into the eurosterling market (i.e., a market where sterling is bought and sold *outside* the UK). The 'corset' applied only to banks based in the UK. Overseas, banks including UK subsidiary banks, could attract sterling deposits from UK residents. In particular, a UK subsidiary bank in Paris could borrow sterling at attractive rates of interest since these funds were not included in the interest-bearing eligible liabilities of the parent bank. The result was a transfer of sterling to the eurosterling market. Although this transfer would reduce £M3, if it found its way back into the UK, the £M3 would rise again. This, in turn, meant £M3 became a most unreliable indicator of monetary policy.

The incoming Conservative government in 1979 was persuaded of the distortionary effects of the 'corset' and that the regulations were being circumvented (an example of Goodhart's law). Thus, in June 1980 the scheme was finally abandoned.

APPENDIX 10.3 SUMMARY OF THE 1980–81 REFORMS

The main reforms began in 1980 and continued in 1981. The main elements of the changes are summarised in Table A10.3.1.

Table A10.3.1 Summary of 1980–81 UK banking reforms

January 1980	The Bank of England released the special deposits which had been called from banks and larger finance houses, initially as a temporary measure. They have not so far been called, although the facility to do so has been retained
June 1980	Supplementary Special Deposits (the 'corset') were abolished: these had penalised excessive growth of interest-bearing deposits during three successive periods since December 1973
October 1980	The Bank of England ceased to announce dealing rates for eligible commercial bills of over one month to maturity (which banks could hold as reserve assets)
January 1981	The Bank ceased to announce dealing rates for Treasury bills (also reserve assets). Reserve assets ratio reduced from 12% to 10% of eligible liabilities, and temporarily to 8% from 2 March to 30 April
August 1981	Reserve asset ratio abolished: • $1\frac{1}{2}$% cash ratio reduced to $\frac{1}{2}$% of eligible liabilities, but coverage extended from London clearing banks to all authorised banks and licensed deposit-taking institutions • 6% of the eligible liabilities on average to be held as secured money at call, subject to a daily minimum of 4% • the monetary aggregate 'eligible liabilities' to be broadened by the inclusion of deposits of all authorised banks and licensed deposit-taking institutions, but with deposits between this wider range of institutions, and most secured money at call, netted out • the Bank to extend the range of bills in which it will deal to those issued by additional banks, particularly foreign banks (subject to various conditions) • the minimum lending rate (MLR) no longer to be announced, but to be replaced by an unpublished target range for an MLR-equivalent

The purpose of the reforms was to allow the Bank of England to have more discretion in its money-market operations and most particularly, more say in the determination of interest rates. Although the MLR was abandoned, the Bank did retain the option of posting an MLR for short periods of time – which it did in mid-January 1985 when sterling came under pressure.

The result of the 1980 measures has been to leave interest rates as the sole remaining monetary instrument for achieving monetary control. The Bank is basically altering its procedures in order to allow market forces to be a major (but not the sole) factor in determining short-term interest rates.

Chapter 11

EXCHANGE RATE POLICY

Since there has rarely been an explicit policy on the exchange rate, this chapter may appear out of place. However, Britain's history since 1945 quite clearly shows that the exchange rate has influenced policy choices. In a broader context it is not so much the exchange rate but, rather, balance of payments policies. We will pursue some of these in this chapter, leaving the more specific question of UK competitiveness until Chapter 17. It is not our intention in this chapter to present a complete analysis of exchange rate policy – which is impossible within the compass of one chapter. The aim is more limited. After presenting a historical account of UK exchange rate policy within a world context, we turn to *four* topics which have influenced UK attitudes towards the exchange rate. In terms of questions, these are as follows:

1. Now that the UK has a floating exchange rate, is the external sector no longer a constraint on achieving domestic policy aims?
2. Why do governments intervene in the foreign exchange market, and what intervention rules should they follow?
3. What effects has North Sea oil had on the exchange rate, and should these be counteracted?
4. Should the UK join the European Monetary System?

All these are pressing issues, and all influence other macroeconomic policies which are of concern to the UK government.

11.1 THE INTERNATIONAL MONETARY SYSTEM SINCE 1945

It is not possible to understand the post-1945 period without realizing that many of the developments of the international monetary system were designed to avoid the problems which took place in the inter-War period. Three problems were predominant:

(a) competitive devaluations;
(b) exchange rate restrictions; and
(c) lack of international reserves.

The Bretton-Woods System

With regard to exchange and trade restrictions, the International Monetary Fund was set up in 1944 and this set out guidelines for the use of such restrictions. The problem of competitive devaluations was dealt with by countries agreeing to adhere to a particular exchange rate, i.e. the 'parity' rate. The parity rate was declared and registered legally with the IMF. Rates were maintained by countries within a margin of 1% either side of parity. Changes in parity greater than 10% required agreement from the IMF; changes of less than 10% required no such permission. Additional reserves were supplied by creating a pool of gold and national currencies. Quotas were specified for each member country, reflecting size and importance (in some sense). Of the quota, 25% was paid by the country to the Fund in the form of gold and 75% in terms of its own national currency. A country in short-run balance of payments deficit could draw from the pool, subject to various restrictions and costs. An intervention currency (usually dollars) could be obtained automatically, equal to 25% of its quota (the gold tranche) without restriction, thereafter with increasingly more stringent conditions attached – including conditions on the type of *domestic* policies to pursue.

Immediately after World War II, sterling was pegged to the dollar at the rate of £1 = \$4.03, but mounting pressure gave rise to a temporary period of free convertibility. A crisis ensued and Britain abandoned convertibility, and later (September 1949) devalued sterling by 30.5% to £1 = \$2.80, which was maintained until 1967. Sterling's devaluation soon led to ten other countries following suit, which resulted in Britain's effective devaluation being about 15%. However, the system was prevented from settling down because of the Korean War. But even in the mid-1950s, when Harold Macmillan was Prime Minister, there was general resentment of the restricting influence of sterling on British economic expansion.

Throughout most the 1950s, international settlement took two forms, at least in the non-communist world. First, there was the dollar area in which settlement was by means of dollars. The second arose after the establishment of the European Payments Union (EPU), which led to settlements in sterling, or through the machinery of the EPU. However, in December 1958 most currencies became freely convertible for current account transactions, thus the Bretton-Woods System became fully functional.

The free convertibility of sterling for current account transactions lasted from 1958 until 1971. In coming to an understanding of how the system operated it is important to realize that *two* forms of convertibility operated in the system. They were:

(a) market convertibility; and
(b) official convertibility.

Market convertibility means that the holder of any one of the convertible currencies enjoys considerable freedom to convert it into any other by operating through the foreign exchange market. *Official convertibility* means the willingness of the reserve centre to convert its currency into gold at a specified rate. In the Bretton–Woods System (another name for the IMF System) this meant the US's willingness to convert dollars into gold at \$35 per ounce. In this system, official convertibility also meant that central banks, other than the Federal Reserve, would be willing to convert their own currencies into dollars at some specified rate.[1] From December 1958 until August 1971 both types of convertibility operated.

Under the Bretton–Woods System, a parity value was set for the *spot* exchange rate only, none being set for the forward rate (see Appendix 5.1 for an explanation of these two rates). The market rate, determined by demand and supply, was allowed to fluctuate 1% either side of the agreed parity rate. Sterling, for example, was set at £1 = \$2.80 with a margin of fluctuation of $\pm$ 2 cents, i.e. a range between \$2.78 and \$2.82. No band was set for the forward rate, although economies did not allow the forward rate to float freely at all times, and official intervention in the forward market was much less than in the spot market.[2]

We analysed the workings of the foreign exchange market in Chapter 5. In terms of the Bretton-Woods System, if the market exchange rate determined by demand and supply was going to lie above \$2.82, then the authorities would step in and supply sterling (purchase foreign exchange). On the other hand, if the market exchange rate fell below \$2.78, then the authorities would step in and demand sterling (sell reserves of dollars). This second, more common problem for the UK, is illustrated in Fig. 11.1. If unchecked, the free market exchange rate would fall to £1 = \$2.50. This was not allowed under the IMF rules. Accordingly the Bank would step in and demand sterling (the demand curve would become infinitely elastic at the limit of \$2.78). The amount of sterling that the Bank would have to demand is £AB, and the reduction in the level of reserves would accordingly be \$2.78 $\times AB$. (Similarly, a surplus would mean an infinitely elastic supply curve, a rise in the dollar reserves.)

It is clear, therefore, that a deficit on the balance of payments would lead to a fall in the country's reserves as the authorities were forced to maintain the exchange rate; while a surplus would lead to a rise in the country's reserves. Furthermore, the larger the deficit (surplus) the greater the loss (gain) in the reserves. A series of persistent deficits could lead to a situation where a country ran out of reserves! However, a country losing reserves, if it considered the deficits to be temporary, could borrow from the IMF. If, on the other hand, it considered the situation to be one of 'fundamental disequilibrium', then it could, in the case of a deficit, devalue.[3] This Britain did on 18 November 1967, changing its par value from £1 = \$2.80 to £1 = \$2.40, a devaluation of 14.3%. A detailed analysis of the Bretton-Woods System is beyond the scope of this book, but ten features of the system are outlined in Appendix 11.1.

By the late 1950s the typical policy management was by means of 'stop-go' (see Appendix 5.4). As demand was stimulated to achieve full employment, so the balance of payments went into deficit as imports rose. The deficit in turn resulted in a fall in reserves. So long as the exchange rate remained fixed, this could not continue. The result was a deflationary policy aimed at reducing the level of imports. In 1960 there was a large deficit on the current account, but there was also a very large short-term capital inflow at this time which, to a large extent, offset the current account deficit (see Table 5.2). The reserves rose substantially. However, in March 1961 Germany revalued the Deutschmark by 5%. A sterling crisis ensued and the hot money inflows of 1960 flowed out again. By July the situation called for strong corrective measures: Bank Rate was raised to 7% (up by 2%); regulators were imposed (these were across-the-board changes in tax duties imposed by the Treasury at any time to a maximum of 10%); a credit squeeze was implemented and so, too, was a pay pause. In broad terms, a general deflationary package was implemented to correct an external imbalance. This crisis, like later ones, also involved borrowing from the IMF, but such loans had strings. Although a cut in government spending required by the IMF was rejected, the general deflationary programme was undoubtedly a condition of the IMF loan. This crisis

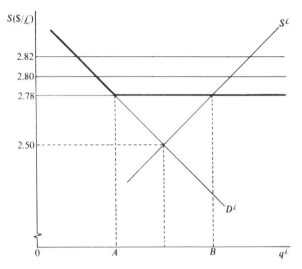

Figure 11.1 Bank of England support for sterling.

was typical. Although there was no direct policy towards the exchange rate and the balance of payments, when the reserves became low it was the domestic economy that was adjusted.

The question arises as to whether devaluation was discussed in Britain at this time. Earlier, in 1961, the Bank warned the government that the large wage settlements already in sight would give Britain an overvalued currency. The policy for this was devaluation. However, the Bank was generally opposed to this, and its advice was usually supplemented (both at this time to Mr Macmillan and in 1967 to Mr Wilson) with comments about the unpredictable effects this would have, especially on the dollar. The implication was that devaluation would weaken Britain's foreign policy, and particularly her relations with the USA. Since Macmillan and Wilson were sensitive about US relations, devaluation was ruled out as a policy alternative. This was a good example of a policy which was economically feasible (and, some might say, sensible) but politically unacceptable – see Fig. 8.1(*d*).

Throughout the early 1960s it was thought that sterling was overvalued, and that this, to a large extent, was accounting for the recurrent sterling crises. When Labour came to power in 1964 it inherited a very large balance of payments deficit, and to outsiders Britain was in 'fundamental disequilibrium' and should have devalued by 10–15%. It was clear, however, soon after Labour took office that it had made a decision not to devalue, largely on political grounds. The reasons were four in number: (1) It would adversely affect the Overseas Sterling Area. (2) There was a wish not to upset the Americans. (3) The Labour Party did not want to be associated, yet again, with a devaluation. (4) Harold Wilson, the incoming Prime Minister, believed that Britain's problems were structural and needed microeconomic intervention. In fact, devaluation became 'the great unmentionable'.

The sterling crisis of 1964 came to a head in November and the policy reactions were varied and mostly introduced under panic conditions, implemented as they were as an alternative to devaluation. The situation became very tense. In December 1964 there was a Joint Statement of Intent by the TUC and the Government. In paragraph 2 of this document it argued that to achieve its objectives there needed to be a strong currency and a healthy balance of payments. It was clear, then, that during this period the balance of payments was seen as a constraint on the achievement of the generally accepted policy objectives. The fact that devaluation had been ruled out meant that the government had to look elsewhere for instruments by which to bring about adjustment in the economy. In this sense, the selective employment tax (SET) was a substitute for devaluation. Although introduced in the April budget of 1966, it took too long to be effective and was therefore too slow as a means of demand management. By the summer of 1967 things had worsened and it was clear that the market considered the UK to be in 'fundamental disequilibrium' at this overvalued rate. Speculation was rife. The pound was accordingly devalued by 14.3% to £1 = \$2.40, resulting in the resignation of Mr Callaghan as Chancellor of the Exchequer.

From a theoretical point of view two features of the period are worthy of note:

1. Were the economic conditions suitable for a successful devaluation?
2. To what extent was Labour's boost to the supply side of the economy thwarted by an overvalued currency?

In answering the first question economists usually turned to the Marshall–Lerner condition. In its most extreme, and simplest, form it states that a devaluation will improve the balance of payments if the sum of the import and export demand elasticities exceed unity in absolute value. Early estimates at the time of the 1967 devaluation set the sum at about 3.[4] Once the J-curve effect had passed,[5] there was some improvement but this seemed short-lived. On the second question of affecting the supply side of the economy there is less agreement. There is some indication that the period of stop–go had a detrimental effect on investment and profitability and had, to some extent, contributed to the low supply elasticities in the UK.

Post-devaluation and the collapse of the Bretton-Woods System

Following the 1967 devaluation, the UK secured a \$1,400 million standby credit. As pointed out earlier, the IMF placed conditions on loans in greater order of severity. At the time the House of Commons was rather slow to realize that these credits were in fact conditional. This became a most important feature of the 1970s, with the IMF imposing a more constraining influence on domestic and exchange rate policy. If in the autumn of 1969 the balance of payments had not improved, Mr Jenkins, the then Chancellor of the Exchequer, was not prepared to be constrained by the IMF because of increased loans; on the contrary, he was prepared to float the pound downwards. Even so, the IMF did impose a ceiling on Domestic Credit Expansion (DCE) of £400 million for the financial year 1969–70 and the 'letter of intent' included a target basic balance[6] of £300 million.

Throughout the 1960s, and especially in the very early 1970s, the Bretton-Woods System was showing obvious strain. The symptoms of disequilibrium were: the persistent UK deficits and the short-lived effects of the 1967 devaluation of sterling; the persistent US deficit, which was leading to excessive world liquidity and to a confidence problem in the dollar; and, finally, the persistent surpluses of Germany and Japan. The mechanism of adjustment *de facto* within the Bretton-Woods System was shown to be inadequate. It is true that under the rules a country could change its par value. In practice, this turned out to be infrequent and when it did occur it was taken as a sign of defeat, and the usual accompanying crisis meant that the changes had to be large. Furthermore, there was a basic asymmetry in the adjustment mechanism which placed onus on the deficit countries rather than on *both* deficit and surplus countries. Because parities were only infrequently changed, adjustment fell on income, output and employment. This, in turn, led to policy conflicts between internal and external balance, see Chapter 8. In addition, the reserve assets transactions balance of the US swung from a surplus in the late 1960s to enormous deficits in 1970 and 1971, which gave rise to the *dollar overhang*.[7] This, it was argued, led to an increase in world liquidity and for some countries large inflows of short-term capital. Such inflows, if not sterilized, resulted in increases in the domestic money supply and to inflationary pressure. The result was that a number of countries imposed capital controls and policies on interest rates to curb such inflows.

The situation came to a head, and on 15 August 1971 President Nixon announced measures to stimulate the US economy and protect the dollar. These measures included the suspension of convertibility into gold, which meant the dollar was officially floating, and a 10% surcharge on imports that are subject to duty but not to quantitative restrictions. The following week most European foreign exchange markets were closed. The London market re-opened on 23 August and announced that, although the official sterling parity remained at £1 = $2.40, the Bank of England had abandoned its buying of dollars at £2.42. At the same time, other currencies were allowed to fluctuate more freely. Thus did the Bretton-Woods System come to an end.

The period 1971 to March 1973 was a limbo period, involving many negotiations and temporary measures. For want of a title it became known as the *dollar standard*, since most currencies were still related to the dollar, while the dollar itself floated. Following the Nixon measures, there was a confused period of managed floating and increased controls. Europe, through the Group of Ten (G-10), attempted to find a common policy towards the US. The discussions centred around a multilateral realignment of exchange rates, and a deal was concluded at the Smithsonian Institute in Washington in December 1971, which became known as the Smithsonian Agreement.

Under the Smithsonian Agreement, the Group of Ten agreed to re-peg on the dollar at target (or central) rates in return for the ending of the US 10% surcharge and other measures. The effect was a substantial devaluation of the dollar. In addition, the band around the central rates was changed from $\pm 1\%$ to $\pm 2\frac{1}{4}\%$. Finally, but less significantly as it turned out, the official price of gold was raised from $35 to $38 per ounce. One unfortunate consequence, at least for Europe, of the Smithsonian arrangement, was that it meant cross-rates between European currencies could fluctuate by as much as 9%. Since at this time Europe had been making progress with European Economic unity, and there were plans to establish fixed rates between the currencies of member states,[8] alternative arrangements were made between European currencies which gave rise to the 'snake in the tunnel', outlined in Appendix 11.2.

The 'snake in the tunnel', including Britain as one member, continued until June 1972, when a further crisis and talk of another devaluation led to increased support for the pound in order to keep within the snake limits. However, on 23 June 1972 the UK announced suspension of all intervention for sterling and the pound left the snake (and the tunnel) and was allowed to float. This was accompanied with exchange controls on capital transactions, which also applied to the Sterling Area, and effectively resulted in the demise of the Sterling Area.

But why did Britain decide to float in June 1972? It has to be remembered that there was a change in government in June 1970 when Mr Heath took over as Prime Minister from Mr Wilson. Throughout most of Mr Wilson's premiership there was a variety of sterling crises. Unemployment was rising and so, too, were wages and prices. There had been a variety of wage freezes and periods of restraint. The Conservative government opposed controls and it abolished the Prices and Incomes Board. The most significant aspect was Mr Barber's dash for growth in 1971–73. It should not be placed, however, solely at the hands of the Chancellor; the Prime Minister undoubtedly had considerable influence on the policies adopted at the time. The growth in the money supply rose sharply and although the government tried to adopt an '$n - 1$ strategy' in public sector wage settlement (i.e., each settlement should be 1% less than the last), early in 1972 it was forced to settle for a 25% wage rise for miners. Others followed and it appeared that inflation would get out of control. It was in this climate that Britain considered itself too constrained by an overvalued currency. If it floated it could, *it was thought*, pay more attention to achieving internal balance and containing domestic inflation. Throughout the remainder of 1972 and 1973 Mr Heath instituted statutory wage controls in three stages (the TUC having refused to endorse a new voluntary incomes policy).

By floating, Britain withdrew both from the snake and the tunnel. In the nine months that followed, to March 1973, other countries also floated. Although the snake survived with reduced membership, the tunnel had been decidedly abandoned: none of the Group of Ten were pegged on the dollar.

The changes agreed at the Smithsonian Institute were insufficient to hold the system (or 'non-system') together. In February 1973 the mounting flood of dollars caused the Japanese authorities to close the exchange market and suspend their market support of the dollar. New central rates for the main currencies were once again negotiated on a multilateral basis, although a number of currencies were left floating, e.g. the lira, yen, Canadian dollar, sterling, Irish punt, and the Swiss franc. Also the official dollar price of gold was raised from $38 to $42.2 per ounce. However, further speculation, more prolonged than that of February, occurred in March 1973. The outcome was the abandonment of pegged rates to the dollar by the major industrial countries. Thus the dollar standard came to an end.

Managed floating: March 1973–present

The floating of most currencies in March 1973 turned out to be more acceptable than some had thought. The debate on fixed versus flexible exchange rates had continued unabated throughout the 1950s and 1960s.[9] But the 'success' of managed floating converted an arrangement from one which was to be temporary to one which was a permanent feature of the international economic order.

One other important event occurred which helped to bring about the permanency of floating rates: OPEC raised its oil prices dramatically in December 1973, initiated by the Yom Kippur war in October of that year. This, and subsequent oil price rises (most notably in 1979), is a story in itself. What it did do, however, was give a fillip to inflation and create larger deficits and surpluses than hitherto on the balance of payments. Adjustment became even more of a problem than before. In addition, the large oil surpluses of the OPEC countries were finding themselves in the eurocurrency market, for instance funds were now called 'petro-dollars'. These petro-dollars raised the level and severity of short-term capital flows. The oil importing countries were demanding dollars on a large scale – the currency used for the purchase of oil, and to some extent sterling – and were thus putting considerable pressure on these currencies. Since March 1973 the widespread recourse to floating has led to considerable discussion on rules for official intervention in the foreign exchange market. If 'managed' floating was to be made official under the IMF rules, then some guidelines would have to be laid down, and this the IMF did in 1974 (see appendix B in Tew, 1977). Briefly, the guidelines indicated that intervention should be based on the following three principles:

1. The exchange authorities should prevent sudden and disproportionate short-term movements in exchange rates.
2. In consultation with the IMF, countries should establish a target zone for the medium-term values of their exchange rates and keep the actual rates within their target zone.
3. Countries should recognize that exchange rate management involves joint responsibilities.

This legalized floating!

The discussion of changes in the IMF Articles concerning exchange rates was made difficult by the many differing views. The major antagonists were France, who considered that floating should only be temporary, and the US, who favoured continued floating. In August 1975 the EEC Monetary Committee failed to support France. This resulted in France and the US being requested to hammer out their differences concerning Article IV dealing with exchange rate regimes. This they did in the Summit Conference of Rambouillet in November 1975 (see Williamson, 1977). The flavour of the new Article IV is conveyed in Section 2(b), which states

> Under an international monetary system of the kind prevailing on January 1, 1976,
> exchange arrangements include. . . .
> (iii) other exchange arrangements of a member's choice.

The article was thus sufficiently liberal to allow a country to peg its currency, if it so wished, to anything other than gold; to another currency; to a composite of several currencies (including SDRs); or by mutual pegging (as in the snake). It could peg within any margins it wished. Alternatively, it could let its currency float, intervening as and when it pleased – only subject to restraint on aggressive intervention laid down in the *Guidelines for Floating*. In other words, the new Article allowed a country to do virtually anything it wished with regard to its exchange rate!

But the arrangements did not prevent crises. For the UK, the sterling crisis of 1976 will be a landmark in its economic history and is a story that was nearly never told. A summary of it is given in Appendix 11.3, taken from Fay and Young (1978). The impact on the exchange rate is shown quite clearly in Fig. 11.2, which shows the dollar–sterling exchange rate since the advent of floating.

An important observation of the 1976 crisis is worth making. Many believed that a floating exchange rate would allow domestic policy to be pursued without being constrained, or even dictated, by the exchange rate. But it is clear that in 1975–76, monetary policy was very much influenced by external conditions. In particular, monetary policy at the time appeared to be very much influenced by considerations of competitiveness (which we will deal with in a later chapter). This was not always the case, however. In 1978 the

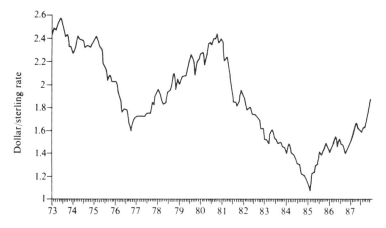

Figure 11.2 Dollar–sterling exchange rate, 1973–87. *Source: Economic Trends.*

exchange rate depreciated, which helped the competitive position of exporters, and it turned out that there was no conflict between monetary policy and movements in the exchange rate. Unfortunately, the measures taken in the Spring of 1978 were not sufficient to restore confidence and so had to be reinforced by further fiscal and monetary measures in June 1978. These had the desired effect, and sterling appreciated, as shown in Fig. 11.2.

In 1979 there was a change in government, with Mrs Thatcher taking premiership in October of 1979. But 1979 was significant in another respect; it was in this year that North Sea oil came on-line. These two events had significant and complicated implications for the exchange rate and UK competitiveness. The incoming Conservative government made it a central policy objective to bring down the rate of inflation, and to do this by means of monetary restraint – coupled with a consistent fiscal policy. The result was a rise in UK interest rates. Such a rise attracted short-term capital from abroad which, as we explained in Chapter 5, led to pressure on the exchange rate to appreciate. However, at the same time, the production of North Sea oil meant that Britain could import less oil than previously and could export some of its North Sea oil.[10] The result of this was also to put pressure on the exchange rate to appreciate. This is exactly what happened. To what extent the appreciation was due to monetary policy and oil-related factors has been much disputed, and we will discuss these briefly in Section 11.4.

It is highly likely that one explanation of the 1979–80 sterling appreciation was overshooting, but, then, it would be necessary to explain *why* the exchange rate overshot during this period. There is some evidence that floating exchange rates have led to greater exchange rate volatility (see Appendix 11.4), which in turn has led to greater uncertainty in economic decision-making. It must be realized that the decision period for exchange rates is very small (less than one day), and that any exchange rate volatility will have considerable effects throughout the economy. Under floating there has been a tendency for the foreign exchange market to overreact to *domestic disturbances*, leading to overshooting.

The dilemma with the exchange rate was becoming apparent in the 1980s. A depreciation, although helpful for the country's competitive position, actually fuelled the inflation which the government had made a top priority to bring down. An appreciation of the exchange rate, although consistent with inflation policy, damaged the competitive position of the economy. Whichever direction the exchange rate went, there was a problem! It was clear, then, that the government could not simply ignore the exchange rate. The budget of 1981 was designed to depreciate the exchange rate, and this it did between January and September of that year. But by late September 1981 things had gone too far and panic ensued. At the same time, interest rates in the US were rising and vast quantities of short-term capital were being attracted away from London, which further extentuated the depreciation of sterling. Thus, the authorities, having initiated policies to depreciate the exchange rate, now began to worry about the fact that it was depreciating both too rapidly and by too much. It was largely this worry that led to further rises in UK interest rates. What became clear in the early 1980s was that the authorities were incapable of preventing a *sustained* movement in or out of sterling and hence of preventing a dramatic movement – both in speed and extent – of the exchange rate.

When judging monetary policy in various versions of the MTFS after 1982, there were various references to the government taking account of exchange rate movements (i.e., monitoring the exchange rate). However, it was only in 1985 that it was clearly spelled out. The budget of 1985 marked a change in policy towards the exchange rate within the Medium-term Financial Strategy. In essence, Mr Lawson, the Chancellor of the Exchequer, was arguing that sound internal policies could be pursued independently of the exchange rate *in the long run*, but that in the short run the exchange rate affected both the price level and inflationary expectations, and that these influences made sound internal policies harder to implement, and thus 'benign neglect is not an option'. He went on to say

> This is why I have repeatedly argued that it is necessary to take the exchange rate into account in judging monetary conditions. There is no mechanical formula which enables us to balance the appropriate combination of the exchange rate and domestic monetary growth needed to keep financial policy on track. But a balance still has to be struck, and struck in a way that takes no chances with inflation. (Quoted from Budd (1985), p. 14)

The statements of 1985 highlighted a typical problem for the authorities with regard to the exchange rate. Mr Lawson's pronouncements just alluded to led to uncertainty and led some in the City to attempt to define the government's target for the exchange rate – in spite of the government's frequent denials that it actually had one. Part of the uncertainty at the time arose because the government indicated that it intended to distinguish between external and internal influences on the exchange rate. If they were external, such as a rise in US interest rates or a rise in oil prices, then these would not necessitate any change in monetary policy. If, on the other hand, the exchange rate was itself responding to changes in the PSBR or monetary growth, then this would necessitate a change in monetary policy. However, as Budd (1985) indicates, there are three problems associated with this, as follows:

1. It is very difficult to tell *why* the exchange rate is changing.
2. Even if the exchange rate change is external, it still affects the price level in the short run.
3. Changes in the exchange rate are seen as signs of fluctuating economic health, whether rightly or wrongly.

In 1985, therefore, there was a switch to take account of exchange rate movements *whatever their cause*.

It is clear from this account that the period of floating can hardly justify the claim that internal policy under a floating exchange rate can be pursued independently of external factors.

11.2 A BALANCE OF PAYMENTS CONSTRAINT?

It would appear from the historical account that whenever Britain attempted to expand the economy the rise in national income would lead to a rise in imports and hence to a deterioration in the current account of the balance of payments. Under a fixed exchange rate, this would usually mean a loss of reserves. Since such a loss could not be sustained for very long, any expansion would need to be stopped, or even reversed. This naturally led to the idea that the balance of payments was a 'constraint' on the demand management of the economy, a view most explicitly expressed by Thirlwall (1978). This view was a reaction to the Bacon–Eltis thesis that there had been a growth of the non-marketable sector at the expense of the marketable sector, thus undermining the industrial base of the economy (Bacon and Eltis, 1976). It is not the intention here to discuss the Bacon–Eltis thesis,[11] but, rather, to consider whether the balance of payments was a constraint in the 1950s and 1960s and to what extent this has been removed by a floating exchange rate.

The view that the balance of payments was a constraint in this early period has been reiterated by Pratten (1985), where he says

> The balance of payments constraint was the main obstacle to the use of expansionary policies during the 1950s and 1960s. As world trade was freed the balance of payments constraint on expansionist policies tightened. (p. 231)

Furthermore, the argument has been applied to the 1970s and 1980s, albeit in a slightly different form, by Hawkins, who says

> It is this tendency for Britain to export relatively cheap, low value-added goods and import more expensive, high value-added products, rather than the growing propensity to import goods *per se*, which is the kernal of the balance of payments constraint. Unless and until this constraint is removed there is not the slightest possibility of achieving a significant and permanent reduction in unemployment and, indeed, unemployment will continue to increase as the manufacturing base of the economy is further eroded.
>
> Hawkins (2nd edn, 1984, p. 93)

As soon as one accepts the view that there is a balance of payments constraint, attention is directed immediately towards ways of removing it, by such means as devaluation or import controls. It is therefore essential to justify the existence of the constraint. In order to do this, however, we must be careful of the use of the word 'constraint', and ask the question of constraint on what? In terms of the policy analysis of Chapter 8, the balance of payments (external balance) is a constraint on achieving domestic demand (internal balance). Thus, one way to define the constraint is to say that external balance is a constraint on the achievement of internal balance. The situation is captured in Fig. 11.3, where IB denotes the internal balance line and XB denotes the external balance line (see Chapter 8 for an analysis of internal and external balance). The economy is positioned at point A. If policies are initiated to achieve internal balance, then the economy can move along such paths as AB, AC or AD. But, whichever path is taken, the economy moves *further* away from the achievement of external balance. Any correction for this will hinder the achievement of internal balance.

If this line of reasoning is adopted, then it is equally valid to say that domestic policies are a 'constraint' on the achievement of balance of payments equilibrium (external balance). No such argument would normally be advanced. But why not? The reason is that, in general,

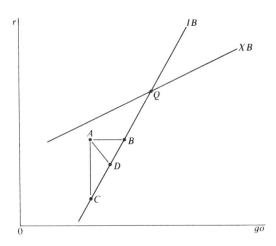

Figure 11.3 External balance constraint on internal balance.

the achievement of internal balance is accorded more importance than that of external balance. But, in the words of Fritz Machlup (1958), this is 'disguised politics'. And this is not the only objection. A glance at Fig. 11.3, and a consideration of policy assignments discussed in Chapter 8, show that it is possible to move the economy to point Q where both internal and external balances are achieved. At point Q there is no constraint! Thus, even if one accepted that external balance was a constraint on the achievement of internal balance, this only makes sense when the economy is at a point such as point A in Fig. 11.3, rather than at point Q. This is an important observation. If one considers that an appropriate response to a balance of payments constraint is to devalue the currency or to impose import controls, then these may be advocated for an economy at point A. But it could be argued that the policy instruments are not at a suitable combination and that what is thus required is to change their levels.

The problem with the 1950s and 1960s was that, in general, fiscal policy was used as the main instrument to achieve internal balance. As such, the economy moved along path AB in terms of Fig. 11.3. This inevitably worsened the balance of payments and under a fixed exchange rate led to a fall in the country's reserves. All this is quite logical. But to move from this to the argument that the balance of payments is therefore a constraint on the achievement of internal balance is simply to accept the policy stance being pursued. As pointed out above, there is no reason *on logical grounds* why policy instruments cannot be assigned in such a way that point Q is attained. Hence, it was not so much that the balance of payments was a constraint in the 1950s and 1960s, but, rather, that policy instruments were either set at inappropriate levels and/or that they were inappropriately assigned. This, of course, does not prevent the problem being exacerbated by a particular level of the exchange rate. Both the internal and external balance lines will depend on the level of exchange rate set. An inappropriate exchange rate could very well mean that the economy is 'far away' from both the internal and external balance lines. This, of course, means that when internal balance is achieved the balance of payments will have a much greater deficit than before: the 'constraint' is even greater.

But does a floating exchange rate make the situation any better? Fig. 11.4 helps to clarify the problem. The only difference between this diagram and the preceding one is that on the

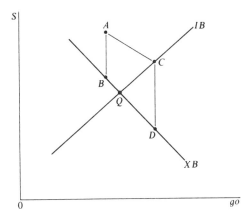

Figure 11.4 Balance of payments constraint on internal balance under a floating exchange rate.

vertical axis we have the spot exchange rate, S, as an instrument.[12] Again position the economy at point A, in this case with unemployment and a deficit. If the exchange rate is free to float, and if there is quick market clearing in the foreign exchange market, then the economy will quickly move to the external balance line, path AB. But this in no way removes the 'constraint', as used in our earlier discussion. It certainly means that the balance of payments can achieve an equilibrium. But, and here again 'disguised politics' arise, it does not necessarily achieve internal balance. If internal balance is still the main objective of the two, this will not be achieved. Alternatively, if the economy were taken, for example, along path AC in order to achieve internal balance, the quick depreciation of the exchange rate would move the economy to point D along path CD. It would thus appear once again that the external account (now through the exchange rate) was a constraint on domestic policy – even though the exchange rate was free to float. Furthermore, a movement along paths AC and CD could be much worse for the achievement of internal balance than under a fixed exchange rate, at least as shown here (Goldstein, 1980).

But a consideration of Fig. 11.4 demonstrates once again that it is the use of the word 'constraint' which is misleading. It is quite possible to have no constraint if the level of government spending was set at the appropriate level, namely the level where the IB and XB lines intersect. The 'constraint' then, is, the appropriate mix of policies being pursued by the authorities. If the number of objectives grows, it is highly likely that a conflict of objectives will ensue, and one or other of the objectives will act as a 'constraint' on the achievement of the rest. The constraint is within the policy formation rather than attributable to one particular source.

11.3 GOVERNMENT INTERVENTION IN THE FOREIGN EXCHANGE MARKET AND EXCHANGE RATE TARGETS

Under the Bretton-Woods fixed exchange rate system that operated until 1971, intervention by the authorities was fairly well defined. An authority agreed (1) the parity rate, and (2) the currency it would use to intervene in the foreign exchange market (i.e., its intervention currency). It further agreed to maintain its currency $\pm 1\%$ either side of the parity rate. In general, the parity rate was defined with respect to the dollar. In the case of the UK this meant, in practice, 2 cents either side of the parity rate. Thus, after 1967 when the parity rate was set at £1 = \$2.40, the band was \$2.38–\$2.42. As we explained in Section 11.1, this would be achieved by the Bank selling dollars (buying sterling) when the market exchange rate fell to the lower limit of \$2.38 and buying dollars (selling sterling) when the market exchange rate reached its upper limit of \$2.42. In general, most intervention was done in the spot market, and only during crisis situations was intervention also carried out in the forward market.

Difficulties over intervention only really became a problem with the advent of floating. Under a truly freely fluctuating exchange rate there is no government intervention in the foreign exchange market and no reason to hold reserves. But this has never been the situation in practice: governments have nearly always intervened in the foreign exchange market and this has given rise to 'dirty floating'. It is thus necessary to discuss *why* a government would wish to intervene. If there is some justification for intervention, then the obvious next question is: 'What are the appropriate rules for intervention in the foreign exchange market?' Even if there is no theoretical justification for intervention, it is still necessary to consider what *actual* intervention policies have been pursued and what have been their implications. The question of appropriate intervention rules is a theoretical question, while the issue of what intervention rules have actually been followed is country-specific. In this section we will confine ourselves to the UK.

Why, then, do governments intervene in the foreign exchange market? A number of reasons have been advanced, as follows:

1. To reduce exchange rate volatility arising from capital flows which do not reflect the underlying real economy and increase the level of uncertainty.
2. To avoid too great an appreciation because this will reduce the competitive position of exporters and import substitute industries.
3. To avoid too great a depreciation because this will hinder policies for bringing down inflation.
4. To counter disturbances (shocks) either domestically or externally.

The first reason is a mixture of concerns. The degree of exchange rate volatility is an empirical question, and we give some brief remarks about this in Appendix 11.4. But if exchange rate volatility in and of itself is a 'bad' thing, then the answer is not intervention but, rather, a fixed exchange rate. A second concern is that capital flows are responding to expectations, whether about government policy, external events or institutional changes. This has led to investigations into how exchange rates change in response to news (Frenkel, 1982). Finally, if the exchange rate changes are uncertain, then pricing and investment decisions become more difficult for many firms.

The second reason arises from the possible conflict between the current and capital account. The exchange rate is determined by the demand and supply of foreign exchange, and this demand and supply is responding both to the trade in goods and services *and* to flows of capital. As we outlined in Section 11.1, it is possible for tight monetary policy or the production of North Sea oil to lead to an appreciation of sterling, which in turn raises export prices and lowers import prices. Although helpful in the fight towards reducing inflation, it does have the unfortunate consequence of reducing export competitiveness and making it difficult for import substitute industries to compete. If the government feels that such effects are detrimental, then it can deliberately intervene in the foreign exchange market to reverse the movement.

The third reason is the opposite of this. A depreciation may arise which raises import prices and lowers export prices. Although beneficial for competition, it could undermine the government's attempt at reducing inflation. It is even possible that in a few weeks of exchange rate depreciation, months of domestic policy are nullified. To prevent this, the government may consider itself justified in the intervening in the foreign exchange market.

The fourth and final reason has also become prominent in the 1970s and 1980s, and we take this up in more detail in Chapter 16.

There is, however, a very practical problem regardless of why the government may wish to intervene. Namely, the government must (1) ascertain what the trend in the exchange rate is; and, (2) establish the reason for the movement away from the trend. Neither of these are easy to do, as Nigel Lawson discovered in the early 1980s. It is especially difficult to associate particular exchange rate movements with particular disturbances. There is also a further problem that the authorities must face. If the movement in the exchange rate is large and/or persistent, then it may not have sufficient reserves to carry out the required intervention. It is, of course, possible for the Bank to supplement the reserves by *swap* arrangements, but even these may not be sufficient. On the other hand, all the Bank may wish to do is indicate the *direction* in which it would like to see the exchange rate go, and hope that this will have sufficient influence on expectations that they achieve their aim.

Having said all this, it still remains for us to discuss the *form* the intervention should take, or has taken. However, this is no easy task, not least because it depends on two things. First, it depends on what model is considered appropriate for exchange rate determination. The different models of exchange rate determination have very different adjustment mechanisms, and hence exchange rate movements have different implications for the domestic economy.[13] Second, it depends on the source of disturbance. These two factors are too involved to examine here, see Blundell-Wignall and Chouraqui (1984). What can be said is that rules for intervention fall into two broad categories as follows, Argy (1981):

1. Those that mandate some form of 'leaning against the wind'.
2. The setting of exchange rate targets.

The first category is the one which has largely been taken by the UK, and discussed in detail in Tosini (1977). However, it implies that private transactors cannot achieve the desired stability of exchange rates and that the government can. It is also possible that the policy to stabilize the exchange rate is counter to the stabilization of income (output). Finally, the rule is very vague and could be open to abuse.

The second category of setting of target exchange rates involves two steps, (1) setting the target, and (2) specifying the rule for intervention in relation to that target. Discussion of the rules proposed is beyond the scope of this book, but see Mikesell and Goldstein (1975). However, one is worth mentioning: this is a rule based on purchasing power parity (see Section 5.3), and was embodied in the OPTICA Plan.[14] Under this rule a country that has a high rate of inflation and whose currency is depreciating would intervene at the lower end of the band in order to prevent further depreciation, but would not be allowed to intervene at the upper end of the band. Conversely, a country that has a low rate of inflation and whose currency is appreciating would intervene at the upper end of the band but would not be allowed to intervene at the lower end of the band. (Notice in this proposal that a band for the exchange rate is still envisaged.) But this, too, is not without its critics (for an example see Bigman, 1984; and Niehans, 1984).

On a more practical level, the Conservative government since 1979 has had a rather unclear intervention policy. At one level it perceives the foreign exchange market to be like any other market. As such, the less government interference the better. In this case the only intervention is to iron out excessive movements in the exchange rate, 'leaning against the wind'. Here the objective is to reduce exchange rate volatility. However, as our historical outline in Section 11.1 has revealed, the government at various times has had to monitor the exchange rate more carefully. Furthermore, in crisis periods it is difficult to believe that it did not try to intervene to reverse either a rapid and too great an appreciation or a rapid and too great a depreciation. In this case there would be a temporary switch in objective towards the exchange rate: a switch from monitoring it to setting it as an intermediate target – even if the authorities did not disclose what that target was! Consideration of the exchange rate as a target was also apparent in September 1985 when the finance ministers of the Group of Five (G-5, the US, the UK, Germany, France and Japan) attempted an 'orderly appreciation of the non-dollar currencies against the dollar'. Ministers agreed on a target but gave no explanation of how such targets would be met (see Sachs, 1986).

As far as the SDP and the Labour Party are concerned, both support the idea of setting a target for the exchange rate. Labour is quite clear that the target should be based on some measure of competitiveness. The SDP, however, favour both a target exchange rate and entry into the European Monetary System (EMS), which we will deal with in Section 11.5. This has two implications: first, the target must be in relation to the effective exchange rate; second, it may not be compatible with a target based on competitiveness. Even so, the SDP see targeting of the exchange rate as desirable both in the short run and in the long run. Both parties recognize that setting exchange rate targets means abandoning monetary targets. Monetary policy becomes a means of regulating the exchange rate (Tomlinson, 1986).

11.4 EXCHANGE RATE POLICY AND NORTH SEA OIL

There are basically two extreme forms of exchange rate policy which can arise from North Sea oil (NSO) exploration.[15] One extreme is to assume a freely floating exchange rate with no change in UK reserves or, alternatively, a fixed exchange rate and a change in UK reserves. We can look at these in terms of the demand and supply of sterling.

Prior to 1974 we have the initial demand and supply curves $D_0^£$ and $S_0^£$, shown in Fig. 11.5. The early period was typified by substantial imports both of goods and related services. These were largely financed by large capital inflows. The costs of exploration were relatively small but the purchase and installation of platforms was by far the major component. The high capital inflow led to a shift to the right in the demand for sterling, while the related imports also led to a rightward shift in the supply curve, shown by curves $D_1^£$ and $S_1^£$ respectively. The overall impact on the exchange rate was small and probably swamped by other short-term factors. The turning point was 1976–77 when oil production began to rise substantially. The situation is illustrated in Fig. 11.6. The rise in oil exports led

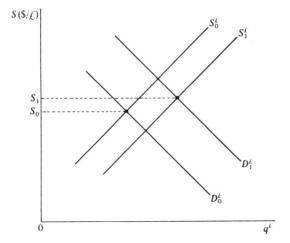

Figure 11.5 NSO impact on the exchange rate after 1977 during oil exploration.

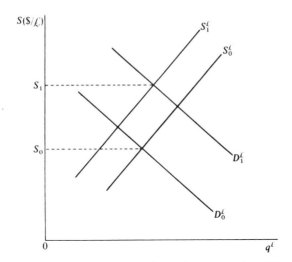

Figure 11.6 NSO impact on the exchange rate after 1977

to a rightward shift in the demand for sterling, while the reduced level of imports of oil led to a leftward shift in the supply curve. The combined effect was an appreciation of sterling from S_0 to S_1.

Although there was an appreciation of the dollar–sterling exchange rate (and of the effective exchange rate) during the period 1977–80, as shown in Fig. 11.2, this cannot be attributed solely to North Sea oil. The fight against high inflation in the UK led to a rise in interest rates, which also attracted short-term capital into the UK, with the result that the dollar–sterling exchange rate was pushed up. To put the issue in the form of a question: Was the sterling appreciation since 1977 largely a result of (1) North Sea oil, (2) government policy in fighting inflation, or (3) both (or possibly neither)?

In 1980 the general opinion seemed to be that the appreciation of sterling was due to North Sea oil. Alan Walters, economic advisor to Mrs Thatcher, doubted this, and thus an independent report was commissioned under Professor Niehans. The Niehans Report (published in 1981) argued that tight monetary policy was the main cause of the sterling appreciation.[16] There has been general support for the argument that tight monetary policy, leading to high interest rates, certainly was a contributory factor in sterling's appreciation (the 'Thatcher factor'), but there has been some doubt cast on the significance of North Sea oil as a significant contributory factor, Spencer (1986). The reason is that it was quite clear once North Sea oil had been discovered and was being produced that it would improve the UK balance of payments position significantly and that the exchange rate would appreciate. These events, it is argued, should have been anticipated and markets should have adjusted instantaneously to such expectations, Minford (1977). The simulations undertaken by Spencer (1986) seem to support this. Further investigations into the impact of North Sea oil on the exchange rate point to the importance of the assumption of the degree of substitutability between domestic and foreign assets. If substitutability is poor, then a depreciation is possible, which arises from lower interest rates when debt is retired, which in turn leads to a large increase in domestic demand. Thus, an appreciation is more likely only if substitutability between domestic and foreign assets is high (Wallis, 1985). On the other hand, the tight monetary policy of the incoming Conservative government could not have been so readily anticipated. These arguments are a clear expression of the rational expectations thesis that was gaining ground during this period (outlined in Chapter 4). But Spencer goes as far as saying that neither monetary policy nor North Sea oil could have been the main reason for the appreciation, and that we are little the wiser even now.

An alternative strategy could have been to hold the exchange rate fixed, say at S_0 in Fig. 11.7, which would have meant that North Sea oil would have increased the reserves by dR. This policy was not followed, however. Since the crisis of 1976 when the dollar–sterling rate fell dramatically, to as low as 1.651 in the fourth quarter of 1976, the rate, it is claimed, has not been deliberately managed and the government has pursued a policy of 'leaning against the wind'. Furthermore, the appreciation of sterling was a help to the government in its fight against inflation. The appreciation led to a fall in import prices whose effect on the general price level has more than swamped the effect resulting from the rise in export prices. The concomitant effects, however, have been the rise in import penetration and the loss of export competitiveness, both of which we discuss in Chapter 17.

There are basically five interacting factors which can lead to an appreciation of sterling. If inflation at home is less than that abroad, then exports will become more competitive on world markets and import substitutes relatively more attractive. This will stimulate net exports and put pressure on sterling to appreciate. A second factor arises from a rise in the North Sea oil price. North Sea oil, like OPEC oil, is quoted in dollars. Since the demand for oil is relatively inelastic, a rise in the dollar price of oil will improve the balance of payments and put pressure on sterling to appreciate. A third possibility occurs through the capital account. If UK interest rates rise relative to those abroad, then there will be an increase in the net capital inflow and pressure on sterling to appreciate. A fourth reason why sterling might appreciate is because of short-term market conditions which are responding to news, for example. Or, fifthly, because of a rise in the expected rate of appreciation. This final influence will attract funds into the UK until the appreciation occurs which will be then taken out again if and when the appreciation occurs. However, it is extremely difficult to

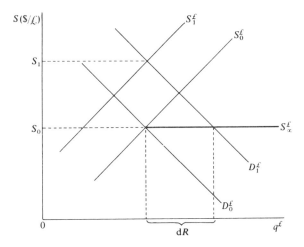

Figure 11.7 NSO, the exchange rate and policy options.

disentangle these influences. For whatever cause, the government has the option of letting the exchange rate appreciate or letting its reserves rise (or some combination of the two). In debating these two alternatives, monetarists favour an appreciating exchange rate, while neo-Keynesians point to the loss of competitiveness and the loss of employment that this will cause. In the event the exchange rate was allowed to float, and the change in the reserve position was minimal.

11.5 THE EUROPEAN MONETARY SYSTEM: BRITAIN IN OR OUT?

The snake arrangements, outlined in Appendix 11.2, were not very successful, and there was a more determined effort within Europe to move towards monetary union. It was thought to be a feasible strategy that would allow inflation-free growth, full employment and greater economic unity within the EEC. As originally envisaged, the European Monetary System was just a first step; later would come a European Monetary Fund (similar to the International Monetary Fund) and a European Currency Unit (ECU), which would be more than just an accounting unit. However, to date, only the first step has been taken. The European Monetary System (EMS) was set up in March 1979.

The initial negotiations were dominated with rather technical arrangements surrounding the question of who bears the adjustment burden, and whether the system should be based on a basket formula or a parity grid. As it turned out, a compromise between the two was set up. A European Currency Unit (ECU) was established for accounting purposes, which comprised a basket of currencies of member countries. (At the time Britain was part of the basket but did not become a member of the EMS.) In addition, a rather complex system was set up to act as an indicator of divergence from the norm. In essence the divergence threshold was a fraction (0.75) of the fluctuation allowed within the parity grid (i.e., the divergence of any currency of the system *vis-à-vis* the ECU) weighted by the importance of the country within the basket.[17] This gave a band for any given currency around the central ECU rate within the system. If the *divergence indicator* came close to or beyond the threshold, then the Central Bank had to intervene to bring the currency back towards the norm. The divergence indicator arrangements dominated the negotiations, but a number of policy issues were left unresolved, such as arrangements for currency realignments, clear intervention rules, and attitudes towards third parties (especially the US dollar).

Britain did not join the EMS, although the issue was much debated, especially in the First Report of the Expenditure Committee, Session 1978–79 (HMSO, 1978). In fact, the Committee saw the following four problems particular to the UK in relation to the EMS:

1. Sterling was still a reserve currency and hence was subject to marked pressure additional to those which other EEC countries are subject.
2. North Sea oil would lead to an appreciation under floating; if the exchange rate was fixed, then all the impact would fall on domestic prices, so leading to a higher rate of inflation in the UK than in other EEC countries.
3. Exchange controls in the UK were more severe than those in other EEC countries, so if they were removed (as they were) Britain would face particular problems.
4. If Ireland entered and Britain did not, the pound sterling and the Irish punt would diverge, with detrimental consequences for Northern Ireland.

The UK agreed that stability of exchange rates was important, but it decided to opt out, largely because it saw the basket formula as more appropriate and because of its trade with the USA. The link between the UK and the USA meant that the dollar–pound rate was very important, and without a policy towards the USA, the UK would be left in an uncertain situation. However, this point of view substantiated Britain's anti-European stance in the eyes of some people. Britain's relative trade with the USA as against other EEC countries has played a large part in the debate of Britain's entry into the EMS. However, since 1973 Europe has increasingly become a much more important market for UK exports, with the US remaining more or less stable. The EEC share rose from 32.6% in 1975 to 49.4% in 1987, while the US share was 9.2% in 1975 and 9.6% in 1980, but rose to 13.8% in 1987, see Table 17.1.

The EMS was set up just prior to the incoming Conservative government in the UK. With oil output now rising and the removal of capital controls, pressure on sterling mounted and the possibility of the UK joining the EMS became more remote. However, in 1986 the issue was debated once again, but at the time of writing the UK is still not a member. Nor is there general agreement on the issue between the major political parties. The Labour Party is very against Britain's entry into the EMS: 'Essentially, the attitude here mirrors that of the Labour Party towards European Community institutions generally: they restrict Britain's freedom of action, and hence are disadvantageous'. (Tomlinson, 1986, p. 74). This view has been put more forcibly by Jay (1986)

> All schemes for limiting the basic freedom to influence the exchange rate of one's own currency should be treated with the greatest scepticism. Indeed almost the only mistake in economic policy which British governments have not made since 1970 is to join the European Monetary System (EMS). The broad guiding principle should be to treat the exchange rate as a consequence of other desirable policies and not as an instrument for enforcing them, still less as an end in itself. (p. 236)

Such a view, however, is not shared by the SDP, which is pro-Europe and favour Britain joining the EMS. It sees the following three advantages of being in the EMS:

1. It would provide an appropriate framework for pursuing an exchange rate policy.
2. It would provide participants with access to greater resources to deploy in foreign exchange markets.
3. It would create a zone of greater currency stability, at least with Britain's major trading partners.

In conclusion, there is still a 'wait and see' attitude from Britain in response to entry into the EMS.

NOTES

1. In the case of the Sterling Area the intervention currency was sterling.

2. Forward intervention for sterling was particularly strong in the early 1960s when capital flows were great. See Chalmers (1971) for a discussion of the forward intervention of sterling during the period 1964–67.

3. The IMF laid particular stress on the fact that a country had to be in 'fundamental disequilibrium' in order to alter its parity rate. However, it did not define what this meant, and thus it was difficult for countries to know exactly when they were in 'fundamental disequilibrium'. For an early discussion of this problem see Nurkse (1945) and Machlup (1958) and, more recently, Thirlwall (1980).

4. A subsequent study by the National Institute of Economic and Social Research (1972) placed the sum at about 1.65.

5. The J-curve effect denotes the response of the value of the current balance consequent on a devaluation (or depreciation). The fall in the exchange rate raises import prices and lowers export prices. However, volumes are not affected initially. Hence, the value of imports rise and the value of exports fall until quantities adjust to the price changes. Thus, the initial impact is a *worsening* of the current balance, which improves as quantities adjust to the price changes.

6. The basic balance was a popular concept in the 1960s and 1970s, and refers to the current account balance (goods and services) plus long-term capital. The balance of payments accounts no longer distinguish short- and long-term capital flows.

7. See Tew (1977).

8. A number of plans are discussed in Coffey and Presley (1971), but the one which received the most attention was the Werner Report, which outlined a series of steps towards monetary unification of the EEC. Unfortunately the events of the early 1970s meant that any such moves were impracticable.

9. See Friedman (1953), Johnson (1969), and Sohmen (1969).

10. North Sea oil is of superior quality to Arabian crude oil, so it is quite sensible to both import and export oil: importing the lower quality oil and exporting the higher quality oil.

11. On the Bacon–Eltis thesis see Bacon and Eltis (1976), Thirlwall (1978) and Section 17.5 of the present book.

12. The shape of the IB and XB lines can be established as follows. Begin at point Q and consider a depreciation of sterling (a fall in S). First consider IB. A depreciation will improve the balance of payments and lead to a stimulus of the economy (income rising above the full employment level).

Hence, to re-establish internal balance, income must be reduced, and this can be accomplished by reducing government spending. Hence, the *IB* line is positively sloped. Now consider the *XB* line. The fall in the exchange rate, as just indicated, will lead to an improvement in the balance of payments and, since we begin with a balance, a surplus will occur. To eliminate the surplus and re-establish equilibrium on the balance of payments, government spending can be increased which will raise income, raise imports and eliminate the surplus. Hence, the *XB* line is negatively sloped.

13. On the different exchange rate models, see Krueger (1983) and Williamson (1983, chapter 10).

14. The OPTICA proposal is discussed in Basevi and de Grauwe (1978).

15. For a theoretical discussion of the impact of North Sea Oil, see Corden (1980).

16. For a discussion of the issues surrounding the Niehans Report, see Holmes (1985, pp. 59–61) and Keegan (1984, pp. 159–61).

17. See Bank of England (1979).

APPENDIX 11.1 TEN FEATURES OF THE BRETTON-WOODS SYSTEM

The Bretton-Woods System had ten features which are worthy of brief discussion:

1. The system did allow for changes in parity rates, but only in periods of 'fundamental disequilibrium'. However, the IMF nowhere defined what constituted a 'fundamental disequilibrium', and in practice changes in parity rates were infrequent. When they did occur, they were often forced on an economy and tended to be large. Furthermore, both devaluations and revaluations were considered to represent, rightly or wrongly, a failure of the government in its management of the economy.

2. Throughout the post-war period all foreign exchange markets were managed to some degree by means of official intervention, and official transactions were carried out by the Central Banks.

3. Central Banks, or the monetary authorities, besides being responsible for intervention, also undertook two other forms of transactions:
   (a) transactions with each other, e.g., credits, swaps and gold sales; and
   (b) transactions with international institutions such as the IMF and the Bank of International Settlements (BIS).

4. All Central Banks, when they intervened in the market, had to do so by means of their specified *intervention currency*. In most cases this was dollars.

5. The Bretton-Woods System contained two asymmetries:
   (a) *the nth country problem.* Suppose the system contains n different currencies, and let the nth be the US dollar. Then the remaining $(n-1)$ currencies are pegged to the dollar at the agreed par values. This means the US has no say in the level of the par value of any of the $(n-1)$ countries; nor does the Federal Reserve need to intervene, since this, too, is undertaken by the $(n-1)$ members' Central Banks. The reserve currency country, the US, acts purely passively in this system; and,
   (b) *asymmetry between deficit and surplus countries.* We have already established that a deficit country loses foreign exchange reserves and a surplus country gains foreign exchange reserves. In the absence of borrowing, a deficit country is limited in the number and size of deficits it can finance from its reserves, since, ultimately, they cannot fall below zero.

6. Operating official convertibility required all countries to hold reserves of the asset into which they undertook to convert their national currencies. Invariably, these were dollars. As US dollar liabilities grew, its gold backing diminished in proportion. This led to the Triffin dilemma. As the dollar came under pressure, countries diversified their reserves.

7. Currencies were bolstered by *ad hoc* arrangements between the members of the Group of Ten, which supplied reserves in addition to an individual country's reserves, and these became part of international liquidity.

8. In 1961, when the dollar came under pressure, the Federal Reserve Board entered into cooperative

arrangements with foreign Central Banks. Basically, dollars were *swapped* for other currencies, and reversed when the pressure was off. These were reciprocal arrangements which became quite frequent.

9. In the mid-1960s there was growing concern that international liquidity was inadequate. By 1969 the negotiations on a new form of international liquidity came to fruition, and Special Drawing Rights (SDRs) were created.

10. The need for international liquidity also manifested itself through the creation of new capital markets, the most conspicuous and fastest growing of which was the eurodollar market.

APPENDIX 11.2 THE SNAKE IN THE TUNNEL

The *snake in the tunnel* was a nickname given to the currency arrangements that arose from the initial stages of the Werner plan for European monetary reform in the early 1970s. In particular, it was an arrangement which attempted to overcome fluctuations in European currencies arising from the Smithsonian Agreement of December 1971. Under this agreement, currencies could fluctuate *with respect to the dollar* by $\pm 2.25\%$ around a central rate. (Prior to this date the allowed fluctuation with respect to the dollar was $\pm 1\%$ around a parity rate.) It is to be noted that dollars were the intervention currency of most countries, and currency had to be declared as such to the IMF. Hence, from floor to ceiling, a European currency could move 4.5%. This range of 4.5% represented the 'tunnel' in which European currencies could fluctuate. The problem with the arrangement, at least for European countries, was that if one currency moved from floor to ceiling (a movement of 4.5%), while another moved from ceiling to floor (also a movement of 4.5%), then the movement between *themselves* was a total of 9%. A simple arithmetical example is illustrated in Table A11.2.1.

This possible movement of cross-rates between European currencies was disliked, and certainly ran counter to the Werner Report of October 1970, which (in three stages) wanted eventual fixed cross-rates between member countries. The widening of the tunnel (from 2% to 4.5%) which was accepted by the Group of Ten (G-10) was seen by the Community Council of Ministers as a retrogressive step. Consequently, in April 1972 the EEC Central Banks took steps to halve the divergence between member countries. In other words, the difference between the strongest and the weakest currency in the arrangement could not diverge from each other by any more than 2.25% when compared with the dollar (which would give a maximum cross-parity rate of 4.5%). This accordingly gave rise to a snake-like figure, as illustrated in Fig. A11.2.1. Between 1972 and 1976 there was even a *worm* in the snake. arising from the 1.5% divergence agreed between Belgium and the Netherlands.

The snake began in April 1972 with Belgium, France, Germany, Italy, Luxembourg, and the Netherlands as members. In May the UK and Denmark joined the arrangement. The snake, with Britain as a member, continued until June 1972, when a further crisis and talk of another devaluation led to increased support for the pound in order to keep within the snake limits. However, on 23 June 1972, the UK announced suspension of all intervention for sterling and left the snake. Denmark followed shortly after, but then returned in October 1972. As Table A11.2.2 shows, however, the snake had a very unsettled period. with countries leaving and then returning, and with yet others joining. Even so, it did form the basis of later negotiations for the formation of a European Monetary System (EMS), which came into being in 1979. Britain did not join this system (at least not formally, even though sterling was part of the basket which made up the ECU). At the time of writing, Britain is still not a member.

APPENDIX 11.3 THE STERLING CRISIS OF 1976

Following the resignation of Harold Wilson (16 March) and the subsequent success of James Callaghan (5 June), there was a deliberate policy to let the pound float down – but it went out of control!

Table A11.2.1 An example of a possible 9% cross-parity
variation within the snake arrangements

DM–$ situation
Initial position 2DM = $1
New position   2.09DM = $1
Change = 4.5%

FF–$ situation
Initial position 20FF = $1
New position   19.1FF = $1
Change = 4.5%

DM–FF situation
Initial position 2DM = $1 = 20FF or 1DM = 10FF
New position   2.09DM = $1 = 19.1FF or 1DM = 9.1FF
Change = 9%

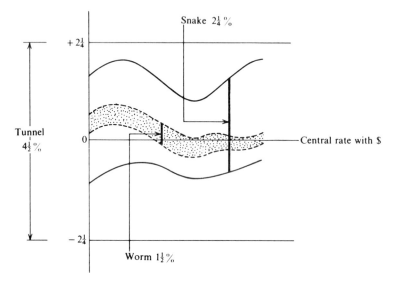

Figure A11.2.1 The snake in the tunnel.

The Treasury were in favour of devaluation, the Bank of England favoured swap loans. The problem with loans was (1) whether they were forthcoming, and (2) what strings they attached in regard to changes in domestic policies. By 4 June a standby credit of $3.3 billion was arranged from European banks and the Bank of International Settlements. The US Treasury and Federal Reserve advanced $2 billion (totalling $5.3 billion). The government preferred this because it did not incur IMF interference. The Americans, however, were not happy and were determined that some deflation would be adopted on the lines of the IMF requirements. The Americans, through Edwin Yeo, forced Denis Healey into accepting a time constraint on the loan, a period of 6 months. If the loan could not be repaid after this time then the government would approach the IMF. Denis Healey, however, announced to the Commons: 'There are no strings to this money at all.'

During the lead up to the loan there was a great deal of policy manipulation of the exchange market, and quite a conflict of views between the Treasury and the Bank of England. The Americans, too, were very worried and saw the possibility of another world depression if Britain lost control. The American view was that the Tories had lost control of monetary policy and, after 1974, that Labour had lost control of budgetary policy.

Table A11.2.2 European monetary chronology, 1972–79

1972		
April	24	Basle Agreement (10.4.72) comes into force forming the 'snake in the tunnel'; participants: Belgium, France, Germany, Italy, Luxembourg, The Netherlands
May	13	The UK and Denmark join snake
	23	Norway becomes associated
June	23	The UK withdraws from snake and tunnel
	27	Denmark withdraws from snake but remains in tunnel
October	10	Denmark returns to snake
1973		
February	13	Italy withdraws from snake
March	19	Transition to joint floating; interventions to maintain tunnel margins against the dollar discontinued; Sweden becomes associated; DM revalued by 3%
April	3	Establishment of European Monetary Cooperation Fund (EMCF) approved
June	29	DM revalued by 5.5%
September	17	Dutch guilder revalued by 5%
November	16	Norwegian krone revalued by 5%
1974		
January	19	France withdraws from snake
1975		
July	10	France returns to snake
1976		
March	15	France withdraws from snake
October	17	Frankfurt realignment: Danish krone devalued by 6%, the Dutch guilder and the Belgian franc by 2% and the Norwegian and Swedish krone by 3% each
1977		
April	1	The Swedish krone devalued by 6%, the Danish and Norwegian krone by 3% each
August	28	Sweden withdraws from snake; Danish and Norwegian krone devalued by 5% each
1978		
February	13	Norwegian krone devalued by 8%
July	6–7	Bremen summit
October	17	DM revalued by 4%; Dutch guilder and Belgian franc by 2%
December	12	Norway withdraws fron snake
1979		
March	13	Brussels Agreement (4–5 December 1978) enters into force – EMS begins functioning. Participants: Belgium, Denmark, France, Germany, Ireland, Italy, Luxembourg, The Netherlands.
September	24	Realignment of EMS currencies; the DM revalued by 2%, the Danish krone devalued by 3%
November	30	Danish krone devalued by 5%

It was hoped that the $5.3 billion loan, coupled with another mini-budget and a newly negotiated Phase II of incomes policy, would restore confidence in the market. In addition, it was hoped that at the very least this would not displease the Labour Party, who did not want strong deflation because of its likely unfavourable impact on employment. After much debate, an original £1 billion cut was raised to £2 billion by Healey (an unprecedented move because the second £1 billion came without discussion) in the mini-budget of 22 July 1976 – this extra £1 billion coming from a 2% rise in the national insurance contributions paid by employers.

Events really began to move when on 9 September the Bank was instructed not to support the pound. Of the $5.3 billion loan, $1.1 billion had been spent by the last week in August and a further $0.4 billion was spent in the first week in September to hold the exchange rate at £1 = $1.77. It must also be recalled that the entire loan had to be repaid in December. In addition, M3 rose sharply towards the end of August. At this time no clear money supply target, as a weapon against inflation, was laid down. This, however, would require changes in the interest rate but it was summer and Parliament was in recess, and so no decision was made. The professionals, however, took this indecision as further proof that the government had lost control of the economy. The interest rate was raised to 13% on 9 September.

By 28 September the pound reached an all-time low of £1 = $1.64 and next day Healey announced that he would apply for a loan from the IMF. There was also pressure to raise the Minimum Lending Rate to 15%; otherwise 'the pound would go down the drain'. There was a lot of toing and froing and innumerable telegrams. On 6 October James Callaghan fought off both the Chancellor of the Exchequer and the Governor of the Bank of England, who were demanding a rise in the MLR. Late in the same day, however, Healey saw the Prime Minister again and claimed that if interest rates did not rise, he would not be responsible for the currency. Grudgingly, Callaghan agreed to raise the interest rate to 15%, which was announced on 7 October. October 6 was 'The day the £ nearly died'.

The seriousness of the situation was not apparent to most – even those in the Cabinet. Fay and Young (1978) put the position clearly

> The Bank of England could support the pound, but with the pound so weak and confidence so low the Bank never knew how much it would have to spend. If it supported the pound at any price the cost could run to $1 billion a day or even more, and when the reserves and the standby loan had been used up, Britain would have nothing left with which to pay her way. In October 1976 the men at the Bank and Treasury felt there was that real possibility: the money would actually run out. (p. 21)

With the raising of interest rates, Callaghan decided to take over the running of the economy personally. In this he assumed he could rely on the support of Anthony Crosland. Fay and Young argue there were the following three strands in developments over the next weeks:

1. Callaghan's conviction that both his and the US Treasury were in league to force deflation.
2. Britain could not pursue independent economic policy while sterling was still a major reserve currency.
3. The only way to deal with the situation was to start an international political offensive – that is, bring others round to his way of thinking.

On 1 November the IMF team arrived, under assumed names and very nervous, to discuss the terms of the loan. This was the biggest single loan in the Fund's 30-year history. Crucial to the discussions was the Public Sector Borrowing Requirement, but this was very difficult to forecast. There was a belief that the figure was 'cooked' by the Treasury. The IMF team felt that the PSBR should be reduced by £4 billion in two years, stricter control over the money supply and stricter control over domestic credit expansion (DCE). Furthermore, it favoured a fall in the exchange rate, possibly to a target rate of £1 = $1.50. All suggestions of low targets for the exchange rate were hotly denied, but it was undoubtedly a major debating point. There was considerable fear in the US that the whole system would collapse and economies would be sent on quite divergent and unforeseen courses. A large part of the debate concerned sterling balances.

By 21 November rumours were widespread about the IMF intention, which inevitably resulted in the Cabinet meeting of 23 November being a heated one. The two camps divided on the evening of 22 November, and presented their cases at the Cabinet meeting the following day. The second Cabinet meeting occurred on 25 November. This resulted in a change of strategy away from Anthony Crosland's side and in favour of Tony Benn's alternative strategy of import restrictions. This was feared, however, especially if retaliation was forthcoming and the Treasury's view was that Britain was too weak to fight. It became clear, once Callaghan indicated he would support Chancellor Healey, that if Crosland stood by his views the Cabinet would be defeated, and a Tory majority of 200 was forecast. During the talks the possibility of an import deposit scheme was mooted which was not so stringent as import restrictions. Even so, Shirley Williams was adamant that they were protectionist and would damage the Third World. While these discussions continued, fears in the Treasury mounted as protectionism became more of a reality. On 2 December Callaghan made his support for Healey public. Crosland succumbed rather than risk bringing down the government.

The problem now was where should the cuts in public spending occur. One aspect is vital to understand: the cuts would have to be in areas where no new laws were required because they would never be accepted by parliament. This set the tone and direction of later talks. Thus, it was announced that the PSBR would be cut by £3 billion over two years. The letter of intent also contained promises to restrict DCE and (in private) the Chancellor had promised the IMF that tax cuts would be forthcoming.

The last stage in the negotiations concerned sterling balances. The safety net agreement for sterling was announced in the Commons on 11 January 1977. This allowed an orderly reduction in the role of sterling as a reserve currency.

APPENDIX 11.4 EXCHANGE RATE VOLATILITY

Since sterling was floated in June 1972 there has been a general impression that exchange rates have been more volatile; certainly more volatile than under the fixed exchange rate system that prevailed under Bretton-Woods. Considering for the moment the dollar–sterling exchange rate only (the most important for the UK), it is clear from Fig. 11.2 that there has been major movement in this rate since floating began.

In the Bretton-Woods period the dollar–sterling exchange rate could move only within a 4-cent range ($2.78–$2.82 prior to 1967 and $2.38–$2.42 after 1967). The range and standard deviation for the sterling–dollar exchange rate for the period 1972–87 using monthly data is given in Table A11.4.1. What is certainly shown is a range far in excess of $0.04 for all the years of floating. The range goes from a low of $0.1081 in 1972 to $0.5650 in the crisis year of 1981. Although the mean level of the range is certainly greater since floating began, there is no obvious indication that the spread is rising generally. Of course, the range simply considers the maximum and minimum monthly rates. However, a similar result is indicated by considering the standard deviations, which are also presented in Table A11.4.1 for the dollar–pound exchange rate. The standard deviation for the period since floating began has risen substantially in comparison with the fixed rate period (the maximum standard deviation for the $/£ during the fixed rate period being 0.0433 in 1971).

But both the range and the standard deviation does not allow comparison across the eight exchange rates *vis-à-vis* sterling (since they involve units of measurement). Therefore, in order to consider relative volatility; in Table A11.4.2 we present the *coefficient of variation*, which is a statistical

Table A11.4.1 Range and standard deviation for the dollar–sterling rate, 1972–87

Year	Range	Standard deviation
1972	0.1081	0.0508
1973	0.2585	0.0809
1974	0.1468	0.0448
1975	0.4090	0.1584
1976	0.4432	0.1398
1977	0.2057	0.0649
1978	0.2597	0.0797
1979	0.2675	0.0937
1980	0.2735	0.0769
1981	0.5650	0.1868
1982	0.2689	0.0813
1983	0.1541	0.0423
1984	0.3335	0.1042
1985	0.4084	0.1320
1986	0.1450	0.0443
1987	0.3725	0.1093

Table A11.4.2 Coefficient of variation of currencies against sterling, 1972–87

Year	US dollar	Belgian franc	Swiss franc	French franc	Italian lira	Dutch guilder	Deutschmark	Japanese yen
1972	2.1171	1.9120	1.9984	1.7193	1.8480	1.8447	1.7841	2.0279
1973	3.2946	5.2140	5.2726	4.9037	3.0424	7.1171	9.0047	3.0129
1974	1.9053	3.2272	6.1618	3.5838	1.4142	3.0891	3.0328	2.5085
1975	7.1728	2.2446	4.4712	5.2867	4.0522	2.6338	2.7411	5.5548
1976	7.7915	10.1841	10.0282	4.2726	5.2406	10.2983	10.4087	9.1216
1977	3.6913	1.5280	4.2649	2.1113	3.2155	1.6070	1.2614	2.9166
1978	4.1265	3.1212	6.4512	3.6199	2.4132	3.1584	3.2808	8.7849
1979	4.3912	3.8492	3.4533	3.7559	3.0046	3.8765	3.5769	9.4654
1980	3.2981	5.3714	4.1937	5.1397	6.2708	4.9635	5.6046	4.1950
1981	9.2636	4.6117	14.8403	3.7755	3.2267	5.7300	5.8427	5.3939
1982	4.6705	3.4184	3.7288	4.3957	2.7077	3.3629	3.5295	5.1487
1983	2.7939	4.5869	2.5973	5.4882	4.8270	3.9838	3.6767	3.7655
1984	7.8581	2.5942	2.1015	2.0724	1.9858	2.0283	2.0469	4.9216
1985	9.9771	3.8515	3.5613	3.7967	5.5692	3.8143	3.9580	5.7709
1986	3.0083	6.4607	8.2289	5.5528	6.8916	7.3586	7.5037	6.9494
1987	6.6038	2.7175	1.7808	2.8956	3.4637	2.3222	2.4320	1.5898

measure independent of currency units. The coefficient of variation is given by the ratio of the sample standard deviation to the mean, multiplied by 100 to bring it to a percentage (i.e., $CV = 100 \cdot s/\bar{x}$, where s is the sample standard deviation and $\bar{x}$ the sample mean). Once again, there is a marked rise in the level of the coefficient of variation in comparison with the fixed rate period (the maximum CV for the \$/£ during the fixed rate period being 1.8457 in 1971). In a number of the rates there is just a discernible trend, but what is more revealing are the crisis years: 1975–76; 1980–81 and 1985–86.

Although the measures presented here are fairly crude (other measures take account of trends, e.g. Cuddy and Della Valle, 1978), and show no obvious upward trend, they do indicate that the volatility is much greater than that under a fixed exchange rate system. Also, that in each crisis period volatility was substantially higher than in the intervening years. Also revealed in Table A11.4.2 is that the 1976 crisis was a European exchange rate crisis, while the 1981 crisis was a crisis of the dollar!

Chapter 12

INFLATION POLICY

Inflation has become the major problem of most western countries in the 1980s, and as such has become the centre of much policy debate. In Britain the government sees inflation as the major ill of the economy and have made the reduction of inflation its number-one priority. Nor is the UK the only country to see inflation as the major economic problem, and it is not just politicians who see it that way. Trevithick (1980) in the opening sentence of his book, *Inflation*, writes

> In the last few years inflation has been accelerating at an alarming rate in most of the countries of the western bloc, to become for the first time by far their most pressing economic problem. (p. 9)

Because the issue of inflation has taken such a prominent place in policy discussion it is necessary to stand back and ask a few pertinent questions concerning it, such as:

1. What exactly *is* inflation?
2. What is (are) the cause(s) of inflation?
3. Is inflation the problem it is made out to be?
4. What policies have been advocated for eliminating inflation?
5. Is inflation more difficult to control in an open economy?

These are just some of the questions which we will deal with in this chapter – and the five questions just raised form the basis of the sections to follow. The one major question missing from this list is whether internal and external shocks have been a major cause of inflation. We only touch on this in the present chapter, returning to it in more detail in Part III, Chapter 16.

However, a word of warning is in order. The discussion of inflation is not straightforward, and its analysis depends upon much economic reasoning. The underlying economic analysis was presented in Part I of this book, and there is no intention to repeat it here. On the contrary, we assume a full understanding of Part I and simply *use* the theory in our discussion of the issues surrounding inflation. The most relevant chapters, however, are Chapters 2, 3, 4, 5 and 8.

12.1 WHAT IS INFLATION?

With so much attention given to inflation, both by governments and in the media, it may be thought that 'inflation' is well defined. Unfortunately, it is a *concept* which is not easily defined. In general it is defined to be a sustained increase in the price level. It must be appreciated, however, that this is a symptom-based definition (see Frisch, 1983). There are other definitions which are based on the *cause* of inflation (assuming, of course, that the cause is known!). Consider the following common monetarist definitions:

> Inflation is a condition where there is general excess demand in which 'too much money is chasing too few goods'.

Or,

> Inflation is always and everywhere a monetary phenomenon . . . and can be produced only by a more rapid increase in the quantity of money than in output.
>
> (Friedman, 1970, p. 24)

It is clear that Friedman gives a *monetarist causal* definition of inflation. Suppose, for example, that a country has a large volume of imports and import prices are generally rising. Suppose, further, that imports are a large input into the country's manufacturing (all of which are typical of the UK), then it follows that the general price level will also rise. This would be inflation under the symptom-based definition but not under Friedman's monetarist causal definition. The causal definition is problematic in that it presupposes the cause is known. Furthermore, if there is more than one cause of inflation, then there will be as many causal definitions as there are causes of inflation! We will take up the issue of the causes of inflation in the next section.

Since inflation is concerned with an increase in the price level, we begin by simply stating that we *measure* inflation by the percentage change in the price level – leaving Appendix 12.1 to make this more explicit. Thus, if P_t denotes the price level at time t, then inflation (as a percentage) is defined as

$$\hat{P}_t = (P_t - P_{t-1}) \times 100 / P_{t-1}$$

It is to be noted that the inflation rate is in respect of the period $t-1$ to t, which may be a month, a quarter or a year. It is, however, common to express inflation as a percentage per annum.

What is certainly the case is that inflation is not simply a rise in the price level; it is a *sustained* rise in the price level. This is quite important. A one-off shock can raise the price *level*, but the economy will settle down at this higher price level unless a further shock is administered. In practice the difficulty with one-off shocks is that they have effects which are *distributed over a period of time* and could thus give the appearance of inflation. The situation is illustrated in Table 12.1. In each of the situations considered, we assume a shock occurs between periods 4 and 5, to the value of 100, this being the only shock. In the first situation, therefore, there is a 100% increase between periods 4 and 5 followed by a 50% decrease in the next period. Therefore, the percentage change is zero. In the second situation there is a new higher level after period 4. In this case, there is a 100% increase between periods 4 and 5, and thereafter the percentage change resumes at zero. In the third situation we have a more complex situation. Again there is a one-off shock between periods 4 and 5 but now we assume that in each period the market adjusts according to a fraction of the forecast error. It is apparent that in this third case the percentage change is *distributed* over the following periods – although its impact will diminish over time.

The data in Table 12.1 can be represented in diagrammatic form using the model outlined in Chapter 2, as shown in Fig. 12.1. Here we have the aggregate demand curve, *AD*, and the

Table 12.1 One-off shocks and the rate of inflation

Period	Situation 1		Situation 2		Situation 3	
	Price level	Inflation	Price level	Inflation	Price level	Inflation
1	100		100		100	
2	100	0	100	0	100	0
3	100	0	100	0	100	0
4	100	0	100	0	100	0
5	200	100	200	100	150	50
6	100	− 50	200	0	175	16.7
7	100	0	200	0	187.50	7.1
8	100	0	200	0	193.75	3.3

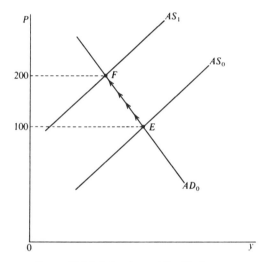

Figure 12.1 Inflation in an AD – AS diagram.

aggregate supply curve, AS. The initial situation is shown by AD_0 and AS_0. Suppose AS is shocked and moves in period 5 to AS_1 (periods 1–4 being AS_0). In period 5, therefore, the price level rises to 200 with 'inflation' of $\hat{P} = 100\%$. In period 6, AS falls back to AS_0 with 'inflation' falling by 50%, with zero inflation thereafter.

In the second case, AS_1 remains at the new level; inflation in period 5 is 100% and then drops to zero thereafter.

The third case is shown by the *path EF*, which appears to create a *continuous* rise in the price level; continuous, but diminishing, inflation. The reason for this is because we have not clearly laid out price expectations and long-run equilibrium.

It is necessary, although difficult in practice, to distinguish between a one-off event which has a distributional impact over time, from a sustained increase which repeats itself each period.

If we *measure* the rate of inflation as the percentage change in the price level, there is the difficulty of deciding which price level to choose, see Appendix 12.1. Whether the Retail Price Index (RPI) or the GDP deflator is used, the pattern is roughly the same. Using the

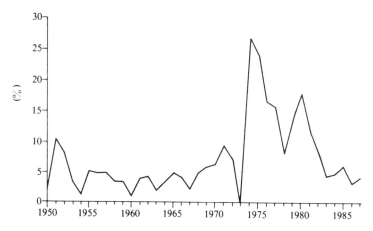

Figure 12.2 UK inflation, 1950–87 *Source: Economic Trends.*

RPI the pattern of inflation in the UK since 1950 is shown in Fig. 12.2. The graph illustrates a number of features. First, it is quite clear that inflation has been positive throughout the post-War period, and hence the price level has been rising continuously. Second, the inflation averaged around 4% over the period 1950–70 (4.7% for 1950–59 and 3.6% for 1960–69), but rose markedly in the 1970s (averaging 12.8%), and has been generally falling in the 1980s (the average for the period 1980–87 being 7.7%). Third, the inflation rate has shown fairly erratic movements around the average, but that these movements became much larger in the 1970s and 1980s (the standard deviations for the 1950s and 1960s were 2.7 and 1.4 respectively; while they were 8.3 and 5.0 for each of the periods 1970–79 and 1980–87). Fourth, inflation reached an all-time peak in 1975 when it rose to 24.2%; although a second high-peak occurred in 1980. Fifth, inflation accelerated in the periods 1970–71, 1973–74 and 1978–79, while there were marked decelerations in the periods 1975–76 and 1980–81.

12.2 THE CAUSES OF INFLATION

'What causes inflation?' is a question that is asked repeatedly and one for which there is no clear answer. There is a variety of theories to explain inflation, which we will discuss briefly in this section. This is necessary because these differing theories not only account for the difference in the costs of inflation, but also for the different policy solutions for reducing it.

Classical theory of inflation

In Chapter 7 we discussed the quantity theory of money. Under the assumption of full employment and a constant income velocity of circulation of money, there was shown to be a direct association between increases in the money supply and rises in the price level. In classical economics, output in the long run is determined by non-monetary factors – most particularly by features of the labour force and working practices (including social conditions). Thus, income is assumed to be constant at the full employment level. Although classicists recognized that under certain circumstances the velocity of circulation of money would change, such changes would only occur when there were major structural changes in the economy or if the velocity rose as the rate of inflation rose. Under these assumptions, and as shown in Chapter 7, an increase in the money supply will lead to an equal proportionate rise in the price level. From this it follows that a *persistent* rise in the price level (inflation) will occur if there is a *persistent* increase in the money supply.

This, of course, is a monetarist causal definition of inflation. It is important, however, to realize that it assumes two things. First, it assumes that inflation is caused by an excess of aggregate demand over aggregate supply, and that the cause of this excess demand is too much money in the economy. If this explanation of inflation is historically correct, then it is asserting that inflation is caused by demand pressure and that it could not be caused by supply-side factors. Second, it assumes that the *causation* goes from the money supply to the price level. Precisely how the increase in the money supply leads to an increase in the price level requires consideration of the *transmission mechanism*. Given the assumption of market clearing, and beginning from an equilibrium position in the money market, then an increase in the money supply will lead to disequilibrium in the money market. In order to re-establish equilibrium, some part of the extra cash balances will be used to purchase goods and services. Since, however, the volume of goods and services is determined independently of money, being associated with the labour supply, then this will give rise to excess demand in the goods market. This, in turn, will put pressure on prices to rise in order to establish equilibrium in the goods market. However, there is no general agreement on the transmission mechanism, see Chick (1977). In terms of the analysis given in Chapter 2, the rise in the money supply leads to a rightward shift in the aggregate demand curve, and with the aggregate supply curve fixed and upward sloping, prices will rise. However, for a persistent rise in prices to be established it would be necessary to explain a repeated increase in the money supply in each period.

Keynesian theory of inflation

Keynes' *General Theory* was more of an explanation of employment (or unemployment) than of inflation, and we deal with this aspect in Chapter 14. A crucial element of his theory was the deficiency in effective demand. On the other hand, inflation was attributable to too high a level of effective demand. Unfortunately, the term 'effective demand' is not at all clear and must be distinguished from 'aggregate demand', which refers to a *schedule* that relates the level of expenditure at each level of income. On the other hand, effective demand refers to a *point* on the aggregate demand schedule which is made effective by what firms, whose decisions are based on what they think the level of demand is going to be, decide to produce (Chick 1983, chapter 4). It could be said more accurately, that 'effective demand' is what is supplied!

According to Chick (1983), Keynes did not assume fixed prices and he asserted that prices will rise whenever there is a rise in aggregate demand in the short run. However, 'true inflation', according to Keynes, occurs only when there is a rise in prices with no expansion of output. One way to interpret this is to assert that if aggregate expenditure is raised such that the equilibrium level of income is above the full employment level, then inflation will occur; and the extent of the inflation is dependent on the *inflationary gap*, i.e. the value of desired expenditure at the full employment level of income less the value of aggregate supply. Hence, the cause of inflation is too high a level of effective demand.

It is to be noted that this, too, is a causal definition of inflation, and that it also attributes inflation to too high a level of demand, but that the reason for the excess demand is explained by the economic system attempting to spend more than the value of output produced. However, for this to be a reasoned definition of inflation it is necessary to explain why expenditure is *persistently* in excess of the value of what is produced. In order to do this, Keynesian economists have therefore carried out detailed studies of the components of aggregate expenditure, especially consumption and investment; they have also considered the level of government spending and the net export position of the economy, all of which we discussed in Chapter 2. As with the classical model, in terms of aggregate demand and aggregate supply, which we developed in Chapter 2, Keynes attributed inflation to a rightward shift in the aggregate demand curve arising from an increase in some component of expenditure. What is not so clear in this model is why there is a *persistent* shift to the right of the aggregate demand curve. With the Keynesian emphasis on fiscal policy, this would require a persistent rise in government spending.

Further developments of demand-pull inflation

The two theories just enunciated are part of the corpus of theories which have been labelled *demand-pull*: they differ only in explaining what causes the increase in demand which puts pressure on prices to rise. It is apparent that the model of the inflationary gap developed by Keynes refers to demand pressure in the goods market only. Bent Hansen (1951) took the analysis one stage further and considered two gaps, one in the goods market and a second in the labour market. In essence, pressure can arise either in the factor market or in the goods market. He assumed that labour was fixed (at, say, the full employment level). Under a number of assumptions, it is possible to have equilibrium in the goods market but to have excess demand in the labour market. In this case there will be pressure on wages to rise. Alternatively, it is possible to have equilibrium in the labour market but excess demand in the goods market. In this instance there will be no pressure on wages to rise, but there will be pressure on prices to rise. All-round (dynamic) equilibrium is possible when the rate of wage increase is equal to the rate of price increase.

Inflation studies took a totally different direction following the publication of Phillips' famous paper (1958). It must be pointed out that this did not provide a theory of inflation, but, rather, presented a statistical regularity – a *trade-off* – between inflation and unemployment. However, later papers, for example by Lipsey (1960), attempted to give a theoretical explanation of the trade-off. These explanations were along the lines of demand-pull, where excess demand in the labour market (proxied by unemployment) was related to the change in the price level (inflation). The attraction of the Phillips curve had nothing to do with its underlying theoretical basis, which has always been very weak, but, rather, as a *stable* relationship it had tremendous policy implications. In short, it meant that governments could choose a suitable combination of inflation and unemployment. In fact, the Phillips curve is consistent with virtually any causal explanation of inflation but, to repeat, it is not in itself an explanation of inflation. However, this relationship has become so entrenched in the various theories of inflation that some comment on it is necessary, and we provide this in Appendix 12.2.

All the developments discussed so far have one implicit assumption, namely, that price expectations are constant. For periods of fairly low inflation, as experienced in the early 1950s and 1960s, this is a reasonable assumption. However, once inflation takes off, it is no longer a reasonable assumption. As we demonstrated in Chapter 2, price expectations are embodied in the aggregate supply curve, arising as they do from the fact that labour bases its supply on the expected real wage. Consider, then, an increase in aggregate demand (whether from a rise in effective demand or a rise in the money supply), as illustrated in Fig. 12.3. This will shift the aggregate demand curve to the right, to AD_1, and prices will rise, from P_0 to P_1. The rise in prices will, if they persist, lead to an upward revision of price expectations. This, in turn, will shift the aggregate supply curve to the left (upward), to AS_1, which will lead to a further rise in prices. A more dynamic version is also possible, as shown in Fig. 12.4. The short-run Phillips curve is based on a given expected rate of inflation. If the demand-pressure curve shifts to the right, leading to a rise in the rate of inflation, then there will be a revision upwards in the expected rate of inflation. This will shift the short-run Phillips curve to the left, which will increase the actual rate of inflation still further. It is apparent, therefore, that the introduction of price expectations is not to explain the cause of inflation, but, rather, to explain the *acceleration* in the rate of inflation (and the clockwise movement of inflation and unemployment), and that such an explanation is independent of the theory underlying the cause of inflation. It does, in fact, apply to some of the cost-push theories of inflation which we will now discuss.

Cost-push theories of inflation

There are a number of cost-push theories of inflation, but basically these can be reduced to different explanations as to the cause in the shift in the aggregate supply curve and/or the short-run Phillips curve, and as such are causal definitions of inflation. It must be pointed out that it is in these arguments that the distinction between a one-off shock and a persistent change in the price level is important. Consider the situation in Fig. 12.5. A shift to the left of the aggregate supply curve, from AS_0 to AS_1, will lead to a rise in the price *level*. But as we explained in Section 12.1, this will not in itself be inflationary. Even where the pressure on prices is distributed over time, inflation will fall to its previous level if there are no further shocks to the system. With this caveat in mind, what has been advanced by cost-push theorists?

A number of sources for increases in costs can be identified, each of which can be the basis of a cost-push theory of inflation. These are as follows:

1. Increases in wages in excess of productivity.
2. Misuse of monopoly and oligopoly powers on the part of firms.
3. A rise in raw material costs.

The first source of cost-push is by far the most common argument. But, even here, a further question is posed; namely, what is the cause of the wage rise in excess of the productivity? Two versions are predominant. First, the reason is laid at the door of trade unions. Second, cost-push inflationary pressure arises from workers attempting to maintain wage differentials. The first explanation asserts that union power has grown to such an extent that unions can exert monopsonistic power on the wage bargaining process. As such, it is argued, they become more ambitious in their wage claims (although what matters is

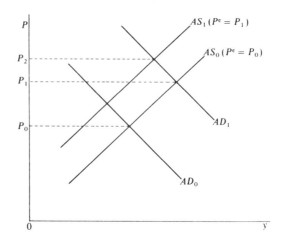

Figure 12.3 Rising AD and rising price expectations.

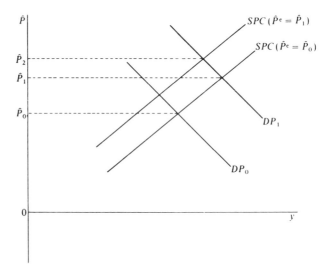

Figure 12.4 Rising AD and the impact on inflation.

whether they succeed in their wage claims). Part of the reason advanced as to why unions, at least in the 1970s, were likely to succeed in getting high wage claims was that governments would maintain full employment, and so any high wage claims which might lead to reduced employment would be 'mopped up' by expansionary monetary and fiscal policy. But even where governments do not pursue expansionary policies, it is still possible for 'selfish' unions to put in for high wage claims. The problem with this whole line of reasoning is that it is difficult to prove! Union *power* is a rather complex multidimensional concept which cannot readily be quantified, see Addison and Siebert (1980) for a summary of early studies. Accordingly, the arguments tend to be based on belief rather than on supported evidence.

The second reason advanced why wages may rise in excess of productivity is because of leap-frogging. Consider the following scenario. Suppose miners get a wage rise, which we

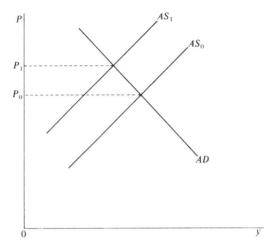

Figure 12.5 Supply shock and a rise in the price level.

will assume is justified on productivity grounds and as such is not inflationary (although it may be the case that the wage increase is in excess of productivity). Now if workers feel that there is a 'fair' wage differential, then some group will now see themselves disadvantaged relative to the miners. Suppose this is policemen. The police force now puts in for a wage claim in order to preserve its differential. Not only has this nothing to do with productivity, but productivity as such is almost impossible to measure for the police force. But the situation does not stop here. Nurses, teachers and firemen possibly see themselves on a par with policemen. They accordingly put in a wage claim to preserve comparability; and so the rounds continue. There are many variants of this line of reasoning, all in some way moving away from the fact that wages are determined by demand and supply in the labour market.

Not all cost-push theories place the blame for wage, and hence price, increases on the monopsonistic practices of trade unions. Modern capitalist society is dominated by monopolies and oligopolies. Under such competition, it is argued, price is set above the competitive price and high profit margins are maintained. But this can hardly be a cause of inflation. It would have to mean that profit margins were continually rising. However, a slightly different argument is that large profits are a stimulus for workers to put in for higher wages. Not only would it be necessary to find an association between wages and profits, but, again, it would be necessary to demonstrate continued rises in profits – neither of which seem plausible for the UK.

One popular cost-push explanation advanced in the early 1970s is that occurring from the rise in raw material prices. The argument has its sources back in the 1967 sterling devaluation. This was followed by a rise in commodity prices on world markets in the early 1970s, a rise in food prices following Britain's entry into the EEC in 1973, and the rise in OPEC oil prices in 1973 and 1975. We deal with these shocks in Chapter 17. What matters for the present argument is that each was a one-off event. In and of themselves they would not be inflationary. The problem is, however, that each of the impacts would be distributed over time, and although each would lead to a fall in the rate of price increase in each subsequent period, the next shock would be superimposed on the earlier ones. As such, all their impacts were spread out over the full decade of the 1970s. This feature of the inflationary process in the UK is analysed in more detail in Appendix 12.3. What this shows is the further problem that any shock which is followed by government policy to reduce the employment effects will be more inflationary, and this too added to the UK inflation of the 1970s.

Monetarist theories of inflation

Monetarism is more than a monetary theory of inflation. However, in this section we confine ourselves to just those aspects of monetarism which have a bearing on the issue of inflation. To some extent we have already dealt with this approach. In the classical analysis developed above, it was shown that the classicists associated inflation with an increase in the money supply, and accelerated inflation with an acceleration in the rate of growth of the money supply. This is a basic proposition of monetarism in its modern form, Laidler (1981). A second feature of monetarism is that in the long run there is no trade-off between inflation and unemployment, i.e. the long-run Phillips curve is vertical at the 'natural rate of unemployment'. Linked with this is the short-run expectations-augmented Phillips curve, which we discussed in Chapter 3. The introduction of the augmented Phillips curve is an attempt to explain accelerated inflation arising from typical Keynesian demand manage-ment. Thus, if governments attempt to keep unemployment below the natural level, then this will lead to a higher rate of inflation, which in turn will lead to an increase in the expected rate of inflation, which will raise the actual rate of inflation still further. An additional element of the monetarist position is that monetary policy has a greater impact on *nominal* income than fiscal policy, but that what has to be further explained is the distribution of this increase in nominal income between increases in the price level (inflation) and increases in real output. However, much of Friedman's analysis is an attempt to explain the growth of nominal income and not worry about the distribution of this increase between inflation and income growth (Friedman, 1971). The main difference between the classical model outlined above and the monetarist model is that the latter includes a Phillips curve relationship and depends on Okun's law (Frisch, 1983), and to a large extent is the version we developed in Chapter 3.

More recently, a modified version of the monetarist model has been developed which relies on the concept of rational expectations, see Chapter 4. (There is also a slight change in Okun's law in that the period change in unemployment is replaced by the difference between the current period's unemployment and the natural rate of unemployment. We used this second version in Chapter 3, but demonstrated the dynamics by using Okun's original formulation.) The crux of this approach is that as long as the growth in the money supply is fully anticipated, then this will be incorporated in individuals' decision-making, and will be fully taken account of in the expected rate of inflation. Thus, although the actual rate of inflation will rise, this will have no influence on the real economy. In essence, the system will settle down on the long-run Phillips curve where the actual rate of inflation is equal to the expected rate of inflation.

Most of the early monetarist models were developed on the assumption of a closed economy. However, there are monetarist models explaining inflation in a world context, referred to as *global monetarism*. In part, such models are aimed at explaining why inflation has risen in many countries at the same time. One such model, the analysis of which was outlined in Appendix 5.5, uses the simple Cambridge equation of classical economics and combines this with purchasing power parity, a central concept in the modern version of open economy monetarism. In Appendix 5.5 we established that the world rate of inflation was equal to the growth in the world money supply less a weighted average of the growth rates of real income. In a two-country model, then, we have

$$\hat{P}w = \hat{M}w - [\beta\hat{y} + (1 - \beta)\hat{y}*]$$

The argument runs that in the late 1960s the US ran large government deficits, which it payed for by increasing the money supply. Since the dollar is a reserve currency, this led to a growth in the world money supply which raised the rate of inflation for the world as a whole. The model was also used to explain the increase in world inflation by arguing that if a number of countries simultaneously expanded their money supply, then world inflation would rise. The model, however, is not without its critics, see Frisch (1983) and Ahmad (1984), and like the closed economy model it is particularly weak at explaining the *transmission* of inflation throughout the world.

Other theories of inflation

The theories so far outlined constitute the main *economic* theories of inflation. But the list is by no means exhaustive. The economic analysis of inflation has undoubtedly had its shortcomings, and a number of writers on inflation concluded that it was more than just an economic problem. Some see inflation as rooted in political and social forces, see Hirsch and Goldthorpe (1978). These alternative approaches see the growth in wages and prices in the 1970s throughout the Western bloc as being endemic in the socio-political structure of Western economies. They argue that the pressures set up within the economic system just led to accommodating monetary growth. It was not the monetary growth which was the cause of inflation, but, rather, the underlying socio-political structure. Two theories are worth mentioning. First, there was the view that it was the growth in the public sector, common throughout the Western world, that led to the increase in cost-push and/or demand-pull inflation (Peacock and Ricketts, 1978). A second theory was based on the idea of an 'aspiration gap', defined as the difference between the target and the actual rate of growth of real disposable income, Baxter (1973) and Panic (1978).

12.3 THE COSTS OF INFLATION

The preceding section clearly indicated that there is no agreement on the causes of inflation. But the varied theories do indicate that there is a major concern in trying to explain it. Does this suggest that inflation really is the 'evil' which it is sometimes made out to be? If it were it would suggest that the economy suffers greatly as a consequence of inflation: that its costs are quite high. Is this in fact the case? Is the reduction of inflation 'at any cost' worth it? These are important questions. Governments have made it their over-riding objective to reduce the rate of inflation. But in doing this they have raised, in the short run, the level of unemployment and created changes in the social fabric of society, especially in the UK. Is the cure worse than the illness?

Why worry about inflation? If wages are rising at the same level as prices, then real wages remain constant. If money income is rising as fast as prices, then real income remains constant. Such a simplistic statement, however, involves a number of assumptions, none of which are true. These include the following:

1. All inflation is anticipated.
2. All income comes from wages and all income is spent on consumption goods.
3. All inflation is distributed evenly across goods and services so that all sectors are equally affected and all people are equally affected.
4. There are no distortions, e.g. taxation.
5. All wage contracts are uniform across sectors and are negotiated to come into force at the same time and for the same duration.
6. All debt contracts are the same.

Anticipated and unanticipated inflation

The first major distinction of importance, therefore, is between *anticipated* and *unanticipated* inflation. A fully anticipated rate of inflation is one where the actual rate of inflation is equal to the expected rate of inflation. If this is the case, then all lending and borrowing can take account of the inflation rate in the contracts agreed. The same applies for wage claims. Does it therefore mean that as long as the inflation rate is fully anticipated it does not matter what level it is at? The answer is, 'no'. What it leads to is the result that an increase in anticipated inflation will result in an equal increase in the *nominal* interest rate. The reasoning behind this result depends on the introduction of the concept of the real rate of interest, and the analysis is given in Appendix 12.4.

Even with fully anticipated inflation, and a process of indexation (discussed in the next section), there may be costs associated with the actual method adopted, Flemming (1976). The costs here, of course, are associated not with the anticipated inflation, but, rather, with the inadequacy of the indexation. Furthermore, since the holding of money involves (in general) no interest payment, and since a fully anticipated rise in inflation raises the nominal interest rate by an equal amount, this would strictly require some compensation for those holding non-interest-bearing assets. Since this is most unlikely, a rise in anticipated inflation would lead to a move out of money and into interest-bearing assets. Since less currency would then be held for transactions purposes, the result would be more frequent visits to the bank or other financial institutions to withdraw currency as and when needed (the *shoe-leather cost of anticipated inflation*). A third cost of anticipated inflation is the fact that even though the price level is rising and is fully anticipated, relative prices are still changing, which will involve changing consumption and investment decisions. Fourth, the presence of taxation will lead to distortions if not appropriately index-linked, or if there are time lags in the payment of taxes and receipts in relation to the inflation. For instance, if tax allowances and tax brackets are not adjusted with the (anticipated) rate of inflation, then as money incomes rise people will move into higher tax brackets, even when their real income may be constant, thus reducing their real disposable income.

When we turn to unanticipated inflation, where the actual rate of inflation differs from the expected rate of inflation, then it means the actual real rate of interest and the expected real rate of interest are different (see Appendix 12.4 for definitions of these terms). If we suppose that the actual rate of inflation is greater than the expected rate of inflation, then this implies that the actual real rate of interest is less than the expected real rate of interest. This means that for the saver the return on his savings is less than he expected, while the borrower pays back less than he expected. Of course, the converse is also true. The most significant net borrower in the country is the government. Hence, during inflation in excess of anticipated inflation, the debt interest payment by the government is less than people would be expecting. What all this means is that there is a re-distribution during inflation from creditors to debtors arising purely as a consequence of the unanticipated inflation. (However, if the actual rate of inflation were less than the expected rate, then the re-distribution would be from debtors to creditors.)

One cost of inflation is incurred by firms. However, it is necessary to distinguish the problems associated with (1) level, (2) variation, and (3) acceleration. In general, a high level of inflation makes long-term investment uncertain, and raises labour and raw material costs. If, however, the inflation were fully anticipated, then investment should not be adversely affected, and neither should the rising costs of labour and raw materials. All wage contracts could, in theory, incorporate the correct adjustment for inflation, as well as other contracts. All decision-making could incorporate adjustment for price rises. What this means is that the problems faced by firms with regard to the level of anticipated inflation are all practical ones involving the appropriate indexation. Once inflation becomes unanticipated, then an extra degree of uncertainty is involved in business decisions. When inflation is *accelerating*, the costs are associated more with frequent changes in prices and costs of production. Wage contracts will need to be settled more frequently and this may lead to greater militancy if there is disagreement over the appropriate adjustment.

The cost of reducing inflation

Although there are costs to inflation *per se*, there are also costs involved in reducing it. It is simply not enough to say inflation incurs costs and therefore must be reduced. It is quite possible that the costs of reducing inflation exceed the costs of the actual inflation. But a more difficult political issue is that those who suffer from high inflation are not those who bear the cost of reducing inflation. This distributional question aside, another issue is whether a policy implemented to reduce inflation, some specific ones of which we will discuss in the next section, will fall mainly on prices or mainly on output. The point, of course, is that nominal income can be reduced either by a reduction in inflation or a reduction in real income (output). Associated with this question is a further question of whether the policy which is implemented should be such as to bring inflation down quickly or whether it should be gradual.

To illustrate these issues, let us consider the Conservative government's strategy. The situation is illustrated in Fig. 12.6. A reduction in the *growth* of the money supply along with a reduction in the public sector borrowing requirement (PSBR) will shift the demand-pressure curve from DP_0 to DP_1. One drastic policy is to reduce the money supply growth and the PSBR necessary to achieve the target inflation rate of $\hat{P}*$. In this case the economy will move to point B, at least in the short run. The policy involves reducing output, thereby reducing aggregate demand, which brings pressure on firms to lower prices, and creates unemployment, and so brings pressure on the labour market to accept lower wage increases. A deep recession is caused in order to 'cure' inflation. Once point B is achieved the

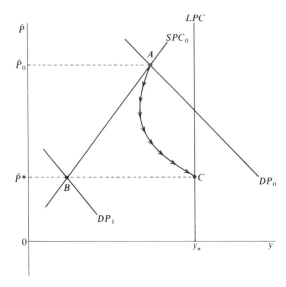

Figure 12.6 The Conservative government's strategy for reducing inflation.

aim is then to move to point C, maintaining inflation at the desired level and raising real income to its natural level. One difficulty here is in moving from point B to point C without once again creating inflation. It certainly cannot be achieved solely by monetary or fiscal policy, since this will simply shift the DP curve to the right and, once again, raise the rate of inflation. What is clear is that some supply-side policies are required which will also shift the short-run Phillips curve to the right. Fig. 12.6 illustrates an additional worry. If the aim is to reduce the rate of inflation to zero, which has been suggested by Nigel Lawson, then the recession will need to be greater unless policies to shift the short-run Phillips curve are simultaneously pursued and are relatively successful.

Under a gradualist strategy the aim would be to reduce the money supply growth by a certain percentage each year. At the same time, other supply-side measures could be implemented. The type of path envisaged is that shown by the curve linking A to C. Under this strategy, in comparison with the sharp shock, real income (and hence unemployment) does not fall by as much. On the other hand, it could take longer to reach point C. Unemployment, although less in each period, may, when taken over the whole adjustment period, involve a greater cost.

It is clear from Fig. 12.6, that a policy to reduce inflation will reduce *both* inflation and real income. Furthermore, an attempt to reduce the rate of inflation down to zero may have a crippling effect on output. There is some difference of opinion as to the relative impacts on inflation and output with regard to a reduction in the money supply. This difference is illustrated in Fig. 12.7. Assume the economy is at point A. Suppose some policy is implemented to bring down inflation (although it does not have to be by means of a reduction in the growth of the money supply). Monetarists generally assume that the economy will move along path MM, with most of the adjustment falling on a reduction in the rate of inflation and some reduction in the growth of real output. But as Hicks (1976) argues, this may not in fact be the path that the economy follows: it may follow the path

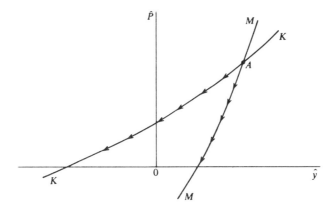

Figure 12.7 Monetarist and Keynesian impacts of monetary contraction.

along the curve KK, which is what neo-Keynesians assume is more likely. Along path KK, output responds relatively more than prices. In fact, as drawn, zero growth in real income occurs before inflation is brought down to its target level; and had the target level been a zero rate of inflation, it is possible that the economy could be crippled before this was achieved. At the moment, however, we have too little information on these relative dynamic adjustment paths. If the government insists on reducing inflation 'at any cost', then as far as it is concerned, it does not matter whether the economy follows path AM or AK. However, political credibility will demand that the path is monitored. The government must gauge the extent to which output falls and unemployment rises, and then adjust its policies accordingly. This uncertainty about which is the most likely path for the economy to follow also gives some support for the gradualist strategy, which would allow for some 'fine tuning' along the way.

12.4 POLICIES FOR REDUCING INFLATION

The numbers of policies for reducing inflation are almost as numerous as theories of inflation; and, not surprisingly, the policies which have been suggested for reducing it are very closely linked with the underlying theory about what causes inflation. What is quite clear from our discussions of the theories is that if one treats inflation as truly being concerned with a *persistent* rise in the price level, then the only shock to the economy which is not temporary is that arising from increasing the money supply. Hence, in the *long run* a persistent rise in the price level must be a monetary phenomenon and must arise from too high a level of monetary growth. But this is hardly interesting. What about the short and medium terms? In these periods other factors will impinge on the inflationary process, and may in fact be (temporarily) more important. Thus, if there is to be control of inflation in the short and medium terms, simply controlling the growth of the money supply may not be the solution. What policies, then, have been advocated for reducing inflation? Five broad policies can be identified as follows:

1. A reduction in the growth of the money supply.
2. Prices and incomes policy.
3. Indexation.
4. Restriction of aggregate demand through fiscal policy.
5. Exchange rate policy.

In this section we shall deal with the first four, leaving the final policy to the next section.

A reduction in monetary growth

From our discussion of the theories of inflation, it is clear that a reduction of monetary growth is a means of reducing demand pressure, and will shift the demand-pressure curve to the left. The initial impact of this shift is to move down the short-run Phillips curve but not to move it. This is, of course, a monetarist solution which depends on the direct link between inflation and monetary growth. If monetary growth in excess of the growth in real output is the cause of inflation, then it follows that to bring down the rate of inflation all one needs to do is reduce the rate of growth of the money supply. As far as monetarists are concerned, this policy will not only bring down the rate of inflation to some desired level (even zero if this is a policy objective), but will do so such that in the *long run* the level of unemployment is at its natural level. Thus, the reduced output and the rise in unemployment which such a policy will entail is purely a *transitory* one and is an adjustment cost. Furthermore, the process will be aided in the medium term by a reduction in inflationary expectations which will shift the short-run Phillips curve to the right, helping to ensure that the long-run solution is at the natural rate of unemployment.

But why should monetarists advocate a monetary rule? We discussed monetary rules in Chapter 7, but it is worth recalling that such a policy would not take account of feedbacks. Whatever is happening within the economy, the rule is followed. Part of the argument for such a strategy is the contention that it is preferable to fine tuning, an issue we take up in the next chapter. But why advocate a *fixed* monetary rule ($\hat{M}_s = \lambda$ say)? Once again, this follows from the quantity theory of money. With a constant k, in the Cambridge form of the quantity theory, and with clearing in the money market, we have the growth relationship

$$\hat{M}_s = \hat{P} + \hat{y}$$

Assuming a constant rate of growth of real output, and with a target rate of inflation of $\hat{P}*$ (which may be zero), then it follows that money supply should grow at the constant rate of $\hat{P}* + \hat{y} = \lambda$. A less rigid rule, but a rule all the same, is to admit that the money supply is prone to random fluctuations and so the growth rate will vary. If s_m is some measure of the random fluctuation of the money supply (e.g., the standard deviation), then a less rigid rule is:

$$\lambda - s_m < \hat{M}_s < \lambda + s_m$$

This implies a target range for the growth of the money supply, which is the policy procedure in the UK.

On a more pragmatic note it may be asked: Why announce such a target range when the growth of the money supply has very rarely been contained within it? The reason is that this will bring down inflationary expectations. However, if the aim is to bring down inflationary expectations, the real question is what is the best way to do so. If a reduction in monetary growth does not bring down expectations and, for that matter the inflation rate, what it certainly will do is reduce the level of real income – increase unemployment and increase the rate of bankruptcies. What is being hinted at here, of course, is that this particular country's inflation at this particular time may not be caused by excessive monetary growth. If this is the case, then whatever monetary rule is followed will not bring down the rate of inflation. What may bring it down, however, is the prolonged depression which could result from such a policy. It is clear, therefore, that the success of this policy is very dependent on the assertion that inflation is caused by too high a level of monetary growth.

Prices and incomes policies

Prices and incomes policies, and there are more than one, Blackaby (1980*b*), are concerned on the one hand with the increase in consumer and producer prices, and on the other with the wage bargaining process. It is, of course, possible to have an incomes policy without a prices policy, but ultimately the aim is to control inflation, the change in the general price level. But even to approach the issue of inflation from this perspective presupposes that a major cause of inflation is wage increases in excess of productivity growth. Hence, attention is generally focussed on incomes policy.

One of the difficulties with incomes policies has always been whether they are voluntary or statutory, both types of which have been tried in various forms in the UK since 1945. Labour have generally favoured voluntary arrangements with trade union cooperation, for example the 'Declaration of Intent' in 1964 where both unions and management accepted a 3–3.5% wage norm (roughly equal to the growth in productivity), the 'Social Contract' of 1975 involving a flat rate increase in wages and the 'Guidelines' soon after (the whole policy collapsing in the 'winter of discontent', 1978–79). However, Labour has also implemented less voluntary policies, such as the six-month wages and price freeze in 1966. Conservatives have tended towards statutory policies, for example the statutory wage controls begun in 1972 and to be implemented in three stages (the policy being brought to an end in Stage III by conflict between the government and the miners).

Any analysis of the history of prices and incomes policies will highlight the following ten issues:

1. Should the policy be voluntary or involuntary?
2. What penalties should be imposed if the rules are violated?
3. What monitoring agency, if any, should be set up?
4. Will there be an upsurge in wage claims when the policy is removed?
5. Should the policy explicitly obtain the unions' cooperation?
6. What distortions will the policy lead to?
7. Will the policy lead to a differential between public and private sector pay?
8. Is there a possibility of misjudging public sympathy (either by government or by trade unions)?
9. Will the policy be short-lived because of inevitable conflicts?
10. Have there ever been any years when some form of restraint on wages and/or prices has not operated?

We cannot possibly answer these questions here, but they do highlight the complex issues surrounding such a policy. For the remainder we will discuss the *aim* of such policies and their *effectiveness*.

Ultimately their aim is to reduce the rate of inflation. But how is this achieved? On the incomes side, the various types of wages freeze, wages norm, etc., are all designed to affect wage increases. Theoretically, we can think of this as affecting the reaction function relating wages to unemployment, either in terms of the position of the curve (reducing the intercept d_0 in equation (3.16)), or in terms of the reaction coefficient (decreasing the coefficient d in equation (3.16)). This will, if successful, shift the short-run Phillips curve to the right and/or tilt it clockwise in the $P-y$ space. If this is accomplished, then with a fixed demand-pressure curve the rate of inflation will be reduced. This result is shown in Fig. 12.8, where the new short-run Phillips curve is SPC_1, which has both moved down and tilted at the same time.

Have the policies been effective? This is not an easy question to answer and there is still considerable dispute over the issue. In a formal sense all that is required is to demonstrate that SPC_1 is below SPC_0 in the relevant range of actual income and inflation. But this relationship is not easy to derive empirically. Its more usual mirror image, the Phillips curve in the $P-U$ space, has been estimated for periods when the policy is on and when the policy is off. But the evidence is conflicting, see Parkin, *et al.* (1972), Henry and Ormerod (1978), Burrows and Hitiris (1972), Dean (1981) and Holden, Peel and Thompson (1987). However, one of the most common damaging criticisms of an incomes policy is that once removed there is a surge in wage claims. This, of course, will shift the short-run Phillips curve back to the left. It is even possible for the short-run Phillips curve to move back beyond the original curve, as shown by SPC_2 in Fig. 12.8, in which case inflation (and unemployment) will be worse than if the policy had not been instituted in the first place, Batchelor *et al.* (1980).

Indexation

Indexation refers to an arrangement whereby monetary contracts involve a clause which compensates for any price increase which occurs after the commencement of the agreement. Thus, wage indexation would be a contractual arrangement whereby a nominal wage would be agreed plus a premium which would be linked to (or equal to) the inflation rate. In this case the wage would be inflation-proof. Of course, any monetary contract could in principle have such an inflation-proof clause built into it. For example, tax brackets and tax thresholds could be changed in line with inflation, as could social security payments and pensions. Contracts involving the payment of interest could also be index-linked. In this case the agreement would be on the *real* interest rate, and then this would be adjusted to take account of inflation, which would lead to a nominal interest rate equal to the real interest rate plus the rate of inflation.

What is the purpose of indexation? Earlier in this chapter we pointed out that one problem is with unanticipated inflation. Indexation is a means of overcoming this problem. If all monetary contracts are index-linked, then (in principle) unanticipated inflation is not an issue. In effect, indexation is a means of *living with inflation*, of reducing the cost of inflation; it is not a means of *reducing* inflation. Monetarists, on the other hand, argue that indexation *is* a means of reducing inflation. The crux of their argument is that wage contracts are based on what workers expect the rate of inflation to be over the period of the contract, and not on what it actually is. Indexation, it is argued, will break the link between

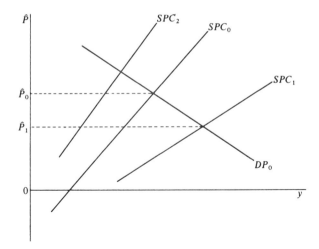

Figure 12.8 Prices and incomes policy and a movement in SPC.

current wage bargaining and expected inflation. However, for such indexation to be successful in reducing inflation it must be assumed that workers always expect a rate of inflation greater than what it turns out to be. If the opposite is the case, then indexation will be inflationary under this argument! The monetarist argument is that indexation will reduce price expectations which in turn will shift the short-run Phillips curve to the right, reducing inflation and raising income and employment. It is clear, however, that indexation operates only on expected inflation and not directly on the rate of inflation. Thus, monetarists insist that to reduce the rate of inflation requires monetary restraint, aided by indexation.

The supposed benefits of indexation just outlined do, however, depend on a belief that inflation is caused by excessive monetary expansion. If, on the contrary, it is caused by external shocks to the economy or excessive wage demands in excess of productivity, then it is possible that index-linking contracts, most especially wages, will simply increase the rate of inflation. Some see the practical difficulties as being especially great. For instance, which index should be used and over which period should the index of inflation be measured? Furthermore, the costs of implementing indexation would be quite considerable, and it could be argued that benefits of such a scheme would only outweigh such costs if inflation was high – a point emphasized by the issue over inflation accounting.

Like any proposed policy change, until it is implemented, its benefits and costs are difficult to establish. Although in many Western countries some indexation is present, it is not on the scale envisaged by monetarists and so cannot be used in evidence either for or against their proposal. To the extent that policy-makers believe the inflation in their particular country at that particular time is not simply due to excessive monetary expansion, then the benefits of indexation become that much less attractive. Even the Conservative Party in Britain have not implemented indexation on any major scale.

Fiscal contraction

On this we can be brief because it acts in a very similar way to monetary contraction. Fiscal contraction will shift the demand-pressure curve to the left. This will reduce inflation, but it will also reduce output and employment. Its long-run success depends on two factors. First, that deflation can be maintained, otherwise the demand-pressure curve will shift back. Second, which is closely associated with the first, whether the government is prepared to return a high level of unemployment for long periods of time. The general mistake with fiscal contraction *as a policy on its own* is that it will lead to unemployment. The rising unemployment will soon lead to pressure to reverse the policy. What this suggests is that it is necessary to pursue a policy of fiscal contraction along with policies to stimulate output and shift the short-run Phillips curve to the right. However, this is no easy task since the fiscal contraction will not in general encourage firms to expand their output without some positive stimulus from the government, say in the form of tax concessions. We will, however, deal with industrial policy more fully in Chapter 15.

12.5 INFLATION IN AN OPEN ECONOMY

This section is inevitably selective, but our main purpose is to demonstrate that whether a country is under a fixed exchange rate system or a floating exchange rate system, the end result with regard to income of some exogenous shift in demand is no different; what is different is the means by which the domestic price level is changed, and hence has different implications for inflation.

Floating exchange rates

Assume a system where exchange rates are freely floating. We assume that the system is initially in equilibrium with inflation equal to the growth in the money supply, expectations are fulfilled and a balance of payments of zero, as shown in Fig. 12.9. In Fig 12.9(a) the initial position is given by point A and in Fig. 12.9(b) by point Z.

Now consider a rise in real government spending. This will initially shift IS to IS_1. Given the BP curve shows a fair degree of capital mobility (see Appendix 5.3), the balance of payments goes into *surplus*. This is a crucial observation. The rise in income increase imports and worsens the country's net export position, but the rise in interest rates attracts more than enough capital inflow to compensate and to lead to a surplus on current and capital account. The economy has in the first period moved to point B in the upper diagram and to point Q in the lower diagram. What do we now observe?:

(a) a surplus on the balance of payments;
(b) a deterioration in net exports;
(c) an appreciation of the home currency; or
(d) a rate of inflation of $\hat{P}_1$.

Since the price level is rising, the LM curve will shift to the left as real money balances decline. If the appreciation of sterling is quick, then there is no reason for the level of reserves to change and hence there is no reason for the nominal money supply to alter on this account. Hence, the leftward shift in the LM curve arises from the increase in the rate of inflation only. Furthermore, the appreciation of sterling raises export prices and lowers import prices. (This will temporarily shift the *SPC* upward, but it will then return to its

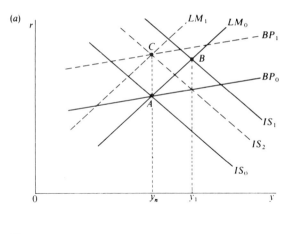

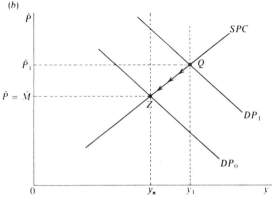

Figure 12.9 Inflation under a flexible exchange rate.

former position – we will ignore this to keep the treatment manageable.) This deterioration in the competitive position of the home country is reinforced by the increase in the home rate of inflation to $\hat{P}_1$. The result is a further decline in the UK's net export position, i.e., over and above the decline arising from an increase in domestic income. The result is to shift *IS* leftward, to IS_2 and *BP* upward (leftward) to BP_1. The process will in fact continue until income returns to the initial level. This is at point *C* in the upper diagram.

Comparing the new position with the old we note the following six observations:

1. Real income has not changed.
2. During the adjustment period inflation has risen so that the new price level is higher.
3. Real balances have declined, so causing a rise in the interest rate.
4. During the adjustment period the currency has appreciated so that the new rate of exchange is higher.
5. A deterioration in the net export position of the country has occurred.
6. The balance of payments is again in equilibrium but with greater net capital flows.

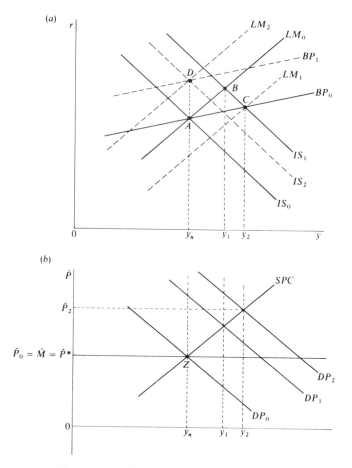

Figure 12.10 Inflation under a fixed exchange rate.

Fixed exchange rate

The situation under a fixed exchange rate is shown in Fig. 12.10(a,b). Again we begin with positions A and Z. The only new element we have added is that the world inflation rate is given by $\hat{P}*$, which is equal to the domestic rate of inflation in the initial position. Throughout the analysis we hold the world inflation rate constant.

Real government spending again increases, shifting IS to IS_1 and DP (temporarily) to DP_1. Again the net export position deteriorates, due to the rise in income, and the rise in interest rates attracts short-term capital. There is pressure on the exchange rate to appreciate. In order to maintain the exchange rate the Bank of England must sell sterling and buy dollars. The sale of sterling increases the domestic money supply so shifting LM to the right, to LM_1 at point C. But this shifts DP still further to DP_2. The result is the domestic inflation rate rises relative to that abroad. Two effects follow from this rise in the domestic rate of inflation. First, real money balances decline, so shifting LM to the left. Second, there is a decline in the competitive position of the UK, so shifting BP up (to the left) and *IS* to the left. The process will come to a stop when *LM* cuts *BP* on the new IS curve. In other words, at point *D*. Point *D* must be at income level y_n because only this income level is consistent with a domestic inflation rate equal to the world inflation rate.

The end result must be a higher nominal interest rate. Why? Because throughout the whole adjustment period the net export position deteriorates. Since balance of payments equilibrium has to be maintained at a fixed exchange rate this could only come about by an increase in net capital inflows. This in turn is only possible if domestic interest rates rise relative to those abroad.

Two important conclusions follow from the analysis of fixed and floating exchange rates in response to a rise in government spending; these are as follows:

1. An increase in demand pressure over what the market can bear will have no lasting effects on real income and will lead to a rise in interest rates and a deterioration in the net export position of the country. This result is very dependent on the fact that the BP curve is less steep than the LM curve.
2. The type of exchange rate regime is not important to the *final outcome* as regards interest rate and the level of income. What is affected is the means by which the domestic price level is changed. This can be seen by considering the real exchange rate, *R*, defined as SP/P^*. Taking percentage changes we have,

$$\hat{R} = \hat{S} + \hat{P} - \hat{P}^*$$

For a given change *R*, and with P^* constant, then under a fixed exchange rate regime, all adjustment must fall on domestic prices. This is accomplished by an accommodating increase in the money supply. Under a floating rate regime, the real exchange rate change is a combination of a change in the domestic price level and a change in the nominal exchange rate.

Thus, what is different is the *adjustment path* and the sectors in the economy which are adversely/beneficially affected by such adjustment. As far as inflation is concerned, this is likely to be greater under a fixed exchange rate than under a floating exchange rate because the domestic price level must bear all the adjustment burden.

APPENDIX 12.1 MEASURING INFLATION

Laidler and Parkin (1975) opened their survey article with the statement: 'inflation is a process of continuously rising prices, or equivalently, of a continuously falling value of money.' (p. 741) Although a symptom-based definition, it does indicate that in order to measure inflation it is necessary to measure the price level. But the price *level* can only be a construction from individual prices of commodities, and as such must involve the use of an index of prices. This immediately begs the question of what type of index and which prices should be used as the basis for the index. It is not the intention here to discuss the 'index number problem', but simply to state that in the UK there are two price indices which are used to measure inflation:

(a) the retail price index (RPI); and
(b) the GDP deflator.

The RPI is a base weighted price index constructed by the Central Statistical Office using information from the Family Expenditure Survey. Because it is a base weighted index, the weights used are the expenditure on a particular item in the base period divided by the total value of expenditure in the base period, see Croxton *et al.* (1968) and Fox (1968). This means that the base period bundle of goods is held constant. In other words, new goods cannot be handled by this index (and goods no longer sold are still included) unless the index is re-based, which is done periodically. The UK retail price index has recently been re-based from 1975 to 1980.

Inflation is measured as the percentage change in the index number over a specified period of time, which is usually taken to be one year. In general terms, if P_t is the price index at time period t (say June 1986) while P_{t-1} is the price index in period $t-1$ (say June 1985), then price inflation is measured by

$$\hat{P} = (P_t - P_{t-1}) \times 100/P_{t-1}$$

which in the example given would be in % per annum, or generally % per period (where the period is the difference between $t-1$ and t).

The same formula would be used to measure inflation even where the retail price index was replaced by the GDP deflator. The GDP deflator is not based on the Family Expenditure Survey, and attempts to find an index for *all* goods and services in the economy. The GDP deflator is calculated by taking the GDP at factor cost at current prices and dividing this figure by GDP at factor cost at constant prices. Thus.

$$\text{GDP deflator} = \frac{GDP \text{ at factor cost at current prices}}{GDP \text{ at factor cost at constant prices}}$$

The GDP deflator uses current weights (i.e., it is a Paasche price index). It is an implicit price index constructed from figures supplied in the National Income Blue Book. Unlike the RPI, which is available monthly, the GDP deflator is only available on a quarterly basis. However, it is sometimes used for measuring inflation when a more comprehensive set of goods and services is considered appropriate.

It is clear that there is no 'right' way to measure inflation because there is no 'right' price index number. However, once the index number is chosen, inflation is measured as the percentage change in that index number over a specified period of time.

APPENDIX 12.2 THE PHILLIPS CURVE

The Phillips curve is a relationship between inflation and unemployment: either wage inflation and unemployment or price inflation and unemployment. It was first outlined by Phillips (1958), and has since then been the most widely used and the most investigated relationship in macroeconomics. Given its weak underlying rationale, this in itself is surprising. But the Phillips curve appealed to all groups of economists. In its original formulation it was theoretically weak, which led to further theoretical investigations, e.g., Lipsey (1960). It appealed to policy-makers because it indicated a trade-off between inflation and unemployment. Phillips' original investigation was crude from an econometric point of view, and so the relationship appealed to the econometricians, who attempted more sophisticated testing. But the relationship, especially from a policy point of view, illustrated that its usefulness depended on its stability (in other words, the relationship needed to be stationary and not 'jumping around'). Like many other economic relationships, the Phillips curve appeared to become totally unstable ten years after Phillips published his results. Although there is dispute over the usefulness of the Phillips curve in macroeconomics, there is no getting away from the fact that it has become an integral part of macroeconomic analysis.

Phillips began with the idea that if there was excess demand in the labour market, then there would be pressure on wages to rise. The basic idea, therefore, is a relationship between excess demand and wage inflation. However, excess demand is not an observable quantity. Phillips thus postulated a relationship between unemployment and excess demand. The greater the excess demand the smaller the level of unemployment in the economy; in other words, there is an inverse relationship between unemployment and excess demand. Unemployment, then, became a proxy measure for excess demand. The greater the level of unemployment (the smaller the level of excess demand for labour) the smaller would be pressure on wages to rise. Hence, there is an inverse relationship between wage inflation and unemployment. This gives rise to the first basic equation, namely,

$$\hat{W} = g(U) \qquad g'(U) < 0 \tag{A12.2.1}$$

Phillips plotted observations on $\hat{W}$ and U for the period 1861–1913, which he used to 'estimate' the relationship g. He then superimposed this relationship on the period 1948–57, and found the observations to lie very close to the 'estimated' curve. (We have deliberately used quotation marks around 'estimated' to highlight the fact that Phillips' estimation methods were extremely crude and involved some dubious practices to find the 'best' fit. Furthermore, the equation used was simply imposed.) The importance of Phillips' results was that it appeared to show a stable relationship, stable for a period of nearly 100 years! Furthermore, the stability of this relationship was for a market which had involved tremendous institutional changes – the most important being the rise of trades unions. Given this stable relationship, a zero wage inflation can then be established where the Phillips curve cuts the unemployment axis. This is shown in Fig. A12.2.1, and Phillips found that the intersection point was at $5\frac{1}{2}\%$ unemployment.

Phillips linked the wage inflation to price inflation by subtracting the rate of change of labour productivity from wage inflation. (This is readily seen in terms of equation (2.32) of Chapter 2. Since μ is a constant, then the rate of change of wages is equal to the rate of change of productivity plus the rate of change of prices. Or, price inflation is wage inflation minus productivity growth.) In Phillips' original paper he took productivity growth to be 2%. Hence, the relationship between price inflation and unemployment is,

$$\hat{P} = g(U) - \hat{a}_L = f(U) \tag{A12.2.2}$$

With a 2% *rise* in productivity, $g(U)$ is shifted down by 2% points. The result is a Phillips curve (now relating price inflation and unemployment, i.e., $\hat{P} = f(U)$) cutting the unemployment axis at $2\frac{1}{2}\%$. Thus, maintaining unemployment below this level by demand-management policies, would imply a predictable level of price inflation for the policy-makers. Put another way, the objective of 'full employment' (approximately 2% unemployment) would have a stable and predictably low rate of inflation associated with it.

From these simple beginnings mushroomed a voluminous literature. The negative relationship between unemployment and inflation needed justification, especially since unemployment may not be the best proxy for excess demand in the labour market. Certainly better estimation techniques were required. In this respect it was soon noted that wage increases may give rise to price increases, and that these price increases may give rise to further wage increases. Although these were sequential on a fine division of time, they were simultaneously determined with the available data. Hence, it was necessary to simultaneously determine a wage equation and a price equation. Returning to the original problem, the main interest was between excess demand in the labour market and wage inflation. However, not only was unemployment used as a proxy for excess demand, but it was the *only* variable. For example, much attention in later years centred on whether trades unions were a source of pressure on wages, Hines (1964). However, this in turn required a proxy for 'trade union power'. But this was not the only problem. Phillips originally noted that the data points moved in a counterclockwise movement around the Phillips curve. This too required investigation, see Knowles and Winsten (1959), Lipsey (1960), Hansen (1970) and Hines (1971).

The next major development in the literature came from monetarists, and new classicists. As inflation took off it was clear that market participants (especially in the labour market) took account of inflationary *expectations*. Friedman (1968) and Phelps (1967, 1968) in particular, argued that the Phillips curve would move as a consequence of such inflationary expectations. This, in turn, led to the expectations-augmented Phillips curve; namely,

$$\hat{P} = f(U) + \hat{P}^e \tag{A12.2.3}$$

(Phelps introduced $\hat{P}^e$ into equation (A12.2.1) rather than equation (A12.2.3), where equation (A12.2.3) is more in line with Friedman's argument.) Of particular significance is the coefficient of $\hat{P}^e$, which in equation (A12.2.3) is unity. First, for each level of expected inflation there is a *different* Phillips curve.

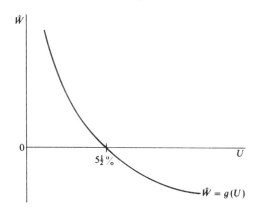

Figure A12.2.1 The Phillips curve.

So long as inflationary expectations are changing, then so too is the Phillips curve (it is unstable!). Second, by introducing the concept of the natural rate of unemployment (see Chapter 14), Friedman argued that in the long run unemployment could not deviate from the natural level. In other words, if $U = U_n$ (a constant), then inflation in the short run could take any value. Attempting to maintain the level of unemployment, for example, below its natural level would simply raise actual inflation in the short run and this, in turn, would sooner or later lead to a revision of inflationary expectations upwards. In other words, in the long run the Phillips curve was vertical at the natural rate of unemployment.

The introduction of inflationary expectations introduced a totally new dimension into the argument. Furthermore, with the rise of rational expectations (see Chapter 4), it provided a new avenue of debate between Keynesians and monetarists (including new classicists). Keynesians, for example, although conceding that price expectations were important, did not accept that the coefficient of $\hat{P}^e$ was unity. In other words, they did not accept a vertical long-run Phillips curve at the natural rate of unemployment. This has important policy implications. If the long-run Phillips curve is vertical, then any increase in aggregate demand which is used to maintain high levels of employment is, according to monetarists, doomed to failure, All it will do in the long run is raise the rate of inflation; it will have no effect on employment or output. If, however, there is a positive long-run Phillips curve (as predicted by the Keynesians), then there is still a role for demand management in the long run. Unfortunately, the question of the nature of the long-run Phillips curve has not yet been resolved.

Equation (A12.2.1) indicated a relationship between wage inflation and unemployment. Equations (A12.2.2) and (A12.2.3), which are by far the most popular specifications of the Phillips curve, show a relationship between price inflation and unemployment. In the present book, however, we have repeatedly used the Phillips curve as a *relationship between price inflation and real income*. It is important to realize that in order to do this we need to take a *second* relationship into account; namely Okun's law, which relates the unemployment gap to the output gap (equation (3.17) in Chapter 3). There is a major weakness in doing this. In this appendix we have attempted to briefly highlight the problems surrounding the original Phillips curve. In Appendix 3.3 we pointed out the *empirical* nature of Okun's law. It follows, therefore, that if both the original Phillips curve *and* Okun's law are based on weak foundations, it is even more true to say that the relationship between price inflation and output is *not* a strong relationship.

APPENDIX 12.3 SUPPLY SHOCKS IN THE 1970s: AN ANALYSIS

The 1970s saw a number of shocks to the supply side of the economy. Each one would not be inflationary in itself, in the sense that all were one-off events. Once the economy settled down, then

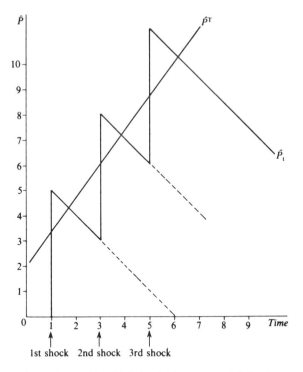

Figure A12.3.1 Trend inflation in the presence of shocks.

inflation would return to its former level. Three observations can be made with regard to this assumption. First, the assumption is that the shock comes from the supply-side, and so constitutes a cost-push analysis of inflation. Second, although an individual shock may be a one-period shock, the effects are likely to be distributed over a number of years. Third, if there is more than one shock, then the effect will be superimposed on whatever remains of previous shocks. The situation is illustrated in Fig. A12.3.1. For simplicity we assume a uniform shock of 5% initially on the rate of inflation and a uniform distribution over a five-year period (i.e., inflation will return to its former level by the fifth year, and decrease by one-fifth for each intervening year). Hence, a shock in period 1 leads to a rate of inflation of 5% in period 1 and this reduces to zero by period 6. All shocks follow the same form, as shown by the downward portions of the path of inflation, $\hat{P}_t$. But, as illustrated in Fig. A12.3.1, suppose there is an initial shock in period 1, a second shock in period 3 and a third shock in period 5. Although the path of inflation in this hypothetical situation is that shown by the saw-tooth, and denoted $\hat{P}_t$, the *trend* in inflation, $\hat{P}^T$, is upward.

Although cost-push theorists present their arguments in terms of AD and AS, most especially a shift up in AS, the analysis is still very much that of Fig. A12.3.2, when looked at in terms of the rate of change of prices (inflation). Turning now to the sequence of historical events, they were as follows for the UK, where for simplicity of exposition we take each event independently. In the late 1960s and early 1970s AD was shifting to the right with both monetary and fiscal expansion, shifting the economy from A to B, where the initial situation is given by AD_0 and AS_0. In the early 1970s the commodity price boom shifted AS upward, so shifting the economy from B to C. The Barber boom shifted the AD curve to the right, moving the economy from C to D. The rise in food prices as a result of Britain's entry into the EEC in 1973 and the rise in OPEC oil prices at the end of 1973 shifted AS upward, moving the economy from D to E. Three effects now contributed to further upward shifts in the AS curve: (1) a further rise in OPEC oil prices in 1975; (2) wage increases in excess of productivity; and, (3) a rise in price expectations. The combined effect was to move the economy from point E to

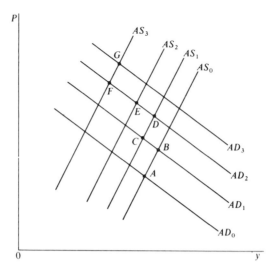

Figure A12.3.2 Shocks to the UK economy, 1960–79.

point *F*. However, because of the deleterious effects on output and employment of these events the governments (prior to 1979) shifted the AD curve to the right in order to alleviate the situation on output and employment. This moved the economy from *F* to *G*. Of course, in practice there would be further shifts in the aggregate supply curve at various stages in the adjustment process as workers tried to maintain their real wages as prices rose. The combined effects, although ambiguous as regards income, pushed prices up persistently so leading to ever higher rates of inflation.

APPENDIX 12.4 THE RELATIONSHIP BETWEEN THE NOMINAL INTEREST RATE AND ANTICIPATED INFLATION

Closed economy

There is a basic result that if inflation is fully anticipated, then the *nominal* interest rate will rise by the full change in the rate of inflation. In establishing this result a number of interest rates must be distinguished as follows:

1. The *nominal* (or market) rate of interest, r
2. The *real* rate of interest, μ. The nominal rate of interest is equal to the real rate of interest plus the rate of inflation. However, since there are two rates of inflation (one actual and one expected), then there are two nominal rates of interest, the actual rate (r^a) and the expected rate (r^e), thus

$$r^a = \mu + \hat{P} \tag{A12.4.1}$$

$$r^e = \mu + \hat{P}^e \tag{A12.4.2}$$

3. The *natural rate of interest*, r_n. This rate is a concept introduced by Wicksell and denotes the real rate of interest at which there is no excess demand in the market for goods and services, see Patinkin (1965).

When inflation is fully anticipated, then the actual rate of inflation is equal to the expected rate of inflation; this in turn means that the actual and expected nominal interest rates are equal.

The result of a higher rate of inflation is illustrated in Fig. A12.4.1. The initial situation is given by IS_0 and LM_0 intersecting at point *A*. We assume initially that there is no inflation and that this is

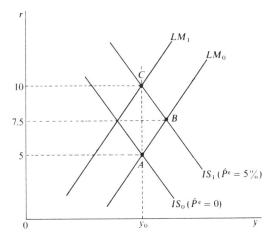

Figure A12.4.1 Result on nominal interest rates of a rise in expected inflation.

expected, $\hat{P} = \hat{P}^e$. At point A the nominal rate of interest (actual and expected) is equal to 5%, which is also equal to the real rate of interest. Now suppose for some reason that everyone expects the rate of inflation to rise to 5% and that these expectations are fulfilled (i.e., the actual rate of inflation does rise to 5%). What is the result?

First it must be noted that the IS curve shifts up vertically by 5% points. Why is this? For any given level of income, income will remain constant when expected inflation changes if the nominal interest rate rises by the same percentage, so leaving investment unchanged (and hence income unchanged). Given, then, a movement of the IS curve to IS_1 and a movement of the economy to point B, this must mean a rise in nominal interest rates by less than 5% points. In Fig. A12.4.1 we have assumed that the nominal interest rate at point B is 7.5%. Given this situation there is now a difference between actual inflation ($\hat{P} = 0$) and expected inflation ($\hat{P}^e = 5$). If the result is to be fully anticipated then the actual rate of inflation will rise to 5%. But this results in a fall in real balances (a fall in M/P). This shifts the LM curve leftward. But by how much? To determine this it is necessary to incorporate into the analysis the natural rate of interest. The natural rate of interest is assumed to be 5% and, in line with Fisher, it is assumed to be independent of the expected rate of inflation. As the LM curve moves left the nominal interest rate will rise, as will the expected real rate. Once the expected real rate is equal to the natural rate, then there is no reason for any further change. This must be at LM_1 where the nominal rate of interest is equal to 10%. This is so because then the real rate of interest is 5% which is equal to the natural rate of interest. This is represented by point C in Fig. A12.4.1.

The conclusion is, therefore, that the nominal interest rate rises by the same amount as the rise in inflation. The economy adjusts nominal values in order to preserve real interest rates equal to the 'natural' level. Hence,

$$r^e = \mu + \hat{P}^e$$

and where inflation is fully anticipated ($\hat{P} = \hat{P}^e$), then

$$r = \mu + \hat{P} \tag{A12.4.3}$$

Open economy

Assume that inflation is fully anticipated in both the home country and the foreign country, where the overseas country is distinguished by an asterisk. Then

$$r = \mu + \hat{P} \qquad \text{in the home country (equation (A12.4.3))}$$

$$r^* = \mu^* + \hat{P}^* \qquad \text{in the foreign country} \tag{A12.4.4}$$

In Chapter 5 we considered two results: one with respect to purchasing power parity (PPP) and the other with respect to interest rate parity (IRP). Purchasing power parity was given by equation (5.13), while interest rate parity was given by equation (5.23); these are presented here as equations (A12.4.5) and (A12.4.6) respectively:

$$\hat{S} = \hat{P}* - \hat{P} \qquad \text{PPP} \tag{A12.4.5}$$

$$z = r* - r \qquad \text{IRP} \tag{A12.4.6}$$

If PPP holds and expectations are fulfilled, then from equation (A12.4.5) we have

$$\hat{S}^e = \hat{P}^{e*} - \hat{P}^e \tag{A12.4.7}$$

If, in addition, we assume market efficiency, then the forward rate is equal to the expected spot exchange rate. This allows us to write equation (A12.4.6) in the form

$$\hat{S}^e = r* - r \tag{A12.4.8}$$

It follows, therefore, from equations (A12.4.7) and (A12.4.8) that

$$r* - r = \hat{P}^{e*} - \hat{P}^e \tag{A12.4.9}$$

or

$$r - \hat{P}^e = r* - \hat{P}^{e*} \tag{A12.4.10}$$

Equation (A12.4.10) is no more than saying expected real interest rates must be equal. Equation (A12.4.9), on the other hand, indicates that nominal interest rates will differ so long as inflation rates differ. Hence, the difference of nominal interest rates will not in itself lead to capital flows because, as we have just demonstrated, if interest rates differ by the inflation differential, then there is no reason for capital to flow. However, this result does require the appropriate change in the exchange rate. Any attempt to control any of the three variables (r, P or S), either at home or abroad, will lead to adjustments elsewhere in the system. In an open economy, interest rates, inflation and the exchange rate are all closely locked together, and are also locked to the same variables abroad.

Chapter 13

STABILIZATION POLICY

13.1 THE ECONOMIC SYSTEM: STABLE OR UNSTABLE?

Government stabilization of the economy has always led to difficulties, and has at various times in history required justification. Even when there has been agreement that some form of intervention is required, there have still been disputes over the precise form such intervention should take. What separates stabilization from other forms of intervention is the fact that it is concerned largely with the overall performance of the economy while intervention is usually concerned with specific markets. This distinction in itself is very revealing. Macroeconomics, as we now understand it, arose largely out of Keynes' *General Theory of Employment, Interest and Money*. It was this book which supplied a macro-economic justification for government intervention. Prior to this publication, and to a large extent today, the reasons given for government involvement in the economy have been on microeconomic grounds, namely:

(a) market failure;
(b) externalities; or
(c) public goods.[1]

But it should be noted that these three reasons for government involvement are concerned with economic *efficiency* and not with macroeconomic objectives. They lie behind the idea of *laissez-faire*, and any intervention requires strong justification. In addition, ever since Adam Smith's *Wealth of Nations*, there has always been a strong belief in the efficacy of the 'invisible hand'. In other words, the best way to allocate resources in society is by leaving the market mechanism alone and letting it do the job of allocation. Implicit, if not explicit, is the belief that the market mechanism can do the job of resource allocation better than any government, and that any interference from the government will simply lead to incorrect signals, and hence to a misallocation of resources.

The invisible hand, however, operates only where markets exist. For example, there is no market for pensioner payments, for future generations (which means that the market is biased towards presently existing consumer preferences), etc. Government intervention in cases of market failure, externalities and public goods are a means of patching up certain weaknesses in the workings of the invisible hand, but that is all. Furthermore, markets are about demand and supply, which in turn refer to the ability to pay and the ability to supply, and not merely to wishes. Demand patterns are therefore dependent upon income

distribution, while supply is dependent upon the present structure, conduct and performance of industry – most particularly its power base (*à la* Galbraith).[2]

One other general observation is worth making. We talk of the economic *system*, for it is a
system. But two views about the economic system run through the debate of stabilization
policy:

1. The economic system is *stable*.
2. The economic system is *unstable*.

It is difficult to prove either of these opposing views about the economic system, but it is
important to realize that classical economists, and the present-day new classicists, believe
that the economic system is stable – but subject to random shocks (a feature we will discuss
in more detail in Chapter 16). Hence, what matters in their view is how the system copes
with such random shocks. Other economists believe that the economic system is inherently
unstable, and so requires constant control by the government . This latter view is partly,
although not wholly, related to the idea that government policy is a means of achieving
macroeconomic objectives.

However, *two* concepts of stability/instability, and hence *two* concepts of stabilization, are
not always distinguished in such discussions. It is useful to distinguish static from dynamic
stability, and static from dynamic stabilization. Static models involve economic relationships which establish an equilibrium of the system. The system can then be altered by
changing the value of some exogenous variable or some parameter and considering the *new*
equilibrium in comparison with the old. This is the familiar comparative static analysis. In
this approach time plays no part. On the other hand, dynamic analysis considers the *time
path* of the variables. If the endogenous variables approach their new equilibrium values
over time then the system is dynamically stable; on the other hand, if the endogenous
variables do not approach their new equilibrium values over time, then the system is
dynamically unstable (even though it may be statically stable).[3]

In regard to the issue of government intervention there is a further distinction to make,
even if we are considering purely static stability. If the economy is statically stable and
suffers no random shocks, then it will (or may), when left alone, settle down at an
equilibrium. This equilibrium, however, may not be a desired position. If it is not a desired
position, then either the government must accept this or it must set things in motion to
move the economy to a position which is desired. If the equilibrium position is *not* a desired
position then the government will be required to implement other policies in order to *keep*
the economy at this desired position; while if the new position is one of equilibrium, then
further policies to maintain the system at this position are unnecessary – unless the system
suffers a shock.

The issue, therefore, is not simply about stable and unstable systems, but also about
equilibrium versus desired positions. By stating it in this way we immediately notice the
explicit values.

> A *free market supporter* is stating a belief that he prefers the market equilibrium to any
> other (a policy of 'do nothing').

> An *interventionist* states his desired objectives and the policies necessary to achieve and
> maintain them (a policy of 'do something').

The free market supporters argue that the market mechanism is efficient, that market-
clearing occurs quickly (a point we emphasized in Chapter 4), and that the economy will, if

not suffering a random shock, settle down at an equilibrium. The equilibrium is stable and can therefore be maintained without government intervention. The only unknown is that of random shocks. Any attempt at intervention by the government will simply lead to a greater variation of economic variables and to even greater uncertainty. Implicit, rather than explicit, is the belief that any government intervention will result in a lower economic welfare than will no intervention. Interventionists point to the failure of the market mechanism, and the presence of externalities and public goods; but they also openly state (usually) what they would set as targets for macroeconomic variables. Interventionists would argue, therefore, that the welfare of society consistent with the target economic variables is greater than the level of these variables when the economy is left to its own devices.[4]

We will deal in more detail with static stabilization in the next section, where we pay particular attention to the use of monetary and fiscal policy to achieve a target (desired?) level of income.

To a large extent, however, the debate over whether governments should stabilize the economy is concerned not with static stabilization, but, rather, with dynamic stabilization. In this framework main economic variables are known to oscillate over time. Thus the purpose of dynamic stabilization is to reduce the extent of such oscillations. Policies for reducing oscillations of variables over time need not be the same as those necessary to achieve a static equilibrium of the same variable. Accordingly, we will deal with dynamic stabilization in Section 13.3.

It will become apparent that a main element in the discussion of *dynamic* stabilization is the use of rules rather than the more traditional policy of 'fine tuning'. We take up this debate in Section 13.4. However, a more technical opposition to fine tuning has come via the rational expectations theorists, and we deal with this in Section 13.5. Although the early debate simply argued for 'rules', it was rarely made clear precisely what rules were called for. The rule put forward by Friedman was a simple fixed rule, but it does not follow that, even if rules are called for, they will be either simple or fixed. A discussion of alternative rules is thus presented in Section 13.6. Most of the debate concerning stabilization has been conducted in terms of a closed economy, but it is necessary to consider the issue from the point of view of an open economy and this is dealt with in the final section.

13.2 STATIC STABILIZATION

Stabilization policy, fine tuning or counter-cyclical policy are all terms meaning short-term intervention by the government, either to counterbalance some trend in an economic variable or to speed up (slow down) its natural time path or to achieve some target value for a variable. Although demand management is sometimes used synonymously with stabilization, it is not the same. Demand management is a *method* for achieving stabilization. As the term 'demand management' indicates, stabilization is carried out through changing aggregate demand.

It is important from the outset to distinguish static stabilization from dynamic stabilization. In the remainder of this section we deal with static stabilization and take up the question of dynamic stabilization in Section 13.3. Static stabilization is concerned solely with the achievement of a *desired level* of an endogenous variable in a comparative static model. Thus, in Chapter 2 we developed a static aggregate demand and supply model which determined the price level and the level of real income (assuming inflation was zero), these being two particular endogenous variables of this model. Equilibrium in this model is where aggregate demand intersects aggregate supply. A change in any exogenous variable or parameter of the model will shift either the aggregate demand curve or the aggregate supply curve and so establish a new equilibrium. Static stability simply considers the necessary conditions for the new equilibrium to be achieved, and does not refer to any passage of time. The major concern of static stabilization is to move the equilibrium from an equilibrium position which is *not desired* to one which *is desired*.

In Section 2.6 we established an unemployment equilibrium in a typically Keynesian macroeconomic model. In other words, the equilibrium level of income leads to permanent (involuntary) unemployment. The purpose of static stabilization, then, is to use government policy to move the economy from its present position to one where income is at the full employment level. When stated in this way, two characteristics stand out. First, the equilibrium is not at its desired level. Second, the variable of concern is real income.[5] The question that was usually posed at this stage was whether monetary policy or fiscal policy was the best way of achieving the desired level of income. However, this is too restrictive. It was based largely on an IS–LM model and therefore only considered the demand side of the question. In terms of our static aggregate demand and aggregate supply model, a rise in government spending (fiscal expansion) or a rise in the money supply (monetary expansion) will shift aggregate demand to the right and so raise the level of income to its target level. As long as the aggregate supply curve is upward sloping, monetary or fiscal expansion will raise the price level when such policies are used to stabilize income.

The above discussion was, of course, in terms of income stabilization. But it is not only income that concerns governments. The choice of variable to be stabilized is a normative question. Consider, then, the situation shown in Fig. 13.1 with the economy initially at point A where AD_0 intersects AS_0. Suppose for some reason that aggregate supply shifts to AS_1, say because the fixed money wage accepted by labour is higher or because there is a deterioration in the competitiveness of the economy. The result will be a rise in the price level to P_1 and a fall in the level of real income to y_1, the economy having moved from point A to point B. Under income stabilization, policy-makers can shift the aggregate demand curve, through monetary or fiscal means, to AD_1, thereby moving the economy to point C. Alternatively, if the policy-maker was concerned about price stabilization he could shift aggregate demand to AD_2, moving the economy from point B to point D. It is clear, therefore, that income stabilization is at the expense of price stability, while price stabilization is at the expense of achieving the full employment level of income. What is also shown in Fig. 13.1 is that income stabilization will lead to the highest rise in prices (point C compared with point B), while price stabilization will lead to the biggest fall in real income (point D compared with B).

It clearly matters, therefore, which variable the policy-makers choose to stabilize. In general those who gain from income stabilization (those who would have been unemployed had the stabilization policy not been pursued) will differ from those who gain as a consequence of price stability (asset holders and fixed income earners in particular).

It is not always clear which variable the policy-maker does wish to stabilize. In a more elaborate model, many variables will be moving away from their desired positions beside income and prices. In Chapter 7, where we discussed money demand and supply, we noted

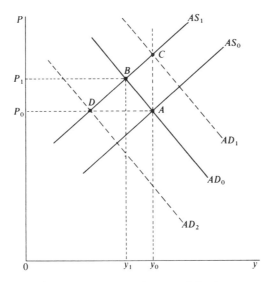

Figure 13.1 Income and price stabilization.

that in the UK the Treasury has often targeted the interest rate. In other words, the Treasury has (rightly or wrongly) stabilized interest rates which, in this case, is at the expense of the money supply. At other times, exchange rate stability has been the over-riding concern of the government. Often these concerns have a dynamic element, which we discuss in the next section, but in so far as the authorities have some target exchange rate in mind, they will be pursuing exchange rate stabilization in the static sense used here.

In the case of some of the main economic variables, monetarists have argued that there is little point in attempting to stabilize them, in either a static or a dynamic sense, because the economic system has *automatic stabilizers*. It is argued that if the system is left to adjust, these automatic stabilizers will ensure an equilibrium is established. Furthermore, since these automatic stabilizers operate on private sector spending, then they are also used as an argument for the stability of the private sector.

Before discussing what the automatic stabilizers are and how they operate, it is important to bear in mind that they will only establish an equilibrium position of the system (or in a dynamic sense, to be discussed in the next section, to reduce oscillations of key indicators); they will not necessarily establish a *desired* equilibrium position. Much of the Keynesian static government stabilization policy which we have so far discussed is attempting to establish a desired equilibrium, usually at the full employment level of income. The presence, or effectiveness, of automatic stabilizers is not necessarily in dispute. Where the difference of opinion lies is in respect of the consequences of stabilizing the economy at some equilibrium which may be different from that which would result without government stabilization and where automatic stabilizers were left to work through the system. With this caution in mind, what are the automatic stabilizers and how do they work?

Three automatic stabilizers are put forward by monetarists. First, according to mone-tarists consumption is not a source of instability because, they argue, consumption is based on permanent income rather than current income (see Appendix 2.2). Thus any change in income will not necessarily lead to major changes in consumption. Any transitory changes in income will, on the contrary, lead to changes in current *savings*. Hence, savings are volatile, but savings are not part of aggregate demand.

Second, taxes and transfers depend on income. A rise in income will raise tax receipts and will reduce the level of disposable income. A rise in income will reduce the level of unemployment and hence reduce the level of unemployment benefits. To a large extent this was analysed in Chapter 6. In the realistic case where taxes are related to income, the multiplier is smaller than if taxes were autonomous (i.e., independent of income). This means that for any shock to the system, leading to a rise or fall in autonomous expenditure, income will rise or fall by less than it would have done had taxes been autonomous. However, this is more important for dynamic income stabilization and can conflict with static income stabilization. Since the change in income is less for any change in government spending, then the size of government spending necessary to achieve a particular desired level of income will be greater.[6]

The third automatic stabilizer is more problematic and is based on whether or not prices are flexible, both upwards and downwards. A rise in aggregate demand will, in general, raise prices. The rise in prices will reduce the level of real money balances (i.e., M/P will fall) and the level of real wages (i.e., W/P will fall) if the money wage level remains fixed. The fall in real money balances will (or may) reduce the level of consumption and the fall in real wages will do likewise. Both effects will reduce the impact of the rise in aggregate demand and will lead to a smaller rise in income and a smaller rise in the price level than would otherwise have been the case. Conversely for a fall in aggregate demand. However, if this is the case, then the effect of the automatic stabilizers arising from a fall in aggregate supply leading to a rise in prices and a fall in income will be to shift the aggregate demand curve to the left, which will stabilize prices but will lead to an even greater fall in income.

13.3 DYNAMIC STABILIZATION

In the preceding section it was stated that a distinction must be made between static stabilization and dynamic stabilization. It is well known that many key economic variables oscillate over time, i.e., they show a cyclic pattern either around an equilibrium value or around some trend. Dynamic stabilization refers to economic policies which are implemented in order to reduce the oscillations in certain key economic variables over time. There is a variety of possible dynamic paths, and a number of cycle characteristics which are detailed in Appendix 13.1. But even if a dynamic path is convergent (i.e., dynamically stable) the question still remains whether it is possible for the government to reduce oscillations. Of course, the implicit assumption here is that the economy will be better off by such a reduction. Since the real world economy is very rarely in equilibrium, stabilization is more usually directed at dynamic stabilization.

For the present let us consider in more detail the meaning we give to dynamic stabilization, and in particular to the meanings of stable and unstable countercyclical policies. To carry out this clarification we must distinguish a number of possible time paths that a variable can take. For the sake of illustration let us suppose we are dealing with real GDP, denoted y. Three time paths must be distinguished:

(a) $y^e(t)$ = the equilibrium time path of income without government intervention and with market-clearing;

(b) $y^a(t)$ = the actual time path of income without any government intervention;

(c) $x(t)$ = the path of income in the presence of government intervention.

In theory we are concerned with two deviations: first, the deviation of the actual time path, $y^a(t)$, from the equilibrium time path, $y^e(t)$, i.e. $y^a(t) - y^e(t)$ is referred to as the *pure cycle deviation*, and denotes how far an unregulated economy is from its equilibrium path. The second deviation is the time path of income in the presence of intervention, $x(t)$, from the equilibrium time path, $y^e(t)$, i.e. $x(t) - y^e(t)$. We will refer to this second deviation as the *government-induced cycle deviation*, and it denotes how far a regulated economy is from its equilibrium path. The debate for and against fine tuning is thus concerned with a comparison between the pure cycle deviation, $y^a(t) - y^e(t)$, and the government-induced cycle deviation, $x(t) - y^e(t)$. If the latter shows less variation than the former, then government policy is stabilizing, while if it shows greater variation, then government policy is destabilizing.

Having established that the main comparison is between the pure cycle deviation and the government-induced cycle deviation, let us concentrate on what the government must do to bring about perfect stabilization. First we note that the time path of income in the presence of government intervention, $x(t)$, must equal the time path of income without intervention, $y^a(t)$, plus an adjustment (positive or negative) for government policy, $a(t)$, i.e.

$$x(t) = y^a(t) + a(t)$$

For perfect stabilization, then, the time path of income in the presence of government intervention must be the same as the time path of equilibrium income, i.e. $x(t) = y^e(t)$. If this is to be the case then we must have

$$y^e(t) = y^a(t) + a_p(t)$$

or

$$a_p(t) = -[y^a(t) - y^e(t)]$$

where $a_p(t)$ denotes perfect adjustment, and is to be distinguished from some general adjustment, $a(t)$. In other words, for perfect stabilization the policy-induced change must be exactly equal to the pure cycle deviation with the opposite sign. The situation is shown in Fig. 13.2. The pure cycle deviation is given by $y^a(t) - y^e(t)$, while the government is pursuing a policy, adjusting by this factor with opposite sign, namely $a_p(t) = -[y^a(t) - y^e(t)]$. The result is that the economy follows a path $x(t) = y^e(t)$. In other words, if the government achieves perfect stabilization then the economy will move along its equilibrium path.

With perfect stabilization we have

$$x(t) - y^e(t) = 0$$

which is preferable to the pure cycle deviation

$$y^a(t) - y^e(t) \neq 0$$

But what if government stabilization is not perfect? The adjustment, $a(t) \neq a_p(t)$, undertaken by the government may be too large (small) or mistimed. In Fig. 13.3 we illustrate a case of mistiming, where the government takes a number of periods before adjusting. The

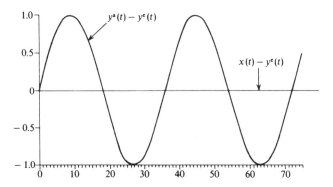

Figure 13.2 Pure cycle deviation and perfect stabilization.

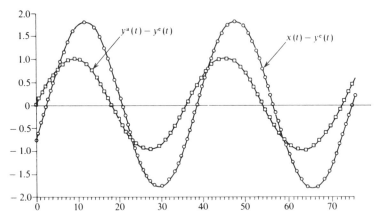

Figure 13.3 Mistiming of stabilization policy.

pure cycle deviation is given by the curve $y^a(t) - y^e(t)$, while the government-induced cycle deviation is given by $x(t) - y^e(t)$. It can be seen that the government-induced cycle deviation shows greater amplitude than the pure cycle deviation. In other words, government intervention is destabilizing. It is not difficult to see why this is so. The adjustment by the government is in the *same direction* as the pure cyclic deviation, and so the induced policy change *reinforces* the cycle rather than countering it.

The discussion highlights two difficulties that the government can encounter when undertaking stabilization:

(a) the *timing* of intervention; or
(b) the *amount* of intervention.

We will take each of these in turn. Why is the timing of economic policy such a problem? Consider the situation where a shock happens to the economy. The first difficulty is to decide whether the shock is a one-off event (i.e., is transitory) or is going to persist some time into the future. Stabilization policy is largely directed at shocks which lead to persistent changes. But the government at some point must decide whether it is or is not persistent.

Having decided it is persistent, then it must make a decision as to what to do. These two lags, the *recognition lag* and the *decision lag*, both make up what is referred to as the *inside lag*. Once action has been taken, there will be a first-round effect on the economy; that is to say, the immediate impact of the policy. Suppose, for example, the government lowers taxes in order to stimulate the economy and increase the level of employment. As the (dynamic) multiplier takes effect, there will be second-round effects which will be distributed over time. The time period taken for the target variable to be affected (both first- and second-round effects) by the policy instrument is referred to as the *outside lag*. The inside lag refers to the period of time taken for decisions to be made by the bureaucratic machinery (hence, inside government), while the outside lag refers to the time the policy takes to influence the actual economy (hence, outside government).

The recognition lag is more important than it first appears. In some cases the recognition is straightforward – such as the requirement for extra liquidity at Christmas time (this is a negative lag in the sense that it is known before the event itself takes place). More usually the lag is positive and arises from taking time to recognize that something must be done, e.g. that a devaluation is necessary. The difficulty here is that market participants may themselves recognize that the government must do something even sooner than the government itself recognizes this.[7] This means that, by the time the government recognizes that something must be done, the time path of the variable concerned has already begun to change as the expectations of market participants begin to take effect. The decision lag depends on which particular policy instrument is being used (e.g., a monetary, fiscal or employment instrument) and the particular institutional set-up. Suppose, for instance, that the government recognizes the need for a tax change in November. Does it wait until the budget of April the following year or does it have a mini-budget in November? (Interesting observations on the decision lag, especially in the case of the Treasury, will be found in S. Brittan's *Steering the Economy* (1971) and W. Keegan and R. Pennant-Rea's *Who Runs The Economy?* (1979).)

In large part, difficulties with outside lags reflect our ignorance of the precise workings of the economy. Take, for example, a policy to deal with unemployment. Unemployment is seen to rise. There is the inside lag involving the recognition of a problem and a decision to do something about it. Suppose a policy such as the Youth Opportunities Programme (YOP) is decided upon. How long is it before YOP has any appreciable effect on the level of unemployment? Let us suppose the inside lag is six months. Further, let us suppose the outside lag is 18 months (which is not unreasonable). Then the total lag is two years! By the time the programme begins to have its full impact, the economy could already have changed direction. This may be true. It does not imply that the policy should not be undertaken, however; it merely indicates that the question of timing is a very complex issue. (It almost suggests that when the economy is booming, an *expansionary* policy should be pursued, because by the time it begins to take effect the economy is likely to be in the downswing of the business cycle!)

Even if the timing is correct, there is still the amount (and hence direction) of the change to be considered. This in turn implies agreement on the type of policy required – for example whether it should be monetary or fiscal policy. Suppose a fiscal expansion is agreed on. What amount of fiscal expansion is required? If too much it could be inflationary. If too little it will not solve the problem. In this case it is not simply that it could be extended if too little, since the inside and outside lags may mean that the two attempts together could sum to four or more years! Furthermore, the amount depends very much on the assessment of the problem. This assessment in turn rests on the various macroeconomic models in existence. The Treasury model, the London Business School model and the National Institute model (not to mention the few other large models around the country) all assess the economic climate differently. Which one does the government choose – if any? A brief summary of the main UK macroeconomic models is provided in Appendix 13.2.

It must be recognized that there will always be uncertainty about the economic system. Given this uncertainty, the issue is: What is the best way of managing the economy (where we include 'doing nothing' in the term 'management')?

13.4 THE TRADITIONAL ARGUMENT FOR RULES

Before we begin discussing rules versus fine tuning it is important to realize that the discussion about rules has two quite distinct elements (which are often taken as one, and so leading to confusion). They are:

(a) arguments in favour or against rules; and
(b) arguments about the choice of rule to follow.

The confusion arises from the fact that the original discussion in favour of rules posed the argument in terms of simple fixed rules. It is possible to be in favour of rules only where the rules are of a particular form, where the form may or may not be a simple fixed rule. In this and the next section we shall deal only with point (1), leaving point (2) to Section 13.6.

In Section 13.3 we pointed out that one of the arguments against fine tuning was the fact that, if the policy was mistimed or involved too much or too little adjustment, it was possible for the policy to be destabilizing. Section 13.3 demonstrated that uncertainty is increased because of an unknown lag structure (both inside and outside lags). When we consider monetary policy more explicitly – within which most of the debate has taken place – we find that the following two characteristics are agreed upon:

(1) Behaviour of the money stock is important for real income and money income.
(2) Money influences the economy with:

    (a) a *long* lag; and
    (b) a *variable* lag.

If these two points are accepted, and notice that they are both *empirical* observations, then monetarists argue that fine tuning should not be undertaken. Any fine tuning could very well destabilize the economy. But is this claim justified?

We noticed in the preceding section that this claim rests on comparing the pure cycle deviation, $y^a(t) - y^e(t)$, with the government-induced cycle deviation, $x(t) - y^e(t)$. Monetarists are claiming that fine tuning leads to greater variation in the government-induced cycle deviation than in the pure cycle deviation. But both deviations are *unobservable* because the equilibrium time path of income (or any other equilibrium variable) is unobservable. Short of setting up a full dynamic macroeconomic model which will supply the equilibrium time path of the endogenous variables, the only simple operational equivalent in the present case for $y^e(t)$ is the deviation of income from a (logarithmic) trend. The (logarithmic) trend of income, $y^T(t)$, is acting as a proxy for the equilibrium time path of income. But even doing this only allows us to compute $x(t) - y^T(t)$, since the government does step in. The actual time path of income without any intervention is not known because the government did not choose to remain passive. The *proximate* pure cycle deviation, $y^a(t) - y^T(t)$, is accordingly unknown. It is possible to construct a second proxy, this time for $y^a(t)$, by using a simulation model and assuming that the economy moves along a path governed by the situation at some base period and assuming that the government no longer intervenes (at least not in the money market).[8]

It should be apparent that things are now getting complicated, and that we seem to be moving far away from the initial comparison. It is no longer clear what, in fact, we are testing. This arises not only from the inherent uncertainty in the economic system, but also from the fact that the questions being posed involve counterfactual information (i.e., what would the state of the economy be if the government did not do what it is doing but did something else?).

Notwithstanding these practical difficulties, there is also a conceptual difference of opinion. An essential feature of fine tuning is that there is constant monitoring of the economy, and, in the light of this information, further adjustment is made. In other words, fine tuning involves closed loops, or what is elsewhere referred to as a feedback mechanism. Given the difficulties discussed above, monetarists argue that it is this constant adjustment which destabilizes, because by the time the policy becomes effective the situation has changed. Monetarists have therefore advocated the use of rules. The point about rules, at least the simple fixed variety, is that they do not take account of any temporary reaction on the economy; in other words, they involve no feedback mechanism.[9] No matter what is happening to the economy, the rule is followed.

Notice the implicit importance of the assumption about the stability of the economy in this argument. Assuming the economy is stable, a fixed rule will not disturb this stability, while fine tuning can – and, according to monetarists, does. Consequently, the debate of rules versus discretion is not just about lags and uncertainty, but also about whether you believe that the economic system is stable or unstable. Even more, it rests on the *degree* of belief you have in the stability or otherwise of the economic system.

The point is that both monetarists and non-monetarists agree that there are long lags and uncertainty in the economic system. Non-monetarists, however, argue that if the economy is left to its own devices the adjustment will be painfully slow in reaching a solution. Fine tuning is then applied, not so much to reach some desired position, but to speed up the workings of the economic system. In other words, fine tuning is used to *reinforce* the workings of the market mechanism and not to replace it.

This discussion highlights the following two totally different reasons for fine tuning:

1. As a means of reaching some desired goal, which may or may not be the equilibrium solution.
2. As a means of reinforcing the workings of the market mechanism.

The argument in favour of rules is largely (although not totally) a counter to (2). The argument for rules to achieve (1) is more ambiguous.

Those in favour of rules tend to argue their case by appealing to the facts: 'Look at the evidence, does it not show that fine tuning has failed!' Let us assume that fine tuning has not

succeeded in achieving what it set out to achieve. This does not, however, suggest that rules
are the solution. Consistent with this 'evidence' is that a 'better' approach to fine tuning is
necessary. (Suppose your leg is plagued with boils and you are taking some medication
which is not helping the matter: does this mean that you should amputate, or try a 'better'
medication?)

The conclusion we draw from the traditional arguments for rules is that they are weak.
They are difficult to support because they involve unobservable variables and pose
counterfactual questions. In addition, they rest on the assumption that the economic system
is stable – which can only be a matter of belief.

There has, however, been a growing interest in rules arising from work being undertaken
by new classical economists and to this we now turn.

13.5 NEW CLASSICAL ARGUMENTS FOR RULES

Rational expectations theorists have also argued against fine tuning – but for totally
different reasons than those traditionally put forward. Their basic contention is that any
attempt at fine tuning will already be embedded in rational expectations behaviour. What
this means is that, in a world of rational expectations, the model is known (or people behave
as if the model were known) and, consequently, the parameters of the system will already
incorporate any response on the part of the government. Put another way, fine tuning is
based on the assumption that the structural model will remain the same both before and
after the policy change; i.e. the structural parameters will remain the same. Because of this
there will be a resultant change in the endogenous variables of the model. Rational
expectations theorists argue that the structural parameters will not remain the same, that
they will change as account is taken of the government policy. This will mean no change in
the equilibrium values of the endogenous variables, a point we developed in Chapter 4,
especially in Appendix 4.1. Any feedback policy will therefore fail.

Thus any attempt by the monetary authorities to affect the level of income will
be unsuccessful. In the same way, systematic fiscal policy is fully anticipated by
market participants and, according to rational expectations, cannot bring about any
divergence between actual and expected price level changes. Since aggregate supply is dependent on the expected price level, no change in the aggregate supply curve will result
and hence no change in output – in the long run. All such fine tuning is therefore ineffective.

Of course, the conclusion rests on the confidence you place in the rational expectations
model. The problem is that this model assumes not only that expectations are rationally
formed, but (more significantly) that markets clear quickly. The conclusions of rational
expectations depend more on the assumption of quick market-clearing than they do on how
expectations are actually formed. (The point is that, in a given model, the same long-run
solution will occur with either rationally formed expectations or with adaptive
expectations – only the actual time path of the endogenous variables will be different.) But
the assumption of quick market-clearing is just another aspect of the assumption that the
economic system is basically stable. The difficulty with the new classical reasoning is in
trying to separate those arguments which involve only an assumption about the formation

of expectations from the (often implicit) assumption that markets clear quickly. The former is an issue in model construction, while the latter is an empirical question.

13.6 WHAT TYPE OF RULES?

We have frequently referred to rules, but have not specified any so far. It is now time to be somewhat more specific about what type of rules are being advocated. (It is like debating for or against punishment without specifying the type of punishment being advocated: imprisonment or the death penalty!) The early rules were monetary rules and had the characteristics of being *fixed* and *simple*.

Consider the simple Cambridge version of the quantity equation:

$$M_d = kPy$$

Assuming quick market-clearing so that $M_d = M_s$, then with k assumed constant, the price level change, $\hat{P}$, is given by:

$$\hat{P} = \hat{M}_s - \hat{y}$$

It is now clear from this result that, if the money supply growth is set equal to the growth of real income, inflation will be zero. The *monetary rule* is to set the rate of growth of money supply equal to the rate of growth of real income. (An extreme form is a stationary economy in which there is no growth of real income and hence no change in the money supply, i.e. $\hat{M}_s = 0$.) This is the simple fixed monetary rule advocated by Friedman.

Does there exist any simple fixed fiscal rule? This is less straightforward. Let us approach it by first considering a very extreme case of a long-run stationary economy. We discussed this in some detail in Section 9.5, but we can summarize as follows. In a stationary economy income is at its natural level and so is the rate of interest. With no shocks to the system these will continue at the same levels. With income at its natural level then $\hat{y} = 0$, according to the monetary rule just discussed, implies that $\hat{M}_s = 0$ (or $dM = 0$). Furthermore, if the interest rate is to remain at its natural level, then the bond issue must remain unchanged. This implies $db/r = 0$. From the government budget constraint (discussed fully in Chapter 6) we therefore have

$$go - t = dM + db/r = 0$$

The *simple fixed fiscal rule* advocated is therefore one of a balanced budget. Whether this is the rule to be followed for a situation where real income is growing is not made clear.

The monetary and fiscal rules just outlined are both simple and fixed. They are based on typical monetarist analysis with its emphasis on the long-run stationary state. Two questions naturally arise:

1. Is the 'best' rule necessarily a *simple* rule?
2. Is the 'best' rule necessarily a *fixed* rule?

These two questions are not in fact independent of each other. To see this consider the difference between fixed and flexible monetary rules. Consider being at some point in time t. The information at time t will suggest some growth of real income at time $t + 1$. Based on this information, the money supply under a fixed monetary rule will be allowed to grow at the same rate as real income. Regardless of what actually happens to real income at time $t + 1$, the growth of money supply remains at its fixed rate determined by the information at time t. On the other hand, a flexible monetary rule recognizes that the situation at time $t + 1$ is uncertain and may take a variety of forms, often referred to as contingent states of the world. Continuing with our present example, income growth in each of these states is assumed to be different. For each state the same fixed policy rule is advocated, namely, money supply growth must equal the growth of real income. The only difference now is that different contingent growths of real income are taken into consideration. As further information becomes available to determine which state of the world applies, only then is the growth in money supply determined. In other words, further information is taken into account in a flexible policy rule.

The difficulty with the flexible policy rule is that there is an infinite number of future possible states of the world. It is difficult enough to carry out a single forecast of real income growth without having to do so for all possible contingencies. This might suggest that a simple policy rule may be the most suitable in such an uncertain situation.

The discussion so far has been carried out in an apolitical world. It has been argued that political parties in a democracy are often required to state in their manifestos what they would do if they took office. Since rules can be stated fairly clearly, certainly in comparison with the vagueness of demand management, then such political considerations also give support for rules. Even more, the rules are likely to be simple ones that the voting population can understand.

13.7 STABILIZATION IN AN OPEN ECONOMY

So far our discussion has been conducted in the context of a closed economy. The question we now need to consider is whether stabilization is easier under fixed or floating exchange rates. Once again, however, we must keep a distinction between static stabilization in an open economy and dynamic stabilization in an open economy. We will consider each of these in turn.

It will be recalled that static stabilization policy is directed at some desired level of a variable, most usually full employment income or stable prices (zero inflation). Consider the situation in Figs 13.4 and 13.5. Initially the economy is at point A with equilibrium in the goods market, the money market and the balance of payments. Suppose the government wishes to achieve a target level of real income y^*. The question is whether fiscal policy or monetary policy is the 'best' means of achieving this. However, in order to answer this question for such an open economy, we must stipulate what type of exchange rate system is operating. We consider two extreme situations: a fixed exchange rate system, illustrated in Fig. 13.4, and a perfectly flexible exchange rate system, illustrated in Fig. 13.5.

Consider, first, the fixed exchange rate system, shown in Fig. 13.4. As well as assumption of a fixed exchange rate, we make a further simplifying assumption that the price level is also constant (both at home and abroad). This means that the real exchange rate $(R = SP/P^*)$ is also constant. Now a fiscal expansion is undertaken shifting the IS curve from IS_0 to IS_1, moving the economy from point A to point B. However, at point B the economy is in

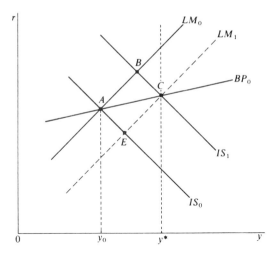

Figure 13.4 Income stabilization and fiscal and monetary policy under a fixed exchange rate.

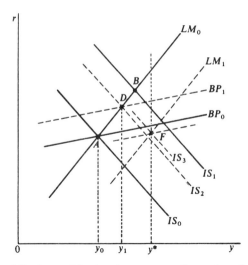

Figure 13.5 Income stabilization and fiscal and monetary policy under a flexible exchange rate.

surplus on its balance of payments. Although the rise in income has led to a worsening of the current account, the rise in the rate of interest has led to an increased net inflow of capital which more than swamps the current account deterioration. But, as we outlined in Chapter 5, a rise in the net capital inflow will put pressure on the exchange rate to appreciate. The exchange authorities, being committed to a fixed exchange rate, will accordingly supply sterling and demand foreign exchange. The result will be a rise in the domestic money supply. This will continue until the LM curve moves from LM_0 to LM_1, moving the economy from point B to point C.

What about monetary policy? Monetary expansion moves the LM curve from LM_0 to LM_1, thus moving the economy from point A to point E. The rise in income will lead to a deterioration in the current account, while the fall in the rate of interest will lead to a reduction in the net capital inflow. The result is a deficit on the balance of payments. This will put pressure on the sterling exchange rate to depreciate. Since the authorities are committed to a fixed exchange rate, however, they accordingly demand sterling and supply foreign exchange. The result will be a decrease in the money supply. This will continue until the LM curve moves back to LM_0, returning the economy to point A. The conclusion, therefore, is that under a fixed exchange rate system, fiscal policy is more effective than monetary policy in achieving a desired level of a real income.

Consider, next, the same fiscal expansion, but now the exchange rate is perfectly flexible. The situation is shown in Fig. 13.5. We continue to make the assumption that the domestic (and foreign) price level is constant, which means that the real exchange rate, R, will vary directly with the spot exchange rate. The fiscal expansion will move the IS curve once again to IS_1, moving the economy from point A to point B. However, at point B the economy would, under a fixed exchange rate, have a surplus on its balance of payments. This will put pressure on sterling to appreciate. The appreciation of sterling will shift the IS curve to the left, to IS_2, and the BP curve to the left (upwards), to BP_1. The end result is to raise income to level y_1, which is below the target level y^*. But how will monetary policy fare? A monetary expansion will move the LM curve to LM_1. Under a fixed exchange rate this will result in a balance of payments deficit. The deficit will lead to a depreciation of the exchange rate which, in turn, will lead to a movement right in the IS curve, from IS_0 to IS_3, and a movement right (down) in the BP curve, from BP_0 to BP_2. The result is an eventual movement of the economy to point F, at the target real income. Thus, under a flexible exchange rate system, monetary policy is more effective than fiscal policy in achieving the target rate of income.

It should be noted that all the analysis so far presented in this section is done under the assumption that capital is fairly interest elastic. In other words, the BP curve is less steep than the LM curve. We discussed this problem in Appendix 5.3, and the reader would do well to reconstruct the analysis of this section under the alternative assumption that capital is not interest rate elastic.

It is also important to note that we assumed throughout that the domestic price level is fixed. In other words, we considered income stabilization under a rigid system where there was also, by assumption, price stabilization. However, in the more general case, this will not be the situation. The question then arises, will fiscal policy be more or less price destabilizing than monetary policy? Furthermore, a fixed exchange rate system, by definition, has exchange rate stability. However, when exchange rates are floating, which is more destabilizing with respect to the exchange rate, monetary policy or fiscal policy? In general, therefore, we should ask the question: what is the result (cost of!) in the rest of the system of stabilizing one particular variable? We do not have the space to deal with this complex issue here, but it can be observed to some extent in terms of Fig. 13.4. We noted in terms of this diagram that fiscal policy was more effective at achieving the target income level than monetary policy. However, this will be at the expense of interest rate stability. The final result under a fiscal expansion is point C, while that under a monetary expansion remains point A. Hence, fiscal policy will raise the rate of interest.

When exchange rates are fixed, all adjustment must fall on income and prices. When exchange rates are flexible, adjustment will fall on prices, exchange rates and income. This means that under a fixed exchange rate system, income stabilization will lead to greater price destabilization, while price stabilization will lead to greater income destabilization. Under a floating exchange rate system, stabilization/destabilization is spread across more sectors of the economy. Greater price stability will almost certainly result in greater income and exchange rate instability. In a dynamic sense, the time path of income and exchange rates will show greater amplitude. This will be inevitable if stabilization of prices is pursued by governments, *and* market forces in *other* sectors are allowed to operate.

Basically, what monetarists state is that governments should not manipulate the economy at all; that they should follow rules (as outlined in earlier sections), which are announced and kept to. If this is done, so they argue, the time path of the main economic variables (income, prices and exchange rates) will be less than if governments try to intervene. But the point of rules is largely, if not wholly, to stabilize price expectations, which in turn will stabilize prices. It would appear, then, that a normative judgement has been made, namely, that the stabilization of prices is more important than the stabilization of, say, income or exchange rates. The UK government, in particular, has found to its cost that it cannot simply ignore the variation that rules will give rise to in such variables as income (employment) and exchange rates.

The obvious conclusion one comes to from this brief section is that concentration on the stabilization of *one* economic variable will inevitably lead to destabilization elsewhere in the economy. There is no getting away from the normative judgement of having to choose which to stabilize – whether this be one economic variable or a combination of economic variables.

NOTES

1. See Shone (1981), Part III.

2. See Hahn (1982) for a caution on unjustified faith in the 'invisible hand' based on a perfectly competitive model with no market distortions.

3. For the distinction between static and dynamic stability see Takayama (1974) and Henderson and Quandt (1971).

4. In the international trade literature this distinction was well recognized in the form of internal and external equilibrium versus internal and external balance (see Chapter 8). The failure to distinguish equilibrium from desired positions led to much confusion and to what Machlup (1958) called 'disguised politics'. The same is true of the present debate, which is about internal equilibrium as distinct from internal balance.

5. In the present analysis it is important to note that the target variable is *real* income. A number of economists have suggested that the appropriate target variable for stabilization should be *money* income, e.g. Brittan (1981).

6. This follows immediately from the multiplier formula, $dy = kdgo$. The multiplier (whether for constant interest rate or variable interest rate) will be smaller the higher the marginal rate of tax, t_1. Hence, for any change in government spending, dgo, the change in income, dy, will be smaller. Conversely, to achieve any particular target income the change in government spending necessary to achieve this, $dgo = dy/k$, will be greater the smaller the multiplier.

7. The stock market crash of late 1987 indicated a number of features. First, the market recognized a problem sooner than did the politicians. In fact, the market expected some policy change but the

US president (Ronald Reagan) did not see this as necessary. Second, the force of the market was too strong for the politicians to ignore, especially as the stock market decline moved rapidly around the world. Third, the decision time (although quicker than usual) was still very long. It was difficult for President Reagan to achieve the necessary cuts in the government budget, which was clearly expected by the market.

8. This is the basis of the simulation exercises undertaken to assess the success or otherwise of UK demand management, see Posner (1978).

9. Early work on government policy adjustment rules, based on the ideas of control theory, was that by Phillips (1954); see also Allen (1965) and Turnovsky (1977). These rules are for government spending and should not be confused with monetary and fiscal rules advocated by monetarists.

APPENDIX 13.1 CYCLES AND THEIR CHARACTERISTICS

This appendix is concerned with outlining and clarifying a number of dynamic concepts used when discussing cycles, and, in particular, countercyclical policy. However, here we will deal with the formal aspects only.

Dynamic stability/instability

Suppose for some economic system that one of the endogenous variables is X, where $X(t)$ denotes the variable at time t. Further, suppose it can be shown that the equilibrium of the system will give an *equilibrium* value for X of $\bar{X}$. If the system begins from some value X_0, say, and is then disturbed, $X(t)$ may or may not *converge* on the equilibrium value $\bar{X}$ as time tends towards infinity. If $X(t)$ converges on the equilibrium value $\bar{X}$, then the equilibrium is said to be *dynamically stable*. If the variable $X(t)$ diverges from the equilibrium value $\bar{X}$, then the equilibrium is *dynamically unstable*. If the divergence of $X(t)$ from the equilibrium value $\bar{X}$ becomes smaller for each subsequent period, then the variable $X(t)$ converges asymptotically on the equilibrium. Fig. A13.1.1 illustrates convergent and divergent series.

Phase diagrams

A more modern way to represent convergent and divergent series is by means of *phase diagrams*. In simple terms this considers the change in the variable X (in mathematical terms, dX/dt) for each level of $X(t)$ at different points in time. By way of example, consider the following example (taken from Neal and Shone, 1976):

$$dX(t)/dt = -X^2(t) + 7X(t) - 10$$
$$= [X(t) - 2][5 - X(t)]$$

The graph of this is drawn in Fig. A13.1.2. First we note that the equilibrium of such a variable will occur when the value remains constant. In other words, equilibrium is where $dX(t)/dt = 0$. In the present example, therefore, there are two equilibria:

$$\bar{X}_1 = 2 \quad \text{and} \quad \bar{X}_2 = 5$$

However, the system behaves differently in the neighbourhood of the two equilibria. The behaviour can be summarized as follows:

1. For $X(t) < 2$, $dX(t)/dt < 0$ implying that $X(t)$ decreases as t increases.
2. For $2 < X(t) < 5$, $dX(t)/dt > 0$ implying that $X(t)$ increases as t increases.
3. For $X(t) > 5$, $dX(t)/dt < 0$ implying that $X(t)$ decreases as t increases.

In terms of Fig. A13.2.2, these results are shown by the path of the arrows, which indicates the

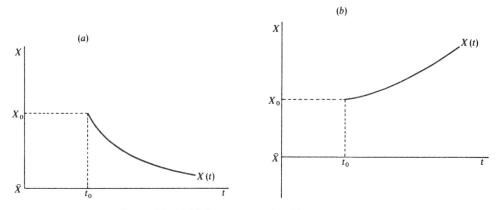

Figure A13.1.1 (a) Convergent series. (b) Divergent series.

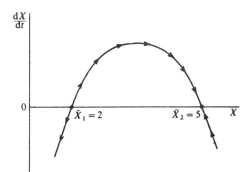

Figure A13.1.2 Phase diagram.

movement of the variable as time passes. It is apparent from the phase diagram that equilibrium $\bar{X}_1$ is *unstable*. Any point in the neighbourhood of the value 2 will mean that the system will move away from the equilibrium value of 2 as time passes. On the other hand, $\bar{X}_2$ is a *stable equilibrium* in the sense values of X in the neighbourhood of 5 will bring the system back to the value 5 over time.

It is to be noted that we said in the neighbourhood of the equilibrium points when referring to the situation shown in Fig. A13.1.2. This is because the starting point makes a difference. In Fig. A13.1.3, however, we have a situation where the equilibrium of the variable X is dynamically stable. In addition, it does not matter what the initial value of X is; over time the system will converge on the equilibrium $\bar{X}$. The value $\bar{X}_1 = 2$ in Fig. A13.1.2 is said to be *locally unstable*, while $\bar{X}_2 = 5$ is said to be *locally stable*. The situation in Fig. A13.1.3 illustrates a situation of *global stability*.

The lines drawn in Figs A13.1.2 and A13.1.3 are called *phase lines* and it is to be noted from what we have said so far that the stability or instability of the equilibrium can be ascertained by the slope of the phase line in the neighbourhood of the equilibrium. A positively sloped phase line gives rise to an unstable equilibrium, while a negatively sloped phase line in the neighbourhood of the equilibrium is dynamically stable. A globally stable system, therefore, will have a negatively sloped phase line for all possible values of the variable.

Cyclical variables

A number of economic variables do not show a regular decline or movement away from equilibrium; on the contrary, they cycle. In other words, the variable rises and falls in some regular manner: it

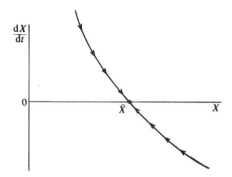

Figure A13.1.3 Phase line for a globally stable variable.

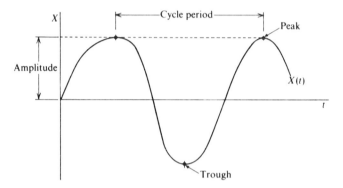

Figure A13.1.4 Characteristics of periodic variables.

exhibits *periodicity*. Fig. A13.1.4 illustrates the various terms used in describing periodic variables. The *peak* denotes the value of the variable when it is at a maximum, a *trough* denotes the value when the variable is at a minimum. The *period* of the cycle denotes the length of time between one peak and the next. The *amplitude* denotes the change in the variable from some base. In Fig. A13.1.4 we have a regular periodic variable with constant amplitude, constant period, and peaks and troughs of equal value.

Figs A13.1.5 and A13.1.6 illustrate a *damped fluctuating* variable and an *explosive fluctuating* variable respectively. In other words, in Fig. A13.1.5 the deviations from equilibrium, although positive and negative, get smaller as time passes (i.e., the amplitude declines). In Fig. A13.1.6, on the other hand, the amplitude increases as time passes.

Consider two periodic series $X(t)$ and $Y(t)$. If the two series have the same length of period but differ only in the location of their peaks and troughs, then they are said to differ only in their *phase*. Put more pictorially, if one series was moved along so that the two series were *in* phase, then they would look alike – differing possibly only in their respective amplitudes. In economics such cycles are important in so far as one series will lead and another will follow (lag).

It is possible for a series to fluctuate around a constant equilibrium value, as shown in Fig. A13.1.7. In this instance there is no trend in the equilibrium value. On the other hand, it is possible for the equilibrium value itself to be a function of time. In other words, the equilibrium exhibits a time trend. Fig. A13.1.8 illustrates a series which fluctuates around a rising trend.

Finally, it is worth noting that a series which shows cycles will have a phase 'line' which is a closed loop, as illustrated in Fig. A13.1.9.

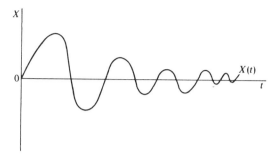

Figure A13.1.5 Damped fluctuations.

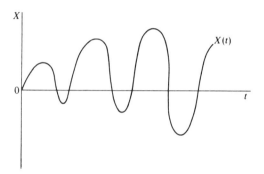

Figure A13.1.6 Explosive fluctuations.

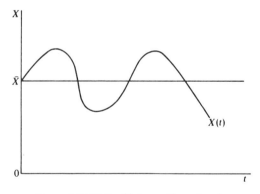

Figure A13.1.7 Equilibrium with no trend.

APPENDIX 13.2 THE MAIN UK MACROECONOMIC MODELS: A SUMMARY

The Economic and Social Research Council in its second review of *Models of the UK Economy*, Wallis (1985) says

A macroeconometric model is a mathematical representation of the quantitative relationships among macroeconomic variables. Its equations comprise technical relations and accounting ident-

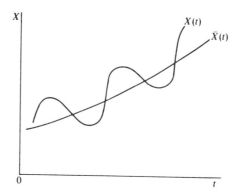

Figure A13.1.8 Equilibrium with rising trend.

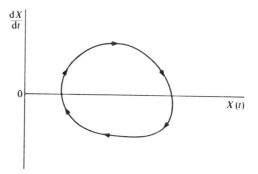

Figure A13.1.9 Phase line for a cyclic variable.

ities that reflect the national income accounting framework, and behavioural equations that describe the aggregate actions of consumers, producers, investors, financial institutions, and so forth. Models are constructed as aids to forecasting and policy-making, also as aids to understanding. Different models, constructed for different purposes and in accordance with different views of the economy, at different levels of aggregation, both sectoral and temporal, and with different relative weights on economic theory and statistical evidence, may give different answers to important questions, without the reasons for these divergencies being well understood. (p. 1)

This quotation is a fair comment on the state of the art at the present time.

Basically there are six macroeconometric models of the UK economy, and these are divided into two main groups according to whether they are quarterly models (Group 1) or annual models (Group 2):

Group 1	London Business School (LBS)
(Quarterly)	National Institute of Economic and Social Research (NIESR)
	The Treasury model (TM)
Group 2	Cambridge Growth Project (CGP)
(Annual)	City University Business School (CUBS)
	Liverpool University Research Model (LURM)

The main characteristics of the six models are set out in Table A13.2.1. Of course, given that such models are often very large, this Appendix can only give a cursory knowledge of these models.

Not only do the models vary considerably in size (in terms of equations, variables and parameters), they also differ as to the basic framework that governs the way they were set up. Hence, Keynesians set up a Keynesian model, while monetarists set up a monetarist model. The Liverpool model

Table A13.2.1 UK macroeconomic models

	LBS	NIESR	TM	CGP	CUBS	LURM
Variables (exog.)	~ 700 70	~ 275 100	~ 1000	~ 8000 3000	~ 130 70	~ 50 20
Equations	~ 100	~ 90	~ 700		~ 10	~ 20
Basic framework	International monetarist	Keynesian	Income–expenditure model	Input–output model	Supply-side model	New classical model
Monetary sector	General portfolio approach	Minor role	Deals with four sectors	Derives sectoral surplus/deficits	Not explicitly modelled	Allows substitution – goods & financial assets
Labour market	Included	Included	Included	Included	Included	Included (market clearing)
Expectations	Various (mainly adaptive)	Included (labour market only)	Included			Rational

epitomizes the new classical modelling involving rational expectations and market clearing (especially the labour market). The NIESR tends to be more pragmatic, while the City University Business School model emphasizes the supply side of the economy. The Cambridge model is quite different from the rest in being based on input–output tables. Undoubtedly, the largest model is the Treasury model. This is in essence an IS–LM–BP model which incorporates a labour market and a Phillips curve. The London Business School is referred to as 'International Monetarist' because the exchange rate is determined within the system by domestic and foreign asset holdings (and not simply by money stocks).

In the LBS, the NIESR and the TM, the North Sea oil sector is modelled separately. In the Cambridge model this sector is treated as an industry and has a full accounting framework. However, it does not occur in the Liverpool model.

The City University Business School model comes closest to the model developed in Chapters 2 and 3. The short-run aggregate supply curve is positive, while aggregate demand is negative (in the *P–y* space). In the long run the model *assumes* a vertical aggregate supply curve, although aggregate demand can have short-run influences on real income (output). Although labour market clearing results in the long run, this is not so in the short run. The model, however, is supply-side dominated, with no explicit modelling of the monetary sector. By assuming sluggish price adjustment, this model is basically a (Keynesian) disequilibrium model.

The Liverpool model is monetarist, with monetary factors feeding directly into price rises and no role for cost influences on the price level. Labour market clearing is built into the model by construction. In addition, unlike most of the other models, expectations are assumed to be rational. Only this model 'imposes' a theoretical ideal on the econometric estimation process. It assumes rapid price adjustment, leading to market clearing, and hence constitutes an equilibrium model.

The Cambridge model and the NIESR model are both quantity adjustment models. However, there is no mechanism within these models to re-establish equilibrium. Hence, these, too, are disequilibrium models. The same could be said about the LBS model and the Treasury model, except that price play a slightly greater role than in the Cambridge and NIESR models.

In the past the exchange rate has not been treated very fully in macroeconometric models. But in almost all cases here the exchange rate plays an important role. It is treated as endogenous (i.e., determined within the model itself), but in each case the determination is different. (See chapter 4 of Wallis, 1985, for a more comprehensive treatment of the exchange rate in these models.)

Chapter 14

UNEMPLOYMENT POLICY

In the 1970s and 1980s the most pressing problem for many countries was inflation, but the most pressing problem in the 1980s and 1990s is the high levels of mass unemployment.

While the fight to bring down inflation brought a higher level of unemployment in its wake, the extent to which such policies were the *cause* of the rising unemployment is difficult to establish. It must be recalled that inflation *itself* was considered to be one of the main causes of unemployment. If this contention were true, reducing inflation should also be accompanied by a reduction in unemployment. The difficulty is that other things were happening at the same time. It could very well be that unemployment may have been worse if inflation had not been brought down. But if inflation (either its rise or its fall) is not the cause of all unemployment, then why is unemployment rising in most Western countries? In this chapter we concentrate on UK unemployment. But the UK pattern of unemployment is not drastically different from other OECD countries. In the context of the UK economy the typical questions that must be raised, and answered, are as follows:

1. What are the characteristics of UK unemployment?
2. What are the causes of unemployment?
3. Is UK unemployment largely structural in nature?
4. What policies have been proposed for reducing the level of unemployment in the UK?

These are just some of the issues we will be dealing with in this chapter.

'Unemployment' is not an easy concept to get to grips with. On the face of it, it appears straightforward – a person is either employed or unemployed. If it were as simple as this there would not be such a dispute over the causes of unemployment, the theoretical analysis of unemployment, the policy prescriptions for reducing unemployment, or even the 70-odd different categorizations of unemployment to be found in the literature. As will be noted shortly, unemployment can be categorized in a number of ways; no one way is better than another, each simply serves a different purpose. However, a particular categorization may be undertaken because of the theoretical interest of the investigator. In other words, the theoretician may already have in mind some heuristic model of the cause of unemployment which he then attempts to clarify and justify. But in doing this he will be directed to a particular system of defining or classifying unemployment. Thus, if a theorist believes that unemployment is caused by a deficiency in demand (which we will clarify shortly), then he may exclude certain kinds of unemployment because this may give rise to an unnecessary expansion in aggregate demand. Similarly, the policies towards unemployment will depend very much on the view of what causes it. If it is argued that a large element of the unemployment is due to inefficiencies in the search for a new job, then, clearly, the policy recommendations will be directed more to improving the efficiency of search than to raising the level of aggregate demand, since the latter will have no effect on the efficiency of search (and may make the search process even more inefficient). However, the categorizations just alluded to are based on the *cause* of unemployment. But it is possible to categorize unemployment in terms of its *cure*. These, in turn, will differ from purely statistical categorizations.

After discussing some of the characteristics of UK unemployment in Section 14.1, in Section 14.2 we discuss some of the main theories which have purported to explain unemployment. It is important to go through these because they form the basis for the policy proposals which have been advanced for reducing the level of unemployment. We discuss briefly: (1) the classical theory; (2) Keynesian theory; and (3) search theories. In Section 14.3 we take up the issue of whether UK unemployment is largely demand-deficient or structural. In doing this we pay particular attention to the 'natural rate of unemployment', which we have so far avoided discussing in any detail. In the light of these three sections, we turn in Section 14.4 to some of the policy recommendations which have been advanced for reducing UK unemployment.

14.1 SOME CHARACTERISTICS OF UK UNEMPLOYMENT

On the face of it, if a worker has a job he appears to be employed; and if a worker does not have a job, then he is unemployed. However, this does not clearly distinguish between being 'out of work' and being 'without a job' (Hughes and Perlman, 1984). A person who is out of work will consider himself without a job only if he wishes to work, i.e. has some attachment to the labour market. If he does not wish to work, i.e. has no attachment to the labour market, then he will be out of work but will not consider himself unemployed. Because there is a blur between joblessness and unemployment, there is no direct correspondence between a fall in the number of unemployed and a rise in the numbers employed. Another blur arises from whether an individual is in part-time employment or full-time employment. Finally, there may (as in the case of women) be a change in the participation rate over time.[1]

Before presenting some of the figures, it is important to distinguish between the *stock* of unemployed and the *flow* of unemployed. The stock of unemployed is the number of individuals counted as being unemployed on a specific day. Prior to October 1982, the official count consisted of those individuals who had registered themselves at the local offices of the Employment Services Agency or the Youth Employment Services as being both unemployed and 'capable and available' for work. Since October 1982 the count has been based on computer records at Unemployment Benefits Offices. Hence, only those claiming benefit will be counted as unemployed.[2] Although this leads to a discontinuity in the stock series, the stock of unemployed still refers to the numbers unemployed at a point in time on a specific day. The change in this stock between two points in time denotes the *flow* of unemployed. It represents the change in the stock level. Thus, if the inflow into the pool of unemployed equals the outflow from the pool of unemployed, the stock of unemployed remains constant. Of course, the composition of the stock is very likely to be different: different in terms of age, sex, occupation and unemployment duration. On the other hand, if the inflow exceeds the outflow, then the stock of unemployed will rise. Once again, however, there is no reason to suppose that the characteristics of those flowing into the unemployment pool are the same as those flowing out of the unemployment pool.

Unemployment stocks and flows provide information on the supply side of the labour market. It is also possible to ascertain stock and flow figures for vacancies, which give information on the demand side of the labour market. Although there is more reason for claimants to register for unemployment benefit, there is no basic reason why firms should register their vacancies at Job Centres. Probably less than half the existing vacancies are recorded at Job Centres.[3] In general, vacancies are filled very quickly, but where they are not it is far from obvious that they are due to a requirement of skills beyond the majority of unemployed (e.g., hotels and catering, retailing and warehouse work).

Notwithstanding the various definitional changes in the official statistics on unemployment (and the working population), there has been a dramatic increase in the level of unemployment since about 1966, as can be seen in terms of Fig. 14.1. Between 1948 and 1966 the average level of unemployment was below 2% (approximately 1.7%), while since that date the rate has never fallen below 2%, and since 1981 it has risen dramatically, with rates each year in excess of 10%. Nor is this pattern of rising unemployment peculiar to the UK; it has occurred in all OECD countries. The obvious question to ask is why this is so.

A second characteristic of the unemployed is the increase in *duration* of unemployment. Table 14.1 sets out the figures for long-term unemployment in the UK for the period 1948–87, where long-term unemployment is defined to be a duration of unemployment of 52 weeks or more. It has further been established that the duration of unemployment increases with age and that the prospects of finding employment decreases with the duration of unemployment. However, to what extent the latter is due to a decrease in the motivation of the individual seeking employment or to employer discrimination against the long-term unemployed is difficult to establish. But the increase in long-term unemployed is undoubtedly a most serious problem.

The rising proportion of young and older workers among the unemployed is a third characteristic of UK unemployment. In particular, youth unemployment since 1980 has risen sharply. More important, especially for the young, is that the length of time spent unemployed has also increased substantially. Thus, the under-25s account for a growing proportion of the total unemployed. When we turn to the older worker, say 50 and above, the major proportion of this group unemployed have become so through redundancy. When this is broken down in more detail, it appears that those unskilled and semi-skilled who are made redundant are generally anxious to seek further employment, but find this difficult (if not impossible). On the other hand, workers in management and professional jobs may have taken early retirement on quite favourable terms and are not necessarily anxious to seek employment. In addition, the major proportion of the over-50s who are unemployed tend to be men (which, of course, partly reflects the fact that unskilled and semi-skilled jobs have been dominated by men).

A fourth characteristic of the unemployed in the UK is the predominance of unskilled and unqualified labour. Although by no means a new phenomenon, what is new is the extent to which the proportion of the unemployed made up of such workers has been rising, and that they constitute the major part of the long-term unemployed. This observation, along with the fact that there has been an increase in the youth unemployed who, by their very nature, have little experience, is of major concern. Such a rise in unskilled and semi-

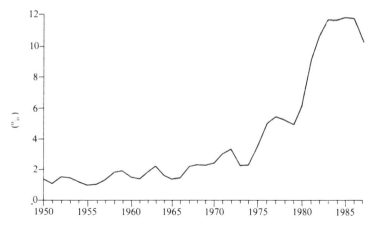

Figure 14.1 UK unemployment, 1950–87 *Source: Economic Trends.*

Table 14.1 Long-term unemployment in Great Britain, 1948–87

Year	52 weeks and longer (% of unemployed)	Year	52 weeks and longer (% of unemployed)
1948	12.9	1968	18.6
1949	11.6	1969	17.6
1950	12.4	1970	17.8
1951	10.5	1971	15.9
1952	8.5	1972	22.5
1953	10.8	1973	27.7
1954	11.1	1974	20.5
1955	10.3	1975	14.7
1956	8.3	1976	20.0
1957	9.2	1977	22.3
1958	9.7	1978	24.4
1959	15.7	1979	25.9
1960	17.0	1980	19.2
1961	13.5	1981	22.0
1962	12.4	1982	33.6
1963	17.0	1983	36.5
1964	18.8	1984	39.8
1965	16.7	1985	41.0
1966	12.9	1986	41.1
1967	13.7	1987	42.6

Source: Miller and Wood (1982), table XI and the Employment Gazette

skilled workers is probably symptomatic of structural changes in the employment pattern. Of major concern here is the degree to which one form of labour (or capital!) is substitutable for another: the extent to which labour can be re-deployed either within the same organization or within the same economy. The general move of employment away from manufacturing is illustrated in Table 14.2, and since male employment predominates this leads to a more significant effect on male unemployment. Any attempt to solve such an occupational mismatch will require a policy of manpower training and retraining.

The changing pattern of female participation, and in female unemployment, is a fifth characteristic of the unemployed in the UK. Although the level of female employment has

Table 14.2 The changing structure of UK employment, 1978–87

Industrial sector	Employees in employment, males and females (thousands) Annual averages										% change
	1978	1979	1980	1981	1982	1983	1984	1985	1986	1987	1978–87
Manufacturing	7131	7034	6618	5948	5641	5551	5421	5438	5154	5046	−29.2
Construction	1227	1247	1218	1097	1020	998	967	948	971	987	−19.6
Transport and communication	1459	1471	1460	1400	1355	1310	1282	1281	1322	1331	−8.8
Distribution	2758	2782	2712	2588	2662	3200	3282	3383	3285	3314	20.2
Insurance, banking, finance	1191	1225	1240	1216	1298	1816	1871	1961	2192	2321	94.9
Professional and scientific services	3585	3616	3601	3580	3648	2827	2822	2855	2859	2904	−19.0
Miscellaneous services	2330	2391	2401	2310	2435	1302	1334	1369	1529	1585	−32.0
Public administration	1553	1555	1539	1520	1493	1833	1814	1828	1936	1983	27.7
All industries and services	22 274	22 359	21 773	20 631	20 534	20 759	20 720	21 008	21 125	21 344	−4.2

Source: Employment Gazette, various issues

risen in the UK, the number of females officially registering as unemployed has also increased. The rise in the general level of unemployment is partly explained by the number of women now registering as unemployed. However, it is certainly the case that as the general level of unemployment rises there is a fall in the female participation rate.[4] Throughout much of the 1960s and 1970s the industries which grew most tended to be relatively large employers of females, e.g. professional and scientific services and the services sector as a whole. However, it must be realized that a large part of this increase in employment was in the form of part-time workers, which was most attractive to married women. The picture since 1977, however, is not at all clear. The reduction in the manufacturing base (which we deal with in more detail in Chapter 17), has not only led to a rise in male unemployment, but has also led to a fall in the demand for clerical and service staff, who tend to be women. The result is a rise in the female unemployment which was not so characteristic of the 1960s. The growth of information technology has also displaced many unskilled (full-time and part-time) women. However, it has simultaneously led, for example, to an increase in microprocessor operators, who tend to be women.

A sixth characteristic of UK unemployment is its regional distribution. In almost all countries unemployment tends to affect some regions more than others, a feature illustrated in Table 14.3. This, of course, is associated with the distribution of population and the distribution of firms. For instance, if staple industries are located in certain areas and these decline very markedly, then unemployment in these areas will rise relative to the country as a whole. Furthermore, the rise in unemployment in such regions occurs because, generally speaking, labour is more immobile than firms. But this need not necessarily be the case. There has always been a longstanding debate as to whether *work should be moved to the workers or workers to the work.* But either approach is founded on the belief that regional unemployment should be counteracted.

Brief as this section is, it highlights the six main characteristics of UK unemployment, namely:

(a) the dramatic rise in unemployment, especially since 1966;
(b) the rise in the duration of unemployment;
(c) the rising unemployment in youth and older age groups;
(d) the rise in unskilled and semi-skilled unemployment;
(e) the changing pattern of female employment and unemployment; and
(f) the regional changes in unemployment.

It is these features which the various theories attempt to explain, and it is these features which policies have been advocated to eliminate.

14.2 THEORIES OF UNEMPLOYMENT

One of the great difficulties in analysing unemployment is that the different theories use different categorizations of unemployment. Even the concept of 'full employment' is not at all obvious. Thus classical economics deals only with frictional unemployment. Keynes distinguished voluntary from involuntary unemployment. Monetary economists refer to the natural rate of unemployment. Modern classicists refer to the non-accelerating inflation

Table 14.3 Regional unemployment rates, 1965–87 (%) (average of quarterly figures, seasonally adjusted)

	1965	1970	1975	1980	1987
North	2.4	4.5	4.8	8.6	14.5
Yorkshire and Humberside	1.0	2.8	3.2	5.8	11.8
East Midlands	0.8	2.2	2.9	4.8	9.4
East Anglia	1.2	2.1	2.7	4.1	7.1
South East	0.8	1.6	2.2	3.3	7.3
South West	1.5	2.8	3.6	4.8	8.5
West Midlands	0.6	1.9	3.3	5.9	12.2
North West	1.5	2.7	4.4	7.0	13.2
Wales	2.5	3.8	4.5	7.3	13.0
Scotland	2.8	4.1	4.3	7.5	13.4
Great Britain	1.3	2.5	3.3	5.3	10.1

Source: Economic Trends, Annual Supplement 1988 and May 1988

rate of unemployment (NAIRU). While, more recently, Malinvaud (1984) emphasizes disequilibrium unemployment. In Appendix 14.1 we present some of the various definitions and categories of unemployment which have been used in the literature – this being by no means exhaustive.

In dealing with the various theories of unemployment it is useful to note the following terms:

D_L = demand for labour
S_L = supply of labour
E = employment
V = vacancies
    V_s = suitable vacancies
    V_u = unsuitable vacancies
U = total unemployment
    U_v = voluntary unemployment
    U_f = frictional unemployment
    U_s = structural unemployment
    U_d = demand-deficient unemployment
    U_n = natural rate of unemployment (same as NAIRU)
    U_j = job-search unemployment
    U_r = residual unemployment
N = working population

Classical theory of unemployment

In Chapter 2 we established that in real terms the labour market can be written in the following way:

$$D_L: w = f(L)$$

$$S_L: w = g(L)$$

where no distinction is made between actual prices and expected prices because these are identical in classical economics. With the assumption of flexible wages and prices, then it follows that equilibrium labour demanded and supplied is determined in the labour market independently of the rest of the economy. In terms of Fig. 14.2, real wages will always alter to ensure that the demand for labour is equal to the supply of labour. In this case the only unemployment is the difference between the equilibrium labour employed, E_0, and the total working population, N. It follows that this difference, $N - E_0$, must be composed of those who do not choose to work at the ruling equilibrium wage, i.e. $N - E_0$ denotes voluntary unemployment at the equilibrium wage.

In this model the demand for labour is determined from some idea of a production function which assumes firms are profit maximizers and will employ labour only up to the point where the marginal cost of hiring the last unit of labour is equal to the marginal revenue product of selling the output produced by that marginal labour input. This does not mean that classical economists did not recognize that additional unemployment was possible; what it does mean, however, is that any additional unemployment was due to frictional reasons. The frictional nature of (involuntary) unemployment in classical economics can be clarified as follows. Since the demand for labour is employment plus vacancies ($D_L = E + V$) and the supply of labour is employment plus (involuntary) unemployment ($S_L = E + U$), then equilibrium in the labour market ($D_L = S_L$) will mean $V = U$. Hence, the only (involuntarily) unemployed are those temporarily unemployed and waiting to be matched up with an equal number of vacancies.

Furthermore, the equilibrium labour employed, determined by D_L intersecting S_L, is totally independent of aggregate demand. Put another way, there is no way that any manipulation of aggregate demand would change the demand curve for labour or the supply curve of labour when expressed in real terms – and it is this that determines employment in the labour market.

The implication of classical analysis was that the aggregate supply curve was vertical at the level of employment determined by the intersection of D_L and S_L. Why was this? The demand and supply curves of labour are relationships which depend only on the real wage (equal to the expected real wage). The level of output is related, via the production function, to the level of employment. Since the real wage is independent of the price level, and both money wages and prices are completely flexible, the level of employment is determined solely in the labour market and independently of any other market – specifically the market for goods and services and the money market (not to mention the foreign exchange market). Put another way, the labour market is segmented from the remainder of the economy. The other variables in the system depend on the wage rate and on the level of employment, but the wage rate and the level of employment do not depend on other macroeconomic variables – such as consumption, investment and interest rates. Therefore, given the level of employment, the level of real income is determined immediately from the aggregate production function. This level of real income occurs regardless of the level of prices: i.e. the aggregate supply curve is vertical.

In this model the only unemployment is frictional unemployment and the difference between the total working population and the equilibrium level of employment (which is voluntary in nature). Furthermore, the equilibrium level of employment, E_0 in Fig. 14.2, denotes 'full employment'. It is important to realize that 'full employment' is not the same as the working population, and that 'full employment' is determined by the equilibrium wage and the supply of labour. Thus, a shift in the demand curve for labour will raise the equilibrium wage and raise the full employment level (and, with a fixed population, reduce the level of voluntary unemployment).

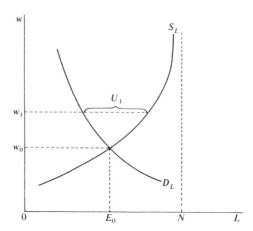

Figure 14.2 Classical unemployment.

Also note that both the demand and supply of labour is defined for a zero rate of actual and expected inflation; hence E_0 is not only the equilibrium level of employment, but constitutes what is now referred to as the natural rate of employment, i.e. $N - E_0$ denotes the *natural rate of unemployment*, U_n.

When a vertical aggregate supply curve is combined with a downward sloping aggregate demand curve, it follows that expansion of aggregate demand will only have a temporary impact on output and employment. In the long run all it will do is raise prices. Even in the classical model there is no presumption that the equilibrium rate of unemployment, the natural rate of unemployment, is desirable. All that is argued is that with market clearing taking place, monetary and/or fiscal policy will not be able to do anything about this level of unemployment in the long run.

But classical economists, such as Pigou, did recognize that unemployment (other than frictional unemployment) could arise if the real wage was set above the market clearing wage, and this would occur if minimum wages were set or if trade unions could negotiate such wages. In terms of Fig. 14.2, if the real wage was set at w_1, then unemployment, U_1, would result. This idea that trade unions could establish a real wage above the market clearing wage and so 'price workers out of jobs' was one of the reasons advanced by Pigou for the high unemployment in the inter-War period.[5]

Keynesian theory of unemployment

Keynes disputed the classical interpretation of unemployment. He could not accept that the unemployment of the 1930s was all frictional and could not be eliminated by government policy. Keynes hypothesized that employers could predict the expected price (i.e., for them the actual price and the expected price were one and the same). This meant that the demand curve for labour could be expressed in *money* wages as

$$W = P \mu a_L$$

The supply curve of labour, however, he contended depended on the expected real wage, w^e $= g(L)$. Hence, in *money* wages we have

$$W = P^e g(L)$$

In this version we immediately see an important implication. Since expected and actual prices are not necessarily equal to one another, then a change in aggregate demand, in so far as it creates or increases this divergence, means that the labour market equilibrium is influenced by the level of aggregate demand. The level of unemployment is, therefore, also affected by the level of aggregate demand. But Keynes introduced a second reason for unemployment and how aggregate demand may influence it.

The model is set out in Fig. 14.3. In part (*a*) we have the goods and money market. In part (*c*) we have the economy's short-run production function relating labour input, L, to output, y. The labour market is captured in parts, (*d*) and (*f*). Part (*d*) shows the labour market relating labour demanded and supplied to the *real* wage; part (*f*) shows the labour market relating labour demanded and supplied to the *money* wage. Since the real wage, w, is equal to the money wage deflated by the price level, W/P, we can relate the real wage and the money wage for a *given* price level, as shown in part (*e*). Notice that the price level is given by the angle of the price line measured from the vertical axis. A higher price is shown by a price line to the right. So the price line P_0 denotes a *higher* price than P_1. Finally, there are two parts at 45°. Part (*b*) allows us to move from parts (*d*) and (*f*) to the production function shown in (*c*). Notice that all horizontal axes in parts (*b*), (*d*) and (*f*) are the same. This means the employment level E_0 in part (*d*) or (*f*) is the same level of labour denoted as L_0 in part (*b*). Similarly for E_1 and L_1. These levels of labour employed are converted to levels of labour input in part (*b*), i.e. L_0 on the horizontal axis is equal to L_0 on the vertical axis. Similarly for L_1. On the other hand, part (*g*) allows us to move between parts (*d*) and (*f*) via part (*e*).

The classical situation is shown by employment E_0, where the labour market is cleared, and income is at y_0 (or what is now called the natural rate of income, y_n). Income level y_0 is derived by taking the level of employment of E_0 in part (*d*) (or (*f*)), moving up to part (*b*) to determine the level of labour input, namely L_0, and moving across to part (*c*) to find the output of y_0.

Keynes believed that wages were set in monetary terms and that they were, to a large extent, rigid downwards. Why wages were what they were is historical and thus cannot be explained within the framework. Furthermore, the price level was assumed to be rigid downwards but could rise. The Keynesian situation is also illustrated in Fig. 14.3. The price level is initially at P_1. The demands and supply of labour, relating the *money* wage to labour, are given by $D_L(P_1)$ and $S_L(P_1)$ respectively. In terms of Fig. 14.3, such a fixed money wage is given by W_1 in part (*f*). At this money wage, labour employed is not determined by the intersection of demand and supply but is, on the contrary, determined by the demand for labour. This is shown in parts (*d*) and (*f*). In part (*f*) we have $D_L(P_1)$ and $S_L(P_1)$ denoting the demand and supply of labour. At the money wage W_1 employment is determined by the demand for labour, namely E_1. The same information is supplied in part (*d*). At money wage W_1 and price level P_1 the real wage is w_1. Again, labour employed is determined by the demand for labour. Hence, only E_1 will be employed. At this level of employment, labour input is only L_1 and hence real income (output) will be y_1. Furthermore, it is quite possible for the economy to be in equilibrium at this level of output, i.e., *IS* intersects *LM* at real income level y_1, as we have illustrated in Fig. 14.3. There is, then, what Keynes called an *underemployment equilibrium*.

Given this situation, Keynes attempted to distinguish two kinds of unemployment:

(a) voluntary unemployment; and
(b) involuntary unemployment.

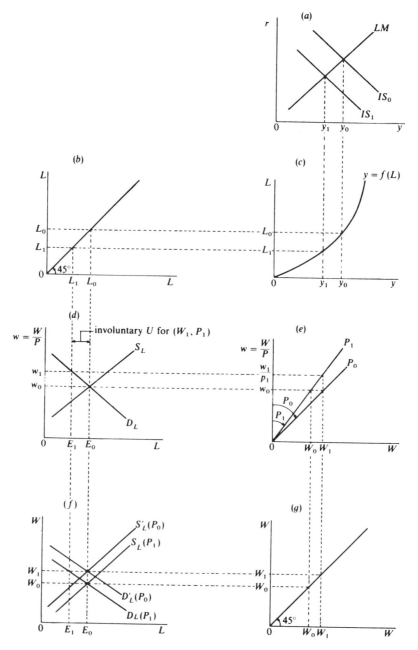

Figure 14.3 Keynesian unemployment.

The former was defined as in the classical model, namely those at the wage W_0 who decided not to supply themselves onto the labour market. The remainder $(E_0 - E_1)$ Keynes called involuntary unemployment. (Notice that involuntary unemployment is *not* the gap between the supply curve of labour and the demand curve of labour at the wage rate W_1, but, rather, the gap between the demand for labour at the wage W_1 (E_1) and what it would have been in the classical situation (E_0). Also note that the level of involuntary unemployment is in relation to a given money wage and a fixed price level, i.e. (W_1, P_1).)

Keynes argued that given this situation there was nothing inherent in the economic system to move it to the classical solution. Only intervention by the government could move the economy from y_1 to y_0. Suppose, then, that the government pursued some expansionary policy. This would shift the IS curve from IS_1 to IS_0. Income would rise from y_1 to y_0, and prices would rise from P_1 to P_0. The result would be equilibrium in the labour market at employment level E_0, which is the labour necessary to produce output level y_0. Notice, there is no change in the *money* wage, it remains at W_1. There is, however, a fall in the real wage from $w_1 = W_1/P_1$ to $w_0 = W_1/P_0$ (since $P_0 > P_1$).

Neo-Keynesians emphasize that the level of income, y_1, in the goods market sets a *quantity ration*. The income this generates gives rise to a certain demand for goods and services. No matter how much firms produce they cannot sell beyond this amount. Such a quantity ration allows a range of real wages consistent with the rationed output, y_1. If the real wage is 'high' (above the classical market clearing wage of w_0), then this is a *consequence* of the quantity rationing and not a cause of the low employment (high unemployment). This is to be contrasted with the classical model where a 'high' real wage is a *cause* of the low employment (high unemployment).

Search theories of unemployment

Even in the classical model, both unemployment *and* vacancies can exist at the 'full' employment level. The unemployment arises from workers *searching* for jobs, while vacancies exist because employers are *searching* for new workers. Thus, this version explains both U and V as *frictional* unemployment arising from very special features of the labour market which involve workers and employers searching for suitable jobs and employees respectively.

Models vary according to their emphasis, but two aspects stands out:

1. the person searching – worker or employer; and
2. the uncertainty surrounding W or P.

But the modern version, monetarist and/or microeconomic approach, the natural rate of unemployment (U_n), or the non-accelerating inflation rate of unemployment, NAIRU, underlies much of the reasoning. If one accepts the natural rate of unemployment hypothesis, then no amount of raising aggregate demand can, in the long run, reduce this level of unemployment. Thus, any reduction in the unemployment rate below U_n will only be temporary and in the long run will simply lead to accelerated inflation. *During* this process three types of unemployment can occur:

1. unemployment arising from the income–leisure choice of households;
2. unemployment arising from job search;
3. unemployment arising from labour market imperfections.

We will consider only (2) and (3), taken from Parkin and Bade (1982).

The analysis begins with the idea that work and leisure are two out of three activities, the third being job search. Searching for a job is costly, requires time and effort, and may or may not be undertaken while the person is presently in a job. Where job search becomes a full-time pursuit, then the person becomes registered as unemployed.

There are two interrelated functional relationships, as follows:

1. $U_j = h(S_L, c)$ where c is a given cost of labour search, U_j is job-search unemployment.
2. $S_L = g(L)$ the supply curve of labour.

The situation is shown in Fig. 14.4 *(a,b)*.

This even at the equilibrium real wage, w_0, there is still U_j^0 unemployment. Notice, in particular that U_j, as read off Fig. 14.4 *(a)* is added horizontally to S_L to obtain $S_L + U_j$. Parkin and Bade define this as the labour force, which is misleading. If N denotes the working population, then total unemployment can be broken down into the following three parts:

1. Excess demand (ED_L) (or deficient-demand).
2. Job-search unemployment, U_j.
3. Residual unemployment, $U_r = N - (S_L + U_j)$.

At equilibrium, wage w_0, then $ED_L = 0$ while U_j and U_r are both positive, but *both* denote voluntary unemployment, i.e. in this model

$$U_v = U_r + U_j$$

Notice that in this version the search is confined to workers and involves the idea of a *reservation wage*. For wage w^r, the reservation wage, the marginal unemployed person becomes part of the searches. For a slightly higher wage he chooses to be employed. (If the person is truly indifferent he may or may not be working at wage w^r.)

The analysis can be taken further than Parkin and Bade do by incorporating search on the management side. A vacancy may exist which is not filled if managers cannot find suitable employees. Let D_L represent total demand for labour – including current employment plus unfilled vacancies, i.e.

$$D_L = E + V$$

then the employment curve, where we assume that employment reflects the management wishes for wages above the equilibrium, is

$$E = D_L - V$$

Thus the E-curve is to the left of D_L above w^0, as shown in Fig. 14.5. Even at a wage w^0 we have vacancies of V^0 and search unemployment of U_j^0. These may remain in the long run if there is, say, a mismatch of job skills to those required by industry (i.e. $U_j^0 - V^0 = U_s$).

Monetarists in particular have argued for a cut in unemployment benefits. The reasoning is fairly clear within the present analysis. Unemployment benefit is a contribution to the cost of searching for a job. It acts like a subsidy to job searches. It also, so they argue, leads to more people opting not to work at all. The argument is that the introduction of a benefits scheme shifts S_L to the left. Parkin and Bade claim that with benefits people will remain job searching *longer*, so lowering the labour supply in aggregate (i.e. shift S_L to the left and raise U_j). Hence, if benefits raise unemployment by raising the level of search unemployment, then a cut in such benefits will reduce the level of unemployment.

However, the evidence is far from conclusive. In the US, such benefits did increase job search time, but the scale and timing was limited. In the case of the UK, Nickell (1979) found

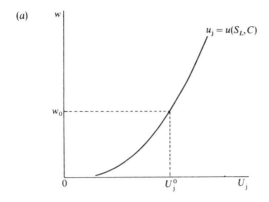

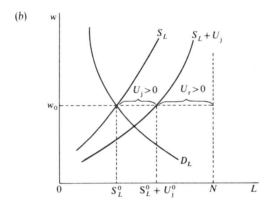

Figure 14.4 Job-search unemployment and the supply curve of labour.

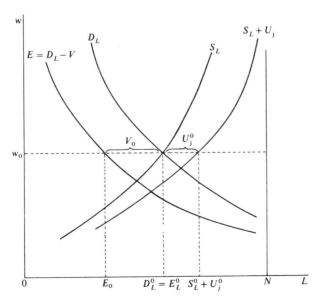

Figure 14.5 Job-search unemployment and vacancies.

that unemployment increased by 13% for the period 1964–65 and 1973 as a result of higher benefits, but that measured unemployment over the same period rose by 92%. Furthermore, unemployment has continued to rise even though compensation benefits have not changed.

In the monetarist model the rate of inflation is determined by the rate of growth in the money supply, but the natural rate of unemployment is determined by *real* factors independently of the equilibrium rate of inflation. Friedman puts it as follows

> At any moment of time, there is some level of unemployment which has the property that it is consistent with equilibrium in the structure of real wage rates .... . The 'natural rate of employment' in other words, is the level that would be ground out by the Walrasian system of general equilibrium equations, provided there is imbedded in them the actual structural characteristics of labor and commodity markets, including market imperfections, stochastic variability in demands and supplies, the cost of gathering information about job vacancies and labor availabilities, the costs of mobility, and so on.
>
> 'The role of monetary policy' *AER* (1968)

Hence, there are two reasons why unemployment can differ from its natural level:

(a) job search; and
(b) forecasting errors between P and P^e.

As well as search unemployment, Phelps in particular refers to speculative and precautionary unemployment – both defined in Appendix 14.1. Again it is to be noted that these are forms of voluntary unemployment and are *frictional* (and possibly structural) in nature.

All the different forms of search theories do, however, mean that unemployment over-and-above the natural level is voluntary in nature. One problem is that these theories encounter difficulty in explaining *persistent* levels of unemployment above or below the natural level. In defending search theory some authors have made the point, however, that it is a reason not for mass unemployment over long spells, but an explanation of low, though above normal, levels of unemployment.

More recently, criticism has been directed at the observation that many of the search theories attribute all entry into the unemployment pool to voluntary quit decisions. In other words, all such unemployment is voluntary. But this means that there is no explanation for unemployment arising from firings and layoffs. In this case, attention is directed away from price surprises as a means of explaining unemployment and towards consideration of the microeconomic optimizing behaviour which gives rise to wage and price contracts. This has led to a growth of literature concerned with 'implicit contracts'. Contracting models (see Frank, 1986) are based on quantity adjustment, unlike search models which are based on price adjustment. In a contracting model, for instance, a firm will hold wages constant but will lay off workers if demand should fall. The reason behind this (optimizing) behaviour is that the firm is attempting to maintain its reputation in employment practices – hence the term 'implicit contracts'. Some see such contracting models as a microeconomic justification of wage rigidity in Keynesian economics, and hence as a justification for Keynesian involuntary unemployment.

Some economists argue, however, that profit maximizing entrepreneurs and rational workers would not enter into such contracts. Be this as it may, they do, and so other economists are attempting to see what types of contract exist in the labour market and how they may be included in economic theorizing. In brief, the following three reasons can be advanced for such contracts, other than unionization:

1. It is a rational way to ensure that risks in respect of future incomes are borne by the employer rather than by the employee.
2. It may allow employers to retain their quality workers.
3. It prevents workers from undercutting fellow workers in order to take over their jobs.

What this work will do is account for the shape and movement of the aggregate supply curve, and hence the short-run Phillips curve.

Before leaving this section on theories of unemployment a word of caution is in order. Unemployment is often categorized as either classical (real wages too high) or Keynesian (aggregate demand too low). But this dichotomy may be very misleading, as Solow (1986) warns. If both unemployment and real wages are endogenous to the system, then it makes no sense to say that 'unemployment is high because the real wage is too high'. Change in the exogenous variables is the cause of the unemployment, and these, in turn, depend on the model that is set up.

14.3 STRUCTURAL OR DEMAND-DEFICIENT UNEMPLOYMENT?

A major difference of opinion about the present high levels of unemployment in the UK and elsewhere concerns whether it is structural in nature or whether it is demand-deficient. Thus, Hughes and Perlman (1984) say

> . . . unemployment remains perhaps the most chronic economic problem facing the industrial economies of the UK and US, and requires an expansion in aggregate demand for its reduction. (p. xi)

Clearly, they see it largely as a deficiency of demand. On the other hand, Hawkins (1984) sees the problem as a structural one. He says

> The plain fact is that employment in British manufacturing industry has fallen sharply and no other sector of the economy has been able to take up the resulting slack in the labour market. There is no prospect of a significant or sustained recovery in manufacturing employment – indeed there will almost certainly be a further decline over the next few years. While some forms of service employment will probably expand, the kind of jobs created are unlikely to resolve the growing problem of structural unemployment which . . . the UK now faces. The appearance of large-scale, long-term unemployment among male manual workers is directly due to the contraction of manufacturing employment, not to the provision of generous welfare payments nor any other such diversionary nonsense. (p. 5)

While Bean, Layard and Nickell (1986) take a more middle view

> The decline in demand, relative to potential, seems to have been an important proximate cause of the rise in unemployment, especially in the European Community. However, it is clear that supply-side factors have also played a significant role. (p. 819).

These three quotations are typical of the diversity of opinion surrounding the causes of the growing and high levels of unemployment. The demand-deficient argument is a direct result of viewing unemployment from a Keynesian perspective. The high levels of unemployment are largely involuntary and arise because of the low level of aggregate demand. Hence, to eliminate such a problem all that is required is to raise the level of aggregate demand, usually by means of fiscal policy. However, since in the past this led to inflation, it is now recognized by Keynesians that this must be undertaken without generating future inflation. Perlman and Hughes, therefore, argue that it is futile to attempt to cure unemployment by means other than demand stimulation, but add that demand stimulation must be combined with income and manpower policies in order to contain any inflationary pressure that such a stimulation may cause.

When we turn to structural arguments about the present unemployment situation, a distinction must be made between those who base their analysis on observations about the structure of an actual economy and those who argue in terms of a rise in the natural rate of unemployment. In this latter case it is first necessary to establish the connection between the natural rate of unemployment and structural unemployment, and second to establish that the natural rate of unemployment has been rising. The two views converge to the extent that arguments advanced as to why the changing structure of the economy is leading to higher levels of unemployment, is also the reasoning that lies behind the rise in the natural rate of unemployment. It is therefore necessary to discuss in more detail what is meant by the 'natural rate of unemployment' (NRU).

The natural rate of unemployment has been defined in many ways. Not only does it denote the difference between the working population and the level of employment consistent with equilibrium in the labour (the classical view discussed in Section 14.2), but such an equilibrium is the outcome of a Walrasian auction. This view is most clearly associated with Friedman (1968, see p. 332). In more simple terms it is a model which is based on market clearing (see Barro, 1984).

Putting the Walrasian auction on one side, a number of authors have concluded that the natural rate of unemployment is that level of unemployment where there is no deficient-demand unemployment, since this will occur when the labour market is in equilibrium. Thus, if seasonally adjusted unemployment (U) is broken down into frictional unemployment (U_f), structural unemployment (U_s) and demand-deficient unemployment (U_d), then the natural rate of unemployment is given by

$$U_n = U_f + U_s \qquad U_d = 0$$

But the question arises, under what conditions will $U_d = 0$? At a particular wage, the supply of labour is the amount of labour employed plus (disequilibrium) unemployment. The demand for labour, on the other hand, is the level of employment plus the level of vacancies in the economy. Hence,

$$S_L - D_L = (E + U) - (E + V) = U - V$$

If $U - V$ is zero or positive, then this represents demand-deficient unemployment, i.e.

$$U_d = U - V \geqslant 0$$

$$U_d = 0 \quad \text{for} \quad U - V < 0$$

Although on the basis of this analysis it is possible to establish the level of demand-deficient unemployment, this cannot be said for the natural rate of unemployment. Although we have established that $U_n = U_f + U_s$, it is not possible to obtain separate estimates of U_s and U_f. The reason for this is because where the number of vacancies exceed the numbers unemployed, then U_f can be considered as the number of *right* types of vacancies ($U_f = V_r$), while structural unemployment can be considered in terms of the *wrong* types of vacancies ($U_s = V_w$), and we do not have knowledge on the right and wrong types of vacancies which exist in the economy. However, this approach does highlight the frictional and structural nature of the natural rate. It indicates that structural unemployment is more serious and more long term than frictional unemployment. However, it does not indicate why inflation is not germane to the definition.

It will be recalled that one of the reasons Keynes proposed for involuntary unemployment was worker expectations about prices which may not be correct. However, monetarists and new microeconomists have argued that in the long run, expectations must be satisfied: that labour cannot be fooled in the long run. Hence, when actual inflation is equal to expected inflation, actual prices will equal expected prices in all time periods. When looked at in this way, the NRU is the level of unemployment consistent with the long-run level of unemployment where price expectations are fulfilled (actual and expected inflation rates are the same). Put yet another way, e.g. by Phelps, there is a rate of unemployment in the long run which is consistent with a non-accelerating rate of inflation – dubbed NAIRU. It is to be noted, then, that the natural rate of unemployment is:

(a) a long-run concept;
(b) not 'natural' in the sense of inevitable;
(c) consistent with clearing in the labour market;
(d) consistent with a non-accelerating rate of inflation; and
(e) can be influenced by shifts in the demand for or supply of labour.

One approach to the estimation of the natural rate of unemployment is to consider the relationship between unemployment and vacancies. When there is no demand-deficient unemployment, then $U_n = V$ (since $U_d = 0$ and $U_n = U_s + U_f$). Consequently, if there is a relationship between unemployment and vacancies, the natural rate should lie on a straight line through the origin for which $U = V$. The natural rate of unemployment can therefore be estimated by finding where the U–V relationship cuts the 45° line. Furthermore, if the U–V curve moves towards the origin, then the natural rate of unemployment will be falling, while if it moves away from the origin, then the natural rate of unemployment will be rising. There has, therefore, been a fair amount of interest in estimating the U–V curve, which is considered in more detail in Appendix 14.2.

But why is the natural rate of unemployment so high? In explaining the high level of the NRU, one is really attempting to explain why structural and frictional unemployment is high. Even when vacancies exist it does not mean unemployment will be absent or lowered. The point is that it takes time to match labour with the available jobs, and this will lead to frictional unemployment. Being short run in concept, it usually means vacancies in the same occupation and in the same location as the unemployment. What it also means is that given the existence of vacancies, a worker simply requires time to find the job which does not require him or her to change occupation or location, or to change his or her reservation wage.

More persistent mismatch, and hence a long-run concept, is where the unemployed are mismatched with job vacancies because they do not possess the required skills or do not live in the location in which vacancies occur. Clearly, correcting structural unemployment of this type requires retraining and relocation – which is far more complex than simply searching for the right job in the same location and in the same occupation. The dividing line between frictional and structural unemployment is a hazy one, but it occurs because of mismatches between job vacancies and individual abilities and location. A variety of reasons have been put forward as to why such mismatches occur, as follows:

1. Inflexiblity of relative wages (especially minimum wage legislation).
2. Lack of training incentives by firms.
3. Employer discrimination in favour of experience.
4. Pure discrimination.
5. Hit-and-miss availability of training in school.
6. Difficulty of borrowing.
7. Long adjustment lags in education.

Not only is it necessary to account for the high level of the natural rate of unemployment, but it is also necessary to explain why the natural rate has been *rising*, which appears to be the case. The following five reasons have usually been advanced for the rise in the natural rate of unemployment in the UK:

1. Deindustrialization.
2. A decline in UK competitiveness.
3. Too little investment.
4. A growth of the non-market sector at the expense of the market sector (the Bacon–Eltis thesis).
5. A growing balance of payments weakness (the balance of payments constraint on growth).

14.4 POLICIES TOWARDS UNEMPLOYMENT

What is quite clear from the preceding sections is that policies which have been advocated for curing unemployment will depend very much on what is thought to be the cause of unemployment. Since there is no agreement on what is the cause of unemployment, then it follows there will be no agreement on how to go about solving this particular problem. However, what is also clear from earlier sections is that the two main explanations for high unemployment attribute high unemployment to demand-deficiency or to structural changes. This is because monetarist and modern classical arguments are basically statements to the effect that unemployment is structural in nature; the only difference is how they account for this. However, the difference is not the only element of importance. The increase in the duration of unemployment, no matter what has caused it, is of major concern. Furthermore, young people leaving school are entering this pool of long-term unemployed on an increasing scale. If these individuals are not to be too disadvantaged relative to others, then some policies will need to be directed specifically at the young. Whether the same can be said about the unemployment of the over-50s (or even over-40s) is not so obvious.

Any policy concerning the reduction in the level of unemployment is predicated on the view that high, or 'full', employment is a policy objective. Keynesian macroeconomics gave a theoretical basis for governments to stimulate the economy in order to achieve the objective of full employment. Monetarism and, more recently, modern classicism, has undermined the belief in the ability of governments to achieve such an objective. If the 'full employment' target is less than the natural rate of unemployment, then, monetarists argue, this will simply lead to inflation – and inflation which will accelerate. Modern classicists go further. Basing their arguments on rational expectations, they argue that the government is totally impotent in achieving its full employment target because market participants will take account of their influence on the economy and so nullify it (see Chapter 4). Although some argue that this is only true in the long run, others contend that it is both true in the long run and true in the short run. Of course, monetarists and modern classicists place great emphasis on the market mechanism. If the market mechanism is allowed to work 'properly' and efficiently, then the only unemployment will be the natural rate of unemployment. Being structural in nature, policies should be directed at reducing this natural rate. However, it is not at all clear from the arguments of modern classicists whether they would countenance *any* policies towards unemployment other than those which improve the efficiency of the market mechanism.

Keynesians have adapted their view towards unemployment since Keynes' *General Theory* (see, for example, Frank, 1986). But still they see a role for government in reducing unemployment stimulating aggregate demand. Thus, not only do they see the major component of total unemployment as demand-deficient unemployment, they also see a positive role for government in reducing such unemployment. For example, Hughes and Perlman (1984), although recognizing that occupational mismatch requires manpower policies (to solve a structural problem), say that 'retraining is no substitute for aggregate demand policies'. (p. 50) Their point is that vacancies for the retraining will arise only if accompanied by a rise in aggregate demand.

Because of the diversity of views about the cause of and cures for unemployment, we present a summary of measures proposed for dealing with UK unemployment in Table 14.4. The suggested policies are very extensive and include stimulating aggregate demand, income policies of various types, and legislative reform of the labour and the housing markets. In some cases the proposals only refer to long-term unemployment or to youth unemployment.

Although Table 14.4 sets out a variety of proposals to alleviate unemployment, the question still remains as to which is the more dominant: demand-deficient unemployment or structural unemployment. This, however, is a difficult question to answer. Here we consider just some of the empirical investigations which have been carried out.

One estimate is presented by Bean, Layard and Nickell (1986). They construct a model composed basically of four equations: (1) labour demand; (2) a price-setting equation; (3) a wage-setting equation; and (4) an aggregate demand equation. Thus, equations (1)–(3) establish an aggregate supply equation and equation (4) specifies an aggregate demand equation. These four equations are used to solve for the employment rate, demand, the real wage and the price level, each in terms of the exogenous variables. Using this model they

Table 14.4 Policies for correcting UK unemployment

Metcalf (1982)	1. Expand demand
	2. Abolish NIS
Core policy wage	3. Impose an incomes policy
subsidies and job	4. Pursue special employment measures (e.g., early retirement and reduction
creation schemes	in working hours)
	5. Implement wage subsidies and job creation schemes
Minford (1983) (2nd edn 1985)	1. Changes in the benefits system
	2. Changes in tax and income supplements for those in work
Improve market efficiency	3. Change in law and institutions regulating the labour and housing markets
Hawkins (2nd edn 1984)	1. Improvement in competitiveness (a) shift resources into wealth creating
	sector by reducing business costs not related to market forces (e.g., NIS)
Main policy supply oriented	2. Reduce wage-push elements (a) reduce bargaining power of TUs
	(b) increase market sector determined wages.
	3. Subsidize employment
	4. Increase public employment
	5. Reduce labour supply (increase withdrawals and reduce entrants).
Hughes and Perlman (1984)	1. Public employment programmes (limited)
	2. Reduce labour supply (limited)
Favours demand policies	3. Reduce hours worked (limited)
	4. Expand aggregate demand
	5. Active manpower policy (Implement 4 and 5 together)
	6. Incomes policy
NIER (1984)	1. Fiscal reflation (gradual)
	2. Raise direct public expenditure on goods and services
Favours gradual reflation	3. Abolish NIS
Marsden, Trinder and	Youth Training Scheme (YTS), Young Workers' Scheme (YWS) and the
Wagner (1986)	Community Programme (CP)
Describes the measures	
actually taken	
Knight (1987)	Discusses in general terms reducing (a) non-natural (disequilibrium)
	unemployment, and (b) natural (equilibrium) employment
Favours policy package	Suggests a policy package since no single cause of unemployment
Jackman and Layard (1987)	1. Job guarantees for the long-term unemployed (e.g. by MSC on Community
	Programme and on a new Building Improvement Programme) – subsidized
TIP central to proposal	programmes envisaged for 1 year only
	2. Tax based incomes policy (TIP)
Beenstock and Minford (1987)	1. Replace collective bargaining with competitive bargaining
	2. Legal reform necessary (a) remove legal immunity of TUs from tort action,
Favour market solutions	(b) extend brief of Monopolies Commission
Junankar (1987)	Considers 4 ways to affect the labour market:
	1. Increase aggregate demand (AD)
Concentrates on youth, favours	
raising AD	2. Decrease labour costs of young people
	3. Increase skills of the young
	4. Change incentives of work/leisure choice of young

establish the following breakdown for UK unemployment for 1956–66 to 1980–83, where all figures are percentage points.[6]

Taxes	2.06
Import prices	−0.05
Search	2.25
Demand	5.33
Total	9.60
Actual	8.33

The authors present estimates for many of the OECD countries, and the results (both for the UK and for the other OECD countries) confirm the importance of demand as a reason for the rise in unemployment – most especially in the EEC. To the extent that unemployment is due to a deficiency of demand, therefore, the appropriate policies listed in Table 14.4 for dealing with *this particular type* of unemployment are those which will stimulate aggregate demand. However, there is also a significant contribution from reduced search activity and from a higher tax burden. Hence, the policies required for reducing *this type* of unemployment are those that basically improve search and reduce market imperfections. The impact from import prices seems to play a small role, with the exception of the period when commodity prices rose on world markets and when the two oil shocks occurred.

Layard and Nickell (1986) attribute most of the rise in UK unemployment since 1979 to the fall in demand. They argue that unemployment benefits have not played an important role, as Minford makes them out to be. Considering the outward shift in the $U–V$ relationship (see Appendix 14.2), they attribute 3 percentage points of the extra unemployment to a combination of social security benefits and employment protection. Mismatch, they establish, only accounts for 1 percentage point in the unemployment. On the other hand, they estimate that union militancy (measured as the mark-up of union over non-union wages) has risen and accounts for about 3 percentage points of the increase in unemployment. In contrast to Bean, Layard and Nickell discussed above, in the present study Layard and Nickell found little evidence for income taxes and indirect taxes influencing unemployment.

However, these studies also argue that the main reason for the increase in unemployment is the increase in the *duration* of unemployment. If this is the case, as it seems to be, then there is a good reason to argue that long-term unemployment, at least, is structural. This is certainly the basis of Hawkins' (1984) contention. The rise in the duration of unemployment would also support the contention that there has been an increase in the natural rate of unemployment (e.g., an outward shift in the $U–V$ relationship). Accordingly, the appropriate policies for dealing *with this particular category* of unemployment are supply-side policies.

The conclusion one can draw from this brief review is that there is *no single reason for the rise in unemployment*. Aggregate demand and supply have individually and together been contributory factors. If, therefore, unemployment is going to be tackled as a policy objective – and it is not clear that the Conservative government under Mrs Thatcher sees its role in this way – then the problem will have to be approached on at least two fronts: raising aggregate demand and pursuing supply-side policies. This is not only essential to reduction of unemployment, but it is also necessary if inflation is not to re-assert itself as a consequence of such policies. For this reason, unemployment policy must be seen as part of an economic strategy and not in isolation.

NOTES

1. The participation rate (or activity rate) is defined as the supply of labour relative to the working population. Let

   $S_L(t)$ = supply of labour
   $N(t)$ = working population
   $U(t)$ = level of unemployment
   $E(t)$ = level of employment

all defined at time t, then the unemployment *rate*, $u(t)$, and the activity rate, $a(t)$, are defined:

$$u(t) = U(t)/[E(t) + U(t)]$$

$$a(t) = S_L(t)/N(t)$$

Since $S_L(t) = E(t) + U(t)$, then it follows that

$$u(t) = U(t)/[a(t)N(t)]$$

Hence, the unemployment *rate* depends not only on the level of employment but also on the participation rate and the level of the working population. The working population variable is only important when looking over long periods of time.

If we distinguish between men and women, then we can define their respective participation rates as

$$a_m(t) = S_{Lm}(t)/N_m(t)$$

$$a_w(t) = S_{Lw}(t)/N_w(t)$$

and the respective unemployment rates as

$$u_m(t) = U_m(t)/[a_m(t)N_m(t)]$$

$$u_w(t) = U_w(t)/[a_w(t)N_w(t)]$$

2. After October 1982 voluntary registration for unemployment benefit is the basis for the unemployment count. Hence, those who choose not to claim are not part of the count (but disabled are now included). This does mean that there is a stock of unregistered unemployed which are part of labour supply but are not counted as unemployed in terms of official statistics.

3. In some local labour markets jobs are so quickly taken up that they would rarely be counted. Furthermore, there is some evidence that services in particular are more likely to advertise vacancies in the local newspaper and not register them at the local Job Centre.

4. Between 1961 and 1977 the female participation rate in the UK increased from 37 to 50%. However, after 1977 it began to decline as the level of unemployment rose sharply.

5. A justification for such a non-clearing real wage is the possible preferred distribution of income that it entails.

6. See Bean, Layard and Nickell (1986), table 4, p. S11.

APPENDIX 14.1 VARIOUS DEFINITIONS OF UNEMPLOYMENT

seasonal unemployment: unemployment which arises from activities that have well-defined seasons, such as construction and tourism.

frictional unemployment: unemployment which arises from unfilled vacancies in the same occupation and the same place. It arises because it takes time to match jobs and workers appropriately. It arises because of short-run search.

structural unemployment: unemployment arising from the mismatch between job applicants and the skills required or because of locational mismatch. The difference between structural and frictional unemployment is that structural requires retraining or relocation, which is a long-run problem.

demand deficient unemployment (or cyclical unemployment): unemployment arising from the fact that the level of aggregate demand in the economy is not at such a level as to provide work for everyone no matter how they are trained or located.

job-search unemployment: unemployment arising through individuals who cease work temporarily in order to search for another job. (This will not include those who are searching for another job while still in employment.)

natural rate of unemployment: that rate of unemployment which occurs when the labour market is in
  equilibrium – the equilibrium being the outcome of a Walrasian system of general equilibrium.

non-accelerating inflation rate of unemployment (NAIRU): the unemployment that prevails if price
  expectations are fulfilled. (This is an alternative but consistent definition of the natural rate of
  unemployment.)

involuntary unemployment: the difference in the level of employment that would occur in a freely
  operating labour market and the level of employment that actually occurs. (It is *not* the same as
  excess supply in the labour market.)

voluntary unemployment: denotes those individuals in the working population who choose not to work
  at the ruling wage.

speculative unemployment: unemployment that arises from the family unit withholding labour either
  part-time or full-time on the expectation that wages will rise.

precautionary unemployment: unemployment which arises from the act of not taking a job at the
  present time on the anticipation of getting a (more suitable) job in the near future.

APPENDIX 14.2 THE *U–V* RELATIONSHIP

The *U–V* relationship is derived by first postulating that vacancies are related to excess demand in the
labour market. Basically, as excess demand rises the level of vacancies we would expect would also
rise. When excess demand is zero, vacancies would equal the natural rate of unemployment. Further
restrictions are imposed: (1) vacancies cannot be negative; and (2) vacancies cannot exceed the level of
excess demand. Together these all imply a relationship, as shown in Fig. A14.2.1, where the curve is
asymptotic to the two axes and cuts the 45° line at the natural level of unemployment. For a real wage
rate above the equilibrium, we have stated earlier that employment is determined by the demand for
labour. On the other hand, for a real wage below the market clearing wage, employment is determined
by the supply of labour, since employers cannot force individuals to work. In terms of Fig. A14.2.2(*a*),
this would imply an *employment curve* shown by the heavy lines. However, such an argument ignores
the presence of vacancies. To the extent that vacancies exist, the level of employment will be to the left
of the heavy lines. In practice, therefore, the employment curve is shaped something like *EE* and the
level of vacancies is the gap between *EE* and the heavy lines. As real wages vary, it will be noted that
there is an inverse relationship between *V* and *U*.

Although it has never been the case in the UK that $U = V$, the data indicate that the natural level
of unemployment, using such a relationship, has been rising.

The *U–V* relationship is not a clear one. Its dynamic features have been investigated by Bowden
(1980). His main conclusion is that the *U–V* scatter diagram can be conceived of as a 'temporary
equilibrium' locus and, more importantly, cannot be derived from a demand/supply model of the
labour market. However, he did show that a reduction in the speed of market clearing will shift the
U–V curve to the right. The same is likely to be true with regard to the industrial composition of the
demand for labour, leading to a greater mismatch of skills. A limitation of this model, as others, is that
it pays very little attention to quits, firings, hirings and retirements.

The reasons advanced for the outward shift in the *U–V* relationship (after 1966) are as follows:

1. Individuals remaining in unemployment for longer than necessary because of unemployment
   benefits.
2. A reduction of employment in the services sector because of the selective employment tax (SET
   started in 1966).
3. A reduction in labour hoarding.
4. An increase in the birth rate in the late 1940s.

There has, however, been no generally accepted explanation.

The study by Evans (1977) attempted to look at both males and females (many earlier studies
considering only males). He concludes that some of the explanations of the *U–V* shift cannot be
supported. Although the *U–V* for males shifted to the right, that for females shifted to the left. This, for

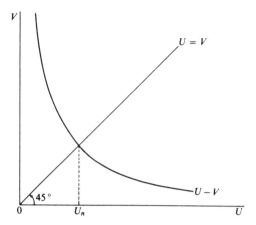

Figure A14.2.1 The *U–V* relationship.

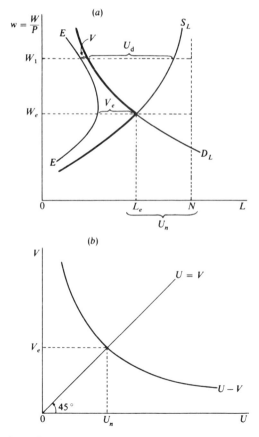

Figure A14.2.2 Construction of the *U–V* relationship.

example, would rule out the increase in birth rate because this would mean that *both* curves would move to the right. The same is true for redundancies. Evans largely attributed the shift in 1966 to the earnings-related unemployment benefit that was introduced in that year.

Evans' analysis supports Gujarati's (1972) view, which is contained in the most widely quoted empirical paper on the $U-V$ relationship. Basically, Gujarati was interested in knowing (correcting for) the September 1966 changes. To do this he ran a regression for the period 1958.4–1966.3, thus

$$\text{Log } U_t = a_0 + a_1 \text{ Log } V_t + a_2 t + e_t$$

He then used this to predict the values of U_t, $U_t(p)$, say, for given values of V_t in any period after 1966.3, i.e. the correction factor is:

$$U_t(a) - U_t(p)$$

where $U_t(a)$ is the actual unemployment in period t. He estimated the general 'correction factor' to be 1.44 in each quarter, i.e.

$$U_t(c) = U_t(a)/1.44$$

where $U_t(c)$ denotes 'corrected' unemployment. However, the relationship still requires further investigation.

Chapter 15

INDUSTRIAL POLICY AND SUPPLY-SIDE ECONOMICS

Industrial policy is usually confined to microeconomics or, most especially industrial economics, but very rarely to a macroeconomics textbook. But the very subdivision into microeconomics and macroeconomics breaks down when considering supply. We have already noted the obvious point that a shift of the aggregate supply curve to the right, assuming aggregate demand stays fixed, lowers the price level and raises output. In a dynamic context, a shift to the right of the Phillips curve will lower inflation and raise output – and whether this is a short-run result or a long-run result depends on whether it is the short-run or the long-run Phillips curve which is being shifted. But how can governments do this, or even, can governments do this? What is quite clear is that, at the macroeconomic level, there is very little that governments can do to shift either the aggregate supply curve or the Phillips curve to the right. This is basically because there are no macroeconomic *instruments* with which the government can operate as far as supply is concerned. Assuming that the government does wish to stimulate supply (and that it is possible to do so, which we will discuss later), then this can only be done at the microeconomic level. Although not a view shared by all (see the CLARE group's discussion in Midland Bank, 1982), it is an inevitable conclusion when considering policy from an instruments–targets framework (as outlined in Chapter 8).

We begin with a discussion of post-War industrial policy, paying particular attention to the legislative process because this emphasizes what *actually* took place, rather than to the rhetoric that accompanied such legislation. What this legislation emphasized was the policy towards competition and mergers, which we take up in more detail in Section 15.2. However, neither of the first two sections gives a flavour of the underlying rationale – or even discusses whether there was one. This we do in Section 15.3. Although many Conservative governments in the UK have advocated the benefits of free markets, it is really only the Thatcher government since 1979 that has put such ideals into practice. The most crucial element in this strategy is privatization, and we will deal with this separately in Section 15.4. Privatization, however, is only one aspect of supply-side economics, and we turn to this in Section 15.5.

15.1 POST-WAR INDUSTRIAL POLICY

Of all government policies in the UK, industrial policy is the least well-defined and the least coherent. It has no clear objectives and no clear instruments. It has its roots in the formation of the Monopolies Commission in 1948 (see Appendix 15.1), which set the scene for specific legislation.[1] This was followed by the 1956 and 1968 Restrictive Trade Practices Acts and the abolition of resale price maintenance as a means of enhancing competition. In 1965 attention turned to mergers, with the Monopolies and Mergers Act, which allowed cases to be referred to the Monopolies Commission. Of some significance is the 1973 Fair Trading Act, which extended the powers of the Director General of Fair Trading (his powers were extended still further in the Competition Act of 1980). The legislative history is briefly laid out in Table 15.1. What this table reveals is a persistent series of Acts to deal with four things:

1. Monopolies.
2. Mergers.
3. Restrictive practices (e.g., price-fixing).
4. Resale price maintenance (i.e., the situation whereby a retailer must sell a product at a price laid down by the manufacturer).

What is also quite clear is that industrial policy up to 1980 has been very interventionist in the UK, and that this has been so under both Labour and Conservative governments.

But why has there been this general tendency for intervention? Intervention under Labour has always been one of philosophical justification: Labour favours planning and the state control of industry. But industrial policy under various Conservative administrations was also interventionist – at least until Mrs Thatcher's term of office. One reason advanced for this general tendency is that it was a response to the persistent failure of governments to achieve their major *macroeconomic* objectives. The UK was lagging behind her major competitors, and this was not simply a question of reconstruction after the Second World War. As the UK continually failed to match her rivals on productivity and growth, the balance of payments became weaker, and this placed even greater constraints on growth (see Chapter 18). Thus, in a 1961 report the Council on Prices, Productivity and Incomes urged the setting up of a planning institution (along French lines). When Labour came to power in 1964, the report became the basis for establishing the National Economic Development Council (NEDC). However, the actual work of carrying out indicative planning was not undertaken by the NEDC, but, rather, by the newly formed (1964) Department of Economic Affairs (DEA), which cooperated with the Economic Development Committees (the 'little Neddies') to check with individual industries on the implications for them of a predetermined growth target. Once again there was an emphasis on the microeconomic. This microeconomic emphasis, and the type of indicative planning envisaged in the UK, was embodied in The National Plan (1965), but this was virtually abandoned the moment it was published.

At this time, growth became an important macropolicy objective. However, it was being pursued largely by microeconomic means and by government intervention. There was a general belief at this time (at least on the part of Labour), that markets could not bring about the greater efficiency or growth necessary to compete internationally. Not only that, markets would not bring about the reorganization and rationalization that government considered necessary for growth. Thus in 1966, it set up the Industrial Reorganization Corporation (IRC). This was to bring about industrial reorganization by encouraging mergers which were considered justified on the grounds of economies of scale, better management and improved international competitiveness. Further selectivity was taken

Table 15.1 Competition legislation

UK – Principal Acts

1948	Monopolies and Restrictive Practices Act (Monopolies Commission created)
1956	Restrictive Trade Practices Act (Restrictive Practices Court and Registrar of Restrictive Trading Agreements created. Register of restrictive agreements relating to goods)
1964	Resale Prices Act (Cases to be referred to Restrictive Practices Court)
1965	Monopolies and Mergers Act (Provision for mergers to be referred to Monopolies Commission)
1968	Restrictive Trade Practices Act (Provision for registration of information agreements)
1973	Fair Trading Act (Director General of Fair Trading to replace Registrar of Restrictive Trading Agreements)
1976	Restrictive Trade Practices Act (Restrictive agreements relating to services to be registered)
1980	Competition Act (Director General to investigate anti-competitive practices. Provision for public bodies to be referred to Monopolies Commission)

EEC

1973	Treaty of Rome Article 85 Agreements prohibited which affect trade between member states and prevent, restrict or distort competition Article 86 Abuse of a dominant position within the Common Market prohibited

---

with the Industrial Expansion Act of 1968, which allowed departments to finance investment schemes in industry without the need to enact separate legislation each time.

When Heath came to power in 1970, the initial statement on belief in markets that has dominated the rhetoric of all Conservative administrations was issued. Certainly, he dismantled much of Labour's apparatus set-up under Harold Wilson, most especially the Industrial Reorganization Corporation (abolished 1971) and the Industrial Expansion Act (in large part reversed). However, he had to face two situations, each involving a financial crisis to the companies concerned: namely, the Upper Clyde Shipbuilders and Rolls-Royce. In solving the first, the government formed Govan Shipbuilders by combining three shipping yards; while in the case of Rolls-Royce, the government nationalized the company's aero-engine division. The result was a U-turn on industrial policy. What was particularly significant about these two episodes was the reason for the intervention: to avoid high levels of unemployment. In fact, this became the focus of much industrial policy throughout the 1970s. However, maintaining employment was not the only reason. Additional reasons were to maintain international competitiveness; to bolster the balance of payments; to satisfy defence requirements; to maintain strategic industries; to cater for the special needs of high technology industries; and, finally, to satisfy social needs (including employment).

The main ideas of the Labour government (1974–79) on industrial policy were set out in the White Paper, *The Regeneration of British Industry* (Cmnd 5710) and put into effect by the Industry Act of 1975. It involved a planning agreement system and the setting up of a

National Enterprise Board (NEB). The planning agreements were envisaged as providing consultation between government and individual companies in the planning of such things as investment, exports, output, employment, etc. It was envisaged that union officials would be involved in such consultations. After some debate, the agreements were to be voluntary rather than compulsory. But nothing really came of these agreements.[2] The influence of the Board had been limited, in large part because it lacked any compulsory powers. Labour made further attempts after the removal of Mr Benn in mid-1975,[3] by taking a tripartite approach to industry (management – labour – government), which was to be based on agreement and not compulsion. Labour's ideas were set out in the 1975 White Paper, *An Approach to Industrial Strategy* (Cmnd 6315). However, the policy became largely institutionalized in terms of Sector Working Parties under the aegis of the NEDC. Again the emphasis of the 'new industrial strategy' was microeconomic in order to achieve macroeconomic objectives of improved productivity, growth and competitiveness. The result was a series of *ad hoc* interventions which occurred as a result of immediate expediency. In addition, a whole plethora of aid was implemented in the period 1974–79.

15.2 COMPETITION POLICY AND MERGERS

Section 15.1 concentrated on the legislative aspect of policy throughout the post-War period, but what it does not do is give any real idea of the changing views towards mergers and towards competition which formed the underlying rationale for much of this legislation. In this section we will briefly discuss each of these topics, beginning with competition, where we include under this title both monopoly and restrictive practices.

Competition policy

The inter-War period was a time of increased industrial concentration and cartelization. But following the Second World War there was a strong anti-trust movement, both in the UK and, more especially, in the US. It must be emphasized that the working definition of a monopoly bears very little connection with the theoretical textbook version, and in practice (in the UK) refers to a firm which has a 25% share of the market (prior to 1973, one-third). It was considered that the formation of monopolies was against the public interest, and the lack of competition would allow such firms to take advantage of their monopoly power. Of course, not all monopolies are necessarily against the public interest and thus regulation was required. The establishment of the Monopolies Commission was to see that any monopolies were not detrimental to the public interest. Thus, central to the workings of the Monopolies Commission was the idea that a situation should not oppose the 'public interest', which was clarified in the Fair Trading Act of 1973. The main clause of the Act is set out in Table 15.2, and it can be seen that the interpretation of 'in the public interest' remains rather vague. However, it has meant that a number of situations have been referred to the Commission for investigation. But although around 150 cases have been dealt with by the Commission, little notice has been taken of its deliberations.

The case-by-case approach to monopolies and cartels has been typical of the post-War period, and is based on the structure – conduct – performance paradigm. In other words,

Table 15.2 The public interest: the Fair Trading Act 1973, Section 84

---

1. In determining for any purposes to which this section applies whether any particular matter operates, or may be expected to operate, against the public interest, the Commission shall take into account all matters which appear to them in the particular circumstances to be relevant and, among other things, shall have regard to the desirability:

   (a) of maintaining and promoting effective competition between persons supplying goods and services in the United Kingdom;

   (b) of promoting the interests of consumers, purchasers and other users of goods and services in the United Kingdom in respect of the prices charged for them and in respect of their quality and the variety of goods and services supplied;

   (c) of promoting, through competition, the reduction of costs and the development and use of new techniques and new products, and of facilitating the entry of new competitors into existing markets;

   (d) of maintaining and promoting the balanced distribution of industry and employment in the United Kingdom; and

   (e) of maintaining and promoting activity in markets outside the United Kingdom on the part of producers of goods, and of suppliers of goods and services, in the United Kingdom.

---

you can affect performance by doing something about structure and conduct. Although policy in the UK is aimed at controlling both structure and conduct, most emphasis has been on market conduct, Shaw (1984). However, there has been a growing dissatisfaction with the structure–conduct–performance paradigm. Some arguments point out the endogeneity of market structure (Dasgupta and Stiglitz, 1980); while others emphasize the importance of contestable markets,[4] which stress *potential* competition. But these developments have yet to make any impact on policy.

What appears to have been more effective, certainly in fostering more competition, is the policy towards restrictive practices. The main purpose of the Restrictive Practices Court (see Table 15.1) is to deal with cartel practices such as price fixing. A pivotal case before the Court was that of the Cotton Yarn Spinners' Agreement in 1959, which was deemed to oppose the public interest. Following this case a large number of cartels were abandoned. Equally significant was the 1964 legislation dealing with resale price maintenance. Like the Restrictive Practices Court, this generally went against prevailing cases. The success of these courts in dealing with cartels may have been one of the reasons for the large increase in mergers in the 1960s.

Mergers

There have been four periods of 'merger mania' in the UK: (1) at the turn of the century, (2) during the inter-War period, (3) 1960–70, and (4) in the mid-1980s. Studies of industrial concentration in the UK, see Appendix 15.2, have revealed a rise in industrial concentration, and higher levels of industrial concentration than in the US, West Germany and other industrial countries.

Mergers account for about 50% of the change in the concentration ratio. However, the mergers which have taken place in the mid-1985 period differ from those in the 1960s and 1970s in two respects: first, the average size of acquisition is much larger in real terms; and second, the occurrence of 'hostile bids' has increased. In addition, the pattern of the transfer of ownership has changed. There are three identifiable aspects to the transfer of ownership (Chiplin and Wright, 1987):

1. the acquisition of independent companies;
2. the sale of subsidiaries between parent groups (parent-to-parent divestments);
3. management buy-outs (whereby managers buy-out the business for which they were employed).

Information on all three aspects is presented in Table 15.3, which not only indicates that acquisitions account for the major proportion of transfers of ownership (both by number and by value), but that over the last decade there has been a dramatic rise in management buy-outs.

Although since 1965 all proposed mergers involving a minimum market share of 25% being supplied by one firm[5] had to be considered by the Mergers Panel for possible referral to the Monopolies and Mergers Commission (the Monopolies Commission was renamed in 1973), the eventual decision was taken by the Secretary of State, who was not bound by the Commission's recommendations. In 1984 Mr Norman Tebbit, the then Secretary of State, made the point that the government regarded mergers as part of competition policy, and that competition both at home and abroad would be the basis for referral – but the reference of Elders IXL and Allied – Lyons in December 1985 cast doubt on this because it was made on the basis of finance. In spite of this, there has so far been a very low referral rate, as shown in Table 15.4, which indicates that the relevant percentage of referrals barely exceeded 3%.

What this reveals in general is a bias on the part of ministers in *favour* of mergers. This bias in favour of mergers has been a bias in favour of large firms and a presumption that mergers are generally in the public interest. The point is that the onus is on the Commission to demonstrate that the proposed merger is *against* the public interest in order to prevent it. In other words, the firms concerned do not have to demonstrate that the merger is *in* the public interest. Government studies do seem to have shown that high concentrations are necessary for firms to reap the benefits of economies of scale. Using minimum efficient scale measures, sixteen from a total of twenty-five producer groups required a market share of 25% in order to achieve minimum efficient scale! Even so, there has been a suggestion that the burden of proof should be reversed, but the 1985 Green Paper, *A Review of Monopolies and Mergers Policy*, did not see any need to reverse the burden of proof. What it did suggest was a shift in policy from one favouring mergers to one which was neutral towards mergers. But at the present time there is no evidence that this has happened.

Although mergers can take a variety of forms (vertical, horizontal or conglomerate), what is revealing about the mergers that took place in the 1960s and 1970s in the UK was the dominance of *horizontal* integration. Table 15.5 shows that during the period 1970–85, vertical integration played very little role in mergers. The significance of this, of course, is that horizontal integration raises the dangers of the misuse of market power.

The general policy towards mergers (both Labour and Conservative) has therefore been one of indifference and a general disinclination to dissolve monopolies.

15.3 CAN AND SHOULD THE GOVERNMENT INTERVENE IN INDUSTRY?

In the last two sections we indicated how UK governments have intervened in industry for one reason or another. The three main areas have been in monopolies, restrictive practices

Table 15.3 Acquisitions, divestments and buy-outs, 1969–1986/Q3

Year	Acquisition of independent industrial companies			Sales of subsidiaries between industrial parent groups			Management buy-outs		
	No.	Av.	£m	No.	Av.	£m	No.	Av.	£m
1969	742	961	1.30	102	100	0.98	..	..	..
1970	608	954	1.57	179	126	0.70	..	..	..
1971	620	745	1.20	264	166	0.63	..	..	..
1972	931	2337	2.51	272	185	0.68	..	..	..
1973	951	1057	1.11	254	247	0.97	..	..	..
1974	367	459	1.25	137	49	0.36	..	..	..
1975	200	221	1.11	115	70	0.61	..	..	..
1976	242	348	1.44	111	100	0.90	..	..	..
1977	372	730	1.96	109	94	0.86	13	..	..
1978	441	977	2.22	126	163	1.29	23	..	..
1979	414	1438	3.47	117	186	1.59	52	26	0.50
1980	368	1265	3.44	101	210	2.08	107	50	0.47
1981	327	882	2.70	125	262	2.10	124	114	0.92
1982	296	1373	4.64	164	804	4.90	170	265	1.56
1983	302	1783	5.90	142	436	3.07	205	315	1.54
1984	396	4253	10.74	170	1121	6.59	210	255	1.21
1985	339	6281	18.53	134	793	5.92	229	1176	5.02
1986/Q3	349	10 000	28.65	93	914	9.83	201	944	4.70

.. indicates data not available
Source: Chiplin and Wright (1987), table 2, p. 17

Table 15.4 Merger referrals to the Monopolies and Mergers Commission, 1965–85

Period	Within legislation (No.)	% of all mergers	Referred (No.)	% of relevant mergers
1965–69	466	10.5	10	2.1
1970–74	579	11.4	19	3.3
1975–79	903	36.5	19	2.1
1980–84	987	38.6	31	3.1
1985	192	38.3	4	2.1

Source: Chiplin and Wright (1987), table 5, p. 31

Table 15.5 Types of acquisition/merger with legislation 1970–85 (%)

	Horizontal		Vertical		Diversifying	
	by number	by value	by number	by value	by number	by value
1970–74	73	65	5	4	23	27
1975	71	77	5	4	24	19
1976	70	66	8	7	22	27
1977	64	57	11	11	25	32
1978	53	67	13	10	34	23
1979	51	68	7	4	42	28
1980	65	68	4	1	31	31
1981	62	71	6	2	32	27
1982	65	64	5	4	30	32
1983	71	73	4	1	25	26
1984	63	79	4	1	33	20
1985	58	42	4	4	38	54

Source: Chiplin and Wright (1987), table 6, p. 34

and mergers. But why have an industrial policy at all? Why not simply let market forces operate unhindered? In a pure market system no industrial policy is required. But even in the US there has been a long history of anti-trust policy. So long as it is possible for monopolies to take advantage of their monopoly power, then some form of regulation is required. Although there is general agreement on this aspect of policy, why should governments go further and try to intervene in industry on a greater scale?

The more usual arguments for government intervention – market imperfections and the divergence between private and social costs – do not provide a sound basis on which to discuss the post-War industrial policy in the UK. For example, the 1972 Industry Act emphasized the basis for intervention as being for reasons of 'national interest' and of 'benefit to the UK economy'. Under Labour, concern surrounded control of the abuse of monopoly power more than the fostering of competition. Competition, it could be argued, played very little role in the rationale for intervention.

A survey of the 1960s and 1970s indicates that reasons for intervention were manifold. They included:

(a) the pursuit of growth;
(b) a desire to maintain external balance;
(c) a desire to reduce unemployment;
(d) a desire to control inflation; and
(e) a desire for public control.

Furthermore, the measures were often short-term, were implemented to deal with particular problems, and discriminated against small firms. There has never been any clear long-run policy towards industry. Although there has been a view that firms must compete internationally – that this is necessary and healthy – the same basic theme has not been pursued domestically!

What is quite clear is that the policies which have been pursued have not given rise to a thriving, productive and efficient industrial sector. One view now being expressed is that this was inevitable because government just cannot stimulate industry. A less extreme version of this is that in the post-War era there was an exaggerated view of the potential of government to stimulate industry, but at the end of the day, governments cannot do management's job, they can only change the situation with which managers are confronted.[6] This view is now being expressed by the Conservative Party – who believe that all government can do is to "create a climate" in which industry can thrive and grow.

However, there is some degree of inconsistency in its industrial policy to the extent that it does believe it can help small industry and that Britain's future will be better served by the growth and stimulation of the small-firm sector. Furthermore, the small-firm sector is being seen as a useful means of alleviating the high levels of unemployment. There is a number of other roles envisaged for the small firm:

(a) to fill the gap of declining demand for large-firm products;
(b) to provide a more flexible industrial base with faster response time to market changes;
(c) to satisfy those markets where minimum efficient scale is small;
(d) to fill those markets where entry is easy and where capital requirements are low;
(e) to cater for the specialist niche, in both product and factor markets;
(f) to provide the potential for innovation; and
(g) to bring about an urban/rural shift.

The list is long, and not even complete, and reveals the exaggerated hopes of what small firms can do for the UK economy. It seems to reflect the dissatisfaction with large size and reveals the swing in the pendulum to the opposite extreme. It will provide no panacea for Britain's industrial problems.

However, the stimulus of the small-firm sector is not the only aspect of the present government's industrial strategy. A major element (and a growing one) is that of privatization, to which we now turn.

15.4 PRIVATIZATION

There are the following three strands to the policy of privatization, Kay and Silberston (1984):

1. Liberalization – in order to increase competition.
2. Transfer of ownership of assets to the private sector.
3. Encouragement of the private provision of services which are currently provided collectively.

These are distinct and can be pursued separately, but can easily be in conflict. The transfer of ownership to the private sector is now considered to be a far too narrow interpretation of privatization. It is neither necessary nor sufficient for greater efficiency: and it is improved efficiency which is constantly being stressed by the present government.

It is not our intention here to discuss the whole issue of privatization, of which there is now a growing literature.[7] But, rather, to point out in broad terms this change in direction of industrial policy. The underlying economic rationale for privatization has only recently received attention in terms of principal-agency theory, imperfect competition and regulatory theory. There is also some analysis arising from public choice theory, most particularly the study of bureaucracies. However, these theories were not the basis on which the wave of privatization was pursued, especially in the UK: it was more a question of belief. But belief in what? It is a belief in the workings of the market, that the private sector is fundamentally more efficient than the public sector. Given this line of reasoning, it follows that privatization (if pursued) should be directed towards those areas where competition is presently limited but where it can be raised through the act of privatization. Thus, Beesley and Littlechild (1983) argue that most benefits would arise from privatizing electricity, coal, railways, telecommunications, and the Post Office.

It could be argued that the recent theories of contestable markets do give some underlying rationale for privatization, but this theory is abstract and has yet to be tested against the real world. What it does do is direct attention away from market structure, on the grounds that even one firm can be in competition with potential entrants. Like the arguments advanced for rational expectations, which we outlined in Chapter 4, this theory tends to support the view that markets work well — but only if they are unregulated and left to do their job efficiently. In other words, competition (or contestability) is a 'good thing' so long as the industry concerned is not a natural monopoly, where competition (potential or actual) is difficult to conceive.

An additional argument for privatization is concerned with the reduction in the size of the public sector. As we pointed out in Chapters 6 and 9, there is a belief that the present size of the government sector is too large and that this should be reduced. One way to reduce the size of the public sector is de-nationalization – or, more generally, privatization. Even so, with the present scale of privatization, there will still be only about a 10% reduction in the size of the nationalized sector!

Although the 1970s stressed the importance of competition, this was stimulated by government through appropriate legislation, as outlined above. Even though Conservatives have always been opposed to public ownership, it was only after 1979 that there was any positive move in its reduction. In the 1970s, neither Labour nor Conservatives really saw competition policy as having an important role to play. Although the theory of contestable markets is being discussed in the literature, it is hard to believe that this has had any bearing on the programme of privatization, which is dominated more by a Conservative philosophy about the public/private balance of a modern capitalist economy. At the same time, however, privatization is consistent with the view that government cannot directly stimulate industry and make it more effective, it can only provide the 'climate'; and part of this climate is a competitive private sector.

It was initially thought that privatization was likely to be insignificant. Certainly in the early period the firms to be denationalized were generally peripheral to the core role of government. However, as Table 15.6 indicates, the degree of privatization has become quite extensive, and during Mrs Thatcher's third term of office the extent of privatization is expected to increase right into the core of government provision, with privatization occurring (or proposed) in gas, electricity and water.

In the final analysis, nationalization or privatization is a question of how to organize business. If one form of organization (public or private) best achieves the aims laid down, then this form should prevail. A blanket statement in favour (or against) privatization (nationalization) is not helpful to the industrial development of the UK economy.

15.5 SUPPLY-SIDE ECONOMICS

The programme of privatization is only part of the Conservative government's overall strategy. Its strategy has three interlocking parts which are to set the scene for recovery, as laid down in the 1985 paper, *Employment: The Challenge for the Nation*, and outlined in Table 15.7. Taken as a whole, there is great emphasis on the supply side of the economy. More to the point, there is a major change in emphasis by the Conservative Party over the demand management which typified most of the post-War period. Mr Lawson, the Chancellor of the Exchequer, put their approach as follows

> There are two strands of policy, each of fundamental importance. On the one hand a macroeconomic policy designed to conquer inflation. And on the other, a microeconomic policy, indeed a whole range of microeconomic policies, designed to improve the operation of markets so that the economy can perform better and generate more jobs. These two policies have to progress in parallel; they are complementary.
>
> (Quoted in Coates and Hillard, 1987, p. 8)

Table 15.6 Privatization, 1979–87

Company	Date of first sale	What was sold	Subsequent events/intentions
British Petroleum	Nov 1979	5%	5.6% Jun 1981; 7% Sep 1983; remaining 31.5% Oct 1987
ICL	Dec 1979	25%	
Fairey Holdings	Jun 1980	private sale	
Ferranti	Jul 1980	50%	
British Aerospace	Feb 1981	50%	Remainder sold May 1985
British Sugar	Jul 1981	24%	
Cable and Wireless	Oct 1981	49%	Further 22% sold Dec 1983, remainder sold Dec 1985
Amersham International	Feb 1982	100%	
National Freight	Feb 1982	100%	
Forestry Commission	1982	Small sections	No further sales anticipated
British Steel	Apr 1982	Redpath Dorman Long	Other piecemeal divestments to follow
Britoil	Nov 1982	51%	Other 49% sold Aug 1985
Association British Ports	Feb 1983	51.5%	Remainder sold April 1984
British Airways	Mar 1983	International Aeradio	BA Helicopters Sep 1986
British Rail/Hotels	Mar 1983	10 hotels	Other sales in progress
British Rail/Hoverspeed	Feb 1984	100% of Hoverspeed	
Wytch Farm	May 1984	private sale	
Enterprise Oil	Jun 1984	100%	
British Leyland/Jaguar	Jul 1984	100% of Jaguar	Unipart sold Jan 1987; Leyland Bus Jan 1987 and Trucks April 1987
British Rail/Sealink	Aug 1984	100% of Sealink	
British Telecom	Nov 1984	50.2%	
British Shipbuilders	Jun 1985	private sale	Piecemeal sales of individual yards
Trustee Savings Bank	Feb 1986	100%	
Royal Ordnance Factories	Apr 1986	private sale	
National Bus Company	Aug 1986	private sale	
British Gas	Dec 1986	100%	
British Airways	Feb 1987	100%	
Rolls-Royce	May 1987	100%	
British Airports Authority	Jul 1987	100%	
Short Bros and Harland	?		Future prospect?
Water Authorities	?		Future prospect?
Naval Dockyards	?		Future prospect?
Crown Suppliers	?		Future prospect?
Hospital catering and cleaning	?	private sale	Future prospect?

Source: Adapted from Curwen (1986), table 6.3

The present government, therefore, assigns macroeconomic policy to the achievement of inflation and microeconomic policy to the achievement of employment. Prior to 1979 it was the reverse of this.

That aggregate demand *and* aggregate supply must be influenced simultaneously has been recognized by all parties. Where they differ is on whether demand or supply is the *driving* force behind the recovery. In the case of the Labour Party it is aggregate demand; while in the case of the Conservative Party it is aggregate supply. Furthermore, as Table 15.7 reveals, the emphasis on the supply side is in terms of the efficient and unhindered functioning of markets, most especially the labour market.

In Part I we made a point of constructing the aggregate supply curve in some detail. But even this treatment is fairly limited when trying to understand the present strategy. But, first, let us consider what can be noted in terms of our theory. The first point to make is that

Table 15.7 The government's strategy for jobs (Cmnd 9474)

---

1. 'The government's strategy for guiding and supporting the national effort for jobs has three interlocking parts;
   - First and most important is a sound and stable framework and economy and industrial policy. Sustained employment growth needs an economic setting in which enterprise can flourish and industry and commerce can compete successfully and raise output. The first priority has to be the control of inflation.
   - Secondly, within the economic framework, the government is encouraging jobs in particular ways, for example by removing obstacles which hamper employers taking on workers or prevent individuals using their potential, and by helping to modernise training so that jobseekers can acquire the right skills.
   - Thirdly, the government is taking direct action, as with its Community Programme, to tackle severe and deep-seated problems of unemployment for groups particularly hit by the changes in industry.'
2. '. . . Since 1979 clear government leadership and a steady course have laid a firm foundation for lasting recovery:

in *financial and economy policy*:
   - by bringing inflation under sustained control and maintaining a sound financial framework on which business planning can rely;
   - by restraining public expenditure, and so not weighing down the business on which all jobs ultimately depend;
   - by removing distortions in the tax system which weakened the incentive to work and wealth-creation, and hindered jobs;
   - by lifting bureaucratic controls on pay, prices, dividends, credit and foreign exchange;

in *industrial policy*:
   - by giving help and incentives to enterprise, especially in small firms;
   - by supporting innovation and the exploitation of new technology;
   - by reshaping regional policy, so that help to the most disadvantaged parts of Britain will give far better value for the taxpayer's money in creating jobs;
   - by easing the burden of regulation and simplifying the planning system;
   - by breaking up monopolies and fostering competition;
   - by releasing as much business as possible out of public-sector constraints into the challenge and opportunity of a free commercial setting;

in *labour market policy*:
   - by providing a surer and better balanced framework of law for responsible and constructive industrial relations;
   - by removing the National Insurance Surcharge tax on jobs;
   - by removing or easing impediments to taking on workers or taking up work;
   - by stimulating the reform of our education and training systems to meet the needs of a competitive modern economy;
   - by financing major new efforts in training for young people and adults;
   - by programmes which give unemployed people not just short-term help but better chances of getting jobs afterwards;
   - by modernising the information and support services for those seeking work.'

Source: Employment: The Challenge for the Nation (Cmnd 9474) 1985

aggregate supply is derived by combining the workings of the labour market and the aggregate production function (see Chapter 2). Any policy, therefore, which attempts to shift the aggregate supply curve to the right must operate, directly or indirectly, through the demand or the supply of labour, or by shifting the aggregate production function. Second, as outlined in Chapter 2, there is no obvious *policy instrument* by which the government can influence the labour market. The only instrument which is readily incorporated into the analysis is taxes on income (see especially Appendix 2.5). In Part I we pointed out that the *supply* of labour was dependent on the net expected wage. Putting expectations aside for the moment, the net wage is the gross wage adjusted for tax. Of course, income tax *is* an instrument of government. But in what way is a reduction in income tax supposed to shift the aggregate supply curve to the right?

In his budget speech of 1979, Sir Geoffrey Howe said

> We need to strengthen incentives, by allowing people to keep more of what they earn, so that hard work, talent and ability are properly rewarded.

And the same theme has been put forward by subsequent Chancellors. From micro-economics we know that a reduction in the rate of tax on incomes has both a substitution effect and an income effect, and that these work in *opposite* directions.[8] At the individual level a reduction in the tax rate will raise hours worked if the substitution effect outweighs the income effect (and assuming there are no complications from the standard working week). But there is no clear evidence that this is true at the individual level. There is even less evidence that it is true at the macroeconomic level. The evidence available for the UK would, if anything, suggest that at the aggregate level the income and substitution effects cancel each other out (Brown, 2nd edn, 1983). If this is indeed the case, then the aggregate supply curve is independent of the change in the tax rate. It may be argued that at the lower tax rate (with greater take-home pay) people work harder, that is to say individuals put in more *effort* so that effective labour hours have risen. But this would be very difficult to prove (and hence to refute!).

Even granting that a reduction in the tax rate increases the *supply curve* of labour, it does not follow that this will in fact shift the aggregate supply curve. What matters for the aggregate supply curve is not the amount of labour supplied at any particular wage, but, rather, the level of *employment* at a particular wage. To take an extreme example, suppose a reduction in the marginal rate of tax shifts the supply curve of labour to the right (downward). If prior to the reduction there was excess supply of labour at the ruling wage, then one possible outcome of the policy would simply be to increase the amount of demand deficient unemployment – employment would remain the same because nothing has altered the demand for labour and hence aggregate supply would remain the same. We return to the point that aggregate supply would only alter if those in employment put in more effort and became more efficient because of their greater take-home pay.

But this is too simplistic an interpretation of the present government's policy. It can be seen in terms of Table 15.7 that great stress is placed on improving the functioning of the labour market. The aim here is to create a situation where the ruling wage is the market clearing wage (where demand equals supply). At such an equilibrium wage, all those who wish to work can work. Furthermore, as we outlined in Part I, the aim would also be to establish the natural rate of employment. However, this policy will raise output and shift the aggregate supply curve to the right to the extent that the policy can bring about a reduction in the real wage. This will entice management to take on more workers, raise employment and hence raise aggregate supply. Although there is no obvious *instrument* of policy, it is undoubtedly a policy which, if successful, will shift the aggregate supply curve to the right. Any success the government may have in raising aggregate supply will not come from a reduction in the tax rate, but, rather, in the improved workings of the labour market (even though it may attribute the improvement to the tax reductions!). Tax changes should be seen for what they are: a redistribution of income.

What the theory in Part I does not develop in any way is how government policy can stimulate employment and output by influencing the *demand* curve for labour. It has to be recalled that the demand curve for labour is derived from equating the marginal revenue product with the money wage. From this relation a number of potential policies can be outlined. First, by increasing the degree of competition, as outlined in earlier sections, firms will have lower prices and greater employment and output. Second, the marginal revenue product of labour depends on the capital stock. Any policy which raises the capital stock will in all likelihood shift the marginal revenue product curve to the right, and hence raise the level of employment and output. Third, tax policies on profits could stimulate investment, as could a reduction in (or removal of) the national insurance surcharge. Finally, the government could influence investment through its policy towards interest rates and exchange rates.

The policies just alluded to directly or indirectly influence the demand for labour, but there are also policies which can influence the production function itself: namely, policies towards research and development. We will deal with this topic more fully in Chapter 18. Suffice it to say that such policies could be aimed at raising the level of output for any given level of input, which would mean a shift to the right in the long-run aggregate supply curve (and the long-run Phillips curve).

What is quite clear from our discussion of supply-side policies is that they are not as well defined as policies towards demand management, either in terms of policy instruments or in terms of government institutions. Although this does not necessarily mean that they are any less effective, it does mean that it is difficult for government to deliberately go out and influence aggregate supply. On the other hand, simply stating that the only role for government is to 'create a climate' for industry to thrive is tantamount to having no industrial policy at all, and to taking no responsibility for shifting aggregate supply to the right. A benign industrial policy can hardly be said to be a supply-side policy!

NOTES

1. This was in marked contrast to the inter-War period, when government policies encouraged the formation of cartels and the increased concentration of industry. It was a means of dealing with excess capacity and the structural decline of staple industries, and with the depression.

2. Only one planning agreement was concluded in the private sector.

3. Largely because he made financial support available for workers' cooperatives.

4. See Spence (1983) and Baumol (1982).

5. Or were assets to exceed a certain value.

6. Cairncross, Kay and Silberston (1977).

7. E.g., Kay and Silberston (1984), Beesley and Littlechild (1983), Bailey (1986), Hammond, Helm and Thompson (1985), Kay and Thompson (1986), Shackleton (1984), Curwen (1986), and Dodgson (1987).

8. See Shone (1981), Chapter A1, Brown (2nd edn, 1983) or any intermediate microeconomics textbook.

APPENDIX 15.1 THE MONOPOLIES AND MERGERS COMMISSION

It has generally been assumed that monopolies are a 'bad thing' if they take advantage of their monopoly power. Therefore, most capitalist countries have regulated the behaviour of monopolies. In the UK this was initiated in 1948 by the setting up of the Monopolies Commission under the Monopolies and Restrictive Practices Act. In 1965 the Commission's powers were extended to mergers, and in 1973 the body became known as the Monopolies and Mergers Commission (MMC), a term we use throughout this appendix. Following the Competition Act of 1980 the emphasis (in terms of the work undertaken) of the MMC shifted very much towards mergers.

The MMC deals with a number of situations as follows:

1. It investigates situations where one firm (the *dominant firm*) supplies 25% or more of the market share for a good or service (this was one-third prior to 1973).
2. Where *parent and subsidiary* company control 25% or more of the market.
3. Where two quite distinct companies *collude* in such a way as to restrict competition without a formal agreement.
4. To investigate *mergers* where assets are in excess of £5 million (£30 million after 1984) or where the market share is 25% or more.
5. After 1980, to investigate '*anti-competitive practices*' which have the effect of restricting. distorting or preventing competition.

In all cases the main criterion is whether the situation is against the public interest, although as Table 15.2 makes clear there are a number of other considerations to be taken into account by the Commission.

Reference to the MMC is normally made by the Director General of Fair Trading (DGFT). Thus, unlike the Restrictive Practices Trade Court, companies do not have to notify the MMC of their dominant position or intention to merge – it is up to the DGFT to find this out and recommend that the situation be investigated by the MMC. The recommendation by the Director General to the MMC does not carry with it a presumption that the monopoly is against the public interest; this has to be demonstrated by the MMC. Furthermore, the MMC itself does not have the power to enforce its decision if it considers the firm does have a monopoly. It makes a recommendation to the Secretary of State for Trade and Industry based on its findings, and it is the Secretary of State who makes the final decision. (In the past the relevant minister has included that for Prices and Consumer Affairs and for Trade.) In regard to the Policy towards 'anticompetitive practices', if the Office of Fair Trading find such practices, and if they persist, then a reference is made to the MMC, who will determine whether it is against the public interest. The 1980 Act also extended such powers to the investigation of certain public bodies, e.g. the nationalized industries, agricultural marketing boards, water operators and some bus operators.

The MMC's approach to monopolies and mergers has been said to be pragmatic. It takes a case-by-case approach, sometimes coming out against the firm (as with Kodak and Roche Products), while in other situations coming out in favour of the monopoly on efficiency grounds (as in the case of Pedigree Petfoods and the London Brick Company). More recently, the Commission has come out in favour of some companies on the grounds of risk in new innovation (as in the case of Rank-Xerox, Pilkingtons, and Redland and Marley), where such monopoly profits are expected to be transitory. Under the 1980 Act, there have been investigations of 'anti-competitive practices' (as in the case of TI Raleigh and Sheffield Newspapers). The extension to public sector bodies has led to a number of investigations. These have often involved a whole series of recommendations for improvements (as in the case of London Transport and the Civil Aviation Authority). The review by Ferguson (1985) suggests that 'the largest benefits to society may come from investigating the activities of government, since government-imposed entry barriers are the greatest hinderance to change and statutory monopolies are largely protected from the forces of competition'. (p. 39)

APPENDIX 15.2 INDUSTRIAL CONCENTRATION

A crucial concept in the structure–conduct–performance paradigm (see Scherer, 2nd edn, 1980) is that of industrial structure. But how is structure measured? Monopoly is distinguishable from monopolistic competition and perfect competition either in terms of the number of firms in the industry or because of barriers to entry which exist in the case of monopoly. Furthermore, monopolistic competition can be distinguished from perfect competition by the presence of product differentiation – giving rise to a downward sloping demand curve for the firm in the case of monopolistic competition

Table A15.2.1 Examples of 5-firm concentration ratios (gross value added),
UK manufacturing industry, 1982

Industry	5-firm concentration ratio (%)
Food, drink and tobacco	62
Coal and petroleum products	67
Chemicals and man-made fibres	55
Metal manufacture	74
Mechanical engineering	36
Electrical engineering	65
Telecommunications and electronic components	52
Shipbuilding and repairs	80
Vehicles	91
Aerospace equipment	76
Ordinance small arms and ammunition	92
Textiles	49
Leather and leather goods	38
Clothing and footwear	27
Bricks, pottery, glass	50
Timber and furniture	8
Domestic electrical appliances	56
Paper, printing, publishing	35

Source: Caslin, T. (1987), table 7.1

but a horizontal demand curve for the firm in perfect competition. Although market structure is often distinguished by the number of firms in the industry, what matters from a theoretical point of view is *potential* competition. Thus, even if an industry has only one firm it may still be perfectly competitive if the number of potential competitors is very large. Unfortunately, there is no way in practice to take account of potential competitors, and so measurement must be based on *actual* competition.

By far the most dominant form of market structure in the UK (and other capitalist countries) is oligopoly. Such industries are dominated by a few large (often very large) firms. The degree to which an industry is concentrated in the hands of a very few large firms can be measured in a variety of ways. Three measures are fairly common. Let s_i denote the share of firm i in whatever measure of economic activity is being used, e.g. sales, employment (where the firms are ranked so that (1) denotes the largest, (2) the next largest, etc.) for an industry with a total of T firms. The three common measures of industrial concentration are defined as, Sawyer (1981):

1. *5-firm concentration ratio*

$$C_5 = \sum_{i=1}^{5} s_i$$

2. *Herfindahl index*

$$H = \sum_{i=1}^{T} s_i^2$$

3. *Entropy*

$$E = \sum_{i=1}^{T} s_i \, \text{Log}(1/s_i)$$

Some indications of UK industrial concentration, using the most popular 5-firm ratio, are provided in Table A15.2. 1, although they are only a rough guide.

It is generally assumed that a higher concentration ratio means a lower level of competition, and possibly lower efficiency and poorer performance. However, care must be exercised in coming to such a conclusion because the 5-firm concentration ratio has a number of shortcomings as a measure of structure. In particular, it does not take account of entry barriers or the demand side of the market.

However, if such things remain constant over time, then trends in the concentration ratio can at least be fairly indicative of changes in industrial structure. Thus, Aaronovitch and Sawyer (1974), Hart and Clarke (1980) and Curry and George (1983) have studied the trend in concentration between 1935 and 1975. What does this evidence show? It shows that in the post-War period the degree of industrial concentration in the UK steadily increased until about 1975, and that there was a particularly rapid rise in industrial concentration in the period 1960–70.

In many cases, the 5-firm concentration ratio does not include imports or exports. This may be very significant for the UK. As we shall show in Section 17.3, the degree of import penetration into the UK has been steadily growing over the post-War period. Hence, the most effective form of competition is not necessarily coming from other firms situated in the UK, but, rather, from firms situated abroad, which do not enter the concentration ratio.

Part III

UK PROBLEMS

Chapter 16

DEALING WITH SHOCKS

One of the most striking features of the 1970s was the fact that many countries suffered major shocks to their economies. In our policy discussion in Part II, there were repeated references to shocks to the UK economy and also policy suggestions on how to deal with them. It was hinted in Part II that an *external* shock to an economy might require some different policy than an *internal* shock. But is this the case? Furthermore, the question arises as to whether the way in which an economy deals with shocks is dependent on *where* in the economic system the shock originates. For instance, if we consider only internal shocks, does it make a difference to policy whether the shock arises in the money market or in the goods market? There are the additional questions of whether shocks are anticipated or unanticipated and whether they are temporary or long-lasting. When explicitly considering the policy approach to take to shocks, the question of whether policy should be neutral, accommodating or extinguishing becomes important. In attempting to answer this question, we also need to consider the aim of stabilization, which we discussed in Chapter 13. For instance, if we consider a policy to cancel the effects of a shock, does it make a difference whether the policy is designed to eliminate the adverse effect on real income (output) or whether the policy is designed to eliminate the adverse effect on the rate of inflation? Undoubtedly, when considering external shocks, the question arises as to whether policy would be different under a fixed, floating, or managed exchange rate system. It is these sorts of questions which this chapter is addressing.

However, before discussing some of the more formal aspects of shocks it will be useful to begin by outlining some actual shocks which have occurred to the UK economy so that the analysis can be put in perspective.

16.1 SHOCKS TO THE UK ECONOMY

In this section we will discuss the following five major shocks to the UK economy:

1. OPEC oil price rises.
2. North Sea oil.
3. Prices and incomes policies.
4. Tax changes.
5. Productivity decline.

In this chapter we concentrate only on those aspects which give us some insight into the importance and difficulty of dealing with shocks.

1. OPEC oil price rises

One of the most significant structural changes in the 1970s was the dramatic rise in the price of crude oil of the OPEC countries – a rise from below an average of $2 per barrel prior to 1973 to an average of over $9 per barrel of South Arabian crude oil at the end of 1973. There was a second major increase in OPEC oil prices in 1979, when the average price per barrel rose from just under $14 to just over $19. The impact of these changes on the UK, as on other countries, was dramatic. It is important to realize that prior to 1973 there had been a steady movement away from domestic coal as a source of fuel and towards imported oil. To put the 1973 change in perspective, the net cost of UK fuel imports rose from about 1.5% of GDP to over 4%. Furthermore, the short-run elasticity of demand for oil is very low, and is even fairly low in the long run.

Three immediate results followed from the OPEC oil price rise. First, the UK value of fuel imports rose substantially. Second, as the same problem was faced by all non-OPEC countries, they in turn reduced the volume of their demand, which led to a fall in UK exports. The result of these two events was a deficit on the current account of the balance of payments. Third, because oil was a major input (either directly or indirectly) into many UK products, there was a general rise in the costs of production. The deflationary effect of the deterioration in net exports led to a reduction in aggregate demand, while the rise in the costs of production for many UK industries meant a decline in aggregate supply. Although the OPEC oil price rise is thus often seen as a supply shock, it incorporates *both* supply and demand components.

The adjustment faced by the UK was compounded by the fact that it was known that the North Sea contained oil reserves. The unknown factors were: (1) how much oil, (2) if produced, when it would come on stream, (3) whether OPEC intended any further price rises, and (4) what pricing policy should be applied to the oil from the North Sea. Important as these are, they have little bearing on the fact that the OPEC oil price rise was a major shock to the economy which, in the short- to medium-term, had to be dealt with.

2. North Sea oil

The first North Sea oil (NSO) strike was made in Norwegian waters when the Ekofisk field was discovered by the Phillips group in November 1969, while later discoveries were concentrated in the British sector. Oil itself began to flow in 1975, but major production did not begin until about 1977. The increased production of NSO was intended to replace a high proportion of OPEC oil imports. However, NSO is of a higher quality (it is light and has a low sulphur content), and so commands a higher price on world markets. Generally, however, the NSO price is determined after the OPEC price is set – where the margin depends on (1) quality, (2) location, and (3) political security.

When considering NSO in relation to a shock to the economy, it is worth bearing in mind that there are basically three main stages in the life of an oil province: (1) exploration, (2) development, and (3) production. Each of these has a different time profile, involve different activities, and has different effects on expenditure and employment.

The discovery of any deposit, certainly one as major as NSO, is a rise in the productive potential of the economy.[1] Consequently, this would lead to an increase in long-run aggregate supply. There is also, however, the effect on the net export position of the country. Britain has exported much of the higher quality NSO and, to some extent, reduced its imports of OPEC oil. The result is an improvement in the oil sector of the balance of payments accounts. In the medium term, however, the result on net exports is less. Why is this? The improvement in the net oil sector results in a net demand for sterling; this in turn leads to an appreciation of sterling, which itself leads to a deterioration in the non-oil sectors. If, as seems likely, the benefits of net oil exports outweigh the deterioration of the non-oil sectors, then there will be a rise in aggregate demand. Hence, the NSO shock affects both aggregate demand and aggregate supply.[2]

3. Prices and incomes policies

We have already dealt with these in Section 12.4, and so we can be fairly brief here. Prices and incomes policies can either be seen as a distortion to the economy or as a shock. In essence they are introduced to contain the rate of inflation. They accomplish this either by shifting the short-run Phillips curve down or tilting it (where a wages freeze would be an extreme form of tilting the Phillips curve in the $W - U$ space). Since a prices and incomes policy is intended to operate either directly on prices or on incomes, then it follows that such a policy affects only the aggregate supply curve directly (or Phillips curve). Such policies in the UK were frequently imposed in the 1970s, but whether they were effective or not is still being debated.

4. Tax changes

There has been a number of tax changes in the UK in the post-War period, some of which are outlined in Section 9.2. Like prices and incomes policies, tax changes can either be considered as distortionary changes, or as a shock to the economy – which can either be a favourable shock or an unfavourable one. When looked at from the point of view of shocks to the economy, what matters are major tax changes. For instance, the imposition of an indirect tax, such as VAT (especially at a fairly high rate and over a substantial range of products and services), will raise the costs of production and so lead to a decrease in aggregate supply (a shift left in the AS curve). However, if this is simultaneously combined with direct tax cuts, then the result of this latter tax change can in itself have two possible results. First, the reduction in the marginal rate of tax will increase disposable income and so lead to an increase in aggregate demand (AD will shift to the right). Second, if the substitution effect of a tax change on labour outweighs the income effect on labour, then this may lead to a favourable movement in aggregate supply (AS will shift to the right). Although the outcome on real income is uncertain, the likely result on the price level is that it will rise.

A rise in such items as profits tax, or the imposition of the selective employment tax (SET), will raise the costs of production and in all likelihood will lead to a decrease in aggregate supply (a shift left in AS); conversely for a reduction in the rate of profits tax or a reduction in the rate of SET. At the present time, however, the major debate is over the effect of reducing direct taxes. As just pointed out in the preceding paragraph, this will have two effects: one raising aggregate demand, and the other affecting the aggregate supply curve. The problematic response is on the aggregate supply curve. Even though a reduction in the rate of tax may increase the supply of labour (and then only if the substitution effect outweighs the income effect), the position of the aggregate supply curve is governed more by the *demand* for labour. Only if the labour market is clearing does it follow that a rise in labour supply will lead to a fall in the wage and a rise in the demand and supply of labour. Since this is highly unlikely for the UK at the present time, then it does not necessarily follow that a tax reduction will lead to a shift to the right in aggregate supply. However, given that tax cuts of this nature are combined with policies to improve labour market clearing, then the possible favourable effects on aggregate supply are more likely to be realized.

5. Productivity decline

There was a general view that UK productivity has declined since the Second World War, and has declined relative to other industrial countries. Such a view highlights *two* aspects to productivity decline. First, there is the decline in UK output per unit of labour (a decline in a_L in terms of the model of Chapter 2). Second, there is the decline in UK labour productivity relative to that abroad. Since this usually means that UK labour costs are rising relative to those abroad, this results in a decline in UK competitiveness (a fall in R in terms of the model of Chapter 2). Since we deal with UK competitiveness in some detail in the next chapter, all we will concentrate on here is the decline in output per unit of labour.

   Taking the period since 1960, there has been no obvious declining trend in labour productivity for the economy as a whole. In fact, the average change, using index numbers for labour productivity on annual data, gives a figure of about 2% increase for this period. However, there were significant declines in labour productivity in 1974 and 1975 (a decline of 1.8% and 1.5% respectively) and in 1980, the latter decline being over 2% relative to the previous year. These two periods indicate a major shift in the aggregate supply curve (and the short-run Phillips curve) to the left, and can be considered as significant shocks to the supply side of the economy.

16.2 SHOCKS AND STABILIZATION

In Chapter 13 we discussed automatic (or built-in) stabilizers. The argument is basically that the greater such things as income tax, VAT, employment benefits, etc., the smaller the size of the multiplier. Hence, for any autonomous change in aggregate demand, the impact on *equilibrium* income (and output) will be less. (Recall that the change in equilibrium income is the multiplier multiplied by the autonomous change.) The significance of automatic stabilizers is that they are *automatic*. Why is this so important? It means that for any shock to the economic system, these automatic stabilizers will reduce the impact of the shock on equilibrium income without any person or institution having to decide that there is a shock; or to decide whether to do something about it.

   It is important to bear in mind that the interest and significance of automatic stabilizers arises from concern about *demand* shocks: usually shocks to the autonomous components of aggregate demand, in fact. This analysis grew out of Keynesian economics, and with the aggregate supply curve assumed horizontal at some price level, the main focus of attention was the impact on income arising from a demand shock: either through some fiscal change, such as a change in income tax or VAT, or through monetary policy, such as a call by the Bank of England for an increase special deposits from the clearing banks.

Within this analysis it is, of course, possible to consider shocks from the world economy. With exports treated as exogenous, an international shock would be seen as a change either in autonomous exports or in the autonomous component of imports. However, lumping together all autonomous components of aggregate demand can be misleading. It gives the impression that the *source* of the disturbance to aggregate demand does not matter. This in turn leads to the mistaken view that the *solution* to a demand shock is independent of its source. The question arises, however, of whether the source of the shock makes a difference to its solution? In analysing this, consider three possible sources of shock:

(a) a disturbance in the goods market;
(b) a disturbance in the money market; and
(c) a disturbance in the trade sector.

A goods-market disturbance. Suppose there is a decline in business confidence which leads to a fall in investment at all levels of interest rate. The situation is illustrated in Fig. 16.1. The decline in autonomous investment leads to a shift left in the IS curve, from IS_0 to IS_1, with a resulting fall in real income (y_0 to y_1) and a fall in interest rates (r_0 to r_1). One possible adjustment (correction) to this real shock is for the government to increase government spending. This will shift the IS curve back to IS_0. Alternatively, it could have used monetary expansion to raise the money supply so shifting the LM curve from LM_0 to LM_1. Although such a policy would stabilize income at level y_0, it would lead to a fall in interest rates to r_2. Even if the aim of the government was to stabilize interest rates at r_0, which it could do by decreasing the money supply and so shifting LM from LM_0 to LM_2, this would lead to a major fall in income (to y_2). Thus the most sensible strategy for a real disturbance is to correct the disturbance at the source and raise autonomous expenditure.

A money-market disturbance. Suppose there is a general rise in liquidity preference so that individuals increase their demand for money at all levels of interest rate. This will shift the LM curve from LM_0 to LM_1 in Fig. 16.2. Once again, the authorities could correct this by raising the level of money supply, so shifting the LM curve back to LM_0. If, on the other hand, it had pursued a fiscal correction, then it would have raised spending if it wished to stabilize income (shifting IS to IS_1); or reduced spending to stabilize interest rates (shifting IS to IS_2). Again the most sensible strategy is to correct the shock at source: namely, to correct a monetary shock by means of monetary policy.

A trade sector disturbance. Suppose there is a general depression in world markets. This will lead to a decline in UK exports. On the face of it, this appears to be like a real disturbance. The fall in exports shifts the IS curve to the left, just as in the case illustrated in Fig. 16.1. It is possible to correct this by the government pursuing an expansionary policy. However, the simplest solution is to correct at source, and carry out a trade policy which expands exports – such as an export guarantee. This policy has the further advantage that it does not distort other sectors of the economy in order to correct a trade distortion.[3]

The general result can be formulated in terms of a proposition.

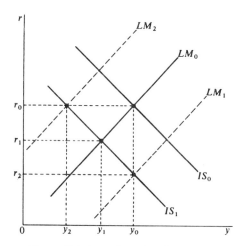

Figure 16.1 A goods market disturbance.

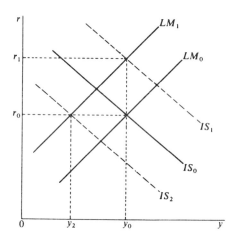

Figure 16.2 A money market disturbance.

Proposition
A demand shock to the economy should be corrected at source: a real shock should be corrected by adjustment to the goods market; a monetary shock corrected by adjustment to the money market; a trade shock corrected by a trade policy.

Of course, this is a matter of degree. It could be taken still further depending on the sectoral breakdown. For instance, suppose a real shock is in terms of a decline in investment, then it could be argued that the appropriate policy is a stimulus to investment and not a general rise in government spending. Similarly, a rise in autonomous consumption could be corrected by a constraint on consumer spending, and so on. However, what matters in the present analysis is that the major sector breakdown is in the goods market, the money market and the trade sector (and, later, the labour market). These sectors will thus categorize the sources of disturbances.

What is also clear from our discussion of shocks so far is that the appropriate policy solution is not dependent on which variable is being stabilized. There is one difficulty with this analysis which should not be overlooked. The *appropriate* policy may not be the same as the most *effective* policy. When policy-makers are concerned with the effectiveness of policy, their attention is often directed to the stabilization of just one variable, income say. Thus, although a disturbance may arise in the goods market, if monetary policy is more effective than fiscal policy, then income stabilization can be achieved by correcting a real shock by means of monetary policy. The difficulty with this approach is that a shock in one sector is corrected by means of distorting a *different* sector. Over time it is no longer clear which distortions are correcting for which shock, and whether the distortions themselves are engendering inefficiencies within the economy.

16.3 AGGREGATE SUPPLY SHOCKS

It will be recalled that in Section 16.1 we outlined a number of shocks which occurred in the 1970s, and it is quite clear that all these are supply shocks. In other words, they shift the aggregate supply curve and the short-run Phillips curve, generally upwards (to the left) and could, in the long run, shift the long-run aggregate supply curve to the left. In this section we will deal only with the short-run effects of supply shocks, leaving consideration of the long run effects until the next section.

What is the appropriate policy solution (correction? for supply shocks?) In Fig. 16.3 we have a shift left in the aggregate supply curve from AS_0 to AS_1; for example, due to a rise in OPEC oil prices, which occurred in 1973, or a rise in world raw material commodity prices, which occurred at the beginning of the 1970s. One solution, of course, is to do nothing. The result of this would be to raise prices from P_0 to P_1 and reduce real income from y_0 to y_1. If no policy correction was undertaken, the rise in unemployment would bring down money wages. This fall in money wages, along with the rise in the price level, will reduce real wages. The decline in real wages will increase the demand for labour, and hence employment. This leads to a shift down (to the right) in the aggregate supply curve. The adjustment will be complete when AS_1 returns to AS_0.

If, however, the aim is to stabilize income in the short run, then this may suggest a policy of raising aggregate demand and so shifting AD to AD_1. However, the result of this policy solution is to raise the price level to P_2. The *inflationary* impact of this policy is illustrated in Fig. 16.3(*b*). The oil price rise shifts the short-run Phillips curve from SPC_0 to SPC_1. Inflation rises to $\hat{P}_1$. If this is offset by government policy, shifting the demand-pressure curve to DP_1, then the result is a higher rate of inflation, namely $\hat{P}_2$, This increase in inflation can only be a long-run solution if the stimulus to demand is a rise in the growth of the money supply to $\hat{M}_1$ (the original level being $\hat{M}_0 = \hat{P}_0$).

An alternative policy solution is to shift the aggregate supply curve back to AS_0. Not only would this stabilize income, it would also stabilize prices. The obvious conclusion we arrive at, then, is that for a supply shock the appropriate policy is a supply-side policy. This is in conformity with our analysis on the demand side. Once again it suggests that the appropriate policy is to implement a correction at the source of the disturbance.

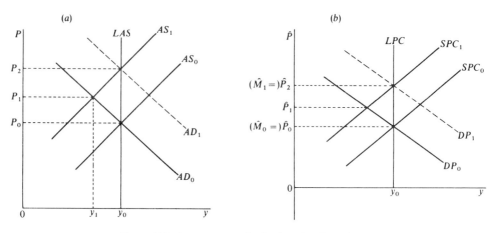

Figure 16.3 Aggregate supply shock and policy solutions.

If supply-side adjustment is the appropriate response to a supply shock, then why was it not undertaken in the 1970s? The reasons are many. First, it was not obvious what *cumulative* impact the supply shocks would have. The point is that these shocks were largely unanticipated. Not only were they unanticipated, but it took time to recognize many of them – with the exception of the OPEC oil price rise. Second, Keynesian demand management was still dominant. Policy-makers had a tendency to stabilize income by means of demand management no matter what the source of the disturbance to income. As we have outlined elsewhere, this simply increased inflationary pressure for the future. Third, a number of attempts at shifting aggregate supply and the short-run Phillips curve to the right failed. The most obvious were the whole variety of prices and income policies which were implemented throughout the 1970s.[4] The point is that even with a supply shock, it is *easier* to stabilize income by implementing a policy of demand management. However, the very act of stabilizing income by this means, when the source of the shock is on the supply side, is to *destabilize* prices!

So far we can establish the following three policy requirements with regard to shocks, whether on the demand side or the supply side:

1. It is necessary to identify their *source*.
2. It is necessary to establish their *magnitude*.
3. It is necessary to decide on the instrument(s) to *correct* them.

16.4 LONG-RUN RESULT OF A SHOCK

What is the long-run result of a shock to the economy? Consider first a demand shock, which shifts the aggregate demand curve from AD_0 to AD_1, illustrated in Fig. 16.4. The short-run result is to move the economy from equilibrium point A (on the long-run aggregate supply curve) to point B. Prices rise from P_0 to P_1 and income rises to y_1. However, the rise in prices reduces real wages, since nominal wages in the short run remain

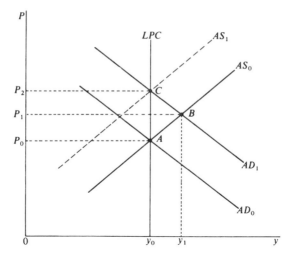

Figure 16.4 Long-run result of a demand shock.

unchanged. This fall in the real wage leads workers to negotiate for a higher money wage, which has the result of shifting the AS curve upward. So long as actual prices and expected prices do not coincide, adjustment will continue. As we indicated in Part I, the results are a shift in aggregate supply to AS_1, a rise in the price level to P_2 and a fall in real income from y_1 back to y_0, hence moving the economy from point B to point C. Thus, a demand shock which raises aggregate demand will, in the long run, result in no change in output but will lead to a higher price level.

Consider next a supply shock which shifts the short-run supply curve up from AS_0 to AS_1, but leaves the long-run aggregate supply curve unaffected, as shown in Fig. 16.5. Just as in the demand shock, prices rise from P_0 to P_1; however, income falls from y_0 to y_2. In the short run the economy moves from point A to point C. But what happens in the longer run? Over time, the rise in unemployment associated with the lower level of income will lead to a decline in money (and real) wages, which will lead to a shift down in the aggregate supply curve. As this takes place the economy moves down the aggregate demand curve until point A is reached once again.

In the long run, therefore, the economy if left alone will return to its long-run equilibrium point A. But two considerations are worth bearing in mind. First, in the case of both a demand shock and a supply shock, the adjustment of the economy over time is dependent on the change in real wages. In the case of the demand shock, the adjustment depends on how workers alter their money wages as a result of the decline in the real wage; while in the case of the supply shock, the adjustment depends on real wages declining as a result of the unemployment. To the extent that either of these adjustments do not occur, or occur only very slowly, then the adjustment of the economy to such a demand or supply shock will not take place, or will take place only very slowly. Second, the actual rise in prices could result in a revision of price expectations upwards. If this happens, then the aggregate supply curve will shift up for both types of shocks. In the case of a demand shock this is likely to speed up the adjustment process; while if the shock is on the supply side, then the revision of price expectations upwards will prolong the adjustment period.

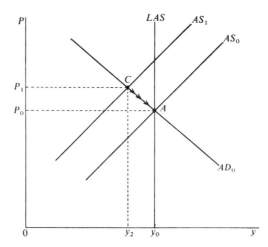

Figure 16.5 Long-run result of a supply shock.

What is the long-run result of a supply shock which in fact shifts the long-run aggregate supply curve?[5] Suppose the rise in oil prices (along with the rise in world commodity prices) moves the short-run aggregate supply curve from SAS_0 to SAS_1, *and* the long-run aggregate supply curve from LAS_0 to LAS_1, as shown in Fig. 16.6. But the shift up in the short-run aggregate supply curve is on the assumption of *no* change in expectations. As workers revise their expectations upwards, then we have a new *set* of curves, one of which is labelled SAS_2 in Fig. 16.6. In the short run, before expectations are revised, the economy moves from point A to point B. If the government does nothing, then the rise in unemployment will eventually bring down money wages (and, with the rise in prices, real wages also). Expectations will also be revised. Hence, the short-run supply curve will shift down until it reaches SAS_3, and the economy moves to point C.[6]

16.5 ACCOMMODATING POLICIES

We have pointed out that the 1970s saw a number of adverse supply shocks. Although it is possible for the economy to return to long-run equilibrium if left alone, this may involve prolonged periods of high unemployment *and* high levels of inflation. Such a situation is sometimes referred to as a *neutral demand policy*. However, it is possible for the authorities to accommodate an adverse supply shock by raising the level of aggregate demand. Such accommodation can either be *partial* or *total*. We have already illustrated a total demand accommodation to an adverse supply shock in terms of Fig. 16.3, where aggregate demand is raised to AD_1 in order to counteract the adverse affect of the supply shift from AS_0 to AS_1. Similarly, in Fig. 16.6 a movement of aggregate demand from AD_0 to AD_1 is fully accommodating (and note that expectations are fulfilled). However, the policy-makers should avoid returning income to the original level by shifting AD to AD_2 and the economy to point F, since this is 'over-accommodating' and will be highly inflationary. A partial accommodation would be the same but the magnitude of the change would be less (hence

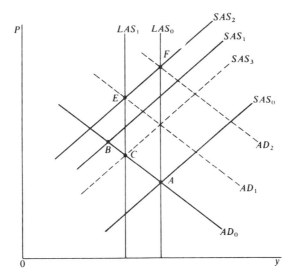

Figure 16.6 Long-run result of supply shock which also shifts LAS.

the shift in aggregate demand would be less than AD_1). It is clear, however, that both a partial and a total demand accommodation will lead to inflationary pressure – with total accommodation giving rise to the greater pressure.

Note that neutral and accommodating policies are with reference to real income, i.e. real income is not stimulated through demand in the case of a neutral policy; or real income is stimulated through demand in the case of accommodating policy (both partial and total). However, a policy correction may concentrate more on the problem of inflation than on real income. This is illustrated in Fig. 16.7, where we now concentrate on the dynamic aspects. The initial situation is given by the short-run Phillips curve, SPC_0, and the demand-pressure curve, DP_0. Suppose a supply shock leads to a rise in the short-run Phillips curve from SPC_0 to SPC_1. In the absence of any policy correction the economy will, in the short run, move from point A to point B, and inflation will rise from $\hat{P}_0$ to $\hat{P}_1$. However, suppose the government is more concerned about inflation than about unemployment. It may wish to *extinguish* the inflationary affect of the supply shock. To do this it would reduce the growth in demand and shift the demand-pressure curve from DP_0 to DP_1, moving the economy, in the short run, to point C and so returning inflation to level $\hat{P}_0$. This has thus been called an *extinguishing policy*,[7] Gramlich (1979).

In the neutral and extinguished policies the eventual rate of inflation remains constant at the initial level, although it will rise during the adjustment period. However, in the case of accommodating policy, whether partial or total, the rate of inflation will rise. This will mean that individuals' inflationary expectations will be incorrect. There will thus be a revision of expectations upwards. The result of this is higher prices and a decline in real aggregate demand towards its previous level. To eliminate this problem a government would have to accommodate once more. The conclusion we come to, therefore, is that accommodating demand policy to reduce the effects of a supply shock will simply lead to inflation in the long run, while an extinguishing policy will lead to a greater recession. Neither alternative is appealing!

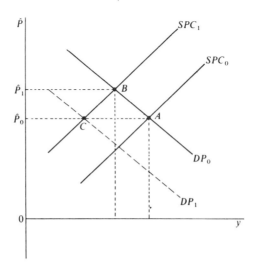

Figure 16.7 Extinguishing policy towards inflation.

16.6 TEMPORARY AND PERMANENT SHOCKS

A number of the shocks which occurred world-wide in the early 1970s were a result of crop failures. In general, these are one-off events: they are temporary in nature. Thus, for one period only, the aggregate supply curve shifts upward, since the crop failure leads to an increase in grain prices. The price level will rise, as will the rate of inflation. However, in the next period the aggregate supply curve returns to its former level and so does the rate of inflation. In the case of such a temporary shock, and assuming no government intervention to offset the shock, there is no reason why consumers should adjust their expectations. They will be aware that the rise in prices (or inflation) is purely temporary.

However, the rise in OPEC oil prices is slightly different. In this case oil prices would be raised but not lowered. The intention was to raise the price of oil and maintain the higher prices. In this instance, therefore, there was every expectation of higher prices. However, there was no real necessity to change the level of expected inflation. Why not? The inflation level would rise initially after the price rise, so raising the general price level. But thereafter the inflation rate should return to its former level. In this instance policy-makers can raise demand pressure to eliminate unemployment, and then reverse the policy when inflation returns to its former level. Inflation would only rise if in each period OPEC raised its oil price, or if people expected further price rises. In the mid-1970s, although OPEC raised its prices (on two occasions), this was not expected.

16.7 FAVOURABLE SUPPLY SHOCK: NORTH SEA OIL

Not all supply shocks need to be adverse. The discovery of North Sea oil was a favourable supply shock to the British economy; as was gas for the Dutch economy, shifting the long-run aggregate supply curve to the right. However, even this statement must be treated with caution. If the result of the discovery is to appreciate the exchange rate, which in turn leads to a loss of competitiveness in the non-oil sector, then it is just possible that the long-run result is adverse. Even so, the discovery of oil and gas is an autonomous increase in factor endowments, and hence a potential increase in the economy's output.

The result of a North Sea oil shock is not simply a shift in the long-run supply curve to the right, as illustrated in Fig. 16.8. This shock, analysed in terms of the diagram, is best thought of as a domestic shock, such as some major change in taxation – either on labour or on company profits. This would shift the long-run aggregate supply to the right, as shown in the diagram. However, the presence of North Sea oil has a major impact on the balance of trade, which in turn affects the exchange rate.

Consider first the impact on the trade balance. Oil is a major import. The discovery of North Sea oil allows the UK to import less oil and/or to export oil, which it did not formerly do. In the case of the UK it imports less oil but it also exports oil, since North Sea oil is of a higher quality than Arabian oil. The result of this is a rise in net exports. The rise in net exports will shift the aggregate demand curve to the right, to AD_1 in Fig. 16.8. However, the long-run results depend on *two* further impacts. First, the reduction in net exports arising from the oil account leads to an *appreciation* of sterling. The appreciation raises export prices and lowers import prices. This, in turn, will lead to a decline in the non-oil net export situation, which will shift the aggregate demand curve to the left, from AD_1 to AD_2. The second result depends on what happens to the price level. On average this should fall. The favourable shift in the aggregate supply should lower the overall price level. Although export prices are rising the price of imports is falling. The fall in import prices, at least for the UK, should dominate the rise in export prices, so leading to a fall in the overall price level. Hence, the price level is most likely to fall, with the economy reaching a final point B in Fig. 16.8. Once again we see that the result of a shock depends very much on its source.

16.8 SHOCKS UNDER FIXED AND FLEXIBLE EXCHANGE RATES

The preceding section highlighted the fact that the result of a foreign shock depends on the impact on the exchange rate. However, there can only be an impact on the exchange rate if it is floating or is managed. Under a perfectly fixed exchange rate there can be no impact from this source. Of course, a shock – whether domestic or foreign – will still have an impact. Exactly where that impact will be depends on the source of the shock.

Consider first a domestic shock under a fixed exchange rate. The situation is illustrated in Fig. 16.9, where the initial situation is at point A in Fig. 16.9(a) and at point E_0 in Fig. 16.9(b), with AD_0 and AS_0 being the initial aggregate demand and supply. Suppose there is a rise in autonomous consumption. This will shift the IS curve to the right, to IS_1, and will also shift AD to the right, to AD_1. Given that point A was a point of balance of payments equilibrium, then the result of this shock is to create a surplus on the balance of payments. Although the rise in income leads to a deterioration in the current account balance, the rise in interest rates leads to a capital inflow which more than compensates for the deterioration in the current account. The capital inflow raises the money supply, shifting the LM curve to LM_1. However, the resulting rise in prices to P_1 will create adjustments,

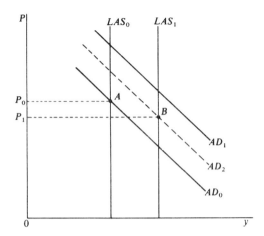

Figure 16.8 North Sea oil shock.

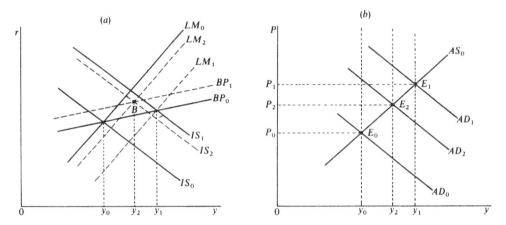

Figure 16.9 A domestic shock under a fixed exchange rate.

shifting the IS curve left and the BP curve up as competitiveness deteriorates, while the LM curve shifts left as real money balances decline. These changes will continue until a new equilibrium is established at point B in (a) and point E_2 in (b).

Next, consider a foreign shock, say a rise in US interest rates. This will not affect the aggregate supply curve, nor will it *directly* influence the aggregate demand curve. The aggregate demand curve is related to net exports. The foreign interest rate, as Chapter 5 made clear, affects only the net capital inflow. Therefore, a rise in the US interest rate will reduce the net capital inflow (or increase the net outflow of capital). This will shift the BP curve up to BP_1 and reduce the money supply, so shifting the aggregate demand curve to the left, to AD_1 in Fig. 16.10(a). The resulting fall in the price level to P_1 will improve the competitive position of the home country. This in turn will shift the BP curve down to BP_2 and the IS curve right to IS_2, with the eventual result that the aggregate demand curve shifts to AD_2 (Fig. 16.10(b)).

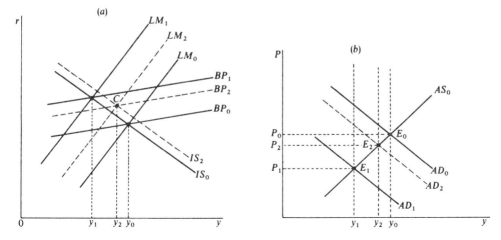

Figure 16.10 A foreign shock under a fixed exchange rate.

Return now to the same two shocks but assume that the exchange rate is floating. The situation is illustrated in Fig. 16.11. In the case of the domestic shock, the shift in IS to IS_1 and the consequent surplus on the balance of payments will lead to an appreciation of the exchange rate. This will shift the BP curve up to BP_1 and shift the IS curve left to IS_2. The eventual equilibrium is B' and E_2' in terms of Fig. 16.11(a and b).

The situation under floating is illustrated in Fig. 16.12. The initial impact of arise in overseas interest rates is to shift the BP curve to BP_1. Since money flows out of the home country, the exchange rate depreciates. The depreciation shifts the BP curve down; but simultaneously, the depreciation stimulates net exports and so shifts IS to the right. Since these impacts shift the AD curve to the right, there is a rise in the price level. The rise in the price level reverses the impact of the depreciation to some extent. The end result is B'' in Fig. 16.12(a) and E_2'' in Fig. 16.12(b).

What can we conclude from the analysis? The first point is that shocks will lead to adjustments of the domestic economy – whether the shock is domestic or foreign. Second, the adjustments that take place depend fundamentally on two things: (1) the source of the shock, and (2) whether the exchange rate is fixed or floating. Third, if income stabilization is taken as a goal of policy, then it is not obvious that either a fixed or a floating exchange rate *for all circumstances* is the 'best' exchange rate regime to accomplish this. It follows, therefore, that a policy of management is likely to be the appropriate policy for achieving such stabilization. The same is true if inflation stabilization is the goal of policy. The policy conclusion we come to from an analysis of shocks is that management of the exchange rate is a possible sensible strategy to follow.

NOTES

1. However, only in the longer term. In the short-term exploration involves costs with little benefit. Only when the oil comes on stream will the benefits outweigh the costs.

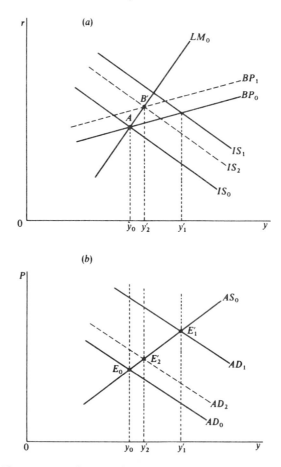

Figure 16.11 A domestic shock under a flexible exchange rate.

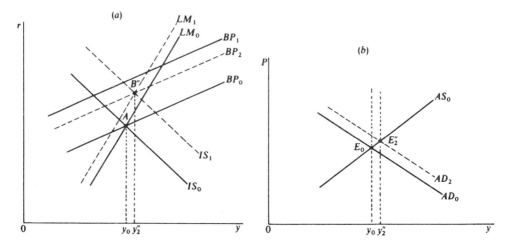

Figure 16.12 A foreign shock under a flexible exchange rate.

2. Whether NSO actually was the cause of sterling's appreciation in the late 1970s, see Fig. A.11.4.1 in Appendix 11.4, is problematic. At the time the government's attempt to deal with inflation resulted in high interest rates and consequently large capital inflows. These capital inflows also put pressure on sterling to appreciate. It has become extremely difficult to disentangle the individual effects on the exchange rate. See Spencer (1986).

3. This is basically the familiar result in international economics: namely, domestic distortions should be corrected by a domestic policy and trade distortions by a trade policy. Only recently have macroeconomists come to recognize the same proposition.

4. See Chapter 12.

5. Factors likely to shift the long-run aggregate supply curve are: (1) growth in factor inputs, e.g. labour, capital and natural resources; (2) a permanent change in productivity; (3) a permanent change in competitiveness.

6. If B is to the right of LAS_1, then price expectations will continue to rise until the new SAS curve cuts AD_0 on LAS_1.

7. Had wage contracts been 100% index-linked, then any policy reducing demand pressure by *less* than the move to DP_1 will result in an inflationary spiral, since the increase in inflation will be matched by an increase in money wages.

Chapter 17

DECLINING UK COMPETITIVENESS

One of the most serious problems facing the UK is the decline in its competitive position in world markets. Declining competitiveness would not be a serious problem if the UK was not such an open economy and its trade (and the rest of the economy) was not so dependent on manufacturing. But the UK is a manufacturing nation, and has been since the Industrial Revolution. What we are attempting to address in this chapter are the reasons for the decline in UK competitiveness, whether such decline is inevitable and what it means for the manufacturing base of the economy.

One feature of the international economy that has been stressed throughout this book is the fact that the exchange rate is determined both by the flow of goods and services *and* by capital flows. Monetarist arguments suggest that in the long run the exchange rate is determined by purchasing power parity (going as far as to argue this in absolute form, see Chapter 5). In this case capital flows have very little bearing on the issue of competitiveness. But this view is too simplistic. Capital flows influence interest rates which in turn influence investment decisions – unless investment is totally interest inelastic. Such investment, in turn, will partly determine what goods are produced in the future, the price they sell at, and the quality at which they are produced. The fact that such influences are *indirect* makes it that much more difficult to demonstrate the cause of the decline in competitiveness.

Important as the exchange rate is in determining UK competitiveness, it is not the only reason for its decline. Competitiveness, of course, can be measured in a variety of ways, as we will see in Section 17.2, but to the extent that it is the ratio of prices of goods sold at home and abroad (denominated in a common currency), differing rates of inflation at home and abroad will thus be important determining factors. However, for this to be a major reason for the decline in UK competitiveness it would be necessary to demonstrate that the rate of inflation in the UK has persistently been above that of her trading partners. Such an explanation would not only explain a decline in UK exports, but would also explain a rise in UK imports: a rise in *import penetration*. It is important to realize that a decline in competitiveness can come about from either a decline in exports and/or a rise in imports (a decline in import substitute industries). Although the major part of this chapter is concerned with the decline in UK export competitiveness, in Section 17.3 we will deal briefly with the rise in import penetration.

One purpose of this chapter is an attempt to sort out short-term from long-term explanations for the decline in UK competitiveness. A number of writers have emphasized the declining manufacturing base of the economy,[1] which has led to a declining performance in world markets. When attention is directed to this as an explanation, we turn away from price factors and concentrate on such questions as investment, quality, after-sales service, the commodity composition of trade and the geographical distribution of trade. The change, when put into historical perspective, has led to the view that Britain is going through a process of *deindustrialization*. We will discuss the decline in the manufacturing base, as emphasized by Bacon and Eltis, in Section 17.5, and in Section 17.6 we will take up the 'Cambridge' view on deindustrialization.

Although the 'Cambridge' view directs attention to declining price competitiveness, a number of economists have emphasized the decline in non-price competitiveness. Furthermore, attention has been directed to why the UK is uncompetitive in non-price factors. We take up this issue in Section 17.7, where we also consider some of the policies which have been suggested for reversing the decline in UK competitiveness.

From the list of issues that this chapter will be addressing it is clear that no reason is readily agreed upon for the decline in UK competitiveness. Furthermore, the reasons that have been advanced range over the whole spectrum of macro *and* microeconomics. In order, therefore, to put the issues in some sort of perspective it is essential that we begin this chapter with some observations about the changing pattern of UK trade and UK manufacturing.

17.1 THE CHANGING PATTERN OF UK TRADE AND THE DECLINE IN UK MANUFACTURING

In the post-War period a number of changes have occurred in the pattern of UK trade, most of which point to the decline in the competitive performance of UK manufactures. In this section we simply set out the facts and trends, leaving interpretation to later sections.

Following the Industrial Revolution, the typical pattern of UK trade was the export of manufactures and the import of foodstuffs and other raw materials. Britain traded mainly with the Commonwealth and the overseas sterling area countries. The geographical pattern of UK merchandise trade (excluding, as it does, services) has switched from these locations to the countries of Western Europe, especially those of the EEC. This change is shown dramatically in Table 17.1. Britain joined the EEC in 1973. Just prior to entry, the current nine members accounted for about 30% of UK exports and imports. By 1987 the export share had risen to 49.4%, while imports had risen to 52.7%.

Two other features are shown in Table 17.1. First, Japan has been a growing source of imports for the UK, rising from 0.6% in 1955 to 5.8% by 1987. On the other hand, the share in UK exports to Japan rose slightly between 1955 and 1970, falling throughout the 1970s, but rising to 1.9% by 1987. Second, there has been a major decline in imports from the oil-exporting countries. This has clearly been a direct result of North Sea oil. However, the oil-exporting countries have become a more significant market for UK exports, although exports fell from 10.1% in 1980 to 6.5% in 1987.

The switch in geographical location just outlined was also accompanied by a change in the commodity structure of UK trade, which is illustrated in Tables 17.2 and 17.3. Table 17.2 shows the changing commodity structure of UK imports. The major decline has been in food, beverages and tobacco. There has also been a fairly significant decline in industrial

Table 17.1 UK merchandise trade by source and destination, 1955–87

	(%)				
	1955	1970	1975	1980	1987
Imports (cif)					
Western Europe	25.7	41.5	51.1	55.9	66.4
EEC	12.6	27.1	36.9	41.3	52.7
North America	19.5	20.5	13.5	15.0	11.5
USA	10.9	12.9	9.8	12.1	9.7
Other developed countries	14.2	9.4	8.0	6.8	7.7
Japan	0.6	1.5	2.8	3.4	5.8
Total developed countries	59.4	71.4	72.6	77.7	85.6
Oil-exporting countries	9.2	9.1	13.6	8.5	1.8
Other developing countries	28.7	15.3	11.2	11.4	9.9
Centrally planned economies	2.7	4.2	2.4	2.1	2.2
Exports (fob)					
Western Europe	28.9	46.2	47.9	57.6	58.9
EEC	15.0	29.4	32.6	43.4	49.4
North America	12.0	15.2	12.1	11.3	16.3
USA	7.1	11.6	9.2	9.6	13.8
Other developed countries	21.1	11.8	9.6	5.6	5.1
Japan	0.6	1.8	1.6	1.3	1.9
Total developed countries	62.0	73.2	69.6	74.5	80.2
Oil-exporting countries	5.1	5.0	11.7	10.1	6.5
Other developing countries	31.2	17.2	15.1	12.3	10.7
Centrally planned economies	1.7	3.8	3.4	2.8	1.9

Source: Annual Abstract of Statistics, various issues

Table 17.2 Commodity composition of UK imports, 1955–87

		(%)						
	SITC group	1955	1960	1965	1970	1975	1980	1987
Imports (cif)								
Food, beverage and tobacco	0, 1	36.2	33.1	29.7	22.6	18.0	12.4	10.8
Fuel	3	10.4	10.3	10.6	10.4	17.9	13.8	6.5
Industrial materials and semi-manufactures	2–6	47.9	55.1	53.7	42.7	51.6	35.2	39.4
Finished manufactures	7, 8	5.2	11.1	15.3	22.9	28.2	35.6	48.6
Manufactured goods	5–8	23.2	32.7	39.2	51.0	52.4	62.6	75.5
Unclassified	9	0.3	0.7	1.2	1.4	2.3	3.0	1.2

Source: Annual Abstract of Statistics, various issues

materials and semi-manufactures. But the most dramatic rise is in finished manufactures, rising from 5.2% in 1955 to 48.6% in 1987.

Although changes in the commodity structure of UK exports are less dramatic, they are significant. Textiles and metals have declined, as have motor vehicles, albeit less so. With the development of North Sea oil, there was a substantial rise in fuels after 1975.

Of particular note is the net export of manufactures. This is illustrated in Fig. 17.1. What is most significant is the fact that Britain became a net *importer* of manufactures in 1983 for

Table 17.3 Commodity composition of UK exports, 1955–87

	SITC group	(%)				
		1955	1970	1975	1980	1987
Exports (fob)						
Non-manufactures	0–4, 9	21.2	15.3	18.1	26.4	23.6
Food, beverages and tobacco	0, 1	6.5	6.3	7.3	6.9	7.0
Basic materials	2	5.6	3.0	2.6	3.1	2.4
Fuels	3	4.6	2.6	4.2	13.6	11.0
Other	4, 9	4.5	3.4	4.0	2.8	3.2
Engineering products	7, 87	36.5	43.6	44.2	37.5	39.0
Machinery	71–7	21.1	27.4	29.5	25.3	25.3
Road motor vehicles	78	8.9	10.7	9.5	6.7	6.1
Other transport equipment	79	5.7	3.7	3.4	3.5	4.7
Scientific instruments	87	1.2	1.8	1.9	2.0	2.9
Semi-manufactures	5, 65, 67–9	29.7	26.4	24.1	22.7	22.1
Chemicals	5	7.8	9.5	10.9	11.2	13.2
Textiles	65	10.1	5.1	3.7	2.9	2.4
Metals	67–9	11.8	11.8	9.4	8.6	6.5
Other semi-manufactures and manufactures	Remainder of 6, 8	12.6	14.7	13.6	13.4	15.4

Source: Annual Abstract of Statistics, various issues

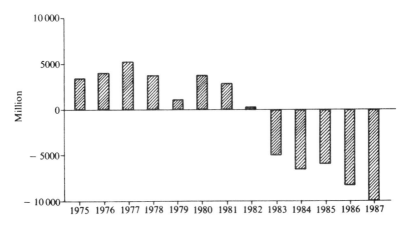

Figure 17.1 UK net exports of manufactures, 1975–87 *Source: Annual Abstract of Statistics.*

the first time since the Industrial Revolution. Although too soon to tell, it may be that this is a trend for the future. Certainly, every year since 1983 the UK has been a net importer of manufactures, and this has been increasing.

In brief, then, we may conclude that the UK trades manufactured goods for manufactured goods, largely to and from other developed countries, mostly the EEC, North America and Japan.

Having established the changing pattern of trade, it is clear that this must have had a major impact on the manufacturing industry, and although it is not the only cause of change, it is useful to consider the changing pattern of the manufacturing industry. Fig. 17.2 shows the average annual growth of industrial production in selected countries for the two periods 1960–73 and 1973–85. Two features are clear from this diagram. First, average

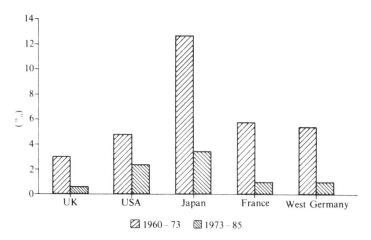

Figure 17.2 Growth of industrial production, 1960–85.

annual growth in the second period was significantly lower than that in the first period for all countries as a result of the oil-price shocks (see Chapter 16). The UK's performance was the lowest in both periods. The low figure of 0.6% average annual growth for the UK in the period 1973–85 is even more significant because during this period she joined the EEC and increased North Sea oil and gas production substantially.

What Fig. 17.2 shows is the decline in manufacturing growth relative to other countries. But a major concern has been the resulting decline in employment in UK manufacturing (shown dramatically in Table 17.4). However, there are a number of indicators of the decline of manufacturing which could be considered and some of these are also given in Table 17.4. In general, Table 17.4 reflects the loss of competitiveness in manufacturing exports and the fall in home demand that is supplied by UK producers (illustrated in earlier tables).

17.2 MEASURING COMPETITIVENESS

In this section we will consider measures of competitiveness for both exports and imports. In general terms, competitiveness refers to the 'advantage in price, speed of delivery, design, etc., which enables a company or country to secure sales at the expense of its competitors' (Enoch, 1978, p. 181). Given this definition, it is useful to distinguish between price-competitiveness and non-price-competitiveness. However, the price charged depends on the nature of the market – whether perfectly competitive, oligopolistic, etc. Why is this the case? Take the usual definition of price competitiveness given by the ratio of relative export prices, which we will clarify in a moment. Under perfect competition a firm can sell what it likes at the going price, whatever that price, so that this measure says very little about how much will be sold. Similarly, in the case of a kinked demand curve, costs may change but the price ratio remains unaltered. With mark-up pricing, although the downward sloping demand curve is not irrelevant, it is not at all clear that the ratio of relative prices indicates changing competitiveness. This is the basic reason why there is a variety of measures of export and import competitiveness.

Table 17.4 Indicators of UK manufacturing decline, 1960–87 (1980 = 100)

Year	Index of employment	% change	Index of output per person employed	% change	Index of output per person hour	% change
1960	122.6	..	63.2	..	..	..
1961	123.8	1.0	62.7	−0.8	..	..
1962	122.7	−0.9	63.5	1.3	..	..
1963	121.3	−1.1	66.5	4.7	..	..
1964	123.0	1.4	71.6	7.7	..	..
1965	124.5	1.2	72.6	1.4	..	..
1966	124.6	0.1	73.9	1.8	..	..
1967	121.1	−2.8	76.5	3.5	..	..
1968	120.2	−0.7	82.5	7.8	..	..
1969	121.8	1.3	84.6	2.5	..	..
1970	121.5	−0.2	85.1	0.6	80.6	..
1971	117.6	−3.2	86.9	2.1	83.7	3.8
1972	113.8	−3.2	92.0	5.9	89.0	6.3
1973	114.4	0.5	100.0	8.7	95.2	7.0
1974	114.7	0.3	98.5	−1.5	95.8	0.6
1975	109.6	−4.4	95.9	−2.6	94.0	−1.9
1976	106.2	−3.1	100.9	5.2	98.9	5.2
1977	106.5	0.3	102.5	1.6	99.8	0.9
1978	105.9	−0.6	103.6	1.1	101.0	1.2
1979	105.3	−0.6	104.1	0.5	101.5	0.5
1980	100.0	−5.0	100.0	−3.9	100.0	−1.5
1981	91.0	−9.0	103.5	3.5	104.8	4.8
1982	85.5	−6.0	110.4	6.7	110.4	5.3
1983	81.0	−5.3	119.8	8.5	118.9	7.7
1984	79.8	−1.5	126.5	5.6	124.4	4.6
1985	79.5	−0.4	130.6	3.2	128.1	3.0
1986	77.9	−2.0	133.8	2.5	131.5	2.7
1987	76.8	−1.4	142.8	6.7	139.7	6.2

.. indicates data not available
Source: Economic Trends, Annual Supplement, 1988 edn and May 1988

The first major measure of competitiveness is *relative export prices*, column (1) in Table 17.5. This is defined as the ratio of the export prices (unit values) of UK manufactured goods to a weighted average of the export prices of manufactures of the UK's main competitors expressed in a common currency (US dollars). The measure is expressed as an index number, with base year presently at 1980. A reduction in the index shows that UK export prices of manufactured goods are falling relative to those abroad, which indicates an improvement in export competitiveness. However, the index concentrates only on export prices and does not take account of the decision of whether to supply on the home market or to export. In addition, what matters for competition is the wholesale price. Thus, a second measure of export competitiveness is the *relative producer prices*, column (2) in Table 17.5. This denotes the UK producer price index for home sales of manufactures, divided by a weighted average of the indices of competitors' output prices, all expressed in US dollars. The base year is presently 1980, and a fall in the index indicates an improvement in export competitiveness.

Because of the problems of market structure and the possibility that the price ratios just discussed may be poor indicators of competitiveness, attention has focused on *cost* measures of competitiveness. The advantages of such a measure are as follows:

1. It covers all manufacturing industries.

Table 17.5 Measures of UK trade competitiveness, 1963–87 (1980 = 100)

Year	Relative export prices	Relative producer prices	IMF index of relative unit labour costs		Relative profit-ability of exports	Import price competitiveness
			Actual	Normalized		
	(1)	(2)	(3)	(4)	(5)	(6)
1963	81.2	91.9	79.1	84.1	..	..
1964	81.3	93.4	78.0	84.5	..	..
1965	83.5	96.3	81.1	87.8	..	..
1966	85.3	96.6	83.1	90.6	..	..
1967	86.2	94.5	79.1	87.0	..	..
1968	79.7	83.6	67.2	76.2	..	..
1969	79.2	84.6	70.2	77.5	..	..
1970	80.1	85.0	72.5	79.5	103.4	86.8
1971	81.9	89.1	74.6	83.0	98.8	90.3
1972	82.0	86.9	72.7	82.1	98.4	91.3
1973	75.5	75.7	64.7	74.1	101.3	85.2
1974	74.2	75.7	64.7	73.7	101.3	83.1
1975	77.9	79.0	70.0	78.3	103.5	85.8
1976	75.5	74.2	63.6	70.3	104.7	82.7
1977	79.7	79.0	62.8	67.7	106.4	83.9
1978	84.5	81.7	67.9	72.2	106.5	86.0
1979	90.4	89.4	80.7	83.3	102.5	93.0
1980	100.0	100.0	100.0	100.0	100.0	100.0
1981	98.0	100.8	101.4	105.7	100.5	100.5
1982	92.2	97.7	95.1	101.9	101.8	98.5
1983	89.2	91.0	86.7	95.9	105.0	94.3
1984	87.6	87.7	81.9	93.0	108.0	92.0
1985	89.7	90.0	81.8	93.6	110.0	91.8
1986	87.5	87.9	76.8	89.5	111.1	91.4
1987	90.3	89.4	76.0	92.8	111.1	91.6

.. indicates data not available
Source: Economic Trends, Annual Supplement, 1988 edn and May 1988

2. It is not affected by whether changes in costs are reflected in prices or in profit margins.
3. It would relate better to export quotations, both in terms of timing and of coverage.

The main difficulty with a cost measure of competitiveness is in the construction of a suitable index. Two are supplied in published figures, columns (3) and (4) in Table 17.5. Both refer to the ratio of unit labour costs per unit of output in the UK divided by a weighted geometric average of competitors' unit labour costs. Column (3) gives the ratio of actual labour costs, while column (4) adjusts the indices to allow for estimated short-term variations in productivity from its long-term trend. Hence, the 'normalized' ratio should be independent of cyclical variations. The indices relate only to manufacturing and are based on information compiled by the International Monetary Fund. The base year is presently 1980, and a fall in the index indicates an improvement in export competitiveness.

The final index of export competitiveness is the *relative profitability of exports*, shown in column (5) in Table 17.5. It denotes the unit value of UK exports of manufactures divided by a weighted index of UK producer prices of home sales of manufactures. It excludes, however, some erratic items (ships, North Sea installations, aircraft, precious stones and silver). The base year is presently 1980, and a *rise* in the index indicates an improvement in export competitiveness. This is because exports are now becoming more profitable in comparison to the supply of goods on the home market.

Column (6) in Table 17.5 gives a measure of *import price competitiveness*. It denotes the weighted index of UK producer prices of home sales of manufactures divided by the unit value index of imports of manufactures, adjusted for tariff changes. This index also excludes the same erratic items as listed in the relative profitability of exports. The base year is presently 1980, and a fall in the index indicates an improvement in import price competitiveness.

So far we have simply listed the various definitions of export and import competitiveness. However, in Appendix 17.1 we supply a formal connection between these definitions and the analysis of Part I. The main conclusion from the appendix is that a change in export competitiveness is a result of the following four factors:

1. The change in the spot exchange rate.
2. The difference between the change in wages at home and abroad.
3. The difference between the change in labour productivity at home and abroad.
4. The difference between the change in the profit mark-up at home and abroad.

Specifically, there will be an improvement in competitiveness if (1) the exchange rate depreciates; (2) wages rise less at home than abroad; (3) labour productivity rises more at home than abroad; (4) the profit margin at home falls; conversely for a worsening in competitiveness.

What, then, do the various measures tell us about the UK's competitiveness? First, the major competitive measures, although having different indices, show roughly the same pattern over time. Second, competitiveness has not declined uniformly. It has cycled throughout the period, with a general improvement up to mid-1975 and then a dramatic deterioration up to about 1981, with some improvement thereafter. Third, for most of the period the normalized unit labour cost measure of competitiveness was below that of the other measures, but it rose most after its turning point in 1977. Fourth, all series identify the turning points within one year of each other.

17.3 IMPORT COMPETITIVENESS AND IMPORT PENETRATION

We can see in terms of Table 17.5, column (6), that there has been a decline in UK import competitiveness, especially in the second half of the 1970s. This would suggest that there has been an increasing supply of home demand provided by imports in a particular product group: in other words, there has been an increase in *import penetration* for that product group. The two common measures of import penetration are, first, the ratio of imports to home demand and, second, the ratio of imports to home demand plus exports (the denominator also equalling sales plus imports).[2] The first is the most common, and it attempts to measure the share of the home market for a product group captured by imports. However, if a particular industry also exports, then this can compensate, to some extent, for a higher level of imports, and is taken into account in the second measure of import penetration.

The trend in import penetration of manufactures as a whole, for both measures, is illustrated in Fig. 17.3. This shows quite clearly that an ever-increasing amount of home demand for manufactures is supplied from abroad. Although fairly steady up to about 1965,

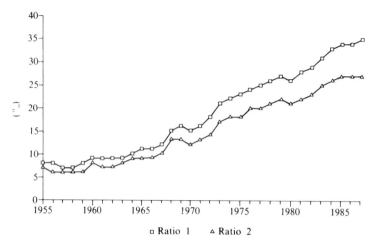

□ Ratio 1   △ Ratio 2

Figure 17.3 UK import penetration of manufacturing industry, 1955–87
Source: Annual Abstract of Statistics, various issues.

Table 17.6 UK import penetration for manufacturing, 1975–86

Manufacturing industry	Ratio 1			Ratio 2		
	(%) 1975	(%) 1986	Points change	(%) 1975	(%) 1986	Points change
Metals	32	48	16	27	36	9
Other minerals	11	15	4	10	13	3
Chemicals and man-made fibres	23	41	18	17	27	10
Metal goods n.e.s.	8	16	8	7	14	7
Mechanical engineering	26	37	11	16	25	9
Office machinery etc.	71	100	29	44	56	12
Electrical and electronic engineering	25	47	22	19	33	14
Motor vehicles and parts	26	51	25	17	41	24
Other transport equipment	49	45	−4	33	26	−7
Instrument engineering	47	56	9	31	40	9
Food, drink and tobacco	18	18	0	17	17	0
Textile industry	23	45	22	19	36	17
Leather and leather goods	27	46	19	22	36	14
Clothing and footwear	21	36	15	19	31	12
Timber and wooden furniture	24	31	7	23	30	7
Paper, printing and publishing	20	21	1	18	19	1
Rubber and plastics processing	14	27	13	12	22	10
Other	27	39	12	20	31	11
All manufacturing	23	34	11	18	27	9

Source: Annual Abstract of Statistics, 1988 edn

the trend thereafter has been upwards, rising from 11% in 1965 to 35% in 1987 (ratio 1). Of course, different industries have shown different degrees of import penetration. Table 17.6 gives some indication of this. The most striking observation about this table is that import penetration has risen for all groups, with the single exception of other transport equipment. The major industry groups affected are office machinery, electrical and electronic engineering, motor vehicles, leather and leather goods, textiles and instrument engineering. However, when account is taken of UK exports in these groups (ratio 2), the major group to be affected is motor vehicles. But textiles, leather and electrical and electronic engineering still have substantial import penetration.

Although the literature includes much in the way of statistics, hypotheses are few. One hypothesis which has been examined, however, is the following

> *Hypothesis* Are deviations from the trend of import penetration related to the pressure of demand for labour in particular industries?

This is not easy to test because of the difficulty in measuring 'demand pressure for labour'. Hughes and Thirlwall (1977) in their test of this proposition use the vacancy–unemployment ratio (see Appendix 14.2). They conclude that: 'Over the period 1963–74 foreign manufactures penetrated the British market quite markedly.' (p. 316) The annual average growth in imports relative to domestic sales for all manufacturing was 3.6% over the period, and in several important industries it was over 10% (being over 20% in the motor vehicle industry). The study further showed that import penetration for certain sectors was more pervasive than that revealed by the aggregate studies. In terms of the above hypothesis, they concluded that cycles in import penetration were related to demand pressure in the labour market in 21 industries (accounting for 16% of total imports).

17.4 COMPETITIVENESS AND THE BALANCE OF PAYMENTS

So far we have been fairly descriptive in our discussion of competitiveness and it is now time to delve deeper into the problem. We return to the definition of export competitiveness in terms of the ratio of prices (for the moment ignoring whether we are dealing with export prices or producer prices). Letting $P^\$$ denote the domestic UK price in dollars, P the domestic UK price in £s, S the dollar/pound exchange rate and P^* the overseas price in dollars, then export competitiveness is expressed as the ratio

$$P^\$/P^* = SP/P^* = R \tag{17.1}$$

where R is the real exchange rate (as used throughout this book). What the alternative measures indicate is that we can use different price indices in measuring such competitiveness.

Equation (17.1) indicates that a reduction in R is an *improvement* in the competitive position of the economy in export markets and import competing industries. It is more revealing, however, to consider percentage changes. Thus,

$$\hat{R} = \hat{S} + (\hat{P} - \hat{P}^*) \tag{17.2}$$

Equation (17.2) indicates that competitiveness improves either if there is a depreciation of the spot exchange rate ($\hat{S} < 0$) or if prices at home rise less than they do abroad ($\hat{P} - \hat{P}^* < 0$).

Turning to the net export position, as outlined in Chapter 2, we have

$$nx = x(R) - im(y, R) \tag{17.3}$$

An improvement in the competitive position (a fall in R) will raise exports and lower imports. Hence, for a given level of real income, a fall in R will improve the net export position of the home country.

What is important to bear in mind, however, is the complex interconnection between the *balance of payments* and competitiveness. The balance of payments is given by

$$bp = nx + cf$$

The net capital flow (cf) is not directly related to R but, rather, to the interest differential plus the expected change in the exchange rate ($r - r^* + \hat{S}^e$), as we outlined in Chapter 2. But there is an *indirect* association. Changes in interest rates will influence the flow of capital. As we demonstrated in Chapter 5, for example, an increase in the UK interest rate (r) with that abroad (r^*) held constant, will attract more capital into the UK. This in turn will lead to an appreciation of the currency (a rise in S). If the appreciation is not offset by price changes, then this will lead to a deterioration in the competitive position (a rise in R). This will then influence the net export situation adversely. Monetarists often argue that *in the long run* the appreciation of the exchange rate will lead to an equal fall in the price level which will offset the change (leave R constant). However, the change in the spot exchange rate will lead to changes in exports and imports in the short and medium terms. Whether these are offset when prices fall depends on at least two things. First, whether the price does, in fact, fall by the same percentage as the exchange rate appreciates. Second, whether firms respond in the same way to an exchange rate change as to a price change. Neither of these two points involve the complex lag response that will inevitably be involved in such changes. Since the exchange rate change is observable and immediate, there is a strong case for arguing that the deterioration in competitiveness arising from the appreciation will be realized and immediate, while the improvement in competitiveness arising from the price fall is problematic and will take place only over the medium and long terms (if at all). Furthermore, there may be an asymmetry. A depreciation may be offset (or even more than offset) by a price rise, since prices are not so sticky in an upward direction.

What is partly being advanced here is that a *major* reason for the changes in competitiveness is changes in the exchange rate (whether an appreciation or depreciation). If this is the case, then it is possible to test it – at least superficially – by regressing the change in competitiveness, $\hat{C}$, on the change in the exchange rate, $\hat{S}$ (or $\hat{E}$, the percentage change in the effective exchange rate), i.e. run a regression of the form

$$\hat{C} = a + b\hat{S} \tag{17.4}$$

We present some of these results using various measures of competitiveness in Appendix 17.2.

The conclusions drawn from the analysis in Appendix 17.2 are as follows:

1. Generally, whether dealing with yearly or quarterly data, the change in the effective exchange rate is more important in explaining changes in competitiveness.
2. For yearly data, changes in the effective exchange rate explain relatively more of relative producer prices and relative unit labour costs (actual and normalized) than relative export prices. For quarterly data, however, the most significant correlation is with relative producer prices ($R^2 = 0.92$).
3. For yearly data, the change in the effective exchange rate is significantly correlated with the changes in the relative profitability of exports. This is not the case for quarterly data.
4. For yearly data, the change in the effective exchange rate is significantly correlated with the changes in import price competitiveness, but is slightly less significant when considering quarterly data.

17.5 DEINDUSTRIALIZATION: BACON–ELTIS THESIS

Britain is a manufacturing nation, and as such depends very much for its growth, development and welfare on the manufacturing sector. This, of course, does not mean that other sectors of the economy are unimportant, or that the service sector, in particular, is a 'drain' on the manufacturing sector. What it does mean is that a large part of the economy's wealth is generated by this sector. But because manufacturing has been such an important sector since the Industrial Revolution, it also means that the type of products the economy is geared to (see Table 17.2), the type of markets the economy sells to (see Table 17.1), and the type of employment that dominates many sectors has been to a large extent determined by historical circumstances. It is quite clear that Britain's dominance in shipping, textiles, steel and coal, to name the most obvious, arose from the fact that it was one of the first countries to industrialize. But each of these industries had characteristics which, to a large extent, determined where in the economy they were located, and the type of markets they would be looking at in order to sell what they produced.

What some economists are worried about is whether, over the last two decades or so, the manufacturing base of the economy has not only declined, but declined to such an extent that there is a serious problem for the future. The point about this argument, if true, is that no 'tinkering' with the macroeconomy will solve this underlying *structural* problem. In the remainder of this section we will pursue just one argument for the decline in manufacturing, namely that put forward by Bacon and Eltis (1976). In the following section we will consider the Cambridge arguments for deindustrialization.

Bacon and Eltis base their argument on the decline in 'marketable output' relative to 'non-marketable' output. They drew attention to the decline in the level of employment in UK manufacturing, arguing that this was a serious problem and needed to be halted, if not reversed. They argued that Britain's relatively poor economic performance, *and* the reason why successive governments could not achieve internal and external balance (see Chapter 8), was because of the decline in the economy's manufacturing base. This decline became more rapid after 1960 *because* of the growth in the non-marketable sector – largely services, most especially central and local government controlled services. The 'marketable sector', on the other hand, referred to goods and services whose value was determined in the market place: the price being determined by the forces of demand and supply. A central precept of their argument was that real wealth can only be provided by the marketable sector. Since the non-marketable sector 'starved' the marketable sector of labour, the marketable sector had to compete for labour, which forced wages up. The rise in wages led to a rise in prices which, in turn, led to a loss of price competitiveness.

There appears to be a supposition in their reasoning that only what is 'marketable' contributes to wealth! What must be kept in mind in this debate is the distinction between wealth and welfare. There is an implicit view that a rise in wealth 'is a good thing'; that a rise in wealth leads to a rise in welfare. But welfare is a much broader concept than wealth, and is by no means independent of the distribution of wealth.[3] Thus, the authors point to the fact that a growing proportion of profits, wages and salaries are taken in the form of 'deductions' which are then used for 'non-marketable' items, such as social services. This, in turn, leads to a reduction in corporate profits and to a decline in industrial investment. Furthermore, they argue that certain groups within the economy, in order to preserve their standard of living in the presence of such deductions, turned to 'aggressive union leaders to produce results'. Their concentration on manufacturing as the basis of welfare is clearly brought out by their statement: 'With a halving of the rate of growth of industrial production, less has been available to raise living standards.' (1978, p. 8). Their essential point is that the growth of the service sector was at the *expense* of the manufacturing base, and this declining manufacturing base has led to problems in growth and employment. However, a counterargument is that manufacturing was simply not demanding the labour, and the services sector, far from crowding out employment from manufacturing, was simply mopping up the surplus. Certainly, before mid-1970 the argument was more one of overmanning rather than an inability to acquire labour. In addition, services employed relatively more women while manufacturing was shedding male labour, Moore and Rhodes (1976). Taking this line of reasoning, the argument is that the growth of services was a means of preserving full employment at a time when manufacturing was demanding less (male) labour, and the participation rate of women increased.

There is a further aspect to the Bacon–Eltis thesis: as successive governments attempted to expand the economy, the net export position of the economy deteriorated as the level of imports rose. This often led to a deflationary package being imposed in order to curb the deterioration in the net export position (see Appendix 5.4 on stop–go). However, the continued growth in the non-marketable sector, and especially the rising level of employment in this sector, meant that wages and salaries in the aggregate could sustain continually high levels of imports. What this would suggest, therefore, is a continued rise in import penetration, as illustrated in Fig. 17.3. However, this aspect of the discussion led to a different view being expressed by Thirlwall (1978). He points out that the world income elasticity of demand for British exports is less than Britain's income elasticity of demand for imports and it was this that was Britain's fundamental problem. The growth in the non-marketable sector was a *consequence* of the inability of the marketable sector to grow without hitting a balance of payments constraint. Hence, once this constraint was hit, the only outlet for labour was in the non-marketable sector. Whatever the cause of the growth in the non-marketable sector, what is undoubtedly true is the continued growth in import penetration in the UK.

A number of observations come from this discussion including the following:

1. There has been a growth in the service sector, especially in terms of employment.
2. There has been a decline in employment in UK manufacturing (especially of men).
3. There has been an increase in 'deductions' from wages and salaries.
4. There has been a rise in import penetration.
5. There has been a decline in UK exports of manufactures relative to total OECD exports (see Fig. 17.4).

Although a number of academics have attacked the Bacon–Eltis thesis,[4] it has generally found favour with governments, most especially with Conservative governments. It could be said that one reason for the move towards privatization is to increase the marketable sector of the economy. Not only is this supposed to be more efficient, but it is supposed to reverse the decline in manufacturing. However, even a 'free' market operates within a given structure and it is not at all clear that privatization will in any way fundamentally alter the structure of the British economy. Whatever the merits of the Bacon–Eltis thesis, there is still the problem of dealing with the decline in UK competitiveness.

17.6 DEINDUSTRIALIZATION: THE 'CAMBRIDGE' VIEW

The Bacon–Eltis thesis just put forward is only one *explanation* for the decline in manufacturing. But the worry about such a decline goes much further, sufficient to have given rise to the term 'deindustrialization'. But the term itself is not at all clear. Some authors simply use it to mean a decline in employment in manufacturing. But, as Cairncross (1979) points out, this is inadequate. Nor is the concentration on the level of output in manufacturing (possibly along with employment) a suitable alternative. Singh (1977) pointed out earlier that there are conceptual difficulties with the term 'deindustrialization', which include the following:

1. What is so special about industry that requires the term 'deindustrialization'? (We do not hear of 'de-ruralization').
2. It may be a structural feature of all advanced industrial countries (the 'mature economy' in Rostow's terms).
3. In an *open* economy, it may simply be a normal adjustment to changing domestic and world market conditions.

Looking at the longer term (1860–1970), Singh does not find strong evidence in support of a decline (relatively) in employment in manufacturing; however, there is a definite trend to decline since the 1960s and it is this decline which is presently of major concern. What Cairncross emphasizes is that deindustrialization is meaningful not so much in terms of a trend, but, rather, in terms of an *explanation* for the trend, although this does presuppose that there *is* a trend. As Singh's paper seems to point out, even this is not so clear – unless one concentrates on the post-War period.

Accepting the decline since the 1960s, what other explanations have been advanced? Singh provides a typical 'Cambridge' view. He interprets deindustrialization as a progressive failure to achieve a sufficient surplus of exports over imports of manufactures to keep the economy in external balance (see Section 8.2 for a discussion of internal and external balance). Put another way, Britain's decline in the export of manufactures has meant that, more and more, it is becoming unable to pay for its (full employment) level of imports. Thus, this view explains deindustrialization as a consequence of declining competitiveness: defining deindustrialization as the contribution of manufacturing industry to the balance of payments.[5]

In Section 17.3 we pointed out the association between competitiveness and the exchange rate. It might be thought, therefore, that the deterioration in competitiveness could be reversed simply by an appropriate devaluation, as was suggested by Beckerman and Associates (1965). However, both Singh (1977) and Cairncross (1979) disagree that a one-off devaluation would be adequate. Part of the reason given is that on the supply side there is a vicious circle operating: namely, a declining market share, declining profits and investment, and declining competitive power. This is borne out to some extent by a glance at Fig. 17.4, which shows UK exports of manufactures relative to 'world' exports of manufactures. The steady decline in this ratio could not be halted by a one-off devaluation. Policies concentrating only on demand are unlikely to succeed because they ignore supply-side difficulties. Such a vicious circle is often compared with a virtuous circle which operates abroad. In

Figure 17.4 UK exports of manufactures relative to 'world' exports, 1960–85.
Source: National Institute Economic Review, various issues.

some versions of the argument, e.g. Stout (1979), Beckerman and Associates (1965) and Moore and Rhodes (1976), great stress is laid on dynamic economies of scale and the advantages enjoyed by other countries supplying expanding markets, able to invest more and innovate more, reinforcing their competitive position – with Japan as the oft-cited example. On the other hand, Posner and Steer (1979) argue that price competitiveness, which is the basis of much of the 'Cambridge' view, cannot explain the UK's falling share in world manufacturing output. They argue that the explanation must lie in non-price factors, a point we will pursue in the next section.[6]

Thus, far from Britain having too few producers, it is more likely that producers were not producing enough, not exporting enough and not investing enough. This 'Cambridge view' was the reason advanced for the causes of the 'British disease'. In particular, it directed attention to supply-side factors for Britain's decline in competitiveness. Of special note was the (mis)allocation of research and development (R&D). In absolute terms, R&D was quite high on European comparisons. The main criticism was that over half of it was on defence and less than one-third was funded by private industry. Much of the R&D expenditure was concentrated on the aircraft industry, and much was government sponsored. Furthermore, this sponsorship was directed to areas of high technology (notably defence), see Freeman (1979). However, the return from such 'high prestige' activities was low.

17.7 OTHER FACTORS IN BRITAIN'S MANUFACTURING DECLINE

The Bacon–Eltis thesis and the 'Cambridge view' place the decline of manufacturing, respectively, in the hands of the growth in the non-marketable sector at the expense of the marketable sector and to declining competitiveness. Although most economists accept that a decline in UK competitiveness has been a major reason for the decline in UK manufacturing, there still remains the question of why there has been such a decline in competitiveness. The discussions on devaluation generally revealed that this would have only a limited affect on UK exports. Posner and Steer (1979) argued that *if* price competitiveness could be improved, then it would raise manufacturing output only in the order of 5–10%. But the diagrams and tables presented in earlier sections would suggest that a much more significant improvement is required. On the other hand, there is some improvement to output and employment arising from exchange rate devaluation, especially in the medium term. According to a CBI inquiry (Oppenheimer *et al.*, 1978), UK businessmen recognize the advantages of a low exchange rate, and hence if the authorities do bring about a depreciation, then it is believed such businessmen would take advantage of it. Both Posner and Steer (1979) and Stout (1979) express concern that a devaluation will adversely affect non-price competitiveness by failing to encourage exporters' aggression and by failing to carry out necessary investment.

Because of the unlikely benefits from a devaluation, and also because some economists believe the problem of Britain's declining competitiveness lies elsewhere, attention has centred on non-price competitiveness. To put these arguments in perspective, and to set out a framework for policy solutions, it is useful to consider some of the important links in the economic process. These are shown in Fig. 17.5, adapted from Stout (1979). In this diagram the solid lines connecting the boxes denote fairly well-established links, with the causation going in the direction of the arrows. The more tenuous links are shown by the dashed lines joining the various boxes – in other words, these influences are possible but not necessary.

The important features of Fig. 17.5 are the arrows in the centre linking product quality, productivity, prices, and net exports; and the direct link between product quality and net exports. The diagram places product quality in a central position for improving (or worsening) competitiveness – either directly or indirectly. The view that non-price factors are the underlying cause of Britain's industrial decline was strongly argued by a National Economic Development Office (NEDO) report, Connell (1980), and was supported by Posner and Steer (1979). The latter conclude that 'over a ten-year period, what happens to non-price factors must be more important than any gains that can be got from increases in price competitiveness.' (p. 160). Stout (1979) makes a similar point. He argues that where dynamic economies of scale exist, and are taken advantage of by companies abroad, then the policy for reversing this is *not* manipulation of the exchange rate but, rather, conditions for a faster rate of innovation. He points out that the UK disadvantage is not in the broad product structure of her exports, rather the main reason is because 'equivalent industries in rival economies have taken advantage of the existence of a technological gap to grow unusually fast in the process narrowing it' (p. 178). In other words, Britain's rival competitors have benefited from the virtuous circle.

The difficulties over policy recommendations are also illustrated in Fig. 17.5. The decline in UK exports of manufactures will only be halted or reversed if it acts on one or both of two links:

(a) the link between product quality, productivity, prices and net exports; and
(b) the link between product quality and net exports.

What this suggests is that some policies will be ineffectual while others will be more likely to succeed. The probable successful policies are shown in diamonds while probable ineffectual policies are shown in 'clouds'. Since the two links emanate from product quality (by construction!), then policies directed at improving product quality will have the most

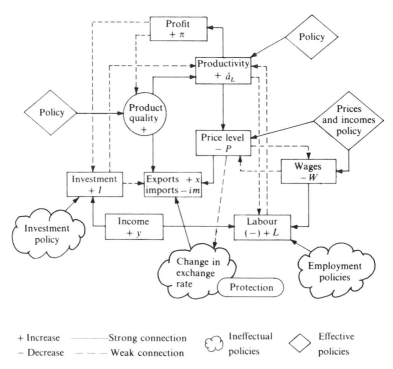

+ Increase ——————Strong connection ⬭ Ineffectual ◇ Effective
– Decrease   – – – Weak connection   policies   policies

Figure 17.5 Policy solutions to Britain's manufacturing decline (from Stout, 1979).

beneficial affects: operating both directly (link 2) and indirectly (link 1). Other likely successful policies are those to do with productivity and a prices and incomes policy. The PIP not only enters the circle directly by affecting prices, but also indirectly by affecting wages.

The less successful policies are those which do not affect the circle, although they may have short-term effects. Thus, investment policy has only a tenuous link with net exports and with productivity. If it can be established that there is a strong link between investment and productivity, this will become more important. Hence, policies which argue for improved R&D may have only limited impact. The same can be argued for employment policy. Although this may halt the decline in employment in manufacturing, the result on export competitiveness is less certain, and will have an impact only if it improves productivity. We have already discussed policies with regard to the exchange rate, but an even less successful policy for dealing with the *long-term* decline of UK manufacturing is by means of protection. None of these policies will enter the circle to create the 'virtuous circle' claimed to be so typical of Britain's trading competitors.

Thus, when attention is directed at product quality and improved productivity, the question that has been raised is: Why is Britain so poor in these areas? The usual supply-side difficulties which are listed include the following:

1. Lack of mobility in the labour force.
2. Poor industrial relations.

3. Lack of innovation.
4. Inability to predict demand.
5. Inappropriate skills, both management and workers.

It has been noted that a number of these have been attributed to poor management – both top and middle management.

The inevitable conclusion we draw from this chapter is that the main reason for Britain's decline is not yet known, and that it simply may be an amalgam of causes.

NOTES

1. Along with Bacon and Eltis (1978) and the articles concerned with deindustrialization in Blackaby (1979), there are relevant studies by Kilpatrick and Lawson (1980), Thirlwall (1982), Williams *et al.* (1983), and Rowthorn and Wells (1987). Also a summary of the general views concerned with Britain's decline can be found in Coates and Hillard (1986).

2. For a discussion of the various measures of import penetration see *Economic Trends* (1977).

3. Although here we refer to wealth and welfare, the arguments about the relationship between growth and welfare are equally applicable. See Mishan (1967, 1977) and Nordhaus and Tobin (1972).

4. See Singh (1977), Cairncross (1979) and Chrystal (1979).

5. Singh points out that invisible trade, which gives rise to marketable services, will be insufficient to finance essential imports.

6. Another version of the vicious circle is given by Thirlwall (1982).

APPENDIX 17.1 EXPORT COMPETITIVENESS: A FORMAL STATEMENT

In Appendix 3.1 we established the following result for price inflation,

$$\hat{P} = \hat{W} - \hat{a}_L - a\hat{R} + b\mathrm{d}\pi \qquad (A17.1.1)$$

where a and b are positive constants. A similar result holds for abroad, namely,

$$\hat{P}^* = \hat{W}^* - \hat{a}_L^* - a^*\hat{R}^* + b^*\mathrm{d}\pi^* \qquad (A17.1.2)$$

But

$$\hat{R}^* = -\hat{R}$$

therefore

$$\hat{P}^* = \hat{W}^* - \hat{a}_L^* + a^*\hat{R} + b^*\mathrm{d}\pi^* \qquad (A17.1.3)$$

From the definition of R, we have

$$R = SP/P^*$$

Hence, taking percentage changes, we have

$$\hat{R} = \hat{S} + (\hat{P} - \hat{P}^*) \qquad (A17.1.4)$$

Substituting equations (A17.1.1) and (A17.1.3) into equation (A17.1.4) and making the simplifying assumption that $b = b^*$, we obtain

$$\hat{R} = \frac{\hat{S} + (\hat{W} - \hat{W}^*) - (\hat{a}_L - \hat{a}_L^*) + b(\mathrm{d}\pi - \mathrm{d}\pi^*)}{1 + (a - a^*)}$$

So long as $(a - a^*) > -1$, the real exchange rate will fall, i.e. there will be an improvement in competitiveness for the home country if:

(a) the spot exchange rate depreciates;
(b) wages at home are rising less than those abroad;
(c) productivity at home is rising more than that abroad;
(d) the profit mark-up falls more (or rises less) at home than that abroad.

APPENDIX 17.2 ASSOCIATION BETWEEN COMPETITIVENESS AND THE EXCHANGE RATE

Much has been made in the literature of the likely effect that changes in the exchange rate have on competitiveness. A depreciation will lower export prices and raise import prices, so leading to an improvement in competitiveness, and conversely for an appreciation. In terms of our formal analysis, this means that a fall (rise) in the spot exchange rate, S, will lead to a fall (rise) in the real exchange rate, R. From equation (17.2) we see further that the percentage change in the real exchange rate, the percentage change in competitiveness, is equal to the sum of the percentage change in the spot exchange rate and the inflation differential at home and abroad. It is possible to break down the inflation differential further, as we did in Appendix 17.1, into differences in wage inflation, differences in productivity growth and differences in the change in the profit mark-up.

But how important is the percentage change in the spot exchange rate in explaining movements in competitiveness? One difficulty in establishing this is the fact that there are different measures of competitiveness, as we outlined in Section 17.2, and the spot exchange rate is meaningful only if we are considering two countries. Where the exchange rate is floating against a variety of currencies, it makes more sense to think of competitiveness being related to the effective exchange rate.

We begin, therefore, with a straightforward statement that the percentage change in competitiveness ($\hat{C}$) is related to the percentage change in the exchange rate, either the spot exchange rate ($\hat{S}$) between sterling and the dollar, or the effective exchange rate ($\hat{E}$). Finally, we assume that the relationship takes the form

$$\hat{C} = a_0 + b_0 \hat{S} \tag{A17.2.1}$$

or

$$\hat{C} = a_1 + b_1 \hat{E} \tag{A17.2.1a}$$

The results of such regressions for the UK, using the various measures of competitiveness against either the dollar–sterling spot exchange rate or the effective exchange rate for the period 1971–87 using annual data, are shown in Table A 17.2.1.

Since the period is dominated by floating (generalized floating taking place after 1973, while the UK began floating in 1972), we would expect the more significant results to be reflected in regression equation (A17.2.1a). This is indeed the case. Changes in the effective exchange rate account for over 50% of changes in competitiveness, and in the case of normalized unit labour costs, it is as much as 82%. All coefficients of $\hat{S}$ and $\hat{E}$ are significant, as reflected in the t-statistics shown in brackets. Of particular note is that for yearly data the least significant association between the effective exchange rate and competitiveness is the relative profitability of export competitiveness. In addition, although the most significant association is between the effective exchange rate and normalized unit labour costs, this is less significant when using the spot exchange rate.

Table A17.2.1 Association between competitiveness and the exchange rate, 1971–87

Competitive measure	Spot exchange rate			Effective exchange rate		
	Constant	Coefficient	R^2	Constant	Coefficient	R^2
Relative export prices	1.308 (1.269)	0.284 (2.766)	0.338	2.728 (2.770)	0.611 (4.036)	0.521
Relative producer prices	1.002 (0.735)	0.306 (2.555)	0.253	3.091 (2.876)	0.837 (5.070)	0.632
Relative unit labour costs – actual	1.546 (0.757)	0.507 (2.492)	0.293	5.015 (3.560)	1.390 (6.420)	0.733
Relative unit labour costs – normalized	1.959 (1.139)	0.439 (2.561)	0.304	5.106 (5.230)	1.249 (8.327)	0.822
Relative profitability of exports	0.264 (0.521)	−0.117 (−2.488)	0.292	−0.397 (−0.905)	−0.271 (−4.014)	0.518
Import price competitiveness	0.780 (0.963)	0.228 (2.832)	0.384	2.073 (3.103)	0.540 (5.258)	0.648

Table A17.2.2 Association between competitiveness and the exchange rate, 1975/Q2–1987/Q4

Competitive measure	Spot exchange rate			Effective exchange rate		
	Constant	Coefficient	R^2	Constant	Coefficient	R^2
Relative export prices	0.675 (2.017)	0.552 (8.991)	0.623	0.939 (4.476)	0.884 (16.916)	0.854
Relative producer prices	0.656 (1.770)	0.589 (8.670)	0.605	0.966 (5.652)	0.992 (23.305)	0.917
Relative unit labour costs – actual	0.698 (1.161)	0.622 (5.640)	0.394	1.040 (2.191)	1.073 (9.075)	0.627
Relative unit labour costs – normalized	0.778 (1.853)	0.580 (7.530)	0.536	1.108 (5.306)	1.020 (19.600)	0.887
Relative profitability of exports	0.084 (0.642)	−0.050 (−2.102)	0.083	0.057 (0.444)	−0.085 (−2.669)	0.127
Import price competitiveness	0.290 (1.363)	0.227 (5.807)	0.408	0.409 (2.350)	0.380 (8.775)	0.611

A similar set of results are provided in Table A 17.2.2, where quarterly data are used. The period taken is from the second quarter of 1975 to the last quarter of 1987. Most R^2s are much higher than for annual data (as are the *t*-statistics). Once again, the effective exchange rate is a better explanatory variable than the spot exchange rate, which is to be expected in a period of floating. Although normalized unit labour costs are highly correlated with the effective exchange rate, the greatest correlation is between relative producer prices and the effective exchange rate.

Finally, it is to be noted that import price competitiveness is more highly correlated with exchange rate changes in the longer term than in the short term.

These results do seem to indicate the importance of exchange rate changes for changes in competitiveness. If over 50% of the change in competitiveness is accounted for by changes in the exchange rate, then the other factors *combined* will account for the remainder. Certainly in the short run the changes in the exchange rate account for a sizeable proportion of the change in competitiveness.

Chapter 18

ECONOMIC GROWTH

A large part of this book has been concerned with the short- and medium-term macroeconomy. In particular, we have assumed that investment takes place but that this is such a small increment in the capital stock that we can effectively assume capital stock is constant. If we think of an economy producing its output with labour and capital (other factor inputs will be considered later), then to assume the stock of capital is fixed is the very same assumption as that made in microeconomics which allows a distinction to be made between the short run and the long run – the short run is that period of time for which at least one factor input is constant. However, in macroeconomics, the time periods are not so readily distinguishable as this. In our theoretical development in Part I, we made the point that in the short run an economy can diverge from the natural rate of income (or the natural rate of unemployment), but that in the long run it would gravitate to its 'natural' level. One of the driving forces in the economy which accomplishes this adjustment to the long-run solution is the change in expectations. On the other hand, this very same analysis which includes long-run changes in expectations does not include changes in the capital stock! Put another way, a change in the capital stock will shift the long-run aggregate supply curve – to the right for a rise in the capital stock. This shift in the long-run aggregate supply curve is our concern in this chapter, since it reflects a change in the economy's productive potential.

In the next section we begin by considering why we should be concerned about growth. Given this concern, in Section 18.2 we turn to the theories of economic growth. Here we limit ourselves to the Harrod–Domar model of growth and to the neoclassical theory of growth. Our intention is a pragmatic one. It is to lay the foundation for some of the discussions which have taken place surrounding the sources of economic growth (Section 18.3) and the concern over the decline in labour productivity (Section 18.4). Furthermore, the analysis in this section concerns both demand and supply. But which determines growth more (Section 18.5)? In addition, can we identify any constraints on the growth process (Section 18.6)? In the final section we return to the policy aspect of growth and raise the question of whether economic growth should be an objective of government policy.

18.1 WHY BE CONCERNED ABOUT ECONOMIC GROWTH?

But why be so concerned about economic growth? In simple terms this means an increase in the average rate of output produced per person (i.e., real *per capita* output growth), usually measured on a per annum basis. Of course, this increase in output could have come about simply because of increased capital, increased productivity of the labour force or the discovery of some new resource deposit. But this is an explanation of the *source* of the increase, which we will deal with in Section 18.3; it does not explain *why* growth in itself is necessarily a good thing. With labour held constant, a greater output means, potentially, that an individual can become better off without anyone else becoming worse off – a Pareto improvement. In other words, someone can receive the extra output. Since the extra goods and services provide welfare for individuals, then it is a short step to say that the increase in output leads to an increase in welfare, i.e. that society is better off with the growth in output than with no growth (or negative growth).

Although an increase in growth can lead to an increase in welfare, this is not always the case. The concentration on the growth of *output* fails to take account of the impact on the environment. The increase in output has led to the felling of trees, the mining of minerals, the fishing of the rivers, lakes and seas, etc.; the production of industrial products has led to pollution of various sorts (some degradable and some non-degradable). In the early days of industrial development, however, the environment could *absorb* all this. But as development progressed, and as populations expanded greatly, the absorptive capacity of the environment diminished considerably. Because the environment itself provides amenities, and therefore contributes to welfare, it is now possible for the welfare increase associated with the increase in goods and services to be swamped by the decrease in welfare from the reduced amenities.[1] This particular debate is beyond the scope of this book, but what it does do is remind us not to confuse growth with welfare improvement, or growth with development.

Closely associated with the observation that growth can contribute to welfare is the fact that with increased *per capita* output it is possible for the *absolute* level of government spending to increase without necessarily altering the *relative* size of government spending, a point we touched on in Chapters 6 and 9. This increase in government spending can re-distribute the benefits of the increased output to various members of society – or by engaging in major social works, such as increasing the supply of houses, schools, and hospitals. However, it is also possible for the increased growth simply to be channelled into extra defence – more missiles, more rockets and more submarines! To the extent that some people see this as a 'good thing', then welfare has improved; but not everyone sees defence expenditure in this light. The issue here is one of distribution – both between defence and social services and between the rich and poor. But the issue goes beyond defence, it is a question of how *can* society reap the benefits of the increased growth and take full account of all the costs of providing this growth? One possibility is for the government to undertake this on behalf of the community – i.e. engage in a major social programme. Another possibility is to let the market mechanism do the job – even in many of those areas which were formerly considered to be the role of government. We touched on these issues in Chapter 15 on Industrial Policy, and the issue is one of political and philosophical (not to say moral) attitudes, which cannot be gone into here. Very few would argue that economic growth *per se* is a 'bad thing', only that it can lead to both gains and losses in welfare; and that the distributional questions of increased growth are not easily resolved.

18.2 THEORIES OF ECONOMIC GROWTH

In the preceding section we pointed out that growth is concerned with the increase in the natural rate of real income. This being so, it follows that we are making the bold assumption that an economy is always achieving its natural rate of employment, that its full potential is being achieved, and that what we are concerned about is the growth in this potential.[2] Although emphasis is usually placed on labour, the same assumption applies to all factor inputs, for only then can we concentrate on the growth in potential output.

The *level* of output is determined by the relationship between the economy's factor inputs and its output. However, there is no single output for the economy as a whole, so how can we analyse the growth of output? Much of the literature on economic growth assumes an *aggregate production function*, which relates an economy's factor inputs to an index of output. There is one important difference between the use of the aggregate production function and that used in microeconomics. In microeconomics, whether dealing with the short or the long run, technical progress is usually assumed constant. However, when dealing with growth, one of the very causes of such growth is a change in the technology. To make these points more explicit, assume the economy has three factors of production: labour (L), capital (K), and a third factor which we simply label X (but could be considered as a basic resource). Then

$$y = G(L, K, X; A) \tag{18.1}$$

where A is an index of technical progress.

Equation (18.1) is a great oversimplification, but it does show in idealized form, what the level of output, y, depends upon: namely, labour, capital, factor X, and technical progress. It is not surprising, therefore, that this is the basis of considerable investigation into the sources of economic growth, which we will deal with in the next section. Different theories of economic growth make, among other things, different assumptions concerning equation (18.1). Many, for example, assume only two factor inputs: labour and capital; or that technical progress is not taking place (the change in A is zero); or that factor inputs are used in fixed proportions, etc. These are merely technical aspects of the production function and are pursued further in Appendix 18.1. But we can summarize some of the main results here.

1. If the input factor X is ignored and technology is assumed constant, then

$$y = F(L, K) \tag{18.2}$$

2. If there is Hicks-neutral technical progress which grows at a constant rate μ, then[3]

$$y = A_0 e^{\mu t} H(L, K)$$

3. In the Harrod–Domar model, output is assumed proportional to the capital stock, i.e.

$$y = \sigma K \tag{18.3}$$

which implies that the capital–labour ratio (K/L) is constant.

4. If, for both equations (18.1) and (18.2), the production functions G and F exhibit constant returns to scale, there is perfect competition, and factors are paid their marginal products, then

$$\hat{y} = \mu + S_L \hat{L} + S_k \hat{K} + S_x \hat{X} \tag{18.4a}$$

or
$$\hat{y} = \mu + S_L \hat{L} + S_k \hat{K} \tag{18.4b}$$

where S_L, S_k and S_x denote the shares of these factors in total output and μ denotes the growth of productivity.

The Harrod–Domar growth model

One of the first theories of economic growth was that put forward by Harrod and Domar.[4] Although rather a simplistic model, it does give some insights. Harrod and Domas assume that output supplied is proportional to the capital stock, equation (18.3). On the demand side, investment is simply the change in the capital stock ($i = dK$). In equilibrium (in a *closed* economy), saving is equal to investment ($s = i$ in the notation used in Part I). A further simplifying assumption is made that savings are proportional to income:

$$i = s = \gamma y$$

or
$$y = i/\gamma \tag{18.5}$$

where γ denotes the marginal propensity to save. Hence, in equilibrium, the change in aggregate demand ($dy = di/\gamma$ from equation (18.5)) is equal to the change in aggregate supply ($dy = \sigma dK = \sigma i$ from equation (18.3)), so that

$$di/\gamma = \sigma i$$

or
$$di/i = \hat{i} = \gamma\sigma \tag{18.6}$$

Furthermore,
$$\hat{y} = dy/y = (di/\gamma)/(i/\gamma) = di/i = \gamma\sigma$$

That is, the growth in income, $\hat{y}$, is constant and equal to the product of the marginal propensity to save and the output–capital ratio,

$$\hat{y} = \gamma\sigma \tag{18.7}$$

In interpreting equation (18.7) it is important to consider what, in this model, can be said about the rate of growth of investment (di/i). It is clear from the foregoing analysis that the rate of growth of income is equal to the rate of growth of investment, namely $\gamma\sigma$. The conclusion of the model is, therefore, that economic growth is determined by the growth in investment, and that this in turn is dependent on the marginal propensity to save and the output–capital ratio, a rise in either of which will lead to an increase in the rate of growth of the economy. The result is fairly straightforward. The increase in savings will lead to funds being made available for investment, which will raise the capital stock, and hence the output of the economy. A rise in the output–capital ratio denotes a rise in capital productivity. Hence, even with the same capital stock, if this is more productive the economy can produce more. Harrod called the constant rate of growth, denoted in equation (18.7), the *warranted* rate of growth, i.e.

$$G_w = \gamma\sigma \tag{18.8}$$

But how does labour fit into this analysis? Does it mean that the labour force is totally irrelevant to the growth of the economy? The assumption embodied in equation (18.3) does not of course mean that labour is not used in the production process. It is simply making the assumption that whatever the labour and capital employed, the level of output will be proportional to the capital stock. Suppose for a moment that 1 unit of capital and 2 units of labour produce 10 units of output. If there were only 1 unit of capital, then it would not matter how much labour was available, only 10 units of output could be produced. Similarly, if there were 2 units of capital available and 4 units of labour, then 20 units of output could be produced. Once again, it would not matter whether more than 4 units of labour were available, they would not be utilized. It follows, then, that labour and capital must be used in a fixed proportion – in this example the capital–labour ratio is 1/2 while the output–capital ratio is 10.

In this model, two further assumptions are made concerning population growth:

1. Population growth is biologically determined.
2. The growth of population is assumed constant.

Given these two assumptions, along with the assumption of a fixed capital–labour ratio, it follows that capital utilization must grow at the same exogenous rate as the labour force. In other words, investment and output must grow at the same rate, or less, as that of the labour force. The growth of labour in the Harrod–Domar model is referred to as the *natural rate* of growth, denoted G_n. Hence[5]

$$G_w \leqslant G_n \quad \text{or} \quad \gamma\sigma \leqslant G_n \tag{18.9}$$

In this model, therefore, the growth process is determined by the warranted rate of growth, which is itself determined by the marginal propensity to save and the output–capital ratio.

Growth equilibrium, or a *steady state*, in this model is where the rate of growth of output, the warranted rate of growth, is just matched by the rate of growth in the population, the natural rate of growth, i.e.

$$G_w = G_n \tag{18.10}$$

Only when this is true will there be full employment of *both* labour and capital over time.

What would happen if this growth path were not established? Suppose, for instance, that the warranted rate of growth exceeded the natural rate of growth ($G_w > G_n$). In this case, industry would be demanding capital for investment purposes in excess of what industry could use because of the more limited growth of labour. Labour would be fully employed but there would be a surplus of capital. The surplus capital would mean the marginal product of capital was zero. It would not, then, be worthwhile for businessmen to undertake any new investment. Over time, therefore, there would also be a drop in capital utilization from the full employment position. This would reinforce the situation, and investment would decline still further. The economy would go into permanent decline. If, on the other hand, the warranted rate of growth were less than the natural rate of growth ($G_w < G_n$), then the demand for capital would be less than the growth of labour. Capital would be fully employed but there would be a surplus of labour. Since the marginal product of labour would decline, less labour would be employed over the next period. Over time, therefore, unemployment would continue to rise. Thus, the equilibrium condition shown by equation (18.10) denotes a 'knife edge'.

Neoclassical theory of growth

One of the main distinguishing features of the neoclassical theory of growth, especially as compared to the Harrod–Domar model, is that the production function is assumed continuous. This in turn implies a whole variety of possible capital–output ratios, and not just one as in the Harrod–Domar model. But does this change the conclusions of the Harrod–Domar model in any substantial way?

What it does do is lead to a stable solution to the growth process. In Appendix 18.2 we outline the mathematical reasoning behind this conclusion. Here we will illustrate the result graphically. In doing this, however, the capital labour ratio (K/L) plays a major role. It will be recalled that in the Harrod–Domar model the actual capital–labour ratio either rose without limit or declined to zero if there was *no* equality between the warranted and the natural rate of growth. Stability, therefore, can be established if we can demonstrate that the economy will move to a single capital labour ratio *no matter where the economy starts*, and that, once achieved, the economy can maintain this level.

The situation is shown in Fig. 18.1. On the horizontal axis we measure the capital–labour ratio (K/L). On the assumption that the production function exhibits constant returns to scale, it can be shown[6] that the output–labour ratio (y/L) is related to the capital–labour ratio, as shown by the curve $f(k)$, where

$$k \equiv K/L \text{ and } y/L = f(k) \tag{18.11}$$

From the information given in Appendix 18.2, we can use the result that the *change* in the capital labour ratio is given by

$$dk = \gamma f(k) - nk \tag{18.12}$$

where n is the rate of growth of the population. Since γ, the marginal propensity to save is less than unity, then the curve $\gamma f(k)$ is below that of $f(k)$. Finally, the line nk denotes the second term in equation (18.12) and is a straight line (with slope n), as shown in Fig. 18.1.

It follows from equation (18.12), that there will be no change in the capital–labour ratio if $dk = 0$; in other words, where the curve $\gamma f(k)$ intersects the line nk. Hence, k_e represents the equilibrium capital–labour ratio. But is this ratio stable?

In order to explain this, first note that $\gamma f(k)$ denotes saving per unit of labour, which is equal to investment per unit of labour. On the other hand, nk denotes the growth in capital (investment) required per unit of labour which is necessary to preserve a particular capital–labour ratio. Consider, then, a capital–labour ratio below k_e, namely k_1. At this ratio the level of investment per unit of labour that is generated, Oa, is greater than the investment required to maintain k_1, namely Ob. The additional investment will raise the capital–labour ratio (raise k). But as k rises, the additional capital involves diminishing returns to capital (the slope of $f(k)$ falls as k rises).[7] Thus, there will come a point where $\gamma f(k) = nk$. If $k > k_e$, say k_2, then more investment is required per unit of labour to maintain k (Od) than is being generated (Oc). Then k will fall. As k falls, the marginal product of capital rises. This will continue until $\gamma f(k) = nk$. Hence, the very stability of this growth process is established because of the variable capital–labour ratio!

In this model the capital–labour ratio is constant at the equilibrium level. Put another way, for equilibrium to be maintained, the rate of growth of capital must equal the rate of growth of labour. Furthermore, at the equilibrium capital–labour ratio, output per person

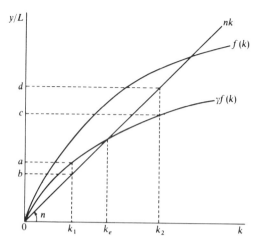

Figure 18.1 Neoclassical growth.

(y/L) is constant, which implies that the rate of growth of output is equal to the rate of growth of labour, i.e.

$$\hat{y} = n$$

What is not so obvious is that this equilibrium growth is *independent* of the marginal propensity to save, γ, which played such an important role in the Harrod–Domar growth process. This conclusion can be readily seen in terms of Fig. 18.2. A rise from γ_1 to γ_2 in the marginal propensity to save shifts the $\gamma f(k)$ function upward. The new equilibrium is at point *B* rather than point *A*. Although the equilibrium capital–output ratio has risen from k_1 to k_2, the rate of growth is still determined by the population growth, namely *n*. The only result of a rise in the rate of savings is to alter the rate of capital investment in the short run, which in turn will alter the capital–labour ratio until it reaches k_2.[8] There will be a one-off increase in *per capita* income.

If savings do not have an impact on the rate of growth of the economy, what does give rise to an increase in the growth rate? If *per capita* income is to grow continuously, then we must look for something other than one-off events. The most obvious candidate is technology. Throughout the discussion so far we have assumed a given technology. An improvement in technology will shift the production function upward, i.e. more output can be achieved by the same inputs. However, if *per capita* income is to grow *continuously*, then this means that technological progress must itself be continuous. The situation is illustrated in Fig. 18.3. The point about the process of technological progress is that this *offsets* the decline in the marginal product of capital which results as the capital–labour ratio rises (with fixed technology). This has naturally led to some important investigations into technological progress which we shall consider in the next section.

Before leaving such theories of economic growth, it must not be assumed that these are the *only* theories of growth. Growth economics is quite advanced and fairly mathematical and requires a fuller treatment than can possibly be given here.[9]

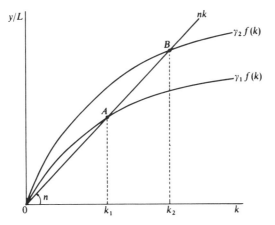

Figure 18.2 Neoclassical growth and the marginal propensity to save.

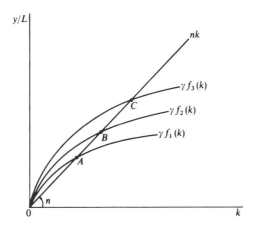

Figure 18.3 Neoclassical growth and technological progress.

18.3 SOURCES OF ECONOMIC GROWTH

As indicated in the preceding section, it is possible to account for the *sources* of economic growth in output by considering the growth in the factors of production (labour, capital and any other factor inputs considered relevant) and in the rate of technical progress. Furthermore, the analysis indicated that this is possible, in theory at least, by considering the aggregate production function.

The first major study using this approach was that by Solow (1957), who attemped to fit a Cobb–Douglas production function, allowing for a constant rate of change in technical progress, to a set of observations on the US economy for the period 1909–49. The basic form that he used for his equation was

$$y = A_0 e^{\mu t} L^a K^b \qquad (18.13)$$

where μ is the rate of technical change, a is the elasticity of output with respect to labour and b is the elasticity of output with respect to capital (see Appendix 18.1). It is to be noted that in this formulation no other factor of production was considered, and that constant returns to scale are assumed to hold $(a + b = 1)$. Furthermore, equation (18.13) assumes that technical change is *Hicks-neutral*, i.e. it simply shifts the production function outward for any given capital–labour ratio.[10]

Using equation (18.13), or at least one very similar to it, he obtained estimates of μ, a and b. Having done this he could then break down the growth in income into its component parts. To see the procedure, consider the following stylistic facts. Labour's share in income is found to be 0.75, while capital's share is 0.25. The growth of labour and capital over some period is 1.5% and 5% respectively. By regression, the growth in technical change, μ, is found to be 1.2%. Finally, output has been growing at 3.575%. From Appendix 18.1 we know that

$$\hat{y} = \mu + S_L \hat{L} + S_k \hat{K} \tag{18.14}$$

Using the information provided we can establish the results shown in Table 18.1, where output per person is $\hat{y} - \hat{L}$. Although in this example, the contribution of each element to the growth in income is fairly equal, this is simply a result of the figures used.

A major criticism was the assumed nature of the technical progress: namely, that it was of the disembodied form. In a later paper Solow (1962) undertook the same analysis, but assumed that technical progress was capital-embodied technical progress, where more recent additions to the capital stock were more productive than earlier ones – what are now called *vintage growth models*. The result was to raise substantially capital's share in income from what he obtained earlier. The most obvious conclusion we can draw from this particular study is that the assumptions made about the form that technical progress can take makes a vast difference to the results, and hence to any conclusions that can be derived. It is not surprising, therefore, that Solow's work sparked off a whole series of studies into technical progress.[11]

A different approach, but one still based on an aggregate production function of the Cobb–Douglas type, was taken by Denison in his major investigations into the sources of growth in the US and, later, in Europe.[12] He assumes that output can be represented by a Cobb–Douglas production function exhibiting constant returns to scale. He makes the further assumption that factors are paid their marginal product, i.e. he assumes perfect competition. Under these assumptions, growth in output is simply a weighted average of factor inputs, where the weights denote the relative shares of each factor in production (see Appendix 18.1). Having established this, Denison then takes a base period, deriving an index for labour in the base period, capital in the base period and output in the base period. There is, of course, the further assumption here that in the base period there is full employment. Next Denison considers a period in the future. He can of course measure the change in the index to the quantity of labour and to the quantity of capital. Using the same weights as in the base period, he can calculate what this would give rise to in terms of the growth of output. If the actual growth of output is greater than this amount, then the difference is attributable to technical change.

Using the same notation as in equation (18.14), and for the moment assuming only two factors of production, labour and capital, then their contribution to growth is given by

$$S_L \hat{L} + S_k \hat{K} \tag{18.15}$$

Table 18.1 A breakdown in the growth of output

	Absolute contribution	Percentage contribution
Technical change (μ)	1.2%	34
Labour ($S_L\hat{L}$)	1.125%	31
Capital ($S_k\hat{K}$)	1.25%	35
	3.575	100
Growth of output per person	2.075%	

Given the growth of output is recorded as $\hat{y}$, it follows that the rate of technical progress is given by

$$\mu = \hat{y} - (S_L\hat{L} + S_k\hat{K}) \tag{18.16}$$

This approach not only allows the source of growth to be attributed to each factor input; it also allows a more detailed breakdown of the exact source of the increase. In a more recent study, Maddison (1987), undertook a similar procedure to that of Denison for six major countries: France, Germany, Japan, Netherlands, UK, and US. Before looking at Maddison's results, it is worth noting that two further refinements have been made to equation (18.16). First, labour and capital have been 'augmented' in various ways in order to obtain a better estimate of the growth of these factors. For example, labour has been adjusted for hours worked, for sex, for education, etc. Capital, although less refined, has also been 'augmented', in particular to take some account of age. We can distinguish such 'augmented' variables by L^* and K^* respectively. Second, because there is still a major unexplained element, supplementary phenomena are considered. As a group, these can be represented by the growth term $\hat{S}$. Hence, taking account of these two refinements, we can rewrite equation (18.16) as

$$\mu = \hat{y} - (S_L\hat{L}^* + S_k\hat{K}^*) - \hat{S} \tag{18.17}$$

In fact, both Denison and Maddison break $\hat{S}$ down into a variety of elements. Maddison's results for the UK economy showing sources of GDP growth over three periods are shown in Table 18.2. Taking account of other sources, technical progress (the 'residual') accounts for a rising percentage of the growth in income in the UK over the period 1913–1984, rising from 29% to 46%. The contribution to growth by labour quantity has persistently declined, while augmented capital rose in the growth period after the Second World War and then declined in 1973–84 period.

Denison's work is a valiant attempt (as is that of Maddison) at breaking growth down into its component parts. Furthermore, as a basis for policy, he attempts to provide a 'menu of choices' for the policy-maker, distinguishing between those policies which would give a one-off fillip to growth and those which would allow a more sustained growth. Maddison is more cautious, arguing that such analysis does identify which facts require ultimate explanation. However, the method does give a basis for discussing the present Conservative party's approach to growth. The reduction in the power of the unions, assuming this is successful, will in all likelihood just give a one-off fillip to the growth process. On the other hand, an improvement in the level and type of education undertaken in the UK could give a

Table 18.2 UK sources of GDP growth, 1913–84

	1913–50	1950–73	1973–84
GDP	1.29	3.02	1.06
Labour quantity	−0.20	−0.11	−0.93
Labour quality	0.32	0.09	0.20
Labour hoarding	0.00	0.00	0.00
Residential capital quantity	0.12	0.21	0.16
Non-residential capital quantity	0.22	0.78	0.61
Capital quality	0.45	0.52	0.38
Capacity use effect	0.00	0.00	0.00
Catch-up effect	0.00	0.14	0.29
Structural effect	−0.04	0.10	−0.26
Foreign trade effect	0.00	0.16	0.06
Economies of scale	0.04	0.09	0.03
Energy effect	0.00	0.00	−0.12
Natural resource effect	0.00	0.00	0.22
Regulation/crime	0.00	−0.02	−0.07
Total explained	0.91	1.96	0.57
Residual	0.38	1.06	0.49
Percentage 'explained'	71	65	54

Source: Maddison (1987), table 20

more sustained impetus to growth. Whether the actual policies being pursued by the Thatcher government will in fact do this remains to be seen – especially in terms of the major educational reforms which they are carrying through.

18.4 TECHNICAL PROGRESS AND PRODUCTIVITY SLOWDOWN

Measurement difficulties aside, the preceding section indicated the importance of technical change as an explanation of the source of growth. However, it makes no attempt to classify the sources of technical change; it simply measures it as a constant rate of growth of the production function. One major source of technical change is that arising from *innovation*, i.e. the process by which an idea is incorporated into the production process (as distinct from invention, which is simply the discovery of some new process). Innovation can in turn take place by accident, or because of 'learning by doing', or it can take place as a result of research and development, R & D. However, for innovation to lead to an improvement in growth it is necessary for the innovation to *diffuse* itself throughout the economy. These considerations have spawned a whole literature on innovation and diffusion.[13]

These issues are too broad to go into here. What we wish to investigate is the narrower question of why UK growth is poor relative to other industrial countries and why there has been a slowdown in productivity in these countries in the 1970s. One possible explanation for the poor relative performance of the UK economy is its poor innovation. In establishing whether this is the case, it is necessary to have a measure of innovation. A fairly common proxy for innovation is the expenditure on R & D. As a percentage of GNP, R & D has been fairly constant in the US and the UK, while rising in France, Germany and Japan. It appears from aggregate figures that the UK is not particularly failing on this score.

However, when a more disaggregated level is undertaken, especially distinguishing between R & D directed towards defence from that towards non-defence, a different picture emerges. Germany and Japan spend relatively less of their R & D expenditure on defence than the UK, and the UK's expenditure is the highest outside that of the US (at least of the OECD countries). Freeman (1979) concludes

> The peculiar British paradox of the postwar period was thus one of a completely inappropriate allocation of government and industrial R and D resources at a time when the total British R and D effort was temporarily greater than that of any of our major competitors except the US. Whereas the US at least derived substantial trade advantages from its world dominance in military-related technologies, British trade and industrial performance gained little from the heavy UK investment in these areas and may indeed have been weakened by it. (In Blackaby, 1979b, p. 70)

When we turn to the productivity slowdown, it is useful to clarify which productivity we are referring to. In Denison's work, which we discussed above, he refers to the difference between income growth and the contributions of labour and capital as 'productivity'. This productivity denotes the increase in output relative to *all* factor inputs (since he only considers labour and capital!). It is thus often called total productivity or joint factor productivity. This is to be distinguished from labour productivity (output per unit of labour) or capital productivity (output per unit of capital).[14] It is often the case that labour productivity is used as a proxy for total productivity. Certainly it is the case that capital is notoriously difficult to measure and so there is undoubtedly a greater emphasis on labour productivity. However, Maddison (1987) provides a whole series of productivity measures, and those for the UK over the period 1913–84 are provided in Table 18.3. It can be seen immediately that all measures in the period 1973–84 are down on the previous period, and that this phenomenon is not special to the UK. In particular, labour productivity is down by 0.80 percentage points, while capital productivity is down by an even greater amount, 1.19 percentage points.

Additional identifying causes of the slowdown in economic growth in the post-1973 period can be seen in terms of Table 18.2 above. Although the OPEC oil price rises did have some affect (calculated in terms of the 'energy effect'), this was more than offset by the 'resource effect' in the case of the UK. Of possibly more concern is the 'structural effect' and the 'trade effect'. We dealt with the latter in some detail in Chapter 17. The 'structural effect' is a sort of measure of deindustrialization. The major structural changes in the UK can be seen in terms of Table 18.4, which shows employment as a percentage of total employment in the three main sectors agriculture, industry and services, for the period 1870–1984. The decline in agriculture is dramatic. The bell-shaped pattern of relative industrialization and deindustrialization has affected not only the UK but also all other industrial countries, the only major difference being the time when the deindustrialization began. Equally obvious is the rise in the services sector.

It is well known that the income elasticity of demand is such that growth leads to a move away from agriculture (having a demand which is income inelastic) and towards industry and services (where demand tends to be income elastic). Furthermore, there has been a differential pace of technological advance between the sectors, with productivity in the service sector being slower. Whether the major decline in labour productivity growth in UK services, as shown in Table 18.5, is due to the intrinsic nature of many services, or simply because of measurement difficulties, is not easily determined. However, the magnitude of the

Table 18.3 UK measures of productivity (reducing the residual), 1913–84

	1913–50	1950–73	1973–84
GDP	1.29	3.02	1.06
Labour productivity	1.60	3.20	2.40
Capital productivity	0.13	−0.26	−1.45
Joint factor productivity	1.15	2.14	1.22
Augmented joint factor productivity	0.38	1.53	0.64
Residual	0.41	1.06	0.49

Source: Maddison (1987), tables 19, 2, 5, 11a, 11b, 20

Table 18.4 UK employment structure as a percentage of total employment, 1870–1984

	Agriculture	Industry	Services
1870	22.7	42.3	35.0
1913	11.0	44.8	44.2
1950	5.1	46.5	48.4
1960	4.6	46.7	48.7
1973	2.9	41.8	55.3
1984	2.6	32.4	65.0

Source: Maddison (1987), table A.13

Table 18.5 UK sectoral labour productivity growth (value added per person employed), 1913–84

	Agriculture	Industry	Services
1913–50	2.5	1.4	0.7
1950–73	4.6	2.9	2.0
1973–84	4.2	2.9	0.6

Source: Maddison (1987), table A.6

fall in labour productivity growth between 1950–73 and 1973–84 in the service sector in the UK is quite dramatic.

The cross-country studies, and especially the studies done on the US economy, have not revealed any obvious single reason for the slowdown in world growth in the post-1973 period. The reasons appear to be complex and diverse.

18.5 DEMAND OR SUPPLY?

We pointed out at the beginning of this chapter that economic growth could be envisaged as a movement to the right of the long-run aggregate supply curve, indicating that the economy's potential output had increased. This would, however, suggest that growth was no more than a supply-side policy, that demand was not relevant to the issue. In order to take this line of reasoning, however, it must be assumed that aggregate demand and aggregate supply are *independent*. In other words, shifting one curve has no impact on the other. But is this assumption realistic?

Undoubtedly in the UK a number of Labour and Conservative governments have believed that it is possible to stimulate growth through raising aggregate demand. Although this has often led to balance of payments problems and to inflationary pressure, it only indicates that pursuing this approach is difficult. It in no way deems it impossible Certainly, those who argue for an export-led growth (e.g. Kaldor, 1975; and Thirlwall, 1980) clearly see growth from the point of view of demand. Supply-siders, of course, argue that the way to stimulate growth is through supply-side policies – such as reducing taxation (both on individuals and firms), stimulating savings and investment, and promoting efficiency through unregulated markets.

The role of demand in growth is a difficult one. The argument starts from basic Keynesian economics. If it is possible for the economy to be in underemployment equilibrium, then it is also true that the economy is not working at its full potential. The aim of Keynesian demand management, therefore, is to ensure that the economy *does* operate at its full potential. But what about the long run? Here the argument may be that the long run is simply a collection of short-run periods! But this is inadequate since it does not explain the transition from one short run to the next, and so cannot explain either the long-run nature of the economy, or whether the long run depends on the particular short-run paths taken. Neoclassical analysis, in which we include monetarism and the new classicists, is also fairly limited. It goes some way towards explaining the long run, but only after making some heroic assumptions. To some extent, the failings of this approach can be seen in terms of our earlier analysis, where there is still almost 50% of growth in GDP to be explained.

One point does come out of what we have just said. Neoclassical growth is concerned with raising the economy's potential level of output, but if this potential is not being reached in the first place, will this not simply create a greater gap between the actual rate and the potential rate of growth? Consider just one aspect of this. Suppose the government pursues supply-side policies which raise the level of hours *supplied* by workers. However, suppose the economy is such that the *demand* for labour remains the same. Potential output will have risen, since there is a rise in hours per person, but actual output will have remained the same. The counterargument to this is that tax incentives have to be *combined* with policies to improve the workings of the market so that the full potential can be achieved. Arguments such as those just given have led some commentators to put forward strategies which include both expansionary policies to achieve full potential and industrial policies to raise the potential level of output.[15]

What is quite clear is that the theory developed in Part I (even if one takes a very monetarist stance with a vertical long-run Phillips curve) does not explain why the long-run Phillips curve shifts. There is no basis, therefore, to argue that growth is a question of supply. If, in the aggregate, demand and supply are *interconnected*, then the question of whether growth is determined by demand or by supply is a nonsense question!

18.6 CONSTRAINTS ON GROWTH

The policies pursued by a number of Labour governments in the post-War period, and the attempt by Anthony Barber, the Conservative Chancellor of the Exchequer in the early

1970s,[16] indicated that whenever there was an attempt to expand the economy this inevitably led to either a balance of payments problem or to inflation. Under a fixed exchange rate system that operated prior to 1972, the expansion of demand led to a rise in imports which led to a deterioration in the current account balance. When the pound floated, the rise in aggregate demand led to a depreciation of sterling, which in turn put pressure on prices to rise. Whatever the exchange rate system, some problem arose from the trade sector when demand was expanded. Since reserves could not be allowed to shrink to nothing, or the exchange rate allowed to depreciate indefinitely, this meant that any attempt to expand the economy was halted. Put another way, the balance of payments was a constraint on any attempt at growth.[17]

It is worth pointing out, however, that this argument only applies to the expansion of demand necessary to reach the short-run potential of an economy. If, as we argued in the preceding section, it is possible to expand supply along with aggregate demand, then such a constraint would not be binding. Nevertheless, as our analysis in earlier chapters makes clear, it is not at all easy to raise aggregate supply. On the other hand, it does indicate that pursuing demand-side policies independently of supply will very soon reach a balance of payments constraint. Furthermore, if this constraint is persistently hit, and if this results in repeated 'stops' to the economy, then the result is businessmen's reduced expectations about future potential growth. This, in turn, leads to lower levels of investment, which does reduce the rate of growth and creates self-fulfilling expectations!

Constraints on growth have also been voiced from other quarters. Kaldor (1966) argued that a constraint on growth arose in the UK because agriculture, the major source of surplus labour for industrialization, had more or less exhausted itself. Manufacturing productivity, he argued, was limited by the size of its labour supply, and any such constraint on labour supply will limit the extent to which manufacturing can reap the benefits of economies of scale. The only other source of labour, therefore, was the service sector. It was partly for this reason that he advocated the selective employment tax (SET), which operated for the period 1966–73. The aim of this tax was to re-allocate labour from services to manufacturing, and hence to stimulate growth. Bacon and Eltis (1978) argued that the expansion in the non-marketable sector was absorbing labour and so constraining growth in the marketable sector. Neither of these arguments is very convincing. Kaldor's 'law' did not stand up to more detailed analysis, and the correlation between productivity growth and employment growth was only significant if Japan was included in the sample, Rowthorn (1975). Kaldor himself abandoned his initial thesis (see Kaldor, 1975). The Bacon–Eltis thesis, too, has come in for strong criticism, as we outlined in Section 17.5. But if labour is not constraining growth, can it be said that capital is a source of constraint on growth? There is no clear evidence that this is true. Although there has been a decline in capital productivity, as shown in Table 18.3, this does not demonstrate that it is a constraint on growth; it could just as easily be reflecting a decline in UK profitability. Alternatively, investment might be low because there is a constraint from the financial sector on the sources of capital. This was investigated by the Wilson Committee (Cmnd. 7937). They concluded that the problem was not that the financial system was a constraint on funds, but, rather, that industry was unwilling to take the required investment. Like most explanations of Britain's economic decline, it is almost impossible to establish whether the fall in capital productivity is a cause or a consequence of the decline.

18.7 ECONOMIC GROWTH AS AN OBJECTIVE OF POLICY

Growth has not always been a major policy objective in the UK. Interest in growth can be traced back to the early 1960s. At this time growth was thought of as a panacea for the many problems afflicting Britain (and other Western economies), such as balance of payments problems, the dollar shortage, underemployment and inflation. The Labour Party, under Harold Wilson 1964–70, was committed to growth as an objective of policy. In particular, growth was seen as a means of breaking out of the stop–go cycle. In order to achieve this growth, great emphasis was placed on planning, and planning became synonymous with growth during this period – 'both remained equally vague' (Tomlinson, 1985, p. 95). Because growth was seen as an objective of government, the slow growth which occurred was ascribed to government failure.

But the attempts at stimulating growth, especially by planning, were thwarted. The 1966 crisis led to a long 'stop' in defence of sterling, revealing most clearly the balance of payments constraint on growth. Furthermore, with the abandoning of the National Plan (in 1966) and the devaluation of sterling in 1967, growth played very little part in policy discussions in the latter part of the 1960s. It returned to policy discussion in the early part of the 1970s under Mr Heath's Conservative administration. In this period growth was primarily seen as a means of reducing inflation in two ways:

(a) by reducing incompatible demands, and
(b) by providing greater resources to reduce social problems.

Unlike the earlier Labour administration, growth under Heath was not tied to anything in particular nor to any institution. It may be thought that the Conservatives, too, would soon face the balance of payments constraint, but they attempted to avoid this difficulty by floating sterling in 1972. At the time, such a floating of the exchange rate was not considered to be too inflationary. On the contrary, it was seen as a means of breaking out of the stop–go cycle and into sustained growth. In addition, this proposed growth was an offering to the unions for an incomes policy. This did mean, of course, that the exchange rate was to become subordinate to that of growth. As we have recorded elsewhere, the Barber boom led to roaring inflation and the expansion was brought to a halt.

Thus two main periods when great stress was placed on growth as a policy objective failed miserably. It appeared in both cases that demand management could not deliver growth. It even led to the view that growth should not be a government objective. This was stated, for example, by Keith Joseph, who said

> 'During 30 years we have tried to force the pace of growth. Growth is welcome, but we just do not know how to accelerate its pace. Perhaps faster growth, like happiness, should not be a prime target but only a by-product of other policies.'
> (Quoted in Tomlinson, 1985, p. 186)

This view, to some extent, was re-iterated by Sir Geoffrey Howe when he was Chancellor of the Exchequer, when he said that his policies were to 'create a climate for growth'. In other words, government policy was not to promote growth *directly*, but, rather, to facilitate the market mechanism and so create growth through competition. This conception of the way to promote growth is central to Mrs Thatcher's policies for the UK economy. It is in marked contrast to the views of the 1960s, when government policy towards growth was directed at correcting for the failings of the market. Under Mrs Thatcher, growth will be achieved through competition, and competition will be achieved by pursuing policies which ensure that markets operate efficiently and unhindered.

In many ways it is not surprising that there are two very conflicting views about policy towards growth. Growth, as this chapter shows, is a complex process which is not fully understood. If we knew what caused it, then it would be a simple step to raise it – if that was thought to be an objective of policy. Even policies directed towards labour and capital productivity, if successful, will only influence part of the growth process. If a major 'cause' of growth is the 'residual' (i.e., is unexplained), then it is difficult to see how policies can be directed towards raising growth. We can only conclude that more investigation is required into explaining economic growth.

NOTES

1. Mishan, in particular, has consistently argued that growth is not necessarily a 'good thing'. See Mishan (1967, 1977).

2. The assumption of an economy always being at its natural rate of employment is in contrast to earlier literature which always assumed 'full employment'. These would be the same only if we use 'full employment' to mean the 'natural rate of employment'.

3. With Hicks-neutral technical progress, both labour and capital grow over time at the same constant rate, μ, and so the capital–labour ratio remains unaffected. Only the production surface shifts (by an amount $e^{\mu t}$) such that the isoquant map remains invariant except that the output level associated with a given isoquant increases over time (by an amount $e^{\mu t}$). Thus, with Hicks-neutral technical progress the production function can be written

$$y = A_0 e^{\mu t} H(L, K)$$

For example, if we have a Cobb–Douglas function of the form,

$$y = A_0 L_0^a K_0^{1-a}$$

and both labour and capital grow at the same rate μ, so that

$$L_0^a = e^{\mu t} L \text{ and } K_0 = e^{\mu t} K, \text{ then}$$

$$y = A_0 (e^{\mu t} L)^a (e^{\mu t} K)^{1-a}$$

$$= A_0 e^{\mu t} L^a K^{1-a}$$

$$= A_0 e^{\mu t} H(L, K)$$

4. Harrod (1939) and Domar (1946). These two famous articles are reprinted in Sen (1970), Readings 1 and 2.

5. The labour force can grow either because man-hours increase (e.g., as population size increases) or because there is an increase in labour productivity. In this case, the natural rate of growth of the population is the *sum* of the rate of growth of man-hours and the rate of growth of labour productivity.

6. See Allen (1967) and Chiang (1984).

7. Given $y = F(L, K)$ and $y/L = f(k)$, then the marginal product of capital is given by $\partial y/\partial K$. Now partially differentiate the second function. Thus,

$$\partial(y/L)/\partial K = [\partial f(k)/\partial k][\partial k/\partial K]$$

or

$$(1/L)(\partial y/\partial K) = f'(k)(1/L)$$

i.e.

$$\partial y/\partial K = f'(k)$$

Hence, the marginal product of capital is the slope of the production function $f(k)$.

8. Since a rise in savings does alter the capital–output ratio, which in turn alters the *per capita* income (y/L), then the question arises as to what is the 'best' rate of savings for such an economy. If 'best' is defined to mean the greatest consumption *per capita*, then it is possible to establish the optimal rate of savings for such an economy. Furthermore, under the assumption of perfect competition, the marginal product of capital is equal to the (real) rate of interest. Hence, the rate of interest must equal the equilibrium rate of growth – which has been referred to as the 'golden rule' of accumulation, see Phelps (1961).

9. See, for example, Jones (1975), Burmeister and Dobell (1970) and Wan (1971).

10. See footnote 3 on the different meanings that can be attached to technical progress, see the survey by Hahn and Matthews (1964).

11. See Hahn and Matthews (1964) and Jones (1975).

12. See Denison (1962, 1967)

13. See Freeman (1974) and Stoneman (1983).

14. See Shone (1981) and Stoneman (1983).

15. See, for example, *The Alternative Economic Strategy*, by the CSE London Working Group, 1980.

16. See the analysis of the Barber boom on p. 217.

17. It could be argued that expansionary policies pursued by earlier Labour and Conservative governments were misguided because they misjudged the capacity of the UK economy to produce the things that people actually wanted to buy at the relative prices created by UK institutions. This, rather than any balance of payments constraint, was the problem of the 1960s and 1970s. (I am grateful to A. Rebmann for this point.)

APPENDIX 18.1 THE AGGREGATE PRODUCTION FUNCTION

In the most general terms the aggregate production function relates output to the factors of production of an economy and to the level of technology. The factors of production usually included are labour, L, and capital, K; sometimes a third factor of production is included, which represents land and resources and which we shall simply denote by X. Finally, various assumptions can be made about the technology: (1) that it is constant; (2) that it is disembodied; (3) that it is disembodied and assumed to grow at a constant rate; (4) that it is embodied (either in labour or in capital); etc. Sometimes additional assumptions are made about the aggregate production function, including (1) it exhibits constant returns to scale; (2) it is continuous and twice differentiable; and (3) marginal products are positive but diminishing. Given such diversity, we cannot possibly deal with all these characteristics in this appendix. What we will do, however, is lay out the bare essentials which are useful in analysing growth. Further analysis can be found in Allen (1967).

In Table A18.1.1 we set out four general specifications of the aggregate production function which occur in the literature on growth. What should be noted from this table is what is assumed about the third factor of production, X, and what is assumed about technology. The table also includes some specific examples of production functions along with just some of their assumptions or characteristics.

Table A18.1.1 The aggregate production function

Function	Comment
$y = G(L, K, X; A)$	Most general
$y = F(L, K)$	X ignored and A constant
$y = AH(L, K)$	X ignored and technology disembodied
$y/L = f(k)$ $(k \equiv K/L)$	Constant returns to scale in $y = F(L, K)$
Examples	
$y = F(L, K) = cL^a K^b$	Cobb–Douglas $(a + b = 1)$
$y = AH(L, K)$	Cobb–Douglas with disembodied
$\quad = A_0 e^{\mu t} L^a K^b$	technical progress changing at a constant rate
$y = \min[L/\alpha, K/\beta]$	Harrod–Domar assumed production function with L-shaped isoquants
$y/L = f(k) = ck^b$	Derived from Cobb–Douglas

Since our particular interest here is in growth, it is useful to consider the aggregate production function in terms of such growth. As usual, a circumflex above a particular variable denotes a percentage rate of growth. We cannot consider all the functions listed above, and so we concentrate only on

$$y = AH(L, K) \tag{A18.1.1}$$

which we assume is continuous and twice differentiable.

Totally differentiating (A18.1.1), we have

$$dy = dAH + A(\partial H/\partial L)\,dL + A(\partial H/\partial K)\,dK$$

Hence,

$$dy/y = (dA/A) + (\partial y/\partial L)(L/y)(dL/L) + (\partial y/\partial K)(K/y)(dK/K)$$

But

$$E_L = (\partial y/\partial L)(L/y) \quad \text{and} \quad \hat{L} = dL/L$$

$$E_K = (\partial y/\partial K)(K/y) \quad \text{and} \quad \hat{K} = dK/K$$

where E_L and E_K simply denote elasticities of output with respect to labour and capital respectively. Letting $\mu = dA/A$ then

$$\hat{y} = \mu + E_L \hat{L} + E_K \hat{K} \tag{A18.1.2}$$

If we make the further assumptions of perfect competition and that factors of production are paid their marginal products, then

$$\partial y/\partial L = w \quad \text{and} \quad \partial y/\partial K = r$$

where w is the real wage and r the real price of capital. Under these assumptions, the elasticities become

$$E_L = (wL/y) \quad \text{which is the share of labour in income}$$

$$E_K = (rK/y) \quad \text{which is the share of capital in income}$$

We denote these shares as S_L and S_K respectively. Under this additional assumption, therefore, we have the rate of growth equal to

$$\hat{y} = \mu + S_L \hat{L} + S_K \hat{K} \tag{A18.1.3}$$

It must be realized, however, that the shares will only equal the output elasticities under *all* the assumptions on p. 408 about the production function and the type of market structure.

Growth of output per worker

In a number of studies, output per worker (or per worker hour) is the major concern. In such studies attention is directed to the relationship between the growth of output per worker ($\widehat{y/L}$) and the growth of the capital–output ratio. The relationship can be derived using equation (A18.1.3) as follows:

$$(\widehat{y/L}) = \hat{y} - \hat{L}$$
$$= \mu + S_L \hat{L} + S_K \hat{K} - \hat{L}$$
$$= \mu + (S_L - 1)\hat{L} + S_K \hat{K}$$

But $S_L + S_K = 1$. Hence,

$$(\widehat{y/L}) = \mu - S_K \hat{L} + S_K \hat{K}$$
$$= \mu + S_K(\hat{K} - \hat{L})$$

But $k \equiv K/L$, and so $\hat{k} = \hat{K} - \hat{L}$. Hence,

$$(\widehat{y/L}) = \mu + S_K \hat{k} \qquad (A18.1.4)$$

Notice in particular that this is a linear equation in ($\widehat{y/L}$) and $\hat{k}$, so that regression analysis can be used to obtain estimates of μ and S_K (and from S_K an estimate of S_L).

Using a Cobb–Douglas production function

Many studies involving growth use a Cobb–Douglas production function of the form

$$y = A_0 e^{\mu t} L^a K^b \qquad (A18.1.5)$$

In this case it is possible to show that the elasticities of output with respect to labour and capital are a and b respectively, and hence under the further assumption of perfect competition, the share of labour in income is a while the share of capital in income is b. These results can be verified as follows:

$$E_L = (\partial y/\partial L)(L/y) = (A_0 e^{\mu t} a L^{a-1} K^b)(L/y) = a$$
$$E_K = (\partial y/\partial K)(K/y) = (A_0 e^{\mu t} b L^a K^{b-1})(K/y) = b$$

Hence, under perfect competition where factors are paid their marginal products.

$$E_L = a = S_L$$
$$E_K = b = S_K$$

APPENDIX 18.2 NEOCLASSICAL GROWTH

We begin with the continuous and twice differentiable production function

$$y = F(L, K) \qquad (A18.2.1)$$

which has positive, but diminishing, marginal products

$$F_L > 0 \qquad F_{LL} < 0$$
$$F_K > 0 \qquad F_{KK} < 0$$

It is further assumed that the production function exhibits constant returns to scale (i.e., is homogeneous of degree one). Thus,

$$y/L = F(1, K/L) = f(k) \quad k \equiv K/L \qquad (A18.2.2)$$

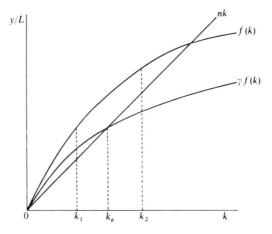

Figure A18.2.1 Equilibrium in a neoclassical growth model.

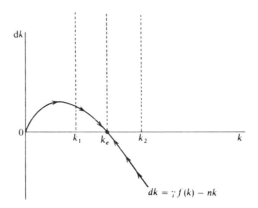

Figure A18.2.2 Phase diagram for neoclassical growth model.

Of special interest in the neoclassical growth model is the capital–labour ratio, k. Taking the growth in this, we have

$$\hat{k} = \hat{K} - \hat{L} \tag{A18.2.3}$$

In discussing the Harrod–Domar growth model, we have already indicated that

$$dK = i = s = \gamma y$$

which implies that

$$\hat{K} = \gamma y / K \tag{A18.2.4}$$

In this model labour is assumed to grow at a constant rate n. Thus,

$$\hat{L} = n \tag{A18.2.5}$$

Substituting equations (A18.2.2), (A18.2.4) and (A18.2.5) into equation (A18.2.3), we obtain

$$\hat{k} = \gamma f(k)/k - n$$

or

$$dk = \gamma f(k) - nk \qquad \text{(A18.2.6)}$$

If capital and labour are fully employed, and if this full employment is to be maintained over time, then there must not be any change in the capital–labour ratio, i.e. we require

$$dk = \gamma f(k) - nk = 0 \qquad \text{(A18.2.7)}$$

The situation is illustrated in Figs. A18.2.1 and A18.2.2, where Fig. A18.2.2 is illustrating a phase diagram (see Appendix 13.1). Beginning from some capital–labour ratio such as k_1, the marginal product of capital, the slope of $f(k)$, is greater than the slope of nk, hence there will be a temporary rise in capital, which will lead to a rise in the capital–labour ratio. On the other hand, if the capital labour–ratio were given by k_2, then the marginal product of capital would be less than the slope of nk, and hence there would be a decrease in investment. The fall in investment would lead to a fall in the capital–labour ratio over time (since labour is growing at the rate n). No further changes in the capital–labour ratio will take place when k_e is reached, i.e. when the phase line in Fig. A18.2.2 cuts the horizontal axis. Hence, no matter what capital–labour ratio prevails in the economy, adjustment will take place until k_e is reached.

BIBLIOGRAPHY

Aaronovitch, S. and Sawyer, M. C. (1974) 'The concentration of British manufacturing'. *Lloyds Bank Review*, No. 114.

Addison, J. T. and Siebert, W. S. (1980) *The Market for Labor: An Analytical Treatment*. Goodyear Publishing Co.

Ahmad, J. (1984) *Floating Exchange Rates and World Inflation*. Macmillan.

Akerlof, G. A. (1979) 'The case against Conservative macroeconomics: an inaugural lecture'. *Economica*, **46** (183), August.

Allen, R. G. D. (1965) *Mathematical Economics*. Macmillan.

Allen, R. G. D. (1967) *Macro-Economic Theory*. Macmillan.

Allin, P. (1976) 'Drawing the line in the balance of payments accounts'. *CSO Statistical News*, No. 36.

Ando, A. and Modigliani, F. (1963) The 'life cycle' hypothesis of saving: aggregate implications and tests. *American Economic Review*, **LIII**, March.

Arestis, M. J. and Hadjimatheou, G. (1982) *Introductory Macroeconomic Modelling*. Macmillan.

Argy, V. (1981) *The Postwar International Money Crisis – an Analysis*. George Allen & Unwin.

Artis, M. J. (1978) 'Monetary Policy', in Blackaby, F. T. (ed.) (1978) *British Economic Policy 1960–73*. Cambridge University Press.

Artis, M. J. and Lewis, M. K. (1976) 'The demand for money in the UK, 1963–1973'. *Manchester School*, **44**, June.

Artis, M. J. and Lewis, M. K. (1981) *Monetary Control in the United Kingdom*. Philip Allan.

Artis, M. J. and Lewis, M. K. (1984) 'How unstable is the demand for money function in the United Kingdom?' *Economica*, **51**, November.

Artis, M. J. *et al.* (1984) The effects of economic policy 1979–82. *National Institute Economic Review*, May.

Attfield, C. L. F., Demery, D. and Duck, N. W. (1985) *Rational Expectations in Macroeconomics*. Basil Blackwell.

Backhouse, R. (1980) 'Fix-price versus flex-price models of macroeconomic equilibrium with rationing'. *Oxford Economic Papers*, **32** (2), July.

Bacon, R. and Eltis, W. (1976) (2nd edn 1978) *Britain's Economic Problem: Too Few Producers*. Macmillan.

Bailey, R. (1986) 'Gas privatization and the energy strategy' *National Westminster Bank Quarterly Review*, August.

Bain, A. D. (1970) (3rd edn 1980) *The Control of the Money Supply*. Penguin.

Bain, A. D. (1973) 'Flow of funds analysis: a survey'. *Economic Journal*, **83**, December.

Ball, R. J. (1978) *Report of Committee on Policy Optimisation*. Cmnd. 7148. HMSO.

Bank of England (1972) *An Introduction to Flow of Funds Accounting: 1952–70*. Bank of England.

Bank of England (1974) 'Credit control: a supplementary scheme'. *Bank of England Quarterly Bulletin*, **14** (1), March.

Bank of England (1979) 'Intervention arrangements in the European monetary system'. *Bank of England Quarterly Bulletin*, **19** (2), June.

Bank of England (1982a) 'Measures of competitiveness'. *Bank of England Quarterly Bulletin*, **22** (3), September.

Bank of England (1982b) 'Venture capital'. *Bank of England Quarterly Bulletin*, **22** (4), December.

Barro, R. J. (1984) *Macroeconomics*. John Wiley & Son.

Basevi, G. and De Grauwe, P. (1978) 'Vicious and virtuous circles and the OPTICA proposal: a two country analysis'. In Frathianni, M. and Peeters, T. (eds.) *One Money for Europe*. Macmillan.

Batchelor, R., Bendle, E. and Griffiths, B. (1980) 'Inflation, unemployment and reform'. In Blackaby, F. T. (ed.) (1980) *The Future of Pay Bargaining*. Heinemann.

Baumol, W. J. (1952) 'The transactions demand for cash: an inventory theoretic approach'. *Quarterly Journal of Economics*, **66**.

Baumol, W. J. (1982) 'Contestable markets: an uprising in the theory of industry structure'. *American Economic Review*, **72** (1), March.

Baxter, J. L. (1973) 'Inflation in the context of relative deprivation and social justice'. *Scottish Journal of Political Economy*, **20**, February.

Bean, C. R., Layard, P. R. G., and Nickell, S. J. (1986) 'The rise in unemployment: a multi-country study'. *Economica, Supplement*, **53** (210), (S).

Beckerman, W. (2nd edn 1976) *An Introduction to National Income Analysis*. Weidenfeld and Nicolson.

Beckerman, W. and Associates (1965) *The British Economy in 1975*. Cambridge University Press.

Beenstock, M. (1979) 'Taxation and incentives in the UK'. *Lloyds Bank Review*, No. 134, October.

Beenstock, M. and Minford, P. (1987) 'Curing unemployment through labour-market competition'. In Minford, P. (1987) (ed.) *Monetarism and Macroeconomics*. IEA, Readings 26.

Beesley, M. and Littlechild, S. (1983) 'Privatization: principles, problems and priorities'. *Lloyds Bank Review*, No. 149, July.

Beeton, D. J. (1986) 'On the size of the public sector'. Queen Mary College, Discussion Paper No. 149.

Begg, D., Fischer, S. and Dornbusch, R. (2nd edn 1987) *Economics*. McGraw-Hill.

Begg, D. K. H. (1982) *The Rational Expectations Revolution in Macroeconomics*. Philip Allan.

Bell, D. and Kristol, I. (eds.) (1981) *The Crisis in Economic Theory*. Basic Books.

Bigman, D. (1984) 'Exchange rate determination: some old myths and new paradigms', In Bigman, D. and Taya, T. (eds.) (1985) *Floating Exchange Rates and the State of World Trade and Payments*. Ballinger Publishing Company.

Bisham, J. (1986) 'Growing public sector debt: a policy dilemma'. *National Westminster Bank Quarterly Review*, May.

Biswas, R. Johns, C. and Savage, D. (1985) 'The measurement of fiscal stance'. *National Institute Economic Review*, No. 113, August.

Blackaby, F. T. (ed.) (1978) *British Economic Policy 1960–74*. Cambridge University Press.

Blackaby, F. T. (1979a) 'The economics and politics of demand management'. In Cook, S. T. and Jackson, P. M. (eds.) (1979) *Current Issues in Fiscal Policy*. Martin Robertson.

Blackaby, F. T. (ed.) (1979b) *De-industrialisation*. Heinemann.

Blackaby, F. T. (ed.) (1980a) *The Future of Pay Bargaining*. Heinemann.

Blackaby, F. T. (1980b) 'An array of proposals'. In Blackaby, F. T. (ed.) (1980) *The Future of Pay Bargaining*. Heinemann.

Blinder, A. S. and Solow, R. M. (1974) 'Analytical foundations of fiscal policy'. In Blinder, A. S. *et al.* (1974) *The Economics of Public Finance*. The Brookings Institution.

Blundell-Wignall, A. and Chouraqui, J. (1984) 'The role of exchange market intervention'. *National Westminster Bank Quarterly Review*, November.

Bond, M. E. and Knoble, A. (1982) 'Some implications of North Sea oil for the UK economy'. *IMF Staff Papers*, **29** (3), September.

Bordo, M. D. and Jonung, L. (1987) *The Long-run Behavior of the Velocity of Circulation*. Cambridge University Press.

Bowden, R. J. (1980) 'On the existence and secular stability of u–v loci'. *Economica*, **47** (185), February.

Brittan, S. (1971) *Steering the Economy*. Penguin.

Brittan, S. (1981) 'How to end the monetarist controversy'. *Hobart Paper No. 90*. Institute of Economic Affairs.

Britton, A. (1986) 'Can fiscal expansion cut unemployment?' *National Institute Economic Review*, No. 113, August.

Brown, C. V. (1980) (2nd edn 1983) *Taxation and the Incentive to Work*. Oxford University Press.

Brown, C. V. and Jackson, P. M. (3rd edn 1986) *Public Sector Economics*. Martin Robertson.

Brown, W. A. (1980) 'The structure of pay bargaining in Britain'. In F. T. Blackaby (ed.) (1980) *The Future of Pay Bargaining*. Heinemann.

Browning, P. (1986) *The Treasury and Economic Policy 1964–1985*. Longman.

Brunner, K. and Meltzer, A. H. (1969) 'The nature of the policy problem'. In Brunner, K. (ed.) *Targets and Indicators of Monetary Policy*. Chandler.

Budd, A. (1979) 'The future of demand management: reviewing the choices'. In Cook, S. J. and Jackson, P. M. (eds.) (1979) *Current Issues in Fiscal Policy*. Martin Robertson.

Budd, A. (1984) 'Macroeconomic aspects of the 1984 Budget'. In Keen, M. (ed.) (1984) *The Economy and the 1984 Budget*. Basil Blackwell.

Budd, A. (1985) 'Macroeconomic policy and the 1985 Budget'. In Kay, J. (ed.) (1985) *The Economy and the 1985 Budget*. Basil Blackwell.

Budd, A., Dicks, G. and Keating, G. (1985) 'Government borrowing and financial markets' *National Institute Economic Review*, No. 113, August.

Buiter, W. H. (1977) '"Crowding out" and the effectiveness of fiscal policy'. *Journal of Public Economics*, **7** (3), June.

Buiter, W. H. (1980) 'The macroeconomics of Dr Pangloss: a critical survey of the new classical macroeconomics'. *Economic Journal*, **90** (357).

Buiter, W. H. and Miller, M. (1981) 'The Thatcher experiment: the first two years'. *Brookings Papers on Economic Activity*, **4**.

Burmeister, E. and Dobell, A. R. (1970) *Mathematical Theories of Economic Growth*. Macmillan.

Burrows, P. and Hitiris, T. (1972) 'Estimating the impact of incomes policy'. *Bulletin of Economic Research*, **24**.

Burton, J. (1985) 'Why no cuts?' *Hobart Paper No. 104*. Institute of Economic Affairs.

Cairncross, A. (1979) 'What is de-industrialisation?' In F. T. Blackaby (1979) *De-industrialisation*. Heinemann.

Cairncross, A., Henderson, P. D. and Silberston, Z. A. (1982) 'Problems of industrial recovery'. *Midland Bank Review*, Spring.

Cairncross, A., Kay, J. A. and Silberston, A. (1977) 'The regeneration of manufacturing industry'. *Midland Bank Review*, Autumn.

Carter, M. and Maddock, R. (1984) *Rational Expectations*. Macmillan.

Caslin, T. (1987) 'Industrial and market structure in the UK'. In Vane, H. and Caslin, T. (1987) *Current Controversies in Economics*. Basil Blackwell.

Chacholiades, M. (1978) *International Monetary Theory and Policy*. McGraw-Hill.

Chalmers, E. B. (1971) (ed.) *Forward Exchange Intervention*. Hutchinson.

Chiang, A. C. (3rd. edn 1984) *Fundamental Methods of Mathematical Economics*. McGraw-Hill.

Chick, V. (1977) (Rev. ed.) *Theory of Monetary Policy*. Basil Blackwell.

Chick, V. (1983) *Macroeconomics After Keynes*. Philip Allan.

Chiplin, B. and Wright, M. (1980) 'Divestment and structural change in UK industry'. *National Westminster Bank Quarterly Review*, February.

Chiplin, B. and Wright, M. (1987) 'The logic of mergers'. *Hobart Paper 107*. Institute of Economic Affairs.

Chrystal, K. A. (1979) (2nd edn 1983) *Controversies in British Macro-economics*. Philip Allan.

Clower, R. W. (1965) 'The Keynesian counter-revolution: a theoretical appraisal'. In F. H. Hahn and F. Brechling (eds.) *The Theory of Interest Rates*. Macmillan.

Coates, D. and Hillard, J. (eds.) (1986) *The Economic Decline of Modern Britain*. Harvester Wheatsheaf.

Coates, D. and Hillard, J. (eds.) (1987) *The Economic Revival of Modern Britain*. Edward Elgar.

Cobham, D. (1981) 'Definitions of domestic credit expansion for the United Kingdom'. *Journal of Economic Studies*, **8**, (3).

Coffey, P. and Presley, J. R. (1971) *European Monetary Integration*. Macmillan.

Coghlan, R. (1978) 'A new view of money *Lloyds Bank Review*, July 1978.

Coghlan, R. (1980) *The Theory of Money and Finance*. Macmillan.

Colander, D. C. and Guthrie, R. S. (1980–81) 'Great expectations: what the dickens do "rational expectations" mean?' *Journal of Post Keynesian Economics*, Winter.

Congdon, T. G. (1984) 'The analytical foundations of the medium-term financial strategy'. In Keen, M. (ed.) (1984) *The Economy and the 1984 Budget*. Basil Blackwell.

Congdon, T. G. (1985) 'Does Mr Lawson really believe in the medium-term financial strategy?'. In Kay, J. (1985) *The Economy and the 1985 Budget*. Basil Blackwell.

Connell, D. (1980) The UK's performance in export markets – some evidence from international trade data. *National Economic Development Office. Discussion Paper 6*.

Corden, W. M. (1977) (3rd edn 1985) *Inflation, Exchange Rates and the World Economy*, Oxford University Press.

Corden, W. M. (1980) 'The exchange rate, monetary policy and North Sea oil: the economic theory of the squeeze on tradeables'. *Oxford Economic Papers*, March.

Coutts, K., Tarling, R., Ward, T. and Wilkinson, F. (1981) 'The economic consequences of Mrs Thatcher'. *Cambridge Journal of Economics*, **5**, March.

Craven, B. M. and Wright, G. A. (1983) 'The Thatcher experiment'. *Journal of Macroeconomics*, **5**, Winter.

Cross, R. (1982) *Economic Theory and Policy in the UK*. Martin Robertson.

Croxton, F. E.. Cowden, D. J. and Klein, S. (3rd edn 1968) *Applied General Statistics*. Pitman. [Chapter 18].

CSE London Working Group (1980) *The Alternative Economic Strategy*. CSE Books.

Cuddy, J. D. A. and Della Valle, P. A. (1978) 'Measuring the instability of time series data'. *Oxford Bulletin of Economics and Statistics*, **40**, (1), February.

Culyer, A. J. (1985) *Economics*. Basil Blackwell.

Currie, D. (1985*a*) 'Macroeconomic policy design and control theory – a failed partnership?' *Economic Journal*, **95**, (378), June.

Currie, D. (1985*b*) 'The conduct of fiscal policy'. *National Institute Economic Review*. No. 113, August.

Currie, D. *et al.* (1985) 'Alternative financial policy rules in an open economy under rational and adaptive expectations'. *National Institute Economic and Social Research, Discussion Paper No. 94*, June.

Curry, B. and George, K. (1983) 'Industrial concentration: a survey'. *Journal of Industrial Economics*, **31**.

Curwen, P. (1986) *Public Enterprise*, Harvester Wheatsheaf.

Cuthbertson, K. (1979) *Macroeconomic Policy*. Macmillan.

Cuthbertson, K. (1985) *The Supply and Demand for Money*. Basil Blackwell.

Dasgupta, P. and Stiglitz, J. (1980) 'Industrial structure and the nature of innovative activity'. *Economic Journal*, **90** (358), June.

Davidson, J. and Ireland, J. (1987) 'Buffer stock models of the monetary sector'. *National Institute Economic Review*, No. 121, August.

Davidson, P. (1981) 'Post Keynesian economics'. In Bell, D. and Kristol, I. (eds.) (1981) *The Crisis in Economic Theory*. Basic Books.

Dawkins, D. J. (1980) 'Incomes policy' In P. Maunder (ed.) *The British Economy in the 1970s*. Heinemann.

Dean, A. (1981) 'Incomes policy and the British economy in the 1970s'. In Chater, R. E. J., Dean, A. and Elliott, R. F. (1981) (eds.) *Income Policy*. Clarendon Press.

De Grauwe, P. (1983) *Macroeconomic Theory for the Open Economy*. Gower.

Demery, D. and Duck, N. W. (1984) 'The macroeconomic implications of the theory of rational expectations'. In Demery, D. *et al.* (1984) *Macroeconomics*. Longman.

Demery, D. and Duck, N. W. (1984) 'Stabilisation policy'. In Demery, D. *et al.* *Macroeconomics*. Longman.

Demery, D., Duck, N. W., Sumner, M. T., Thomas, R. L. and Thompson, W. N. (1984) *Macroeconomics*. Longman.

Denison, E. F. (1962) *The Sources of Economic Growth in the United States and the Alternatives Before Us.* Washington DC. Committee for Economic Development.

Denison, E. F. (1967) *Why Growth Rates Differ.* Washington DC. Brookings Institute.

Desai, M. (1981) *Testing Monetarism.* Frances Pinter.

Dodgson, J. (1987) 'Privatization' In Vane, H. and Caslin, T. (1987) *Current Controversies in Economics.* Basil Blackwell.

Domar, E. (1946) 'Capital expansion, rate of growth and employment. *Econometrica*, **14**.

Dornbusch, R. (1976) 'Expectations and exchange rate dynamics'. *Journal of Political Economy*, **84**.

Dornbusch, R. and Fischer, S. (1981) (4th edn 1987) *Macroeconomics.* McGraw-Hill.

Dow, J. C. R. (1964) *The Management of the British Economy, 1945–60.* Cambridge University Press.

Dow, S. C. and Earl, P. E. (1982) *Money Matters.* Martin Robertson.

Downs, A. (1957) *An Economic Theory of Democracy.* Harper & Row.

Duesenberry, J. S. (1949) *Income, Savings and the Theory of Consumer Behavior.* Harvard University Press.

Eckaus, R. S. (1953) 'The acceleration principle reconsidered'. *Quarterly Journal of Economics*, **67**, May.

Economic Trends (1977) 'The home and export performance of United Kingdom industries'. *Economic Trends*, August.

Edison, H. J. (1987) 'Purchasing power parity in the long run: a test of the dollar/pound exchange rate (1890–1978)'. *Journal of Money, Credit and Banking*, August.

Enoch, C. A. (1978) 'Measures of competitiveness'. *Bank of England Quarterly Bulletin*, **19** (2), June.

Evans, A. (1977) 'Notes on the changing relationship between registered unemployment and notified vacancies: 1961–1966 and 1966–1971'. *Economica*, **44** (174), May.

Fay, S. and Young, H. (1978) 'The day the £ nearly died'. *The Sunday Times*. June.

Feldstein, M. (1986) 'Supply side economics: old truths and new claims'. *American Economic Review, Papers and Proceedings*, May.

Ferguson, P. R. (1985) 'The monopolies and Mergers Commission and Economic theory'. *National Westminster Bank Quarterly Review*, November.

Flemming, J. (1976) *Inflation.* Oxford University Press.

Foot, M. D. W. *et al.* (1979) 'Monetary base control'. *Bank of England Quarterly Bulletin*, **19** (2), June.

Fox, K. A. (1968) *Intermediate Economic Statistics*, John Wiley & Son.

Frank, J. (1986) *The New Keynesian Economics*, Harvester Wheatsheaf.

Frazer, W. (1982) 'Milton Friedman and Thatcher's monetarist experience'. *Journal of Economic Issues.* **16**, June.

Freeman, C. (2nd. edn 1974) *The Economics of Industrial Innovation.* Penguin.

Freeman, C. (1979) 'Technical innovation and British trade performance'. In F. Blackaby (ed.) (1979) *De-industrialisation.* Heinemann.

Frenkel, J. A. (1982) 'Flexible exchange rates, prices and the role of "news": lessons from the 1970's. In Batchelor, R. A. and Wood, G. E. (eds.) (1982) *Exchange Rate Policy.* Macmillan.

Friedman, M. (1953) 'The case for flexible exchange rates'. In Friedman, M. (1953) *Essays in Positive Economics.* University of Chicago Press.

Friedman, M. (1956) 'The quantity theory of money – A restatement'. In Friedman, M. (ed.) (1956) *Studies in the Quantity Theory of Money.* Chicago University Press.

Friedman, M. (1957) *A Theory of the Consumption Function.* Princeton University Press.

Friedman, M. (1968) 'The role of monetary policy'. *American Economic Review*, **58** (1). March.

Friedman, M. (1970) The counter-revolution in monetary theory. *Institute of Economic Affairs, Occasional Paper, No. 33.*

Friedman, M. (1971) 'A monetary theory of nominal income'. *Journal of Political Economy.* **79** (2), March/April.

Friedman, M. and Friedman, R. (1980) *Free to Choose.* Penguin.

Frisch, H. (1983) *Theories of Inflation.* Cambridge University Press.

Gapinski, J. H. (1982) *Macroeconomic Theory. Statics, Dynamics, and Policy.* McGraw-Hill.

Glahe, F. R. (1967) 'An empirical study of the foreign-exchange market: test of a theory'. *Princeton Studies in International Finance, No. 20*, Princeton University, International Finance Section.

Goacher, D. J. (1986) *An Introduction to Monetary Economics*. Financial Training Publications.

Godley, W. A. A. and Shepherd, J. R. (1964) 'Long-term growth and short-term policy'. *National Institute Economic Review*, No. 29.

Goldstein, M. (1980) 'Have flexible exchange rates handicapped macroeconomic policy?' *Special Papers in International Economics*, No. 14, June. Princeton University.

Goodhart, C. A. E. (1975) *Money, Information and Uncertainty*. Macmillan.

Goodhart, C. A. E. (1984) *Monetary Theory and Practice*. Macmillan.

Goodwin, R. M. (1951) 'The nonlinear accelerator and the persistence of business cycles'. *Econometrica*, **19**, January.

Gordon, R. J. (1978) (3rd edn 1984) *Macroeconomics*. Little Brown and Company.

Gordon, R. J. (1981) 'Output fluctuations and gradual price adjustment'. *Journal of Economic Literature*, **19** (2), June.

Gowland, D. (1978) *Monetary Policy and Credit Control*. Croom Helm.

Gowland, D. (1982) *Controlling the Money Supply*. Croom Helm.

Graham, A. W. M. (1977) (2nd edn 1979) 'Objectives and instruments'. In D. Morris (ed.) *The Economic System in the UK*. Oxford University Press.

Gramlich, E. M. (1979) 'Macroeconomic policy responses to price shocks'. *Brookings Papers on Economic Activity*, **10** (1).

Grice, J. and Bennett, A. (1984) 'Wealth and the demand for £M3 in the United Kingdom, 1963–1978'. *Manchester School*, **LII** (3), September.

Greenaway, D. and Shaw, G. K. (1983) *Macroeconomics*, Martin Robertson.

Griffiths, B. (1979) 'The reform of monetary control in the United Kingdom'. *The City University Annual Review*, **I**, October.

Griffiths, B. and Wood, G. E. (eds.) (1981) *Monetary Targets*. Macmillan.

Gujarati, D. (1972) 'The behaviour of unemployment and unfilled vacancies'. *Economic Journal*, **82** (325), March.

Gupta, S. (1967) 'Public expenditure and economic growth: a time-series analysis'. *Public Finance*, **22**.

Haberler, G. (1949) 'The market for foreign exchange and the stability of the balance of payments: a theoretical analysis'. *Kyklos*, **3**. Reprinted in Cooper, R. N. (ed.) (1969) *International Finance*. Penguin.

Hadjimichalakis, M. G. (1982) *Modern Macroeconomics*. Prentice Hall.

Hahn, F. (1982) 'Reflections on the invisible hand'. *Lloyds Bank Review*, No. 144, April.

Hahn, F. H. and Matthews, R. C. O. (1964) 'The theory of economic growth: a survey'. *Economic Journal*, **74**.

Hall, M. (1983) *Monetary Policy Since 1971*. Macmillan.

Hallwood, P. and MacDonald, R. (1986) *International Money*. Basil Blackwell.

Hammond, E., Helm, D. and Thompson, D. (1985) 'British Gas: options for privatisation'. *Fiscal Studies*, **6** (4), November.

Hansen, B. (1951) *A Study in the Theory of Inflation*. George Allen & Unwin.

Hansen, B. (1970) 'Excess demand, unemployment, vacancies, and wages'. *Quarterly Journal of Economics*, **84**, February.

Harrod, R. F. (1939) 'An essay in dynamics theory'. *Economic theory*, **49**.

Hart, P. E. and Clarke, R. (1980) *Concentration in British Industry 1935–1975*. Cambridge University Press.

Hawkins, C. J. and Pearce, D. W. (1971) *Capital Investment Appraisal*. Macmillan.

Hawkins, K. (1979) (2nd edn 1984) *Unemployment*. Penguin.

Hemming, R. and Kay, J. A. (1980) 'The Laffer curve'. *Fiscal Studies*, **1** (2), March.

Henderson, J. M. and Quandt, R. E. (2nd edn 1971) *Microeconomic Theory. A Mathematical Approach*. McGraw-Hill.

Henry, S. G. B. and Ormerod, P. A. (1978) 'Incomes policy and wage inflation: empirical evidence for the UK 1961–77'. *National Institute Economic Review*, No. 85, August.

Hey, J. D. (1979) *Uncertainty in Microeconomics*, Martin Robertson.

Hicks, J. R. (1939) *Value and Capital*. Clarendon Press.

Hicks, J. R. (1974) *The Crisis in Keynesian Economics*. Basil Blackwell.

Hicks, J. R. (1976) 'The little that is right with monetarism'. *Lloyds Bank Review*, July.

Hines, A. G. (1964) 'Trade unions and wage inflation in the United Kingdom, 1893–1961' *Review of Economic Studies*, 31.

Hines, A. G. (1971) 'The determinants of the rate of change of money wage rates and the effectiveness of incomes policy'. In Johnson, H. G. and Nobay, A. R. (1971) (eds.) *The Current Inflation*. Macmillan.

Hirsch, F. and Goldthorpe, J. H. (ed.) (1978) *The Political Economy of Inflation*. Martin Robertson.

Hodgson, G. (1984) 'Thatcherism: the miracle that never happened'. In Nell, E. J. (ed.) (1984) *Free Market Conservatism. A Critique of Theory and Practice*. George Allen & Unwin.

Hodjera, Z. (1973) 'International short-term capital movements: a survey of theory and empirical analysis'. *IMF Staff Papers*.

Holbrook, R. S. (1978) 'The interest rate, the price level, and aggregate output'. In Teigen, R. L. (ed.) (4th edn 1978) *Readings in Money, National Income and Stabilization Policy*. Richard D. Irwin.

Holden, K., Peel, D. A. and Thompson, J. L. (1987) *The Economics of Wage Controls*. Macmillan.

Holmes, M. (1985) *The First Thatcher Government 1979–1983*. Harvester Wheatsheaf.

HMSO (1965) *The National Plan*. Cmnd. 2764.

HMSO (1974) *The Regeneration of British Industry*. Cmnd. 5710.

HMSO (1975) *An Approach to Industrial Strategy*. Cmnd. 6315.

HMSO (1978) *The European Monetary System. First Report from the Committee Expenditure Session 1978–79*, House of Commons 60, 20 November.

HMSO (1985) *Employment: The Challenge for the Nation*. Cmnd. 9474.

HM Treasury (1980) *Monetary Control. Green Paper*. Cmnd. 7858.

Hughes, J. and Thirlwall, A. P. (1977) 'Trends in cycles in import penetration in the UK'. *Oxford Bulletin of Economics and Statistics*, **39**.

Hughes, J. J. and Perlman, R. (1984) *The Economics of Unemployment*. Harvester Wheatsheaf.

Humphrey, T. M. (1976) Some current controversies in the theory of inflation. In Teigen, R. L. (ed.) (4th edn 1978) *Readings in Money, National Income and Stabilization Policy*. Richard D. Irwin, Inc.

Imber, V. (1983) 'Public expenditure: definitions and trends'. *Economic Trends*, No. 361, November.

Jackman, R. and Layard, R. (1987) 'Innovative supply-side policies to reduce unemployment'. In Minford, P. (1987) (ed.) *Monetarism and Macroeconomics*. IEA, Readings 26.

Jackson, P. M. (1982) *The Political Economy of Bureaucracy*. Martin Robertson.

Jay, D. (1986) *Sterling*. Oxford University Press.

Johnson, H. G. (1969) 'The case for flexible exchange rates, 1969'. In Johnson, H. G. and Nash, J. E. (1969) *UK and Floating Exchange Rates*. Institute of Economic Affairs.

Jones, H. G. (1975) *An Introduction to Modern Theories of Economic Growth*. Thomas Nelson.

Junankar, P. N. (1972) *Investment: Theories and Evidence*. Macmillan.

Junankar, P. N. (1987) 'The British youth labour market in crisis'. *International Review of Applied Economics*, **1** (1).

Kaldor, N. (1966) *Causes of the Slow Rate of Growth of the United Kingdom. An Inaugural Lecture*. Cambridge University Press.

Kaldor, N. (1970) 'The new monetarism'. *Lloyds Bank Review*, No. 9, July.

Kaldor, N. (1975) 'Economic growth and the Verdoorn law'. *Economic Journal*, **85**.

Kaldor, N. (1983) *Economic Consequences of Mrs Thatcher*. Duckworth.

Kaldor, N. and Trevithick, J. (1981) 'A Keynesian perspective on money'. *Lloyds Bank Review*, No. 139, January.

Kantor, B. (1979) 'Rational expectations and economic thought'. *Journal of Economic Literature*, **17** (4), December.

Katseli-Papaefstratiou, L. T. (1979) The re-emergence of the purchasing power parity doctrine in the 1970s. *Special Papers in International Economics, No. 13*, Princeton University, International Finance Section.

Kay, J. A. and Silberston, Z. A. (1984) 'The new industrial policy – privatisation and competition'. *Midland Bank Review*, Spring.

Kay, J. A. and Thompson, D. (1986) 'Privatisation: a policy in search of a rationale'. *Economic Journal*, **96** (381), March.

Keating, G. (1985) *The Production and Use of Economic Forecasts*. Methuen.

Keegan, W. (1984) *Mrs Thatcher's Economic Experiment*. Pelican.

Keegan, W. and Pennant-Rea, R. (1979) *Who Runs the Economy?* Maurice Temple Smith.

Keynes, J. M. (1936) *The General Theory of Employment, Interest and Money*. Macmillan.

Kilpatrick, A. and Lawson, A. (1980) 'On the nature of industrial decline in the UK'. *Cambridge Journal of Economics*, **4** (1), March.

King, D. N. (1984) *An Introduction to National Income Accounting*. Edward Arnold.

King, J. (1986) (ed.) *Budget Briefing 1986*. Institute of Fiscal Studies.

Klein, L. R. (1972) 'The treatment of expectations in economics'. In Carter, C. F. and Ford, J. L. (eds.) (1972) *Uncertainty and Expectations in Economics*. Basil Blackwell.

Knight, K. G. (1987) *Unemployment: An Economic Analysis*. Croom Helm.

Knowles, K. G. J. C. and Winsten, C. B. (1959) 'Can the level of unemployment explain changes in wages?' *Bulletin of the Oxford University Institute of Economics and Statistics*, **21**.

Krueger, A. O. (1983) *Exchange-Rate Determination*. Cambridge University Press.

Laidler, D. E. W. (1969) (3rd edn 1985) *The Demand for Money: Theories and Evidence*. International Textbook Company.

Laidler, D. E. W. (1981) 'Monetarism: an interpretation and an assessment'. *Economic Journal*, **91** (1361), March.

Laidler, D. E. W. and Parkin, J. M. (1975) 'Inflation – a survey'. *Economic Journal*, **85** (340), December.

Lawson, T. (1981) 'Keynesian model building and the rational expectations critique'. *Cambridge Journal of Economics*. December.

Layard, R. and Nickell, S. (1985) 'The causes of British unemployment'. *National Institute Economic Review*, No. 113.

Layard, R. and Nickell, S. (1986) 'Unemployment in Britain'. *Economica, Supplement*, **53** (210) (S).

Levačić, R. (1987) *Economic Policy-Making*. Harvester Wheatsheaf.

Levačić, R. and Rebmann, A. (1982) *Macroeconomics*. Macmillan.

Levi, M. (1983) *International Finance*. McGraw-Hill.

Levitt, M. S. (1984) 'The growth of government expenditure'. *National Institute Economic Review*, May.

Lewis, G. R. and Ormerod, P. A. (1979) 'Policy simulations and model characteristics'. In S. T. Cook and P. M. Jackson (eds.) (1979) *Current Issues in Fiscal Policy*. Martin Robertson.

Lipsey, R. G. (1960) 'The relationship between unemployment and the rate of change of money wage rates in the UK. 1862–1957: a further analysis'. *Economica, N.S.*, **27**.

Lipsey, R. G. (6th edn 1983) *An Introduction to Positive Economics*. Weidenfeld and Nicolson.

Llewellyn, D. T. (ed.) (1982) *The Framework of UK Monetary Policy*. Heinemann.

Lomax, D. F. (1982) 'Supply-side economics: the British experience'. *National Westminster Bank Quarterly Review*, August.

Lucas, R. E. Jr and Prescott, E. C. (1974) 'Equilibrium search and unemployment'. *Journal of Economic Theory*, **7**.

Machlup, F. (1958) 'Equilibrium and disequilibrium: misplaced concreteness and disguised politics'. *Economic Journal*, **68**.

Maddison, A. (1987) 'Growth and slowdown in advanced capitalist economies'. *Journal of Economic Literature*, **XXV** (2), June.

Maddock, R. and Carter, M. (1982) 'A child's guide to rational expectations'. *Journal of Economic Literature*, **20** (1), March.

Malinvaud, E. (1977) *The Theory of Unemployment Reconsidered*. Basil Blackwell.

Malinvaud, E. (1984) *Mass Unemployment*. Basil Blackwell.

Marsden, D., Trinder, C. and Wagner, K. (1986) 'Measures to reduce youth unemployment in Britain, France and West Germany'. *National Institute Economic Review*, No. 117, August.

Matthews, R. C. O. (1986) 'The economics of institutions and the sources of growth'. *Economic Journal*, **96** (384), December.

Matthews, R. C. O. and Reddaway, W. B. (1980) 'Can Mrs Thatcher do it?' *Midland Bank Review*, Autumn.

McKinnon, R. I. (1979) *Money in International Exchange*. Oxford University Press.

Meade, J. (1978) 'The meaning of 'internal balance''. *Economic Journal*. **88** (351), September.

Metcalf, D. (1982) Special employment measures: an analysis of wage subsidies, youth schemes and worksharing. *Midland Bank Review*, Autumn/Winter.

Midland Bank (1982) 'Problems of industrial recovery'. *Midland Bank Review*, Spring.

Midland Bank (1986) 'UK manufacturing: output and trade performance'. *Midland Bank Review*, Autumn.

Mikesell, R. F. and Goldstein, H. N. (1975) 'Rules for a floating-rate regime'. *Essays in International Finance, No. 109*, April. Princeton University.

Miller, M. (1981) 'The medium term financial strategy: an experiment in co-ordinating monetary and fiscal policy', *Fiscal Studies*, **2** (2), July.

Miller, M. H. (1982) 'Inflation-adjusting the public sector financial deficit'. In Kay, J. A. (ed.) *The 1982 Budget*. Basil Blackwell.

Miller, R. and Wood, J. B. (1982) 'What price unemployment?' *Hobart Paper No. 92*, Institute of Economic Affairs.

Minford, P. (1977) 'North Sea oil and the British Economy'. *The Banker*, December.

Minford, P. (1983) (2nd edn 1985) *Unemployment. Cause and Cure*. Basil Blackwell.

Minford, P. and Peel, D. (1981) 'Is the government's strategy on course?' *Lloyds Bank Review*, No. 140, April.

Minford, P. and Peel, D. (1983) *Rational Expectations and the New Macroeconomics*. Martin Robertson.

Mishan, E. J. (1967) *The Costs of Economic Growth*. Staple Press.

Mishan, E. J. (1977) *The Economic Growth Debate: An Assessment*. George Allen & Unwin.

Modigliani, F. and Ando, A. (1957) 'Test of the life cycle hypothesis of saving'. *Bulletin of the Oxford University Institute of Statistics*, **19**, May.

Modigliani, F. and Brumberg, R. (1954) 'Utility analysis and the consumption function: an interpretation of cross section data'. In Kurihara, K. K. (ed.) (1954) *Post-Keynesian Economics*. George Allen & Unwin.

Moore, B. and Rhodes, J. (1976) 'The relative decline of the UK manufacturing sector'. *Economic Policy Review*, No. 2.

Mosley, P. (1981) 'The Treasury Committee and the making of economic policy'. *Political Quarterly*, **52**.

Mosley, P. (1984) *The Making of Economic Policy*. Harvester Wheatsheaf.

Mundell, R. A. (1962) 'The appropriate use of monetary and fiscal policy for internal and external stability'. *International Monetary Fund Staff Papers*, **IX**.

National Institute Economic Review (1982) Special Issue on 'Britain's Comparative Productivity'. *National Institute Economic Review*, No. 101, August.

National Institute Economic Review (1984) 'Full employment as a policy objective'. *National Institute Economic Review*, No. 109, August.

National Institute of Economic and Social Research (1972) 'The effects of the devaluation of 1967 on the current balance of payments'. *Economic Journal, Supplement*, **82** (325a), March.

Neal, F. and Shone, R. (1976) *Economic Model Building*. Macmillan.

Nell, E. J. (ed.) (1984) *Free Market Conservatism. A Critique of Theory and Practice*. George Allen & Unwin.

Nickell, S. J. (1978) *The Investment Decisions of Firms*. Cambridge University Press.

Nickell, S. J. (1979) 'The effect of unemployment and related benefits on the duration of unemployment'. *Economic Journal*, **89** (353). March.

Niehans, J. (1984) *International Monetary Economics*. Philip Allan.

Nordhaus, W. and Tobin, J. (1972) 'Is growth obsolete?' In *Fiftieth Anniversary Colloquium V*, National Bureau of Economic Research.

Nurkse, R. (1945) 'Conditions of international monetary equilibrium'. In Ellis, H. S. and Metzler, L. S. (1950) (eds.) *Readings in the Theory of International Trade*. George Allen & Unwin.

Odling-Smee, J. and Riley, C. (1985) 'Approaches to the PSBR'. *National Institute Economic Review*, No. 113, August.

Officer, L. H. (1976) 'The purchasing-power parity theory of exchange rates: a review article'. *IMF Staff Papers*, **23**, March.

Okun, A. M. (1965) 'Potential GNP: its measurement and significance'. Reprinted in A. M. Okun (1970) *The Political Economy of Prosperity*. Brookings Institute.

Okun, A. M. and Teeters, N. H. (1970) 'The full employment surplus revisited'. *Brookings Papers on Economic Activity*, **1**.

Oliver, A. (1980) 'Skill shortages'. *Economic Trends*, September.

Oppenheimer, P. M. *et al.* (1978) *Business Views on Exchange Rate Policy*. Confederation of British Industry.

Panic, M. (1978) 'The origin of increasing inflationary tendencies in contemporary society'. In Hirsch, F. and Goldthorpe, J. H. (ed.) (1978) *The Political Economy of Inflation*. Martin Robertson.

Panic, U. (1975) 'Why the United Kingdom's propensity to import is high'. *Lloyds Bank Review*, No. 115, January.

Parkin, M. and Bade, R. (1982) *Modern Macroeconomics*. Philip Allan.

Parkin, J. M., Jones, R. A. and Sumner, M. T. (1972) 'A survey of the econometric evidence of the effects of incomes policies on the rate of inflation'. In Parkin, J. M. and Sumner, M. T. (1972) (eds.) *Incomes Policy and Inflation*. Manchester University Press.

Patinkin, D. (1948) 'Price flexibility and full employment'. *American Economic Review*, **38**. Revised version reprinted in Mueller, M. G. (ed.) (1967) *Readings in Macroeconomics*. Holt, Rinehart and Winston.

Patinkin, D. (1959) 'Keynesian economics rehabilitated: a rejoinder to Professor Hicks'. *Economic Journal*, **69**.

Patinkin, D. (2nd edn 1965) *Money, Interest, and Prices*. Harper & Row.

Patterson, K. D. (1987) 'The specification and stability of the demand for money in the United Kingdom'. *Economica*, **54** (213), February.

Peacock, A. T. and Ricketts, M. (1978) 'The growth of the public sector and inflation'. In Hirsch, F. and Goldthorpe, J. H. (ed.) (1978) *The Political Economy of Inflation*. Martin Robertson.

Peacock, A. T. and Wiseman, J. (1961) *The Growth of Public Expenditure in the United Kingdom*. Oxford University Press.

Perry, G. (1977) 'Potential output and productivity'. *Brookings Papers on Economic Activity*, **8** (1).

Peston, M. H. (1974) (2nd edn 1982) *Theory of Macroeconomic Policy*. Philip Allan.

Phelps, E. S. (1961) 'The golden age of accumulation: a fable for growthmen'. *American Economic Review*, **51**.

Phelps, E. S. (1967) 'Phillips curves, expectations of inflation and optimal unemployment over time'. *Economica*, *N.S.* **34**.

Phelps, E. S. (1968) 'Money wage dynamics and labour market equilibrium'. *Journal of Political Economy*, **76**.

Phillips, A. W. (1954) 'Stabilisation policy in a closed economy'. *Economic Journal*, **64**.

Phillips, A. W. (1958) 'The relationship between unemployment and the rate of change of money wage rates in the UK, 1861–1957', *Economica*, *N.S.* **25**,

Pierce, D. G. and Tysome, P. J. (2nd edn 1985) *Monetary Economics*. Butterworths.

Pigou, A. C. (1943) 'The classical stationary state'. *Economic Journal*, **53**.

Pike, R. and Dobbins, R. (1986) *Investment Decisions and Financial Strategy*. Philip Allan.

Pliatzky, L. (1982) *Getting and Spending: Public Expenditure, Employment and Inflation*. Basil Blackwell.

Poole, W. (1970) 'Optimal choice of monetary policy instruments in a simple stochastic macro model'. *Quarterly Journal of Economics*, **84**, May.

Posner, M. (ed.) (1978) *Demand Management*. Heinemann.

Posner, M. V. and Steer, A. (1979) 'Price competitiveness and performance of manufacturing industry'. In Blackaby F. T. (ed.) (1979) *De-industrialisation*. Heinemann.

Prachowney, M. F. J. (1985) *Money in the Macroeconomy*. Cambridge University Press.

Pratten, C. F. (1982) 'Mrs Thatcher's economic experiment'. *Lloyds Bank Review*, No. 143, January.

Pratten, C. F. (1985) *Applied Macroeconomics*. Oxford University Press.

Price, R. W. R. (1978) 'Budgetary policy'. In Blackaby, F. T. (ed.) (1978) *British Economic Policy 1960–1974*. Cambridge University Press.

Radcliffe Committee (1959) *Report on the Workings of the Monetary System*. Cmnd. 827. HMSO.

Reddaway, W. B. (1982) 'The government's economic policy – an appraisal'. *Three Banks Review*, No. 136, December.

Robinson, J. (1947) 'The foreign exchange market'. In *Essays in the Theory of Employment*. 2nd edn 1947. Basil Blackwell. Reprinted in AEA *Readings in the Theory of International Trade*. George Allen & Unwin, 1950.

Rowthorn, R. E. (1975) 'What remains of Kaldor's Law?' *Economic Journal*, **85** (337), March.

Rowthorn, R. E. and Wells, J. R. (1987) *De-Industrialization and Foreign Trade*. Cambridge University Press.

Sachs, J. (1986) 'The uneasy case for greater exchange rate coordination'. *American Economic Review, Papers and Proceedings*, May.

Samuelson, P. A. (1939) 'Interactions between the multiplier analysis and the principle of acceleration'. *Review of Economic Statistics*, **21**, May.

Samuelson, P. A. and Nordhaus, W. D. (12th edn 1983) *Economics*. McGraw-Hill.

Sargent, T. J. (1973) 'Rational expectations, the real rate of interest and the natural rate of unemployment'. *Brookings Papers on Economic Activity*, No. 2.

Sargent, T. J. and Wallace, M. (1973) 'Rational expectations and the dynamics of hyperinflation'. *International Economic Review*, **14** (2), June.

Sargent, T. J. and Wallace, N. (1975) 'Rational expectations, the optimal monetary instrument and the optimal money supply rule'. *Journal of Political Economy*, **83**.

Savage, D. (1980) 'Some issues of monetary policy'. *National Institute Economic Review*, No. 91, February.

Savage, D. (1982) 'Fiscal policy 1974/5–1980/1: description and measurement'. *National Institute Economic Review*, February.

Saving, T. R. (1967) 'Monetary-policy targets and indicators'. *Journal of Political Economy*, **75**, August.

Sawyer, M. C. (1981) (2nd edn 1985) *The Economics of Industries and Firms*. Croom Helm.

Sayers, R. S. (1964) (6th edn) *Modern Banking*. Oxford University Press.

Scherer, F. M. (2nd edn 1980) *Industrial Market Structure and Economic Performance*. Rand McNally.

Schiltknecht, K. (1981) 'Targeting the base – the Swiss Experience'. In Griffiths, B. and Wood, G. E. (eds.) *Monetary Targets*. Macmillan.

Sen, A. (1970) (ed.) *Growth Economics*. Harmondsworth. Penguin.

Shackleton, J. R. (1984) 'Privatisation: the case examined'. *National Westminster Bank Quarterly Review*, May.

Shaw, G. K. (1984) *Rational Expectations*, Harvester Wheatsheaf.

Shaw, R. (1984) 'Competition policy in Britain'. In Hare, P. and Kirby, M. (eds.) (1984) *An Introduction to British Economic Policy*. Harvester Wheatsheaf.

Sheffrin, S. M. (1983) *Rational Expectations*. Cambridge University Press.

Shone, R. (1979) 'Internal and external balance: problems of interpretation'. *Journal of Economic Studies*, **6** (2), November.

Shone, R. (1980) 'The monetary approach to the balance of payments: stock-flow equilibria'. *Oxford Economic Papers*, **32** (2), June.

Shone, R. (1981) *Applications in Intermediate Microeconomics*. Martin Robertson.

Singh, A. (1977) 'UK industry and the world economy: a case of de-industrialisation?' *Cambridge Journal of Economics*, **1**, June.

Sohmen, E. (Rev. edn 1969) *Flexible Exchange Rates*. University of Chicago Press.

Solow, R. M. (1957) 'Technical change and the aggregate production function', *Review of Economics and Statistics*, **39**.

Solow, R. M. (1962) 'Technical progress, capital formation, and economic growth'. *American Economic Review*, **52**.

Solow, R. M. (1980) 'On theories of unemployment'. *American Economic Review*, **70** (1), March.

Solow, R. M. (1986) 'Unemployment: getting the questions right'. *Economica, Supplement*, **53**, (210) (S).

Spence, M. (1983) 'Reviewing *contestable markets and the theory of industry structure*'. *Journal of Economic Literature*, **XXI** (3), September.

Spencer, P. D. (1986) *Financial Innovation, Efficiency and Disequilibrium*. Oxford University Press.

Sprenkle, C. M. (1966) 'Large economic units, banks and the transactions demand for money'. *Quarterly Journal of Economics*, **80**.

Stibbard, P. (1985) 'Measuring public expenditure'. *Economic Trends*, No. 382, August.

Stigler, G. J. (1962) 'Information in the labour market'. *Journal of Political Economy*, **70** (*Supplement*), October.

Stone, R. (8th edn 1966) *National Income and Expenditure*. Bowes.

Stoneman, P. (1983) *The Economic Analysis of Technological Change*. Oxford University Press.

Stout, D. K. (1979) 'De-industrialisation and industrial policy'. In F. Blackaby (ed.) (1979) *De-industrialisation*. Heinemann.

Struthers, J. and Speight, H. (1986) *Money. Institutions, Theory and Policy*. Longman.

Takayama, A. (1974) *Mathematical Economics*. Dryden Press.

Tatom, A. (1978) 'Economic growth and unemployment: a reappraisal of the conventional view'. *Federal Reserve Bank of St Louis Review*, October.

Teigen, R. L. (ed.) (4th edn 1978) *Readings in Money, National Income and Stabilization Policy*. Richard D. Irwin.

Tew, B. (1977) *The Evolution of the International Monetary System 1948–77*. Hutchinson.

Theil, H. (1964) *Optimal Decision Rules for Government and Industry*. North-Holland Publishing Company.

Theil, H. (1966) *Applied Economic Forecasting*. North-Holland Publishing Company.

Theil, H. (1970) *Economic Forecasts and Policy*. North-Holland Publishing Company.

Thirlwall, A. P. (1978) 'The UK's economic problem: a balance of payments constraint?' *National Westminster Bank Quarterly Review*, February.

Thirlwall, A. P. (1980) *Balance of Payments Theory and the United Kingdom Experience*. Macmillan.

Thirlwall, A. P. (1982) 'Deindustrialisation in the United Kingdom'. *Lloyds Bank Review*, No. 144, April.

Thomas, R. L. (1984) 'The consumption function'. In Demery, D. *et al.* (1984) *Macroeconomics*. Longman.

Thompson, G. (1986) *The Conservatives Economic Policy*. Croom Helm.

Tinbergen, J. (1956) *Economic Policy: Principles and Design*. North-Holland Publishing Company.

Tobin, J. (1956) 'The interest elasticity of transactions demand for cash'. *Review of Economics and Statistics*, **38**.

Tobin, J. (1958) 'Liquidity preference as behavior towards risk'. *Review of Economic Studies*, **25**, February 1958. Reprinted in M. G. Mueller (1967) *Readings in Macroeconomics*. Holt, Rinehart and Winston.

Tobin, J. (1980) *Asset Accumulation and Economic Activity*. Basil Blackwell.

Tomlinson, J. (1985) *British Macroeconomic Policy Since 1940*. Croom Helm.

Tomlinson, J. (1986) *Monetarism: Is there an Alternative?* Basil Blackwell.

Tosini, P. A. (1977) Leaning against the wind: a standard for managed floating. *Essays in International Finance, No. 126*. Princeton University.

Trevithick, J. A. (1977) (2nd edn 1980) *Inflation*. Penguin.

Turnovsky, S. J. (1977) *Macroeconomic Analysis and Stabilisation Policy*. Cambridge University Press.

Veverka, J. (1963) 'The growth of government expenditure in the United Kingdom since 1790'. *Scottish Journal of Political Economy*, **10**.

Wadsworth, J. E. (1973) (ed.) *The Banks and the Monetary System in the UK 1959–1971*. Methuen and Co. Ltd.

Wallis, K. F. (ed.) (1985) *Models of the UK Economy*. Oxford University Press.

Wan, H. Y. (1971) *Economic Growth*. Harcourt Brace Jovanovich.

Ward, T. (1982) 'Mrs Thatcher's strategy in practice'. *Journal of Post Keynesian Economics*, **4**, Summer.

White, G. and Chapman, H. (1987) 'Long term trends in public expenditure'. *Economic Trends*, No. 408, October.

Wickens, M. R. (1981) 'The new Conservative macroeconomics'. Inaugural Lecture delivered 5 February.

Williams, K., Williams, J. and Thomas, D. (1983) *Why are the British Bad at Manufacturing?* Routledge & Kegan Paul.

Williamson, J. (1977) *The Failure of World Monetary Reform, 1971–74*. Nelson.

Williamson, J. (1983) *The Open Economy and the World Economy*. Basic Books.

Wilson Committee (1977) *Progress Report on the Financing of Industry and Trade*. HMSO. Cmnd. 7937.

AUTHOR INDEX

SUBJECT INDEX